Anonymous

The Present Condition of Mexico

Message from the President of the United States in Answer to Resolution of the

House of 3d of March Last Transmitting Report from the Department of State

Regarding the Present Condition of Mexico

Anonymous

The Present Condition of Mexico
Message from the President of the United States in Answer to Resolution of the House of 3d of March Last Transmitting Report from the Department of State Regarding the Present Condition of Mexico

ISBN/EAN: 9783337813086

Printed in Europe, USA, Canada, Australia, Japan

Cover: Foto ©ninafisch / pixelio.de

More available books at **www.hansebooks.com**

37TH CONGRESS, } HOUSE OF REPRESENTATIVES. { Ex. Doc.
2d Session.   { No. 100.

THE PRESENT CONDITION OF MEXICO.

MESSAGE

FROM THE

PRESIDENT OF THE UNITED STATES,

IN ANSWER

To resolution of the House of the 3d of March last, transmitting report from the Department of State regarding the present condition of Mexico.

APRIL 15, 1862.—Referred to the Committee on Foreign Affairs, and ordered to be printed.
APRIL 21, 1862.—*Resolved,* That ten thousand extra copies of the President's Message of the 14th instant, in regard to the present condition of Mexico, be printed for the use of the members of this House, and one thousand extra copies for the use of the State Department.

To the House of Representatives:

In compliance with the resolution of the House of Representatives of the 3d ultimo, requesting information in regard to the present condition of Mexico, I transmit a report from the Secretary of State and the documents by which it was accompanied.

ABRAHAM LINCOLN.

WASHINGTON, *April* 14, 1862.

DEPARTMENT OF STATE,
Washington, April 14, 1862.

The Secretary of State, to whom was referred the resolution of the House of Representatives of the 3d ultimo, requesting the President, "if not inconsistent with the public interest, to communicate to this house any correspondence or other information in his possession relative to the present condition of Mexico, and especially in relation to the alleged design of the allied powers now invading that country to establish a monarchy there," has the honor to lay before the President the papers containing the information desired as specified in the subjoined list.

Respectfully submitted.

WILLIAM H. SEWARD.

The PRESIDENT.

LIST OF DOCUMENTS

RELATING TO

MEXICAN AFFAIRS,

ACCOMPANYING THE

President's message in reply to the resolution of the House of Representatives of March 3, 1862.

Mr. Seward to Mr. Corwin............................April	6,	1861
Mr. Corwin to Mr. Seward............................May	29,	1861.
Same to same..June	29,	1861.
Mr. Seward to Mr. Corwin............................June	3,	1861.
Same to same..June	24,	1861.
Same to same..July	30,	1861.
Mr. Corwin to Mr. Seward............................June	29,	1861.
Same to same..July	29,	1861.
Mr. La Reintrie to ministers of foreign powers in Mexico..December	20,	1860.
Mr. Seward to Mr. Corwin............................August	24,	1861.
Mr. Corwin to Mr. Seward............................August	28,	1861.
Mr. Seward to Mr. Corwin............................September	2,	1861.
Mr. Corwin to Mr. Seward............................September	7,	1861.
Mr. Seward to Mr. Corwin, (with one enclosure,)........September	23,	1861.
Mr. Corwin to Mr. Seward, (with three enclosures,)......September	29,	1861.
Mr. Seward to Mr. Corwin............................October	2,	1861.
Same to same..October	21,	1861.
Mr. Corwin to Mr. Seward............................October	29,	1861.
Mr. Seward to Mr. Corwin............................November	11,	1861.
Mr. Corwin to Mr. Seward............................November	29,	1861.
Mr. Seward to Mr. Corwin............................December	5,	1861.
Mr. Corwin to Mr. Seward............................December	24,	1861.
Same to same, (with six enclosures,)..................December	24,	1861.
Mr. Seward to Mr. Corwin............................January	24,	1862.
Mr. Corwin to Mr. Seward............................January	12,	1862.

Same to same..January 26, 1862.
Mr. Seward to Mr. Corwin............................February 15, 1862.
Same to same, (with one enclosure,)..................February 28, 1862.
Mr. Corwin to Mr. Seward............................February 18, 1862.
Mr. Seward to Mr. Corwin............................April 3, 1862.
Mr. Romero to Mr. Seward, (with twenty-eight enclosures,).. September 21, 1861.
Mr. Seward to Mr. Romero...........................September 24, 1861.
Mr. Romero to Mr. Seward, (with twelve enclosures,)..... September 30, 1861.
Same to same, (with one enclosure,)...................October 30, 1861.
Same to same, (with one enclosure,)...................November 23, 1861.
Same to same, (with seven enclosures,)................November 28, 1861.
Same to same, (with two enclosures,)..................December 21, 1861.
Same to same, (with nine enclosures,).................January 24, 1862.
Same to same, (with three enclosures,)................February 16, 1862.
Same to same, (with one enclosure,)...................April 10, 1862.
Mr. Seward to Mr. Romero...........................April 11, 1862.
The ministers of Spain, France, and Great Britain, to Mr.
  Seward, (enclosing convention of the allied powers, signed
  at London, October 31, 1861,)......................November 30, 1861.
Mr. Seward to Mr. Tassara, Mr. Mercier, and Lord Lyons..December 4, 1861.
Mr. Seward to Mr. Adams............................August 24, 1861.
Mr. Adams to Mr. Seward............................September 14, 1861.
Same to same.......................................September 19, 1861.
Mr. Seward to Mr. Adams............................September 24, 1861
Mr. Adams to Mr. Seward............................September 28, 1861.
Same to same.......................................October 4, 1861.
Mr. Seward to Mr. Adams............................October 10, 1861.
Mr. Adams to Mr. Seward............................October 11, 1861.
Mr. Seward to Mr. Adams............................October 12, 1861.
Same to same.......................................October 14, 1861.
Same to same.......................................October 19, 1861.
Mr. Adams to Mr. Seward............................October 24, 1861.
Mr. Seward to Mr. Adams............................October 28, 1861.
Mr. Adams to Mr. Seward............................November 1, 1861.
Same to same.......................................November 8, 1861.
Mr. Seward to Mr. Adams............................November 9, 1861.
Mr. Adams to Mr. Seward............................November 14, 1861.
Mr. Seward to Mr. Adams............................November 21, 1861.
Same to same.......................................November 25, 1861.
Same to same.......................................December 18, 1861.
Same to same.......................................January 8, 1862.

LIST OF DOCUMENTS.

Mr. Adams to Mr. Seward..........................January 24, 1862.
Mr. Seward to Mr. Adams..........................February 19, 1862.
Same to same.....................................March 3, 1862.
Mr. Adams to Mr. Seward..........................February 14, 1862.
Mr. Seward to Mr. Adams..........................March 10, 1862.
Mr. Seward to Mr. Dayton.........................September 2, 1861.
Mr. Dayton to Mr. Seward.........................September 25, 1861.
Mr. Seward to Mr. Dayton.........................October 11, 1861.
Mr. Dayton to Mr. Seward.........................September 27, 1861.
Mr. Seward to Mr. Dayton.........................October 19, 1861.
Mr. Dayton to Mr. Seward.........................November 6, 1861.
Same to same.....................................October 16, 1861.
Mr. Seward to Mr. Dayton.........................November 4, 1861.
Same to same.....................................November 23, 1861.
Mr. Dayton to Mr. Seward.........................November 7, 1861.
Mr. Seward to Mr. Dayton.........................December 18, 1861.
Mr. Dayton to Mr. Seward.........................January 15, 1862.
Same to same.....................................February 13, 1862.
Mr. Seward to Mr. Dayton.........................March 3, 1862.
Same to same.....................................March 10, 1862.
Same to same.....................................March 31, 1862.
Mr. Dayton to Mr. Seward.........................March 31, 1862.
Mr. Schurz to Mr. Seward.........................September 7, 1861.
Same to same.....................................September 14, 1861.
Mr. Seward to Mr. Schurz.........................October 14, 1861.
Same to same.....................................October 14, 1861.
Mr. Schurz to Mr. Seward.........................October 4, 1861.
Same to same.....................................October 9, 1861.
Mr. Seward to Mr. Schurz.........................October 28, 1861.
Mr. Schurz to Mr. Seward.........................October 15, 1861.
Same to same.....................................November 3, 1861.
Mr. Seward to Mr. Schurz.........................November 9, 1861.
Mr. Schurz to Mr. Seward.........................November 7, 1861.
Mr. Seward to Mr. Schurz.........................November 11, 1861.
Same to same.....................................November 23, 1861.
Mr. Seward to Mr. Schurz.........................December 6, 1861.
Same to same.....................................December 11, 1861.

Correspondence respecting the affairs of Mexico, presented to both houses of Parliament by command of her Majesty, 1862, containing 123 documents.

CORRESPONDENCE.

Mr. Seward to Mr. Corwin.

No. 2.]
DEPARTMENT OF STATE,
Washington, April 6, 1861.

SIR: The actual condition of affairs in Mexico is so imperfectly understood here that the President finds it very difficult to give you particular and practical directions for the regulation of your conduct during your mission.

Our latest information was, in substance, that the provisional government of President Juarez, so long confined to the sea-coasts of the country, had finally overthrown its adversaries and established itself at the capital; that the opposing armies had been demoralized and dispersed, and that there was no longer any armed resistance in the States; that an election for president had been held, in conformity with the constitution of 1857, and that the now provisional president had probably secured a majority of the votes, although the result was as yet not certainly known. The pleasure which these events have inspired is unhappily diminished by rumors that the government is without sufficient authority or hold on the public confidence to maintain order; that robberies are of frequent occurrence on the high roads, and even that a member of our late legation in the country has been murdered on his way from the city of Mexico to Vera Cruz.

You will apply yourself at once, with energy and diligence, to investigate the truth of this last-mentioned occurrence, which, if found to have been accurately reported, will not only be regarded as a high offence against the dignity and honor of the United States, but will prove a severe shock to the sensibilities of the American people.

The President is unable to conceive that any satisfactory explanation of a transaction so injurious to the character of Mexico can be made. He will, however, wait for your report concerning it, though with the deepest anxiety, before taking action upon the subject.

I find the archives here full of complaints against the Mexican government for violations of contracts and spoliations and cruelties practiced against American citizens. These complaints have been lodged in this department, from time to time, during the long reign of civil war in which the factions of Mexico have kept that country involved, with a view to having them made the basis of demands for indemnity and satisfaction whenever government should regain in that country sufficient solidity to assume a character for responsibility. It is not the President's intention to send forward such claims at the present moment. He willingly defers the performance of a duty which at any time would seem ungracious, until the incoming administration in Mexico shall have had time, if possible, to cement its authority and reduce the yet disturbed elements of society to order and harmony. You will, however, be expected, in some manner which will be marked with firmness as well as liberality, to keep the government there in mind that such of these claims as shall be found just will, in due time, be presented and urged upon its consideration.

While now, as heretofore, it is a duty of this government to reason with that of Mexico, and deprecate a continuance of the chronic reign of disorder there, a crisis has unhappily arrived, in which the performance of this duty is embarrassed by the occurrence of civil commotions in our own country, by which

Mexico, in consequence of her proximity, is not unlikely to be affected. The spirit of discontent seems, at last, to have crossed the border, and to be engaged in an attempt to overthrow the authority of this government in some parts of the country which adjoin the Mexican republic. It is much to be feared that new embarrassments of the relations of the two countries will happen when authority so long prostrated on the Mexican side finds the power of the United States temporarily suspended on this side of the frontier. Whatever evils shall thus occur, it is much to be feared, will be aggravated by the intervention of the Indians, who have been heretofore with difficulty restrained from violence, even while the federal authority has been adequately maintained.

Both of the governments must address themselves to this new and annoying condition of things, with common dispositions to mitigate its evils and abridge its duration as much as possible.

The President does not expect that you will allude to the origin or causes of our domestic difficulties in your intercourse with the government of Mexico, although that government will rightfully as well as reasonably ask what are his expectations of their course and their end. On the contrary, the President will not suffer the representatives of the United States to engage in any discussion of the merits of those difficulties in the presence of foreign powers, much less to invoke even their censure against those of our fellow-citizens who have arrayed themselves in opposition to its authority.

But you are instructed to assure the government of Mexico that these difficulties, having arisen out of no deep and permanent popular discontent, either in regard to our system of government itself or to the exercise of its authority, and being attended by social evils which are as ruinous as they are unnecessary, while no organic change that is contemplated could possibly bring to any portion of the American people any advantages of security, peace, prosperity, or happiness equal to those which the federal Union so effectually guaranties, the President confidently believes and expects that the people of the United States, in the exercise of the wisdom that hitherto has never failed them, will speedily and in a constitutional way adopt all necessary remedies for the restoration of the public peace and the preservation of the federal Union.

The success of this government in conducting affairs to that consummation may depend in some small degree on the action of the government and people of Mexico in this new emergency. The President could not fail to see that Mexico, instead of being benefited by the prostration or the obstruction of federal authority in this country, would be exposed by it to new and fearful dangers. On the other hand, a condition of anarchy in Mexico must necessarily operate as a seduction to those who are conspiring against the integrity of the Union to seek strength and aggrandizement for themselves by conquests in Mexico and other parts of Spanish America. Thus, even the dullest observer is at last able to see what was long ago distinctly seen by those who are endowed with any considerable perspicacity, that peace, order, and constitutional authority in each and all of the several republics of this continent are not exclusively an interest of any one or more of them, but a common and indispensable interest of them all.

This sentiment will serve as a key to open to you, in every case, the purposes, wishes, and expectations of the President in regard to your mission, which, I hardly need to say, he considers at this juncture perhaps the most interesting and important one within the whole circle of our international relations.

The President of the United States does not know, and he will not consent to know, with prejudice or undue favor any political party, religious class, or sectional interest in Mexico. He regrets that anything should have occurred to disturb the peaceful and friendly relations of Mexico with some of the foreign states lately represented at her capital. He hopes most sincerely that those relations may be everywhere renewed and reinvigorated, and that the independence and sovereignty of Mexico and the government which her people seem at last to have accepted, after so many conflicts, may be now universally acknowledged and respected.

Taking into view the actual condition and circumstances of Mexico, as well as those of the United States, the President is fully satisfied that the safety, welfare, and happiness of the latter would be more effectually promoted if the former should retain its complete integrity and independence, than they could be by any dismemberment of Mexico, with a transfer or diminution of its sovereignty, even though thereby a portion or the whole of the country or its sovereignty should be transferred to the United States themselves. The President is, moreover, well aware that the ability of the government and people of Mexico to preserve and maintain the integrity and the sovereignty of the republic might be very much impaired, under existing circumstances, by hostile or unfriendly action on the part of the government or of the people of the United States. If he needed any other incentive to practice justice and equality towards Mexico, it would be found in the reflection that the very contention and strife in our own country which at this moment excite so much domestic disquietude and so much surprise throughout a large part of the world, could probably never have happened if Mexico had always been able to maintain with firmness real and unquestioned sovereignty and independence. But if Mexico has heretofore been more unfortunate in these respects than many other modern nations, there are still circumstances in her case which justify a hope that her sad experience may be now coming to an end. Mexico really has, or ought to have, no enemies. The world is deeply interested in the development of her agricultural, and especially her mineral and commercial resources, while it holds in high respect the simple virtues and heroism of her people, and, above all, their inextinguishable love of civil liberty.

The President, therefore, will use all proper influence to favor the restoration of order and authority in Mexico, and, so far as it may be in his power, he will prevent incursions and every other form of aggression by citizens of the United States against Mexico. But he enjoins you to employ your best efforts in convincing the government of Mexico, and even the people, if, with its approval, you can reach them, that the surest guaranty of their safety against such aggressions is to be found in a permanent restoration of the authority of that government. If, on the other hand, it shall appear in the sequel that the Mexican people are only now resting a brief season to recover their wasted energies sufficiently to lacerate themselves with new domestic conflicts, then it is to be feared that not only the government of the United States, but many other governments, will find it impossible to prevent a resort to that magnificent country of a class of persons, unhappily too numerous everywhere, who are accustomed to suppose that visionary schemes of public interest, aggrandizement, or reform, will justify even lawless invasion and aggression.

In connexion with this point, it is proper that you should be informed that the Mexican government has, through its representative here, recently complained of an apprehended attempt at invasion of the State of Sonora by citizens of California, acting, as is alleged, with the knowledge and consent of some of the public authorities in that State. You will assure the Mexican government that, due care being first taken to verify the facts thus presented, effective means shall be adopted to put our neutrality laws into activity.

The same representative has also expressed to the President an apprehension that the removal of the federal troops from the Texan border may be followed by outbreaks and violence there. There is, perhaps, too much ground for this apprehension. Moreover, it is impossible to foresee the course of the attempts which are taking place in that region to subvert the proper authority of this government. The President, however, meantime directs you to assure the Mexican government that due attention shall be bestowed on the condition of the frontier, with a view to the preservation and safety of the peaceable inhabitants residing there. He hopes and trusts that equal attention will be given to this important subject by the authorities of Mexico.

These matters, grave and urgent as they are, must not altogether withdraw our attention from others to which I have already incidentally alluded, but which require more explicit discussion.

For a few years past the condition of Mexico has been so unsettled as to raise the question on both sides of the Atlantic whether the time has not come when some foreign power ought, in the general interest of society, to intervene to establish a protectorate or some other form of government in that country and guaranty its continuance there. Such schemes may even now be held under consideration by some European nations, and there is also some reason to believe that designs have been conceived in some parts of the United States to effect either a partial dismemberment or a complete overthrow of the Mexican government, with a view to extend over it the authority of the newly projected confederacy which a discontented part of our people are attempting to establish in the southern part of our own country. You may possibly meet agents of this projected confederacy, busy in preparing some farther revolution in Mexico. You will not fail to assure the government of Mexico that the President neither has, nor can ever have, any sympathy with such designs, in whatever quarter they may arise, or whatever character they may take on.

In view of the prevailing temper and political habits and opinions of the Mexican people, the President can scarcely believe that the disaffected citizens of our own country, who are now attempting a dismemberment of the American Union, will hope to induce Mexico to aid them by recognizing the assumed independence which they have proclaimed, because it seems manifest to him that such an organization of a distinct government over that part of the present Union which adjoins Mexico would, if possible, be fraught with evils to that country more intolerable than any which the success of those desperate measures could inflict even upon the United States. At the same time it is manifest that the existing political organization in this country affords the surest guaranty Mexico can have that her integrity, union, and independence will be respected by the whole people of the American Union.

The President, however, expects that you will be watchful of such designs as I have thus described, however improbable they may seem, and that you will use the most effective measures in your power to counteract any recognition of the projected Confederate States by the Mexican government, if it shall be solicited.

Your large acquaintance with the character of the Mexican people, their interests and their policy, will suggest many proper arguments against such a measure, if any are needful beyond the intimations I have already given.

In conclusion, the President, as you are well aware, is of opinion that, alienated from the United States as the Spanish American republics have been for some time past—largely, perhaps, by reason of errors and prejudices peculiar to themselves, and yet not altogether without fault on our own part—that those States and the United States, nevertheless, in some respects, hold a common attitude and relation towards all other nations; that it is the interest of them all to be friends as they are neighbors, and to mutually maintain and support each other so far as may be consistent with the individual sovereignty which each of them rightly enjoys, equally against all disintegrating agencies within, and all foreign influences or power without their borders.

The President never for a moment doubts that the republican system is to pass safely through all ordeals and prove a permanent success in our own country, and so to be commended to adoption by all other nations. But he thinks also that that system everywhere has to make its way painfully through difficulties and embarrassments, which result from the action of antagonistical elements which are a legacy of former times and very different institutions. The President is hopeful of the ultimate triumph of this system over all obstacles, as well in regard to Mexico as in regard to every other American State; but he feels that those States are nevertheless justly entitled to a greater forbearance and more generous sympathies from the government and people of the United States than they are likely to receive in any other quarter.

The President trusts that your mission, manifesting these sentiments, will reassure the government of Mexico of his best disposition to favor their commerce and their internal improvements. He hopes, indeed, that your mission, assuming a spirit more elevated than one of merely commerce and conventional amity, a spirit disinterested and unambitious, earnestly American in the continental sense of the word, and fraternal in no affected or mere diplomatic meaning of the term, while it shall secure the confidence and good will of the government of Mexico, will mark the inauguration of a new condition of things directly conducive to the prosperity and happiness of both nations, and ultimately auspicious to all other republican states throughout the world.

I am, sir, your obedient servant,

WILLIAM H. SEWARD.

THOMAS CORWIN, Esq., &c., &c., &c.

Mr. Corwin to Mr. Seward.

[Extract.]

No. 1.]   LEGATION OF THE UNITED STATES,
             City of Mexico, May 29, 1861.

SIR: *   *   *   *   *   *   *   *

I deem it of the very first importance that our consuls at every port on the Gulf of Mexico should be at their respective posts, with careful and specific instructions as to their treatment of vessels sailing under the flag of the Confederate States, or having papers from ports within those States, made out by officers under their authority.

Should the relations now existing, or which may hereafter exist, between the United States and the seceding States be such as to require of me any specific act in relation to such state of things, I beg to be advised of it by the department as early as possible.

The present government of Mexico is well affected towards us in our present difficulties, but, for obvious reasons, will be unwilling to enter into any engagement which might produce war with the south, unless protected by promise of aid from the United States.

*   *   *   *   *   *   *   *

I am, &c.,

THOMAS CORWIN.

Hon. W. H. SEWARD, &c., &c., &c.

Mr. Corwin to Mr. Seward.

[Extracts]

No. 2.]   LEGATION OF THE UNITED STATES,
             Mexico, June 29, 1861.

SIR: *   *   *   *   *   *   *   *

The present time is most propitious for securing the advantages and preventing the evils which I have suggested. The government here feels the strongest sympathy with the United States.

* * * * * * * *

It has been my constant endeavor since my arrival here to possess the Mexican mind of the true causes of our difficulties, and thus enable them to estimate the danger to this republic which will result from any unfavorable termination of them. I am quite sure that whilst this government will endeavor to preserve peaceful relations with all the European powers on fair terms, it regards the United States as its true and only reliable friend in any struggle which may involve the national existence. That this should be so is somewhat remarkable, when we regard the deep prejudices engendered in the general Mexican mind by the loss of Texas, which they attribute to our citizens, and the compulsory cession of territory which was a consequence of our war with them.

* * * * * * * *

I am, &c.,

THOMAS CORWIN.

Hon. W. H. SEWARD,
Secretary of State, U. S., &c., &c., &c.

Mr. Seward to Mr. Corwin.

[Extract.]

No. 8.]

DEPARTMENT OF STATE,
Washington, June 3, 1861.

SIR: Information, which wears an air of authenticity, leads us to apprehend that a design exists, on the part of the insurgents of this country, to gain possession of the peninsula of Lower California, to cut off our commerce with Mexico, to seize the Panama steamers, and, with the aid of the treasure so to be acquired, to extend their conquests to Sonora and Chihuahua. The design is understood to embrace an ultimate absorption of all Mexico. We are informed that the native-born population of California would, to a man, join the invaders in such a case.

We shall immediately take care to have the commanders of our land and naval forces on the Pacific coast and ocean instructed to prevent this threatened violation of the territory and sovereignty of Mexico. The President desires you to bring the subject at once to the notice of the government of that republic.

You will invoke its energetic and vigorous efforts to the defence of its own sovereignty in the peninsula.

Secondly, you will assure that government of the cordial co-operation of this government, and will ask its consent, if there shall be need for the intervention of our forces, so far as to prevent the invasion, by the insurgent citizens of this country, from being made effectual; it being in no case the purpose of this government to retain any possession, or exercise any political authority within the limits of Mexico, beyond the defeat of the designs before described.

Thirdly, the United States do not desire to acquire any part of Mexico.

* * * * * * * * *

THOMAS CORWIN, Esq., &c., &c., &c.

Mr. Seward to Mr. Corwin.

[Extracts.]

No. 11.]
DEPARTMENT OF STATE,
Washington, June 24, 1861.

SIR: Your despatch (No. 1) of the 29th of May last has been received.
The President approves your speech to the chief magistrate of Mexico, and is gratified with the very just and generous sentiments expressed by him in his reply.
This government is highly pleased with the opinions and sentiments so full of generosity and of hope in regard to Mexico which you have expressed in your despatch. We pray God that they may be vindicated by the restoration of the peace, order, credit, power, and influence of that republic.
Your suggestion to negotiate for religious liberty in behalf of American citizens in Mexico is cordially approved, and you are authorized to make it a subject as prominent as you may think discreet in the negotiations, in regard to which we have left you so liberal a range. We think favorably also of your suggestion to obtain a stipulation against the imposition of forced loans on American citizens in any emergencies, and you will negotiate accordingly.

* * * * * * *

The President expects that you will in every case exercise your best judgment as to the measures necessary to prevent the insurgent armed vessels from finding shelter in Mexican ports, and also to prevent arms and other military stores being carried to the seceding States through Mexico. The consuls will be instructed to confer with you and follow your instructions.
We are attempting to negotiate, through Mr. Romero, a postal treaty with the republic of Mexico. You will be promptly advised of our progress. * *

THOMAS CORWIN, Esq., &c., &c., &c.

Mr. Seward to Mr. Corwin.

[Extract.]

No. 13.]
DEPARTMENT OF STATE,
Washington, July 30, 1861.

SIR: I communicate to you extracts from a despatch which has just been received from Mr. Dayton, our minister in France.
I fear that Mr. Almonte's solicitude about our relations with the present government of Mexico is excited by wishes personal rather than patriotic. I am unable to see how any good could happen to Mexico from overturning the present government and bringing in another which could give no better guarantees of stability and order. But I am too far from the scene to judge safely either for our own government or for that of Mexico.

* * * * * * * * *

THOMAS CORWIN, Esq., &c., &c., &c.

Mr. Corwin to Mr. Seward.

[Extracts]

No. 2.] MEXICO, *June* 29, 1861.

SIR: I have the honor to acknowledge the receipt of your despatches Nos. 3, 4, 5, 6, and 7, with the papers referred to in them.

* * * * * * * * *

Since my last despatches the country here has been in a state of great disorder. Bands of armed men, in numbers varying from fifty to four thousand, have been ravaging the country in this and two or three adjoining States, pushing their operations to the very suburbs of this city. These forces are made up of the fragments of the army commanded formerly by Miramon, and a portion of the worst of the liberal troops disbanded on the final conquest of this city in December last—the latter generally organized for the mere purpose of plunder, and acting under chiefs taken from the forces of the church party, or, as they are called, reactionists. Marquez (the same officer who ordered the infamous massacre at Tacubaya) commands the reactionary forces, and has been hovering in the mountains near Mexico for the last week—sometimes within ten miles of the city. He is reported to have marched now to the neighborhood of Puebla. The government forces have pursued him for several hundred miles within the last two weeks without result. General Ortega commands the liberal forces. He is now in the city. Two days ago the congress (now in session) elected him chief judge of the supreme court. This was a merely revolutionary movement, as the constitution gives no authority of the kind to that body, but expressly provides that the judges of that court shall be elected *by the people*. This act was done to pave the way, however, to make Ortega president, as it was supposed Juarez could be persuaded to resign, and in that event the newly-elected judge (by the constitution) would take his place. Every means of a peaceful nature is now being employed to induce Juarez to resign. I think the project will succeed, and Ortega will be the next revolutionary president. I entertain strong fears that this movement will fail of its intended effect. Having its origin in a revolutionary act, not warranted by the constitution, it will form a plausible precedent for another act of the same nature in favor of some other chief who may attain a temporary popularity in a similar emergency, which is very likely to arise soon unless Ortega shall be more fortunate than his predecessors for the last forty years. The great want of this republic is that *public opinion* which is so omnipotent with us, and this again arises from the want of an *enlightened people.* Hence, in the last forty years Mexico has passed through thirty-six different forms of government; has had seventy-two, or rather, up to this time, has had seventy-three presidents. Still, I do not despair of the final triumph of free government in Mexico. Progress has been made. The signs of regeneration, though few, are still visible. Had the present liberal party enough money at command to pay an army of ten thousand men, I am satisfied it could suppress the present opposition, restore order, and preserve internal peace. These once achieved, the leaders of this party would adhere to the written constitution and enforce obedience to law; and industry, secure in its rewards, would soon take the place of idleness and crime. Education of the right kind begins to be felt as a necessity, which in time would, under such auspices, expel from the minds of the people religious superstition, and make the supremacy of either religions or political despotism impossible. I am persuaded that the pecuniary resources to effect these objects at this time must come from abroad. This country is exhausted, as might be expected, by forty years of almost uninterrupted civil war. She looks now, and has looked for some time in vain, for help from other nations

England presses her, and claims from her the scanty resources at her command, to pay the interest on a debt of about sixty-two millions due to British subjects. France urges with equal pertinacity the claims of French subjects, into whose hands bonds issued by the Zuloaga and Miramon governments to the amount of some fifty millions have fallen. These last were put out at a time when the liberal government was contending against the above-named self-constituted dictators in that struggle which terminated in their final overthrow six months ago. These bonds, it is said, were sold to French subjects here for sums varying from one-half of one per cent. to four or five per cent., and are now claimed as a debt of the republic, to be paid in full. Meantime there is not one dollar from day to day in the treasury, and only yesterday another heavy forced loan was made to raise money to pay troops to protect the citizens of this capital and its neighborhood from pillage and slaughter. I state the foregoing facts as universally admitted, in the hope of obtaining from the department instructions permitting me to negotiate a treaty which, for ample equivalents, may stipulate for the payment by us of a sum varying from five to ten millions in money or United States stocks, to be paid in instalments to this government, which would enable it to keep on foot a sufficient force to save it from ultimate subjugation, perhaps to one of these European monarchies, or, it may be, from a partition of its territory amongst them all. The sale of territory is the last expedient to which this government will resort: perhaps it would be refused under any circumstances. If, however, this could be effected, I presume at present it would not be a popular measure with our government. If this should be adopted, I would strongly recommend Lower California as the most eligible for both parties. This territory is of no value to Mexico; its population does not exceed twelve thousand. A glance at the map will show its importance to us in a naval or military point of view, in the event of an attack upon our Pacific possessions by any naval power, or any attempt upon us or Mexico in that quarter by a lawless force. I have reason to know that this territory is much more valuable than is generally supposed in mineral resources.

Another expedient, and perhaps one more likely to be favored by both governments, is this: The Mexican tariff is now under revision by a committee whose labors will be submitted soon to Congress. In conversation with one of the leading minds here, he suggested that for a sum, to be stipulated in a treaty, to be paid in instalments, Mexico would agree to admit all articles the growth or manufacture of the United States at a rate fifty per centum below the duties to be paid by other nations, with a stipulation that no change shall be made in favor of other nations without a payment by such nations of an amount equal to that paid by us, calculated upon the proportion which the commerce of such nation with Mexico has borne for the last five years to ours. I wish to be understood here as only suggesting the outlines of an arrangement, or rather the leading principle which should be adopted, if a measure of that kind is thought expedient.

It has been supposed that the church property, which has been secularized and made available to the government, would furnish an ample fund to enable the government to preserve itself and pay the interest and principal of the public debt. This fund has been entirely, or almost entirely, exhausted in the last three years' struggle, and is no longer a resource to be calculated upon. If the liberal government here is not sustained, and the church party get possession of the capital again, the following consequences may be calculated on as inevitable: First. It is most probable that, as heretofore, the liberal government will take refuge in some one of the States favorable to it, and wage another protracted war for supremacy, the end of which must be considered as doubtful when we take into view the exhausted condition of the States favorable to the liberal party; or, secondly, the respective States will form combinations regulated by territorial and neighborhood ideas, and set up a number of small confederacies, say four or five. Looking at the geographical and political map of the republic, it is not likely, in the event of a disintegration, that there would be less than four separate political organizations. Each of these would be too weak to stand alone against the temptation to seek a protectorate somewhere. Ambitious chiefs would soon be found, like Santa Anna, of San Domingo, who would throw their power down at the feet of some European government. I have strong reasons for the belief that England, France, and Spain are each looking to such a result. England desires to possess (as she now very nearly does, owing o our neglect of our interests in this quarter) the commerce of the Gulf States as well as that of the western coast. Spain, in her rising fortunes, cannot but desire to repossess herself of her lost American colonies. The recent movement on San Domingo is ample proof of this. The towering ambition of Napoleon to regulate Europe, when it shall have been gratified in that quarter, will seek to dazzle the world by impressing upon this continent the idea of French glory and French supremacy. Indeed, I have seen, in a recent number of a creditable journal, a statement that France and England now have under consideration the project of intervention in Mexican affairs. How will any or all of these ideas, if realized, affect the great idea of free government on this continent? Surely American statesmen should be awake to even a suspicion that such portentous events are possible. Had our madmen allowed the majestic march of freedom to progress, Spain would not now have shown her flag in San Domingo, nor would it ever have been suggested that any possible event could make Mexico again a rich appanage to any European crown. Unhappy as our *domestic* situation may now be, I feel an assured confidence that the northern United States are equal to the successful termination of the struggle at home, and at the *same time* able to secure our interests and promote successfully the cause of human progress on this entire continent. These opinions have led me to regard our present connexions with Mexico as of more importance than they may seem to be to those who are in the midst of the great rebellion which very properly engrosses the chief attention of the government at this time. My duty, I have supposed, was to guard our interests here, as they are connected directly or remotely with those ideas which are now in conflict in the United States.

The present time is most propitious for securing the advantages and preventing the evils which I have suggested; the government here feels the strongest sympathy with the United States. * * * * * It has been my constant endeavor since my arrival here to possess the Mexican mind of the true causes of our difficulties, and thus enable them to estimate the danger to this republic which will result from any unfavorable termination of them. I am quite sure that whilst this government will endeavor to preserve peaceful relations with all the European powers on fair terms, it regards the United States as its true and only reliable friend in any struggle which may involve its national existence. That this should be so is somewhat remarkable, when we regard the deep prejudices engendered in the general Mexican mind by the loss of Texas which they attribute to our citizens, and the compulsory cession of territory which was a consequence of our war with them.

* * * * * * * *

Very respectfully, your obedient servant,

THOMAS CORWIN

Hon. W. H. Seward,
Secretary of State, U. S. of America.

Mr. Corwin to Mr. Seward.

No. 3.] LEGATION OF THE UNITED STATES,
City of Mexico, July 29, 1861.

SIR: In my last despatch to the department under date of 29th ultimo, No. 2, I suggested the probability of an armed European intervention in the affairs of Mexico, or a partition of its territory.

Since that time events here have given greater plausibility to those fears. On the 17th day of this month the Mexican congress passed a decree suspending the payment of all debts of every sort due from the government for the term of two years.

The English and French ministers immediately sent in their protests respectively, copies of which, marked G 1 and 2, I transmit herewith.

At the expiration of the time mentioned in these protests, the legations of both these powers took down their flags and signs, and advised the department of foreign affairs here that all diplomatic intercourse with their respective governments and Mexico was at an end. England and France seem to be acting in concert in this movement. They either intend to frighten Mexico into a repeal of the obnoxious decree, or they take this step as the best and quickest means to initiate such movements as will end in possible occupation of the entire maritime frontier of the republic, which would inevitably lead to the possession of the whole of the interior.

I beg the department to consider whether, *if it be possible,* our duty and interest do not require of us to prevent the consummation of this scheme.

If the interest of the debt due to English bondholders could be secured, say for five years, that alone would put a stop to every attempt of the kind suggested above. The bondholders' debt is now about sixty-two millions, bearing an interest of three per cent. per annum. The interest on this debt would amount to less than two millions a year. If Mexico should offer any equivalent acceptable to our government for the guarantee of the payment of this interest for five years, would it not be our interest to close with such a proposition?

England and Spain are now in possession of the best of the West India islands, (for I consider San Domingo is certain to fall into the hands of Spain before our rebellion is quelled,) and Mexico a colony of England, with the British power on the north of our possessions, would leave on the map of this continent a very insignificant part for the United States, especially should the present unnatural rebellion end in the final severance from us of eight or nine, or all of the slave States.

Mexico, I am persuaded, would be willing to pledge all her public lands and mineral rights in Lower California, Chihuahua, Sonora, and Sinaloa, as well as her national faith, for the payment of this guarantee. This would probably end in the cession of the sovereignty to us. It would be certain to end thus if the money were not promptly paid as agreed on. By such an arrangement two consequences would follow: First, all hope of extending the dominion of a *separate* southern republic in this quarter or in Central America would be extinguished, and any further attempt in all time to come to establish European power on this continent would cease to occupy the minds of either England or continental Europe. If the republics of Mexico or Central America could maintain themselves against southern filibusters or European cupidity, I should not desire either to intermeddle in their concerns or add any of their territory to ours, except, perhaps, Lower California, which may become indispensable to the protection of our Pacific possessions.

The reasons, however, for a departure from this rule, arising out of our present apparent weakness, stimulating aggression, as well by filibusters as Europeans, seem to demaud serious consideration. The United States are the only safe guardians of the independence and true civilization of this continent. It is their mission, and they should fulfil it. This task would have been comparatively easy but for the madness of the south, plunging us into our present difficulties.

Europe is quite willing to see us humbled, and will not fail to take advantage of our embarrassments to execute purposes of which she would not have dreamed had we remained at peace.

I repeat these suggestions as my reasons for desiring instructions on the points stated above, relating to aid to Mexico in some form suitable to her present exigencies.

Her late suspension, leading to the cessation of diplomatic relations with England and France, may, perhaps, have been imprudent. She could not pay the debts, however, and maintain her government; and perhaps it was as well to say she would not pay for two years, as to promise to pay, and subject herself to the mortification of constantly asking further time. She is impoverished to the last degree by forty years of civil war. I cannot find in this republic any men of any party better qualified, in my judgment, for the task than those in power. If they do not save her, then I am quite sure she is to be the prey of some foreign power, and they, I fear, cannot without *our* aid. I say *our* aid, for she will look in vain for help elsewhere.

Mr. J. T. Pickett is here in the character of commissioner from the so-called "Confederate States." I believe the secretary of foreign affairs has given him a private interview at his house. I have the positive assurance of the president that this government will not entertain any propositions coming from that quarter which may seem to recognize these States in any other light than as a part of the United States.

Well-informed Mexicans, in and out of the government, seem to be well aware that the independence of a southern confederacy would be the signal for a war of conquest with a view to establish slavery in each of the twenty-two States of this republic.

I have judged it proper to forward to our ministers at Paris and London the protests of the French and English ministers to the decree of the Mexican congress, in the hope that they will offer their good offices to mitigate the unfriendly feeling of the British and French cabinets towards this country.

I have nearly completed the arrangement for two treaties with the cabinet. They will probably be submitted to congress before its adjournment, which is fixed for the 30th instant, but may be postponed for a few days. I have no doubt of their ratification, but it will come too late for the present mail.

One of these is a treaty for the extradition of criminals, the other is a postal convention. The latter is in all essentials quite the same with that, a form of which reached here from Mr. Romero. The former is, in substance, like those we have concluded with other powers.

I am deeply impressed with the necessity of having our consul at Vera Cruz at his post. I forwarded his exequatur to the vice-consul at that place some weeks since. I am satisfied that the public interests require the best officers at all the ports on the Gulf, as well as in the West India islands.

I beg to call your attention to a paper addressed by Mr. La Reintrie, acting as special agent of this legation under instructions from Mr. McLane, to all the foreign ministers at this place, under date of December 20th last. It must or should be in the State Department, as well as the instructions of Mr. McLane, on which it is based. I wish to know if the government concurs fully in the views and principles therein set forth. I hope the government will immediately take steps to insure a mail twice a month between New York and Vera Cruz. As New Orleans is now a closed port, we can only receive advices once a month— this a British steamer, and that by no means *certain*. The commerce of the

Gulf would be much more secure had we two vessels sailing in those waters once a month.

I must also ask your particular attention to papers forwarded to the department on the 23d March last by Colonel Waller, exculpating Colonel Natzmer, vice-consul at Minatitlan, from the charges on which he was removed. I know Mr. A. C. Allen well, (the consul at that place,) he is a gentleman on whose truth and honor I am sure I can rely. He has satisfied me that Natzmer is not guilty of any act inconsistent with his official duty. His statement is with the papers alluded to. I trust Colonel N. will be restored.

I have received from the department the President's proclamation, under date of April 19, 1861.

I am, very respectfully, your most obedient servant,

THOMAS CORWIN.

29TH, 1 P. M.

P. S.—The mails per British steamer are just at hand, but I have not a single communication or paper. A passenger states (as I am informed by the consul at Vera Cruz) that an American steamer was in sight as the British steamer was leaving Havana.

No mail is expected from Havana until 15th August, when the steamer Union leaves there, her mails reaching this city on the 26th of that month, before which time it will therefore be impossible for me now to get any advices.

My latest despatches from the department are those I acknowledged on the 29th ultimo.

Respectfully,

THOMAS CORWIN.

Hon. WILLIAM H. SEWARD,
Secretary of State, Washington.

Mr. La Reintrie to Ministers of Foreign Powers in Mexico.

SAN ANGEL, (NEAR MEXICO,)
December 20, 1860.

SIR: I have the honor to advise you of my arrival at this place in the character of special agent of the legation of the United States in Mexico, with instructions from the honorable Robert M. Mc Lane, envoy extraordinary and minister plenipotentiary of the United States, to communicate with the representatives of foreign powers now residing in the city of Mexico, and to make known to them the policy of the government of the United States with respect to Mexico, under the present deplorable circumstances which afflict this republic.

You are aware that proposals have already been made by the government of Great Britain to the two parties now contending for political power and ascendency in Mexico, with the object of bringing about a pacification of the country. These efforts, however, have thus far failed of the desired end—both parties declining the proffered intervention and meditation, because neither are willing to compromise the great principles at issue in the pending civil war.

The liberals, who had taken up arms in defence of the right of the people to govern themselves, and to live under a constitution that guarantees political equality to every citizen of the republic, were unwilling to confide the adjustment of these sacred rights to a *foreign intervention and mediation.* On the other hand, the conservatives were unwilling to surrender their organization, or to subject the government of General Miramon to any *foreign intervention* that did not guarantee to them the ascendency and triumph of principles which are in direct antagonism with the equality of the citizen and the form of a republican government.

At a later period the governments of France and Spain have both, with more or less formality, renewed the efforts which Great Britain originally made, and the same obstacles which rendered the efforts of Great Britain unavailing have attended these subsequent efforts.

I am, therefore, instructed to inform you that all these matters have been fully and duly considered by the government of the United States, and that the policy heretofore adopted by the liberals in their intercourse with European powers, in relation to these negotiations for peace, has been approved and adopted by it, and that it has determined to resist any forcible attempt to impose a particular adjustment of the existing conflict against the will and sanction of the people of Mexico, and, also, any forcible intervention, by any power, which looks to the control of the political destiny thereof.

This determination on the part of the government of the United States has already been explicitly, though respectfully, declared to all the powers of Europe.

The government of the United States does not deny to the European powers the right to wage honorable warfare for a sufficient cause, anywhere, or against any nation; nor does it deny their right to demand redress for injuries inflicted on their respective subjects, and, if need be, to enforce such demands; but it does deny them the right to interfere, *directly* or *indirectly*, with the political independence of the republic of Mexico, and it will, to the extent of its power, defend the nationality and independence of said republic.

This settled policy of the government of the United States, I believe, is well understood by all the representatives of European powers in Mexico. It is also fully understood and appreciated by the constitutional government at Vera Cruz; and, under my instructions, it becomes my duty to cause it to be well understood by all those who, from their public character and the circumstances that characterize the political condition of the republic, are charged with the responsibilities of political power and authority, in order that said policy may neither be misunderstood nor misrepresented to the prejudice of either Mexico or of the United States.

I am further instructed to state, in the most explicit manner, that the government of the United States earnestly desires the pacification of Mexico, and that it will recognize and support any government that is adopted and accepted by the free choice of the people thereof, and that it will always encourage the friendly efforts of any foreign power that have for its objects such a result—notwithstanding its resolution to abstain from all *direct participation* in any such mediation, and its adherence to the relations already established between it and the constitutional government of the republic.

Having complied with the spirit of my instructions from the minister of the United States, I have, in conclusion, to request your acceptance of my consideration and respect.

HENRY ROY DE LA REINTRIE,
Special Agent United States Legation in Mexico.

This communication was sent to all the representatives of foreign powers in Mexico, to wit: Mr. Dubois de Saligny, France; Mr. J. F. Pacheco, Spain; Mr. George B. Mathew, England; Mr. E. de Wagner, Prussia; Mr. Clementie, Nuncio of the Holy See; Mr. F. N. del Barrio, Guatemala; F. de P. Pastor, Ecuador.

H. R. DE LA REINTRIE.

Mr. Seward to Mr. Corwin.

No. 16.]   DEPARTMENT OF STATE,
                                        Washington, August 24, 1861.

SIR: In your despatch of the 29th ultimo, numbered 3, you call my attention to a circular from Henry Roy de la Reintre, under date of December 20, 1860, to all the representatives of foreign powers in Mexico, which purports to have been written by direction of your predecessor, Mr. McLane, and you desire to know whether this government concurs in the views and principles therein set forth.

To answer this question broadly in the affirmative would be to commit it to opinions expressed by the writer of that paper concerning the merits of domestic political parties in Mexico, in transactions which, since that paper was written, have been fully completed and ended.

Again, although I am very sure that this government cherishes the actual independence of Mexico as a cardinal object to the exclusion of all foreign political intervention, and is willing to take decided measures favoring that independence, as is seen in another despatch to you of this date, yet the present moment does not seem to me an opportune one for formal reassurance of the policy of the government to foreign nations. Prudence requires that, in order to surmount the evils of faction at home, we should not unnecessarily provoke debates with foreign countries, but rather repair, as speedily as possible, the prestige which those evils have impaired.

Perhaps it will be sufficient for me to say that it is our wish and our purpose, so far as our action may bear upon the question, that the people of Mexico shall, in every case, be exclusive arbiters of their own political fortunes, and remain free and independent of all foreign intervention and control whatever. I hardly know how it can be necessary for the government of the United States to say this in view of the policy and principles set forth in the instructions under which your mission to Mexico was begun.

The postal convention made in this city, on the 31st July, having been ratified by the Senate of the United States, now awaits ratification by the government of Mexico. I send you a copy for your information.

I am, sir, your obedient servant,

                                        WILLIAM H. SEWARD.

THOMAS CORWIN, Esq., &c., &c., &c.

Mr. Corwin to Mr. Seward,

[Extracts.]

No. 4.]   LEGATION OF THE UNITED STATES OF AMERICA,
                                        Mexico, August 28, 1861.

SIR:
   *   *   *   *   *   *   *   *   *

Your instructions touching Lower California, alluded to in your despatch No. 11, have not been received here. If not destroyed on their way I may hope to get them either by the Spanish steamer Union, which passes from Havana to Vera Cruz once a month, the mail from which is due here to-night, or by the British steamer which comes from Havana to Vera Cruz every month, whose mail will be due here the 30th instant.

Nothing has occurred here to change the relations between Mexico and the United States since my last despatch. The liberal government still maintains its power, though its dominion is disputed by armed bands of reactionary troops in different parts of the republic. The pursuit of these robber bands in various directions compels the government to keep up a considerable military force, the expense of which has drained the last dollar from the treasury, and the government has often been compelled to borrow from individuals sums varying from $30,000 to $100,000, at enormous rates, for the purpose of moving a battalion or one or two regiments against the roving bands of the reactionary party. Many plans have been suggested by the friends of the government, and one or two by the department of foreign affairs, in conversation, for present relief of a pecuniary nature. None of these, however, were of a character which I deemed practicable, and therefore I have as yet presented to the government no proposition for a treaty which has for its basis the payment of money to Mexico by the United States. I have no doubt that any treaty which would give the present government from five to ten millions of dollars in monthly instalments of, say, a quarter of a million, would enable it to crush the last hope of the church party as well as to restore comparative safety from robber bands who infest the roads and rob travellers in all directions. Such a sum would also enable the government to arrange the foreign debt, the non-payment of the interest on which has caused the English and French ministers to discontinue diplomatic relations, *till further orders*, with Mexico, and which at present threatens to end in foreign intervention, which was alluded to in my despatch No. 3, under date of July 29, 1861. I am extremely anxious to obtain the views of the department on the subject proposed in that despatch, and hope to receive them by the mails of to-morrow or next day.

Mr. Pickett, commissioner from what he denominates "the Confederate States," is still here. He and three southern persons, sojourning in this city, were engaged last night in rejoicing over the victory at Bull Run and Manassas Gap. The sketch of that battle in the New York Herald of the 23d of July reached here yesterday. The paper came here from Havana by private conveyance. Mr. Pickett has learned that Mexico had granted the United States the privilege of marching troops through Mexican territory to Arizona. He has informed the government here that this will be considered as offensive to the "Confederate States," as New Mexico had placed herself under the protection of those States. He has said in private conversation that "*if this decree is not annulled Mexico will lose the State of Tamaulipas in sixty days.*"

By looking on any map of Mexico it will be seen that Tamaulipas, Nuevo Leon, Coahuila, Chihuahua, and Sonora, all adjoin Texas or New Mexico. Tamaulipas is easily approached by her port, Tampico, on the Mexican gulf, and also by land from Texas. All the others of these States can be reached by land from Texas or New Mexico. Guaymas is the great port on the Gulf of California from and to which shipments are made for the States of Sonora and Chihuahua, and also to our territory of New Mexico, including Arizona. It is, therefore, reasonable enough to conclude that United States troops from California could be landed at Guaymas in seven days by steamers, and with a safe passage through Sonora could confront any rebel force operating in Arizona or New Mexico proper, and also be in a position to act against any fillibustering enemy which might attack any of the Mexican States bordering on Texas. It is no doubt the design of the "Southern Confederation," whenever it can, to seize all of these States, indeed, to possess itself of the entire Terra Caliente of Mexico, that being well adapted to slave labor. If Mexico should be attacked under the pretence that she had justly offended the Confederate States, by the grant of passage through Sonora, every obligation of honor would seem to require that our troops should be ready to enforce our laws against fillibustering expeditions from our territories against the territories of a nation with whom we are at peace. Such troops would at the same time be efficient to restore our lawful dominion in Texas and New Mexico. Upper California, Oregon, and Washington Territory could furnish a respectable force for all these purposes, which could be conveyed by water to Guaymas, and from thence by land, over good roads, to their proper points of operation.

The States bordering on Texan and our New Mexican frontiers are very weak in population and wealth, and could be conquered by a comparatively small force.

Tamaulipas has only one hundred and eight thousand of all ages, races, and sexes.

The entire population of the five Mexican States above named is stated in the most reliable census to be six hundred and twenty-eight thousand, of all ages, sexes, and races, covering an area of sixty-seven thousand five hundred and sixty-three square miles. I am informed that recent discoveries of mineral wealth in Sonora and Chihuahua have invited large bodies of men from California to those two States. It is suspected that they are of a class easily induced to unite with the southern rebels in an attack on these and their neighboring Mexican States, as well as to promote southern pretensions in New Mexico and Texas. I suggest whether a prudent forecast would not invite our government to raise in California and Oregon a force which should pass, from Guaymas through Sonora, to our possessions in New Mexico and Arizona, for the purposes suggested above.

A contract has been concluded here with the government for carrying the mail from New York city to Vera Cruz, via Havana, twice a month, and so twice a month from Vera Cruz to New York; a subsidy of fifty thousand dollars per annum is given for the service. This subsidy is quite small, but if a subsidy from our government, in proportion to its interest in the line, compared with that of this government, is granted, we may hope the enterprize will go into immediate operation. If this, however, should fail, another expedient might be adopted. I understand boats run regularly from New York to Havana three times a month. If the government could put a despatch boat on the line between Havana and Vera Cruz to meet the boats from New York at Havana, this would give us a mail three times a month. This boat, if armed, might supersede the necessity of keeping an armed ship at Vera Cruz, and render valuable service in the protection of our commerce in the Gulf. Something should be done to render the commerce between the United States and this country certain and more frequent. My latest despatch from the department is dated 24th June, 1861, and latest reliable news is dated the 11th July. It is now within three days of the 1st of September. The mail from Washington, if sent by steam to Vera Cruz, could easily reach this city in thirteen days.

I have this day concluded a postal treaty with Mr. Lerdo, the minister appointed *ad hoc*, which will be submitted to the State Department to-morrow. I have no doubt it will be approved by that department and sent to congress for ratification at its second meeting, which is to open next Monday. I hope to conclude with the same minister an extradition treaty, which can be ratified during the coming month.

I have heretofore urged the *necessity* of having consuls on the Gulf, especially at Vera Cruz, the most important, whose fidelity and ability should be beyond even suspicion. The vice-consul at Vera Cruz has served many years there in that capacity, under Mr. Pickett. Mr. Pickett is now here, the agent of the "Confederate States." I know nothing against Mr. Rieken. I am sure some strange accident has happened that important despatch to which you allude in your despatch No. 11.

Why is not Mr. Dunnell at his post? That at Vera Cruz is one of the most important consulates, *just now*, in our service.

* * * * * * * *

Very respectfully, &c.,

Hon. W. H. SEWARD,   THOMAS CORWIN.
   Secretary of State, Washington.

Mr. Seward to Mr. Corwin.

No. 17.]
DEPARTMENT OF STATE,
Washington, September 2, 1861.

SIR: Your despatch of the 29th July last, numbered 3, has just now been received. The account of Mexican complications which it gives is painfully interesting. The President greatly desires that the political *status* of Mexico as an independent nation shall be permanently maintained. The events you communicate alarm him upon this point; and he conceives that the people of the United States would scarcely justify him were he to make no effort for preventing so great a calamity on this continent as would be the extinction of that republic. He has therefore determined to authorize and empower you, and you are hereby authorized and empowered, to negotiate a treaty with the republic of Mexico for the assumption by the government of the United States of the payment of the interest, at three per cent., upon the funded debt of that country due to Mexican bondholders, the principal of which is understood to be about sixty-two millions of dollars, for the term of five years from the date of the decree recently issued by the government of Mexico suspending such payment, provided that that government will pledge to the United States its faith for the reimbursement of the money so to be paid, with six per cent. interest thereon, to be secured by a specific lien upon all the public lands and mineral rights in the several Mexican States of Lower California, Chihuahua, Sonora, and Sinaloa, the property so pledged to become absolute in the United States at the expiration of the term of six years from the time when the treaty shall go into effect, if such reimbursement shall not have been made before that time. This course is rendered necessary by circumstances as new as they are eventful, while the Mexican crisis seems to admit of no delay. The President therefore accepts the responsibility, and will submit his action in the premises to the consideration of the Senate of the United States, so soon as that body shall be convened, for the constitutional sanction, without which the treaty when made would be of no effect.

It must be understood, however, that these instructions are conditional upon the attainment of consent on the part of the British and French governments to forbear from resort to action against Mexico on account of her failure or refusal to pay the interest in question until after the treaty shall have been submitted to the Senate, and, if ratified, then so long thereafter as the interest shall be punctually paid by the government of the United States. I shall immediately instruct our ministers in London and Paris to apply to the British and French governments for their consent to the terms thus indicated. You will see at once the importance of urging the Mexican government to give its best efforts to the support of these applications.

I am to be understood, moreover, as giving you not specific but general instructions, to be modified as to sums, terms, securities, and other points, as you may find necessary, subject to approval when made known to me.

Other matters discussed in your despatch will be treated of in distinct papers.

I am, sir, respectfully, your obedient servant,
WILLIAM H. SEWARD.

THOMAS CORWIN, Esq., &c., &c., &c.

Mr. Corwin to Mr. Seward.

No. 5.]
LEGATION OF THE UNITED STATES OF AMERICA,
Mexico, September 7, 1861.

SIR : I have this moment received your despatch, No. 13, dated 30th July, 1861, covering an extract from Mr. Dayton's despatch, dated at Paris, July 11, 1861.

I have heretofore informed the department that Mr. Pickett, formerly consul at Vera Cruz, was here in the character of commissioner from the "Confederate States." Mr. Cripps, formerly secretary of legation under General Gadsden, is also here, and has resided here ever since General Gadsden's departure from Mexico. The latter gentleman is not engaged in the business of Mr. Pickett in any other character than that of a friend of the south.

Mr. Pickett has learned that Mexico has allowed our troops to pass from Guaymas to Arizona, and has (unofficially of course) advised the government here that this grant to our government will be looked upon as an unfriendly act towards the south. He alleges that Arizona and New Mexico have placed themselves under the protection of the southern States, and that an invasion of the northern frontier of Mexico by the southern forces will probably be the result. He states to his acquaintances here that Colonel Van Dorn, of Texas, is moving towards El Paso with a large force, intended to occupy New Mexico and Arizona, and that if United States troops should advance through Sonora to Arizona war will probably ensue between Mexico and the Confederate States. I mentioned this in my last despatch, No. 4, and gave fully all the information I had on the subject. Nothing has occurred since to change the opinions then expressed. I beg the particular attention of the government to that portion of my despatch No. 4.

The threatened intervention in Mexican affairs by France and England, to which I have so often called the attention of the department, seems now to be quite certain to occur. The main pretext urged for this intervention is, the non-payment of money due the English and French governments, respectively, and to their citizens. I have stated in my former despatches that from five to ten millions of dollars would enable the government here to take away this pretext, and at once relieve them from the threatened guardianship of England and France. I am satisfied that our government would be greatly benefited (not only in reference to the present contest with the southern rebellion, but its permanent advantage in all time to come promoted) by advancing this sum to Mexico at once. It would enable the latter to look southern invasion in the face without fear, and it would bind her to the north by ties never to be broken. I expect, in a day or two, to receive from the minister of foreign relations some propositions which will offer an equivalent on the part of Mexico for the money they so much need. They would gladly reduce their tariff on American goods *fifty per cent.* below the charges on other foreign merchandise, say, for five or ten years, if this would be accepted. I have supposed such an arrangement would be rejected by our government on the same grounds which prevented the ratification of the treaty negotiated by Mr. McLane two years ago. There are other objections to this plan.

First. It might be considered by the English and French governments as giving an invidious preference to American trade, and be used as an additional reason for intervention here, and it would probably not be considered as showing the most friendly dispositions, on our part, towards England and France, with both of whom I consider it expedient, at this time, to preserve the most cordial relations.

Secondly. Mexico is bound by treaty to trade with both these powers on the same terms as those extended to "the most favored nations." If, therefore,

England or France, or either, should propose to Mexico a like equivalent, in proportion to their commerce with this country, she would be compelled to grant the same reduction of 50 per cent. on her present tariff to them, and then no advantage could accrue to us in this trade, and we should pay the money proposed without realizing an equivalent for it. This objection might be overcome by making the payments annual, and providing that payment should cease whenever England or France should obtain the same advantage by treaty with Mexico.

I wish to be *informed and instructed whether the United States would agree to pay, in money, to this country, at this time, any sum—say, five or six to ten millions of dollars*—on receiving for it stipulations of any kind from Mexico.

The present government, so far from being in danger of failing at this time is, in my judgment, stronger than at any former period of its existence. But this remark would not be true if European intervention should take place. The effect of such intervention, in my judgment, would be either to overthrow the constitutional government and substitute another, which would be merely the instrument of the intervening powers, or it might result in a dissolution of the union—each State, or combination of two or three separate States, setting up for themselves. This latter result would be probable in case intervention should only extend to the occupation of the maritime frontier and possession of the custom-houses. Either result would bring upon us consequences highly prejudicial. European influences, once inaugurated here, would encourage and corroborate the hopes of the southern rebels, and would aid them in procuring their recognition by European powers. It would so weaken Mexico that a very inconsiderable southern force could conquer in a very short time four or five Mexican States. For the reasons for this opinion I refer to my last despatch, No. 4.

These views, derived from a careful study of Mexican affairs, have ripened into convictions in my mind, and hence my extreme anxiety to furnish the pecuniary aid to Mexico, to which I have so often called attention, as this aid would, in my judgment, at once remove all possibility of the evils which, without such aid, must come upon Mexico soon, and, as incidents, must so seriously affect the United States.

Very respectfully,

THOMAS CORWIN.

P. S.—I only learned an hour ago that a courier, hired by merchants, would leave at 4 p. m. to-day. I judged it advisable to try this mode of communicating with Washington, as I despair of any regular conveyance between Mexico and the United States.

T. C.

Hon. WILLIAM H. SEWARD,
Secretary of State of the United States.

Mr. Seward to Mr. Corwin.

No. 21.]

DEPARTMENT OF STATE,
Washington, September 23, 1861.

SIR: I send you a copy of an extract of a communication from the Mexican minister in Paris to Mr. Romero, Mexican chargé d'affaires at this capital, which has been presented to me by the latter gentleman. Sympathizing with him and with the Mexican republic in the present emergency, I earnestly invoke your assiduous promotion of the negotiation for an assumption of the interest on Mexican bonds, committed to your care by my recent instructions.

I am, sir, your obedient servant,

WILLIAM H. SEWARD.

THOMAS CORWIN, Esq., &c., &c., &c.

[Translation.—Extract.]

No. 44.] LEGATION OF MEXICO,
Paris, September 4, 1861.

Unhappily, I yesterday saw realized the apprehensions which I mentioned to you in my note No. 41, of the date of 31st of August last past. The measures adopted by the governments of France and England, in consequence of the law approved on the 17th July, are openly hostile towards us, and I think you will be informed about them by the time when this despatch will reach your hands.

You already know, by my note referred to, that I could not obtain the audience which I had asked from the minister here for the 21st August, and that he fixed it for yesterday, (Tuesday,) 3d September. I began by saying that I had received from my government special charge and direction to give to that of his Majesty the most ample explanations upon matters which concerned subjects of France, under the new law, by virtue of which the suspension of payment of the national debt was ordered. Mr. de Thouvenel interrupted me, saying that personally he had no cause to be discontented with me; but he could not listen to such explanations. "We will not receive any," he added, giving way to the greatest excitement; "we have entirely approved the conduct of Mr. de Saligny; we have given our orders, in concert with England, that a squadron composed of ships of both nations demand from the Mexican government the satisfaction due, and your government will know through our minister and our admiral what are the demands of France. I have nothing against you," he repeated, "and I wish that events allowed me to address you in more friendly terms." "But it is much to be regretted," said I, in turn, "that such a reply should be given to an application so proper and simple as that which I have just made in the name of my government. But equitable as that may be, after the language you have addressed to me I should not for a moment urge you to listen to me, nor is there any motive for prolonging this conversation;" and I cut it short, withdrawing without delay.

* * * * * * *

I reiterate to you the assurances of my most distinguished consideration.

JUAN ANTONIO DE LA FUENTE.

The MINISTER FOR FOREIGN RELATIONS, Mexico.

Mr. Corwin to Mr. Seward.

[Extract.]

No. 6.] LEGATION OF THE UNITED STATES,
City of Mexico, September 29, 1861.

SIR: As the mail by the British steamer for this month has not yet arrived, I have nothing to communicate further on the subjects pertaining to my duties here than is to be found in my previous despatches.

The reasons for furnishing pecuniary assistance to this country still remain, and are rather strengthened by the expected forcible intervention of both England and France, which seems to be likely to occur now very soon.

All apology for this intervention would be taken away by an arrangement such as I have already repeatedly suggested.

I have as yet received no instructions from the department on this subject, and am, therefore, left only to conjecture as to the views and wishes of the government of the United States on this point. The subject, in my opinion, is one of deep interest to the United States in its present and remote bearing upon the future of the American continent.

* * * * * * * *

Hon. WM. H. SEWARD,
Secretary of State, Washington.

[Exhibit A, accompanying despatch No. 6]

Unofficial.] LEGATION OF THE UNITED STATES OF AMERICA,
Mexico, September 4, 1861.

SIR: Several citizens of the United States during the last week addressed me a note requesting my opinion as to the legality of a tax recently levied by the President on the inhabitants of the federal district. After consideration carefully given to the subject, I have given them an answer, a copy of which is herewith enclosed. I was compelled to the conclusions contained in this paper. I earnestly desired to find the government in the right; but after much reflection I was obliged to differ from it in this instance.

I renew the assurances of my esteem.

THOMAS CORWIN.

His Excellency SEÑOR MANUEL MA. DE ZAMACONA,
Minister of Foreign Relations.

[Exhibit A 2, accompanying despatch No. 6]

LEGATION OF THE UNITED STATES OF AMERICA,
Mexico, August 30, 1861.

GENTLEMEN: I received your note of the 26th instant on the 27th, asking my opinion as to the legality of a tax of one per cent. on the property of all persons residing in the federal district, where the property of such persons amounts to a sum exceeding two thousand dollars. As the mail for the United States was to leave this city on the 29th, I found myself, from the time I received your note until yesterday at two o'clock in the afternoon, occupied incessantly with other indispensable duties. You will accept this as my apology for delaying an answer to your request till now.

The only question which I think it is useful to consider, when determining the duty to pay this tax, may be stated thus: "Is the tax in question imposed by that power to which the constitution and laws of Mexico have given the right to levy taxes?" If this question, by a fair and liberal construction of the constitution, can be answered affirmatively, then it is a lawful tax, and in my judgment should be paid, unless other objections, which in this instance do not occur to my mind, should forbid its payment.

The powers and duties of the present government of Mexico are (happily in my judgment) defined and limited by a written constitution. Every functionary of this government, whether executive, legislative, or judicial, before he enters upon the duties of his office, binds himself, by a solemn oath, to maintain and support the constitution. In other words, he swears that he will exert the powers and discharge the duties of his office in conformity with those rules which are laid down in and by the constitution.

In the 50th article of the constitution now in force, it is declared that "the supreme power of the federation is divided, for its exercise, into legislative, executive, and judicial. Two or more of these powers can never be united in the same person, nor the legislative power be deposited in one individual."

It will be seen that the various functions necessary to carry on this government are divided into three separate departments. It is expressly declared that the powers of no two of these departments shall ever be united in the same person. Article 72, section 7, defines the powers and duties which are imposed upon congress, or the legislative department, as to taxes. It declares that "congress has the power of approving the federal estimates of expenditures, which shall be annually presented by the executive, and of imposing the taxes necessary therefor."

The power to levy taxes upon the people is here (in language which admits of no equivocation in its terms) given expressly to congress. No clause in the constitution gives congress the power to transfer this duty to any other person or to any other department of the government. It is a discretion very liable to abuse, and, when abused, attended with consequences fatal to the rights as well as prosperity of the people. It is therefore a power which, in all governments, free in form and design, is wisely lodged only in the hands of those who directly represent the people, and who, more than any other department of the government, are responsible to the people.

Wherever the legislative power is elected by the people, the taxing power is given to that department. The present constitution of Mexico, as we have seen, has embodied these principles. In this respect it is in harmony with all modern systems of government, where written constitutions prevail on this continent. This trust cannot be delegated to any one, unless such power is given in express terms, which power, as we know, is nowhere to be found in the constitution.

But another question may arise. Has congress, by any law, either intended or pretended to transfer this power? It may be said, and no doubt the president supposed and believed, that this power was delegated by congress to him. I have endeavored to bring my mind, if possible, to agree with this opinion, for I did wish, in the present condition of this republic, to aid rather than oppose the government in raising money to enable it to crush anarchy and restore peace, security, and order. But I am compelled to come to a different conclusion by reasons which appear to me unanswerable.

First. The law whence this power is said to be derived does not give the power when its language is properly construed, whatever may have been the unexpressed intentions of those who enacted it. The law in question was enacted on the 4th day of June, 1861. It reads in these words: "The government is empowered to raise funds in whatever way it may deem proper for the purpose of destroying the reaction."

The wisest judges, when acting upon subjects like this, have adopted a canon of construction which requires that if you can give effect to a law, under a constitution, you shall (if its words will admit of it) so construe it as not to make it violate the constitution. The law in question authorizes and requires the president to raise money in any way he *may* or *can*, to crush the reactionarios. Can the president raise money, by virtue of his executive power, in other ways than by taxation? Undoubtedly he can. By the 72d article, section 8, in the constitution, he can, as president, raise money by loans. Said section declares that congress has the power "of giving the basis upon which the executive may procure *loans* on the faith of the national credit, and of approving said loans, and of recognizing and ordering the payment of the national debt."

In conformity to the rule above stated, we must presume that congress did intend to authorize the president to loan money; for this they might do, and yet not violate the constitution; and that they did not intend, and have not given the power to tax; for this they could not do, as the constitution expressly forbids it. The law must be so construed as to make congress intend to give the president only such power as by the constitution they could give. The power to loan money they could give. The power to tax they could not give. The words "to raise money in any way he may or can," only mean "in any way he, as president, constitutionally can."

Second. But if we admit (which I do not) that the words of the law do give, in express terms, the power to tax, then I reply that such a law is totally void, as it is clear that congress has no power to give such authority. The constitution gives the taxing power to congress. It therefore denies such power to the executive. It is expressly declared that the powers of no two of the three departments—that is, the executive, legislative, and judicial—shall ever be united in any one. If the President is allowed to exert the taxing power, that being by the constitution a power given to the legislative only, then it follows that legislative and executive powers are united in one, which, as we have seen, is expressly forbidden by the constitution, in plain terms. The imposition of this tax is, in my judgment, a void and nugatory act, and therefore no person, either Mexican citizen or foreigner, is bound *by law* to pay it.

I may here add that, in my opinion, every American citizen resident in Mexico, is bound to pay every tax which any Mexican citizen is bound to pay.

The law of nations permits every independent government to legislate touching the property of foreigners as well as citizens within its territorial limits. One of the most accurate and learned treatises, in modern times, on national law, has thus defined this power: "Every independent State is entitled to the exclusive power of legislation in respect to the personal rights and civil state and condition of its citizens, *and in respect to all real and personal property situated within its territory, whether belonging to citizens or aliens.*"—(See Wheaton's International Law, page 112, part 2, chapter 2, section 1.)

The legislative power here given over the property of foreigners has always been considered as including the power to tax the property of foreigners. It has been the constant practice of the United States government, as well as the governments of the separate States, to tax the property of foreigners just as they tax the property of citizens. This power may, however, be limited by treaty. The only treaty stipulation on this subject between the United States and Mexico is to be found in the 9th article of the treaty of 1831, which is now in full force, that treaty having been revived by the treaty of 1848. That article reads as follows: "The citizens of both countries, respectively, shall be exempt from compulsory service in the army or navy; *nor shall they be subjected to any other charges, or contributions, or taxes* than such as are paid by the citizens of the States in which they reside."

This treaty, in my judgment, obliges citizens of Mexico, resident in the United States, to pay in the United States "*all charges, or contributions, or taxes*" which are paid there by the citizens of the United States, and as clearly binds all citizens of the United States, resident in Mexico, to pay all "*charges, or contributions, or taxes*" which are paid here by the citizens of Mexico. If, therefore, a Mexican citizen is bound by law to pay this tax, then, by the treaty of 1831, the American citizen, resident here, is bound to pay it also.

The treaty makes no distinction between *ordinary* and *extraordinary* taxes—between *local* or *general* taxes. I have no doubt that at this moment taxes that may well be termed "extraordinary" are levied, both by the federal and

State governments, in the United States, which operate alike upon the property of the citizens of the United States and Mexicans resident there. But it is not now necessary to consider this point, as, according to the foregoing reasoning, neither Mexican citizens nor foreigners can be *lawfully* required to pay this tax.

I wish here to add, that it is with great reluctance that I am compelled to differ from the Mexican authorities in a point of so much delicacy and importance. I have no doubt but the government has been actuated by the most patriotic motives. Still, I cannot but hope that, in a moment free from the violent excitements which prevail here, and under the influence of which this act has been done, its unbiased judgment will be brought to concur in the general reasons on which I have founded the opinion here expressed.

I am, gentlemen, your obedient servant,

THOMAS CORWIN.

Messrs. BENNETT, LARA, and others.

[Translation.]

NATIONAL PALACE, *September* 5, 1861.

The undersigned has had the honor to receive the note which his excellency the minister of the United States has pleased to send to him, together with a copy of a communication addressed by him to some of his countrymen, resident in Mexico, in relation to the impost decreed on the 27th August last past. The undersigned intends to submit this note, and the document which accompanies it, to the president of the republic, and meantime may communicate to the minister of the United States the conclusions of the chief magistrate of the nation. He has the honor to express to him his satisfaction with the frank and impartial spirit which manifests itself in the said note, which the undersigned appreciates, notwithstanding the difference there may be between the opinions of his excellency the minister of the United States, and those which the government maintains as to the legality of the impost decreed on the 27th of August.

The undersigned does himself honor in repeating to Mr. Corwin the assurances of his consideration.

MANUEL MA. DE ZAMACONA.

His Excellency THOMAS CORWIN,
Minister Plenipotentiary of the United States.

Mr. Seward to Mr. Corwin.

No. 23.]
DEPARTMENT OF STATE,
Washington, October 2, 1861.

SIR: Your despatch of September 7 (No. 5) has been received.

The attention of this government has been already arrested by the threats of the insurgents of this country to invade the northern frontier of Mexico; but at present it seems wisest to oppose to them the necessary resistance nearer home.

You ask, with marked earnestness, whether the United States would agree to pay in money to Mexico at this time any sum, say from five millions to ten millions of dollars, on receiving for it any kind of stipulation that the republic of Mexico might offer?

I feel myself authorized to assure you that the President is as deeply sensible as you yourself confessedly are of the importance of maintaining the integrity and independence of Mexico. He is prepared to adopt the best practicable means to compass that end, so important to the welfare, perhaps to the security, of the United States and to the success of civilization in this country. But it seems to him that a payment or advance to Mexico of such a sum as you suggest is at this time impossible, even if it would be wise, which is a question that I do not now propose to discuss.

We are now necessarily paying out of the treasury near a million a day, rendered necessary for the organization, all of a sudden, of a great army and a considerable navy. We could not hope to satisfy the country that it would be expedient to send five or ten millions of money into Mexico until our own military and naval preparations shall have been perfected and we shall begin to see the insurrectionary movement distinctly recoil or subside.

Again, the proposition to advance all at once to Mexico so large a sum of money, under the circumstances I have mentioned, would, we apprehend, encounter serious opposition in the Senate of the United States, upon the ground not merely of the present inexpediency in regard to our own country, but also on the further ground of probable improvidence on the part of the Mexican government in applying the subsidy.

You suggest, as one of the means by which Mexico might indemnify the United States for any moneys to be advanced by them, an accommodation of the revenue tariff of Mexico, so as to favor our manufactures.

I should not feel myself at liberty to discuss a proposition of that kind at this time. The Congress of the United States, and even the people themselves, are justly jealous of executive attempts to disturb or modify our revenue system at home or to enter into engagements with foreign countries which may have a bearing upon the export trade of our country. If it should be thought wise to institute negotiations of either kind, it would be best to ask the Senate for its advice in the first instance, and not to negotiate a treaty first and afterwards ask the Senate for its ratification.

I am constrained to say that your first proposition on this subject seems to me the most feasible and expedient one, namely, that the United States shall assume the payment of interest for Mexico for a term of years upon a pledge of sufficient Mexican mineral lands and territory. On this subject I see no reason to modify the instructions which I have already given.

We hear indirectly and believe that Spain has proposed to enter into an arrangement with France and Great Britain for sending an armed expedition to Mexico. Acting upon public rumor, to this effect, we have asked the powers concerned to explain the objects of the contemplated expedition.

Thus far, we have no reply, either from Mexico or from Great Britain or from France, to our overtures for an assumption of the interest on Mexican bonds. Such replies, however, must soon be received. When they shall have come I shall be able to write to you more definitely, and I trust more satisfactorily, than I can write now, when the complication of Mexican affairs is understood only on one side, and when we are acting upon conjecture as to the extent of hostilities meditated by the states which claim to have been injured by the government of Mexico.

I am, sir, your obedient servant,

WILLIAM H. SEWARD

THOMAS CORWIN, Esq., &c., &c., &c.

Mr. Seward to Mr. Corwin.

[Confidential.]

No. 28.]
DEPARTMENT OF STATE,
Washington, October 21, 1861.

SIR: I send you a copy of a despatch just received from Mr. Schurz. You will see, without any effort at elucidation upon my part, the importance of his suggestion that the Mexican people shall not be induced to become betrayers of their own independence.

I am, sir, your obedient servant,

WILLIAM H. SEWARD.

THOMAS CORWIN, Esq., &c., &c., &c.

Mr. Corwin to Mr. Seward.

No. 7.]
LEGATION OF THE UNITED STATES OF AMERICA,
Mexico, October 21, 1861.

SIR: Your despatches Nos. 17, 18, and 19, under date of the 2d, 7th, and 12th of September, were received on the 10th instant from Mr. Otterbourg, the lately-appointed consul at this city. I find, on examination, that your despatches Nos. 14, 15, and 16 have never reached me. They are doubtless in the hands of the "secessionists," or the robbers who infest the mail routes to this country on both sea and land. I shall be gratified could copies of these last despatches be forwarded immediately; they may possibly escape the evil fortunes of the originals. Your despatch No. 8, dated June 3, was delivered to me on the 23d instant by Mr. George Ingraham, to whom the department had intrusted it. Mr. Ingraham's vessel was ninety days in making the voyage from Bangor, Maine, to Vera Cruz.

I beg here to repeat the reasons which have induced me heretofore to urge the *absolute necessity* of having the consuls appointed by the present administration to Vera Cruz and Havana at their posts in person. The vice-consul at Havana served several years under Mr. Helm, who, I believe, is now a "secessionist." Mr. Riehen, vice-consul at Vera Cruz, served three or four years at that place under Mr. Pickett, who is now here, and who, I have reason to believe receives his letters from New Orleans and elsewhere through Mr. Riehen, who sends them from Vera Cruz to this place. Of this latter fact I cannot be certain, but I have strong reasons for suspecting its truth. Both these vice-consuls *may* be very faithful to the government, but the facts relating to their former associations seem to me to constitute sufficient cause for the supervision of those who are known to be faithful, and whose duty it is in these critical times to be at the ports assigned them. It is possible the lost despatches, to which I have referred, may have fallen into treacherous hands. I alluded, in my last despatch, to the necessity of having a consul of high qualifications at Matamoras, on the Rio Grande. It is highly important that the government should be in possession of the earliest and most reliable information of the movements of the rebels in that quarter. It is on that frontier that the first attack (if indeed any is ever made) will be made by the rebel forces upon Mexico. Mr. Pickett throws out (as I learn) threats of such a movement soon to be made, and sometimes, as now in the course of execution, as a measure of retaliation upon Mexico for granting to the United States the privilege of marching troops from Guaymas to Arizona. He has actually proposed to recede to Mexico,

Upper California and New Mexico, including Arizona, on condition of free trade between Mexico and the "Confederate States." He has furnished an opposition member of congress here with a copy of his letter to the Mexican secretary of state, who read it in secret session, as the grounds of a violent attack on the administration, bestowing great abuse upon President Juarez and his cabinet for rejecting both Mr. Pickett and his proposition. The opposition orator was merely laughed at, and not complimented even by a reply. This I learned from one who was present, and deeply interested in the subject.

Mr. Pickett has very formally advised the government here that the Confederate States *cannot consent* to the sale or hypothecation of the public lands of Mexico to any government not in amity with them.

The object of these *informal* communications is to prevent any treaty arrangement by Mexico with either the United States or England or France which would relieve Mexico from her embarrassments, and so insure a hostile interference from abroad, which would so weaken the Mexican government as to render the northern states of Mexico an easy prey to filibusters acting in harmony with the rebel troops.

The motives of the secessionists, being thus clearly disclosed, present at once to both the United States government and that of Mexico the obvious policy of strengthening Mexico by an advance of money to her, to enable her to fight the common enemy of both. The public lands of the entire Mexican republic, mortgaged to the United States, as proposed in your dispatch No. ——, will constitute a justifiable reason for our meeting the rebel forces on our own lands in Mexico, where we could unite the troops of both republics against them, and thus draw off their military strength from Texas, so as to enable the Union party of that State and New Mexico to re-establish in both the legitimate government of the United States. I mention these as incidental advantages growing out of the proposed treaty, which may be worth consideration.

In your last despatch I am instructed to enter into an arrangement to pay the interest on the foreign debt of this republic for five years. You estimate this debt at sixty-three millions of dollars. This sum is exactly the principal of the debt due to what are called "English bond-holders." In addition to this there is what is called the "English convention debt," five millions of dollars; the "Spanish convention debt," eight millions of dollars; and the "French convention debt," the exact amount of which I do not know; but it is small, and will be arranged without difficulty, or be paid off out of other funds.

The interest, therefore, on the foreign debt, which must be provided for, to avoid threatened hostility, is as follows:

"Bondholders'" claim	$63,000,000	
At three per cent. per annum		$1,890,000
"English convention debt"	5,000,000	
At six per cent. per annum		300,000
"Spanish convention debt"	8,000,000	
At three per cent. per annum		240,000
Total amount of interest on foreign debt		2,430,000

In your instructions you say: "I am to be understood, moreover, as giving you not specific but general instructions, to be modified as to sums, terms, securities, and other points, as you may find necessary—subject to approval by me."

The British minister here, having been informed by Lord Lyons of the substance of your instructions to me, immediately proposed that the duties on foreign merchandise, heretofore assigned to foreign creditors, should be collected and paid as agreed upon, and that an equivalent amount received from the

THE PRESENT CONDITION OF MEXICO. 33

United States would place the government of Mexico beyond the necessity of suspending this agreement, which suspension had compelled the British government to resort to forcible intervention. In a conference with the British minister and the Mexican authorities this plan was thought advisable, and, acting within the spirit of my instructions, I have offered the following terms to Mexico, to which the Mexican cabinet has assented.

I propose to loan to Mexico five millions of dollars for five years, at six per cent. per annum, to be paid in monthly payments of five hundred thousand dollars—the first payment to be made in one month after the ratification of the treaty by the United States—and to loan at the same rate for five years the sum of $2,000,000 each year for three years, making an aggregate of eleven millions of dollars ($11,000,000) in all; Mexico to file her bonds corresponding to the above payments before the receipt of the money.

If the sum to be paid by the United States had been limited to interest at 3 per cent. on $63,000,000—which was your estimate of the amount—for five years, the aggregate debt would have been nine millions four hundred and fifty thousand dollars, ($9,450,000,) secured by bonds pledging the public lands in Lower California, Chihuahua, Sonora, and Sinaloa. By the modification which I propose, the aggregate debt will be eleven millions of dollars, secured by pledge of the public faith, and also the entire public lands of the republic, and all the national property formerly belonging to the church. The latter, though not exactly ascertained, is, at the lowest estimate, equal to one hundred millions, ($100,000,000.). In the States of Puebla and Mexico alone the amount not restored is known to be worth twenty-seven millions of dollars. This value consists, in the two States mentioned, in bonds and mortgages taken from purchasers who had bought the church property at a rate so very low that none will risk a forfeiture by non-payment, and all will be due in five years, the payments being annual. It is agreed that a board of five persons shall be appointed, to sit in the city of Mexico—three to be appointed by the President of Mexico, and two by the President of the United States—who shall have all the powers of the government to survey and sell the public lands, and grant mineral rights, and to collect the amounts due on church property, and sell what is not disposed of, and keep the funds thus derived separate from the general treasury, and transmit them to the treasury of the United States, at the risk and expense of Mexico, as often as half a million shall be realized. By this arrangement, I have no doubt, the interest due on the proposed $11,000,000 will be punctually paid after the first year, and interest and principal fully paid in the five years. The amount to be paid Mexico by this plan is only increased $1,550,000, while the securities for payment are such as to render the United States government perfectly secure, and in all probability we shall secure a large portion of the money from Mexico before we have paid it out to her, and be able to close the whole within five years.

I know that the British minister has written to the foreign office in London, by this mail, that his arrangement, when ratified by congress, will be every thing the British government can ask. The French government will be satisfied by arrangements in progress here, and in any event the money to be paid by the United States will be in part pledged to the payment of the interest on the Spanish and French debts, which cannot exceed $150,000 per annum. I am fully satisfied that the amount proposed to be paid by the above plan is absolutely necessary to keep the present government on foot for the next three years, and, if any thing can, *that* will enable the Mexican republic to exist under some form of government limited by written constitution. Both the British and American treaties will be submitted to congress here in all of the next two weeks for ratification.

I hope you will approve my course. The absolute necessity for despatch

H. Ex. Doc. 100——3

prevents me from sending you the proposed modifications before acting on them here; but I have shown the minister of foreign relations my instructions, and advised him that no obligation can be relied on by him till your approval and that of the Senate is obtained.

I have already asked leave to visit home. If the proposed treaty is ratified here, nothing of importance can possibly demand my actual presence here for a month or two, and I therefore renew my request to visit my home and family.

Very respectfully,

THOMAS CORWIN.

Hon. WILLIAM H. SEWARD,
Secretary of State, Washington, D. C., U. S. of America.

Mr. Seward to Mr. Corwin.

No. 29.]   DEPARTMENT OF STATE,
                    Washington, November 11, 1861.

SIR: Your despatch of September 29, which bears no number, has been received.

I notice with regret that important communications from me on the subject of Mexican relations with European nations had failed to reach you before your despatch was written. Owing to this circumstance, it would be unprofitable to reply to your suggestions on that subject.

I am not altogether satisfied that you judged wisely, under the circumstances, in the course you pursued in regard to the claims of American citizens to exemption from the taxes imposed by the government of Mexico. It is our desire, we know it is yours, to see the government of Mexico sustain itself in the crisis through which it is passing. Citizens of the United States residing in Mexico ought to bear their proportion of the burdens necessary to the maintenance of the government whose protection they enjoy. The question of the lawfulness of the tax does not arise out of any rights peculiar to themselves, but out of right common to them with all the citizens of the republic of Mexico. It seems to me that Americans, under such circumstances, might well be left to abide the decisions of the Mexican tribunals in the same manner as Mexican themselves must do. But I write with much hesitation on the subject and await further developments of it.

I am, sir, your obedient servant,

WILLIAM H. SEWARD,
By F. W. SEWARD,
Acting Secretary.

THOMAS CORWIN, &c., &c., &c.

Mr. Corwin to Mr. Seward.

No. 8.]   LEGATION OF THE UNITED STATES OF AMERICA,
             Mexico, November 29, 1861.

SIR: I have to acknowledge the receipt, since my last communication of the 29th of October, of the missing despatches Nos. 14 and 15, and also of your other despatches from No. 20 to No. 28, (of October 28,) inclusive. Despatch No. 16 has not been received by me. Since my last despatch (No. 7) Mexican affairs have assumed a very unfavorable aspect. Sir Charles Wyke, the British minister, having arranged with Mr. Zamacona, the minister of foreign affairs of the republic of Mexico, a treaty on the basis mentioned in my communication to you, and which I considered very favorable to Mexico, and this treaty having been submitted to congress, and rejected by a vote of almost two to one, I have withdrawn my propositions for a loan from the United States, understanding from your instructions that this loan was to be made merely with a view to prevent European intervention in the affairs of Mexico. As this treaty has been rejected, I have good reason to believe that England will take possession of the ports of Mexico, with the intention of paying the debts due to her citizens. The fleets of France and Spain, I have no doubt, will co-operate with that of England. What the views of France may be I cannot say. I agree, however, entirely with Mr. Schurz that it is the desire of Spain to regain her dominion over this country, and to establish here a monarchy. Whether the other powers referred to will consent to this you can judge better than I.

In accordance with the instructions contained in your first despatch on this subject, I made an arrangement with the government of Mexico for a loan of five millions of dollars, payable in monthly instalments of one half million per month, and secured by the pledge of all the public lands, mineral rights, and church property. In addition to this I agreed, on behalf of the United States, to make a further loan of four millions of dollars, (making in all nine millions of dollars,) to be paid in sums of one half million every six months, and to be secured in like manner as the five millions. Since the rejection of the English treaty I have not felt at liberty to complete this arrangement, and shall await further instructions. Should the three European powers referred to take possession of the Mexican ports, and then offer to relinquish all claims upon this country in consideration of the payment of the interest upon their debts, and the securing of the payment of the principal, I shall feel at liberty to renew my propositions unless otherwise instructed.

It will be seen that the treaty now proposed reduces the loan from the sum proposed in my last advices from eleven to nine millions. I transmit herewith a copy of the treaty as drawn by myself and submitted to the cabinet here. I have no doubt it will be ratified here if I shall hereafter be authorized to propose it. On this point I ask the favor of instructions as early as possible.

I entertain a confident belief that when the English, French, and Spanish fleets shall arrive at Vera Cruz, and demand and obtain possession of the Mexican ports on the Gulf as well as Pacific frontier, that Mexico will enter into treaties with all these nations, such as was proposed by the lately rejected British treaty. Her national pride is so great that nothing but actual demonstration of her weakness will subdue it.

From the best judgment I can form as to coming events here, I am inclined to the belief that England will unite in taking possession of the ports and appropriate the proceeds of the custom-houses in some way to the payment of the just claims of the three nations, but will not agree to any intervention in the internal concerns of the republic. I think Spain will desire to seize the entire government of Mexico, and re-establish her power here. If France concurs in this, they can accomplish it. If it is attempted by Spain alone, it will ultimately fail. The hatred of the Spanish race is extreme here, and has been so since 1820. The conflict with the church, which has raged for the last three years, has intensified this feeling greatly.

I think the obvious folly of rejecting the British treaty will be corrected by the events of the coming month, at least, in the realization of this hope consists the only peaceful solution of the questions which threaten the destruction of Mexican independence.

I send herewith copies of the late proceedings of a portion of the diplomatic corps here, in their attempt, by the tender of their good offices, to reconcile the differences between France and Mexico. It will be seen that the French ultimatum required the Mexican government to admit French intervention in the Mexican ports, with power to reduce the Mexican tariff. The organic structure of the Mexican government does not admit the delegation of such power; and as far as I could learn from the Mexican secretary for foreign affairs this was the main objection to his unqualified acceptance of the ultimatum. I endeavored to induce the minister of foreign affairs to give his unqualified acceptance, being satisfied that in any arrangement which would follow the French minister would not insist upon a demand of that kind. The fear of being charged with bad faith prevailed over my suggestions, however, and our efforts ended as the papers I send will show.

The government is now making great efforts to embody fifteen thousand men at Vera Cruz to meet the Spanish troops, should they attempt to land.

The British minister, Sir Charles Lennox Wyke, has, in my judgment, conducted himself here with great prudence, good sense, and perfect equity. He has sought to accomplish the object of his mission without resort to force, and his treaty was in all respects equitable and just towards both nations, but the overweening pride of the Mexican congress, not to say folly, in rejecting that treaty has subjected Mexico to the hazard of finding an enemy instead of an ally in Great Britain.

I have been confined to my bed for several days by a violent cold, and was only permitted by my physician to leave it this morning. This I trust may be received by the department as some apology for the want of more extended details in this despatch. This will leave in two hours by the British courier extraordinary, and be sent by the British steamer to Havana. By the obliging courtesy of the British minister, I am enabled to avail myself of *this, the only safe medium of communication with the coast;* all other mails are sacked and robbed of all their valuable contents by the numerous bands of robbers that infest the roads in all directions.

I have the honor to be your obedient servant,

THOMAS CORWIN.

Hon. WM. H. SEWARD,
Secretary of State of the United States of America.

Mr. Seward to Mr. Corwin.

No. 32.]

DEPARTMENT OF STATE,
Washington, December 5. 1861.

SIR: Your despatch of October 29, No. 7, has been received and submitted to the President.

I have delayed replying to it some days for the reason that I hourly expected the answers of the British, French and Spanish governments to our propositions concerning war. These have come at last in the form of the convention mutually concluded by them for hostilities against Mexico, with an invitation to us to join in the convention. I send you a copy of it, together with my reply to that communication.

I infer from your despatch that you will have signed a treaty with the government of Mexico before this time, and without waiting for new or further instructions. I am hoping every day to receive that convention, and though I have only a very imperfect knowledge of the stipulations which it will contain, I willingly hope and am ready to believe that it may find speedy favor with the President and the Senate.

The President thinks that you cannot properly leave Mexico while the hostilities against the republic are going on, and that your presence there will be needful for counsel and possible negotiation between ourselves and the belligerent parties.

You may look for an immediate response from us, with important despatches, by special messenger, after the expected treaty shall be sent to us. Meantime, there seems to be nothing important to be communicated beyond what this paper and the accompanying documents contain.

Some comparatively unimportant matters contained in your despatch will be entertained in a separate paper.

I am, sir, your obedient servant,

WILLIAM H. SEWARD.

THOMAS CORWIN, Esq., &c., &c., &c.

Mr. Corwin to Mr. Seward.

No. 10.]   LEGATION OF THE UNITED STATES OF AMERICA,
Mexico, December 24, 1861.

SIR: I have deemed it necessary to appoint Mr. Plumb a special bearer of despatches at this time. He will take with him an extradition and postal treaty, which I was not sure could reach the United States by any other mode of conveyance. The present position of England and Mexico renders it entirely uncertain whether any mail, except that of the English legation, will be allowed to go on the English steamer, which is at present the only possible means of communication between Vera Cruz and Havana, at which latter place my correspondence is taken up and delivered in New York by the American steamers, which come and go to and from Havana twice a month.

I have heretofore presented to the department the difficulty of communicating with the United States by conveyances so precarious and tedious as those now at command. If the British mail steamer, which is available only once a month, should be withdrawn, or communication through her be prohibited by the government of Mexico, then I know of no practicable mode of communication between this country and the United States at all, unless a mail can be secured from this city to Acapulco, from which last point letters could be taken twice a month to Panama. I have been laboring for the last week to unite with the merchants of this city to subscribe a sufficient sum which, with a small monthly subscription by the American legation, would enable us to employ a *safe* courier, who would go twice a month to Acapulco and back to this place. I am informed by the government here that if such arrangement should be made, it would endeavor, by every means at its command, to render the route safe from the robber bands which have heretofore infested the roads in all directions. I do not think this plan will be carried out without a subscription on my part of at least fifty dollars per month. I must be guided by particular instructions on this point.

If a vessel of the United States, *armed*, could be employed by our government to carry the mail once or twice a month between Vera Cruz and Havana, the *necessity* for establishing a route from this city to Acapulco would cease.

Additional reasons for employing Mr. Plumb as bearer of despatches at this time will appear in my despatch, No. 11, of this date. If I can find it possible to send despatches through the British courier from this place to Vera Cruz, and from thence to Havana by the *British* steamer, I shall duplicate all the papers sent by Mr. Plumb, and send them by that route, so that the information which they contain may be certain to reach the department.

Very respectfully,

THOS. CORWIN.

Hon. WM. H. SEWARD,
Secretary of State of the United States, Washington.

Mr. Corwin to Mr. Seward.

No. 11.]   LEGATION OF THE UNITED STATES OF AMERICA,
Mexico, December 24, 1861.

SIR: Since the date of my despatch No. 8 the event has happened which I have expected for the last seven months. The Spanish fleet has arrived at Vera Cruz and taken possession of that city without firing a single gun. The Mexican population has all been ordered by the government to leave the city, and we hear that all, or nearly all, have obeyed the order. The castle of St. John de Ulloa has been entirely disarmed and the guns taken up to the difficult passes in the mountains, and there mounted, preparatory to the defence of those places should Spanish or allied troops attempt a march upon this city. From fifteen to twenty thousand troops, now under command of General Uraga, are stationed at these points, with orders to resist to the last.

By reading carefully the correspondence of the Spanish commander with the Mexican authorities, you will perceive that no positive declaration of war has been made by Spain, either for herself or in the name of France or England. The French and English legations here both left Mexico, and are now at Vera Cruz. I was told by the British minister when he left that he should repair to Jamaica, at which point he expected further instructions applicable to the present state of affairs. I have seen it stated in the European papers that a consultation of the three powers was to take place at Jamaica before any decided move would be made upon Mexico. The statement of the British minister, as above, confirmed me in the truth of that made by the European press. If I am right in this, then it follows that the advance of Spain upon Vera Cruz has been made without the consent of France or England, and this is to be inferred from the fact that neither the French nor English fleet has yet been heard of in the Gulf. I am quite sure that the British minister here was surprised when he heard of the arrival of the Spanish fleet *alone.*

You will observe that the Spanish commander does not wish to be understood as making *war* on Mexico, but rather holds out the idea that he comes *to collect a debt*, and has seized Vera Cruz as part of the estate of the debtor, and holds it as a pledge, or by virtue of an attachment. The words *prenda pretoria*, which he has borrowed from the "Civil Law," mean, I believe, when translated into our law language, property held in pledge *by a court* to answer to the judgment to be rendered in a pending cause. Whether such a writ, served in such a way, by such an officer, may be a "*casus belli*," or not, may be a question for diplomatic investigation and decision. Hence you will see that President Juarez in his proclamation does not consider the act of the Spanish commander as a declaration of war, and contents himself with saying "he will resist force by force," if it should turn out that Spain under its financial claims covers aggressive designs upon Mexico.

After carefully considering all the facts within my knowledge which tend to throw light upon the real designs of the three powers, I incline to the belief that Spain secretly entertains a wish to prevent a peaceful adjustment between Mexico and either of the three powers, and that France and England, especially the latter, only intend to *extort* from Mexico treaties conformable to their ideas of justice. Spain desires, by war between Mexico and all the three, to effect the reconquest of her lost American colonies. France, as she thinks, would be willing to aid her in this. England, she has reason to believe, would never agree to the establishment of a vice-regal power here, unless upon such conditions as would take away all motives which prompt Spain to such a course. These are only my own inferences from the few facts which I have been able to learn here. The government of the United States, having a more enlarged knowledge of facts and a higher stand point from which to survey the whole field of probabilities, will be able to form its own better conclusions on the subject.

Mr. Plumb, the bearer of this despatch, will pass through Vera Cruz, and be able to learn much of the state of things there which is unknown at this moment to me. I suggest that you have an interview with him. He will be able to explain to you fully the difficulties likely to arise out of the present state of things touching the communications between this country and the United States. I have been told by M. de Saligny (the French minister) that the United States had been requested by France to join the three powers in their present movement. I desire very much to know whether this has been done, and what answer our government gave to this request. If, as I think probable, this intervention shall end in treaties with Spain, France, and England, *giving away a large portion of the revenue of this government to satisfy the claims of interest due on the foreign debt of Mexico*, it will be important that I should know whether I will be at liberty to contract by treaty to loan Mexico the amounts, more or less, named in your previous instructions, with such guarantees of repayment as those contained in the projet I sent with my despatch No. 8. Such a loan will be absolutely necessary to the very existence of government and law in Mexico, should they treat with all the three powers on a basis similar to that adopted in the treaty with Great Britain recently—I will add, madly rejected by the Mexican congress. The present cabinet has full power to sign and *ratify* treaties, and I *know* each member of it is determined on a peaceful adjustment of all their difficulties with all the European powers, if it can be accomplished by any arrangement approaching to justice. I beg immediate instructions on this point.

I have the honor to be your obedient servant,

THOMAS CORWIN.

P. S.—At this time every republic in South America should be represented here. It would weigh against the European scale, which, at present, is quite too heavy here for the safety of American interest. *I beg you will take measures to insure this.* Ecuador, alone, is now represented here. Spain and France, it is to be feared, have a covetous eye on the weak South American republics. They should meet them *here*, where they make their first demonstration.

THOMAS CORWIN.

Hon. WILLIAM H. SEWARD,
Secretary of State of the United States, Washington.

Mr. Doblado to Mr. Seward.

[Translation.]

NATIONAL PALACE, *Mexico, December* 20, 1861.

The undersigned, minister for foreign affairs of Mexico, has the honor to place in the hands of his excellency the minister of the correspondent department for the United States of America copies of the communication which the commander of the Spanish expedition, upon the invasion of this republic, addressed to the governor of the State of Vera Cruz, calling upon him for the surrender of the fortress and castle of Ulloa; and of what this department has despatched to the said governor in reply.

His excellency the Secretary will also find annexed a printed copy of the decree issued by the chief magistrate of the nation, under date of 17th instant, which, besides other provisions contained in it, declares the port of Vera Cruz closed to the foreign and coasting trade; and another of the manifesto which the president has put forth, and a copy of the circular transmitted to the governors of the States of the confederation, calling upon them all for the defence of the national independence.

The undersigned avails of the occasion to proffer to your excellency the assurances of his very distinguished consideration.

MANUEL DOBLADO.

His Excellency the SECRETARY FOR FOREIGN AFFAIRS
of the United States of America.

Mr. Rubalcava to the Governor of Vera Cruz.

[Translation.]

GENERAL HEADQUARTERS OF THE NAVAL FORCES
OF HER CATHOLIC MAJESTY IN THE ANTILLES.

GOVERNOR: The long succession of injuries inflicted upon the government of her Catholic Majesty by that of the Mexican republic; the repeated outrages committed upon Spanish subjects; and the blind obstinacy with which the government of Mexico has constantly refused to give ear to the just reclamations of Spain, always presented with the moderation and decorum proper to a nation so chivalric, have obliged my government to put aside all hope of obtaining through measures of conciliation a satisfactory arrangement of the grave differences existing between both countries. Notwithstanding, the government of her Majesty resolved upon obtaining full reparation of so many outrages, has ordered me to begin my operations by taking possession of the fortress of Vera Cruz and the castle of San Juan de Ulloa, which will be held as an hypothecated security until the government of her Majesty becomes convinced that in future the Spanish nation will be treated with the consideration which is due to it, and that the treaties which may be concluded between the two governments will be religiously observed. Your excellency will communicate to me through the channel of the French consul, charged with the representation of the commercial interests of Spain, within the limit of twenty-four hours, reckoned from the time at which you may receive this communication, whether you are, or not, ready to surrender to me the fortress and the castle, with the understanding that if the response is negative, or if at the expiration of the time fixed I have received no answer, from that moment you can assume that hostilities are begun, for which purpose the Spanish army will be landed. I ought not to hide from you that although I make this intimation to you in the name of Spain alone, in obedience to the instructions I have received, the occupation of the fortress and castle will also serve as guarantees of the rights and claims against the Mexican government which the governments of France and England may have occasion to establish.

It remains to me to set before you that the mission of the Spanish forces in no way affects the internal policy of the country; all opinions will be respected, no censurable act will be done, and from the moment when our troops occupy Vera Cruz the Spanish commanders will answer for the safety of the persons and property of its inhabitants whatever may be their nationality. It belongs to you and the rest of the Mexican authorities to give guarantees to the foreigners until such occupation may take effect, whether it be pacifically or by active force. If Spanish subjects and other foreigners should be persecuted or maltreated the forces which compose this expedition would see themselves under the hard but unavoidable necessity of recurrence to reprisals. I entertain the hope that you, whatever be your decision, will act with the practical wisdom which is to be desired, being yourself convinced that the Spanish troops, always humane, always noble and loyal even towards their enemies, will not take the first step in the way of reprehensible violence even in case of war—will avoid every species of crime, the only result of which would be to render more difficult the arrangement of pending international difficulties.

I avail myself of this opportunity to offer to you the assurances of my consideration.

Steamer "Isabel la Catolica," at the anchorage of Anton Lizardo, 14th December, 1861.

JOAQUIN GUT'Z DE RUBALCAVA.

The GOVERNOR *of the State of Vera Cruz.*

MEXICO, *December* 20, 1861.

True copy.

JUAN DE DIOS ARIAS.

Mr. Doblado to the Governor of Vera Cruz.

DEPARTMENT OF FOREIGN RELATIONS AND OF ADMINISTRATION,
Mexico, December 17, 1861.

The citizen president to whom I made report of the despatch which the commander of the Spanish naval forces addressed to you, and of that which you directed to that chief in reply, orders me to say to you that you must follow punctually the instructions which were given you beforehand for the event that has already occurred, (the open breaking out of hostilities on the part of the subjects of Spain,) and which, in the military service, leaves free action to the commanding general-in-chief of the Mexican army, General Uraga, to operate in his sphere, as he has been already instructed in detail. It would be improper for the government of the republic to address itself to a chief, who, waiving the formalities of the law of nations, begins by calling for the surrender of a fortress.

The war cry spontaneously shouted forth by the nation marks out to the government the course it ought to follow, and it will not be the president who will fall back before a foreign invasion, with the more reason that in this case Mexico does but repel force by force, in the exercise of an incontestable natural right. I also send to you, by superior order, a copy of the decree and circular which I transmit to-day, by express, to the governors of the States, recommending you to second, with the energy and activity which the circumstances demand, the views of the government, by the faithful carrying out of which the president has no doubt the invasion which menaces the destruction of our liberty and of our independence will be repulsed.

Liberty and reform.

DOBLADO.

The GOVERNOR *of the State of Vera Cruz.*

MEXICO, *December* 20, 1861.

A copy.

JUAN DE DIOS ARIAS

Mr. Doblado to the Governors of the Mexican States.

[Circular.]

DEPARTMENT OF FOREIGN RELATIONS,
Mexico, December 18, 1861.

By order of the president, I have the satisfaction to transmit to you, in copy, the despatches exchanged between the commander of the Spanish force at Vera Cruz and the governor of that State, as well as the decree and manifesto which, to-day, the chief magistrate of the republic has deemed proper to issue, that the States may prepare for the defence of independence. After having exhausted the means of pacific accommodation between Spain and Mexico, the government of the republic, strong in the consciousness of right, and sensible to the impulses of public opinion, pronounced for war, accepts that which the Spanish forces have initiated in a manner so unusual, because its right to repel force by force is incontrovertible, and it protests in the presence of the civilized world that all responsibility for future events will fall solely on the government of the Queen of Spain, which has so inconsiderately made its own the unjust pretexts upon which the enemies of Mexican liberty have attempted to speculate. Notwithstanding our intestine divisions, the love of independence, and hatred of the ancient rulers over the country still keep alive, although the latter has been mitigated by the effects of the culture and civilization of the age. The president, in raising the banner of Mexican nationality, does no more than follow the current of public opinion, and has the pleasure to see arrayed around him, on the day of a national contest, the greater part of those Mexicans, who, by reason of political opinions, remained disunited, but have abandoned intestine divisions on the first call of their native country. Although the government has asserted its right to expel from the territory of the republic Spaniards resident therein, it has omitted to do so at present, because it trusts that they, appreciating the generosity with which it treats them, will continue to keep the strict neutrality which their position enjoins upon them. Thus has the president given another proof of the practical wisdom with which he has conducted his foreign relations, establishing, by irrefragable acts, that he is not to blame if those relations have reached the unfortunate state in which they actually exist. The president, therefore, hopes that by giving prompt and strict fulfilment to the decree, of which mention was made in the beginning, you will put on the march, with the least possible delay, the contingent of armed force allotted to you, and that besides you will make use of all the resources of your government to place the State under your worthy command in the imposing attitude which becomes it, by arousing, by all means in your reach, the patriotism of all the inhabitants of such State, that they may assemble together for the common defence, so that if such unfortunate event should occur as the enemy penetrating to the interior, all the inhabitants may rise in one body and oppose with their swords and their courage an invincible barrier to the daring of our invaders. May the recollection of Hidalgo, of Morelos, and of Guerrero, be the rallying point for Mexicans, as well as the flag which waves over the ranks of our army in the hour of battle. All hail our independence. All hail the republic. Liberty and reform.

MANUEL DOBLADO.

The governor of the State of ———.

MEXICO, *December* 23, 1861.

A copy.

JUAN DE DIOS ARIAS.

THE PRESENT CONDITION OF MEXICO. 43

Decree of President Juarez to the Governors of the Mexican States.

DEPARTMENT OF FOREIGN RELATIONS.

The constitutional president of the republic has seen fit to make the decree which follows:

Benito Juarez, constitutional president of the United Mexican States, makes known to the inhabitants thereof:

That the Spanish forces having taken possession of the port of Vera Cruz, and hostilities having by that act broken out between the republic and Spain, in virtue of the full powers with which I am clothed, I have thought proper to decree the following:

ARTICLE 1. The port of Vera Cruz is closed from and after the 14th of the present month to the coasting trade as well as that of the high seas.

ARTICLE 2. Those Mexicans are traitors to their country, and shall be punished as such, who may take up arms and join the Spaniards, or may in any manner favor their cause.

ARTICLE 3. The time which the act of amnesty of the 2d of the present month conceded to dissidents to accept the pardon offered by the government is extended for fifteen days longer; and the grace is extended to all Mexicans, except those who, in the judgment of the government, are not in condition to receive it, for which purpose a habilitation will be made in each special case.

ARTICLE 4. Governors are empowered to dispose of revenues belonging to the general government in their respective States, so that they may, in the shortest time possible, put on the march the contingent of armed force allotted to them by this decree.

ARTICLE 5. The contingent of the States is as follows:

States.	No. of men.	States.	No. of men.
Federal district	3,000	Chihuahua	2,000
Oajaca	3,000	Guerrero	2,000
Juanajuato	3,000	Yucatan	2,000
Galisco	3,000	Tabasco	2,000
Zacatecas	3,000	Aguas Calientes	1,000
San Luis Potosi	3,000	Queretaro	1,000
Mexico	3,000	Colima	1,000
Michoacan	3,000	Chiapas	1,000
Puebla	3,000	Tlaxcala	1,000
Vera Cruz	3,000	Baja California	1,000
Nueva Leon y Coahuila	2,000	Sonora	1,000
Tamaulipas	2,000	Sinaloa	1,000
Durango	2,000		

ARTICLE 6. Without prejudice to the posting of the contingent designated, at the point which will be designated in due season, the governors will call to arms all the national guard which may be disposable, imposing the extraordinary duties which, in their judgment, may seem proper to obtain the resources necessary for the subsistence of such forces.

ARTICLE 7. The Spaniards resident in the country will continue living under the protection of the laws, and those who, abusing the generosity of the government, may aid the invaders shall only be punished in conformity therewith.

Wherefore I order that this be printed, published, and circulated, and be duly executed.

Given at the national palace, in Mexico, the 17th of December, 1861.

BENITO JUAREZ.

To MANUAL DOBLADO,
   Minister for Foreign Relations.

I communicate this to you for its execution and resulting consequences. God and liberty. Mexico, December 17, 1861.

DOBLADO.

To the GOVERNOR OF THE STATE OF ―――.

Proclamation of President Juarez to the Mexicans.

[Translation.]

The constitutional president of the republic to the nation:

MEXICANS: The announcements of the approaching war which was preparing against us in Europe have unhappily begun to be realized. Spanish troops have invaded our territory, our national dignity is wounded, and our independence perhaps endangered. In circumstances so afflictive the government of the republic deems that it discharges one of its principal duties by placing before you the cardinal idea which will be the basis of its policy in the present affair. The interest of all is at stake, and therefore all are under obligation, as faithful sons of Mexico, to contribute their intelligence, their fortune, and their blood to the safe-keeping of the republic. All have equal right to inform themselves of the action and of the policy of the government.

On the 14th of the present month the governor of the State of Vera Cruz received a summons from the commander of the Spanish naval forces to evacuate that port and the fortress of Ulloa, which the same commander announced that he would hold in pledge until the government of the Queen of Spain should be assured that in the future the Spanish nation will be treated with the consideration due to it, and that the treaties which may be concluded between the two governments will, be religiously observed. The Spanish commander also announces that the occupation of the port and castle will serve as a guarantee of the rights and claims against the Mexican government which France and Great Britain may have occasion to establish.

The foundations of this aggression are inexact, to wit: the offences offered to the government of her Catholic Majesty by the government of the republic, and the blind obstinacy with which the government of Mexico has constantly refused to give ear to the just claims of Spain.

The invariable conduct of the Mexican government does not allow the impartial eyes of justice to give assent to such imputations. The Spanish government, since the treaty of peace of 1836, has always been regarded as that of a friendly power, connected with Mexico by means of especial ties, without that, against this truth there can at this day be alleged, as a well-founded objection, the fact of the expulsion of the Spanish ambassador. As the special circumstances of that case are well known, and no less well known is the disposition which the government entertained, and still entertains, to give upon this particular explanations the most rational and proper; reduced, in a few words, to the necessity of excluding from the national territory a foreign functionary, who came decidedly to encourage the principal fosterers of the rebellion against the legitimate authorities of the republic. The government then made use of a right which all nations hold and exercise, and which Spain has on repeated occasions put in force; but manifesting at the same time that that determination in nowise affected the good relations which existed, and which it desired to maintain with the Spanish nation.

The outrages committed against Spanish subjects are not either acts which can be presented in contradiction of the purpose of maintaining the best agreement with that government, because those outrages were only the inevitable consequences of the social revolution which the nation initiated and consummated, in order to extirpate those abuses which had been the perennial causes of its misfortunes—consequences which, in their turn, natives and foreigners have endured without any distinction of their respective nationalities. And if somewhat the greater portion of these mischances has fallen upon Spanish subjects, may not this have arisen from the fact that the number resident in the republic is also larger than that of those of another nationality? May it not have sprung from the fact that the Spaniards, more than any other foreigners, have taken and take sides in our dissensions, in which many of them have displayed a fierce and sanguinary disposition?

Notwithstanding, the various administrations which have succeeded to each other have always listened to the claims of the Spanish legation, and have received with favor those which seemed to be supported by any principle of equity. A long time anterior to the recognition of our independence the Mexican congress made national the debt contracted by the Spanish government, although a great part of its amount had been spent in fighting against that very independence, and another part, no less considerable, was appropriated to the European obligations of the Spanish monarchy. Subsequently the character of agreement was given to the arrangement of Spanish claims; but it being afterwards made apparent that some of the Spanish subjects interested in them, abusing the kind disposition of the government of the republic, presented immense amounts which evidently had not the characteristics required by the convention, the Mexican government took measures, by virtue of which this operation might be set right, reducing them within just and equitable bounds.

For the rest the government has been and is disposed to satisfy all just claims as far as the resources of the nation may permit, well known as they are to the power which is now invading it. All nations, and Spain most especially, have passed through epochs of want and penury, and almost all have had creditors who have waited for better times for their protection. It is only from Mexico that sacrifices are required which are beyond its power.

If the Spanish nation cloaks other designs beneath the financial question, and because of offences which are unfounded, its intentions will soon be known. But the government whose duty it is to prepare the nation for any event, announces, as the basis of its policy, that it does not declare war, but will repel force by force so far as its means of action may permit. That it is disposed to satisfy claims made upon it which are founded in justice and equity, but without accepting conditions that cannot be admitted without offending the dignity of the nation, or calling in question its independence. Mexicans, if such just purposes should not be appreciated; if it should be attempted to humiliate Mexico, to dismember its territory, interfere with its administration and internal policy, or perchance extinguish its nationality, I appeal to your patriotism, and I conjure you that, laying aside the hatreds and enmities to which the diversity of our opinions has given origin, and making sacrifice of your property and your blood, you gather yourselves around the government and in defence of the cause, the greatest and most sacred to men and to nations—the defence of our native land.

Exaggerated and sinister statements by the enemies of Mexico have presented us to the world as rude and degraded.

Let us maintain war with those who provoke us to it, strictly observing the laws and usages established for the benefit of humanity. Let the unarmed enemy, to whom we have granted a generous hospitality, live tranquil and secure under the protection of our laws. Thus shall we repel the calumnies of our enemies, and shall prove ourselves worthy of the liberty and independence which our fathers bequeathed to us.

BENITO JUAREZ.

MEXICO, *December* 18, 1861.

Mr. Seward to Mr. Corwin.

No. 36.]
DEPARTMENT OF STATE,
Washington, January 24, 1862.

Your very interesting despatch of December 24 (No. 11) has been received. You are already aware that the President, early during the present session of Congress, submitted to the Senate your project of a treaty with Mexico, by which provision would be made for a loan to that republic, and asked the Senate's advice upon the subject.

Hitherto the Senate has not acted upon the subject. It is understood that this delay has been made because it was thought desirable to have such information from you of the condition of affairs in Mexico as you should be able to give after the then expected hostilities of the three powers allied against Mexico should be actually begun. A copy of your despatch has been submitted by the President to the Senate, with a request that it would act upon the whole subject at the earliest possible day. Under the circumstances, the President deems it his duty to wait for the Senate's reply, which, of course, must have an important bearing upon the nature of the instructions to be given to you for the regulation of your conduct in the existing emergency. I trust, however, that no long delay will now be found necessary.

I am, sir, your obedient servant,

WILLIAM H. SEWARD.

THOMAS CORWIN, Esq., &c., &c., &c.

Mr. Corwin to Mr. Seward.

No. 13.]
LEGATION OF THE UNITED STATES OF AMERICA,
Mexico, January 12, 1862.

SIR: The last British steamer which arrived at Vera Cruz, the 26th of November, brought nothing from the department to me. Mr. Proctor writes me from Vera Cruz that he was directed to bear to this city important despatches for the legation, but the despatch agent at New York did not furnish them to him, and he went on board the steamer without them.

Under circumstances existing here, this failure is a subject of deep regret. The Spanish fleet, with from seven to ten thousand land troops, are in possession of Vera Cruz, while the French and English forces are hourly expected to join them, making the land forces altogether from fifteen to twenty thousand. If the commissioners, when they arrive, adhere to the avowed objects of the triple treaty, every question pending with either of the three powers will be adjusted without a war. If, as many suspect, there are secret orders to establish a government here under European auspices, then this country is doomed to a long, desultory, and bloody war, and finally to complete subjugation. From all the information in my possession, I incline strongly to the belief that the present European movement will end without war.

All *reliable* means of communication with the United States are entirely cut off. The British courier no longer carries *my* mail to Vera Cruz, or any other. The Mexican mail cannot be relied on, and will probably soon entirely cease to take the mail to the city of Vera Cruz, and Mr. Proctor writes that since the affair of the Trent the British steamer will not carry any mail between Vera Cruz and Havana. I am left, therefore, to find means to write to the department, or not write at all. I send this by a courier (employed by the Prussian minister) who, I learn from Mr. Wagner, will go to Vera Cruz to-morrow. I send to the American consul at Vera Cruz, with instructions to send it, if possible, by the Spanish steamer which goes every week to Havana, at which latter place our consul, I hope, will find some conveyance to New York. I have engaged Captain Stoeker, a brave and honest American, to carry my despatches to Vera Cruz, as often as I deem necessary, at a very moderate compensation, and have yesterday arranged with the president here to allow him to carry letters for the merchants here, at such rates as can be agreed on between him and those who wish to correspond through him. I have some hope that our consul at Vera Cruz will be able to send a mail by the Spanish steamer to Havana. General Gassett, the commander of the Spanish forces, has, so far, been very accommodating towards our consul and people who have been within the district under his control.

I shall duplicate this despatch by Captain Stoeker, who will leave for Vera Cruz on Wednesday, (three days hence,) as it is not *entirely* certain that any courier will reach Vera Cruz safely, and without loss of his mail.

I earnestly entreat that the *important* despatches, said to be left in the hands of the agent at New York, may be forwarded (if this be not already done) at the earliest possible moment.

General Doblado is now secretary of foreign relations, and entertains the best dispositions towards the United States. From all I have yet seen and known of him, I think he is the man for the present times in this country.

I have the honor to be your obedient servant,

THOS. CORWIN.

Hon. WILLIAM H. SEWARD,
Secretary of State of the United States, Washington.

Mr. Corwin to Mr. Seward.

[Extracts.]

No. 14.]   LEGATION OF THE UNITED STATES OF AMERICA,
Mexico, January 26, 1862.

SIR: I have to acknowledge the receipt, on the 19th instant, by means of a special courier from Vera Cruz to the Prussian legation in this city, of your despatches, Nos. 14, 16, 31, 32, and 33; No. 14 enclosing the duplicate of the commission of Marcus Otterbourg, as United States consul at this city, and No. 31 enclosing the commission of Peter Lott, of New Jersey, as United States consul at Tehuantepec.

Since my last despatch nothing of a decided character has been done touching the relations of this republic with Europe. Enough, however, is known to satisfy me that neither of the three powers expect the expedition to result in the establishment of a throne in Mexico. It was thought by many, and I at one time entertained a fear that such was the secret design of Spain. I am now entirely at ease on that point. * * * * * I know further, that the government here were gratified when they received the despatch from the commissioners at Vera Cruz, three days ago. So far everything promises a speedy and safe solution of the present imminent difficulties of Mexico.

The commissioners of the three powers will be in this city by the first of February, and I have little doubt that treaties with them all will soon follow.

I have heretofore informed the department that I had been assured, by both the French and English ministers here, that neither France nor England thought proper to treat directly with the United States for the payment of the interest on their Mexican debt, assigning as a reason that such a course might possibly lead to a disagreement with us, which they very much desired to avoid. Knowing this to be the case, the Mexican government asked me whether, if she gave away her revenue to obtain a peaceful settlement of her European debt, the United States government would lend her a sum equivalent to that proposed to be paid to the European claimants, to wit: three per cent. annually, for five years, on $63,000,000. To this I assented, as being, in my judgment, within the spirit of my instructions. In conformity with these views, I submitted the project of a treaty, a copy of which I transmitted to the department. The entire cabinet were satisfied with that project, in every particular. But I did not deem it proper, under my instructions, to make this treaty until I was assured that England and France were satisfied. The rejection of the British treaty by congress obliged me to withdraw mine for the time. The same treaty, in substance, will now be ratified with England, and I have little doubt, as I have already stated, that similar satisfactory arrangements will be made with France and Spain. When this is done, I shall feel bound, unless instructed to the contrary, to submit a treaty in substance such as I have already sent to the department.

* * * * * * * *

Yours, respectfully,

THOMAS CORWIN.

Hon. W. H. SEWARD,
Secretary of State of the United States.

Mr. Seward to Mr. Corwin.

No. 37.]
DEPARTMENT OF STATE,
Washington, February 15, 1862.

Your despatch of January 26 (No. 14) has been received. The Senate, as I have reason to suppose, is largely occupied with our own domestic affairs, and at the same time is somewhat perplexed by the extraordinary state of affairs in Mexico, and so it has not yet come to any conclusion upon the questions submitted to that body by the President for its advice. Under these circumstances, it seems to me best that if the occasion shall offer for Mexico to make a treaty with her invaders, and if Mexico shall at the same time and with a view to her aid in that emergency, apply to you for some financial aid from the United States, then you shall exercise your best discretion in making a treaty which will be useful to her and as little embarrassing to our own country as possible, and send the treaty here without delay for the consideration of this government.

There are, however, very unmistakable indications that the Senate will require two things in any treaty you may negotiate, namely: 1st. That the aid to be rendered to Mexico shall be in the form of an assumption of payment of interest. 2d. That the aid so rendered shall be guaranteed to be effectual in securing Mexico a release from all her complications with the allies now making war upon her.

THE PRESENT CONDITION OF MEXICO. 49

This seems to be your own view of the subject, and it meets the President's approval.

The views you express concerning a probable escape of the Mexican republic from the embarrassments which surround it, without the loss of independence, are full of interest, and we hope that they may be justified by events.

Desirous to act in good faith with the allies now invading Mexico, as well as with Mexico, and believing that such a course on our part will result beneficially to Mexico, I have informally communicated the general effect of these instructions to the governments of Spain, Great Britain, and France, as you will of course make them known to the president of the Mexican republic.

The consul at Minatitlan had been replaced before your despatch was received.

I am, sir, your obedient servant,
WILLIAM H. SEWARD.

THOMAS CORWIN, Esq., &c., &c., &c.

Mr. Seward to Mr. Corwin.

No. 40.] DEPARTMENT OF STATE,
Washington, February 28, 1862.

SIR: I enclose to you a copy of a resolution of the Senate of the 25th instant relative to your negotiations with the government of Mexico. You will consider your instructions upon the subject referred to modified by this resolution, and will govern your course accordingly.

I am, sir, your obedient servant,
WILLIAM H. SEWARD.

THOMAS CORWIN, Esq., &c., &c., &c.

IN EXECUTIVE SESSION.

SENATE OF THE UNITED STATES,
February 25, 1862.

Resolved, That in reply to the two several messages of the President with regard to a treaty with Mexico, the Senate expresses the opinion that it is not advisable to negotiate a treaty that will require the United States to assume any portion of the principal or interest of the debt of Mexico, or that will require the concurrence of European powers.

Attest: J. W. FORNEY, *Secretary.*

Mr. Corwin to Mr. Seward.

[Extract.]

No. 16.] LEGATION OF THE UNITED STATES OF AMERICA,
Mexico, February 18, 1862.

SIR: *   *   *   *   *   *   *   *   *

I have deemed it my duty to keep the United States government advised of events here as promptly as possible, until the results of the present intervention shall fully appear. Nothing has, as yet, transpired between the intervening powers and Mexico to enable me to say, with certainty, whether war will or will not be waged by the three powers as a means of enforcing their claims against Mexico.

H. Ex. Doc. 100——4

Mr. Doblado, the minister of foreign relations, left here on Friday morning (the 14th instant) to meet the foreign commissioners at Soledad, a small village about thirty miles from Vera Cruz. The object of this meeting is to agree, if possible, on certain points preliminary to treaties settling the claims of each power. In a conference with Mr. Doblado the night before his departure, he informed me that the points he should insist on were :

First. The recognition by each and all of the three powers of the present government of Mexico.

Second. A pledge not in any event to attempt a dismemberment of the present territory of Mexico.

Third. A pledge not to interfere in the domestic government of Mexico, or make any effort to change the existing fundamental laws of the republic.

These propositions seem to me to embody precisely the engagements entered into by these powers with each other in the treaty which has been published by themselves; and if there be no secret understanding behind the treaty, I doubt not Mr. Doblado will succeed in securing the proposed preliminary arrangement. If he fails in this, however, hostilities are inevitable. Should these points be satisfactorily arranged, then no difficulty can arise except such as may grow out of the details to be adjusted as to the amounts due to each of the intervening powers, and the securities to be given by Mexico for their future payment. The amounts may, I think, be easily and fairly adjusted, but the security for the payment of present dues and future interest will be more difficult of adjustment.

The only security acceptable to any of the claimants is a mortgage on the revenues from imposts. To make this security such as will no doubt be earnestly insisted on, Mexico will be required to surrender, for a limited period, a very great proportion of this class of her revenues, which she cannot do without imminent danger to her internal peace, unless the United States will step in and make her the loan proposed in the proposed treaty, a copy of which I have heretofore transmitted for the criticism of the government at Washington. If the parties here shall not agree as to the securities to be received by each, and Mexico shall not be able to give what is demanded for want of the loan proposed by us, then war may ensue, and the subjugation of this country to European domination may and (in such case) probably will be the result.

In the project of the treaty which I forwarded to the department, I had strict regard as to the whole amount, to the sum named in my instructions, that is the payment of the interest at three per cent. on sixty-three millions for five years, making a total of nine millions four hundred and fifty thousand dollars, to be secured on the public lands in four of the States of Mexico. In the treaty I proposed, about the same amount would be loaned to Mexico, payable in instalments, so as to answer the exigencies of the government here, and at the same time secure both governments against any prodigality in the use of this loan, whilst the security given for it included all the public lands and mineral rights in the whole republic, as also the entire unadministered national property, called the "church property," estimated here at not less than twenty millions. To secure the faithful appropriation of this security to the payment of interest and principal of the loan, a mixed commission to administer and apply properly the proceeds of these two funds was provided. In order not to distress the United States treasury, I insisted on the option to advance this loan in cash, or in bonds at par, bearing an interest of six per cent., believing, as I then did and do now, that the proceeds of the lands, mineral rights, and church property would, after the first year, either pay the *cash* to be advanced, or, if the government chose to advance the loan in bonds, to take up these bonds as fast as issued. In the meantime I further provided that Mexican bonds should be deposited in the treasury, equivalent in amount to each advance by our government, bearing six per cent. interest, which, if the funds provided to take them up should be as available, as I believe they would, for their redemption, would readily sell in the market at par, so that if the entire arrangement should be faithfully carried out, the proposed loan could operate no injury to our national credit, whilst the great end in view, the security of the national life of Mexico, would be attained. I am thus particular in stating the points of interest in the treaty I proposed, because I wish the government to see that I have kept in view the substance of my instructions, and because I am sure the time is approaching when we may be obliged to do in substance what we first proposed, that is, to pay the interest on the sum stated above, or abandon Mexico to such a fate as the three powers, now here in force, shall choose to award her. The prompt and friendly manner in which the government here granted us the right to march troops and convey provisions and munitions of war over her territory, to aid in quelling the rebellion on our frontier, contiguous to hers, furnishes, I think, a strong motive to a return of this generous act. Such has been the conduct of this government towards the commissioner of the "Confederate States," that Mr. Pickett recently sent here, from Vera Cruz, a letter which, I am informed, was so abusive in its terms that it was forthwith returned without a reply.

* * * * * * *

I am, very respectfully, your obedient servant,

THOS. CORWIN.

Hon. WILLIAM H. SEWARD,
Secretary of State of the United States, Washington.

Mr. Seward to Mr. Corwin.

No. 43.]
DEPARTMENT OF STATE,
Washington, April 3, 1862.

SIR: Your very interesting despatch of February 28 has been received. You have already been informed that the Senate advised the President adversely to the projected treaty with Mexico, in both of the forms in which it was submitted to them. Under these circumstances the President is unable to suggest to you any other mode for contributing to the deliverance of our sister republic from the embarrassments by which she is surrounded which would be acceptable to the Senate.

The House of Representatives has called for the papers relating to the case, and we may perhaps find some plan for rendering assistance not incompatible with the rights of other parties in the debates which the report from this department may elicit.

Meantime I desire to direct your most earnest attention to the necessity of guarding, if possible, against any such pledge of the resources of Mexico to foreign powers as might affect our cause injuriously, or impair the ability of the people of Mexico to sustain the free government established by their own choice.

You will not leave the government of Mexico in doubt for a moment that the government and people of the United States are indifferent concerning the perils by which they are menaced.

I am, sir, your obedient servant,

WILLIAM H. SEWARD.

THOMAS CORWIN, Esq., &c., &c., &c.

Mr. Romero to Mr. Seward.

[Translation.]

MEXICAN LEGATION IN THE UNITED STATES OF AMERICA,
Washington, September 21, 1861.

Mr. SECRETARY: I have the honor to transmit to you the copies, which are mentioned in the enclosed index, of the documents to which I referred in the conference with which you favored me this morning, and in those held on previous days, relative to the attitude that the ministers of France and England, residing in Mexico, and their respective governments have taken towards that republic.

I avail myself of this opportunity to renew to you, sir, the assurances of my very distinguished consideration.

M. ROMERO.

Hon. WILLIAM H. SEWARD, &c., &c., &c.

[Translation.]

MEXICAN LEGATION IN THE UNITED STATES OF AMERICA.

Index of the documents which, on this date, this legation transmits to the Department of State of the United States in regard to the suspension of relations by the French and English ministers residing in Mexico with the government of that republic.

No.	From whom and to whom.	Date.	Contents.
		1861.	
1	Mr. Zamacona to Mr. Romero	July 29	Instructions.
2	Mr. Zamacona to Mr. Fuente	....do....	Do.
3	....	July 17	Law of suspension of payments.—(See British Parliamentary Document.)
4	....	July 18	Circular explanation of said law, containing the programme of the new cabinet.
5	Sir Chas. Wyke to Mr. Zamacona.	July 19	Asking if the law was authentic which had appeared in the newspapers.—(See British Parliamentary Document.)
6	Mr. de Saligny to Mr. Zamacona.	July 20	Do. do.
7	Mr. Zamacona to Sir C. Wyke and to Mr. de Saligny.	July 21	Enclosing copy of the law, and explaining its contents.
8	Mr. Zamacona to Mr. de Saligny.	....do....	In reply to the note as to whether the law was authentic.
9	Mr. Zamacona to Sir C. Wyke	....do....	In reply to the note as to whether the law was authentic.—(See British Parliamentary Document.)
10	Sir C. Wyke to Mr. Zamacona	July 22	In reply to note No. 9.—(See British Parliamentary Document.)
11	Same to same	July 23	Asking the repeal of the law of the 17th of July within 48 hours.—(See British Parliamentary Document.)

THE PRESENT CONDITION OF MEXICO. 53

Index of documents—Continued.

No.	From whom and to whom.	Date.	Contents.
		1861.	
12	Mr. de Saligny to Mr. Zamacona.	July 23	In reply to note No 7.
13	Same to same................	July 24	Asking the repeal of the law within 24 hours.
14	Mr. Zamacona to Mr. de Saligny.	July 25	Saying that only the congress can repeal the law.
15	Mr. Zamacona to Sir C. Wyke...	....do....	Saying that only the congress can repeal the law.—(See British Parliamentary Document.)
16	Mr. de Saligny to Mr. Zamacona.	....do....	Cutting off relations.
17	Mr. Zamacona to Mr. de Saligny.	....do....	In reply to No. 16.
18	Sir C. Wyke to Mr. Zamacona...	....do.,..	Suspending relations.—(See British Parliamentary Document.)
19	Mr Zamacona to Sir C. Wyke...	....do....	In reply to No. 18 —(See British Parliamentary Document.)
20	Sir C. Wyke to Mr. Zamacona...	July 26	In reply to No. 19.—(See British Parliamentary Document.)
21	Mr. Zamacona to Sir C. Wyke...	July 27	In reply to No. 20.—(See British Parliamentary Document.)
22	Mr. de Saligny to Mr. Zamacona.	July 26	In reply to Nos. 14 and 17.
23	Mr. Zamacona to Mr. de Saligny.	July 27	In reply to No. 22.
24	Mr. Zamacona to Mr. Romero...	Aug. 29	Instructions.
25	Mr. Zamacona to Mr. Fuente....	....do....	Do.
26	Mr. Fuente to Mr. Romero......	Sept. 5	Informing him of the determination of the French government.
27	Mr. Fuente to Mr. Zamacona....	Sept. 4	Interview with Mr. de Thouvenel.
28	Mr. Fuente to Mr. Thouvenel...	....do....	Suspending relations.

WASHINGTON, *September* 21, 1861.

No. 1.

[Translation.—Extract.]

MEXICAN REPUBLIC, MINISTRY OF FOREIGN RELATIONS.

No. 32.]   NATIONAL PALACE, *Mexico, July* 29, 1861.

The copy which I enclose to you of the instructions that on this date are transmitted to the plenipotentiary of the republic at Paris will acquaint you with the present state of the diplomatic relations of this government with the representatives of France and England. You will notice that these instructions have principally two objects: to rectify the inexact reports which the two functionaries mentioned will make to their governments in regard to the political situation of Mexico and the character of the measures recently adopted, and to facilitate the success of the labors which will be undertaken by our representative at Paris, so that they may be seconded by the diplomacy of friendly nations. For a favorable result to these two objects your services may be very useful in your sphere of action, since there are within it springs which may be applied to the prosperous termination of our efforts in Europe; and there are also means by which the question to which the decree of the 17th instant has given rise may not be rendered unnatural to the view of friendly nations. Some documents accompany this note, whose publicity in the country where you are would be very proper, and a copy of the correspondence which this department has lately had with the English and French legations also accompanies it. Although

a copy of this correspondence has been furnished to Mr. Corwin, and I suppose that he will transmit it to his government, it would be proper for you to procure a conference with the Secretary of State, and to give him an idea of the diplomatic question which has just arisen in Mexico, by showing him the documents in relation thereto and making to him the appropriate explanations. * *
* * * * * * * *

In addition to which, it is excusable to recommend to you to cultivate with care the sympathies of the government near which you reside, and to strengthen in it a conviction in regard to the similarity of interests which, in questions with the powers of Europe, binds Mexico and the United States to each other.
* * * * * * * *

I reiterate to you the assurances of my respectful consideration.

MANUEL M. DE ZAMACONA.

THE CHARGE D'AFFAIRS OF THE MEXICAN REPUBLIC,
at Washington.

WASHINGTON, *September* 21, 1861.

A true copy.

ROMERO.

No. 2.

[Translation.—Extract.]

MEXICAN REPUBLIC, MINISTRY OF FOREIGN RELATIONS.

Instructions addressed to his excellency Señor Don Juan Antonio de la Fuente, minister plenipotentiary of Mexico at Paris.

The decree of the 17th of July and the circular accompanying these instructions will acquaint Mr. Fuente with the measures by which the new ministry formed on the 13th of the same month has deemed it its duty to begin the administrative reorganization of the republic. The necessity for temporarily suspending payments, and for giving unity and regularity to the national debt, has been felt not only by the government, but by the whole country; and hence it happened that the idea which had been broached at the time that the government resided at Vera Cruz was proposed at the beginning of the year by the press of the capital, and was recognized as so proper that several writers disputed with each other as to the originality of the proposition. While this was going on in the discussions of the press, Mr. de Saligny confidentially began them with the minister of relations by offering him, although in exchange for important condescensions, to afford to the republic not only a truce for the payment, but even a relief as regarded the most important of the debts due to France.

The great extremities in which the government has found itself, through the necessity of undertaking a campaign on a grand scale against the reaction, have compelled it to reflect on all the means suitable for affording it resources; and, as one of them, it proposed in the congress, at the close of May, the suspension of all payments, including that arising from diplomatic conventions. The chamber recoiled at that time from the idea of interrupting the fulfilment of international compacts, and only voted for the suspension of other ordinary payments, and ample authority to the government to provide resources for itself.

The public situation at that period had rendered this very difficult. The reactionary bands, concentrated under the command of Marquez, had gathered in the valley and state of Mexico, and the public mistrust and the paralyzation of all business concerns rendered very difficult to the government expedients for obtaining resources. There was, therefore, no other salvation for society and public order but by employing its authority in extreme and hateful measures, which extended to the imprisonment of the leading capitalists, for the purpose of compelling them to make heavy exhibits. The reaction, meanwhile, braced up by some small triumphs, threatened at a short distance even the capital of the republic, whose suburbs some of its small lurking bands succeeded in penetrating.

The government, of its own impulse, and on account of public opinion, which was strongly excited, had to put in motion numerous forces in pursuit of the rebels, and to organize the national guard of the district, in order to take into the field the garrisons of regular troops. The costly expenses of equipping and setting in motion the forces, and of arming the national guard, absorbed enormous sums, and this at a time when the ordinary resources of the government were uncollectible, and the chief part of them absorbed by the appropriations for the payment of the foreign debt. The character of the political situation rendered unavailable, also, the revenues from nationalization, the amount of which is in proportion to the probabilities of consolidation which are offered by the reform.

The enemies of this government, meanwhile, do not confine themselves to devastating the richest and most populous districts of the republic, while organized into numerous movable bands, but bring into play very ramified machinations, one of which is to involve in their influences the diplomatic representatives. This was very easy with respect to the one from the French empire, who, having inherited the relations of Mr. Gabriac, keeping in his own house several personages of the reaction, and interested, as is asserted, in the success of some of the business engagements entered into with the usurpers of the public authority, had many points of contact and many affinities with the persons who personified at the capital the retrograde principle. Hence it has happened that within the last few months all the embarrassments which ill will could suggest have been stirred up against the government, and that the attempt has been successful in having his views innocently seconded by the minister of England, who, although without any sufficient cause, is found involved in a political atmosphere rather uncongenial to the principles which this government is developing. In order to render the minister of England an instrument to the views of Mr. Saligny and of the reactionary party, it has been sufficient to strongly imbue him with prejudices in regard to what is called the anarchical character of the progresista party, and to the propriety of a system of compromise which he thinks suitable for giving stability to liberal institutions. Seeing the policy of Mexico through the deceitful prism of the society which forms around the two diplomatists an exceptional and eccentric minority, both predict the inevitable advent of a neutral party, which in reality does not exist in the republic; and not seeing beyond the capital, they do not take into account the interests which the reform has established over the whole surface of the nation, nor the tenacity of the states in maintaining certain principles, nor the promptitude with which they unite and harmonize when they believe these principles to be attacked.

Be this as it may, under the inspiration of that erroneous policy and of the interests before mentioned, the two ministers referred to have maintained within the last two months an attitude rather unfriendly towards the government, and their bad disposition has even had the effect to defeat an arrangement which had recently been made with the parties interested in the English and French conventions, by appropriating to them the revenues from nationalization.

At the middle of this month the situation of the government had become exceedingly difficult. Its exertions to place considerable forces in the field had exhausted its resources. A long ministerial crisis, which kept the cabinet incomplete, rendered languid the action of the government. The pressure of the public spirit and of the congress, which demanded, not without reason, movement and activity, was very strong; and the president, in conjunction with the members with whom he completed at last his ministry, comprehended that the time had arrived for setting about the administrative reform with firmness and resolution, as the only means of re-establishing the prestige of the revolution, and of providing the government with the elements necessary for restoring to the country the peace and security which it has so long needed.

Under the influence of this determination, a proposition, expressed, with very little variation, in the same terms as the decree of the 17th, annexed to these instructions, was drawn up and presented to the congress on the same day (July 13) on which the cabinet was completed. Before the proposition was perfected there was no failure to discuss the propriety of preparing for the suspension of payments on diplomatic ground. But two considerations inclined opinions to the opposite extreme. In the first place, the recent conduct of the ministers, most especially that of Mr. Saligny, led to the presumption that, instead of condescension and prudence on their part, there would be resistance and impediments, created purposely, and that, in case of the measure having finally to be carried into effect, they might give to it a most aggressive and shameful character. On the other hand, the circumstances in which the government was found on the 13th day of July were extreme. The resources with which it had fitted out General Gonzalez Ortega for the field—thanks to forced exactions imposed on many capitalists—gave out on the 15th day of the same month, and the troops of the government, who pursued the reactionary masses in their course to the south, would have had at least to remain immovable, and to abandon Cuernavaca and the neighboring towns, no less than the federal district and State of Mexico, to the depredations and atrocities of the rebels. The subsidies obtained by force and by imprisonment could no longer be depended on; and the government had no other reliance for preventing the catastrophies and anarchy which were threatening the most interesting portion of the republic than the funds existing in Mexico and in Vera Cruz, intended for the payment of the foreign debt. A momentary seizure of them would have produced a like alarm, and would leave the government in the same complications, and deprive it of the excuse which is afforded it by the purpose determined on of attacking the radical arrangement of the treasury and of the public debt. The government believed that it ought not to lose a moment in proceeding to that reform which was the complement of all the others, and that the idea of putting order in the administration, and of re-establishing legal boundaries between the financial powers of the confederacy and of the States, had arrived at such a seasonable juncture that it should not delay one moment in carrying it into practical operation. The government was not deceived. The national representation—a faithful expression of all liberal shades of opinion—carried the proposition of the executive by a vote of one hundred and two against four. The government had resources; it was able to provide General Ortega with them, and to reduce the rebels to the extreme condition in which they are now placed at the south, dwindled down to an insignificant number, and surrounded by the constitutional forces in a district which is hostile to them, and where it is probable they will be brought to an end by desertion and the want of resources. The government has been enabled to breathe, and to devote itself immediately to the arrangement of the offices and to the formation of the estimates, which will be published next week.

The present minister of relations, immediately after going into the cabinet, entered into frank and confidential relations with all the diplomatic representatives, especially with those of France and England, but without speaking to them concerning the proposition which was under discussion in the congress, although it was a public matter. As soon as the decree was communicated by the department of the treasury to the department of relations, the minister of this department proceeded to have a confidential talk with Messrs. Wyke and Saligny before communicating to them by official letter the suspension of payments which had been decreed. The minister of relations reached the English legation at the moment in which Mr. Wyke had just sent him a communication expressing surprise that the decree should have been promulgated without giving him previous notice. In regard to Mr. de Saligny, the minister of relations found him shut up, and preparing, probably, the communication which he soon afterwards addressed to him, to the same effect. By means first of a visiting card, and then of a brief note, the minister of state made known to Mr. de Saligny that he desired to have a private conference with him before communicating to him officially the decree in regard to the suspension of payments. This conference took place on the following day after Mr. de Saligny had on the evening previous sent an official expression of surprise in the same terms as that which had been sent by the English minister. In the conference with the minister of France, he began by laying down, as a question preliminary to all others, the delivery, which he had claimed for some days back, of the funds proceeding from the Penaud convention, which had been deposited in the depository of the provident fund. The correspondence relative to this affair, copies of which are transmitted to Mr. Fuente, will sufficiently enlighten him on the matter; but it should be added that Mr. de Saligny, feigning not to understand the true reasons which have prevented the delivery of that fund, claims it by alleging a verbal promise which he says was made to him by the minister, Mr. Guzman, and even by Mr. Juarez, and by attaching importance to an order which he asserts that he obtained from Mr. Zarco. Mr. Guzman and Mr. Juarez deny having ever made such a promise, and they protest that they merely promised the replacement in the depository of the provident fund of the Penand money, which on a day of urgency had been temporarily withdrawn. As to the order of Mr. Zarco, there is no evidence of it in the department, and the present secretary of relations promised Mr. Saligny that, in case that order should be shown, the funds which he claimed would be delivered to him, and would not be included in the suspended payments.

This took place at the conference which has been referred to, between the minister of relations and Mr. de Saligny, before the suspension was communicated officially to the latter, and the French minister left it to be understood in that conference that, on this preliminary question being adjusted, it would not be impossible to enter into colloquy in regard to the other points respecting the debt to France, and repeated the intimations which he had already given to Mr. Zarco, in regard to the need of Mexico for a breathing spell in order to pay her debt, and to the strong disposition which he, Mr. Saligny, had previously had to second the government in this respect.

The day on which this conference took place was a holiday, and on the following day there was a dissension in the government relative to the delivery of the Penaud fund, it being taken for granted that the decree in regard to the suspension of payments had already been communicated to the English and French legations on the preceding evening. When the secretary of relations was preparing to make known to the minister of France the terms on which the delivery of the thirty-nine thousand dollars proceeding from the Penaud convention could be arranged, the insulting and threatening reply of Mr. de Saligny to the first note which the department of relations had addressed to him was received, and the character of that reply at once rendered all cordial understanding impossible. That reply was followed by others which Mr. Fuente will find in the correspondence, of which a copy is transmitted to him, and which terminated in the suspension of official relations between the two legations and the government, and in the exchange of private notes, of which copies are also transmitted.

In this correspondence Mr. Fuente will find disclosed the principles which justify the conduct of the government as regards the suspension of the diplomatic conventions. It not having been possible to adjust this question in a reasonable way with the representatives of France and England in Mexico, the direct efforts which are being made for this purpose near the governments of those two countries assume a great importance; and the government of Mexico, on seeing this necessity spring up, has had occasion to congratulate itself on the suitable choice which it has made, of Mr. Fuente, to represent it in France at a juncture like the present, when so much is expected of his proverbial patriotism and intelligence.

The government, being in need of a representative at London, and it not being possible for it to send one with the promptitude which this case demands, has gone so far as to expect from the condescension of Mr. Fuente that, in addition to his present important functions, he will accept those of envoy extraordinary and minister plenipotentiary ad interim at London, especially accredited for the adjustment of the question to which the decree of the 17th of July has given rise. The government earnestly desires that Mr. Fuente may be able to make the personal fulfilment of this trust compatible with the duties which he is discharging at Paris, and which now have an important application to the efforts that the suspension of payment under the French convention renders necessary near the government of the Emperor. * * * *
* * * * * * * * * *

The preliminaries relative to what is personal in the matter being thus arranged, the following suggestions in regard to the steps which are rendered necessary in France and England, in the present state of the relations of Mexico with those two countries, have been deemed appropriate.

First of all, it is important to modify the impression which may be made on the governments of England and France by the adulterated reports that their legations will transmit by this packet. In regard to this matter, the English and French ministers, but more especially the latter, besides picturing to their governments the suspension of payments in the hues of an actual spoliation, will endeavor to misrepresent the other provisions of order and economy which are contained in the decree of the 17th of July, and to weaken the confidence which the new system might inspire with respect to the Mexican government.

The two ministers, whose estimates in regard to the condition of the country are singularly inaccurate, will assuredly say to their governments, for they say so even here, that the liberal party in Mexico is incapable of governing and administering the republic; that there are symptoms of dissolution in the existing government; and that the early advent of some entity which shall personify compromise and the principle of order is inevitable. To Mr. Fuente, who fortunately knows so well the policy of Mexico, it is not necessary to point out how artificial, unsubstantial, and impracticable is this policy of compromise which was imposed by the *coup d'état* of 1857 and the events of Christmas, 1858, nor to say that the interests which have been created by the reform and the aspirations of the states which maintained the revolution for three years and made it triumph over colossal resistance form an insuperable obstacle to its development.

They will likewise exaggerate the extortions and atrocities of which they may imagine the foreign residents in Mexico to be victims. Mr. Fuente must know that the government has hastened to afford reparation for damages which may have been occasioned to a few foreigners by the seizures of property for public use which have taken place during the late period; and that the assassination of Mr. Beale, an English subject, which occurred at Napoles, and what a few foreigners may have suffered in their persons, are the work of the reaction, which atrocities the government is very anxious to put an end to, in providing itself with the necessary means of action.

Mr. Fuente will try to correct the exaggerated idea which will not fail to be transmitted to Europe in regard to what is called the squandering of the national estates. Mr. Fuente is very well aware of the depreciation which these have suffered during the three years of the revolution; the considerable portion of the debt which, agreeably to law, has been extinguished with them; the deductions which it has been requisite to make in order to obtain some redemptions for cash, and which in the federal district alone and in two other dioceses amounted to ten millions of dollars; and the existing rates for the payment of the public debt contained in the new decree. If Mr. Fuente deems it opportune, he can call attention to the circumstance that the men who have called loudest in the press for purity in operations of nationalization are exactly those who now form part of the ministry, and can remark that to obstruct now their reparatory action would be equivalent to obstructing the correction of the abuse in the name of the abuse itself. The representative of Mexico should bear in mind that the French residents in the republic are those who have gathered the best fruits of nationalization, and that at this time, beginning with some of the rich bankers of the capital, they deplore the conduct of the French minister, and are even talking of drawing up a representation against him if the complications which he is exciting on purpose are increased.

It should not be forgotten that, in order to have him do this, Mr. de Saligny is moved by the influences of the clerical party, some of whose members are yet sheltered in the French legation, and keep up a regular correspondence with Marquez and other leading rebels.

It is of great importance that a correct idea should be formed in Europe of what the reaction in Mexico is, of its absolute want of political tendency, and of the hateful excesses to which it has abandoned itself, among which figure a series of assassinations that, though committed on obscure persons, are not less odious than that of Mr. Ocampo.

It would conduce also to the object of these instructions if the position in which this government was placed at the middle of this month were well understood, and how its purpose to provide means of action under every event has been the salvation of the capital and of the neighboring States, threatened with an inundation in which nobody would have suffered so much as the foreigners, who are the especial object of hatred to the clerical party.

No more than justice will be done to the government; but it is very important that it should be done, if the sovereigns of Europe are convinced of the firm and decided purpose which animates the present administration of the republic to shun the inveterate abuses which have rendered political revolutions in Mexico barren. It is important to place strongly in relief the spirit of order and morality which preceded the promulgation of the decree of the 17th, as well as to vindicate the decree against those who ascribe to it despoiling tendencies. It is very proper to call attention to the character of the institution created under the name of the *Treasury Board*. In the appointment of its members (the approval of whom is pending in the congress) the government has disregarded political shades, and has only sought integrity and business talent. In the hands of this board the revenues of nationalization will not be barren; and since among them there are many bills which have reached maturity, and capitals of chaplaincies which will mature in a short time, the suspension of payments may be nominal for foreign creditors, and if they second the exertions of the board they may begin to make early collections of much importance. It would be well to let those who are interested in the debt, and their respective governments, understand that the government of Mexico is not blindly smitten with the idea which pervades the decree of the 17th, and that it will accept any other that is compatible with its views of order and general adaptation, and with its need of resources for the pacification of the country. In discussing the means of providing them, the idea may have evolved from the necessity under which the government found itself of increasing the duties of importation in case the revenue from maritime customs continued to be appropriated for the public debt, making the most of the contrary measure which the government has adopted in its liberal amendment to the tariff, and which it is going to submit for the approval of the congress.

As the English and French legations have no confidence in its justice at the bottom of the question, it is not strange that they should be anxious to present it in the light of an outrage on France and England to publish the decree without any previous notice. Mr. Fuente's intelligence is too great to render it requisite to insist on the necessity which has existed on one part to act thus, and on the right, on the other, which every debtor has to declare, without the previous consent of his creditor, the simple fact that he suspends his payments for want of ability to make them, designating at the same time certain guarantees of security. In regard to this it will not be useless to repeat to Mr. Fuente that every step of the government and every private conference which has taken place in the matter has been marked by the same moderation and forbearance as are to be observed in the written correspondence. The foregoing directions are applicable to the question, as well in its relations to the government of England as in those to the government of France; but there are some duties to be performed by you which have a respective fitness for each of these two countries. In England, besides correcting the erroneous ideas which may be conveyed by Sir Charles Wyke in regard to the condition of Mexico and to the future and tendencies of the present government, it would be very proper to present the question in its true light to the view of the bondholders and English merchants. The attention of the former might be called to the great inequality existing between the parties interested in the English convention and the bondholders by exhibiting the prospect that a general adjustment of the public debt could not but remedy to some extent this inequality. It would not be impossible to imbue the minds of the holders of Mexican bonds with the idea that the prosperity of this republic and the consolidation of its government are intimately allied with their interests.

* * * * * * *

As to what relates to France, it would be very proper to render evident the paltriness of the remainder to which the French convention is reduced, this being the only acknowledged and liquidated debt, as the Penaud agreement relates in great part to claims whose amount has not yet been fixed; and the convention recently made with Mr. Zarco has not even been approved by the congress. It may contribute much towards counteracting the ill offices of Mr. Saligny to represent them as the continuation of Mr. Gabriac's system and as part of an intrigue, with the design that a diplomatic complication may bring matters to the recognition of the shameful Jecker business. In this there is an interested effort in behalf of an individual, who is not even a Frenchman, contrary to the real interests of others who are subjects of the empire, creditors of Mexico, and settled in this country.

* * * * * * *

For the completion of these instructions an idea must be given to Mr. Fuente of the political situation in which this country is placed at the present time.

* * * * * * *

The reaction is represented in the bands of suspicious persons whom Mejia yet keeps in his hiding places in the mountain, and in those led by Marquez, who is still surrounded by the forces of the government, with the commanders of which some of the rebel chieftains have begun to enter into understanding. Some other parties, which appear here and there, are nothing more than bandits, who will come to an end now, when the government, provided with resources, can organize a pursuit of malefactors. The reaction, as a political tendency, is not very perceptible, and it is even suspected that it has been trans-

formed by invoking principles less equivocal and names less hateful than those of Marquez and Zuloaga.   *   *   *   *   *
While the forces of the government are intimidating or pursuing the reaction, the ministry, in permanent council, is occupied with the administrative details, to which the decree of the 17th and the circular that accompanies it have relation.   *   *   *   *   *

MANUEL MA. DE ZAMACONA.
MEXICO, *July* 29, 1861.
A true copy.
LUCAS DE PALACIO Y MAGAROLA.
WASHINGTON, *September* 21, 1861.
A true copy.
ROMERO.

No. 3.

[Translation.]

Decree.

The citizen Benito Juarez, constitutional president of the United Mexican States to the inhabitants, know ye: That the sovereign congress of the union has deemed it well to address me the following decree:

ARTICLE 1. From the date of this law, the government of the union will recover the complete product of the federal revenues, deducting from them only the expenses of the administration of collecting, and all payments are suspended for two years, including the assignments for the loan made in London and for the foreign conventions.

ART. 2. The maritime custom-houses and all the other collecting offices of the federal revenues will surrender all their products into the general treasury, being exclusively subject to the orders of the ministry of finances. On the 15th and on the last day of each month, they will forward to the ministry a statement of their receipts and disbursements.

ART. 3. Within the term of one month, the government will form and publish an economical estimate of all public expenses, based on the estimate of the 31st December, 1855, conveniently reduced. The government is to subject itself to this economical estimate from the day of its publication, and congress only has the faculty of making changes afterwards.

ART. 4. The payments in this estimate are to be made in the following manner:

1. The armed force in campaign and in garrison; the material of war; the invalids and disabled soldiers. These payments are to be made complete, but no surplus can be admitted.

2. The civil list in active service, and the military list not in service. These payments, if under $300, are to be made complete; if above $300, they are to be made in strict and equal proportion.

3. The classes pensioned by the nation are to be paid in strict and equal proportion, if the classes above mentioned have been paid before, as is ordered by the decree.

ART. 5. If an order, not included in the estimates, is sent to the general treasury by government, an observation must be made by a communication of the government; if repeated, the treasurer is to communicate it immediately to congress. If the treasurer does not make the observations here mentioned, he is to be destituted immediately.

ART. 6. A superior committee of hacienda is instituted, composed of one president and four members named by government, with the sanction of congress. Two of them, at least, must be creditors of the nation.

ART. 7. The attributes of the junta are the following:

1. To pay the loan made in London and the foreign conventions.
2. To pay the creditors not comprised in the law of the 30th November, 1850.
3. To pay legal and posterior credits against the nation up to the 30th June of this year, including those comprised in the law of the 17th December, 1860.
4. To receive the payment of what is due to the nation, if it be unknown to the collecting offices.
5. To administer and sell the nationalized clergy property, and to execute all the attributes of the law of disamortization and nationalization.
6. To make arrangements, with the sanction of government, with all the persons interested in, or that have any business relative to, nationalized property.
7. To distribute all the funds collected amongst the creditors of the nation. The product of the suppressed convents is to be applied to the creditors of the conducta of Laguna Seca, and after covering the estimates of the nunneries, the remainder is to be distributed to the creditors in the foreign conventions.

ART. 8. In order that the junta may be able to fill the attributes conferred upon it by government, the following is assigned to it:

All the "pagarés" existing in the special disamortization office; the product of all pending redemption; the capitals not redeemed belonging to the nation, the buildings of the suppressed convents, the lands, and all existing materials. In the States and territories all the lands, convents, and buildings comprised in the law of nationalization, and all the products, except the 20 per cent. belonging to the same States and territories. The buildings and capitals expressly excepted by government are not comprised in this article.

ART. 9. All this property will form a fund distinct of public credit; the employers in the district, the chiefs ("gefes superiores") of the finance department in the States and territories are to forward immediately to the junta the titles, deeds, notices, and corresponding documents.

ART. 10. In the special law published for the conversion of public debt, the part to be delivered by the States is to be fixed and regulated.

ART. 11. The government is authorized to publish a decree taxing tobacco; this tax is to be collected for the federal treasury in all the republic.

ART. 12. The government is authorized to increase, during the remaining months of this year, the alcabala of one-half per cent. more on national products, excepting the articles of agricultural and manufacturing industry specified in the decree of the 24th September, 1855.

ART. 13. The duty of "contra-registro" on foreign goods is increased to double in the district; this increase is to be paid as long as the government may deem it necessary to fulfil the object of the following article.

ART. 14. With the new product of the acabala, the "contra-registro" and the tax imposed upon tobacco, the government will pay with preference all the debts contracted from the 29th of last May, and all those that it may contract for the re-establishment of public tranquillity, leaving extant all the orders that have been given on account of "refacciones" for the payment of the money taken in Laguna Seca.

ART. 15. The governors of States, and the employés of the collecting department, have no intervention whatever in the federal revenues.

ART. 16. The government is authorized to reform and organize within one

month all the offices on such a base that their estimates be reduced, and is authorized to increase the salaries of some employés, and to reduce their number.
Given in the sessions hall of the congress of the union on the 17th of July, 1861.
GABINO BUSTAMANTE, *Deputy President.*
FRANCISCO CENDEJAS, *Secretary.*
E. ROBLES GIL, *Deputy Secretary.*

For which I order that it be printed, published, circulated, and given due respect.
Given in the national palace in Mexico, the 17th July, 1861.
BENITO JUAREZ.

No. 4.
[Translation.]

SECRETARYSHIP OF STATE
AND OF THE OFFICE OF FOREIGN RELATIONS,
Mexico, July 18, 1861.

MOST EXCELLENT SIR: The persons whom the most excellent the president of the republic has honored by calling them to form his present cabinet esteem, as is just, this mark of confidence; but they comprehend that they need besides that of the nation, in order to labor with a probability of success in the development of reform, in the arrangement of public administration, and in the pacification of the country; and they wish, therefore, that their practical views for obtaining these results may have the greatest publicity.

Neither the most excellent the president nor his ministers deceive themselves in regard to the public situation; but, on the contrary, they believe that the bold purpose of confronting it in all its difficulties is the chief title which they can present to the sympathy of the nation. In order to form this purpose, the present ministers have had an example in the serene and fervent faith of the chief magistrate of the republic in the future of Mexico, and an incentive in the conviction which they entertain that there are not wanting in the country elements to raise it from its present prostration, and that it only needs the work of organization which accidental circumstances had hitherto rendered impossible for the government. The present one has now a very firm will to undertake it; and, seconded, as it doubtless will be, by the good sense of the country and by the kindness of friendly nations, it expects finally to overcome the obstacles which have heretofore prevented administration from being organized and consolidated in Mexico, and the fruits of political revolutions from being witnessed. The confidence, therefore, and hope of the government to control the present situation is not alone based on the firmness of its purposes, but on the acknowledged patriotism of the representatives of the nation, and on the prudence of Mexicans and of foreigners who have linked their interests with the fate of the republic. The new cabinet, in laying down the ideas which are to serve as a rule for their administrative movement, cannot lay claim to the merit of originality, nor do anything else than give official form to the instinct of reorganization, morality and economy which for some time past has been developing itself among the majority of Mexicans. In vain have the people washed with their blood all the political principles; in vain have they sought from them fruits of prosperity and welfare; in vain have they just effected a great revolution which shall in the future be an escutcheon of pride for Mexico as honorable as that of her independence. The instinct of the nation, enlightened by deceptions and frustrated hopes, has comprehended that revolutions will be barren, and that the elements conquered on political and social ground will afford no fruit unless the work be crowned with administrative revolution. The reform which the Mexican people have proclaimed and put in practice leads to the conquest of great material and moral measures for the public prosperity; but the revolutionary and reformatory labor has still to enter its last and final, its organic period, in which the great Mexican revolution will yield fruit to the country, to civilization, and to mankind.

The revolution must now assume a new phase; it is no longer characterized by the antagonism of two political principles. An immense majority of the nation is on the side of liberty and progress; and the monuments of tyranny and fanaticism having disappeared, the reform places its foot on the ground of administration. Administrative questions of order, of safety, almost of police, are those which occupy the public mind to the exclusion of others. To exterminate the reactionary bands whose number is not sufficient to give them political character, they themselves not claiming this, and who are now reduced to bodies of rascally conspirators against the property, honor and lives of the citizens; to reorganize and expedite the administration of justice, in order that the law may be inexorably applied to the enemies of the public peace; to re-establish security on the principal routes of communication; to regulate the postal service; to abolish, as soon as possible, all irregular and vexatious imposts; to give encouragement to all branches of the national prosperity; and to render visible and palpable the revolution which the Mexican people have effected—these are the objects which at present preoccupy the national mind.

For the attainment of them the treasury question has a special importance. Generalized as are opinions and interests throughout the republic in favor of liberal reform, it is only requisite to provide the legitimate power, with efficient means of repression against certain interests, in a minority, which are opposed to the national tendency. The country does not lack those elements of action which the government needs, and all that is necessary is to organize them under a foreseeing, methodical, and economical administration.

For this eminently practical work the government has not to go back into the speculative sphere, nor will follow any other inspiration than that of a solicitous and honored father of a family, who wishes in good faith to put the domestic finances in order. The nation has material and moral elements enough to prevent its leading a life of anxieties and discredit; it needs nothing more than order, economy, uprightness, to escape from these troubles and disgraces; and the government, in adopting resolutely this system, has no other merit than that of taking for the rule of its future conduct a determination which the blows of adversity have commanded to the general approval of the nation.

The new ministry does not believe in the necessity of making a profession of political faith, because, in its judgment, the period is beginning to arrive when politics is no longer to be the question of the day. Mexico belongs decidedly and irrevocably to reform and democracy, and it will be sufficient for the government to declare, although the antecedents of the citizen charged with the executive power would excuse him even from this, that it professes all the principles of the progresista creed and which are contained in the constitution and in the laws of reform. This is already a fact, and it has only been necessary that it should be drawn from the confusion and elevated to the rank of a solid and regulated institution.

In order that the legitimate power may not descend to the level of the vandalic bands who destroy the republic, it will not contend against them by devastating and destroying, but by repairing and organizing. It is an error to suppose that every attempt at organization ought to be postponed until society has no enemies to battle against. The labors of organization are exactly those which will bring about a final triumph over the enemies of society; and only the power which succeeds in organizing society will place on a secure basis the conquests of the revolution.

The government, therefore, instead of contending from revolutionist to revolutionist—instead of adopting robbery and spoliation as a means of action, wishes to confine itself to the system of tutelary powers which save society without harming it.

The peculiar character of the epoch into which the revolution has entered and of the cabinet which has just been organized consists in this, and the government earnestly desires that this character may be put as much in relief as possible in the eyes of the nation. Notwithstanding this, and that the ministry professes with faith, with plenitude, and with fervor the principles of reform, this will not be the only word which it will inscribe on the frontispiece of its work, but it will add those of *reorganization, order, economy, and morality.*

But it does not write them as they have been so often written in political programmes; it employs them as the outcry of national opinion, which has opened a road for itself at last to official regions; it utters them not as a mere word, but as the echo of an intimate and vehement conviction, not as a promise, but as a fact, as a series of measures which from this very day begin to be put in practice. If the government succeeds in having the firmness, depth, and penetration of its resolutions for creating and moralizing the public administration understood from the tone of its voice; if it succeeds in causing to be perceived the novelty of this tendency from its dominant and almost exclusive character; if it succeeds in having its labors considered as a powerful effort to satisfy the instinct of order and reorganization which has been formed in the country under the influence of experience and of misfortunes; if it obtains that in this manifestation may be seen the announcement of the day, long waited for, and which must arrive at some time, in which the spirit of economy and reparation may transform what for a long while has been in our society a chaos in which no political principle could fructify, it is certain that the measures with which it inaugurates its new march, after the halt which circumstances have compelled it to make for a few days, will be considered not as a new revolutionary convulsion, but as the first sign that matters in Mexico are beginning to be composed and to be placed on a solid basis.

It has heretofore sufficed that the nation, plunged into a morass, should make unusual exertions to get out of it, but succeed only in sinking deeper at every step. It is now time that it should seek a firm spot whereon to place its foot, so as to gather up all which it has been able to save from the flood, and to secure its own interests and those of the foreigners who have confided in its integrity.

The government cannot furnish peace, safety, and progress to the inhabitants of the republic, nor observe hereafter scrupulous fidelity in its compacts, if it is not allowed to breathe for a moment free from the burdens which have oppressed it, to gather up its resources, and to regulate those sacrifices which it has never ceased to make, but which have been barren to the country and its creditors for want of regularity. Between chaos and administrative reorganization, between the revolutionary tempest and the prosperous future which the reform promises to the republic, it is necessary that there should intervene a day of reclusion, of review, of classification, in which the country might unite all its elements and organize them, in order to apply them immediately to the fulfilment of its engagements. This work, far from alarming any legitimate interest, ought to inspire faith and to tranquillize everybody, since it is equivalent to placing the obligations of the republic on a solid and permanent guarantee, which they have never had. The creditors of Mexico have been living in an edifice without foundations, and the government now wishes not to dislodge them, but that they should leave the place disencumbered for a few days, in order that the building may be strengthened, which was threatening ruin.

This is the meaning and this will be the practical result of the annexed decree, which, on the proposition of the ministry, has just been carried by a vote of the federal congress. It tends to put in play the means which intelligent opinion has for some time past indicated as the only efficacious ones for creating a public treasury in Mexico, and for rendering the exertions of the government in re-establishing order and peace not unfruitful; it tends to render impossible hereafter the abuses which have made barren for the people, properly so called, the reforms proclaimed and carried into effect during the late period; it tends to turning to profit the treasures which yet remain of the national states by applying them to the important object of paying off the public debt; it tends to place on the government itself a wholesome restraint by means of the formation of a budget which will be the most economical of all which have been prepared; it tends to impose restrictions and conditions on the administrative power, as far as reason will permit; it tends to pass the level of proportionate distribution over all citizens whom the nation has to remunerate for any service; it tends to abolish every preference which is not based on the public convenience; it tends to limit the powers of the states and of the federal government in treasury matters by re-establishing the legal bounds which disappeared during the revolution, and without which there is no possible order or administration; and it tends, finally, to insure the compensation of the judicial power, without which civil guarantees will be ever nominal, and impossible that stern and inexorable justice which should be applied to the disturbers of the public peace.

Society, for whom these advantages are in preparation, for which it has hungered and thirsted for some time, will not complain if, in return, some sacrifice is demanded of it. Nor will the susceptibilities of the local authorities be hurt, if they are inspired alone by their patriotism, to which the republic appeals through the voice of the federal government, and if they consider that this is the first which begins by imposing restraints and clogs on itself in order that it may be quick only for the welfare of the nation and in economising its revenues.

The government has succeeded in having the national representation do justice to these views, and it experiences more pleasure than it would feel in speaking of a beneficent proposition exclusively its own in declaring that the movement to which the annexed decree is due has done nothing more than anticipate the chamber's inclination for order, morality, and economy. In this it naturally reflects national opinion, which sees that the time has arrived for measures suitable for guarding against the ruin to which the republic has been drawing nigh, and from which no merely political revolution could save it. The congress not only has accepted, but has completed and perfected this idea of the government, which may be called revolution in administration—administrative reform which comes to crown political and social reform. If the idea be seconded by the state authorities, if it be seconded by public opinion, which has preluded it for some days past, if it be seconded, as is to be hoped, by the friendly nations whose experience has counselled Mexico for so long a time to enter into the path of economy and order, this country, from which other nations of the earth have expected so much, will commence finally to pay its contingent to universal civilization. There will be security, peace, and prosperity in Mexico; the administration of justice, properly organized and compensated, will render the laws effective; the reactionary bands, placed between the energetic pursuit of the armed force and the inflexible action of the courts, will cease to devastate the land; the general police will re-establish security on the public roads; trade and commerce will be revived; capital, which in some countries cannot aspire to more than a paltry interest, and which in others is at present threatened by great convulsions, will move without fear to the republic, at the same time that colonists are coming to settle in it and to render fruitful a thousand schemes of material improvement which the public insecurity keeps barren. The government does not wish to flatter the nation with pleasing prospects only, nor must it speak further than of the first labors undertaken after the reorganization of the cabinet, because its purpose is that deeds shall serve as a programme.

At the very time of proposing the annexed decree, it has taken steps that before long will afford security on the roads of the interior and Vera Cruz, and will re-establish the regular postal service on these two highways. Into the purposes of the ministry enter measures of security on a large scale, and the realization of which is intertwined with that of the annexed decree, because the question of security is also a question of resources.

For the purpose of using all the regular force to pursue the remains of the reaction, the government is laboring earnestly in perfecting the establishment of the national guard in the district, and in purging it from the abuses which on other occasions have corrupted it, and which lately began to be visible. The government, which has the firm purpose of extirpating forever from the army of the republic the thousand corruptions which have made of the military budget the cask of the Danaides, and of putting an end to the shameful contracts which only have served to build up great fortunes on the ruins of the public treasury, could ill permit those same abuses to be implanted in the order of citizen militia.

Yielding to the indications of public opinion, and wishing to lose not a minute in giving impulse to the branches of public prosperity, at the same time that it is engaged in forming propositions and in gathering statistical data necessary to put in practice the constitutional principle in regard to the abolition of internal custom-houses in the republic, the government has proposed in the congress to suspend that part of the decree of the 8th of April of this year, in which it has been provided that the payment of duties of importation may be made with fifteen per centum additional in shares of the interoceanic railroad, and it has formed a plan for the amendment of the tariff in a liberal sense, setting out most especially to improve in good faith the condition of commerce, which has been so much damaged by smuggling. The ulterior labors of the ministry will have reference to reforms equally modest, but no less absolute and important.

The government is confident of realizing them, and is firmly resolved to do so by organizing, so to speak, the reform, and by making it fruitful through the medium of administration, provided it meets with support and sympathy in the country, and with kindness and a spirit of equity in friendly nations, as is to be expected from their own interest and from that which they take in the civilization of the human race. Should it be thus, the government will have contributed in its sphere to the salvation of the republic; in the contrary case, it will succumb with the consciousness of having embarked in a noble enterprise, and with the dignity of taking no step backward in its radically organizing tendencies.

The federal government relies, for the realization of the measures to which the annexed decree relates, and of others which are to follow, on the efficient co-operation of your excellency, whose patriotism cannot but impel you to unite in a reform which will render fecund all the others that the nation has conquered, and whose practical barrenness is being made an argument of bad faith against the progresista revolution.

The undersigned avail themselves of this opportunity of tendering to your excellency the assurances of their distinguished consideration.

God, liberty, and reform.

ZAMACONA.
RUIZ.,
BALCARCEL.
ZARAGOZA.
NUÑEZ.

His Excellency the GOVERNOR OF THE STATE OF ———.

WASHINGTON, *September* 21, 1861.

A true copy.

ROMERO.

No. 5.

Sir C. Wyke to Señor Zamacona.

MEXICO, *July* 19, 1861.

SIR: A printed paper, as strange in compilation as in the nature of its contents, was this day hawked about the principal thoroughfares of the city, and has now, I see, been reprinted in the columns of this evening's "Siglo."

According to the wording of this document, it would appear that congress has thought fit to make a free gift of other people's property to the government of the republic, by suspending, for the space of two years the payment of all assignments, as well to the London bondholders as to the parties interested in the foreign conventions.

Until I hear from you to the contrary, I am bound to consider this announcement in the light of a falsehood; for I cannot bring myself to believe that a government which respects itself could sanction a gross violation of its most sacred obligations to other nations, and then proclaim the fact of their having done so in a manner which, if possible, aggravates the offence.

That the representatives of those nations who are thus slighted and injured should be allowed to learn, in the first instance, by handbills circulated in the streets, that you have repudiated your engagements, is as unaccountable as the policy which could dictate a measure alike fatal to the character and credit of the republic.

I will not dwell on other obnoxious paragraphs of this publication, as at present I cannot believe it to be authentic; for when your excellency did me the honor of calling on me to-day you in no way alluded to a subject which would otherwise surely have formed the chief topic of your conversation.

Awaiting a reply at your earliest convenience, I avail, &c.

C. LENNOX WYKE.

No. 6.

[Translation.]

MEXICAN REPUBLIC, DEPARTMENT OF INTERIOR AND FOREIGN RELATIONS.

LEGATION OF FRANCE IN MEXICO,
Mexico, July 20, 1861.

Mr. MINISTER: There has for thirty-six hours been circulating through the principal streets of the capitol, under the signature of his excellency the president of the republic, a printed document, as extraordinary in form as in substance, and which has been republished by several dailies among others, by the "Siglo XIX" of yesterday.

It treats of nothing less than a law approved the 17th July, by congress, and sanctioned on the same day by the president, in which, by the first article, without making mention of other completely inadmissable provisions, the suspension of payment upon the foreign conventions for two years is ordered.

It seems to me superfluous to say to you, Mr. Minister, that I have had no hesitation in considering this document as apocryphal and false.

In fact, I would have thought that I was doing injustice to your government by believing it capable of acting thus, disregarding its most sacred obligations in regard to the lawful property of another, and taking part in an attempt, as audacious as insensate, upon the rights and dignity of France; an attempt the more insulting even, if that be possible, because of the absolute silence observed by the government towards the minister of his imperial Majesty upon this pretended law of the 17th of July, before and after the vote in congress, and the approval by the president.

I am, therefore, persuaded, Mr. Minister, that you will hasten to disavow an act which, without speaking of the terrible and inevitable consequeuces to which it will expose Mexico, will only compromise in the gravest manner its character for loyalty and its credit. And in the hope of prompt and satisfactory reply from your excellency I avail myself of this occasion to renew to you my assurances of most distinguished consideration.

A. DE SALIGNY.

His Excellency Mr. ZAMACONA,
   Minister for Foreign Relations of the
     Republic of Mexico.

MEXICO, *July* 27, 1861.

True copy.

LUCAS DE PALACIO Y MAGAROLA.

WASHINGTON, *September* 21, 1861.

Copy.

ROMERO.

No. 7.

[Translation]

MEXICAN LEGATION AT THE UNITED STATES OF AMERICA.

MEXICAN REPUBLIC, DEPARTMENT OF FOREIGN AFFAIRS,
National Palace, Mexico, July 21, 1861.

The undersigned, &c., has the honor to inform his excellency Sir C. Lennox Wyke, &c., that the decree which forms the enclosure to this note has passed the federal congress of the republic, and that the undersigned brings it to the cognizance of his excellency on account of its connexion with the diplomatic conventions and their payments.

From the known ability and sound sense of her Britannic Majesty's minister, the Mexican government are led to hope that his excellency, so far from seeing in the above decree any cause for alarm on account of those interests which are under the protection of the British legation, will, on the contrary, perceive in this act of the legislature a proof that the republic is anxious to arrive at an estimate of their resources; to organize those resources in the most profitable manner; to cut at the root of such abuses as have hitherto brought censure upon the government, the supreme power being the first to submit to the restrictions and other conditions necessary for this object; and at the same time to place the engagements and obligations of the nation upon such a footing as will insure them in future a sure and lasting inviolability.

To fulfil faithfully their international compacts the Mexican government have made almost superhuman efforts, and can show results of no ordinary kind, such, for instance, as the present balance-sheet of the Mexican debt, whereby it is seen that no very notable change has been brought about therein by the continuous state of revolution. During this crisis, on the contrary, the position of foreign creditors has improved; in the midst of its greatest embarrassments the nation has gone even so far as to increase the rate of interest for paying off the public debt, and has thus deprived itself of the very means which were at its disposal for terminating the civil war; in other words, the nation has paid its creditors their gold with the blood of its citizens.

Since the revolution began the republic has been thirsting after peace, order, and security; yet the government, fully convinced though they were of being able to right themselves if only they could count upon any means that would really admit of action, hesitated long before laying hands upon the funds destined for the payment of their foreign debt. So great, indeed, was their respect for these funds, that they preferred to sacrifice their obligations to Mexicans, to trample under foot the most cherished principles of their country, nay, even to imprison persons of the highest respectability, in order to obtain resources from the sums paid for their release, rather than touch a cent of the assignments destined for the diplomatic conventions and the London debt.

So hateful an expedient, although it has served to prove their good faith toward other nations, has not been and never can be efficacious; so that the government has now to start afresh, as they should do, upon different principles, and with the fixed purpose of thoroughly reorganizing their plan of administration, and of having recourse, not to temporary expedients, but such a system of taxation as from its nature will, while adding fresh vigor to government, abolish once and for all the old system of forced imposts.

To carry out this principle the republic has need of its entire revenue, and of conscientious and practical persons to administer the same, and this is the intention of the law which the undersigned has the honor of placing in Sir Charles Wyke's hands.

The present government of the republic has to meet, on the one hand, the demands of society and civilization for order, and guarantees, on the other, those of the foreign creditors for nearly the entirety of the public revenue. So circumstanced, no government could hesitate as to the course to be taken.

The nation, then, has yielded to the cry of society and civilization, has given way before a pressure too heavy for it to bear, but it has done so merely in order to recover strength and then return to the charge.

The government of the undersigned originated the measures contained in the enclosed decree, and possibly they are the first rulers in the country who have religiously and honestly undertaken seriously to consider the nature of their obligations, and to discover the best means of meeting them.

It is impossible for Mexico to attempt any administrative reform or the reestablishment of peace and order if she has to support the burden of the national debt.

To enable her, however, to remove whatever has led to those numerous questions which have so incessantly occupied the attention of foreign representatives and the finance department, and to do away with the system of forced imports; to enable her to free herself from the necessity of breaking through her own liberal principles and overtaxing foreign imports; to enable her, in short, to procure some portion of the money now paid by the maritime custom-houses toward the extinction of the debt, it is necessary she should be allowed a short respite wherein to recover herself, as well as the full use for a few days of her entire revenue. In that case, by proper management and economy, public order and tranquility would be re-established, and the revenue of the country, with the exception of what was absolutely requisite for the proper protection of society, set apart to meet the payment of arrears.

The government of the undersigned considers that a debtor, so long as he is actuated by honorable feelings and a full determination to carry out his engagements, does not forfeit his dignity in presenting himself to his creditor and frankly confessing he is, though temporarily so, unable to pay his debts; and the sole object which that government now has in view is, to prove to the world that they are really and truly resolved upon attempting administrative reforms in the country, as the only means left likely to produce any amelioration in its political condition. They perfectly understand that they have to struggle against the unfavorable impression caused by the abuses and irregularities allowed in former times, yet it does not escape them that they have inherited this fresh difficulty in addition to the others which they have now to combat, though they are not ashamed of such difficulties, inasmuch as this is no exceptional case in the annals of Mexican revolutions, nor is it the work of the present administration.

A nation, like an individual, has the right to ask to be judged by its own acts, and not according to preconceived prejudices or partial comparisons.

When the president of the republic convened the members of the present government, they each and all, with heartfelt sincerity and honesty of purpose, hailed the idea of at once fearlessly grappling with the difficulties of the problem, upon the solution of which depended the great question of reform. They saw that the nation lacked not the material elements of such a work, but merely their proper organization. Nor were moral elements wanting; for were there not proofs to the contrary in the general longing for the time when, upon the spurious and self-interested promises of a frivolous and corrupt minority, there should be built up lasting institutions, under whose protecting influence Mexicans and foreigners alike would deem their honor, lives, and property secure? The government saw that the nation was weary of its state of anarchy, that it cursed the abuses and the recklessness which had brought upon it discredit and ruin; they saw, in fact, that the majority in the country asked but honesty of purpose from the ruling power, and they did not hesitate to consecrate their efforts exclusively to respond to so just a call.

The cabinet of which the undersigned is a member takes pride in its firmness of purpose, and considers that it merits the sympathy and co-operation of foreign representatives, whose presence in the republic is not solely for the protection of specified interests or nationalities, since their mission is equally one dedicated to the cause of humanity and civilization.

Sad indeed would it be if history had one day to recount how that this country, after the most trying vicissitudes, came to be ruled over by men who, without any supernatural gifts and animated solely by their patriotism and their experience, shrunk not from making one final effort—an effort such as never yet had been made—to establish in Mexico the rule of reason and morality, yet that this effort was shipwrecked on the prejudices and scepticism of the most enlightened nations of the world in respect to Mexico's future and Mexico's capabilities for reform.

Every impartial person must look upon what is now passing as a proof of the energy and loyalty which Mexico is displaying in her endeavors to attain that position which reason and prudence dictates. Government, at the outset, has procured and dedicated to the interests of the public debt all the national property. They have initiated a system of economy which is already in operation; and, as a result thereof, have imposed upon themselves and their subordinates such restrictions and self-denial as have never yet been imposed by any former administration. They have further been occupied with the details of a programme based upon those principles of economy which experience has proved to be necessary. Great progress, too, has been made toward establishing public order and tranquility by the steps taken by government, for tracing out clearly the position which the States hold in respect to the supreme federal power. Moreover, the departments of state now are denied to those who would hold office simply to speculate in the gains of the reigning disorder and confusion, and the present rulers of Mexico would sooner sink under their difficulties than yield an inch of the ground on which they have taken their stand in defence of reform and morality.

All those who have interests in the country—all, indeed, who would see civilization on the increase—should aid the government in attaining the objects they have in view, instead of throwing obstacles in their way. The great European powers are extending their sympathies at the present hour to those countries who are striving to join the rest of mankind in the great work of civilization, and Mexico would fain hope that she is not alone to be excepted.

The very creditors of Mexico themselves should, the undersigned thinks, in their own interests, feel that great encouragement is given to them at the present moment; for it is not the republic alone that is now concerned in the proper regulation of the public debt under surer guarantees, and in the necessity of consolidating the same. The creditors of the nation have even a higher interest at stake, inasmuch as by no other means than those already mentioned can they expect to obtain greater advantages than those they now possess, notwithstanding that they have gradually acquired for themselves almost the entire revenue of the country.

This very circumstance is regarded, and with reason, as a proof of non-stability, while it equally produces distrust in people's minds, a state of things no less prejudicial to the republic generally than to its creditors.

Upon this point natural instinct cannot be deceived. As matters now stand, whether in respect to the country or the creditors, it might be possible that the drain upon the revenue could be continued for the space of a few months, but it would be possible only at the price of certain ruin alike to the country and the creditors.

Had the government hesitated to adopt the measures for a radical financial reform, to which sufficient reference has already been made, they would have been either compelled, against their principles and inclination, to impose fresh taxes upon foreign importations, or quietly to submit to every interest connected with social order being swallowed up in the flood of anarchy—an idea too horrible to be thought of.

To avoid either of these extremes the government, guided by their conscience and feelings of patriotism, suggested the plan contained in the enclosed decree. If, as it is to be hoped, it should meet with support and sympathy from other nations, Mexico would be able to raise her voice and proclaim aloud that she had entered upon the one road that could lead to her salvation. Should it be otherwise, the nation must perish, and with her all those interests which are so closely connected with her future prosperity. Be this as it may, the government that in these stormy days rules over the destiny of Mexico will have had the honor and glory of initiating and doing battle for the only means left that could save their country.

The undersigned would feel obliged to her Majesty's envoy extraordinary if his excellency would transmit a copy of this note to his government, and avail himself, &c.

         MANUEL DE ZAMACONA.

True copy.   MEXICO, *July* 29, 1861.

      LUCAS DE PALACIO Y MAGAROLA.

       WASHINGTON, *September* 21, 1861.

True copy.

           ROMERO.

[Translation.]

No. 8.

MEXICAN REPUBLIC, MINISTRY OF FOREIGN RELATIONS.

NATIONAL PALACE, *Mexico, July* 21, 1861.

The undersigned, minister for foreign relations, has the honor to answer the note which his excellency the minister of France has been pleased to address to him in relation to the decree passed on the 17th instant by the federal congress, and in which provision is made for the suspension of all payments, including that of the debt contracted in London, and that of the diplomatic conventions.

This decree is perfectly authentic, and his excellency the minister of France would have had no occasion to express his doubt upon this point in the note to which this serves for answer, if his occupations would have allowed him to receive the undersigned, who went yesterday to the French legation as soon as the decree mentioned was communicated to his department by that of finance, in order to make to his excellency Mr. de Saligny some confidential explanations before officially communicating to him the resolution of congress.

The undersigned had the ill-fortune to find his excellency the minister of France occupied and invisible, and had to return to this department to solicit, as he did, a private conference by means of a note which he despatched to the French legation before receiving the note which Mr. de Saligny pleased to send him at the close of the afternoon, and to which I have now the honor to reply.

The undersigned flatters himself with the hope that the reading of the law, which he remitted in a separate note to his excellency the minister of France, will suffice with his excellency to rectify the opinion which he expresses in his letter of yesterday on the ground that the decree of congress does not arbitrarily dispose of any property, nor break any of the ties of obligation which bind the republic. The said decree and the note with which the undersigned had the honor to send it to the French legation, are, on the contrary, a virtual ratification of the international engagements of Mexico, accompanied, also, by a frank and loyal declaration that she could not at once fulfil them without prejudice to public order and to peace, and without endangering the very existence of the nation. In this declaration, Mr. Minister, is neither audacity nor folly; but, on the contrary, a melancholy submission to the law of necessity, and a prudent recourse to the only expedient which can save the republic from anarchy.

Truly, the undersigned does not comprehend in what manner the dignity of France can be offended by this protest made by an impoverished nation; that it is not possible for it without some breathing time to continue carrying, at heavy costs, the weight of debt by which it is oppressed.

This declaration refers only to a fact which has long since been proclaimed. There is no reason for considering as an insult that the republic, reduced to the last extremities, has declared the fact officially and solemnly, without previously asking the consent of its creditors.

His excellency the minister of France has the goodness to give the undersigned a hint of the terrible results to which the step which occasions this note may give place, and upon the influence it would have on the credit of the nation and on the belief in its loyalty; and the undersigned must frankly answer that the government, full of a confidence which it does not fear will be disappointed in the good will and equity of friendly nations, has not supposed that a greater evil could threaten the republic than social dissolution and anarchy, and that this act of menace does more injury to its credit than the frank and honest declaration that its obligations, which it new holds in greater respect and acknowledges more than ever, exceed at this moment its ability to meet them.

The undersigned takes the liberty to refer to the note which he addressed to his excellency Mr. de Saligny, transmitting with it the decree of the 17th instant, and concludes by renewing the assurances of his distinguished consideration.

MANUEL MA. DE ZAMACONA.

His Excellency Mr. A. DE SALIGNY,
*Envoy Extraordinary and Minister Plenipotentiary
of his Majesty the Emperor of the French.*

MEXICO, *July* 29, 1861.

True copy.

LUCAS DE PALACIOS Y MAGAROLA.

WASHINGTON, *September* 21, 1861.

True copy.

ROMERO.

No. 9.

[Translation]

Señor Zamacona to Sir C. Wyke.

MEXICO, *July* 21, 1861.

The undersigned, minister for foreign affairs, has had the honor of receiving from his excellency Sir Charles Lennox Wyke, her Britannic Majesty's envoy extraordinary and minister plenipotentiary, the note in which his excellency requests to be informed whether the decree of the federal congress providing for a total suspension of payments, not excepting those of the London bondholders and diplomatic conventions, is or is not authentic.

His excellency's request might have been looked on as anticipated by the explanation the undersigned had the pleasure of making yesterday at the legation only a few minutes after the note, to which this is a reply, had been sent to the foreign office—indeed while it was yet on its way there; but the private character of that explanation renders it incumbent upon the undersigned to recapitulate a portion of it in the present communication.

In the first place, he begs to assure Sir Charles Wyke that so soon as the decree of yesterday was made known to him through the department of finance, he proposed to bring it at once to the cognizance of his excellency, though anxious that this step should be preceded by a visit, at which it was the intention of the undersigned to give Sir Charles Wyke a fuller and more detailed explanation of the decree in question, its purport and probable results, than was compatible with the limits of an official note. In the meanwhile, however, the decree was duly and formally published and printed in the daily newspapers, and this will account for his excellency the British minister having seen it before he received either an explanatory communication or visit from the undersigned.

Sir Charles Wyke will now allow the undersigned the liberty of stating that he does not consider his excellency has formed a correct estimate of this decree when he says the congress therein makes a free gift to government of other people's property. Her Majesty's worthy representative likewise goes on to qualify the act of congress as a total suspension of payments for the space of two years; still, it will not escape his keen judgment that the application of the term "free gift" to what is merely the act of ratifying certain obligations, and specifying the mode of fulfilling the same, amounts to a misnomer.

Neither can the undersigned agree with Sir Charles Wyke in his opinion that the decree in question is a violation of Mexico's most sacred obligations toward other nations. Such a phrase would imply the idea of a voluntary and deliberate act; whereas the republic, in suspending the payments due to the diplomatic conventions, yielded not to the dictates of its own free will, but solely to the force of circumstances, which have rendered it morally and physically impossible for the nation to continue making those payments which have hitherto been made by means of the most strenuous exertions. When, then, such efforts have been unavailing, the government may be permitted to say so without any want of respect either for itself or for those nations with whom they may have engagements.

To every obligation there is attached the tacit condition of possible fulfilment or non-fulfilment, and nobody has ever been judged faithless to his engagements for having, when compelled to suspend payment, stated the simple fact of such engagements being incompatible with possibility.

Of such a nature is the statement contained in the decree that has now passed congress, and her Majesty's minister should not be astonished that it did so pass congress, or that it was afterwards published without the previous consent of the diplomatic representatives in their character of protectors to foreign creditors, for it must be treated of as the mere declaration of a simple fact, in no way tending to the modification or prejudice of the interests connected with the public debt.

It will not have escaped the clear judgment of Sir Charles Wyke, acquainted as is his excellency with the actual situation of the republic, that the suspension of payments which has lately been decreed, which only expresses what has long been the public feeling, and has formed the subject of confidential conversations with some members of the corps diplomatique, as well also as with some of those most interested in the foreign debt, has been brought about by an imperious necessity which did not admit of any preliminary arrangement or adjustment. The government had to choose between two evils—either to respond to public opinion by adopting the only existing means of preserving order and reorganizing the whole administrative system, or to look quietly on and leave society to become an easy prey to the prevailing anarchy.

Government, considering the preservation of order to be its first duty, and believing that for the positive good of all who had interests at stake in the country some one plan should be undertaken which would tend to consolidate those same interests, presumed they might count, to a certain extent, upon the assent of the creditors.

Sir Charles Wyke, then, will thus understand why the undersigned, holding, as he does, these opinions, can neither look upon the decree originating this note, as repudiating national engagements, nor as prejudicial to the good fame and credit of the republic.

In order the better to understand the true force and purport of the decree, the undersigned would beg to refer her Majesty's minister to the note which has been addressed to the legation for the purpose of announcing to his excellency the act of congress; and if Sir Charles Wyke considers that, in the visit which the undersigned had the honor of paying yesterday at the mission, he was only performing such an act of courtesy as should always precede any official or confidential conferences upon matters of business, his excellency will cease to wonder at the absence of special reference to the subject of this communication during the conversation which then took place.

The undersigned, &c.

MANUEL DE ZAMACONA.

No. 10.

MEXICAN LEGATION AT THE UNITED STATES OF AMERICA.

MEXICAN REPUBLIC, DEPARTMENT OF FOREIGN AFFAIRS,
Mexico, July 22, 1861.

SIR: In reply to your communication bearing yesterday's date, which I have just had the honor to receive, I will endeavor to answer seriatim the objections you have to offer to the statements contained in my note to your excellency of the 19th instant.

You state the reasons why the financial decree was not sooner communicated to this legation, and say that you were anxious personally to explain to me the motives which had originated it; but what I complained of was that it should have passed into a law without the intention even of carrying it into execution ever having been announced to me.

When two parties bind themselves to perform certain stipulations, neither of them has the right to free himself from such obligations without having first of all obtained the consent of the other contracting party. With regard to what you say about the impropriety of my calling this act of congress a giving away of other people's property without their consent, permit me to observe that I am perfectly justified in making that assertion, for in matters of this nature time is often equivalent to money, and the arbitrary act of stopping all payments for the space of two years is depriving the parties interested of their money for that space of time, which is a dead loss of so much value to them.

The imperious necessity which you urge as an excuse for the act cannot in any way justify the manner in which you have made yourself sole judges of that necessity, without first of all urging it on the forbearance of your creditors, in order to obtain their consent to what you were about to do.

A starving man may justify, in his own eyes, the fact of his stealing a loaf, on the ground that imperious necessity impelled him thereto; but such an argument cannot, in a moral point of view, justify his violation of the law, which remains as positive, apart from all sentimentality, as if the crime had not had an excuse. If he was actually starving, he should have first asked the baker to assuage his hunger, but doing so of his own free will, without permission, is acting exactly as the Mexican government has done towards its creditors on the present occasion.

Although, as your excellency truly observes, the law just published does not certainly affect the rights of the parties interested, yet it does most positively touch their material interests by depriving them of payments on which they had counted to fulfil their other engagements.

With regard to the hope of immediate relief which you seem to entertain from the operation of this measure, I am convinced that it will, on the contrary, greatly aggravate the actual difficulties under which you are now laboring, and that for reasons so evident that I will not now advance them.

I am not aware that the project of this law was shown to other diplomatic agents, but I certainly never heard of it before under its present form, and, therefore, as far as I am concerned, the case stands exactly as I have stated it.

With regard to the light in which your excellency views this question, as expressed in your above-named note, you will, I am sure, excuse me for stating that it cannot be treated of partially without also taking into consideration the opinions of those who directly suffer from the practical operation of such ideas as emanating from yourself and the other members of the government who submitted the project to the congress.

With respect to what you mention about a note addressed by your excellency to this legation with reference to this matter, I must inform you that it has never reached me, and that, therefore, I had a full right to complain, as I did in my communication to you of the 19th, of having first of all heard of this extraordinary measure of the government by seeing it in printed bills placarded through the public streets of the capital.

I have, &c.,

C. LENNOX ·WYKE.

His Excellency SEÑOR DON MANUEL M. DE ZAMACONA,
Minister of Foreign Affairs.

P. S.—Since writing the foregoing lines the note of your excellency, alluded to above as missing, has been put into my hands, it having reached this legation an hour and a half later than the one to which this is a reply.

C. L. W.

MEXICO, *July* 29, 1861.

True copy.

LUCAS DE PALCINO Y MAGAROLA.

WASHINGTON, *September* 21, 1861.

True copy.

ROMERO.

No. 11.

Sir C. Wyke to Señor Zamacona.

MEXICO, *July* 23, 1861.

SIR: Your excellency's note of the 21st instant reached me yesterday afternoon, by which I learn that the decree forming its enclosure has passed the federal congress of the republic, and that you forward it to me as directly bearing on the stipulations of the diplomatic convention for the payment of British claims concluded between Great Britain and Mexico in the year 1851.

I have already so fully explained to you in my notes of the 19th and 22d of this month what I think of this decree and the manner in which it has been issued, that any further observations of mine with reference to it would only be superfluous, and prolong a correspondence which should never have been called for at all.

As to the appeal you make to the indulgence and forbearance of her Majesty's government, in order to obtain their sanction to a measure which is of itself sufficient for ever to deprive you of their confidence, I need only remind you that such indulgence has already been too far abused by the utter failure of all your engagements in the affairs of the Calle de Capuchinas and the Laguna Seca for it to be again extended to those who, instead of feeling grateful for it, only seem to count on its exercise in order to free themselves from every obligation, however binding it may be.

Apart from these considerations, however, the carrying out of this financial law, so far from benefiting the nation, will only plunge it into tenfold greater difficulties by largely increasing its obligations to its creditors, and at the same time striking at the root of its credit and commercial prosperity.

That which is in itself wrong can never come right, for it is a well-known axiom that spoliation as a source of revenue soon exhausts itself.

It is not by such means that the resources of the country can be augmented, but by a determination to make every sacrifice and incur every privation with a view of maintaining your honor and fulfilling your engagements. This determination once adopted and manfully put into practice would at once inspire confidence and rally round you those whose sympathies you now appeal to in vain, because they doubt from past experience both your prudence and your sincerity.

In using language thus strong you must not attribute to me a desire to offend, which is indeed far from my intention, but I have a duty to perform both to my own government and to that to which I am accredited, which impels me fearlessly to tell the truth and warn you against the inevitable consequences of a step alike fatal to your own interests as well as to those of my countrymen affected by this law.

It now only remains for me to protest most solemnly, as I hereby do, against this decree, at the same time that I hold the republic responsible for all and every damage and prejudice caused by it to the interests of those whom I represent in this matter; and further to warn your excellency that unless the said decree is withdrawn within forty-eight hours from this present time I shall, until I receive fresh instructions, suspend all official intercourse with the Mexican government, as any longer maintaining such under existing circumstances would be incompatible with the dignity of the nation I have the honor to represent.

In compliance with your request I will transmit a copy of your excellency's note of the 21st instant to her Majesty's government.

I avail, &c.,

C. LENNOX WYKE.

[Translation.]

No. 12.

MEXICAN REPUBLIC, DEPARTMENT OF INTERIOR AND FOREIGN RELATIONS.

LEGATION OF FRANCE TO MEXICO,
Mexico, July 23, 1861.

MR. MINISTER: I received yesterday, at 4 o'clock in the afternoon, the two notes you have done me the honor to address to me under date of 21st July. I am now causing a translation to be made of that of the two notes by which you give me official cognizance of the decree of the 17th of this month; but while awaiting this, that I might reply and in my turn inform you of my determination on the substance of the business, I cannot pass without answer the observations by aid of which you seek to reply to my communication of July 20.

I had declared to you, Mr. Minister, that independently of the fact that the measure was in itself an outrage upon the interests and dignity of France, the silence observed upon the subject by your government towards the minister of the Emperor, as well before as after the vote of congress and the approval by the President of the decree of the 17th July, rendered this act still the more insulting, if that were possible. To-day, and after having read your explanations, I persist more than ever in seeing in the silence of your government a fresh insult, gratuitous and premeditated, addressed to France.

To justify your government, you tell me that so soon as you were informed by the minister of finance of the existence of the decree in question you came to my house to give me confidential explanations before communicating to me officially the decision of congress, but that you were so unfortunate as to hit upon a moment in which I was engaged and invisible.

It is very true that through a misunderstanding for which I feel bound to express to you all my regrets, and which is explained by the fact that you did not make yourself known to my chancellor, Mr. de Morineau, I was deprived of the honor of receiving your visit on the 20th of this month. But allow me to remark that this circumstance, apart from the personal regrets I experienced, is without any importance. A simple collation of dates will be sufficient to convince you. The decree voted upon the 17th, and approved on the same day by the executive authority, was on the 18th, by order of the authorities, posted on the corners of the principal streets of the capital, and published in various journals. But it was on the 20th, at four o'clock in the afternoon, at the moment when I had just despatched to you my note, that you called at my house to give me some *confidential explanations!* Shall I add that it must seem very strange that the chief of the cabinet should not have been informed by the department of finance of a measure of such weight until three days after it had been adopted by the executive power, and published for forty hours through the street criers and the journals? Such a fact would not be of a nature to give a high opinion of the manner in which your governmental machinery is managed.

This is not the time to refute the reasoning by aid of which you undertake the impossible justification of an inexcusable measure. But I will not pass unnoticed certain expressions in your note intended to portray in the most touching hues the sad condition of your country, and which seem to imply an appeal to the feelings and to the generosity of the government of the Emperor. France, Mr. Minister, I can say, to its eternal honor, has never been insensible to the sight of a government contending with unmerited misfortunes, and bravely striving to preserve social order and civilization. But such is not, I say it with profound regret, the situation of your government. The difficulties under which it succumbs are only the inevitable result, the forced and foreseen consequence of unheard of waste, of plunder and prodigality without name, of unbridled disorder, of abuses without example, of which since its accession it gives a sad spectacle. To permit at this time that, arming itself with its delinquencies even, against which the minister of the Emperor has not in vain endeavored to place it on its guard, it should lay hands on the lawful property of our subjects, on the resources devoted, in virtue of international conventions of the most sacred character, to supply a tardy and inadequate reparation to Frenchmen, innocent victims during so many years of a system of depredation and spoliation without example in any other country, would be on the part of France, not generosity, but veritable self-deception, an improvidence the more unpardonable, because if I have not much faith in the efficacy of the remedy proposed, I could not, let me frankly avow it to you, have any greater confidence in the hands intrusted with its application.

I pray your excellency, Mr. Minister, to accept the assurances of my very distinguished consideration.

A. DE SALIGNY.

His Excellency Mr DE ZAMACONA,
   Minister of Foreign Relations, National Palace, Mexico.

JULY 29, 1861.

True copy.

LUCAS DE PALACIO Y MAGAROLA.

WASHINGTON, *September* 21, 1861.

Copy.

ROMERO.

[Translation.]

No. 13.

MEXICAN REPUBLIC, DEPARTMENT OF INTERIOR AND FOREIGN RELATIONS.

LEGATION OF FRANCE TO MEXICO,
Mexico, July 24, 1861.

Mr. MINISTER: I have to answer the communication which your excellency did me the honor to address to me the 21st July to bring officially to my knowledge the decree of the 17th of this month, of which I shall hasten to transmit a copy to the government of the Emperor.

I have experienced, perhaps, more regret than surprise on learning, Mr. Minister, that this measure of the 17th July, in the existence of which I refused to believe for the honor of Mexico, was in sooth an authentic act, adopted by your government with deliberate purpose, but in the shadow of concealment, as if, through a final revolt of its own conscience, it might itself shrink back in the blaze of daylight from the avowal of such an enormity. The impression which the government of his imperial Majesty will receive on learning this fresh assault on the rights and dignity of France, as well as all the circumstances connected with it, will not be different, I am convinced, from what I have myself felt.

Your excellency certainly does not expect from me that I should here enter into a discussion of the decree of July 17. It belongs to things that are not discussed. What need have I, moreover, to give myself to useless efforts to convince your excellency that in our conversations you have not hesitated to blame almost as energetically as myself this deplorable measure, even at the moment when, by a contradiction for which I cannot account, you undertook to justify it by means of arguments, more specious than solid, deduced from I know not what pretended considerations of necessity and public safety.

The measure of which we treat worthily crowns the system by the help of which, after several months, your government has wrought itself up to elude, to deny, or to violate its obligations towards the government of the Emperor.

In the situation in which you have just placed it, nothing will remain to France than one single means of defending and avenging her rights and her honor, outraged with indignity—immediate resort to force. It is for your government to decide if it will leave affairs to come to this extremity.

Awaiting its decision, I have, Mr. Minister, a last duty to discharge; that is, solemnly to protest in the name of France, as I here do, against your decree of the 17th July, declaring to you that I hold the republic responsible for all the damages it may cause to the subjects of his imperial Majesty, and that, in fine, if this measure be not recalled and annulled within twenty-four hours from this instant, I shall break off all official relations with your government, these relations having become incompatible with the dignity of the government which I have the honor to represent.

I pray your excellency to accept the assurance of my very distinguished consideration.

A. DE SALIGNY.

His Excellency Mr. ZAMACONA,
Minister of Foreign Relations, National Palace, Mexico.

MEXICO, *July* 29, 1861.
A true copy.

LUCAS DE PALACIO Y MAGAROLA.

WASHINGTON, *September* 21, 1861.
A true copy.

ROMERO.

No. 14.

[Translation.]

MEXICAN REPUBLIC, DEPARTMENT OF INTERIOR AND FOREIGN RELATIONS.

NATIONAL PALACE, *Mexico, July* 25, 1861.

The undersigned minister of foreign relations believes that he ought to make some remarks to his excellency the minister of France on the subject of the two last notes which he has thought proper to address to this department because of the decree of the 17th instant.

Before all, the undersigned should explain that whatever may have been his private information of the measure stated, and of the initiative which was the origin of it, he could not officially communicate it to his excellency Mr. de Saligny before it could be communicated to him by the department of finance, a step inevitably posterior to the promulgation of the decree spoken of. This will put an end to the astonishment which his excellency the minister of France exhibits, and will obviate the possibility of perversion of the meaning of the explanations which the undersigned has given upon this point.

The surprise and sorrow which his excellency the minister of France states that he experienced on learning officially the publication of the decree referred to are things which the undersigned does not undertake to comprehend in treating of a measure which has rested a long time on the public attention, which has been discussed•by the press, and whose unavoidable necessity has passed into a proverb. The undersigned considers himself excused from further remark when the very representative of the French empire has had the frankness to recognize this necessity in private conversations, in referring to some that he had had with one of the predecessors of the undersigned about the arrangement not only of a delay in favor of Mexico for the payment of the debt to France, but even of an alleviation of the enormous weight with which the foreign debt oppresses the republic.

The undersigned must also set in proper light the allusion which his excellency Mr. Saligny makes to the blame which in private conversations he says he had cast upon and now reduces to writing upon the measure which is the cause of these communications. What the undersigned has stated to the minister of France is the decided preference which he would have given to a conventional arrangement for the suspension of payments enacted by congress, and the regret with which he has had to submit to the hard law of necessity which did not give the time needed by the government for entering upon previous conventional arrangements, which, though initiated with this intent, could not effect an immediate result, on account of accidents foreign to the essence of the business; and meantime the extreme moment arrived in which the government literally could not do any other thing than suspend payments, and trust for some general arrangement of the public debt to the presumed consent of the parties interested. This is what the undersigned has constantly said to his excellency the minister of France, and thus it falls out that, while deploring the impossibility of entering into previous arrangements, he may have influenced the conduct of the government upon the overmastering considerations of necessity and of public safety.

The government of the undersigned protests against the imputation thrown upon it of having systematically endeavored, in these latter times, to elude, disregard, and violate its engagements with the government of the Emperor. The facts and the correspondence of this department with the French legation bear witness to the contrary. For three years past Mexico, notwithstanding she found herself in the midst of difficulties and complications without example, in place of eluding her liabilities has ratified them, has confirmed them, has given strength to them by means of acknowledgments in which there has been, perhaps, somewhat of improvidence, and which have contributed much to the difficulties with which the government now contends. At this very moment the nation acknowledges all the rights which are derived from its international engagements, but finds itself compelled to declare that those rights cannot, for a certain period, be regularly provided for by the receipts from the maritime custom-houses, because these constitute the only available and immediate resource of the government, and are not sufficient to meet the serious, although temporary, dangers with which the public is threatened, and the interest upon and funding of the public debt.

The decree of the 17th instant does not repudiate any obligation, nor do anything but place in their appropriate order those which the government maintains towards civilization and society, and those which it is under to its creditors. In all this decree there is not a single word that can reveal any tendencies to spoliation. It is nothing but a declaration on the part of the Mexican people, in the same terms in which such is made daily by traders and merchants who find themselves under actual impossibility to fulfil their engagements. The only difference is, that between individuals the disputes between creditors and debtors are, in such event, carried before the courts, and between nations are brought before the supreme tribunal of justice and of equity. His excellency Mr. de Saligny in his last note declares that he declines this jurisdiction, and prefers to carry the matter before the tribunal of force.

It is strange that the minister of France, to whose intelligence the rules which preside over human revolutions must be familiar, should regard as an exceptional characteristic of that of Mexico the irregular course of public events in the months immediately close upon the downfall of the reaction, and that, arming himself with those recollections, now that the double quick step of reform has slackened, as well as the impetuosity which the revolution brought from the fields of battle—now that we hear the voice of those who claim to organize and direct it, should declare the Mexican people to be unworthy of all equitable consideration, and should oppose the advent of order and regularity precisely in the name of that inevitable disorder. On the other hand, if that has existed, it must be that Mr. de Saligny ought to reflect that, far from having brought prejudice to French interests, it is proverbial that his fellow-countrymen have been the most benefited by what the minister of France calls the prodigalities of the revolution; and in reference to this, the undersigned takes the liberty to ask Mr. de Saligny to look into his conscience and search whether the violent language with which he enforced his criminations of Mexico is worthy of the noble country which he represents, and in whose sentiments it is impossible there should exist a wish to abuse its position as a creditor; and this when France is not so with respect to Mexico, unless for a relatively small amount, and when out of this affair there cannot, on the other hand, any question of dignity be raised, because that would be equivalent to saying that the poverty and the embarrassments of Mexico may affect the dignity of France.

The nation has restricted itself to declaring, by means of the decree of the 17th, the condition of its complication and its penury, without repudiating any of the rights created in favor of its creditors, and, on the contrary, by coming forward and offering new guarantees.

It cannot be unperceived by the practical wisdom of his excellency the envoy of France that he asks an impossibility from the government of the undersigned in requiring from it, within twenty-four hours, the abrogation of the decree of the 17th instant. Neither the government could initiate this abrogation, because that would be to initiate anarchy and social dissolution; nor could congress, which passed that law almost by acclamation, convinced that it was of vital importance to the republic, listen to the initiative.

The protest with which his excellency the minister of France closes his note appears to the undersigned so much the more superfluous, because he has himself anticipated it, so to say, by protesting, even from his first notes upon this business, that the ultimate resolutions of congress can in nowise affect the legitimate rights of parties interested in the foreign debt.

The undersigned permits himself, moreover, to remark, saving his respect for the sound judgment of Mr. de Saligny, that far from seeing an act becoming the honor and dignity of the French empire in the suspension of relations, which its representative announces he believes it to be very possible that impartial nations should look upon this step as absolutely without motive, and hopes, from the prudence of the minister of France, that until he receives instructions he may keep up the cordial understanding, for whose interruption no cause whatever exists, and which may so much contribute to the satisfactory solution of this business.

The undersigned is gratified to offer, on this opportunity, to his excellency Mr. de Saligny the assurances of his very distinguished consideration.

MANUEL M. DE ZAMACONA.

His Excellency Mr. A. DE SALIGNY, &c., &c., &c.

MEXICO, *July* 29, 1861.

A copy.

LUCAS DE PALACIO Y MAGAROLA.

WASHINGTON, *September* 21, 1862.

A copy.

ROMERO.

No. 15.

Señor Zamacona to Sir C. Wyke.

[Translation.]

MEXICO, *July* 25, 1861.

The communication which his excellency her Britannic Majesty's minister was pleased, under yesterday's date, to address to the undersigned upon the subject of the decree of the sovereign congress proclaiming a total suspension of payments, not excepting those of the diplomatic conventions and the London debt, has rendered it incumbent upon the undersigned to make certain explanations, without which it might be supposed that his government had accepted as irrefutable some of the facts and statements therein adduced by Sir Charles Wyke.

Once and for all, then, the undersigned rejects the notion entertained by his excellency in his notes of the 19th and 22d instant, that the decree of the 17th implies an act of spoliation.

This act of the legislature carries with it no legal right whatever to rob foreign creditors of what belongs to them. The nation, in whose house of representatives the decree in question was carried with scarcely a dissenting voice, has never sought to disavow the rights which have accrued to others from international compacts. Still she has been forced to declare that, for some time to come, such rights cannot continue to be a drain upon the revenue of the maritime custom-houses, for that revenue—the only one government possesses for immediate purposes—does not suffice for the actual exigencies, temporary though they be, of the country and society, and at the same time for the payment of the interest and principal of the public debt. Government have obligations to perform both towards society and their creditors. They cannot perform both at once, and consequently, by the decree which has originated this note, government have done nothing more than place those obligations in their legitimate order, without attacking or disavowing any of them.

His excellency her Majesty's envoy extraordinary, while attempting to clothe the act of congress in the garb of spoliation, has in one of his former notes employed a simile, the inaptitude of which is strikingly perceptible. His excellency compares the government at this moment to a person who, impelled by hunger, assaults and robs a provision merchant. Now, two ruling principles are implied in such an act—one of aggression, the other of robbery—neither of which can even be assumed in respect to the conduct of government towards its creditors. Of not a sixpence have these same creditors been deprived; and if one had to employ a simile to qualify the conduct of government, it would be rather that of a father overwhelmed with debts, who, with only a small sum at his disposal, scarcely sufficient to maintain his children, employed it in the purchase of bread instead of in the payment of his bills. Were her Britannic Majesty's representative a member of the family, would his excellency be eager to qualify his father's conduct by the name of spoliation?

In every-day life one is accustomed to see people who suspend payment owing to pecuniary embarrassments, yet nobody seeks to call them thieves. Now, in the decree, upon which her Britannic Majesty's minister passes so severe a sentence, not a single word is there which can give rise to the idea of thieving propensities. Payments, it is true, are stopped because government cannot pay out of the funds assigned to it. They are stopped because the nation, to be orderly, and at the same time methodical in the accounts of the public debt, wants as soon as possible a government; yet still, with feelings of loyalty, and with a solicitude worthy both of being more justly appreciated, she has given her creditors a twofold guarantee; firstly, in the plan itself, so complete, so impartial, a plan wherein looms a prospect of solid stability; and secondly, in the assignment of a special fund of several millions, (most of which can shortly be realized,) whereby, even during the period of suspension, (in their case nominal,) the foreign creditors will obtain even better security than what was given them in the maritime custom-houses.

It is not, M. le Ministre, about sacrifices or money that Mexico is haggling; that which she is defending are the principles of order; that which she is longing for is system and organization, without which she is lost; and she is searching after prudence and method, so that she may never again be accused of slovenliness and mismanagement by those who regard as a national vice what is but a phenomenon inseparable from a state of revolution.

It is well, too, to state accurately the attitude of Mexico before her creditors, both as it was and is; for it is not such a one as his excellency her Majesty's envoy describes in his last note. To judge therefrom, our republic has never been aught than an indigent debtor, who from time immemorial has responded with ingratitude and bad faith to the undeniable generosity and indulgence of her creditors.

The undersigned shuts his eyes purposely to the history of the foreign debt, for neither would he wish to employ the bitter tone of Sir Charles Wyke's note, nor give the slightest indication of Mexico's belonging to the set of faithless debtors who, to avoid payment, dispute the legality of their obligations. Mexico, on the contrary, recognizes in a high degree her engagements, and will abide by them, moreover, without taking exception at the antecedents of the original contract.

But the undersigned is convinced that, when this correspondence shall have come to light, all who are familiar with the history of our external debt, all who are acquainted with the primary elements of the British convention, and know how the parties interested therein were allowed the advantages of increased interest in the midst of a ruinous civil war, and in the days of Mexico's hardest struggle, will see something strange in the allusion of his excellency her Majesty's minister to the indulgence of which the foreign creditors were so prodigal, but which the republic so systematically abused.

Had the demands of the creditors been somewhat fewer, then, perhaps, the fulfilment of international engagements might have come within the range of possibility. Mexico, however, has been like those fields where the harvests have been out of proportion to the fertility of the soil, and the day comes when the land becomes impoverished, yields nothing, and is obliged to lie fallow for one or two years.

The undersigned considers he should not pass over in silence the charge which is made against his government of having failed to fulfil their engagements in respect to the funds seized at the British legation by functionaries of the reaction, and to the money-convoy "occupied" at Laguna Seca.

In the first case, government, with the consent of the legation, engaged simply to make the perpetrators of the act responsible, and if such means did not lead to the desired result, viz., indemnity, to discuss others which might do so. No one, then, can say that until now government has not fulfilled their engagement in this case.

As for the affair of Laguna Seca, when government undertook to repay, within the space of four months, what remained unpaid of the amount "occupied" out of the "conducta," they did so at a time when they could not foresee that the remnant of the reaction would turn refractory, and oblige them to enter upon an expensive campaign, which would upset all their financial calculations.

Notwithstanding this, however, they have made every kind of sacrifice, monetary and otherwise, to keep intact this special debt; to an extent, indeed, that has left them in possession of but a small available surplus. No one who does justice to the Mexican nation can refuse to acknowledge the exemplary manner in which she has endeavored to satisfy her creditors, to the unstable disparagement of national interests.

The actual amount assigned for the payment of the foreign debt during the residence of the constitutional government at Vera Cruz, and that, too, at a time when the re-establishment of peace was being laboriously worked out, and when, consequently, the country could ill sustain the heavy demands made upon it, speaks volumes in itself.

The little faith manifested by his excellency Sir Charles Wyke as to the results of the financial law and the small value he puts upon the guarantees it gives to foreign creditors, do not seem to be shared in by the parties themselves who are interested in the diplomatic conventions, since it is only within the last few days that government had all but concluded an arrangement with them, the basis of which would not have interfered with their present rate of interest, but it could not be perfected owing to her Majesty's envoy extraordinary having refused to sanction it.

The same may be said of the creditors in the matter of the Laguna Seca "conducta." Guided by natural instinct—so infallible a rule where individual interests are concerned—they did not, like Sir Charles Wyke, entertain any doubts about the prudence and sincerity of the government. And touching these said doubts, amounting, as they do, to an insult, his excellency will permit the undersigned to exhort him to commune with his conscience, and ask it whether or not the tone of his excellency's last communication is such as should be used by a creditor, calling himself generous and indulgent, towards a friend who is in his debt and overwhelmed by difficulties.

It cannot escape the enlightened understanding of his excellency the representative of Great Britain that, in demanding from the government of the undersigned the withdrawal, within forty-eight hours, of the late decree, he simply demands an impossibility. Neither could the government initiate the withdrawal, for it would be equivalent to initiating the reign of anarchy and a general dissolution of society; nor could congress, who had carried this law almost by acclamation, and who were convinced of its vital importance to the republic, listen for a moment to such a proposition

The protest with which his excellency her Majesty's envoy extraordinary concludes his note appears to the undersigned so much the more superfluous, as in his very first note upon this subject the undersigned had, so to speak, also protested, but against the supposition that the last act of congress in any way affected the lawful rights of the persons interested in the public debt.

The undersigned will further take the liberty of stating, with all due deference and respect to Sir Charles Wyke's sound judgment, that, very far from seeing in the suspension of relations, now announced by his excellency as representative of Great Britain, an act due to the honor and dignity of England, he thinks it not improbable that all nations, who consider the matter impartially, will look upon this step as absolutely uncalled for; and he therefore trusts that his excellency, while awaiting the instructions to which he alludes, will continue his friendly relations to this government, for the interruption of which there can be no possible cause, while their maintenance will surely contribute to the satisfactory solution of the present difficulty.

The undersigned, &c.

MANUEL DE ZAMACONA.

No. 16.

[Translation.]

LEGATION OF FRANCE IN MEXICO,
Mexico, July 25, 1861.

Mr. MINISTER: I announced, in a note which I had the honor to address to your excellency yesterday, that if the decree of the 17th of July was not withdrawn and annulled within the period of twenty-four hours I should break off all official relations with your government.

The term fixed by my note having expired without my receiving a satisfactory reply, I must regard your silence as a refusal to accede to my request.

Consequently, I have the honor to inform you that from this moment all official relations are broken off between the legation of his Imperial Majesty and your government.

I beg you to accept, Mr. Minister, the assurance of my very distinguished consideration.

A. DE SALIGNY.

His Excellency Mr. M'L DE ZAMACONA,
Minister of Foreign Relations, National Palace, Mexico.

WASHINGTON, *September* 21, 1861.

A true copy.

ROMERO.

No. 17.

[Translation.]

MEXICAN REPUBLIC, DEPARTMENT OF FOREIGN RELATIONS.

NATIONAL PALACE, *Mexico, July* 25, 1861.

The undersigned, minister of foreign relations, has the honor at this instant to receive the note which his excellency the minister of France has pleased to address to him, announcing the suspension of his relations with the government of Mexico. His excellency Mr. de Saligny must have received the note which, at five o'clock yesterday afternoon, the undersigned had the honor to send to him, showing the absolute want of motive for a suspension of relations between the government of the Emperor and that of the Mexican republic; and as little can there serve for cause of the resolution which Mr. Saligny announces that lapse of twenty-four hours, which it pleased him to fix upon in his last note but one, inasmuch as that was not received at this department until seven o'clock last night.

The undersigned refers to what is contained in the last communication, and avails himself of this opportunity to repeat to his excellency the minister of France the assurances of his most distinguished consideration.

MANUEL MARIA DE ZAMACONA.

MEXICO, *July* 24, 1861.

A true copy.

LUCAS DE PALAIOS Y MAGAROLA.

WASHINGTON, *September* 21, 1861.

A true copy.

ROMERO.

To his Excellency Mr. A. DE SALIGNY,
Envoy Extraordinary and Plenipotentiary, &c., of France.

No. 18.

Sir C. Wyke to Señor Zamacona.

MEXICO, *July* 25, 1861, 5 *p. m.*

SIR: The day before yesterday, at this hour, I had the honor of informing your excellency that if the decree of the 17th instant was not withdrawn within forty-eight hours I should feel it my duty to suspend all official intercourse with the Mexican government until I should receive instructions from her Britannic Majesty's government as to the next step to be taken in a matter which not only implies the breach of a solemn international compact, but also carries with it so great a slight as almost to amount to a direct insult to the nation I have the honor to represent.

The term having now expired within which I should have received a reply, and none having reached me, I take your silence as a refusal of my demand; and I therefore from this time forward suspend all official relations with the government of this republic until that of her Majesty shall adopt such measures as they shall deem necessary under circumstances so unprecedented.

I have, &c.

C. LENNOX WYKE.

No. 19.

Señor Zamacona to Sir C. Wyke.

[Translation.]

MEXICO, *July* 25, 1861.

The undersigned, &c., has this moment had the honor of receiving from his excellency Sir C. Lennox Wyke, &c., the note in which his excellency is pleased to announce the suspension of his relations with the government of Mexico.

Sir Charles Wyke must have received the communication which the undersigned had the honor of addressing to him at 5 o'clock this afternoon; this will prove the utter absence of any motive for a suspension of relations between the government of Great Britain and that of the Mexican republic.

Neither can there be any cause for the resolution taken by Sir Charles Wyke, in the expiration of the forty-eight hours fixed by his excellency in his note of the 23d instant, (as the term to be allowed to government for answering the ultimatum,) inasmuch as it was only 7 o'clock in the evening of the 23d that the above note was received at government house.

The undersigned, in calling attention to his last communication, avails, &c.

MANUEL DE ZAMACONA.

No. 20.

Sir C. Wyke to Señor Zamacona.

[Private.]

MEXICO, *July* 26, 1861.

DEAR SIR: At 7 o'clock yesterday evening, that is, two hours after the expiration of the forty-eight hours in which I had required a reply to my note of the 23d instant, I received yours dated the 25th, to which, consequently, I can only reply by a private letter, as its contents have in no way changed the resolution which both the French minister and myself have been driven to adopt by the extraordinary and unjustifiable conduct of the Mexican government with reference to the decree of the 17th instant.

A careful perusal of your above-mentioned note has convinced me that mine of the 23d, to which it is a reply, has not been properly translated to you, as you put some things into my mouth which I never said, and so twist the sense of others as to give them a totally different meaning from what they really convey.

Passing by this, however, I will only revert to the really essential part of your note, which is the refusal to rescind a financial scheme, the maintenance of which, besides plunging the republic into further pecuniary difficulties, will have the effect of bringing it into collision with the two first maritime powers of the world, and that, too, in a quarrel which you have originated, and where, permit me to say, you are quite in the wrong.

As I am, in thus writing to you, unfettered by the reserve imposed in an official corronespdeuce, I may tell you frankly that you are leaning on a broken reed when you trust to the sympathy of those whose interests Mexico has systematically sacrificed to her own. This is proved by the history of the foreign debt as applicable to the bondholders, which it would be well that you should carefully study, and you will then see that the repeated engagements made with them have up to the present moment always been either entirely evaded or only partially executed, as, for instance, when after consenting to a reduction of interest of from 5 per cent. to 3 per cent. on the condition of receiving certain payments from the duties levied in the Pacific ports, they do not receive one sixpence from that source, and are only very partially paid from the Atlantic custom-houses.

I will not dwell on the long and dreadful list of murders committed on my unfortunate countrymen, which, with one exception I believe, have remained unpunished from the date of your independence down to the recent dreadful butchery of poor Mr. Beale at Napolis.

Do you think that these lamentable facts are calculated to gain our sympathy or inspire us with confidence in a people who thus violate their engagements with us, and kill our fellow-subjects with perfect impunity?

It is really time that the government of Mexico should open their eyes to the natural consequences produced by such conduct, and should become aware of the unfavorable opinion entertained of them in Europe.

Whose fault is it that the country has been deluged in blood ever since the declaration of its independence, but that of its own citizens, in constantly making revolutions and carrying on a series of fratricidal wars amongst themselves, which have reduced one of the finest countries in the world to misery, and so degraded its population as to make them dangerous, not only to themselves, but to everybody coming into contact with them?

You appeal to the generous sentiments of creditors towards an unfortunate debtor bowed down by his difficulties, forgetting that that debtor, with only common prudence within the last six months, might at this moment be actually free from debt, had he not wilfully and recklessly squandered the millions he then had at his disposal.

As to the mode of payment proposed to certain British claimants, to which you allude in your yesterday's note, it was so impracticable as to be unacceptable to all of them, when its real nature was pointed out to them.

With regard to what you say about the Laguna Seca robbery and the legation outrage, it is useless for the Mexican government to deceive itself, by calling the former an "occupation of funds," and the latter a deed performed by the "functionaries of the reaction." The first was a theft, and the second an unheard-of violation of international law, committed by a government recognized by every European nation, and for both these crimes, as yet unatoned for, Great Britain will surely hold this republic fully responsible.

I have already extended this letter to an undue length, and must therefore conclude, but, before doing so, let me again urge you, for your own sakes, to retrieve the fatal error you have made with regard to this decree, by immediately withdrawing it; for otherwise all official intercourse between this legation and your government becomes impossible, and you will remain with the responsibility attaching to an act which, both in form and substance, is perfectly unjustifiable.

Trusting that you will receive what I have now written in the spirit which really dictated these lines, I will take leave of a subject which is a much more serious one than seems to be supposed by the Mexican government.

In a second note of yours, received yesterday, you complained that my note, written at 5 o'clock on the 23d, only reached you at 7 o'clock on that day, and that consequently, in writing to you yesterday at 5 o'clock, you had had only forty-six instead of forty-eight hours' delay before the suspension of official relations.

This I regret, but it was not my fault, as on both days I despatched my note from here at half-past five in the afternoon. In point of fact, however, the two

hours thus lost are of no importance, as you refuse to withdraw the obnoxious decree.
Believe me, &c.,

C. LENNOX WYKE.

No. 21.

Señor Zamacona to Sir C. Wyke.

[Translation]

MEXICO, *July* 27, 1861.

MY DEAR SIR: I have had the honor of receiving your letter of yesterday, and I am glad that it gives me the opportunity of asking you to listen once more to the voice of one who is as sincere as he is honorable; of one whose love for his country is only excelled by his love of justice and reason; of one who is confident that you will be brought to do justice to the intentions of the Mexican government, for, as if by inspiration, he knows you to be possessed of similarity of sentiment with himself.

It cannot be that, talented and generous as you are, you have yet thought it strange that government should refuse to withdraw the decree of the 17th instant. Your conscience must tell you, M. le Ministre, that it is an impossibility you ask of government, for how could they entertain your proposition? The mere preliminaries for the suspension of a law which had passed congress would take up more time than what you have allowed for deciding whether or not our official relations were to be maintained. This single fact would account for the position taken up by government, as well as for their determination to meet boldly dangers and difficulties, even greater than those which you have had the goodness to warn me against.

Such a step as the one you now propose, if taken by Mexico, could not but prove suicidal to her political standing as a nation, for it would be equivalent to the surrender of her constitution and her sovereignty into the keeping of the foreign diplomatic body, and that, too, in a matter where my inmost conviction tells me that justice is on our side.

Still, as in the correspondence which has passed between us during the last few days, I had seen the opposite doctrine sustained, and heard the conduct of my government qualified repeatedly as unjustifiable, I began to distrust my own convictions about equity and common sense, so much so that I sought to justify myself and my country by a reference to international law, and I can only say, now that the work of reference is over, that my former convictions are only the more confirmed.

I perceive, M. le Ministre, that writers on international law hold it to be a general principle, that any change of circumstances, or the positive inability of one of the parties in a contract to fulfil the same, does of itself nullify a bond; and since I likewise, in my turn, may be permitted to avail myself of the advantages of a private letter, I will take the liberty of doing what might be considered in the light of pedantry were I writing to you officially, and make certain quotations which bear upon this question.

Grotius and Corcellus hold that "the obligation which results from a compact becomes null and void so soon as its fulfilment becomes impossible." Wheaton, too, has the following passage: "Treaties may be avoided, even subsequent to ratification, upon the ground of the impossibility, physical or moral, of fulfilling their stipulations. Physical impossibility is where the party making the stipulation is disabled from fulfilling it for want of the necessary physical means depending on himself." In Martens we read, "Physical impossibility in a nation to fulfil treaty engagements absolves it from the obligations of the compact, but not from the obligations to make indemnity, should it be proved that the physical impossibility could have been foreseen, or that it was caused by the nation itself." And Heffter has the following remarkable sentence: "The contracting party may refuse to fulfil his engagements, when their fulfilment becomes impossible and is likely to remain so, even though the contract be violated; more especially if private duties, or the rights and wellbeing of a people are concerned."

I could go on quoting, but I should exceed the limits of this note were I to bring forward the numerous authorities upon this recognized principle of international law.

There is, M. le Ministre, something inexplicably harsh in denying the right of Mexico to the sympathy of her creditors, and in saying that she has systematically sacrificed their interests to her own.

I had already, before receiving your advice, studied the history of the English debt, and my research has shown me that from the very date of the London loan the republic has been a loser, its actual loss amounting to something like 8,000,000 dollars; that when bonds were issued in the year 1824 she did nothing less than make good at par what she could have made good at 50 per cent.; that later on she lost several millions in the failure of those British firms who had been mixed up in the business; yet, that still, notwithstanding the civil war which has for years been raging in the country, she has made the bondholders such remittances as cannot but have filled their pockets beyond what could have been expected, considering the circumstances of the country. But this refers solely to the exterior debt, which perhaps has suffered less than anything else from the vicissitudes Mexico has had to undergo, since, at all events, this particular debt has been attended to with something like the very care and method which the government is desirous of employing in respect to the entire public debt.

While her Majesty's legation is talking about the history of the exterior debt, it would be well if, instead of turning their attention solely to the question of the London loan, which has no diplomatic character whatever, they looked into the matter of the British convention, and stated frankly who really have been the sufferers in this business, and who have had to make sacrifices and undergo hardships. Let them say whether or not the republic has come off scot-free, when in the midst of her difficulties she has gone on punctually paying the assignments of the British convention, and even increasing the rate of interest on those assignments.

In one of my last official communications I mentioned to you that feelings of delicacy prevented my entering into the details of the convention question. I can, however, in a private letter call your attention to the kind of elements composing this diplomatic arrangement, and to the consequences resulting therefrom; indeed, it is only a few days ago that an English paper in this capital brought the matter to light, and proved nothing less than that Mexico had been paying for some tobacco concern at the rate of two ounces for each box of cigars.

As to the complaints which you have made about the robberies and murders that of late have been committed in the republic, though they have not solely been committed upon the persons of Englishmen, but equally upon Mexicans, nobody need have less cause to blush than those who, like the present government, are giving the most positive proofs of how much they are taken up with this subject, and of their anxiety to put a stop, at any price, to such atrocities, and who were actually on the point of procuring the means of carrying out their intentions, when those means were protested against by the British legation.

Who, you ask, is to blame for the present state of affairs, and for the wars which have been desolating the republic? I will tell you in all frankness, M. le Ministre, and you must not be astonished at what I am going to say.

If, as I suppose, you are well acquainted with what has happened since the date of our independence, you will find that the origin of the evil can be traced to circumstances over which neither our race in general, nor this generation in particular, had any control. It was no work of theirs; while, as for what has taken place within the last few years, foreign diplomatic agents are, in a great measure, responsible, for having recognized and given moral support to a handful of rebels who were utterly repudiated by the nation at large. Such, at all events, is public opinion.

In your last letter you still hold to the general but exaggerated notion, that many millions of the late church property have been needlessly squandered away. My opinion upon this point, M. le Ministre, may be considered worth something, for no journalist has advocated more strenuously than I have done the necessity of a proper and organized administration of the property in question, yet I am sure that if the matter were reduced to figures, and the actual value of the church property put on paper, with the positive depreciation that value has undergone, owing to the civil wars; and if, moreover, there be taken into consideration the sums paid from this source towards the extinction of the national debt, the discount at which government has been compelled to transact their negotiations in order to realize this property, and the surplus which still remains, I am sure, I repeat, that the charge of having squandered away millions will be found exaggerated.

I cannot understand why you should qualify as impracticable the arrangement which the parties interested in the British convention had entered into with government. This, or any other analogous one, would be very feasible upon the bases laid down in the decree of the 17th for the guidance of the special finance committee. This decree has in no way sacrificed the rights of the public debt; and nothing is asked for either by the government, the congress, or the country, but the permission to attempt the pacification of the country, and carry out their administrative reform. They claim but this.

With respect to what you are pleased to say about the conduct of the chiefs of the federal army in having "occupied" certain funds at Laguna Seca, I will simply ask you whether you conceive the word "robbery" implies the idea of a future indemnity, such as was made voluntarily and at a great sacrifice on this occasion, as is proved by the trifling sum which still remains unpaid?

As for the outrage at the British legation, I must correct a slight error you have made in referring to this act. It is not true that the authors of this outrage, at the time of its commission, were recognized by the representatives of friendly powers.

I thank you, in conclusion, most sincerely for the kind language you employ, while exhorting me to facilitate the renewal of our relations by the withdrawal of the decree of the 17th instant; but it appears to me that the interest you profess in the matter would have lost none of its weight, and would have gained in dignity, had you accompanied it, by way of incentive, with some proposition for an arrangement not incompatible with the honor of the nation, and less unfeasible than the essentially impracticable one you have already made us.

Hoping that you will have the goodness to consider well the observations I now offer, and flattering myself that they may lead to the re-establishment of our official intercourse, for the interruption of which there is as yet no motive, I beg, &c.

MANUEL DE ZAMACONA.

No. 22

[Translation.]

MEXICAN REPUBLIC, DEPARTMENT OF FOREIGN RELATIONS.

[Confidential and private.]

MEXICO, *July* 26, 1861.

MY DEAR SIR: On the 24th, at five in the afternoon, I addressed you a note, informing you that if, within the period of twenty-four hours, your decree of 17th July was not recalled and annulled I should break off my relations with your government. Yesterday, at half-past five o'clock, not having an answer, I had to address to you another note to notify this rupture to you.

At six o'clock I received from you a first communication, of July, (no date.) In fine, at seven o'clock there was brought to me your second note, of the 25th. In this you tell me that my note of ths 24th, despatched by me at five o'clock, had only reached you at seven. I can the less understand this delay, because at half-past five the envelope was brought to me to serve to note the time.

For the rest your two last communications, containing a refusal to accede to my demand, I find myself, to my great regret, under the necessity of persisting in the resolution of which I notified you officially yesterday.

I pray you to accept, my dear sir, the assurance of my most respectful regards.

A. DE SALIGNY.

His Excellency Mr. MANUEL DE ZAMACONA.

MEXICO, *July* 29, 1861.

A copy.

LUCAS DE PALACIO Y. MAGAROLA.

WASHINGTON, *September* 21, 1861.

A true copy.

ROMERO.

No. 23.

[Translation.]

MEXICAN REPUBLIC, DEPARTMENT OF INTERIOR AND FOREIGN RELATIONS.

SATURDAY, *July* 27, 1861.

VERY ESTEEMED AND RESPECTED SIR: I do not consider that I should add anything to the explanations which I had the honor to make to you officially in regard to the hour at which I received your communication of the 24th instant, beyond the solemn protestation that my answer was sent to the French legation before the expiration of the period which, in your said communication, was fixed upon for the abrogation of the decree of the 17th instant, and the interruption of our official relations.

Although you have thought proper to carry this last measure into effect, I do not yet find sufficient reason to cause it, and this induces me to take the liberty to enclose herein a copy of the reflections which I have addressed in a private letter to the English minister in respect of the resolution he has taken in the

same direction as yourself, the grounds for which he thought proper to state, with some fullness, in a letter which he addressed to me yesterday.
I do myself the honor to subscribe myself your most obedient, humble servant.

MANUEL MA. DE ZAMACONA.

His Excellency A. DUBOIS DE SALIGNY,
    Minister of France, &c., &c., &c.

A copy.

MEXICO, *July* 29, 1861.

LUCAS DE PALACIOS Y MAGAROLA.

A true copy.

WASHINGTON, *September* 21, 1861.

ROMERO.

No. 24.

[Translation.—Extract.]

MEXICAN REPUBLIC, DEPARTMENT OF FOREIGN RELATIONS.

No. 34.]   NATIONAL PALACE, *Mexico, August* 29, 1861.

The political review, and the copies enclosed to you of the instructions addressed under date to Mr. Don Juan Antonio de la Fuente, and of one of the private notes to which they refer, will impress upon you the character of the public situation of Mexico, and of the state of the diplomatic question.

*   *   *   *   *   *   *   *   *   *

As for the rest, you may hold as reproduced the recommendations which a month ago were made to you to resort to all opportune measure, to rectify the opinions which people purposely seek to lead astray in what relates to the acts of the Mexican government.

With this motive I renew to you the assurance of my respectful consideration.

ZAMACONA.

The CHARGE D'AFFAIRES
    of the Republic, at Washington.

A copy.

WASHINGTON, *September* 21, 1861.

ROMERO.

No. 25.

[Translation.—Extract]

MEXICAN REPUBLIC, DEPARTMENT OF FOREIGN RELATIONS.

NATIONAL PALACE, *Mexico, August* 29, 1861.

Among the documents which I send with this communication you will find those which brought to a close the correspondence this department had with the legations of France and England on the subject of the decree upon the suspension of payments, which it was not possible to send you a month since in complete condition, because the last notes, as you can see, are of a date later than the sailing of the packet.

The correspondence being closed, the apparent position of the two ministers of England and France has been that merely of expectation. Under these circumstances, nevertheless, both, and very especially Mr. de Saligny, have displayed during all the month a system of incessant hostility which puts forth plainly their purpose to edge things along to a formal rupture, and to frustrate the efforts which the government, with energy and in good faith, has made and is making to give a worthy and satisfactory solution to the question of the foreign debt.

That you may be thoroughly informed upon this question, and may appreciate accurately the conduct of the representatives of England and France during this last period, it may be convenient to give you a compendious review of the labors of the administration, and of the most important political events in the course of the last month.

In the state in which things stood upon the organization, about the middle of July, of the present cabinet, no question presented so much importance as that of finance. The consolidation of reform, the pacification of the country, the establishment of the national dignity, the abolition of vexatious exactions, and ruinous operations for raising revenue, all depended upon the government bringing them about in a sure and regular mode.

Hence sprung the idea of anticipating the receipt in the general treasury of all the federal revenues without any exception, and of organizing the army and the civil service with the strictest economy, completing this reform by framing an economical estimate as far as possibly could be done. The government, therefore, since the publication of the decree of the 17th of July, has been engaged in dictating the most stringent orders for giving effect to the consolidation of the revenues in the general treasury, in framing the estimate, which it has succeeded in reducing to little more than eight millions, and in regulating the civil service and the armed force upon a footing and groundwork which is given in detail in the said estimate, and which may satisfy all the desires of public opinion on the head of economy. But these labors, fertile for the future, cannot yield any immediate fruits of alleviation and of regularity in the public finance; the disturbed condition of the ordinary communications with the coasts and the frontier States, the habits sprung up among the governments of the States of not respecting the federal revenues, and the pretext at this time given for it by the necessity of exterminating at some points the armed residuum of the reaction, made necessary some interval of measures progressively energetic and effective until Mexico realizes the receipt of all the returns from the custom-houses; on the other hand, the most important savings, which are those connected with the organization of the army, could not for the most part be instantaneously reduced to practice with the forces that are actually in campaign, the estimate for which it was indispensable to provide for in some manner so as not to paralyze operations. It followed from all this that, before reaching the fruits of the administrative arrangement proclaimed in the middle of July, an interval must be passed through of serious difficulties, and that their solution was a preliminary question. The solution on which the government decided was to seek some way by virtue of which the revenues which were scattered among the maritime custom-houses should be gathered in here at once, and to this end an understanding was had with the most influential individuals among the merchants and capitalists, combining arrangements into which very strong inducements entered that could do no less than be of common benefit. Among the documents annexed to this note you will find the conditions of this arrangement. But because of it the systematic and implacable hostility of the French minister, and the efficient aid lent him by Mr. Wyke, has made itself especially noticeable. Both have given foreign merchants to understand, almost at the beginning of the arrangement indicated, that every combination connected with the returns from the maritime custom-houses was very dangerous, because they might be occupied at any moment by the naval forces of England and France. These ill-intended intimations frustrated the combination referred to, and the government, obliged to push forward vigorously the military operations in order to realize the important triumph which it obtained on the 14th over Marquez and his people, found itself under the necessity of ordering the extraordinary contribution from capital, of which the decree, included among the documents annexed, makes mention. Upon the ground of this odious and repugnant measure which was forced upon the government by these same foreign ministers, they have attempted to carry out a new class of hostilities. The legations of England and France, so condescending towards Zuloaga and Miramon on the four occasions when they decreed and collected the like imposts, have been at pains at this time to make of this business a question with the diplomatic body, and, were it not for the impartial and energetic rejection by the minister of the United States, would have attained their object. Failing of this, they have instructed their countrymen to resist by all possible means the collection of the contribution. The minister of Prussia, under the guise of friendly advice, came to make, orally, at this department, a movement against the impost decreed. The chargé d'affaires of Ecuador addressed to me afterwards a note upon the same subject, a note which, with the correspondent reply, you will find among the annexed documents.

The measures Mr. de Saligny has been pleased to take to occasion difficulties to the government have not stopped at this.

The news of the complete rout which Marquez and his followers suffered on the 14th was received in Mexico with spontaneous demonstrations of popular rejoicing, but without any commingling of anything threatening, even against the co-religionists of the conquered faction. Those demonstrations, notwithstanding, lent opportunity to Mr. de Saligny to give the diplomatic corps to understand that he had been the object of an insult, and even of an attempted assassination, and, to induce the other ministers to address the collective note, which, with the reply and the rejoinder to which it gave place, goes also with the annexed documents. As these notes indicate, there took place, on the occasion, a zealously conducted judicial investigation, the principal documents in which I send to you in copy, and which has placed beyond all doubt that the complaint of Mr. de Saligny had not the slightest foundation.

The coincidence of this episode with the triumph of the arms of the government over the factions headed by Marquez was nothing but the merest accident. Mr. de Saligny, who uses his time to give all his moral support to the reaction; who gave asylum to some of its leaders; who has sheltered ex-General Robles until within a few days, when he slipped away furtively from the capital to the interior; who, abusing the immunities of his domicile, has covered the correspondence between the military reactionists and those in refuge at the French legation; who has converted this into a focus of permanent conspiracy, which, published without the least concealment that the advent to power of a party of ultraists was close at hand, naturally took part in the dejection of the reactionary faction, on account of the feat of arms which occurred on the 14th, and perhaps had no other way of neutralizing the effect of that event than to make an unmerited and clamorous imputation against the progressive party. The allusion to the recent triumphs of government over the factions presents an opportunity to call your attention to the fact that, notwithstanding the embarrassments with which the government was to struggle before the fruits of the decree of the 17th of July can be practically realized, this arrangement has already proved to be very salutary, because the advantages obtained over the armed faction are exactly such as what the government, strengthened by the resources which the law cited, placed in its hands, could seasonably expect from the forces of General Ortega, which, otherwise, would have kept in position, giving room for the reaction to gather great increase. In virtue of these very measures it has become possible to re-establish the safety of the road between Mexico and Vera Cruz; it enabled it to move eastwardly a considerable force for the purpose of clearing the States of Tlascala and Puebla from the lingering bands which roam through them, and will be able to cause the main body of the army to set off to-day or to-morrow, in the direction of Queretaro, to give the final blow to reaction, by falling on the body under command of Mejia. The recent rout of Marquez has had a most important political effect. There was before much clamor about the lukewarmness and carelessness which, it was said, was entertained by some of the governors for the authorities of the union. The inaction of Doblado, although he had at Guanajuato nearly six thousand men, appeared to corroborate such rumors; but, since the event at Talatlaco, the spirit of loyalty and of constitutionalism has become very perceptible in the States, and Mr. Doblado himself has addressed to the president protestations of sincerity and of adhesion, and has moved with his forces to Queretaro to operate in the Sierra in concert with the troops which are going from Mexico. The immediate result of these movements will be to re-establish, in a durable manner, communication with the interiorr; to put an end to depredations to which the people of the villages near Sierra have been victims, and to give to the situation a normal character, which will influence public confidence very much, and will put an end to the prostration of trade and the excessive scarcity of a currency. By that time the government will begin to see the fruits of the measures it has dictated for concentrating the revenues, and distributing them methodically and economically; then will be the time when it can be said that the constitution and public order rest on a solid foundation. All this, if Providence permits it to happen, will be the fruit of the law of 17th July, and of the labors half hidden, but substantial and most important, which have occupied the government during the last month. If the prospective which I have laid before you be realized, the nation will never repent having decided to use the funds of the Penaud agreement, deposited in the montepio, (provident fund,) and to send them to the camp of General Ortega, whose forces, now victorious over Marquez, were on the point of perishing with want. But this prospective which I have sketched may be dissipated like a mist if the ministers of France and England come forth successfully from their effort to draw down upon Mexico hostilities on the part of these two nations. The hopes of the republic to avert this danger rest on you, and your patriotism and acknowledged intelligence are essential guarantees of the situation which I have, in a friendly manner, interposed to describe.   *   *   *   *   *   *

In speaking of the measures brought into play by Mr. de Saligny to depreciate our government, and give plausible explanations of his conduct, I forgot to tell you of an incident which it is proper to bring to your knowledge. By a former packet I sent you a copy of the correspondence had with the French legation about the delivery of the funds proceeding from the Penaud agreement. You would perceive that the government steadily refused that delivery, resting on the very text of the said agreement. Upon my coming into the department, Mr. de Saligny stated to me that the delivery of those funds ought to be arranged before any other business, and assured me that he had in his hands an order of the government that they should be delivered to him, and had obtained from the president and my predecessor a verbal promise bearing the same meaning, in presence of all the diplomatic corps. I immediately ascertained that neither the one nor the other was certain. All that the president and minister of foreign relations promised in effect to the minister of France, on an occasion upon which he came to the palace accompanied by others, his colleagues, was that the said fund, which had been for the moment taken on the day of a battle, would again be placed anew in deposit in the montepio before a week's end.

This promise was religiously observed. Mr. de Saligny, notwithstanding, made the other ministers believe that this return was never made, and says publicly that the diplomatic corps is ready to bear witness that the president and minister of foreign relations gave him their word of honor to make to him personally delivery of the fund deposited in the montepio. By means of this confusion of particulars, and of this vile intrigue, he has succeeded in presenting the government to the public, and to the diplomatic corps, as regardless of its word of honor. This imputation may figure among the reports of Mr. de Saligny to his court, and it has appeared to me proper to explain to you the facts in detail. * * * *

In view of what precedes you will not think that I dwell too much upon my recommendations that you should endeavor to rectify the unfaithful and angry reports which Mr. de Saligny will, without doubt, make to his government upon the points to which I have above adverted, and that you may call the attention of the French government strongly to the marked effort of its representative to embitter the relations with Mexico by exciting embarrassment and difficulties in its administration, and inventing and publishing intimations intended to neutralize in public opinion the effect of those labors of organization which engage the government, and the advantages it obtains over its enemies. * * * *

It also seems to be of much importance that in France as well as in England it should be understood that the Mexican government is disposed to accept any equitable and practicable solution on the question of the conventions; that it had thought over various projects to this end, and had set at work all possible means to discover some extraordinary aid that would allow it to meet the public debt without detriment to other administrative measures which cannot be set aside. * * * * * *

It is of equal importance, in the belief of this government, that it should not permit to be passed by without notice the practical advantages which it has attained by the suspension of payment, notwithstanding the resistance which this measure has produced, and the hostility growing out of it, by which the government has been brought to a stand.

It is very proper also to set right the exaggerations relating to the attempts upon the persons and property of foreigners, which are said to be made and making in Mexico, that it should be understood that in enlarging upon the reality of this matter there is a systematic purpose, and that if the government wishes to resort to active measures it is precisely because it is anxious to reestablish security throughout the republic. It is well to call attention to the fact that the greater part of the attacks which are discussed are the work of the rebel faction, to which the representatives of England and France are lending moral aid at this very moment.

It is proper you should know and make it understood in Europe that the two last-mentioned diplomatists have, respectively, procured an organ in the press in this capital, and that the *Estafelle* and the *Mexican Extraordinary* receive the impassioned inspirations of Messrs. Wyke and Saligny, and give the most inexact and malicious versions of passing events. * * *

I protest to you on this occasion the assurances of my distinguished consideration. ZAMACONA.

Don ANTONIO DE LA FUENTE,
   Minister Plenipotentiary of the Mexican Republic at Paris.

MEXICO, *August* 29, 1861.

A true copy.   JUAN DE D. ARIAS.

WASHINGTON, *September* 21, 1861.

A true copy.   ROMERO

No. 26.

[Translation.—Extract.]

MEXICAN LEGATION TO FRANCE,
Paris, September 5, 1861.

Our relations with France and England have come to a very lamentable state. You will see by the copy, no less than by the slips annexed, the disposition of the French government, and what may be presumed of that of England, towards the Mexican republic.

But I must recommend to you very specially the article from the "Times," of London, in which it is assumed that, by giving a certain latitude to foreign intervention, it will appear to be acceptable to the United States; and upon this it appears to me to be useless to press upon your intelligence and zeal what this and that will place before you with clearness. I desire to speak of the importance of doing everything possible to withhold the government of the American Union from any participation in this intrigue, and to incline to get rid of it if it should have been given.   *   *   *   *   *   *

I reiterate the assurances of my special and distinguished consideration.

JUAN ANTONIO DE LA FUENTE.

Don MATIAS ROMERO,
Chargé d'Affaires of the Mexican Republic, Washington.

WASHINGTON, September 21, 1861.

A true copy.

ROMERO.

No. 27.

[Translation.—Extract.]

No. 34.]   MEXICAN LEGATION TO FRANCE,
Paris, September 4, 1861.

Unhappily, I have yesterday seen realized the apprehension which you mentioned to me in your note No. 41, dated 31st August last past. The measures adopted by the governments of France and England, in consequence of the law published the 17th July, are openly hostile to us, and I believe you will be informed of them when this despatch reaches your hands.

You already know, by my note referred to, that I could not obtain an audience which I had asked from the minister here for the 31st August, and that he fixed one for yesterday, 3d of March. The conference took place on the day, and lasted only a few minutes. I commenced by saying I had received from my government special instruction and charge to give to that of his Majesty the most ample explanations, upon what affected the subjects of France, under the new law, in virtue of which suspension of payment of the national debt was ordered.

Mr. Thouvenel interrupted me, by saying that personally he had no dissatisfaction towards me; but he could not hear those explanations. "We will receive none," he added, giving way to the greatest excitement. "We have fully approved the conduct of Mr. de Saligny; we have issued our orders, in concert with England, that a squadron, composed of vessels of both nations, exact from the government of Mexico due satisfaction, and your government shall learn from our minister and our admiral what are the claims of France. I have nothing against you, I again say, and I wish that events would permit me to address you in more friendly language." "But it is very sad," said I, in turn, "that such a reply should be given to so just and simple a request as that which I have now made in the name of my government. But be it as it may, after the words you have addressed to me I ought not to insist for a moment that you should listen to me, nor is there any motive for continuing this conversation;" and I cut it short, withdrawing without delay.

The first consequence of this interview, in respect of the legation which I have the honor to conduct, is the interruption of diplomatic relations with the government of France. The declaration of Mr. Thouvenel, refusing to listen to what I had to say to him in the name of my government, the orders to employ force against my country, and the approval accorded to the conduct of Mr. de Saligny, which broke the relations with the federal government, everything pressed me to close this affair. To this end I addressed a note to-day to Mr. Thouvenel, copy of which I enclose.

The second consequence is, the unsuitableness of my presentation to the government of England for the purpose of being received as minister from Mexico, because it is almost certain that this step would bring with it a new slight, such as we have just had here. I am also impelled to decide in this manner from the notice already sufficiently intelligible that in England, where it originated, and where it is most current, the shameless plot is on-foot for European intervention in the policy and government of our country. You will have the goodness to look at, in my correspondence of to-day, the note in which I discuss this question. * * * * * *

Before closing this note I must say that if I have not asked for my passports, it has been that so serious a measure was not necessary, either in accordance with usage or the condition of things which might, perhaps, be brought about by some occurrence; and on the other hand, I believe that my remaining here may well be of some service to the republic.

I repeat to you, sir, the assurances of my distinguished consideration.

JUAN ANTONIO DE LA FUENTE.

His Excellency the MINISTER OF FOREIGN RELATIONS, *Mexico.*

A copy.

ANDRES OSEGUERA.

A true copy.

WASHINGTON, *September* 21, 1861.

ROMERO.

No. 28.

[Translation.]

LEGATION OF THE MEXICAN REPUBLIC AT PARIS,
Paris, September 4, 1861.

MR. MINISTER: As, in our conference of yesterday, your excellency showed me that you would not listen at all to the explanations which, by express order of my government, I was charged to make to you, having regard to the new Mexican law relative to the suspension of the payment of the national debt so far as this measure affects subjects of France; inasmuch as your excellency added that his Majesty's government had in all points approved the conduct of Mr. de Saligny, who, because of that law, declared his official relations with my government interrupted; and, in fine, according to what your excellency stated to me, that, acting entirely in concert with the government of England, orders had been given that the minister of France in Mexico and his Majesty's admiral should come to an understanding with my government, your excellency will consider it to be very natural and very proper that I should accept the reality of this situation, hard and unexpected as it may appear to me, and should infer the necessary consequence—that the essential purpose of my mission is obstructed; that is to say, regular communication with the government of his Majesty consecrated to the maintenance and cultivation of peace, especially when differences have arisen likely to disturb it; that, in fact, I am no longer the organ of my government with the government of his Majesty; and, in fine, that the suspension of diplomatic relations between France and Mexico, and the nature of those which are about to replace them, place me in the painful but necessary extremity of declaring, as a fact independent of my will, (a fact which I should see put out of the way with intense gratification,) that this legation suspends its relations with the government of his Majesty until that of Mexico give him instructions which may prescribe a different course.

Accept, Mr. Minister, the fresh assurances of my most distinguished consideration.

J. A. DE LA FUENTE.

His Excellency Mr. THOUVENEL, &c., &c., &c.

A true copy.

ANDRES OSEGUERA.

Mr. Seward to Mr. Romero.

DEPARTMENT OF STATE,
Washington, September 24, 1861.

SIR: I have read with much interest and instruction the papers relating to the differences between your country and several of the European States, which you submitted to me with your note of the 21st instant.

It cannot, I think, be improper for me to say that these papers abundantly show that the Mexican government is entitled to very high respect, while the new embarrassments of your country cannot fail to awaken in her behalf a profound sympathy among the American people.

I avail myself of this occasion to renew to you the assurances of my highest consideration.

WILLIAM H. SEWARD.

Señor Don MATIAS ROMERO, &c., &c., &c.

[Translation.]

Mr. Romero to Mr. Seward.

MEXICAN LEGATION OF THE UNITED STATES,
Washington, September 30, 1861.

MR. SECRETARY: It being now beyond all doubt, as is shown by the most recent advices from Europe, that the Spanish government has determined to combine its action with that of France and England in the aggressive measures which those powers are preparing to take against Mexico, and to move hostilely, at once and without them, against that republic, we think proper, in virtue of the relations of friendship and good neighborhood which bind Mexico and the United States, to state to you summarily, for the information of the government of this country, what is the existing state of the questions pending between Mexico and Spain.

Passing by the just and too numerous causes for complaint which Mexico has against the government of her Catholic Majesty as not belonging to the case referred to here, I will restrict myself to enumerating those which the cabinet of Madrid alleges it has against the Mexican republic, because those may probably be what has decided the assumption of the hostile attitude which is now being taken towards Mexico.

These sufficient grievances are reducible to two: the first is, the expulsion from Mexico, decreed in January, 1861, of Don Joaquin Francisco Pacheco, who left Madrid the year before with the appointment of ambassador of her most Catholic Majesty; and the second is, that the Mexican government does not consider itself obliged to fulfil the stipulations of a singular document to which the name has been given, as pompous as inappropriate, of "*Tratado Mon Almonte.*"

In regard to the first, I had the honor to show to your department, under date of February 4, of the year last past, what were the motives which determined the government of Mexico to order the expulsion of Mr. Pacheco whose continuance in the country was considered as incompatible with the maintenance of peace and public tranquillity, from the active participation he had taken in the civil war which then affected the republic, and from the decided measures he took to sustain the rebel faction, which ended in defeat by the people of Mexico.

As, unfortunately, Mr. Pacheco had left his country invested with the high character of representative of her most Catholic Majesty, the enemies of Mexico, who desire to provoke foreign wars, to profit by means of them, availed themselves of the incident to endeavor to cause the belief that by the expulsion of Mr. Pacheco, the government of Spain was insulted, in which opinion the government at Madrid did not hesitate to become a partaker.

The government of Mexico has declared repeatedly, in various official documents, that it was not its intention in any manner to offend that of her Catholic Majesty, with which it sincerely desires to arrange the pending differences, and to re-establish that accordance of good relations which ought to exist between both countries, because no official character, whatever, was observed in Mr. Pacheco, because he had never been accredited near the constitutional government, and was, in fact, nothing else than a foreigner, who, by his imprudent conduct, had placed himself in the category of those whom the Mexican laws denominate as *pernicious*. Among the copies which I have the honor to enclose of documents noticed in the annexed index, you will find two circulars which were published opportunely, and which confirm what I have just said.

The government of Mexico, however, did more; it gave instructions to a minister, whom it sent to Paris in May last, that he might go to Madrid to make these explanations directly to that of her Catholic Majesty, fully empowering him at the same time to conclude a settlement of the differences then pending. It seems scarcely credible that the Spanish government which, for seven months had been writing to hear these explanations, without meantime resorting to violent measures, should take them in hand just when on the eve of receiving such explanations.

The treaty called *Mon Almonte*, was signed at Paris on the 26th September, 1859, by Don Juan N. Almonte, in the name of the rebels who occupied the city of Mexico, but could not represent the Mexican republic, because they had risen in revolt against the constitution of the country, and were evading the observance of its laws to such degree that the constitutional government of the republic, which had been lawfully elected by the people, and had not ceased to exist for a single instant, was sojourning for the time at Vera Cruz; was recognized, strengthened and upheld by three-quarters of the Mexican territory, and an immense majority of the Mexican people, and had been acknowledged as the sole government of Mexico since April, 1859, by the United States. The circumstance of the non-residence of the government in the city of Mexico, which had been before, and is now again the capital of the country, and that the rebels were acknowledged as the government of the republic by three or four European powers, could in no way change the nature of the rebellion, nor cause the fundamental laws of Mexico to lose their power.

The representative of the constitutional government at Paris protested repeatedly against the conclusion of the convention, before and after it was signed. The government of Mexico also solemnly protested against it as soon as it had notice of its conclusion, and in anticipation had formally declared that the rebels lacked the authority to pledge the nation, and that settlements which might be made with them would be null and of no avail. Among the annexed documents, I remit a copy of some of the protests to which that convention gave rise.

I avail of this opportunity to repeat to you, sir, the assurances of my distinguished consideration.

M. ROMERO.

Hon. WILLIAM H. SEWARD, &c., &c., &c.

[Translation.]

Index of documents which, with date of to-day, the Mexican legation remits to the Department of State of the United States, upon questions pending between Mexico and Spain, annexed to note of this date.

No.	From whom and to whom.	Date		Contents.
		1860.		
1	Mr. Ocampo to Mr Pacheco	Jan.	12	Order of expulsion.
2	............"	Jan.	15	Circular to Mexican legations, stating the motive for the expulsion.
3	....	Jan.	25	Circular to the Mexican States.
4	Mr. Zano to Mr. Calderon Collanty.	Feb.	21	Explains the expulsion.
		1859.		
5	Mr. Lafrague to Mr. Ocampo	July	9	Remitting protest.
6	....	June	8	Protest.
7	....	Sept.	26	Monalmonte convention.
8	Mr Ocampo to Mr. Mata	Dec.	5	Instructions.
9	Mr. Lafrague to Mr. Almonte	Oct.	4	Protest.
10	Mr. Lafrague to Mr. Ocampo	Oct.	5	Copy of former protest.
11	Mr. Lafrague to Mr. Ocampo	Oct.	22	With protest No. 6.
		1860.		
12	....	Jan.	20	Protest of Mexican government.

WASHINGTON, *September 30*, 1861.

No. 1.

[Translátion.]

SECRETARY OF STATE AND FOREIGN RELATIONS,
Mexico, January 12, 1861.

His excellency the constitutional president *ad interim* cannot regard you but as one of the enemies of his government for the services you have rendered in favor of the rebel usurpers who have occupied this city for the past three years. For this he orders that you depart from this and the republic without further delay than may be strictly necessary to prepare and make your journey.

As all other friendly nations, his excellency the president respects Spain, but your sojourn in the republic cannot longer continue. The consideration which moves his excellency to this resolution is therefore entirely personal.

OCAMPO.

To Sr. D. FRANCISCO PACHECO.

Certified to by Benito Gomez Farias, under secretary.

WASHINGTON, *September* 30, 1861.

True copy.

ROMERO.

No. 2.

[Translation.]

DEPARTMENT OF STATE AND OFFICE OF FOREIGN AFFAIRS,
National Palace, Mexico, January 15, 1861.

In order that you may bring to the knowledge of the minister of foreign relations of the government near which you are accredited, the reasons why the president has thought proper to order the departure from the republic, of Messieurs Don Joaquin Francisco Pacheco, Don Felipe Nery del Barrio, and Don Louis Clementi, archbishop of Damascus, as you will see by the printed communications which accompany this note. I proceed to make a short statement with regard thereto.

Mr. Pacheco came to the republic not long since, accredited expressly in the character of ambassador of her Catholic Majesty near the government (so called) which occupied this capital, and of which Don Miguel Miramon acted as chief.

A few days after his arrival he caused himself to be officially received by the rebel government, and besides the support which, in his official character, he thus lent to the faction which had succeeded in holding possession of the capital during the past three years, he, by his policy, his expressed opinions and his open influence, lent himself to the maintenance of the rebel government and the prolongation of the civil war.

The constitutional government of the republic, which has never ceased to exist and to discharge its functions during this long period of civil war, notwithstanding its official relations with Spain have been interrupted, does not actually see in Mr. Pacheco the representative of her Catholic Majesty, with whose government the constitutional government of the republic desires to cultivate the best relations, and is ready to terminate existing differences in good will, regulating itself always by the principles of the strictest justice; but in ordering the departure of Mr. Pacheco from the country, the government does so simply in the exercise of its prerogatives, viewing him only as a foreigner falling under the stipulations of the thirty-third article of our constitution.

Mr. Nery del Barrio, for a long time minister of Guatemala, accredited to this republic, has not only had continued official relations with the rebels during the last three years, but has made his open partiality for the reactionary faction— to which he lent his most decided support in the unhappy "*coup d'etat*" of December, 1857—a matter of public notoriety.

This minister was almost the first who hastened to recognize the usurper, Zuloaga, and who mainly induced other members of the diplomatic corps to do the same. Notwithstanding, he took this unjustifiable step with the knowledge that the existing constitutional government was lawfully installed at Guanajuato in January, 1858,

The constitutional government cannot allow this gentleman, thus abusing his position, to continue fomenting civil war. For this reason it causes his departure from the republic, without intending, however, that such a measure of internal policy should in any degree imply a hostile spirit towards the republic of Guatemala, which Mr. del Barrio has represented.

Don Louis Clementi has held in this country the mission of nuncio from his Holiness the Pope. His disposition, and the general tone of the roman court which he has represented, has caused him to figure throughout the civil war as a partisan of the seditious clergy of the republic, who to the greatest degree have stained with blood the past revolution in this country under the pretext of religion.

Now that the Mexican republic has, in the exercise of its sovereign power, declared religious liberty and the absolute independence of each other of church and State, the official representative of the Roman court can have no mission whatever to attend to near the general government of the republic.

Neither of these gentlemen has been officially accredited near the constitutional government for the last three years. Consequently, their expulsion signifies nothing more than an act of public order, which is carried into effect through the provisions of the supreme law of the land, and in the exercise of the prerogatives with which the government is invested.   *   *   *   *

Renewing the expressions of my consideration, I am, etc.,

OCAMPO.

To ——— ———, Mexican Legation, at ———————.

WASHINGTON, *September* 30, 1861.

True copy.

ROMERO.

No. 3.

[Translation.]

Circular.

DEPARTMENT OF STATE AND OFFICE OF FOREIGN AFFAIRS,
Mexico, January 25, 1861.

Upon the establishment again of the supreme government in the capitol of the republic, one of its first acts was to order the departure from the republic of Messieurs D. Francisco Pacheco, D. Felipe Nery del Barrio, and D. Louis Clementi, Archbishop of Damascus.

With respect to Señor Pacheco, it had as a reason for his departure the palpable fact that upon his entry into the republic, by way of the port of Vera Cruz, where was located the legitimate government, this gentleman, far from making known his official character and maintaining a due neutrality, in view of the unfortunate circumstances of the country, which could not escape his attention, directed himself at once to this capitol, although there did not exist here any government until the return to this city of D. Miguel Miramon, when he being replaced in a very strange manner in the presidency of the revolutionary government, Señor Pacheco hastened to present himself to him as ambassador of Spain, recognizing Miramon just in the moments when, defeated at Silao, there only remained to him the shadow of power, which, thanks to the *prestige* lent to him by the recognition of this same Señor Pacheco, he was able to prolong for a few days more, during which the rebellious faction had time to perpetrate new scandals and to still further compromise the peace and good name of the country.

Besides, public opinion revolted at the presence of Señor Pacheco, and the government was obliged to obey its dictates, for it pointed him out as one of the persons whose influence had the most strongly and openly favored the reaction.

With reference to Señor Nery del Barrio, his acts in favor of the so-called government of the reactionary party were a matter of public notoriety, and there applied to him nearly the same reasons which operated to cause the departure of Señor Pacheco, and consequently his departure from the country was also a matter of necessity.

Señor D. Louis Clementi, Archbishop of Damascus, had not any diplomatic character, and being manifest, as it clearly is, the great part which the clergy have taken in the struggle which has now been brought to so happy a termination, it was not only just but a public necessity that he should leave the country. In expelling him, the only consideration was his open intervention in the affairs of the country, and not in any manner his religious character, because the government has proclaimed and will always respect entire freedom of religion.

Such have been the reasons which have actuated these measures, which are purely personal, and need not affect in any manner the amicable relations which Mexico has maintained with friendly powers.

The constitutional government, which is directing all its efforts to the permanent establishment of the peace of the country, and which esteems and respects Spain and Guatemala, and the Pontifical States, the same as all other nations with which it is bound by solemn treaties, will not omit any means whatever to maintain with all the most perfect harmony, and to augment and render more intimate their friendly relations, and will endeavor to act towards all with strict justice, in order that the dignity and good name of the republic shall not be in any way compromised.

In saying this to you for your knowledge and that of the inhabitants of the State over which you worthily preside, it is also my duty to recommend to your excellency, in an especial manner, that all foreigners be fully protected in all the immunities and guarantees which are secured to them by international law and by treaties; that the tribunals administer to them speedy justice, that they extend to them the protection required by our laws, and by the high character of the cause they sustain; and very particularly, under the present circumstances, to Spanish subjects and citizens of Guatemala, in testimony that the government is very far from considering the repulsion of the said Señores Pacheco, Del Barrio, and Clementi in any other manner than a question purely personal.

I take pleasure, with this occasion, in renewing to your excellency the assurances of my esteem and consideration. God, liberty, and reform.

ZARCO.

His Excellency the GOVERNOR OF THE STATE OF ———.

Washington, September 30, 1861.

True copy.

ROMERO

No. 4.

[Translation]

DEPARTMENT OF STATE FOR FOREIGN RELATIONS.

NATIONAL PALACE, *Mexico, February* 21, 1861.

The undersigned, secretary of foreign relations of the Mexican republic, has the honor to address himself to the secretary of state for foreign relations of her Catholic Majesty on the subject of the departure of Don Joaquin Francisco Pacheco from this republic, and of the reasons and circumstances which gave motive for it.

When Mr. Pacheco arrived at the port of Vera Cruz the supreme government of the nation was resident in that city; and whilst from respect for it, and for what is due to impartiality and to justice, and to the laws of neutrality which govern the intercourse of nations, and the conduct of their diplomatic agents abroad as ministers of peace, Mr. Pacheco, endued with a high official character, ought to have recognized and presented himself to this government, whose courtesy observed for him considerations of every kind; the said gentleman had none for the legitimate authority which permitted him to enter the country freely, and he immediately took his way towards the capital of the republic, where he announced his official character at the time precisely in which, in that city, there existed not even the shadow of a government, which the rebel crew that for three years had to no purpose stained the country with blood, had erected.

At the time of the arrival of Mr. Pacheco at this capital, Don Miguel Miramon had broken and lost even what he called titles to authority which had been given him by Don Felix Zuloaga, by assuming the chief authority over the revolutionary faction, an authority which Zuloaga attempted to reassume, and which Don Miguel Miramon refused to give over to him.

Such a state of things, which was the logical and natural result of the principles adopted by the men who sought to arrogate to themselves, and were quarrelling among themselves about the chief power over the nation, without having obtained even for a single day, either its sanction or even its assent, compelled the diplomatic corps which was then in Mexico to disregard them, and in effect they were disregarded, not without one of the foreign representatives having made explicit declarations on which he formed his resolution to leave the capital, breaking off all relations with those who ruled there.

But although in this way Don Felix Zuloaga, as well as Don Miguel Miramon, were themselves absent upon the arrival of Mr. Pacheco, their authority did not extend a foot beyond the precincts of three cities, and Miramon, finally routed at Siloa, lost at that battle every trace of his supposed power. He returned afterwards to the city of Mexico without any force or prestige, and it was precisely at that time, when, to the general astonishment, Mr. Pacheco recognized him as the supreme magistrate of the nation, and presented himself in his official character as the representative of her Catholic Majesty; thus, at least, lending his moral support to the rebel band, and thus contributing, as he best could, to the prolongation of the civil war which was then touching upon its close.

Divine Providence chose, notwithstanding, that the rebellion should succumb a little while after, crushed beneath the weight of its own crimes and by the sovereign will of the entire nation.

This result, assuredly glorious, because it was not stained by any acts such as usually accompany those of its kind, came, nevertheless, with the omnipotent force of truth to place in strong light the acts and vindicate the privileges awhile disregarded, of justice and of legitimacy, and in consequence, precisely because of the loyalty and proper spirit which governs the public sentiment of the country, it demanded on the close of the war that those should depart at once who were considered as causes of its disorders and misfortunes. The knowledge and conviction of those causes dwelt in the consciousness of the nation, and, in that of the government, the obligation to provide at once for what the public advantage required, by thus removing all motives for further disorders and disturbances.

It was however painful, but obligatory, to remember that the conduct of Mr. Pacheco had been partial, as, in consequence of his actions public sentiment had pronounced it to be, and the government, in examining it, neither could nor had any reason to acknowledge him in a public character, because in his recognition of an expiring faction he disregarded the sovereignty of the nation, and its legitimate and ever unbroken government, and thus regarding the matter as entirely personal, his withdrawal was settled upon, providing withal that every accommodation should be at his call.

This true and simple narrative will of itself suffice to explain satisfactorily, the retirement of Mr. Pacheco, and the undersigned discharges the grateful duty of solemnly declaring that, that personal and individual incident in no wise affects or lessens the frank and loyal desire which animates the government of Mexico to maintain, cultivate, and strengthen with that of her Catholic Majesty the closest and most cordial relations. That, if it has indeed protested upon occasion, and repeatedly and publicly, against any treaty convention or arrangement emanating from the faction which, in the city of Mexico, assumed for itself the name of government, because for such treaties, conventions, or arrangements, no individual had any personality or lawful mission derived from the nation, whose great majority not only had never conceded to it the least right, but had striven without ceasing for three years to exterminate it, this does not hinder the government of the republic, firm in its purpose to do justice, from directing, with the efficient co-operation of the enlightened government of her Catholic Majesty, their efforts for the smoothing away to a happy end, the differences which may have arisen between Mexico and Spain, by resorting to whatever means are afforded by sound justice, by the probity, and the mutual respect of the two nations.

Nothing will be more grateful to the Mexican people and its government than to see re-established, frankly and honorably, the perfect understanding and cordial agreement which should never have been interrupted between the two countries, considering the friendly spirit which has always influenced Mexico in her relations with the Spanish nation.

Under these impressions, and in the assurance that the government of her Catholic Majesty is animated by like sentiments and desires, it will be very satisfactory to that of the republic to receive or send one of the many persons of talent, taste, and probity, who abound in both countries, and be able, through his adjustments, to give that strength and elevation to their fraternal relations which shall equal in degree that which their name, their civilization, and their mutual interests demand. The present need of an agent of this kind, who may serve as the medium of communication between the two governments, compels the undersigned to address himself directly to his excellency the minister of state for foreign relations, and in doing so, to make the ingenuous exposition which, precedes, he must, by the assent of the president of the republic, here give utterance to the expression of the sincere wishes formed by the government of Mexico for the prosperity and aggrandizement of the Spanish nation, and for the happy reign of its august sovereign.

At the same time the undersigned has the honor to offer to his excellency the minister of state for the department of foreign relations, of her Catholic Majesty, the assurances of his high consideration,

FRANCESCO ZARCO.

His Excellency THE MINISTER OF STATE
For Foreign Relations of her Catholic Majesty.

MEXICO, *March* 18, 1861.

A certified copy.

ZARCO.

WASHINGTON, *September* 30, 1861.

A true copy.

ROMERO.

No. 5.

[Translation.]

DEPARTMENT OF STATE FOR FOREIGN RELATIONS.

MEXICAN LEGATION, NEAR H. C. M.,
Paris, July 9, 1859.

In compliance with your wish, expressed in your communication of May 3, last, I have the honor to send herewith an authenticated copy of the new protest I have made, which I shall at once print and put in circulation, that it may produce the effect which the constitutional government may desire.

I renew to you the assurances of my distinguished consideration,

J. M. LAFRAGUA.

His Excellency Don MELCHOO OCAMPO,
Minister for Foreign Affairs, Vera Cruz.

WASHINGTON, *September* 30, 1861.

A true copy.

ROMERO.

No. 6.

[Translation.]

DEPARTMENT OF STATE,
Legation of Mexico, near H. C. M.

From the time when, in January, 1858, constitutional order was disturbed in the United Mexican States, the settlement of the differences pending between Mexico, and began to be considered as certain; this opinion was founded on a knowledge of the ideas which the administration that triumphed in the capitol of the republic, professed, and on the conduct, unhappily almost uniform, of all parties in the world which reprehend that done by an adversary, not so much for reasons of intrinsic justice, as upon considerations of political conveniency.

During all the past year European periodicals, those of Spain especially, have announced the settlement indicated, until within a few months it has been affirmed to be a business definitely concluded. The supreme constitutional government kept silent while the convention was more or less probable, but now that it is announced as an act consummated, it has considered that it should speak in the name of the nation, because, although to save the rights and interests of the Mexican people, the protest which, on the 16th March, 1858, I made and published in this capital, and which I repeated on the 6th July, in the city of Berlin, is without doubt sufficient, it is also very proper to reproduce it now that it may not at any time be alleged that the silence of the legitimate government was a tacit consent. In fact, in a note of the 3d of May, the minister of foreign relations notifies me, that I should "at once make a fresh protest, insisting especially against the article upon indemnity."

Wanting in official data about the before-mentioned convention, I am obliged to limit myself in judging of them to the advices published in the journals of Madrid. According to them the government presided over by General Zuloaga had agreed to punish the offenders, to indemnify the losses occasioned, and to fulfil fairly and plainly the treaty of the 12th November, 1853; that is, it has acceded to the three propositions which the Marquis de Pidal presented to me in June, 1857, as bases for the settlement of the differences between both countries. I will say nothing about the first; for its justice being acknowledged by me, I accepted it without any difficulty. As for the third, it is sufficient to reflect that the government of the republic has never refused to fulfil the treaty, and that I offered its fulfilment despite its intrinsic defects, but at the same time remonstrated against the improper introduction of some credits on the Spanish fund. The revision of these credits, which has been and is the only cause of dissatisfaction, was asked and maintained by Mexico from the 24th of March, 1855; the Spanish government even yet does not respond to the note of that date; it is therefore needless for me to dwell further on the demonstration of the magnitude of the consequences the nation must suffer if she precludes herself from such revision, because it not only involves the burdening of the public funds with more than two millions of dollars, but gives the character of a foreign debt to that which is domestic, openly contravening the treaty of 1836, the convention of 1851, and the very treaty itself of 1853.

According to the first, Mexico ought to pay the debt anterior to her independence as "her own and national;" and Spain "desisted from any claim or pretension on this point, and declared the republic free and forever acquitted from all responsibility in this matter." The credits referred to are anterior to the independence.

In conformity to the second, the credits of "Spanish origin," and ownership, "but not those which although of Spanish origin had passed into the ownership of citizens of another nation," could alone enter into the Spanish fund. The credits claim had belonged to Mexican citizens.

According to the third "the credits which had already been examined and liquidated in conformity with the convention of 1851, remain legally acknowledged. Consequently, although credits may have been admitted by Mexico, if t were shown that they were not in conformity with the convention, must be excluded from the fund. This is the foundation and object of revision; this is the cause of the difference between Mexico and Spain; this is the just reason upon which Mexico protests against the convention, and here, in fine, let it be said, is the want of justice with which the Spanish government refuses to admit of revision. The second proposition relating to indemnity for losses has been the fertile pretext for heaping abuse on my country and myself, without a single national foundation. "Mexico will indemnify losses," asked Mr. Pidal in his note of 23d June, 1857. Mexico will indemnify, I suggested on the 7th July, in accord with the representatives of France and England, "if it is proved illegally (legally?) that it is under any of those conditions in which, "according to the laws of nations," rulers are liable for the acts of their subjects. As this was not accepted, Lord Howden, on the same day, proposed, "Mexico will indemnify in conformity with the laws of nations." Mr. Pidal rejected this; I accepted it.

Where, then, is the refusal of Mexico to do justice? Where, then, the iniquitous system which has been imputed to the government of the republic? On which side are morality, the law of nations, and the civil law? Would Spain concede anything more to France, or France to England? Why, then, exact from Mexico what is not sought from any other people? Great or small, rich or poor, well or ill constituted, she is as sovereign as other nations of the earth; and if she has the same duties as others she also has the same rights.

This simple exposition is enough, faithfully accordant with truth, to demonstrate the intrinsic injustice of indemnity in decided terms. Well, then, if this proposition was valid in July, 1857, what will it be in June, 1857? If it was valid while the blood of the victims was still reeking, pending the proceedings, the truth ignored, the criminals living, and the law violated, what will it be when the victims are pacified, the causes disposed of, the facts known, the guilty punished, and the laws satisfied? If it were certain, when at least there was room for doubt, how will it be when there is nothing more than reason to think? If, then, to grant indemnity at such time would be grave wrong done to the republic, what will it be to concede it now?

In the horrible catalogue of crimes gratuitously imputed to Mexico, there figures prominently, participation in attacks upon some Spanish subjects, attributed not merely to secondary agents, but to high functionaries to the government, even of General Comonfort. It was idle to allege on well founded reason that morality, justice, public utility, and even private interests made the act impossible. It was idle to ask what convenience and what object the government could have to operate in such manner, because, even for the commission of crime there is need of a motive, an object, a result. It would be idle, in fine, to offer as proof, the constant prosecution of the criminals, the incessant activity urged upon the magistracy, the appointment of a special judge, the creation of an exclusive police, and the deference sometimes unduly yielded, and never acknowledged by the Spanish agents and parties interested in those lamentable occurrences. It was a question of party, and should be passed upon by party reasoning. It was an arm which mischance placed in the hands of the reactionary party, and which that party yielded without restraint against the government to overthrow it if amid its blood-stained fragments the nationality of the republic should be destroyed.

General Comonfort fell and the government which succeded him in the capital, hailed the journals of Madrid not only as impartial, but as friendly to Spain, upheld in the most perfect manner, the acts of the preceding administration. Composed of persons adverse to constitutional order, and triumphant after a contest of two years, it was natural that, if not out of hate or vengeance, it should at least, as an element of policy, bring about an elucidation of all facts. The suit in the San Vicente case was concluded without any indications appearing of the crimes imputed to the government, and in the month of September, five of the leading assassins suffered death. Here is fresh proof of the injustice with which the republic has been judged, because a sentence carried into execution is a truth.

But by good fortune we can place ourselves on indestructible foundations, because, if every sentence carries in its favor the presumption of being just, that of San Vicente reckons, besides, on two very important circumstances. The first, that the judges who, on those occasions, passed sentence were appointed by General Zuloaga and belonged to the political party which ruled the capital. Therefore, any attenuation of the crime cannot even be suspected, and much less any dissimulation in respect of those who could be regarded as accomplices. The second is that of the five criminals executed, four were convicted and also confessed, and one only convicted. If all had been in this case it might perhaps have happened that, by exaggerating injustice into calumny, the sentence would have been attributed to error or to culpable carelessness, because it could be said that the judge, according to his personal inclination, had unduly weighed the facts. But what proofs can be admitted against confessions? The man who now confesses himself guilty of crime, undoubtedly has committed it because there are no longer tortures to extort from the frail body of man, revelations which his conscience does not dictate. Now then, if the principal criminals were punished, if, from the principal trial, there resulted none of those conditions under which, by the law of nations, governments become responsible, upon what can a claim for indemnity be founded? It is true that some Spaniards have been injured, but is that enough to make the nation responsible, especially when justice has been executed on the guilty? To what would the independence of the republic be reduced if such a precedent could be established?

Offences thus submitted to an unsuitable examination, the public treasury would be at the mercy of ill-intentioned foreigners who, in a traffic as immoral as safe, could speculate not only in merchandize but even in blood, and divide perhaps, portions of the one and the other with thieves and assassins. Will the governments of Europe admit a principle so fatal among those which form the law of nations? Wherefore, then, apply it to Mexico?

It is therefore demonstrated that the convention, said to have been concluded by General Zoloaga with the government of her Catholic Majesty, is intrinsically unjust and eminently prejudicial to the rights and interests of the Mexican republic. But even supposing that it may have been made in express terms, even supposing it settled in accordance with equity, it cannot, for that reason, be maintained. It would, perhaps, be just, it would, perhaps, be suitable enough, if you choose, but it would always be void, because of its being concluded by one party utterly incompetent to act.

Not having attained a settlement of the differences with the Marquis Pinal, I withdrew from Madrid, on the 1st day of August, 1857, after having presented to the Spanish government a memorandum, and when Spain had already accepted the mediation which France and England had offered. There was then already pending in Mexico this new negotiation, when, on the 21st January, 1858, the reactionary government triumphed in the capital, and commenced that horrible civil war which, for seventeen months, has been destroying the republic. But that administration was, from the beginning, very far from being a national government, and so it acknowledged itself, when, on first addressing itself to the Mexican people, it said expressly that perhaps "it would be no more than the government of some of the departments, and its representation would be such as the republic might choose to give it." And in fact it has been no more than a government of some cities, and the republic has not yet bestowed upon it a national representation.

On the same day, March 16, last year, I received two orders diametrically opposed. By one the reactionary government provided that the legation which was in my charge should cease. By the other I was ordered to continue it by the constitutional government, which had lawfully organized at Quanajnato, on the 19th January, that is, before its occupation of the capital, a circumstance which should not be forgotten. Not through any party affiliation, still less through personal interest, but upon an intimate conviction that the government at Mexico was not the government of the republic, I found myself constrained not to comply with its orders, and moreover to, protest against any convention it might conclude with the Spanish government. I knew well this course would be the subject of criticism and of ridicule, but as no act of my life has been taken with better or safer conscience, I determined to face not merely persecutions but somewhat worse—ridicule. I discharged my duty; time has placed its ineffaceable stamp upon my protest, and, after seventeen months, what I wrote therein is true, because if General Zuloaga, in the first ten, could only govern a few States, General Miramon, his substitute, in the seven last, did not obtain recognition except in some cities, finding himself compelled to act on the defensive, even in the streets of the capital.

The constitutional government has to-day the same well-established rights as then, because now, as then, it is law, it is not revolution. But the most important fact is that now it rules over wider territory, because now a majority of the people obey it; because now it holds all the ports; because now it is recognized by one of the principal nations. As I then said, a recognition by foreign ministers does not legalize governments which can only owe their existence to the will of the people, but it is nevertheless a highly significant fact that the United States of America, which recognized in General Zuloaga a government *de facto*, have since recognized the constitutional government; because this act at least proves that this is now more a government *de facto* than then, and as its right has been ever the same it necessarily follows that it is the true government of the republic.

Well, then, can acts done by illegitimate authority be obligatory on the nation? The contracts which weigh upon the public income, the mortgages and sales of ecclesiastical property, made in fraud of the law concerning mortmain, can such subsist when the government which passed these measures is not obeyed by full three-fourths of the Mexican people? Certainly not; and if it is thus in treating of affairs with individuals, what will be the issue when treating of international matters. The first are serious and important, but the second much more serious and important, because such are not questions of money but of honor; because they not only prejudice the interests but also the rights of the republic; because the acceptance of a wrongful act is not only intimated thereby, but also the sanction of a wrong principle; and because, in fine, they give rise not only to present evils, but bring on greater in the future. And as the constitutional government has decided to maintain the interests, the rights, and the dignity of the nation, and desires, in good faith, to arrange the differences with Spain in a manner as substantial as honorable, it deems it in every view necessary to make known its determination in so important a matter. Therefore, in the name of the Mexican republic, I *protest*, in the most solemn manner, against any conventions which the government established in the capital has concluded or may conclude with his Catholic Majesty, the legitimate government, in consequence, continuing at full liberty to act as it may judge convenient, and to reclaim all injuries that may attach to the country. I repeat, also, that this government, complying with what it owes to others, will punish the guilty, will grant indemnities according to the law of nations, and will fulfil the treaty of 1853, always claiming the revision of the credits which were unduly included in the Spanish fund.

No one can foresee the end of the civil war. Victory will give more or less importance to the fact of this protest; but it will, at all events, be an authentic testimonial of the justice and good faith of the constitutional government.

JOSE MARIA LAFRAGUA.

PARIS, *June* 8, 1859.

PARIS, *June* 9, 1859.

A copy.

A. ESCALANTE.

VERA CRUZ, *December* 29, 1859.

A copy certified. In the absence of the chief *ad interim*,

JOSE D. CABRERA Y E,
Fourth Official.

WASHINGTON, *September* 30, 1861.

A true copy.

ROMERO.

No. 7.

[Translation.]

The president of the Mexican republic and her Majesty the Queen of Spain, equally moved by the desire to put an end to the differences which unhappily have arisen between the two countries, and to draw more closely the natural friendship which should exist between them, have agreed upon proceeding to conclude a treaty which may re-establish the former relations between the two states, and have for this purpose appointed as their plenipotentiaries, the president of the Mexican republic, Don Juan Almonte, general of division in the Mexican army, and envoy extraordinary and minister plenipotentiary of the Mexican republic near his Imperial Majesty the Emperor of the French; and her Majesty the Queen of the Spains, Don Alexandro Mon, knight of the grand cross of the royal and distinguished order of Charles III, of the imperial legion of honor of France, of that of Christ, of Portugal, and of the pontificate of Pius IX, deputy to the cortes, ex-minister of hacienda, member of the royal academy of San Fernando, and ambassador extraordinary and minister plenipotentiary of her Catholic Majesty near his Majesty the Emperor of the French, who, after having exchanged their full powers, found in good and due form, have agreed upon the following articles:

ARTICLE 1. The principal criminals in the assassinations committed at the haciendas of San Vicente and Chinconcuaque having already been condemned by the courts and executed, undergoing personally the capital punishment imposed upon them, the Mexican government will continue action in the prosecution and punishment of the rest of the accomplices, who have thus far succeeded in eluding the action of justice, and in hastening all the proceedings, so that those may receive the punishment due for the crimes committed at the mine of St. Dimas, department of Durango, the 15th September, 1855, as soon as said department may return to its obedience to the Mexican government, or when the guilty may be arrested or the advisers of these crimes.

ARTICLE 2. The government of Mexico, although convinced that there was no responsibility on the part of the authorities, functionaries, and others employed for the crimes committed at the haciendas of San Vicente and Chinconcuaque, influenced nevertheless by the desire which animates it to cut through at once the differences which have arisen between the republic and Spain, and for the common and well-understood interests of both countries, so that they may pursue their way together, always united and bound by ties of enduring friendship, consents to indemnify the Spanish subjects who may be concerned for the loss and injury which may have been occasioned to them in consequence of the crimes committed at San Vicente and Chinconcuaque.

ARTICLE 3. Moved by the same desires mentioned in the preceding article, the Mexican government consents also to indemnify the subjects of her Catholic Majesty for the loss and damages they may have suffered in consequence of the crimes committed on 15th September, 1856, at the mines of St. Dimas, department of Durango.

ARTICLE 4. Animated by the same sentiments expressed in the two preceding articles, and full of the same desires, the Spanish government consents that the indemnities referred to shall not serve as the ground or antecedent of any cases of like nature.

ARTICLE 5. The Mexican government and that of Spain agree that the sum or value of the indemnities treated of in the foregoing articles be determined by agreement between France and England, who have shown a willingness to accept this trust, which will be discharged by them or their representatives,

THE PRESENT CONDITION OF MEXICO. 115

taking account of the data the parties interested may bring forward. and hearing the respective governments.

ARTICLE 6. The treaty of 12th November, 1853, shall be re-established in all its force and vigor as if it had never been interrupted, unless by another act of equal force it be not by common accord abrogated or altered.

ARTICLE 7. The loss and damage, claims for which were pending on the interruption of relations, and any that during such interruption may have given origin to fresh claims, shall be the subject of ulterior arrangements between the governments of Mexico and Spain.

ARTICLE 8. This treaty shall be ratified by his excellency the president of the Mexican republic and by her Majesty the Queen of Spain, and the ratifications shall be exchanged at Paris within four months, reckoned from this date, or sooner, if possible.

In faith whereof the undersigned plenipotentiaries have signed and sealed this with their respective seals. Done in triplicate at Paris, 26th day of September, of the year of our Lord one thousand eight hundred and fifty-nine.

JUAN N. ALMONTE.
ALEJANDRO MON.

WASHINGTON, *September* 30, 1861.

A copy.

ROMERO.

No. 8.

[Translation]

DEPARTMENT OF STATE FOR FOREIGN RELATIONS.

No. 61.]   NATIONAL PALACE, *Vera Cruz, December* 5, 1859.

I have the honor to send herewith a copy of the communication and protest of Mr. Lafragua, relative to the convention said to have been concluded between Mr. Almonte and the Spanish government about the questions which the last has pending with Mexico, that, being informed about them, and convinced of the sound reasons which dictated them, you may make them in season available with the government of the United States, as those documents rest on the same foundation as those on which the constitutional government reposes, which permit not now, or any time, any derogation from the interest and dignity of the nation.

On this occasion I reiterate to you the assurances of my esteem.

OCAMPO.

The MEXICAN MINISTER at *Washington.*

WASHINGTON, *September* 30, 1861.

A copy.

ROMERO.

No. 9.

[Translation.]

DEPARTMENT OF STATE FOR FOREIGN RELATIONS.

LEGATION OF MEXICO NEAR H. C. M.,
Paris, October 4, 1859.

The Press, the Journal of Debates, and the National Opinion, and other periodicals at this capital, copying a paragraph from the "Correspondencia

Autografa" of Madrid, have announced that your excellency and Mr. Mon have signed a convention which ends the differences between Spain and Mexico. In compliance with the orders of the supreme constitutional government, I protest in the name of the republic against that settlement, be it what it may, wholly saving and reserving the rights of the nation, and reproducing all the reasons alleged in my protests of the 16th of March, 1858, and the 8th of June of the present year, of which I again send your excellency a copy.

I reiterate to your excellency my very distinguished consideration.

J. M. LAFRAGUA.

His Excellency Lieutenant General of Division DON J. N. ALMONTE.

PARIS, *October* 5, 1859.

A copy.

A. ESCALANTE.

VERA CRUZ, *December* 1, 1859.

A copy certified.

JUAN DE DIOS ARIAS.

WASHINGTON, *September* 30, 1861.

A copy.

ROMERO.

No. 10.

[Translation.]

DEPARTMENT OF STATE FOR FOREIGN RELATIONS.

LEGATION OF MEXICO NEAR H. C. M.,
Paris, October 5, 1859.

I have the honor to send you a copy of the communication which I addressed yesterday to General Don Juan N. Almonte on account of the notice, already so formally made public, of a settlement made with the Spanish government. Perhaps (and I wish it for the honor of the country) there may be some inexactness as to the bases settled on for the convention, and that you will see in the number of the National Opinion which I enclose; but if it should not be so—if the settlement be such as is announced—it must be admitted that the reactionary government has put the seal of contempt to an affair so essentially prejudicial to the rights and interests of the nation.

What becomes of independence if every offence of an individual is to be indemnified? What becomes of the dignity of the nation if she not only pays debts she does not owe, but indemnifies for such as, by the greatest abuses, have been introduced into the convention.

I give many thanks to Providence for having relieved me from taking part in such an unjust agreement, but, as a Mexican, I shall always deplore that there should have been a government, although it might not be legitimate, which should thus have opened up a new source of calamities and entanglements for the republic. * * * * * *

In my opinion, the two solemn protests which I have printed and circulated suffice to place the constitutional government at liberty when the time comes for action. It might be opportune that the department should address a note to the American government, or, by means of a formal decree, should disavow the convention, so that not the least doubt should remain as to its determination. I reiterate to you the assurances of my most distinguished consideration.

J. M. LAFRAGUA.

His Excellency THE MINISTER OF FOREIGN RELATIONS
Of the Constitutional Government.

VERA CRUZ, *December* 1, 1869.

A certified copy.

JUAN DE D. ARIAS,
Chief ad interim.

WASHINGTON, *September* 30, 1861.
A copy.

ROMERO.

No. 11.

[Translation]

DEPARTMENT OF FOREIGN RELATIONS.

LEGATION OF MEXICO NEAR H. C. M.,
Paris, October 22, 1859.

I have the honor to send to you copy of the communication which on the 4th I addressed to General Almonte, and of that which on the 5th I addressed to you by way of the United States.

Until to-day Mr. Almonte has made no answer, any more than to the protests of the 16th March and 6th June of last year, and that of the 8th June of the present. Of the first and last I send you six copies, but not of the second, because that was simply a note, in which I repeated that of March. With all the pains I have taken, I have not been able to get at the text of the agreement; but, according to all the accounts I have, it has without doubt been concluded by yielding to all the pretensions of Spain. "El Pais," in an article decidedly encomiastic of the reactionary government, enters into some details which I think very important, and therefore refer you to them, although they are not said to be from an official source.

Let it be said, then, that Mexico obliges herself to punish offenders yet unknown, and concedes indemnification to Spain without recognition of the principle of indemnity, and that this fact may never be cited as a precedent. From this the author of the article infers that the convention is a very good one, because Spain receives satisfaction and Mexico does nothing contrary to its dignity.

If such are the terms of the convention, it may be thought by those who look superficially at the affair that in effect the rights, if not the interests also, of the republic have been maintained; and, as disinterestedness is the basis of Mexican character, it will also be said that the government, while preserving the national dignity, has acted generously towards the ancient mother country.

But upon this I will allow myself to offer a few remarks. In the first place, nations are not like individuals. These may consent to pay what they do not owe without detriment or prejudice from that generosity, because it is not the case that, if a man pay what he does not owe, the principle is settled so that it may afterwards serve as an argument against other men or himself even. But nations cannot act in this manner, because what they have once granted to an other is claimed in turn by all the rest, partly because, under the law of nations, acts always operate against those who do them, and because they give avail to the axiom, so injurious to us, of granting to all that which is granted to the most favored nation.

Consequently, it means nothing that Mexico may indemnify without recognition of the principle of indemnity in absolute terms, because the fact will always present itself as a proof; resulting from this, that the precedent rests established that I resisted with so much zeal, although the text of the convention may say that it is not established.

But even allowing this false supposition were a truth, the most that could be maintained would be that Spain could not in future base other claims upon the last convention. But shall we be able to answer other nations with this? The day they may have anything to claim from us we shall in vain say to them that in paying Spain we did not recognize the principle, because they will insist on the allegation of the fact, and we will have to pay all, without equity, without obligation, and merely from generosity. How, in fact, deny to France, to England, to the United States, what we have conceded to Spain? Is one nation better worth than another? Are not all equal in reason and in law? Is it not truly written in many treaties that we owe to foreigners protection and security? How then will a phrase written in a convention agreed upon between the representatives only of Mexico and Spain save us against claim, when, in fact, we have conceded indemnity without having been in the situations which the law of nations indicates?

I think, therefore, this diplomatic reserve—which the rather merits the name of a stupid subterfuge to pass off feebleness for generosity of spirit—is a germ sadly prolific of disgusts, prejudices, and losses for the republic which must indubitably be heaped up in every quarter, injurious to its international right, and which records in its annals a fact more deplorable than others of those which form the large catalogue of our errors.

It is said the convention is honorable; in my opinion it is little worthy of either country. It is so for Spain, because she receives by favor what she claimed by right, because she accepts as favor what she maintained as right. It is so for Mexico, because she pays what she does not owe, because she apologizes without having offended, supposing that, the principle of indemnity not being recognized, Spain has confessed that the crime of San Vicente was a common offence, and that Mexico unconsciously has made the cause of the assassins her own. Where and how is the national dignity saved? It would have been less evil to confess we were in the situation indicated by the law of nations, because there would have been frankness in that confession, and because it is nothing new in the world nor degrading to a nation that it should have some functionaries who do not discharge their duties.

But to say that we are not in those situations, and nevertheless to grant indemnity, is an act that cannot be explained except by calling upon that partisan spirit for whose sake principles are sacrificed amid the whirlwinds of passion. And if to this situation of the convention, so little satisfactory, is added that relating to the convention pure and simple, acknowledged as it seems to be, what remains of the justice, of the honor, of the name of Mexico? To what purpose have we thrown away eleven years upon the question of credits unduly assumed and about three upon offences improperly adjudicated upon, if those in fact are not revised and these in fact are certified? We pay money we do not owe, and for blood we have not shed, wasting in both cases the interests and in both trampling under foot the laws of the republic.

I have thought it my duty to present these observations to the supreme government because, although I have no certainty that the settlement has been made in the terms I have referred to, it is very probable it may embrace the

ideas expressed by "El Pais," in which case it is very proper things should be placed in their true light, so that transcendental errors may be avoided in the appreciation of the facts.
I reiterate to you my very distinguished consideration.
J. M. LAFRAGUA.
The MINISTER OF FOREIGN RELATIONS
Of the Constitutional Government.

VERA CRUZ, *December* 1, 1859.
I certify this to be a copy.
JUAN DE D. ARIAS,
Chief ad interim.

WASHINGTON, *September* 30, 1861.
A copy.
ROMERO.

No. 12.

[Translation.]

The constitutional government to the nation:

In the difficult position in which Mexico is placed, when she has most need of patriotism and forecast in the direction of her policy, an act offensive to her dignity and injurious to her interests has occurred, to place in strong light how far the inclinations of the enemies of liberty may do her wrong.

The party which, resting its titles to power on the defection of a part of the army, has established itself in the city of Mexico, calling itself the government of the republic, although that has rejected such representations through more than two years of strife, has concluded, at Paris, with the representative of her Catholic Majesty, in September of last year, a treaty unjust in essentials, foreign to the usages of nations in the principles which it sets forth, illegal because of the manner of its adjustment, and contrary to the rights of our country.

These qualifications are not the offspring of the spirit of party, nor of the passions which this engenders or frequently excites; nor are they either the result of unworthy prejudices against the Spanish nation. Into the noble mission of the lawful government, into the noble and patriotic influences which guide it, enter no other sentiments or desires than the sentiment of justice and the desire for the public welfare. The analysis of the document indicated, the reflection suggested by reading it, are enough to attest the justice and good faith of the same government in this respect, as well as that it was under obligation to prevent its silence upon this serious affair from being construed into a national acquiescence.

Eight articles are contained in the convention concluded between the representative of Don Miguel Miramon and that of the Queen of Spain. By the first of said articles the Mexican government assumes an obligation to continue actively to prosecute judicially and to punish the accomplices in the offences committed on the estates of San Vincente and Chiconcuaque, as well as to be responsible for the occurrences, no less deplorable, which happened, in 1856, at St. Dimas, in the State of Durango.

According to articles 2 and 3, although the Mexican government is convinced that there was no responsibility on the part of the authorities, functionaries, or persons in employ, for the offences referred to, it consents to indemnify Spanish subjects for the loss and damages which may have been occasioned to them by such offences. The Spanish government consents (article 4) that such indemnities shall not serve as the base or precedent for other cases of like nature. France and England shall determine (article 5) the amount of the indemnities conceded.

By article 6 the treaty of the 12th November, 1853, is re-established in full force and vigor, without any mention, even incidental, of a revision of credits which are not the property of Spaniards.

The loss and damage (article 7) for pending claims shall be arranged by ulterior conventions, and the ratifications of this treaty shall be exchanged at Paris (article 8) within four months, reckoned from the day on which it was sealed.

It is clearly obvious that this convention is humiliating to our country. How, in what title, by what right, consent to indemnities thus stipulated, when the government of Don Miguel Miramon declares that it is convinced of the complete blamelessness of the agents of the public authority? Upon what could this consent be founded? If pecuniary responsibility for losses proceeding from offences of ordinary character were a principle of the law of nations, the Spanish nation would not have consented to the declaration that the concessions made on this point by the Mexican government should not serve for precedent in future cases. Thus, then, its acquiescence in that declaration goes to show that it is convinced of the injustice of its demand; nor can it be otherwise, because the representative of her Catholic Majesty could not be ignorant that the obligation of nations, in respect to crimes of ordinary character directly injurious to foreigners, is to prosecute and punish their authors, under the provisions of their respective laws, and not to grant pecuniary indemnities for damages caused by those crimes; and it is certainly extraordinary that the person who figured in the convention alluded to as the representative of the supposed government of Mexico should have admitted, on the part of his country, against all reason and all right, obligations which even the party claimant did not hesitate to declare absolutely unfounded—obligations which, if they could have had existence, would end in the reduction of the national independence to a nullity. To convince oneself that this last asseveration is altogether accurate, it will be sufficient to reflect that no government whatever, and whatsoever may be its means of action, can prevent the perpetration of ordinary crimes; that if it should have to provide indemnities to the subjects of friendly nations for the injuries which such should cause to them. it would finish by draining its treasury and all its elements of subsistence.

Why, then, has this party, which allows itself to hurl against its adversaries even the foul stain of faithlessness to the country, humbled itself to the low degree of consenting to an exigency in every point of view without foundation? Nations can only accede to proper applications; otherwise, their honor being once in question, they would be exposed to the contumely and the exactions of the rest.

As little decorous is it to the nation to permit that, under the shadow of the good faith of treaties, its debt should be adulterated, or that there should be a traffic to its prejudice with credits which cannot lawfully be covered by them. Why should not the cabinet of Madrid consent to the revision of those credits when its good name requires it, and when good faith, and even the interests of the lawful Spanish credits, are calling for it?

It is the duty, therefore, of the legitimate government to oppose the sanction, through the interested condescension of a party void of conscience, of abuses which in any case can be guarded against by the law of nations. The responsibility of the governments can only be founded on the absolute denegation of justice. If Mexico be not in such position, there is no law to subject her to a condition contemptible in the eyes of the civilized world. Independence, honor, good name, the great interests of a people, must not be an illusion to Mexicans, but a substantial reality to ourselves as well as to foreigners.

Happily, the treaty in question will not prejudice the interests of the republic, nor will it cede anything in prejudice of its good name because it was concluded and ratified by persons not authorized to treat in the name of Mexico. A political party whose power proceeds from a rebellion which the great majority of the country condemns—a faction which, by the efforts of the forces it has raised is preventing, in the central cities, the free utterance of public opinion—a party which has inaugurated its power by showing what would be the government of some departments, of some cities, according to the support the nation would give to it—a party, in fine, which, notwithstanding the horrible war which it has continued and excited during two years, availing itself of all sorts of measures, has not been able to attain the representative character it sought, is not, nor can be, the government of the Mexican republic.

The constitutional government will not here dwell upon the titles upon which it rests its authority; they are in the laws and in the public will. In a very short time there will be an end to the disturbances which rend the bosom of the country and endanger its glorious independence, and legitimate power will exert itself irresistibly to maintain the last, and give assurance to all the guarantees of our countrymen and foreigners.

Mexico has the best inclination to do Spain full justice, to grant to her whatever may be due, faithfully to carry out her treaties; but she requires this to be done in conformity with the law of nations; and that the consideration of her feebleness or of her strength, of her good or bad political organism, have no influence upon the settlement of these differences. She desires to be regarded as a free and sovereign people, and that the sense of justice be that which may preside over all her stipulations; in a word, she desires that good faith and reason may govern exclusively in her diplomatic arrangements, and that none may claim the right to undervalue a nation which has known how to conquer independence, and which to-day gives proof, in the midst of misfortunes, that she feels the consciousness of her dignity.

The constitutional government cannot assent to the affront with which a political faction would stain the country. It fulfils its duty then, that this may come to the knowledge of the civilized world, by protesting, as it does protest, in the most solemn manner against the treaty referred to, concluded at Paris in September of last year, by demonstrating that its clauses cannot compromit the interests of Mexico for want of authority in the persons who, on its part, intervened, and by declaring that she reserves the right to settle the differences pending with Spain in conformity with the principles of universal justice, and in a manner worthy of the dignity of both nations.

VERA CRUZ, *January* 30, 1860.

BENITO JUAREZ,
President ad interim.
IGNACIO DE LA LLAVE,
Minister of State.
JOSÉ GIL PARTEAROYO,
Minister of War.
JOSÉ DE EMPARAN, *
Minister of the Interior.
SANTOS DEGOLLADO,
Minister of Foreign Relations.
MANUEL RUIZ, *Minister of Justice.*
MIGUEL LERDA DE TEJADO,
Minister of Finance.

WASHINGTON, *September* 30, 1861.

A true copy.

ROMERO.

Mr. Romero to Mr. Seward.

[Translation.]

MEXICAN LEGATION IN THE UNITED STATES OF AMERICA,
Washington, October 30, 1861.

Mr. SECRETARY: Believing that Mr. Corwin may have informed the department over which you preside of the complaint which was made by the diplomatic body residing in Mexico to the government of that republic in August last, in consequence of an asseveration made to it by the minister of France, that on the night of the 14th day of the same month verbal insults were addressed to him by a popular assemblage, and that his assassination had been attempted, I deem it proper to transmit to you a pamphlet which I have just received, and which contains the judicial investigation made by the authorities of Mexico in virtue of that accusation, this investigation throwing sufficient light on the events to show what really occurred.

There were two counts in the accusation of the French minister: first, the insults which had been addressed to him by speech, and second, the attempt at assassination. With respect to the former, it was proved in the examination referred to that on the night mentioned the triumph obtained by the government forces over the rebels in Jalatlaco was celebrated in the city of Mexico. The people of Mexico, as is their custom on such occasions, having assembled in various groups, with a band of music at the head of each, passed through the city in different directions, sending up rockets and hurrahing for the government, the victors, and the constitution. One of these groups went by the legation of France. Mr. de Saligny asserts that it stopped at the door and shouted, "*death to Frenchmen,*" "*death to the minister of France;*" but, strange to say, nobody else heard such cries. Among the persons examined by the appropriate judicial authorities there are Mexicans of character and foreigners, and among the latter some Frenchmen. Some of them live on the same street on which the house of the legation stands and others in a hotel close by, and all uniformly declare that the group neither stopped before the French legation nor used any insulting expression to France, to her subjects, or to her minister.

In regard to the latter charge, it was found that Mr. de Saligny having stopped in one of the galleries of his house, without hearing any detonation, had a perception of a slight crack near him and then of a light blow on his right arm. Examining afterwards the place where this occurred, he found that a ball had made an impression on the column of the gallery near which he had stopped. From the examination of the place, which was made by the judge, accompanied by two skilful engineers, it was found that the ball could not have originally made an impression in the place where it struck unless it had been fired from the roof of the same house, which was not probable, as the servants of the house, in whom Mr. de Saligny stated he had great confidence, declared that no person had been on the roof on that night.

The said engineers who accompanied the judge in the examination just mentioned afterwards made their report in writing, wherein they express the opinion that, taking all the circumstances of the case into consideration, the projectile was not designedly fired at the column, but that it was aimed at some point near the north of the house, struck the wall of the National Theatre, which is close by it and facing in that direction, and, this producing a movement of irregular rebound, it reached the point where the mark was found. The foundations of this opinion are very much strengthened if it is borne in mind that Mr. de Saligny, as he himself deposes, did not hear the detonation of the piece of arms from which the projectile was fired; and that at the time this event took place rockets were being sent up in various quarters, and probably firearms were also discharged in the air on account of the public rejoicing.

The evidence gathered was such that the judge who instituted the examination declared there was no sufficient reason for continuing it.

The interest which I naturally take in rectifying erroneous opinions which may be formed of Mexico in consequence of inaccurate reports induces me to address you in regard to this matter, and to recommend you to peruse the annexed investigation.

It is very agreeable to me to have this opportunity of repeating to you, sir, the assurances of my very distinguished consideration.

M. ROMERO.

Hon. WILLIAM H. SEWARD, &c., &c., &c.

[Translation.]

MEXICAN QUESTION.

INQUEST AND JUDICIAL SENTENCE ON THE COMPLAINT OF MR. DE SALIGNY, MINISTER OF FRANCE IN MEXICO—1861.

Preface.

Several journals have published as positive news that Mr. de Saligny, minister of France at Mexico, has been the object of an attempt at assassination, and that on an evening when the inhabitants of that city had given themselves up to public rejoicings cries of *death* were uttered against the person of this minister and against foreigners in general. It would be impossible to recall here all the comments which have been made with profusion on this piece of news, that has dropped into the field of European publicity in these days when the question of Mexico is discussed with great warmth. From this attempt, and from these acts, accepted as ascertained facts, there has resulted to that unhappy country a seal of reprobation and of anathema which seems to give some weight to the unjust attacks which the clerical press has for a long while not ceased to hurl against it in France, in Spain, and in Italy.

Nothing, however, is better ascertained than the sad error which has been the first cause of so many virulent recriminations on this subject; for not only is the incorrectness of the facts on which it has been attempted to found a complaint established, but the truth of entirely contrary facts has been demonstrated.

All this is rendered as clear as day by the documents of proof in the judicial inquest made at Mexico in consequence of the complaint of Mr. de Saligny. This inquest we publish *in extenso*, as it was communicated to the *Siglo XIX* of that city, which published it on the 5th of September last.

We shall make neither the synthesis nor the analysis of the probabilities which flow quite naturally from this series of documents. They speak for themselves, and therefore we shall refrain from making the slightest observation on them. We only ask that they may be read, and we await with entire confidence the fiat of public opinion

Inquest and judicial sentence on the complaint of Mr. de Saligny.

DEPARTMENT OF FOREIGN RELATIONS,
Mexico, September 3, 1861.

To the Editor of the Siglo XIX:

MY DEAR SIR: By order of the minister of relations, I send you a copy of some of the proofs which form the judicial inquest in regard to the hostile demonstration and attempt at assassination, of which accusation has been made as having taken place on the night of the 14th of the month of August, at the French legation.

These documents prove that on the occasion of the rejoicings to which the triumph over the disturbers of the public peace gave rise on that night the sentiments of sympathy and of fraternity which have always united the inhabitants of that city to the French who reside there were loudly expressed, instead of the latter being molested.

I trust that, for the satisfaction of both, you will be pleased to give publicity in your journal to the documents which are hereto annexed.

I thank you, in advance, for this service, and am your very humble and very obedient servant,

JUAN DE D. ARIAS.

Deposition of José A. Bucheli, esq.

On the same day (20th August) appeared José A. Bucheli, esq., counsellor at law, who, having promised to tell the truth, deposed that he was a native of Mexico, of mature age, married, and was a lawyer, residing at No. 8 Vergara street.

Being interrogated as to the matters of this inquest, he answered that, according to his recollection, one day last week he had noticed a crowd proceeding, between ten and eleven o'clock at night, to the sounds of martial music, from Primera del Factor street to Vergara street, carrying torches and hurrahing in honor of the government, and particularly in honor of General Gonzalez Ortega, on account of the victory gained by him over the forces of Marquez and his accomplices; having also noticed that in all directions this crowd was sending up a great many rockets, and fearing to be hit by an unlucky mischance, he withdrew from the balcony where he had witnessed this spectacle, and shut the windows, being already convinced that the only object of this promenade was to celebrate the triumph of the constitutional government. He noticed that the voices of the persons who composed these groups were gradually becoming fainter, and he concluded therefrom that they had not stopped in Vergara street. Having read this deposition, he has ratified it, as it agrees with the truth, and he has signed it along with the judge.

J. A. BUCHELI.

Proceedings of inquest drawn up by M. Arrieta, esq., notary.

On the same day the judge, assisted by me, a notary, and two officers of engineers detailed by the military commander of the district at the request of the court, repaired to the house No. 10 Vergara street, where the minister of France, who was present, resides; and the minister having been informed by his secretary of the purpose for which we came, he took his hat and showed the place where he was and to which the ball had gone. This place is at one of the angles of the gallery of the house running from south to north, and facing to the east, on turning to the vestibule; and he placed himself in the same position in which he was when the ball fell. He was looking to the north and had his shoulder towards the south, a little inclined on the left to the north. Then he indicated the spot where the ball had struck; it was on the second column of the space of the part mentioned of the gallery where he was standing, at the distance of about half a yard. It was noticed at this place that the part fractured was about two inches in diameter, and on the side to the south, inclining a little towards the east, where said ball struck, which ball he preserves; and he presented at the same time some fragments of paper which he declared to be wadding; telling us, through his secretary, that he was in the place where he is in the habit of walking up and down after dinner when the noise of rockets and the ringing of bells was heard in the city. It was then between seven and eight o'clock. He heard a slight report on one side of him, and immediately felt a light blow on his right arm—a blow to which he paid no attention, supposing it to be from the stick of one of the rockets which had been heard going up. A short time afterwards he received a visit from the Count de Pierres, who stays at the Hotel of Europe, and after relating to him what had happened he went, on his invitation, to the gallery to look with him for the stick which they supposed to have fallen there They asked a servant for a light, in order to make this search; and it was then that they noticed the mark left by the ball on the column, and at the base the fragments of the wadding which he presented were found, as well as the ball which was in the cornice of the gallery outside of the balustrade, and a few steps distant from said column. The minister then took the ball, which was the one which he held in his hand and which was flattened on one side. When he took it out he discovered that it was still hot, and that it smelt of powder.

Then the judge, with the persons above named, went on the terrace (flat roof) of said house, in order to see and examine for themselves; they made an inspection of it, from which it was found that there was not on the walls of the contiguous terraces any mark which could create a suspicion that any person had been able to slip on by that means; and additionally the said minister expressed a suspicion that some one might have got up by the public baths, which are established in the house, and which are in its interior, but at the back part, it was acknowledged that this was not possible. Moreover, the doorkeeper, a person whom the minister accredits as worthy of his entire confidence, was interrogated, and he deposed that at six o'clock in the evening the baths are closed, no person remaining there afterwards; that this had taken place on the day of the occurrence the same as on every other day, said doorkeeper having his place inside of the vestibule, which at that hour is shut; and, finally, he asserted that no person had entered.

The above-named minister added, through his secretary, that, as regarded the persons in his service, he had absolutely no suspicion, for they all possessed his confidence; and that neither had he suspicions against any other definite person, not knowing that he had or could have any enemies. He added that, on the same evening, at ten o'clock at latest, being in his bed engaged in reading, he heard tumultuous voices in the street, and the sound of wind instruments. He arose, and drawing near the glass windows of the balcony, he saw a group of people who had stopped before the house, and with them some soldiers in undress uniform, who uttered cries of "down with the French! down with the minister of France!" He did not see the musicians in uniform; they had citizens' dress.

Shortly afterwards this group went round the corner of Vergara street, into San Francisco street, and, as he presumes, turned into the small street of Belemitas—a supposition which he forms from the manner in which he heard the sounds of music. After these items of information were obtained the present proceedings terminated. The judge made a request to the two officers of engineers that they would draw up a sketch of what they had seen, and transmit it to-morrow to the court with their report. In testimony whereof the judge has signed, which I certify.

M. ARRIETA.

Report of Messrs. Ignacio Pavon and Augustin Arrellano, officers of engineers.— Corps of Engineers.

In virtue of a verbal order which we received from the citizen military commander, we went together with you to the house No. 10 Vergara street, where Mr. Dubois de Saligny, minister of France in Mexico, resides, in order to make an examination there with a view of determining whence had been fired a shot of a musket or carbine, the mark of which was found imprinted on a column of the gallery of that house, and to give our opinion on the question. Was the shot aimed at this point, or had the projectile arrived there by chance? Together with you, we discovered the mark made by the ball on one of the columns of the gallery which faces the east; and, after examining attentively the state of the place and conferring with you, we proceed to state what has happened according to our view, and to the information on which we have relied in giving the opinion by which this report will be terminated. The mark left by the projectile is of a slight depth; the ball which was presented to us is flattened in an irregular manner, as if it had encountered a sinuous surface; and, from the explanations of the minister, we have learned that, after striking the column, the ball had fallen a very short distance from it.

As it was presumed that the shot might have been fired from one of the neighboring eminences, (house-tops,) we went upon them and made an attentive examination, but could not acquire the certainty that it had come from one of them; on the contrary, we were convinced that it had not been fired from the terraces. The only one which overlooks in part the house of the minister is that of the National Theatre; but on examining the part which would have been most convenient and most elevated, and taking for a basis of our calculations the human stature, the visual ray does not reach the point where the projectile struck; so that if the shot had been fired from that terrace it would have hit higher and not where it left its mark.

Nor can it be said that it was fired from the terrace of the house itself; for the minister says that he did not hear the noise of the detonation, and at a distance so short it would have been impossible not to hear it, whatever was the fire-arm discharged, in spite of the noise made at that hour by the ringing of bells and the sending up of rockets. What confirms this opinion is the slight mark which the ball left, and which must have been much larger by reason of shortness of distance.

The minister giving assurance that the shot had not been fired in the court, and as no certain conclusion can be arrived at from the shape which the cavity presented where the projectile struck, several persons having already changed the form by private examinations, it results, in virtue of the foregoing explanation, that we are of opinion, and so declare by way of report, that the projectile was not of deliberate purpose aimed at the column where the mark was found, but that the arm having been discharged from a point close by and to the north of the house, the projectile struck the wall of the theatre which faces this point; by this there was produced a movement of irregular rebound to the point where the mark was found. We base this opinion as well on the irregular flattening of the projectile, whose shape could not have been so much changed if it had only met with the slight encounter which the mark indicates, as on what we ascertained that there was no point whose position was such that a shot could be fired from it to the place mentioned. Such is our opinion, and such we declare in fulfilment of the order which we have received. Liberty and reform.

IGNACIO PAVON.
AGUSTIN ARRELLANO.

MEXICO, *August* 22, 1861.

Deposition of Mr. Frederick Zophy.

Afterwards appeared, on a summons made to him, Mr. Frederick Zophy. The general questions required by law having been put to him, he deposed that such was his name; that he was from Switzerland, was married, was a shoemaker by trade, aged fifty-five years, living at No. 6 Plateros street.

Being interrogated as to the reason why his name was cited by the Inspector Morali and the chief of police, he deposed that on the evening spoken of by those gentlemen, at about ten o'clock, he heard the noise of music; he went out on his balcony to hear the piece which was being played, and then he noticed that the musicians were accompanied by quite a large crowd, who hurrahed in honor of liberty of France and of the United States. The crowd proceeded to Segunda de Plateros street at the moment in which the deponent returned to his parlor. His deposition having been read, he ratified it as being the truth to his knowledge, and signed it.

FREDERICK ZOPHY.

Deposition of Mr. Paul Leautaud.

On the same day appeared before the judge the citizen Paul Leautaud, who, after protesting his willingness to tell the truth, deposed that he was born in France, was unmarried, thirty-eight years of age, residing at No. 5 Primera de Plateros street.

Being interrogated as to the matters of this inquest, and in virtue of the citation of his name, made by the inspector of the ward, and by the inspector of police, he deposed that from the balcony of his house he had seen, at about 10 o'clock at night, on the 14th instant, a band of music followed by a crowd of people cheering for the French, for the United States, for Mexico, and for liberty; that this crowd passed along Segunda de Plateros street; that having left the balcony, he saw nothing more. He has ratified what is stated as being the truth.

PAUL LEAUTAUD.

Deposition of Mr. Angel de la Pena.

On the 24th of the same month, before the judge, appeared Mr. Angel de la Pena, on a summons made to him personally. After promising to tell the truth, he deposed that such was his name; that he was a native of Mexico, was married, was about fifty-three years of age, a property holder, residing at No. 11 Vergara street.

Being interrogated as to the matter of this inquest, he deposed that on the 14th instant, at 10 o'clock at night, he was on the balcony of his house, taking a view of the public satisfaction which was felt by all the inhabitants of the city on account of the triumph of the arms of the supreme government over the forces of the rebel Marquez; that he saw passing at that hour a band of music, followed by people, going from the north to the south, lighted up with torches, and cheering for liberty, for General Gonzalez Ortega, for the constitution of 1857, and uttering other similar cries; that he absolutely heard no cries uttered against the French or against any foreign nation; that he did not see h em stop before the house of the legation of France, nor at any other place in the street. He observed here that his house adjoined that of the minister of France, and that he, the said deponent, was on his balcony, and that this was why if they had uttered such cries and had stopped in the street, he could not have failed to hear it and see it.

As to the shot which was said to have been aimed on that evening at the minister of France, the first news which he received of that event was from the French newspaper called the *Estafette;* that in his house no person had gone upon the terrace, as there was no communication with it, said terrace being lower than the hotel.

He ratified and affirmed what is above stated as being the truth, after it had been read, and has signed.

ANGEL DE LA PEÑA.

Deposition of Mr. Manuel Pavia.

On the same day, after summons made, appeared Mr. Manuel Pavia, and having the general questions put to him, he deposed that he was so named; that he was a native of Mexico, unmarried, a clerk, thirty-five years of age, living in the principal apartment of the Hotel de Vergara, on the first story. Being interrogated as to the matters of this inquest, he deposed that on the evening of the 14th instant he was at home with his family, and that at 10 o'clock he heard a band of music passing through the street; that he occupied himself in looking at it, and that he saw about twenty musicians, who came with a certain number of people in a direction from north to south; that they passed without halting in any part of the street; they hurrahed for General Gonzales Ortega, for liberty, and for the government; that he positively heard no cries of "Down with the French! down with the minister of France!" cries mentioned in this inquest; that perhaps the minister of France confounded these cries with those which were really put forth, and which were, "Down with the assassins of foreigners!" That, as to the shot which is said to have been aimed at the aforesaid minister at 8 o'clock in the evening of the same day, the first news which he had of it was in the newspapers, which he reads every day, and that since he has heard no one speak of that event.

The witness affirmed, ratified, and signed the above statement as being the truth.

M. PAVIA.

Deposition of Mr. Augustin Michaud.

Afterwards appeared, on summons, Mr. Augustin Michaud, who, on the general questions being put to him, deposed that he was thus named; that he was from France, was married, was twenty-nine years of age, was a merchant, living at No. 10 Segunda De San Francisco street.

Being interrogated, in consequence of the allusion made to him personally by the citizen regidor, Manuel Parada, in his report relative to the present inquest, he said it was true that, after ten o'clock on the evening of the 14th instant, when the triumph of the government forces was being celebrated in this capital, the music of the municipal body stopped before the door of his house; it was accompanied by a crowd of people, and by respectable persons of this city; that with pleasure he heard his fellow-citizens hurrah for Mexico, and heard the Mexicans hurrah for the French and for foreigners; that among the pieces of music which followed was recognized the hymn of the *Marseillaise,* and the song of the country, called *Los Cangrejos.*

The witness ratified this deposition, after it had been read, as being in conformity to the truth.

AUGUSTIN MICHAUD.

THE PRESENT CONDITION OF MEXICO. 129

Deposition of Mr. de Pierres.

On the same day a second summons, by letter, was addressed to the Count de Pierres.

On the twenty-fifth of said month appeared, on summons made, Eugene de Pierres, a French citizen, interrogated through the interpreter, Mr. Miguel de Bustamante, who first declared that he should report in Spanish what the witness would testify to in French. He then said that the witness deposed that he was named as before mentioned; that he was from France; was unmarried; was thirty-four years of age; and was temporarily in this republic.

On the question whether he knew anything of the events which the minister of France had asserted to have taken place in his house on the evening of the 14th instant, he was enjoined to tell what he knew, and how he knew it. He answered, that at ten minutes past eight o'clock of the evening of that day he had gone to pay a visit to the minister of France; that said minister told him that five minutes before eight o'clock, of numerous rockets which were sent up in the capital, it seemed the stick of one had fallen into his house, and that he had felt a very slight blow on his arm; that they both went down stairs and into the court to look for this stick, but that they did not find it; that neither did they find it in the gallery; that on their return from the court a flattened ball was found at the base of the column which forms the arcade next to the staircase of the gallery, where the minister was walking, and on that column, as he learned, and saw at five o'clock in the afternoon of the next day, there was a mark which the ball had imprinted, and the doorkeeper showed him the wad, which had caused the minister to believe that a shot had been aimed at him, for on the night of the event he had thought that the ball might have been attached to one of the rockets; that even on the following evening he had entertained the same opinion, until in consequence of the above-mentioned facts, the mark being seen on the column and the wad shown by the porter, the minister judged that he had been fired at; that he ought to remark that the minister had told him that the wad was found at ten o'clock in the morning, and that the diplomatic body who had called to see him at two o'clock in the afternoon had seen it then, as well as the mark, indicating that the ball had struck the column.

Being interrogated as to the hour at which he left the minister's house on the evening of the 14th instant, and whether he had noticed any alarm among the servants, he answered that he retired about a quarter to ten, or in the neighborhood of ten o'clock; he had not noticed that the servants were in anywise alarmed, for no importance had been attached to this occurrence.

Being interrogated as to whether, when he spoke to the minister at five o'clock in the afternoon of the day following, the latter had manifested any suspicions as to the cause of the event or relative to the person who might have been the author of it, he answered that there had been no mention of this.

Being interrogated as to whether he knew on the said evening of cries having been uttered before the house of the minister of France, and whether, when he came out of the house of that gentleman, he had noticed any groups in the streets, he answered that on the next day he had learned from the minister himself that under his balconies cries of "Down with the French! down with the minister of France!" had been uttered, but that when he came out he saw no group in the street, and the street was in its ordinary condition.

After it had been read by the interpreter, he affirmed that the foregoing was true, and he ratified it and signed it together with him.

            COUNT E. DE PIERRES.
            MIGUEL BUSTAMANTE.

H. Ex. Doc. 100——9

Deposition of M. J. R. Massez.

Afterwards appeared, in room No. 20 of the Hotel de Vergaca, M. J. R. Massez, who, having been first interrogated on the general questions according to law, deposed that he was named John, born in Italy, not married, a musician, aged twenty-five years, and living in that room.

Interrogated upon the points on which this investigations bears, he answered: That on the evening of the 14th instant, about eleven o'clock, he heard some musicians passing, playing on stringed instruments, and accompanied by some common people, and uttering various cries; this arrested his attention, and he went on the balcony, and there heard them crying, "Down with Mejia! live pure religion! live the government!" That he absolutely heard no cries of "Down with the French," or "Down with the French minister;" that this body of musicians halted nowhere; that he had specially noticed that several other musical companies, playing on wind instruments, had passed during the night in question, but they took the route by the corner of San Francisco street, and deponent supposes some Frenchmen were among them, because the Marseillaise was sung; that he has not heard that any one walked on the roof that night; and does not know that any one was found on said roof; that he was absolutely ignorant that on that evening a shot had been fired at the minister of France, because he only learned that event by reading it in the Estafette.

After this deposition had been read by him, he ratified and confirmed it as being the truth, and signed it.

JEAN R. MASSEZ.

Deposition of M. John Janis Laurent.

On the same day, after service of summons, appeared M. John Janis Laurent. The questions required by law having been put to him, he answered that he was called as had been stated, born in France, not married, aged twenty-nine years, merchant, living at the pastry-cook shop in Segunda de Ratevos street, No. 3.

Interrogated as to the facts which caused the summons issued to him by Inspector Morali and the colonel-in-chief of the police, citizen Porssoro G. Leon, he deposed that on the night of the celebration here of the victory gained by General Gonzales Ortega over the bands commanded by Marquez, there passed, about ten o'clock in the evening, a body of musicians, who stopped at the pastry shop, Plaisant, of which the deponent is the manager; that amongst the crowd which accompanied the music there were many well-dressed persons, and that the acclamations which were uttered were all in honor of the French, of the United States, and of Gonzales Ortega; that several of these persons came into the shop, asked for a bottle of champagne, and drank healths in the same terms as their acclamations; that as soon as they went out, with the music and the common people who accompanied them, all took the way to the Profesa house, singing and playing the Marseillaise. After reading made, he ratified what is above as being the truth, and signed it.

J. J. LAURENT.

Written deposition of M. J. M. Urquidi.

MEXICO, *August* 22, 1861.

Through your polite communication of yesterday, I am informed that in the investigation, the conduct of which is confided to your court, touching the criminal acts denounced by his excellency the French minister, and which happened on the evening of the 14th instant, order has been issued to proceed and question upon these facts all the inhabitants of Veogara street, in which is the house where the French minister resides. You add that, as I reside in the same street, you desire that I should inform you of all that I know touching such events. According to the intimations of your communication, on the evening of that day, about ten o'clock, a body of about twenty musicians, accompanied by a group, among whom were some soldiers in uniform, halted before the entrance of the French legation, shouting, " Down with the French!" " Down with the French minister!" and on the same evening, at eight o'clock, that a shot had been fired, aimed at the body of the French minister.

Having rallied my recollections touching what had passed that evening, I now answer to the questions you address to me : that after ten o'clock there, in fact, was a group of people that passed along the street going from north to south; it was composed of persons following musicians. As far as I recollect, I saw no soldiers there, nothwithstanding torches lighted up the group. I heard different cries, vivas, and down with them, but I did not clearly distinguish what was cried save the cry of " Down with Mejia!"

I did not see that on their way they stopped before the hotel of the French legation, although the house where I live almost fronts it. That evening I saw the thoroughfares traversed by groups, who passed along the streets celebrating the victory of General Ortega in the environs of Toluco.

I think it was also on the occasion of this holiday that musket shots were fired, which I heard from the beginning of the night, at times more, at times less frequent; but I am entirely ignorant where they were fired, and whether there was one which was aimed at his excellency the French minister. This is all I can say, in assuring you of my respect and esteem.

JOSE M. URQUIDI.
The SEVENTH CRIMINAL JUDGE.

Written deposition of Mr. Zerecero.

OFFICE OF THE CIVIL REGISTRY OF THE FIRST TRIBUNAL,
Mexico, August 24, 1861.

In reply to your communications of yesterday, in which you ask me if the band of music of the municipal guard, in passing through Plateros street, accompanied by a crowd of people, on the evening of the celebration of the victory gained by the constitutional party under the orders of General Gonzales Ortega at Jalattaco, stopped in front of the French pastry shop of M. Plaisant, crying "Live France, the French, and the United States!" I say to you that as the moon was shining, I remained with my family on the balcony of my house until after midnight; that I saw groups passing one after another shouting vivas in honor of liberty, of reform, of the hero of Calpulalpua, and of the French; that their enthusiasm redoubled when they came in front of the pastry shop of M. Plaisant, whence they went in the direction of the street San Francisco, playing and singing, alternately, the Marseillaise and los Cangrajos. This is all I can say to you, sir, in reply to your communication of yesterday, in renewing to you the assurance of my respect and esteem.

A. ZERECERO.
The Licentiate MARIANO ARRIETA,
Seventh Judge on the Criminal Bench.

MEXICO, *August* 27, 1861.

True copy.

Judgment upon the facts investigated.

MEXICO, *August* 27, 1861.

Regards being had to the direction issued by order of the supreme government, in consequence of the complaint laid before it on the 17th of this month by Messieurs the ministers of the United States and of Russia, and Messieurs the chargé d'affaires of Belgium and Ecuador, on account of Messieur the minister of France having informed them of verbal abusiveness addressed to him when at his hotel on the evening of the 14th instant, and an attempt at assassination, which the minister above mentioned affirms was committed against him personally.

Considering, in the first place, that in denouncing the fact to the public authorities, it is submitted to a procedure in accordance with the universally-adopted principles of all legislation, the purpose of which is to seek for a foundation which can be relied on, and which consists in complete proof of the substance of the offence.

In the second place, that the existence of the substance of the offence is not proven in what touches the two facts which would constitute it in the present case, except by the testimony only of the minister and by that of persons who only had cognizance of the facts from the statement of the said minister, that is to say, from the testimony only of the person aggrieved; that this testimony, although of the most respectable kind, regard being had to the high character of the deponent, is nevertheless, of itself alone, inefficient to constitute perfect proof.

In the third place, considering that if this isolated circumstance would in a legal proceeding suffice to render doubtful the fact of the perpetration of an offence of any kind, such a conclusion is so much more natural, when an offence is in question of so grave importance, as well by its own nature as by the character of the person who has been the object of it, and by the sad and natural consequences which it might have.

In the fourth place, that, if to give to the evidence of witnesses the weight which it deserves, it is indispensable to have regard to the quality of the persons who depose; to the credit, more or less great, that should attach to them, as well for their good repute as for the absence of interest to conceal the truth, it must be concluded that the complaint of Monsieur the minister of France is deprived of any foundation; for, even supposing some of the circumstances averred which have induced him to depose to that concerning the attempt at homicide, they would offer explanations, if not altogether satisfactory, at least deprived of the alarming and odious character which the communication contained on the first page of the papers of instruction; besides this, we are precluded from admitting the certainty of said circumstances, on examining with impartiality the force of the detailed report of the experts Monsieurs Ignatius Paron and Augustin Arellano; it is clear, in fact, from this report, that the projectile could not have been aimed directly at the pillar where its mark is seen; that, adverse to the statement of his excellency are opposed the depositions of residents of Vergara street, all irreproachable people, among whom are found functionaries in high social position.

Considering, in the fifth place, that, among the facts proven by this investigation, many are found which prove the enthusiasm and the harmony which reigned between the Mexican people and the foreigners on the evening of the 14th; enthusiasm and harmony which are at once translated by the cries of "Live the French," and by the cries of " Death to the factions ;" hat it is not difficult that these cries may have been confounded by persons who heard them from a distance. Considering, in fine, that the investigation has been pressed as far as possible; considering the fact that a ball was found in the hotel of the minister of France, it remains, at the most, proven that some one has infringed the injunction of November, 1771, and the ordinances and rules relating to it, by firing a shot, without proof made how, by whom, from what point, and for what purpose.

Considering the laws 40, title 16, third part, and 2, title 16, book 2, of the last collection, I must declare, and do declare, that there is no cause to prosecute the warrant, of which report will be made to the third chamber of the superior court of this district. Full return shall be rendered to the supreme government, through the channel of the department of state to the department of justice.

Ordered and decreed by the citizen Mariano Arrieta, seventh judge of the criminal bench, before me, notary public, who certify this.

A true copy.

J DE D. ARIAS.

Mr. Romero to Mr. Seward.

[Translation.]

WASHINGTON, *November* 23, 1861.

Mr. SECRETARY: I have the honor to invite your attention to the annexed publication, which contains a treaty concluded at London, the 31st October last past, between England, and France, and Spain, for intervention in Mexico, and which was sent to me by the Mexican minister resident at Paris, who assures me of the authenticity of the document.

In the second paragraph of the first article of said convention you will note that the leaders of the allied forces are empowered in the most ample manner to carry out the further operations which, after having occupied the different forts and military positions of the Mexican coast, may appear proper to them, being on the spot, to achieve the object for which the expedition has been agreed upon. In the second article the contracting parties bind themselves not to exercise over the internal affairs of Mexico any influences of tendency to impair the right which belongs to the Mexican nation freely to' choose and determine the form of its government.

The simple declaration that Mexico has the right to choose and determine the form of its government allows the true purpose of the expedition, which it was intended to dissemble precisely in these words to shine forth.

Who questions such right? If the allies are going to guarantee it, do they not give to understand by this that in their views the constitutional government of the republic is an unpopular government which tyrannizes over the nation, and preserves its power only by force of arms, against whose tyranny the allies declare themselves as champions, and undertake the expedition in order to its overthrow? What encouragement will not the constant disturbers of public order receive in Mexico on perceiving that they are almost invited to rise in order to destroy the despotism which it is supposed weighs upon them, and that three of the principal powers of western Europe expressly guarantee to them the liberty to choose and determine the form of government which may suit them? What is that despotic government which weighs upon the Mexican people, which, without other elements than its devoted faith in republican principles, and in strict adherence to the rights of the people, fought and triumphed on the battle-fields and at the electoral ballot-boxes over the privileged classes, who combined the moral and material strength of the country, and whose existence was anterior to that of Mexico as an independent nation? What will be that which the allies once in Mexico may earnestly desire to characterize as the national will, and what the movements they may take in virtue of the terms, purposely vague, of the convention?

It is, in truth, much to be regretted that just at the moment when public order and tranquillity were about to be reduced to system in Mexico, if the country were left to settle its own affairs, a foreign expedition should be organized apparently for the purpose of forcible interference with the internal affairs of that republic, by overthrowing the government and by giving fresh fuel to that civil war which was coming to its close.

As the institutions which at present prevail in Mexico are identical with those of this country, and as, should their subversion in that country be brought about, they would suffer a rude shock that would cause them to totter throughout the other republics of this continent, it seems to me that the dangers which actually threaten Mexico are not exclusively limited to her, but extend to all republican America.

I hope, sir, therefore, that the United States, which were the first to establish such institutions, at the same time that they have thus far derived the greatest benefits from them, and have manifested most zeal for their preservation and propagation, will not look with indifference upon the storm which is brewing not alone against the Mexican nation, but against republican institutions in America and the antonomy of this continent.

It will be very satisfactory to me to transmit to my government the assurances which, upon this important matter, you may be able to give me in the name of the United States.

I avail of this opportunity to renew to you, sir, the assurances of my most distinguished consideration.

M. ROMERO.

Hon. WM. H. SEWARD, &c., &c., &c.

Convention between her Majesty, the Queen of Spain, and the Emperor of the French relative to combined operations against Mexico; signed at London, October 31, 1861.*

Sa Majesté la Reine du Royaume Uni de la Grande Bretagne et d'Irlande, sa Majesté la Reine d'Espagne, et sa Majesté l'Empereur des Français, se trouvant placées par la conduite arbitraire et vexatoire des autorités de la république du Mexique dans la nécessité d'exiger de ces autorités une protection plus efficace pour les personnes et les propriétés de leurs sujets, ainsi que l'execution des obligations contractées envers elles par la république du Mexique, se sont entendues pour conclure entre elles une convention dans le but de combiner leur action commune, et, à cet effet, ont nommé pour leurs plénipotentiaires, savoir:

Sa Majesté la Reine du Royaume Uni de la Grande Bretagne et d'Irlande, le Très Honorable Jean Comte Russell, Vicomte Amberley de Amberley et Ardsalla, Pair du Royaume Uni, conseiller de sa Majesté Britannique en son conseil privé, principal secrétaire d'etat de sa Majesté pour les affaires etrangères;

Sa Majesté la Reine d'Espagne, Don Xavier de Isturiz y Montero, chevalier de l'ordre insigne du toison d'or, grand croix de l'ordre royal et distingué de Charles III, de l'ordre impérial de la légion d'honneur de France, des ordres de la conception de Villaviciosa et Christ de Portugal, sénateur du royaume, ancien président du conseil de ministres et premier secrétaire d'etat de sa Majesté Catholique, et son envoyé extraordinaire et ministre plenipotentiaire près sa Majesté Britannique;

---

* Ratifications exchanged at London, November 15, 1861.

Et sa Majesté l'Empereur des Français, son excellence le Comte de Flahault de la Billarderie, sénateur, général de division, grand croix de la légion d'honneur, ambassadeur extraordinaire de sa Majesté Impériale près sa Majesté Britannique ;

Lesquels, après s'être communiqué réciproquement leurs pleins pouvoirs respectifs, trouvés en bonne et due forme, sont tombés d'accord pour arrêter les articles suivants :

ARTICLE I.

Sa Majesté la Reine du Royaume Uni de la Grande Bretagne et d'Irlande, sa Majesté la Reine d'Espagne, et sa Majesté l'Empereur des Français, s'engagent à arrêter aussitôt après la signature de la présente convention, les dispositions nécessaires pour envoyer sur les côtes du Mexique des forces de terre et de mer combinées dont l'effectif sera déterminé par un échange ultérieur de communications entre leurs gouvernements, mais dont l'ensemble devra être suffisant pour pouvoir saisir et occuper les différentes forteresses et positions militaires du littoral Mexicain.

Les commandants des forces alliées seront, en outre, autorisés à accomplir les autres opérations qui seraient jugées, sur les lieux, les plus propres à réaliser le but spécifié dans le préambule de la présente convention, et notamment à assurer la sécurité des résidents étrangers.

Toutes les mesures dont il s'agit dans cet article seront prises au nom et pour le compte des hautes parties contractantes, sans acception de la nationalité particulière des forces employées à les exécuter.

ARTICLE II

Les hautes parties contractantes s'engagent à ne rechercher pour elles-mêmes, dans l'emploi des mesures coercitives prévues par la présente convention, aucune acquisition de territoire ni aucun avantage particulier, et à n'exercer, dans les affaires intérieures du Mexique, aucune influence de nature à porter atteinte au droit de la nation Mexicaine de choisir et de constituer librement la forme de son gouvernement.

ARTICLE III.

Une commission composée de trois commissaires, un nommé par chacune des puissances contractantes, sera établie avec plein pouvoir de statuer sur toutes les questions que pourrait soulever l'emploi ou la distribution des sommes d'argent qui seront recouvrées au Mexique, en ayant égard aux droits respectifs des trois parties contractantes.

ARTICLE IV.

Les hautes parties contractantes désirant, en outre, que les mesures qu'elles ont l'intention d'adopter n'aient pas un caractère exclusif, et sachant que le gouvernement des États Unis a, de son côté, des réclamations à faire valoir, comme elles, contre la république Mexicaine, conviennent qu'aussitôt après la signature de la présente convention il en sera communiqué une copie au gouvernement des États Unis ; que ce gouvernement sera invité à y accéder ; et qu'en prévision de cette accession leurs ministres respectifs à Washington seront immédiatement munis de pleins pouvoirs à l'effet de conclure et de signer, collectivement ou séparément, avec le plénipotentiaire désigné par le Président des Etats Unis, une convention identique, sauf suppression du présent article, à celle qu'elles signent à la date de ce jour. Mais comme les hautes parties contractantes s'exposeraient, en apportant quelque retard à la mise à exécution des Articles I et II de la présente convention, à manquer le but qu'elles désirent atteindre, elles sont tombées d'accord de ne pas différer, en vue d'obtenir l'accession du gouvernement des Etats Unis, le commencement des opérations sus-mentionnées au delà de l'époque à laquelle leurs forces combinées pourront être réunies dans les parages de Vera Cruz.

· ARTICLE V.

La présente convention sera ratifiée, et les ratifications en seront échangées à Londres, dans le délai de quinze jours.

En foi de quoi les plénipotentiaires respectifs l'ont signé, et y ont apposé le sceau de leurs armes.

Fait à Londres, en triple original, le trente-unième jour du mois d'Octobre, de l'an de grace mil huit cent soixante-un.

[L. S.]   RUSSELL.
[L. S.]   XAVIER DE ISTURIZ.
[L. S.]   FLAHAULT.

[Translation.]

Her Majesty the Queen of the United Kingdom of Great Britain and Ireland, her Majesty the Queen of Spain, and his Majesty the Emperor of the French, feeling themselves compelled by the arbitrary and vexatious conduct of the authorities of the republic of Mexico to demand from those authorities more efficacious protection for the persons and properties of their subjects, as well as a fulfilment of the obligations contracted towards their Majesties by the republic of Mexico, have agreed to conclude a convention with a view to combine their common action, and, for this purpose, have named as their plenipotentiaries, that is to say:

Her Majesty the Queen of the United Kingdom of Great Britain and Ireland, the Right Honorable John Earl Russell, Viscount Amherley, of Amberley, and Ardsalla, a peer of the United Kingdom, a member of her Britannic Majesty's privy council, her Majesty's principal secretary of state for foreign affairs;

Her Majesty the Queen of Spain, Don Xavier de Isturiz y Montero, knight of the illustrious order of the golden fleece, grand cross of the royal and distinguished order of Charles III, of the imperial order of the legion of honor of France, of the orders of the conception of Villaviciosa and Christ of Portugal, senator of the kingdom, late president of the council of ministers, and first secretary of state of her Catholic Majesty, and her envoy extraordinary and minister plenipotentiary to her Britannic Majesty;

And his Majesty the Emperor of the French, his excellency the Count de Flahault de la Billarderie, senator, general of division, grand cross of the legion of honor, his Imperial Majesty's ambassador extraordinary to her Britannic Majesty;

Who, after having reciprocally communicated their respective full powers, found in good and due form, have agreed upon the following articles:

ARTICLE I.

Her Majesty the Queen of the United Kingdom of Great Britain and Ireland, her Majesty the Queen of Spain, and his Majesty the Emperor of the French, engage to make, immediately after the signature of the present convention, the necessary arrangements for despatching to the coasts of Mexico combined naval and military forces, the strength of which shall be determined by a further interchange of communications between their governments, but of which the total shall be sufficient to seize and occupy the several fortresses and military positions on the Mexican coast.

The commanders of the allied forces shall be, moreover, authorized to execute the other operations which may be considered, on the spot, most suitable to effect the object specified in the preamble of the present convention, and specifically to insure the security of foreign residents.

All the measures contemplated in this article shall be taken in the name and on account of the high contracting parties, without reference to the particular nationality of the forces employed to execute them.

ARTICLE II.

The high contracting parties engage not to seek for themselves, in the employment of the coercive measures contemplated by the present convention, any acquisition of territory nor any special advantage, and not to exercise in the internal affairs of Mexico any influence of a nature to prejudice the right of the Mexican nation to choose and to constitute freely the form of its government.

ARTICLE III.

A commission composed of three commissioners, one to be named by each of the contracting powers, shall be established with full authority to determine all questions that may arise as to the application or distribution of the sums of money which may be recovered from Mexico, having regard to the respective rights of the three contracting parties.

ARTICLE IV.

The high contracting parties desiring, moreover, that the measures which they intend to adopt should not bear an exclusive character, and being aware that the government of the United States on its part has, like them, claims to enforce upon the Mexican republic, agree that immediately after the signature of the present convention a copy thereof shall be communicated to the government of the United States; that that government shall be invited to accede to it; and that in anticipation of that accession their respective ministers at Washington shall be at once furnished with full powers for the purpose of concluding and signing, collectively or separately, with the plenipotentiary designated by the President of the United States, a convention identic, save the suppression of the present article, with that which they sign this day. But as by delaying to put into execution Articles I and II of the present convention, the high coutracting parties would incur a risk of failing in the object which they desire to attain, they have agreed not to defer, with the view of obtaining the accession of the government of the United States, the commencement of the above-mentioned operations beyond the time at which their combined forces can be assembled in the neighborhood of Vera Cruz.

ARTICLE V.

The present convention shall be ratified, and the ratifications thereof shall be exchanged at London within fifteen days.

In witness whereof, the respective plenipotentiaries have signed it, and have affixed thereto the seal of their arms.

Done at London, in triplicate, the thirty-first day of the month of October, in the year of our Lord one thousand eight hundred and sixty-one.

[L. S.]   RUSSELL.
[L. S.]   XAVIER DE ISTURIZ.
[L. S.]   FLAHAULT.

Mr. Romero to Mr. Seward.

[Translation.]

MEXICAN LEGATION IN THE UNITED STATES OF AMERICA,
Washington, November 28, 1861.

MR. SECRETARY: As it seems, according to all the appearances by which we may reasonably judge, the real object of the European allies, who signed in London the treaty of the 31st of October, is to subvert the form of government which actually exists in Mexico, and to overthrow the constitution which the people of that republic freely chose for itself, I deem it not inappropriate to transmit to you, for the information of the government of the United States, a copy, in English, of the political constitution of Mexico. You will observe, sir, that this code is founded upon the same bases upon which the Constitution of the United States rests, the work of the thoughts and study of the wise and patriotic sons of this country, who made it independent, and who knew how to lay the foundations of its greatness and development.

The people of Mexico, who have witnessed with surprise the astonishing prosperity at which this country.has arrived in the short period of its existence as an independent nation, have desired to arrive at this same result by pursuing, in order to reach it, the same course, and by availing themselves of the same means. They have believed that this would be to them the more probable, because Mexico abounds in the same elements which nature, with her prodigal hand, has scattered over this land, and because its people, having once enjoyed the blessings of democratic institutions, have determined to maintain them, and to defend their liberties.

Scarcely had the constitution of 1857 been promulgated, when the privileged classes of Mexico—the clergy and the army, accustomed to govern the country by despotism—rebelled against the instrument which recognized and sanctioned the rights of the people and their equality before the law. Then there arose a gigantic and unequal contest, in which on one side fought the organized and disciplined forces, sustained with the money of the clergy, and on the other the popular masses, without discipline, and without the resources to meet the expenses of the war which was carried on throughout the whole extent of the Mexican territory.

The repeated reverses which the people met with at the outset served to discipline them, the guns of their enemies to arm them, and at the end of a bloody and ceaseless contest of three years' duration the popular and constitutional cause obtained, without foreign aid of any nature, the victory to which it was entitled by the justice of the principles which it defended and the constancy and inflexible determination of its defenders.

The supremacy of the law having been re-established throughout the entire Mexican territory, the implacable enemies of the liberties of the people sought to overthrow the constitution, availing themselves of various expedients; but the people of Mexico with an extraordinary unanimity, and manifesting a good sense which would do honor to the most enlightened people in the world, refused peremptorily to resort to the measures proposed to them, under the plea of saving the country, but for the real purpose of subverting the public liberties, and nearly all the legislatures of the States issued decrees renewing their allegiance to the constitution, solemnly protesting not to acknowledge any other authority created outside of said constitution, and threatening to reassume their sovereignty in the event of such revolutionary authority being established.

Perceiving the inefficiency of the measures proposed, others were resorted to. It was sought to present the question as merely a personal one, and it was attempted to make the person who at present fills the executive chair of the nation resign the presidency. Happily the good sense of the country and its devotion to the law were so powerful that this other expedient was confounded also by the determination of the States to sustain the government which had emanated from the popular choice. The legislatures ratified their previous protests against any change whatever. They declared again that they would support the government established by the vote of the nation, and the governors of several of the States did the same.

Among a series of newspapers of the past month, which I have just received from Mexico, I find some of the decrees and protests to which I have referred, and which I have the honor to transmit to you to the number of six, in the order set forth in the index which I enclose herewith.

The efforts made in the interior of Mexico to overthrow the present constitutional government having proved ineffectual, it now appears that the determined and implacable enemies of democratic and liberal institutions have resorted to the last imaginable extreme left them, by seeking outside of the country the means which they could not find anywhere else to effect their desired aim. How far these fears have any foundation is left to events to make known to us within a brief period.

I avail myself of this opportunity to renew to you, sir, the assurances of my very distinguished consideration.

M. ROMERO.

Hon. WILLIAM H. SEWARD, &c., &c., &c.

[Translation.]

An index of the documents transmitted to the Department of State of the United States, with the note from this legation of this date.

No.	Date.	Contents.
1	1857. Feb. 5	Copy in English of the federal constitution of the United Mexican States, adopted and sworn to on the 5th of February, 1857.
2	1861. June 22	Decree of the legislature of the State of Durango, protesting against the establishment of any revolutionary authority.
3	Sept. 30	Decree of the legislature of the State of Chicopas to the same effect as the foregoing, and declaring that it will support the government of Mr. Juarez.
4	Oct. 8	Decree of the legislature of the State of Aguas-Calientes to the same effect as the foregoing, and asking President Juarez not to abandon the presidency.
5	Oct. 1	Remonstrance of the governor of the State of Aguas-Calientes against the project of the resignation of Mr. Juarez.
6	Sept. 22	Remonstrance of the governor of the State of Queretaro to the same effect as the preceding.
7	Sept. 30	Remonstrance of the governor of the State of Jalisco to the same effect as the preceding.

WASHINGTON, *November* 28, 1861.

MEXICO—CONSTITUTION OF 1857.

Ignacio Comonfort, president substitute of the Mexican republic, to the inhabitants of the same.

Be it known that the extraordinary constituent congress has decreed as follows:

In the name of God and by the authority of the Mexican people—

The representatives of the different States, the district and territories that comprise the republic of Mexico, called by the plan proclaimed in Ayutla on the 1st of March, 1854, reformed in Acapulco on the 11th of the same month and year, and published by the convention of October 17, 1855, in order to constitute the nation under the democratic republican form, representative and popular, putting in exercise the powers with which they are vested, comply with their high charge by decreeing the following

CONSTITUTION

Of the Mexican republic, upon the indestructible base of its legitimate independence, proclaimed the 16th of September, 1810, and consummated on the 27th of September, 1821.

TITLE I.

Section first.—Of the rights of man.

ARTICLE 1. The Mexican people recognize that the rights of man are the basis and the object of social institutions. Wherefore it is declared that all the laws and the authorities of the country must respect and sustain the guarantees established by the present constitution.

ARTICLE 2. All are born free in the republic. Slaves that set foot upon the national territory recover by that single act their liberty, and have the right to the protection of the laws.

ARTICLE 3. Education is free. The law shall determine what professions need license for their exercise, and with what requisites relative thereto.

ARTICLE 4. Every man is free to adopt such profession or industrial pursuit as he may prefer, the same being useful and honorable, and to enjoy the products thereof. Neither shall any one be hindered in the exercise of such profession or industrial pursuit unless by judicial sentence, when the same prejudices, the rights of a third person, or by executive order, dictated in terms prescribed by law, in case the same offends the rights of society.

ARTICLE 5. No one shall be forced to give his personal labor without just remuneration and without his full consent. The law shall not authorize any contract having for its object the loss or the irrevocable sacrifice of the liberty of man, whether the same be for labor, education, or religious vows. Neither shall the law authorize agreements by which a man stipulates his own proscription or exile.

ARTICLE 6. The expression of opinions shall not be the object of any inquisition, judicial or administrative, except when the same is an attack upon morals, assails the rights of third parties, incites to any crime or offence, or disturbs public order.

ARTICLE 7. The liberty of writing and publishing works on whatsoever subjects is inviolable. No law nor authority shall establish previous censorship, nor exact bonds from the authors or printers, nor limit the liberty of the press, which has no limits but with regard to private life, to morals, and the public peace. The crimes of the press shall be judged by one jury that shall determine the fact, and by another that shall apply the law and fix the penalty.

ARTICLE 8. The right of petition is inviolable, exercised in writing and in a manner respectful and pacific; but in political matters it can only be exercised by citizens of the republic. To all petitions shall be returned the written opinion of the authority to whom they may have been directed, upon whom the obligation is imposed of making known the result to the petitioner.

ARTICLE 9. To none shall be limited the right to associate or reunite pacifically for whatsoever lawful object; but only the citizens of the republic can assemble in order to take part in the political affairs of the country. No armed assembly has the right of deliberation.

ARTICLE 10. All men have the right to possess and carry arms for their security and legitimate defence. The law shall determine what shall be prohibited and the penalty to be incurred for carrying them.

ARTICLE 11. All men have the right of entering and leaving the republic, of travelling through its territory, and of changing their residence without the necessity of letters of security, passports, salvo conducta, or other similar requisite. The exercise of this right shall not prejudice the legitimate faculties of the judicial or administrative authority in cases of criminal or civil responsibility.

ARTICLE 12. There are not, nor shall there be, recognized in the republic, titles of nobility, nor prerogatives, nor hereditary honors. Solely the people, legitimately represented, may decree recompenses in honor of those that have given or are rendering eminent services to their country or to humanity.

ARTICLE 13. In the Mexican republic no one shall be judged by special laws nor by special tribunals. No person or corporation can have *fueros*, nor enjoy emoluments that are not in compensation for a public service and that are established by law. Martial law shall exist solely for crimes and offences that have exact connexion with military discipline. The law shall prescribe with clearness the cases included in this exception.

ARTICLE 14. No retractive law shall be passed. No one shall be judged or sentenced except under laws of date anterior to the fact and exactly applicable to the case, and by a tribunal which shall have been previously established by law.

ARTICLE 15. Treaties shall never be made for the extradition of political offenders, nor for that of those criminals under the common law, who shall have been held in the country where the offence was committed in the condition of slaves; nor shall conventions or treaties be made by which in any manner are altered the rights and guarantees which this constitution secures to the man and to the citizen.

ARTICLE 16. No one may be molested in his person, family, domicile, papers or possessions, except in virtue of a written order from a competent authority based upon legal cause for the proceeding. In case of high crimes all persons may apprehend the offenders and their accomplices, putting them without delay at the disposal of the nearest authorities.

ARTICLE 17. No one can be arrested for debts of a character purely civil. No one may exercise violence in reclaiming his rights. Tribunals are established for administering justice; this shall be gratuitous, judicial costs are therefore abolished.

ARTICLE 18. Imprisonment shall only take place for offences which merit personal punishment. In whatever stage of the proceedings it shall appear that the accused may not be liable to this penalty, he shall be put at liberty under bail. In no case shall the imprisonment be prolonged for default of payment of fees or whatever other furnishing of money.

ARTICLE 19. No detention shall exceed the term of three days, except upon proof of sufficient reason for imprisonment, in conformity with the requisites required by law. The sole lapse of this time shall render responsible the authority that orders or consents to it, and the agents, officers or jailers, that execute it. All maltreatment in the apprehension or confinement of prisoners, all hardship which shall be inflicted without legal motive, and all taxes or contributions in the prisons, are abuses which shall be corrected by the laws and severely punished by the authorities.

ARTICLE 20. In all criminal trials the accused shall have the following guarantees: First. That of being informed of the motive of the proceeding and the name of the accuser, if there should be one. Second. That of taking his preparatory declaration within forty-eight hours, computed from the time of the order for his arrest from the judge. Third. That of being confronted with the witnesses against him. Fourth. That he shall be furnished with the facts and averments contained in the accusation, in order to prepare his defence. Fifth. That of being heard in defence by himself or by counsel, or by both, according as he may desire. In case of having no one to defend him, he shall be presented with a list of the official counsel that he may select the one or the ones he may desire.

ARTICLE 21. The application of punishment, properly such, belongs to the judicial authority. Political or administrative authorities can only impose, as corrections, fines not exceeding five hundred dollars, and confinement not exceeding one month, in cases and manner expressly determined by law.

ARTICLE 22. There shall be forever prohibited penalties of mutilation and of infamy, branding, flogging, the bastinado, torture of whatever species, excessive fines, confiscation of property, or whatever other unsuitable or unusual punishment.

ARTICLE 23. In order to abolish the penalty of death, the administrative power is charged with establishing, without delay, a penitentiary system. Until then it shall be abolished for political offences, and shall not be used in other than cases of high treason during foreign war, highway robbery, arson, parricide, murder with malice premeditated or for gain, high military offences, and for piracy, as defined by law.

ARTICLE 24. No criminal proceeding may have more than three instances. No one shall be tried twice for the same offence, whether he be absolved or condemned by the judgment. The practice of exempting from the regular course of proceedings shall be abolished.

ARTICLE 23. Sealed correspondence circulating by the mails shall be inviolable. The violation of this guarantee is an offence which the law shall severely chastise.

ARTICLE 26. In time of peace no military authority may exact quarters, transportation, or other service, real or personal, without the consent of the proprietor. In time of war it may only be taken in the manner prescribed by law.

ARTICLE 27. Private property shall not be taken without the consent of the owner, except in cases of public utility and with previous indemnification. The law shall determine the authority that may make the appropriation in such cases, and the requisites for its exercise. No corporation, civil or ecclesiastical, whatever may be its character, denomination, or object, shall have legal power to acquire in proprietorship, or to administer for itself real estate, with the sole exception of edifices destined exclusively and directly to the purpose or object of the institution.

ARTICLE 28. Monopolies shall not be established, nor places for the sale of privileged goods, nor prohibitions in the character of so-called protections to industry, excepting solely those relative to the coining of money, to the mails, and to those privileges which, for a limited time, are conceded by the law to the inventors or perfectors of any improvement.

ARTICLE 29. In eases of invasion, grave disturbance of the public peace, or whatever cause which may put society in great peril or conflict, solely the President of the republic in concurrence with the council of ministers and with the approbation of the congress of the union, and in the recess of this, of the permanent deputation, may suspend the guarantees established by this consitution, with exception of those that assure the life of man; but such suspension shall be only for a limited time, by means of general provisions, and of such a character as not to favor a determined individual purpose. If the suspension take place during the session of congress, this shall grant such authorization as they shall esteem necessary to enable the executive to confront the circumstances. If it shall take place during recess the permanent deputation shall, without delay, convoke the congress for its advice and action.

Section second.—Of Mexicans.

ARTICLE 30. They are Mexicans: First. Who are born within or without the republic, of Mexican fathers. Second. Strangers that are naturalized in conformity with the laws of the federation. Third. Strangers who acquire real estate in the republic, or have Mexican sons; providing always, they do not manifest their resolution to preserve their nationality.

ARTICLE 31. It is obligatory upon all Mexicans: First. To defend the independence, the territory, the honor, the rights, and the interests of their country. Second. To contribute towards public expenses, as well of the federation as of the State and municipality where they may reside, in an equitable and proportional manner, as shall be prescribed by the laws.

'ARTICLE 32. Mexicans shall be preferred to strangers under equality of circumstances for all public employments, trusts, or commissions named by the authorities, when the quality of citizenship shall not be indispensable.

Laws shall be formed for improving the condition of Mexican laborers, providing premiums for those who distinguish themselves in whatever science or art, stimulating industry, and founding colleges and practical schools of art and industry.

Section third.—Of strangers.

ARTICLE 33. Those are strangers who do not possess the qualifications determined in article 30. They are entitled to the guarantees established by section first, title first, of the present constitution, except that in all cases the government has the right to expel those who are pernicious to society.

It is obligatory upon them to contribute towards public expenses in the manner that may be prescribed by the laws, and to obey and respect the institutions, laws, and authorities of the country, submitting to the judgments and sentences of the tribunals, without power to seek other protection than that which the laws concede to Mexican citizens.

Section fourth.—Of Mexican citizens.

ARTICLE 34. Those are citizens of the republic who, having the quality of Mexicans, have also the following requisites: First. Eighteen years of age if married, or twenty-one if not married. Second. An honest means of livelihood.

ARTICLE 35. The prerogatives of citizens are: First. To vote at popular elections. Second. To be voted for for any office subject to popular election, and of being selected for any other employment or commission, having the requisite qualifications established by law. Third. To associate to discuss the political business of the country. Fourth. To take arms in the army or in the national guard, in defence of the republic and its institutions. Fifth. To exercise in all cases the right of petition.

ARTICLE 36. It is obligatory upon citizens of the republic: First. To be registered in the poll-list of his municipality, stating the property of which he is possessed, and the industry, profession, or labor by which he subsists. Second. To enlist in the national guard. Third. To vote at popular elections in the district to which he belongs. Fourth. To assist in the conduct of popular elections; which services, however, shall be subject to remuneration.

ARTICLE 37. The character of citizen is lost: First. By naturalization in a foreign country. Second. By serving officially the government of another country, accepting its decorations, titles, or employments, without previous permission from the federal congress, excepting literary, scientific, or benevolent titles, which may be accepted freely.

ARTICLE 38. The law shall prescribe the cases and the form in which may be lost or suspended the rights of citizenship, and the manner in which they may be regained.

TITLE II.

Section first.—Of the national sovereignty and the form of government.

ARTICLE 39. The national sovereignty resides essentially and originally in the people. All public power springs from the people and is instituted for their benefit. The people have at all times the inalienable right of altering or modifying their form of government.

ARTICLE 40. The Mexican people voluntarily constitute themselves a democratic, federal, representative republic, formed of States free and sovereign in all that concerns their interior government, but united in a federation established according to the principles of this fundamental law.

ARTICLE 41. The people exercise their sovereignty by means of federal officers in cases belonging to the federation, and through those of the States in all that relates to the internal affairs of the States, in the manner respectively established by this federal constitution, and by the constitutions of the States, which latter shall never conflict with the federal compact.

Section second.—Of the integral parts of the federation and of the national territory.

ARTICLE 42. The national territory comprises the integral parts of the federation, and the adjacent islands in both seas.

ARTICLE 43. The integral parts of the federation are: The States of Aguas Calientes, Colima, Chiapas, Chihuahua, Durango, Guanajuato, Guerrero, Jalisco, Mexico, Michoacan, Nuevo Leon y Coahuila, Oajaca, Puebla, Queretaro, San Luis Potosi, Sinaloa, Sonora, Tabasco, Tamaulipas, Tlaxcala, Valle de Mexico, Vera Cruz, Yucatan, Zacatecas, and the Territory of Lower California.

ARTICLE 44. The States of Aguas Calientes, Chiapas, Chihuahua, Durango, Guerrero, Mexico, Puebla, Queretaro, Sinaloa, Sonora, Tamaulipas, and the Territory of Lower California, preserve the limits which they now have.

ARTICLE 45. The States of Colima and Tlaxcala preserve in their new character of States the limits which they had as territories of the federation.

ARTICLE 46. The State of the Valley of Mexico is formed of the territory actually composing the federal district, but the erection into a State shall only have effect when the supreme federal authorities shall be removed to another place.

ARTICLE 47. The State of Nuevo Leon y Coahuila comprises the territory which heretofore composed the two States of which it is now formed, except the part of the hacienda of Bonanza, which is reincorporated in Zacatecas, in the same terms as were established before its incorporation with Coahuila.

ARTICLE 48. The States of Guanajuato, Jalisco, Michoacan, Oajaca, San

Luis Potosi, Tabasco, Vera Cruz, Yucatan, and Zacatecas, recover the extension and limits which they had on the 31st of December, 1852, with the alterations which are established in the following article.

ARTICLE 49. The town of Contepec, which has belonged to Guanajuato, is incorporated in Michoacan. The municipality of Ahualulco, which has belonged to Zacatecas, is incorporated in San Luis Potosi. The municipalities of Ojo Caliente and San Francisco de los Adames, which have belonged to San Luis, as well as the towns of Nueva, Tlaxcala and San Andres del Teul, which have belonged to Jalisco, are incorporated in Zacatecas. The department of Tuxpan continues to form part of Vera Cruz. The canton of Huimauguillo, which has belonged to Vera Cruz, is incorporated in Tabasco.

TITLE III.

Of the division of powers.

ARTICLE 50. The supreme power of the federation is divided for its exercise into legislative, executive, and judicial. Two or more of these powers can never be united in the same person, nor the legislative power be deposited in one individual.

Section first.—Of the legislative power.

ARTICLE 51. The exercise of the supreme legislative power is deposited in one assembly, which shall be denominated the Congress of the Union.

Paragraph first.—Of the election and installation of congress.

ARTICLE 52. The congress of the union shall be composed of representatives elected in their entire number, each two years, by Mexican citizens.

ARTICLE 53. A deputy shall be named for each 40,000 inhabitants, or for each fraction over 20,000. The Territory in which the population shall be less than this shall still be entitled to send one deputy.

ARTICLE 54. For each deputy proper shall be elected also a substitute.

ARTICLE 55. The election for deputies shall be indirect in the first degree, and by secret ballot, in the manner which shall be prescribed by the electoral law.

ARTICLE 56. In order to be eligible as a deputy it is required to be a Mexican citizen in the full exercise of his rights; to have completed 25 years of age on the day of the opening of the session; to be a resident of the State or Territory which makes the election, and not to be an ecclesiastic. Residence is not lost by absence in the discharge of any public trust bestowed by popular election.

ARTICLE 57. The position of deputy is incompatible with the holding of any federal commission or office from which a salary is received.

ARTICLE 58. The deputies proper, from the day of their election up to the day on which their trust is concluded, cannot accept any employment offered by the executive of the union by which pay is received, except with the previous license of congress. The same requisites are necessary for deputy substitutes, when in the exercise of their functions.

ARTICLE 59. The deputies are inviolable for their opinions expressed in the discharge of their trust, and shall never be called to account for them.

ARTICLE 60. Congress shall decide with regard to the election of its members, and determine any doubts that may occur regarding the same.

ARTICLE 61. Congress may not open its sessions nor exercise its functions without the concurrence of more than half of the total number of its members; but those present may convene on the day named by the law, and compel the attendance of absent members, under penalties which shall be designated.

H. Ex. Doc. 100——10

ARTICLE 62. Congress shall have each year two ordinary sessions: the first shall commence on the 16th of September and shall terminate on the 15th of December, and the second, which cannot be prorogued, shall commence on the 1st of April and terminate on the last day of May.

ARTICLE 63. At the opening of the sessions the president of the union shall be present and shall deliver a message exhibiting the state of the union. The president of congress shall reply in general terms.

ARTICLE 64. All resolutions of congress shall have no other character than that of laws or economical bills. The laws shall be communicated to the executive, signed by the president and two secretaries. Economical bills by two secretaries.

Paragraph second.—Of the introduction and passage of laws.

ARTICLE 65. The right of introducing laws belongs: First. To the president of the union. Second. To the deputies of the federal congress. Third. To the legislatures of the States.

ARTICLE 66. A project of law presented by the president of the republic, by the legislatures of the States, or by deputations from the same, shall pass immediately to a committee. Those that may be presented by the deputies shall be subject to such action as shall be prescribed by the rules of debate.

ARTICLE 67. All projects of law which may be rejected by congress cannot be presented again during the sessions of the year.

ARTICLE 68. The second session shall be destined in all preference to the examination of and action upon the estimates for the following fiscal year, to the passage of the necessary appropriations according the same, and to the examination of the accounts of the past year which shall be presented by the executive.

ARTICLE 69. The day before the last of the first session, the executive shall present to congress the estimates for the coming year and the accounts of the last year. Both shall pass to a committee composed of five representatives, which shall be named the first day and which shall have the obligation of examining both documents and presenting a report upon them at the second session of the second term.

ARTICLE 70. The initiatories or projects of laws shall be subjected to the following course: First. The report of a committee. Second. One or two discussions in the manner expressed in the following clauses. Third. The first discussion shall take place on the day that may be designated by the president of congress, in conformity with the rules. Fourth. Upon the conclusion of this discussion a copy of the project shall be passed to the executive, that he may within the term of seven days give his opinion, or state that he does not desire to use this faculty. Fifth. If the opinion of the executive is favorable, the law shall be voted upon without further discussion. Sixth. If this opinion disagrees in whole or in part with the law proposed, the project shall be returned to the committee, that they may examine it *de novo*, taking into consideration the objections of the government. Seventh. The new report shall receive a new discussion, and upon the conclusion of this the vote upon the law shall be taken. Eighth. The approbation of an absolute majority of the deputies present.

ARTICLE 71. In cases of notorious urgency, qualified by the vote of two-thirds of the deputies present, congress may contract or dispense with the regular course prescribed by article 70.

Paragraph third.—Of the faculties of congress.

ARTICLE 72. Congress has the power: First. Of admitting new States or Territories into the federal union, incorporating them in the nation. Second. Of erecting Territories into States when they have a population of 80,000 inhabitants, and are proved to have the necessary elements for providing for their political existence. Third. Of forming new States within the limits of those existing, providing, always, that they have a population of 80,000 inhabitants, and are proved to have the necessary resources for their political existence. In all cases the legislatures of the States whose territory is proposed to be taken shall be heard, and their concùrrence shall be necessary, as well as the ratification of a majority of the legislatures of the States. Fourth. Of arranging definitively the limits of the States, terminating the differences which may arise between them respecting the boundaries of their respective territories, except when these differences have the character of contentions. Fifth. Of changing the residence of the supreme powers of the federation. Sixth. Of the internal government of the federal district and territories, upon the basis that the citizens shall elect, by popular voice, their political, municipal, and judicial authorities, and fix the taxes necessary to meet their local expenditures. Seventh. Of approving the federal estimates of expenditures, which shall be annually presented by the executive, and of imposing the taxes necessary therefor. Eighth. Of giving bases under which the executive may procure loans upon the faith of the national credit, and of approving said loans, and of recognizing and ordering the payment of the national debt. Ninth. Of establishing tariffs upon foreign commerce, and of removing, by means of general laws, onerous restrictions which may be established in the commerce between different States. Tenth. Of establishing general bases for mercantile legislation. Eleventh. Of creating and suppressing public employments of the federation, and of establishing, augmenting, or diminishing their salaries. Twelfth. Of ratifying the appointments that may be made by the executive of ministers, diplomatic agents and consuls, of the higher employees of the treasury, and of colonels, and other higher officers in the army or national armed force. Thirteenth. Of ratifying the treaties, contracts, or diplomatic conventions which the executive may make. Fourteenth. Of declaring war upon the facts which may be presented by the executive. Fifteenth. Of regulating the mode in which privateers may be licensed; of dictating laws according to which captures by sea or land shall be declared good or bad; and also relative to maritime rights during peace and war. Sixteenth. Of permitting or refusing the entry of foreign troops into the territory of the federation, and of consenting to the station of squadrons of other powers for more than one month in the waters of the republic. Seventeenth. Of permitting the passage of the national troops without the limits of the republic. Eighteenth. Of creating and sustaining the army and armed force of the Union, and of regulating its organization and service. Nineteenth. Of making regulations for the purpose of organizing, arming, and disciplining the national guard, reserving to the citizens which compose it the appointment of the commanders and officers, and to the States the power of instructing them in conformity with the discipline prescribed by said regulations. Twentieth. Of giving its consent that the executive may order the national guard without their respective States or Territories, fixing the amount of the force necessary to be so used. Twenty-first. Of making laws regarding naturalization, colonization, and citizenship. Twenty-second. Of making laws regarding general means of communication, and regarding the post office and mails. Twenty-third. Of establishing mints, prescribing the rules of their operation; of determining the value of foreign coin, and adopting a general system of weights and measures. Twenty-fourth. Of prescribing the rules under which the public land may be occupied or sold, and the price of the same. Twenty-fifth. Of conceding pardons for offences cognizable by the tribunals of the federation. Twenty-sixth. Of awarding rewards or recompense for eminent services rendered to the country, or to humanity; and privileges, for a limited time, to inventors or perfectors of any improvement. Twenty-seventh. Of proroguing, for thirty business days, the first term of its ordinary sessions. Twenty-eighth. Of forming rules for its internal regulation, and for compelling the attendance of absent members, and for correcting the faults or omissions of those present. Twenty-ninth. Of appointing and removing freely its secretaries and auditors, and of organizing these offiesc according to law. Thirtieth. Of making all laws which may be necessary and proper to render effective the foregoing powers, and all others conceded by this constitution, to the powers of the union.

Paragraph fourth.—Of the permanent deputation.

ARTICLE 73. During the recess of the congress of the union, there shall be a permanent deputation, composed of one deputy from each State and Territory, who shall be named by congress on the evening of the last day of its sessions.

ARTICLE 74. The powers of the permanent deputation are the following:

First. To give its consent to the use of the national guard in the cases spoken of in article 72, clause 20. Second. To determine by itself alone, or at the petition of the executive, the convocation of the congress in extraordinary session. Third. To approve in the case of appointments, as referred to in article 85, clause 3. Fourth. To receive the oath of the president of the republic, and of the ministers of the supreme court of justice, in the cases provided by this constitution. Fifth. To report upon all the business not disposed of, in order that the session which follows may immediately take up such unfinished business.

Section two.—Of the executive power.

ARTICLE 75. The exercise of the supreme executive power of the union shall be deposited in one sole individual, who shall be called President of the United Mexican States.

ARTICLE 76. The election of president shall be indirect in the first grade, and by secret ballot, in such manner as may be prescribed by the electoral law.

ARTICLE 77. In order to be president it is required to be a citizen of the Mexican republic by birth, in the exercise of his rights, to be thirty-five years of age at the time of election, not to belong to the ecclesiastical state, and to be a resident in the country at the time the election takes place.

ARTICLE 78. The president shall enter upon the exercise of his functions on the first day of December, and remain in office four years.

ARTICLE 79. In temporary default of a president of the republic, and in the vacancy before the installation of the newly elected, the president of the supreme court of justice shall enter upon the exercise of the functions of president.

ARTICLE 80. If the default of president be absolute, a new election shall be proceeded with, according to the provisions of article 76, and the one so elected shall exercise his functions until the last day of November of the fourth year following his election.

ARTICLE 81. The trust of president can only be resigned for grave cause, approved by congress, before whom shall be presented the resignation.

ARTICLE 82. If, from whatever reason, the election of president shall not have been made and published by the 1st of December upon which the change is to take place, or if the newly elected is not able to enter promptly upon the exercise of his functions, the term of the preceding president shall nevertheless cease, and the supreme executive power shall be deposited *ad interim* in the president of the supreme court of justice.

ARTICLE 83. The president, in taking possession of his trust, shall swear before congress, and in its recess before the permanent deputation, in the following manner: "I swear to discharge faithfully and patriotically the trust of President of the United Mexican States according to the constitution, and seeking in all things for the good and prosperity of the union."

ARTICLE 84. The president cannot leave the residence of the federal powers, nor the exercise of his functions, without grave motive, approved by congress, or in its recess by the permanent deputation.

ARTICLE 85. The powers and obligations of the president are the following: First. To promulgate and enforce the laws passed by the congress of the union, attending in the administrative sphere to their exact observance. Second. To appoint and remove freely secretaries of state; to remove diplomatic agents and superior employés of the treasury; and to appoint and remove freely all other federal officers whose appointment or removal is not otherwise provided for in the constitution or by the laws. Third. To appoint ministers, diplomatic agents, and consuls general, with the approbation of congress, or in its recess of the permanent deputation. Fourth. To appoint, with the approbation of congress, colonels and other higher officers in the army and national armed force, and the higher employés of the treasury. Fifth. To appoint all other officers of the army and national navy according to law. Sixth. To dispose of the permanent national armed force by sea or by land for the internal security and external defence of the federation. Seventh. To dispose of the national guard for the same objects, according to the provisions of clause 20th of article 72. Eighth. To declare war in the name of the United Mexican States, after the passage of the necessary law by the congress of the union. Ninth. To authorize privateers, subject to the basis fixed by congress. Tenth. To direct diplomatic negotiations, and to make treaties with foreign powers, submitting them to the ratification of the federal congress. Eleventh. To receive ministers or other envoys of foreign powers. Twelfth. To convoke congress in extraordinary session, with the consent of the permanent deputation. Thirteenth. To extend to the judicial power such assistance as may be necessary for the prompt exercise of its functions. Fourteenth. To open all classes of ports, establish frontier and maritime custom-houses, and prescribe their location. Fifteenth. To grant, in conformity with the laws, pardons to criminals sentenced for crimes cognizable by the federal tribunals.

ARTICLE 86. For the despatch of the business of the administrative departments of the federation that number of secretaryships shall be appointed which may be prescribed by congress by a law, which shall also provide for the distribution of business, and prescribe what shall be the department of each secretary.

ARTICLE 87. To be secretary of state it is required to be a Mexican citizen by birth, being in the exercise of his rights, and having completed twenty-five years of age.

ARTICLE 88. All the regulations, decrees; and orders of the president shall be signed by the secretary of state charged with the branch to which the business belongs. Without this requisite they shall not be obeyed.

ARTICLE 89. The secretaries of state, immediately after the opening of the sessions of the first term, shall render an account to congress of the state of their respective departments.

Section third.—Of the judicial power.

ARTICLE 90. The exercise of the judicial power of the federation shall be deposited in a supreme court of justice and in the district and circuit courts.

ARTICLE 91. The supreme court of justice shall be composed of eleven judges proprietary, four supremary judges, one attorney general, and one solicitor general.

ARTICLE 92. Each one of the individuals composing the supreme court of justice shall hold office during six years, and their election shall be indirect in the first grade, according to the terms prescribed by the electoral law.

ARTICLE 93. To be eligible as a member of the supreme court of justice it is required to be instructed in the science of law according to the judgment of the election, to be more than thirty-five years of age, and a Mexican citizen by birth, in the exercise of his rights.

ARTICLE 94. The members of the supreme court of justice upon entering upon the exercise of their trust shall make oath before congress, or, in its recess, before the permanent deputation, in the following manner: "Do you swear to discharge faithfully and patriotically the trust of magistrate of the supreme court of justice, conferred upon you by the people, in conformity with the constitution, and seeking in all things the good and prosperity of the union?"

ARTICLE 95. The duties of members of the supreme court of justice can only be resigned for grave reason, approved by congress, to whom the resignation shall be presented; in the recess of congress, before the permanent deputation.

ARTICLE 96. The law shall establish and organize the circuit and district courts.

ARTICLE 97. It belongs to the federal tribunals to take cognizance of: First. All controversies which may arise in regard to the fulfilment and application of the federal laws. Second. All cases pertaining to maritime law. Third. Those in which the federation may be a party. Fourth. Those that may arise between two or more States. Fifth. Those that may arise between a State and one or more citizens of another State. Sixth. Civil or criminal cases that may arise under treaties with foreign powers. Seventh. Cases concerning diplomatic agents and consuls.

ARTICLE 98. It belongs to the supreme court of justice to take cognizance from the first proceeding of controversies that may arise between one State and another, and of those wherein the union may be a party.

ARTICLE 99. It also belongs to the supreme court of justice to decide regarding cases of jurisdiction among the federal courts, between these and those of the States, and between those of one State and those of another.

ARTICLE 100. In the rest of the cases comprehended in article 97, the supreme court of justice shall be a court of appeal, or rather of last resort, according to the graduation which the law may make in the jurisdiction of the circuit and district courts.

ARTICLE 101. The tribunals of the federation shall decide all questions that may arise: First. Under the laws or acts of whatever authority which violate individual guarantees. Second. Under the laws or acts of the federal authorities which invade or restrict the sovereignty of the States. Third. Under the laws or acts of the States which invade the exercise of the federal authority.

ARTICLE 102. All the decisions of which mention is made in the preceding article shall take place on the petition of the party aggrieved, and by means of formal judicial proceedings, as shall be prescribed by law. The sentence shall be always such as to affect private individuals only, and is intended as merely a protection in the special cases to which the process refers, without embracing any general declaration regarding the law or act in question.

TITLE IV.

Of the responsibility of public functionaries.

ARTICLE 103. The deputies to the congress of the union, the members of the supreme court of justice, and the secretaries of state, shall be held responsible for ordinary offences which they may commit during their term of office, as well as the crimes, faults, or omissions of which they may be guilty in the exercise of their trust.

The governors of the States are also responsible for infractions of the constitution and of federal law.

So is also the president of the republic; but during the term of his office he can only be accused in case of the offences of treason, express violation of the constitution, attack upon the electoral franchise, and grave crimes against public order.

ARTICLE 104. In case of ordinary crime, congress, sitting as a grand jury, shall declare, by an absolute majority of votes, if there is cause of proceeding against the accused, or not. If the latter, no further proceeding shall take place; if the former, the accused shall immediately be deprived of his office and subjected to the action of the ordinary tribunals.

ARTICLE 105. Official offences shall be cognizable by congress as a jury of accusation, and the supreme court of justice as a jury of sentence. The jury of accusation has for its object to declare, by an absolute majority of votes, if the accused is culpable or not. If the declaration is favorable, the functionary shall continue in the exercise of his trust; if it is condemnatory, the accused shall be immediately deprived of his office and placed at the disposition of the supreme court of justice. This in full court, and sitting as a jury of sentence, in the presence of the offender, the attorney general, and the accuser, if such there should be, shall proceed to apply, by an absolute majority of votes, the penalty which the law may have prescribed.

ARTICLE 106. After the sentence is pronounced of responsibility for official crime, no exercise of the pardoning power can be extended to the offender.

ARTICLE 107. Responsibility for official crimes or errors only maintains during the period of occupation of office and one year thereafter.

ARTICLE 108. With reference to the requirements of civil war there shall be no privileged class, nor exemption for any public functionary.

TITLE V.

Of the States of the federation.

ARTICLE 109. The States shall adopt for their interior regulation the form of popular representative republican government.

ARTICLE 110. The States may arrange among themselves, by friendly agreements, their respective limits, but such arrangements shall not go into effect without the approbation of the congress of the union.

ARTICLE 111. The States cannot in any case: First. Form alliances, treaties, or coalitions with other States, nor with foreign powers, excepting the coalitions which may be formed among the frontier States for offensive or defensive war against the Indians. Second. Grant letters of marque or reprisal. Third. Coin money, or emit paper money, or sealed paper.

ARTICLE 112. Neither may they, without the consent of the congress of the union: First. Establish tonnage duty, or any other port duty, nor impose contributions, or duties upon importations or exportations. Second. Have at any time permanent troops or vessels-of-war. Third. Make war by itself upon any foreign power, except in case of invasion or such imminent peril as admits of no delay. In these cases immediate notice shall be given to the president of the republic.

ARTICLE 113. Each State has the obligation of delivering, without delay, the criminals of other States to the authorities that claim them.

ARTICLE 114. The governors of the States are obliged to publish and cause to be obeyed the federal laws.

ARTICLE 115. In each State of the federation entire faith and credit shall be given to the public acts, registers, and judicial proceedings of all the others. Congress may, by means of general laws, prescribe the manner of proving these acts, registers, and proceedings, and their effects.

ARTICLE 116. The powers of the union shall protect the States against all invasion or exterior violence. In case of internal disorder or rebellion they shall give equal protection, providing always that it be applied for by the legislature of the State, or by the governor, if the legislature is not in session.

Title VI.

General provisions.

ARTICLE 117. The powers which are not expressly conceded by this constitution to the federal authorities are understood to be reserved to the States.

ARTICLE 118. No person can, at the same time, hold two federal elective offices, but, if elected to two, he may select between them.

ARTICLE 119. No payment of money shall be made that is not embraced in the fiscal estimates or determined by previous law.

ARTICLE 120. The president of the republic, the members of the supreme court of justice, the deputies, and other public officers of the federation popularly chosen, shall receive a compensation for their services, which shall be determined by law, and paid by the national treasury. This compensation cannot be renounced, and any law that augments or diminishes it shall not have effect during the period for which the functionary holds the office.

ARTICLE 121. All public functionaries, without any exception, before taking possession of their offices, shall swear to observe and protect the constitution and the laws that emanate from it.

ARTICLE 122. In time of peace no military authority can exercise more functions than are in exact connexion with military discipline. There shall be fixed and permanent military authority in the castles, ports, and storehouses which belong immediately to the federal government, or in encampments, barracks, or depots which may be established without the towns for the station of troops.

ARTICLE 123. It belongs exclusively to the federal powers to exercise in matters of religious belief and discipline the intervention which may be prescribed by the laws.

ARTICLE 124. From the first day of June, 1858, *alcabalas* and interior custom-houses shall be abolished in all the republic.

ARTICLE 125. The forts, quarters, storehouses, and other buildings of the government of the union shall be under the immediate inspection of the federal authorities.

ARTICLE 126. This constitution, the laws of the congress of the union which emanate from it, and all treaties made or that may be made by the president of the republic with the approbation of congress, shall be the supreme law of all the union. The judges of each State in giving their decisions shall do so in conformity with said constitution, laws, and treaties, anything to the contrary that there may be in the laws or constitution of the States notwithstanding.

Title VII.

Of the alterations of the constitution.

ARTICLE 127. The present constitution may be added to or altered. In order that additions or alterations may become part of the constitution, it is necessary that such additions or alterations shall be approved of by the congress of the union by the vote of two-thirds of those present, and that they should also be approved by a majority of the legislatures of the States.

The congress of the union shall take account of the votes of the legislatures and the declaration that the addition or alteration had been approved.

Title VIII.

Of the inviolability of the constitution.

ARTICLE 128. This constitution shall not lose its force and vigor even if its observance be interrupted by any rebellion. In case that, by means of such an event, a government shall have been established contrary to the principles which it sanctions, immediately upon the people recovering their liberty its observance shall be re-established, and according to its provisions and the laws which have been framed in virtue of it, they shall be judged as well those who have figured in the government emanating from the rebellion as those who have co-operated with it.

Temporary article.

This constitution shall be published immediately, and shall be sworn to with the greatest solemnity in all the republic, but with the exception of the dispositions relative to the election of the supreme powers of the federation, and of the States, it shall not commence to have force until the 16th day of September next ensuing, when the first constitutional congress is to be installed. Until then the president of the republic and the supreme court of justice, who are to continue in exercise of their functions until the inauguration of the individuals constitutionally elected, shall govern themselves in the discharge of their obligations and powers by the precepts of this constitution.

Dated in the hall of sessions of congress, at Mexico, the 5th day of February, one thousand eight hundred and fifty-seven, and thirty-seventh of independence.

VALENTINE GOMEZ FARIAS,
Deputy for the State of Jalisco, President.
LEON GUZMAN,

Deputy for the State of Mexico, Vice-President.
For the State of Aguas Calientes, MANUEL BUENROSTRO.
For the State of Chiapas, FRANCISCO ROBLES, MATIAS CASTELLANOS.
For the State of Chihuahua, JOSE E. MUÑOZ, PEDRO IGNACIO IRIGOYEN.
For the State of Coahuila, SIMON DE LA GARZA Y MELO.
For the State of Durango, MARCELINO CASTAÑEDA, FRANCISCO ZARCO
For the federal district, FRANCISCO DE P. CONDEJAS, JOSE MARIA DEL RIO, PONCIANO ARRIAGA, J. M. DEL CASTELLO VELASCO, MANUEL MORALES PUENTE.
For the State of Guanajuato, IGNACIO SIERRA, ANTONIO LEMUS, JOSE DE LA LUZ ROSAS, JUAN MORALES, ANTONIO AGUADO, FRANCISCO P. MONTAÑEZ, FRANCISCO GUERRERO, BLAS BALCARCEL.
For the State of Guerrero, FRANCISCO IBARRA.
For the State of Jalisco, ESPIRIDION MORENO, MARIANO FARANDA, JESUS ANAYA Y HERMOSILLO, ALBINO ARANDA, IGNACIO LOUIS VALLARTA, BENITO GOMEZ FARIAS, JESUS D. ROJAS, IGNACIO OCHOA SANCHEZ, GUILLERMO LANGLOIS, JOAQUIN M. DEGOLLADO.
For the State of Mexico, ANTONIO ESCUDERO, JOSE L. REVILLA, JULIAN ESTRADA, I. DE LA PEÑA Y BARRAGAN, ESTEBAN PAEZ, RAFAEL MARIA VILLAGRAN, F. FERNANDEZ DE ALFARO, JUSTINO FERNANDEZ, EULOGIO BARRERA, M. ROMERO RUBIO, MANUEL DE LA PEÑA Y RAMIREZ, MANUEL FERNANDO SOTO.
For the State of Michoacan, SANTOS DEGOLLADO, SABAS ITURBIDE, FRANCISCO G. ANAYA, RAMON I. ALCARAZ, FRANCISCO DIAS BARRIGA, LUIS GUTIERREZ CORREA, MARIANO RAMIREZ, MATEO ECHAIZ.
For the State of Nuevo Leon, MANUEL P. DE LLANO.
For the State of Oaxaca, MARIANO ZAVALA, G. LARAZABAL, IGNACIO MARISCAL, JUAN N. CERQUEDA, FELIX ROMERO, M. E. GOYTIA.
For the State of Puebla, MIGUEL MARIA ARRIOJA, FERNANDO M. ORTEGA, GUILLERMO PRIETO, J. MARIANO VIADAS, FRANCISCO BANUET, MANUEL M. VARGAS, F. L. ESTRADO, JUAN N. IBARRA, JUAN N. DE LA PARRA.
For the State of Queretaro, IGNACIO REYES.
For the State of San Luis Potosi, FRANCISCO J. VILLALOBOS, PABLO TELLEZ.

For the State of Sinaloa, IGNACIO RAMIREZ.
For the State of Sonora, BENITO QUINTANA.
For the State of Tabasco, GREGORIO PAYRO.
For the State of Tamaulipas, LUIS GARCIA DE ARELLANO.
For the State of Tlaxcala, JOSE MARIANO SANCHEZ.
For the State of Vera Cruz, JOSE DE EMPARAN, JOSE MARIA MATA, RAFAEL GONZALEZ PAEZ, MARIANO VEGA.
For the State of Yucatan, BENITO QUIJANO, FRANCISCO INIESTRA, PEDRO DE BARANDA, PEDRO CONTRERAS ELIZALDE.
For the Territory of Tehuantepec, JOAQUIN GARCIA GRANADOS.
For the State of Zacatecas, MIGUEL AUZA, AGUSTIN LOPEZ DE NAVA, BASILIO PEREZ GALLARDO.
For the Territory of Lower California, MATEO RAMIREZ
JOSE MARIA CORTES Y ESPARZA, for the State of Guanajuato, *Deputy Secretary.*
ISIDORO OLVERA, for the State of Mexico, *Deputy Secretary.*
JUAN DE DIOS ARIAS, for the State of Puebla, *Deputy Secretary.*
J. A. GAMBOA, for the State of Oaxaca, *Deputy Secretary.*
Wherefore, I order that it be printed, published, circulated, and that it be fully complied with in the terms which it prescribes.
Palace of the national government, at Mexico, February 12, 1857.

IGNATIO COMONFORT.

The Citizen IGNATIO DE LA LLAVE,
   Secretary of State and of the Department of Government.

I communicate it to you for its publication and fulfilment. God and liberty.

LLAVE.

MEXICO, *February* 12, 1857.

No. 2.

[Translation.]

Jose Maria Patoni, constitutional governor of the State of Durango, to its inhabitants: Know ye that the honorable legislature thereof has decreed the following:

The legislature of the State of Durango decrees:

ARTICLE 1. The legislature of the State of Durango approves the decree of the honorable legislature of Zacatecas dated the 4th of May last past. Therefore it does not recognize as legitimate, and it protests against, the establishment of all authority foreign to the constitutional order.

ARTICLE 2. Should such revolutionary authority be established the State will consider the federal compact broken, and it will reassume its sovereignty, recalling its representatives in the general congress.

The governor of the State will order this to be published, circulated, and observed.

EDUARDO ESCARZAGA,
Deputy President.
LUIS DE LA TORRE,
Deputy Secretary.
AGUSTIN LEYVA,
Deputy Secretary.

VICTORIA OF DURANGO, *June* 22, 1861.

DURANGO, *June* 23, 1861.

Let this be published, circulated, and communicated to whomsoever it may concern for its strict observance.

JOSE MARIA PATONI.
CAYETANO MASCAREÑAS, *Secretary.*

A true copy.

WASHINGTON, *November* 28, 1861.

ROMERO.

No. 3.

[Translation.]

OFFICE OF THE SECRETARY OF STATE OF THE
GOVERNMENT OF THE STATE OF CHIAPAS.

The citizen governor delegate of the State has been pleased to transmit to me the following decree:

The citizen Juan Chimaco Corzo, governor delegate of the free and sovereign State of Chiapas, to its inhabitants: Know ye that the congress thereof has been pleased to decree the following:

ARTICLE 1. The congress of the State, legitimately representing the people of Chiapas, solemnly declares:

1. That it reaffirms the protest made by it on the 4th day of January of the present year not to recognize as legal any authority whatever foreign to the constitutional order, whatever may be its denomination.

2. That if such authority, evidentally a revolutionary one, should be established, the State will consider the bonds of union dissolved with the power which may arise, and from that moment it reassumes its sovereignty.

ARTICLE 2. The State of Chiapas declares that it will sustain the vote of its citizens and of the majority of the nation cast in favor of the citizen Benito Juarez, the constitutional President of the United Mexican States.

ARTICLE 3. This protest shall be laid before the supreme government, the sovereign congress of the union, and will be transmitted to the legislatures of the States and their governments.

The governor of the State will cause it to be printed, published, circulated, and carried into effect.

Given at the chambers of the congress of Chiapas on the 30th day of the month of September, 1861.

IGNACIO CARDONA,
Deputy President.
J. MANUEL GAMBOA,
Deputy Vice-President.
JOSE MARIA FLORES.
VICTOR DOMINGUEZ.
FRANCISCO AGUILAR.
ABRAHAM ROJAS,
Deputy Secretary.
MANUEL L. SOLORZANO,
Deputy Secretary.

Wherefore, I order it to be printed, published, circulated, and observed. Given at the palace of the government, San Cristobal, September 30, 1861

J. C. CORZO.

The Citizen JUAN JOSE RAMIREZ,
Secretary General of the Department.

SAN CRISTOBAL, *September* 30, 1861.
And I communicate it to you for your information and necessary ends.
God, liberty, and reform.
RAMIREZ.

WASHINGTON, *November* 28, 1861.
A true copy.
ROMERO.

No. 4.

[Translation.]

Manuel Cardona, by law the constitutional governor ad interim of the free State of Aguas Calientes, to its inhabitants: Know ye that the following decree has been communicated to me by the secretary of the sovereign congress of the State:

MOST EXCELLENT SIR: The honorable legislature of the State, under this date, has issued the following decree:

Number 6.

The sovereign congress of the State, in the name of the people whom it represents, decrees:

ARTICLE 1. The State of Aguas Calientes, represented by the legislative house, repel the request made by the disagreeing representatives, in which they ask the citizen president of the republic to divest himself of his power.

ARTICLE 2. The same sovereign congress give a vote of thanks to the citizen governor of the State of Queretaro for the worthy reply which he gave to the dissenting members, upon their requesting him to second their disorganizing and illegal views.

ARTICLE 3. The State of Aguas Calientes, in conformity with its decree number 5, of the 13th of June of the present year, protests that it will defend the legitimate government; and prays the constitutional president not to abandon the chief magistracy of the republic.

To the governor of the State for his approval.

Given in the hall of sessions of the honorable legislature, on the first of October, one thousand eight hundred and sixty-one.

ANTONIO RAYON,
Deputy President.
LUIS TOSCANO,
Deputy Secretary.
JUAN G. ALCAZAR,
Deputy pro Secretary.

Which we communicate to your excellency for your information, renewing our consideration.

God, liberty, and reform. Aguas Calientes, October 1, 1861.
LUIS TOSCANO, *D. S.*
JUAN G. ALCAZAR, *D. P. S.*

His Excellency the GOVERNOR *of the State.*

And that it may come to the knowledge of all persons, I order it to be printed and published by proclamation.

THE PRESENT CONDITION OF MEXICO. 157

Issued at the government hall, at Aguas Calientes, this 3d day of October, one thousand eight hundred and sixty-one, in the fortieth year of the independence and the third year of the reform.
MANUEL CARDONA.
J. IGNACIO MEDINA,
Chief Clerk.

A true copy.

WASHINGTON, November 28, 1861.

ROMERO.

No. 5.

[Translation.]

Constitutional government of the free and sovereign State of Aguas Calientes

BUREAU OF HOME GOVERNMENT,
Aguas Calientes, October 1, 1861.

The government of the State of Aguas Calientes has carefully considered the request which you made asking it to second the petition you have presented to the citizen president of the republic, with the view that he should resign the chief magistracy, and it would be wanting in its frankness and in its most sacred duties if it did not express in this reply all the ideas which that document has suggested.

This government sees such an absurdity in the measure which is proposed by you to the citizen Benito Juarez that it utterly fails to comprehend how it could have entered the minds of persons so enlightened as the signers of the manifestation undoubtedly are. It is undeniable that a giddiness, produced by disappointment, has blinded you to that extent that you cannot see that the fundamental law of the nation is infringed upon; that a wide door is opened to the aspirations which have been germinating ever since the capital of the republic was occupied by the legitimate government, and by which the national independence is placed in imminent danger, by which the bond which the federal system establishes is at once broken and the respect for law abandoned by those who should fearlessly sustain it. Civil war, being organized in factions, will destroy, in the most absolute manner, our beautiful country.

The State of Aguas Calientes, by means of its press, has ever sustained the lawful government; its citizens are fully persuaded that the national vote must be blindly respected, and its supreme legislature has thus manifested it in its decree No. 5, dated June 13, of the present year.

The government believes that Mexico cannot be happy whilst the talents of the country, instead of promoting the interests of illegitimate aspirations, do not seek to inspire the majority with that great republican virtue by which a governor, when once elected, is obeyed and aided, its enemies becoming its most constant and decided supporters.

Perhaps you, in the moment of excitement, have only thought of setting aside what is called an obstacle to the advancement of a policy, without considering that it is not the absence of an individual which is left you, but an abyss—a law overthrown—and a phalanx of aspirants, incapable of conducting the ship of state to the haven selected by the illusions of a few persons.

If, in these circumstances, prudence is not resorted to; if it is not sought in good faith to aid the man whom the law alone should set aside at the proper time, we must despair of ever definitely constituting ourselves, because the means which you have adopted is entirely contrary to the sense of a nation grown weak through insurrections, and which has conquered the sublime right of spontaneously electing the functionary who shall preside over its destinies.

This government, as the faithful interpreter of the voice of the state, replies to you that it cannot and must not second your petition, because it perceives that, by deviating in the slightest degree from the path of legality, it would be to sink itself into the mire of insurrections, and to contribute in that the civilized world should witness the sad spectacle of eight millions of intelligent beings overcome by perpetual insanity.

With the foregoing your petition is answered; and now, renewing to you the assurances of my particular esteem, I am, &c. Liberty, constitution, and reform.
MANUEL CARDONA.
J. IGNACIO MEDINA,
Chief Clerk.

WASHINGTON, *November* 28, 1861.
A true copy.
ROMERO.

No. 6.

[Translation.]

GOVERNMENT OF THE FREE AND SOVEREIGN STATE OF QUERETARO,
Queretaro, September 22, 1861.

I have received the circular which you were pleased to address to the citizen governor of the States under date of the 15th instant, and it becomes my duty to make the reply due thereto, and as you anticipate my frankness, which is most agreeable to me, I have the honor to reply to you.

In addressing yourselves to the citizen president, asking him to relinquish the position in which the national vote has placed him, you give the reasons upon which you base your petition, charging upon the administration of Mr. Juarez all the serious evils which surround our unfortunate country. I declare to you that I see in this petition only the best intentions on your part, and far from me is it to accuse you of a dishonorable object, but I cannot do less than to point out to you the very serious calamities which the realization of your views thus initiated would entail.

As you yourselves admit in your petition, the revolution which has caused the banner of reform to triumph on the fields of battle, has not been one of the many commotions which have agitated the country, and you yourselves desire to convert this revolution, which up to this period you know to be just, into one of the many convulsions which ambition and brutal force have created in this country.

If this revolution, which you sustain, has had up to this day a national—a social—character, it has been because, as you also admit, it has been the only time that the law of legitimacy has prevailed in our country and not that of the sword; nevertheless, even conceding your petition, it would bring with it a principle of anarchy, because it would enable any faction to remove a magistrate whenever it saw fit to do so, and the respect which the laws should have would be lost. Of what use then would be constitutions, electoral laws, and the public vote in a country where the president descends from the high position to which the national will has elevated him, at the simple suggestion of a mere handful who in this or that character desire him to do so?

The citizen Juarez is charged with the evils which afflict the country. I shall neither set myself up as the judge of the accused, nor as the eulogist of him who is in power. I withhold my personal convictions, and I only speak to you as the representative of a State of the Mexican confederation,

The State which has honored me with its confidence, when called upon to cast its vote like the others of the confederation for the presidency, did not do so in behalf of the citizen Juarez, because such was its convictions. But when once the electoral contest had terminated, it was the first to acknowledge the national will, as it will be to sustain it.

No State more than that of Queretaro more deeply deplores the misfortunes which have overwhelmed it, because it has been unfortunately selected by the reaction as the theatre of its operations; and for the sake of justice it confesses that if the inability of the general government has been the cause that the proper remedy has not been applied to its evils, it also knows that this same government on many occasions adopted measures of an efficacious nature, and which did not have their salutary influence because the most urgent orders were frequently disobeyed by those to whom they were directed, perhaps already with the view of preparing the way for that which now occupies our attention.

In a word, fellow-citizens, the evil exists and it is a very serious one, but let not the remedy be sought in the persons; let it be sought for at its true origin; let these men of talents and with good intentions, sustained by the wise laws, seek to find the remedy, and let them not seek for an unfortunate division among ourselves, which would destroy us in times like these; let the sovereign congress unfold the programme of reform, and Mexico will be saved; but let not anarchy be introduced, nor the respect for the laws be relaxed.

I believe, fellow-citizens, that I am in duty bound to make to you one last remark. The thought of the deposition of Mr. Juarez is not a measure dictated by a sincere policy, but it is an artifice, which is fully characterized as the revolt of certain ambitious parties, because I had previously been made acquainted with their labors by an invitation to aid them; and I, comprehending the serious evils which would be entailed thereby upon the country, repelled it with all the energy of my character, because you, in enumerating the evils which the citizen president has caused, forget to make mention of the triumph of the reaction, which the desire to apply to them the remedy which you proposed would bring about.

Such is the sincere expression of my views, and as such I give it to you. I present it to the nation whose name you invoke, that it may pronounce its judgment, and I conclude by declaring to that same nation that in me not individuals but principles will find a defender, and that the arms which have been intrusted to the State under my command shall never be used in breaking up the laws for the benefit of a faction, but, on the contrary, to sustain them with all the energy of him who feels the deep conviction that he complies with his duty.

I renew to you the considerations of my esteem. Liberty and reform.

JOSE MARIA ARTEAGA.

Citizen Deputies JUAN O. CAREAGA, MANUEL O. DE MONTELLANO, AND JOSE LINARES, *Mexico.*

WASHINGTON, *November* 28, 1861.

A true copy.

ROMERO.

No. 7.

[Translation.]

Supreme government of the free State of Jalisco, section of government.

GUADALAJARA, *September* 30, 1861.

I have received the circular communication which you were pleased to address to the government under my charge, dated the 15th of the month now closing, in which, as a committee in behalf of the citizens who signed the memorial addressed to the present depositary of the supreme executive power of the republic, asking him to resign the post which he now occupies, you urge me to second the views contained in that petition.

In due reply, I have the honor to state to you that I do not concur in the mode proposed for obtaining the resignation of the citizen Juarez, nor in the change of this functionary, for reasons which I shall set forth.

1st. Because the mode is illegal, as the petitioners have already been told in reply; for it is opposed to a declaration of the constitution, in virtue of which the citizen Juarez is president of the republic for the period marked out by the fundamental law.

2d. Because fifty-one citizens, whatever may be the character and political representation of the party with which they are united in obtaining a change of this kind, do not form a majority of the nation, whose sovereign will ought to be respected.

3d. Because the change which is desired is not, in the judgment of the undersigned, the radical remedy that ought to be chosen for curing the evils which are deplored, but, on the contrary, is a brand of discord among true liberalists, which, in the present revolutionary circumstances of the country, would drive us into an abyss, from which we could not be withdrawn by the declamations of the press, nor by the conviction of having acted with imprudence on a subject of vital interest.

According to the fundamental code of the republic, the ministry is responsible for the administrative acts of the executive, for which acts the ministers may be arraigned if they are wanting in obedience to the laws, since no order of the executive chief is to be obeyed unless it be authenticated by the secretary of the department to which it belongs, differently from the president, who, notwithstanding, is responsible for infractions of the constitution and laws, but can only be arraigned during his official term for offences of treason to his country, express violation of the fundamental charter, attack on the freedom of elections, and grave offences of the common order.

Therefore, I do not deem it just to reproach the citizen Juarez with the faults, omissions, and evils which are deplored by the fifty-one petitioners in the enumeration of them which they make in the appeal that they have thought proper to address to me. What is right, what is politic, and what is suitable, if there really be faults to charge, is to ask that the responsibility of the ministry be made effective. In any other mode the road is crooked, the evil is aggravated, and the law, the preservation of which has cost so much blood and countless sacrifices on the part of Mexicans, is frustrated.

The undersigned is not a partisan of persons; his convictions are firm for principles; and believing, as he does, that the evils complained of in the country are not to be attributed to the present president in person, he thinks that, while no offence of those provided for in the constitution is committed, he ought to be left in peace to finish his term, to be assisted with the exertions of the truly liberal in the discharge of his painful tasks, to be surrounded with a prestige and a respectability that are interested in the triumph of principles and not of persons, and that meanwhile the person should be sought who is most fit, in the opinion of the nation, to take his place when his term shall be ended.

Such are the convictions of the undersigned, which, with the frankness that characterizes him, he has the honor to make known to you, in responding to the appeal which you have been pleased to address to him.

I assure you of my respectful consideration and particular esteem.

God, liberty, and reform.

PEDRO OGAZON.
IGNACIO L. VALLARTA,
Secretary.

The citizens JUAN ORTIZ CAREAGA, M. M. ORTIZ DE MONTELLANO, and JOSE LINARES, Mexico.

WASHINGTON, *November* 28, 1861.

A true copy.

ROMERO.

Mr. Romero to Mr. Seward.

[Confidential.]

WASHINGTON, *December* 21, 1861.

MY DEAR SIR: I have the honor to send you herewith a copy of the translation I read you in our interview of this morning of some remarks in regard to Mexico contained in the addresses delivered by the presidents of the congress and senate of the Spanish cortes, in reply to the queen's speech on the opening of the cortes.

I am, sir, very respectfully, your most obedient servant,

M. ROMERO.

Hon. WILLIAM H. SEWARD, &c., &c., &c.

Extract from an address of Señor Martinez de la Rosa to Queen Isabella in behalf of the Spanish congress, delivered on the 19th of November last.

Making a parallel between the present Isabella and Isabella the I of Spain, Señor Martinez de la Rosa proceeds as follows:

"In those days, as in the present, the weight of Spain in the political scale of Europe was increased. The Spanish soldiers were crowned with abundant laurels on the African coast, and they are preparing themselves, if necessary, to hoist again in Mexico the standard of Hernan Cortes. What more? Even the first island discovered by Columbus has just now returned to the bosom of the mother country."

The following is an extract from the remarks of the president of the Spanish senate, the Marquis del Duero, in reply to the address of Queen Isabella on the opening of the Spanish cortes:

"The senate has learned with satisfaction that your Majesty is disposed to give an example of wholesome energy and a testimony of a noble generosity, inviting also France and England, who equally have cause to complain of the outrages of the Mexicans, to follow our example, and to associate with us in order to obtain the satisfaction we have the right to exact, and to cause that people, worthy of a better fate, to feel, through the power of arms, the necessity of having a government really in harmony with the requirements of so rich a country."

Mr. Romero to Mr. Seward.

[Translation.]

MEXICAN LEGATION TO THE UNITED STATES,
Washington, January 24, 1862.

Mr. SECRETARY: I have the honor to remit enclosed copies, mentioned in the adjoined index of the documents which I yesterday received from the Mexican government, which show the condition the republic was in at the close of December last past by reason of the Spanish invasion, to which I referred at our interview this morning.

I gladly avail of this occasion to reiterate to you, sir, the assurances of my most distinguished consideration.

M. ROMERO.

Hon. W. H. SEWARD, &c., &c., &c.

[Translation.]

Index to the documents which the Mexican legation to-day transmits to the Department of State of the United States, annexed to the note of this date.

No.	From and to whom.	Date.	Contents.
		1861.	
1	Mr. Rubalcara to Mr. Llave.	Oct. 14	Surrender of Vera Cruz and Ulloa.
2	Mr. Llave to Mr. Rubalcara.	Oct. 15	Answer to above.
3	Mr. Doblado to Mr. Llave.	Oct. 17	Reply of the federal government about surrender of Vera Cruz and Ulloa.
4	....	....	Circular to governors of States about Spanish invasion.
5	....	....	Decree closing the port of Vera Cruz.
6	....	Oct. 18	Manifesto of the President to the nation. (For this manifesto see enclosure in Mr. Corwin's despatch No. 11, of December 24, 1861.)
7	....	Nov. 26	Decree abrogating the law of July 17, relating to suspension of the payment of the foreign debt.
8	....	....	Speech of the president on closing the session of congress.
9	....	....	Reply of the president of the congress.

WASHINGTON, *January* 24, 1862.

THE PRESENT CONDITION OF MEXICO. 163

No. 1.

[Translation.]
COMMANDER-IN-CHIEF OF THE NAVAL FORCES OF HER CATHOLIC MAJESTY
IN THE ANTILLES.

STEAMER ISABEL LA CATOLICO AND ANCHORAGE OF
ANTON LIZARDO, *December* 14, 1861.

SEÑOR GOVERDANOR: The long series of injuries inflicted upon the government of her Catholic Majesty by that of the Republic of Mexico, the repeated violences committed upon Spanish subjects, and the blind obstinacy with which the government of Mexico has constantly refused to listen to the just reclamations of Spain, always presented with the moderation and decorum proper to so chivalrous a nation, have placed my government under the necessity of abandoning all hope of obtaining by conciliatory measures a satisfactory adjustment of the grave differences existing between the two countries.

The government of her Catholic Majesty resolved, however, to obtain full reparation for these many outrages, has ordered me to commence my operations by occupying the city of Vera Cruz and the Castle of San Juan de Ulloa, which will be held as a hostage security, (*prenda pretoria*,) until such time as the government of her Majesty shall feel assured that for the future the Spanish nation will be treated with the consideration which is due it, and that the compacts which have been celebrated between both governments shall be religiously observed.

You will communicate with me through the consul of France, charged with representing the commercial interests of Spain, within the term of twenty-four hours, reckoned from the moment you receive this intimation, whether you are disposed or not to surrender to me the city of Vera Cruz and the castle, with the understanding that if your reply is negative, or if at the expiration of the time fixed I have not received any reply, from that moment you may consider hostilities as commenced, to which end the Spanish force will be disembarked.

It is my duty to inform you that although I make this demand only in the name of Spain, according to the instructions which I have received, the occupation of this city and of the castle will serve equally as a guarantee for the rights and reclamations against the government of Mexico which the governments of France and Great Britain have to make good.

It remains for me to make known to you that the mission of the Spanish forces does not in any way interfere with the internal political questions of the country. All opinions will be respected, no censurable act will be committed, and from the moment that our troops occupy Vera Cruz, the Spanish chiefs will respond for the security of the persons and property of its inhabitants, whatever may be their nationality.

To you and to the other Mexican authorities it belongs to afford protection to foreigners until that occupation shall be carried into effect, whether it be pacifically or by force of arms. If Spanish subjects, or other foreigners, should be persecuted or outraged, the forces which compose this expedition will find themselves under the severe but unavoidable necessity of recurring to reprisals.

I entertain the hope that whatever may be your resolution, you will act with that discretion which is to be expected, and, penetrated with the conviction that the Spanish forces, always humane, always noble and loyal, even with their enemies, will not take the first step in the path of violences, reprehensible even in case of war; will avoid all species of crimes whose sole result would be to make more difficult, if not impossible, the arrangement of the pending international questions. I avail myself of this opportunity to offer to you the assurances of my consideration.

JUAN GUTIERREZ DE RUBALCARA.

The GOVERNOR *of the State of Vera Cruz, &c., &c.*

WASHINGTON, *January* 24, 1862.

True copy.

ROMERO.

No. 2.

[Translation.]

MEXICAN REPUBLIC, GOVERNMENT OF THE FREE AND SOVEREIGN STATE OF VERA CRUZ.

VERA CRUZ, *December* 15, 1861.

SIR: I am in possession of the communication which was delivered to me by your commissioners at 1 p. m. on the 14th instant, and beg to inform you that while I have made myself acquainted with its contents, and forwarded a copy to the commander-in-chief of the eastern forces, I have sent the same by express to the chief magistrate of the nation. As you inform me that it is your determination, after the expiration of twenty-four hours, to attack this city and the fort of Ulloa, and that in demanding their surrender, in virtue of your mission, you are merely desirous of holding them as hostages, I shall retire with the government under my charge to an adjacent point, not only with a view to preserving order, but to transmit to you the reply of my government, on which I depend.

The recommendation which you have made relative to the respect due to foreigners was unnecessary, as in this republic those belonging to other nations are so much respected and enjoy so many advantages that I can assure you the condition of a Mexican citizen is disadvantageous as compared with that of a foreigner. As a proof of what I state, I may cite the testimony of many honorable foreigners who live amongst us, and, above all, the conduct observed by the Mexicans under present circumstances.

The news of the war which Spain has brought upon Mexico has for some days been known among us; and notwithstanding this, and the indignation excited by the injurious articles contained in several of the newspapers of the peninsula, the Spaniards have been respected, and not only have they not in any way been injured, but they have not even in the slightest degree been insulted.

Badly disposed persons, and perhaps even degenerate Mexicans, have given sinister information to European governments; but the truth is what I have stated, and the time may perhaps come when you will see this and judge for yourself.

Whatever may be the lot that awaits this city, I have to inform you that, by order of the federal government, the town council will remain, with a force of police and some neutral foreigners—the latter armed, at my request, with the sole object of preserving order up to the last moment.

As the object of the above-named corporation and the forces belonging thereto is merely as indicated above, I trust in your gentlemanly character and the good discipline of your subordinates to respect the said body and the above-mentioned forces.

In conclusion, I have to inform you that it is much to be regretted that nations who, on account of their origin and identity, as well in language as in customs, ought to remain united and on intimate terms of friendship, should to-day, for groundless reasons, in my opinion, find themselves on the point of opposing each other, and commencing a struggle the end of which cannot well be seen.

I avail myself of this opportunity to offer you my most distinguished consideration.

Liberty and reform.

IGNACIO DE LA LLAVE.

The COMMANDER *of her Catholic Majesty's forces
in the Gulf of Mexico.*

True copy.

WASHINGTON, *January* 24, 1862.

ROMERO.

No. 3.

[Translation.]

SECRETARY OF STATE AND DEPARTMENT OF FOREIGN AFFAIRS AND GOVERNMENT.

MEXICO, *December* 17, 1861.

The citizen president, to whom I have given account of the communication directed to you by the commander of the Spanish naval forces, and of that which you sent to that chief in reply, has ordered me to say to you to follow punctually the instructions which have been given by him beforehand for the case, which has now arrived, of the open commencement of hostilities on the part of the subjects of Spain, and that it is to be now left to the military action of General Uraga, who commands in chief the Mexican army, to proceed in his sphere in conformity with the provisions that have been made.

Far will it be from the government of the republic to direct itself to a chief who, throwing aside all the formalities of the rights of peoples, commences by demanding the delivery of a city. The cry of war that the whole nation has spontaneously uttered marks out to the government the path which it should follow; and it will not be the citizen president who will recede before a foreign invasion, and with all the more reason when in this case Mexico does no more than repel force by force, using its most unquestionable natural right.

I enclose to you, by superior order, a copy of the decree and circular which have to-day been remitted by extraordinary express to the governors of the States, recommending to you to second, with all the energy and activity demanded by the circumstances, the plans of the government, by the faithful execution of which the president does not doubt the invasion which threatens to destroy our liberties and our independence will be effectually repelled.

Liberty and reform.

DOBLADO.

The citizen GOVERNOR *of the State of Vera Cruz.*

True copy.

WASHINGTON, *January* 24, 1862.

ROMERO.

No. 4.

[Translation.]

SECRETARY OF STATE AND DEPARTMENT OF FOREIGN RELATIONS AND OF GOVERNMENT.

MEXICO, *December* 17, 1861.

By order of the citizen president, I have the satisfaction of remitting to you copies of the communications exchanged between the commander of the Spanish forces at Vera Cruz and the citizen governor of that State, as well as of the decree and manifesto which the supreme magistrate has thought proper to-day to issue, in order that the States should arouse to the defence of our independence.

After having exhausted all means of a pacific settlement between Spain and Mexico, the government of the republic, strong in the consciousness of right, and feeling all the impulse of the popular opinion pronounced for war, accepts that which has been initiated by the Spanish forces in a mode so unheard of, because its right is unquestionable to repel force by force; and it protests before the civilized world that the responsibility of all succeeding acts will fall solely upon the government of the Queen of Spain, who so inconsiderately has espoused the unjust charges with which the enemies of the liberty of Mexico have sought to speculate.

Notwithstanding our intestine divisions, the sentiment of independence and the hatred of the ancient rulers of our county is still preserved alive, although the latter is lessened by the effect of education and the civilization of the age. The citizen president, in raising aloft the flag of Mexican nationality, does no more than follow the torrent of public opinion; and he has the pleasure of seeing grouped around him, on the day of national conflict, the greater part of those Mexicans who, from differences of political opinions, remained disunited, who have now abandoned their revolutionary flags at the first call of the country.

Although the government has the full right to expel from the territory of the republic all Spaniards resident within it, it has refrained from doing so for the present, because it believes that acknowledging the generosity with which they are treated they will strictly observe that neutrality which their position requires. The president has thus given another proof of the consideration which he has always exercised in the conduct of his foreign relations, proving by indisputable acts that it is not his fault that those relations should have reached the unfortunate state in which they are now found.

The president, therefore, hopes that giving prompt and exact compliance to the decree of which mention was made at the beginning of this circular, you will place in march within the shortest possible time the contingent of armed force which is therein assigned, and that you will, beside, make use of all the official means within your power, as governor, to place the State which is under your worthy command in the attitude of preparation which is demanded by the nature of the circumstances, exciting by every means in your power the patriotism of all of its inhabitants that they join for the common defence; and if the unfortunate case arrives that the enemy penetrates into the interior, that all the inhabitants of the country rise *en masse*, and oppose with their swords and their constancy an impregnable wall to the presumption of our invaders.

Be the memory of Hidalgo, and of Moralos, and of Cuerrero, the model of the Mexicans, and the standard borne aloft in the ranks of our army in the hour of the combat. Long live our independence! Long live the republic, liberty and reform. DOBLADO.

The citizen GOVERNOR *of the State of* ——.

WASHINGTON, *January* 24, 1862.
True copy. ROMERO

No. 5.

[Translation.]

The constitutional president of the republic has been pleased to direct to me the following decree:

Benito Juarez, constitutional president of the Mexican republic, to the inhabitants of the same maketh known:

That Spanish forces having occupied the port of Vera Cruz, and by the same act hostilities having been opened between the republic and Spain, in use of the ample faculties with which I am invested, I have thought proper to decree the following:

ARTICLE 1. The port of Vera Cruz is closed from the 14th instant to the foreign and coasting trade.

ART. 2. All Mexicans who shall join the Spaniards with arms in their hands, or that in whatsoever manner shall favor their cause, are hereby declared traitors to their country, and shall be punished as such.

ART. 3. The time conceded to the reactionists by the law of amnesty of the 2d of the present month to take advantage of the indulgence offered by the government is extended for fifteen days more, and is made applicable to all Mexicans except those who, in the judgment of the government, are not open to receive it, to which end an examination shall be made in each particular case.

ART. 4. The governors of the States are authorized to dispose of the revenues belonging to the general government within their respective States, to the end that with the utmost possible expedition may be put in march the contingent of armed force assigned in this decree.

ART. 5. The contingent of the States is that which follows:

States.	No. of men.	States.	No. of men.
Federal district	3,000	Guerrero	2,000
Oaxaca	3,000	Yucatan	2,000
Guanajuato	3,000	Tabasco	2,000
Jalisco	3,000	Aguas Calientes	1,000
Zacatecas	3,000	Queretario	1,000
San Luis Potosi	3,000	Colima	1,000
Mexico	3,000	Chiapas	1,000
Michoacan	3,000	Tlaxcala	1,000
Puebla	3,000	Baja California	1,000
Vera Cruz	3,000	Sonora	1,000
Nuevo Leon y Coahuila	2,000	Sinaloa	1,000
Tamaulipas	2,000		
Durango	2,000	Total	52,000
Chihuahua	2,000		

ART. 6: In addition to the placing of the contingent designated in the preceding article at the point which will be opportunely designated by the government, the governors will place under arms all the national guard which they have disposable, providing such extraordinary measures as in their judgment may be necessary for the procuring of the resources required for the maintenance of such forces.

ART. 7. The Spanish residents in the country will continue to live under the protection of the laws, and will only be punished in conformity with the same when, abusing the generosity of the government, they shall afford aid to the invader.

Wherefore, I order that it be printed, published, circulated, and that it be duly complied with.
Dated in the national palace of Mexico, the 17th of December, 1861.
BENITO JUAREZ.
The citizen MANUEL DOBLADO,
Minister of Foreign Relations and of Government.

And I communicate it to you for your compliance and the consequent ends. God and liberty! Mexico, December 17, 1861.
DOBLADO.
The citizen GOVERNOR *of the State of* ———.

WASHINGTON, *January* 24, 1862.
True copy.
ROMERO.

No. 6.

[Manifesto of President Juarez.—See enclosure in Mr. Corwin's despatch No. 11, of December 24, 1861, page 44 of this document.]

No. 7.

[Translation.]

The constitutional president of the republic has been pleased to send to me the decree which follows:

The citizen Benito Juarez, constitutional president of the United Mexican States, to their inhabitants: Know ye that the sovereign congress of the union has judged proper to decree as follows:

ARTICLE 1. The provisions of the law of the 17th July of the present year, which relate to the diplomatic conventions and the debt contracted in London, are abolished.

ARTICLE 2. The government will immediately put in course of payment the respective assignments, in conformity with the provisions and regulations anterior to said law.

ARTICLE 3. The government will at once send to congress notice of the amounts subsisting at the time of the passage of the law, and of what has been received since, pertaining to those assignments, initiating the laws which it may deem necessary to make good such amounts to the creditors under the conventions and of the debt contracted in London, and to supply the treasury with the amount that may be wanted for this purpose.

Given in the chamber of sessions of the congress of the union in Mexico the 23d of November, 1861.

MANUEL DUBLAN, Delegate, *President.*
JUAN N. GUZMAN, Delegate, *Secretary.*
ANSELMO CANO, Delegate, *Secretary.*

PALACE OF THE FEDERAL GOVERNMENT IN MEXICO,
November 26, 1861.

Therefore, I order that this be printed, published, and circulated, and be duly executed.
BENITO JUAREZ.

MEXICO, *November* 26, 1861.
And I enclose it to you for your directions and due consequences.
God, liberty, and reform.
GONZALES.
To Citizen JOSE GONZALES ECHEVERRIAS,
Minister of Finance and Public Credit.

No. 8.

[Translation.]

Speech of the president of the republic at the closing of the sessions of congress, December 15, 1861.

CITIZEN DEPUTIES: You are about to suspend your legislative functions in the midst of the most difficult circumstances which have surrounded Mexico since her independence. Your final resolutions have risen, however, to the grave necessities of the moment, since on retiring you have conceded to the executive all the faculties which are necessary to confront the perils which threaten us.

The government, which sees in these extraordinary faculties an immense increase of responsibility, and which will exercise them only in the name of the national representation, without other title than the imperious emergency of the circumstances, nor other object than the salvation of the republic, feels equal timidity in accepting them, and desires to return them to the sovereign power from whence they are derived.

The supreme emergency of the present moment does not weaken the hope which the government has manifested on another occasion, and which it still entertains, of averting the perils which threaten our nationality, and of re-establishing peace under the protection of law and of liberty.

In this work, so difficult, the government has as guarantees of its success the patriotism of the Mexicans and the spirit of reason and of equity, which must prevail among the other nations. The Mexican government remains faithful to its sentiments of peace and of good feeling toward other people, and of loyalty and moderation toward their representatives, and it hopes to be able to procure that the European governments, whose judgment has been deceived by the enemies of our liberty, with reference to the situation of the republic, will come to see in what they allege as injuries only one of the inevitable consequences of a revolution highly humanitarian in its character, which the country commenced eight years ago, and which has already begun to realize its promises, not only to Mexicans, but also for foreigners themselves.

These can easily comprehend that a revolution of reform, which in its progress has wounded more or less, though occasionally, some interests, will, in the end, place upon a solid basis all that is most desirable in point of moral and material order, for the benefit of all the inhabitants of the nation, and they will acknowledge that it has already substituted religious liberty, freedom of commerce, and fraternity with the emigrants from other countries, for the system of suspicion and of exclusiveness which, until recently, has dominated the interior and foreign policy of the republic.

Other people cannot overlook, except momentarily, the interest which they have in aiding us with their sympathy in consolidating a revolution, the fruits of which they will enjoy as well as ourselves.

For this it is that the government hopes, in the war with which the republic is threatened, that the voice of reason, of justice, and of equity, will still be heard, and that rather than by the power of arms, the peril will be allayed by a just and equitable arrangement, compatible with the honor and the dignity of the nation. But if it shall not be so, if it results that our hopes are frustrated the government will employ all the energy which love of country and a consciousness of right can inspire, to stimulate the people to defend their revolution and their independence, having, as the guarantees of our success, the justice of our cause and the patriotism which, among all the citizens of the republic, has been aroused by the sole announcement that the independence of our country might be in peril.

The government will do its duty, and if, as it does not doubt, Mexico, by a supreme effort of her sons, is preserved through a foreign war, and has the happiness to see peace again re-established, congress, at its next session, will come together to take advantage of this position, and by dictating wise laws will consolidate, and finally establish, our independence, liberty, and reform.

WASHINGTON, *January* 24, 1862.

True copy.

ROMERO.

No. 9.

[Translation.]

Reply of the president of congress.

CITIZEN PRESIDENT: Progress is a law of humanity; but this, to develop itself, has required among all people these terrible crises which are called revolutions. History teaches us that all nations, to reach reform and true civilization, have had to pass through terrible proofs and to suffer unhappy sacrifices, and it has been often seen that the most powerful peoples have touched upon the border of ruin, but have saved themselves, notwithstanding, by the faith and by the union of their sons.

Mexico passes at this moment through one of these difficult situations, because the upturning which it has been necessary to have felt throughout its society to establish the reform and secure the regeneration of the country, has given rise to immense difficulties, as well in the interior as in the exterior relations of the republic. The congress of the union has comprehended this state of things, and its labors have demonstrated that its attention has been divided between the civil struggle which has devoured us and the foreign war which threatens us, and it has issued laws which tend to terminate in so far as possible the former, and which will impede or prepare the nation for the latter.

A law has been passed protecting the citizens in the enjoyment of the guarantees conceded to them by the fundamental code. This law, the fruit of long discussions, is, so to speak, the complement of the constitution, which assures the rights of the man and of the citizen, and opens the tribunal to the complaints of those who shall feel injured in their rights by any of the authorities of the federation or of the States. Without this law these guarantees would not really exist, but only be promised, because there existed neither the mode nor the tribunal which should repair in private cases the abuse of power to the prejudice of the individual, which latter only saw a remote and improbable indemnification for injuries occasioned by the agent of powers which had no judge.

Postal and extradition treaties celebrated with the United States have been ratified. Respecting the principles which for a long time have constituted a phase of the civilization of Mexico, it has been expressly stipulated that neither those responsible for political offences, nor slaves, shall ever be the object of extradition. Thus, by an international compact with the United States will remain sanctioned forever the liberty of the slave by the fact of touching the

Mexican territory, and forgetfulness for those who, for political errors, shall fly to the neighboring nation, pursued by the remorse of having co-operated toward the misfortunes of their country.

At the preceding period of sessions, and by the initiation of the executive, congress decreed the law of 17th July, which, among other provisions, suspended the payment of the diplomatic conventions. The members of the cabinet hoped, and thus intimated to the house, that this law would not produce any conflict with those powers whose payments were to be suspended; and as much for this reason as from the right of self-preservation—for that period was a terrible one for the country—the suspension of all payments for two years was decreed, including those of the conventions. But our diplomatic relations suffered from this law, which was resented by them, and the executive presented to the house, as a solution of the difficulties with England, the treaty arranged between the government of Mexico and the minister plenipotentiary of her Britannic Majesty.

The stipulations of this treaty appeared to the house injurious to the nation, in that it recognized and covered with the British flag, besides the English convention, the debt contracted in London in 1823, and the payment of the sum taken by the so-called government of Miramon from the house No. 1, Calle de Capuchinas.

For the payment of all these credits a very large part of the revenues of its custom-houses was to be sacrificed, and at the same time the tariff of duties lowered and all existing prohibitions removed.

The question as to figures, however, would have been nothing, notwithstanding its great importance, if this treaty had not also contained stipulations humiliating to the dignity of the republic. The national bonds which were to be emitted in virtue of this treaty were required, for their validity, to bear at the side of the signature of our minister of treasury the signature of the agent of our creditors. By such condition the paper which was to be emitted, as it was to be received on account of duties, would have a real monetary representation, and be without value if it lacked the signature of the agent of the creditors.

No nation of the world would have accepted such a humiliation, and Mexico consenting to it would, so to speak, have consented to stamp its money with the arms of England.

The administrators and employers were also to be subject to an affective tutelage, exercised by the consular agents and by the attorneys or agents of the English creditors, who could ask for their revision all the books and documents of the custom-houses.

The congress saw, in all this, *intervention;* it saw, in all, reproach and dishonor for the republic. The sovereignty of a nation cannot be preserved from the moment that it has not an absolute independence in the most unimportant of its acts, because, although the individual in society may be free and yet depend upon an authority and have a judge, a nation can depend upon no one, and can have no other judge of its actions but Providence.

Congress, at the same time, desires peace; it desires it in the name of the republic; it desires it at all costs and with whatever sacrifice; but never at the sacrifice of the national honor, nor of the sovereignty and independence of Mexico. The honor of Mexico was compromised in a shameful manner in this treaty, and congress rejected it without hesitation.

But, as a proof of the morality of the nation always desirous of complying with its compromises, and that it was not interest which moved the national representation to reject the treaty, the law of the 17th of July which suspended the payment of the diplomatic conventions was repealed in this part on the day following the rejection of the treaty, and provision made for the payment of the dividends which would have been satisfied during the time for which the suspension had continued under the law.

War, however, appears certain; Spain hastened with a squadron, the minister of the Emperor of the French asks his passports and retires; and the threat of a league between France, Spain, and England against Mexico is presented in the horizon as a tempest.

In these solemn moments the house believed that it was necessary that the republic should prepare for the combat; Mexico is not a feeble and infirm nation, as it has been sought to paint her in the eyes of European nations; and if the bloody struggles of long civil war have deprived her of part of her strength, the union of all her sons will present her again powerful. Born of this conviction, the law of amnesty comes to procure the union of all Mexicans, with forgetfulness for all political offences.

The defence of the country is the glorious opportunity which Providence has prepared for those who were still combatting with arms in the hand against the legitimately constituted government to cease this useless strife and come to group themselves for the commencement of a national struggle at the side of the flag which our fathers left to us in giving us independence.

Mexico has had political parties whose profound divisions have enveloped the republic in blood; but Mexico has not had, nor will there ever be found, traitors who will join the ranks of the enemies of the country.

By a decree congress, before closing its session, has authorized the executive in the most ample manner to dictate all measures that it may deem necessary, under the present circumstances, to confront the situation, saving only the national independence and integrity of territory, and the principles of the constitution and of the reform.

By this the greatest proof of confidence which a legislative assembly of the country has ever given to the depository of the executive power, the congress confides to this power the salvation of the republic, because it is convinced that in moments so supreme, energy and efficiency depend almost always upon unity of action; and this idea is found also in our fundamental code, in the part which authorizes congress to concede to the executive extraordinary faculties.

Incalculable is the weight which will rest upon the shoulders of the executive; terrible is the responsibility which, from this day forward, he is about to assume upon himself alone; but, also, immense are the resources which are placed at his disposal, and unlimited the facilities which have been given to him.

The sole consideration of the necessity of saving the country decided congress to take this step. Upon the executive it now depends, and upon no other, to save the republic, or precipitate it in the abyss.

The national assembly suspends to-day its legislative labors; but it will remain always on the watch, as the sentinel of the public liberties, and ready to return to meet again at the moment when its presence shall be in any manner necessary for the good of the country. It will then receive from the executive an account of this power which to-day it delivers into its hands with so blind a confidence.

If the foreign question is not settled pacifically; if a scene of war is to be spread out over our country we will enter into the combat, and the justice of our cause and the love of our country will present more or less near, but always true and beautiful, a future for Mexico. God preserve the republic.

WASHINGTON, *January* 24, 1862.

True copy.

ROMERO

THE PRESENT CONDITION OF MEXICO. 173

Mr. Romero to Mr. Seward.

MEXICAN LEGATION IN THE UNITED STATES OF AMERICA,
Washington, February 16, 1862.

Mr. SECRETARY: Recently I have received three important documents which confirm the fears which I have made known to you through various notes and in various interviews with respect to the real designs of the powers who signed the treaty of London.

The first of these documents contains the instructions which the minister of foreign affairs of France gave to Rear Admiral Jurien de la Gravière, on the 11th of November last, a short time prior to the departure of the French contingent for the Mexican waters, and which have been recently published among the documents transmitted to the legislative body by the government of the Emperor. In these instructions, which were written almost at the same time that the treaty of London was being ratified in Paris, the latter was found to be insufficient; and in order to remedy this defect, express authority is granted to the commander of the French forces, when the coasts of Mexico shall have been occupied, to penetrate into the interior of the country and proceed to the capital of the republic. Mr. de Thouvenel furthermore takes upon himself to examine a hypothesis which presents itself to his foresight. "It may happen," he says, "that the presence of the allied forces upon the territory of Mexico may determine the sane portion of the people who is tired of the anarchy, anxious for order and repose, to make an effort to constitute in the country a government which may present the guarantees of strength and stability which have been wanting to all those which have succeeded each other in it since its independence."

Mr. de Thouvenel speaks of the interest which the allies have in carrying out the change which he has had the shrewdness to foresee, and continues by saying: "This interest must induce them not to discourage the attempts of the nature which have just been indicated, and you (Rear Admiral de la Gravière) should not refuse them your encouragement and your moral support, if, from the standing of the men who should initiate them, and from the sympathy they should meet with among the mass of the people, they should offer chances of success for the establishment of a state of affairs of such a nature as to insure to the interests of foreign residents the protection and the guarantees of which they have been deprived up to this time." These instructions are so explicit that it is entirely useless to add a single word more to arrive at the purpose with which they have been dictated, and the end to which they tend. Can there be conceived a more direct appeal to rebellion?

The second document is a proclamation which Rear Admiral de la Gravière, issued in compliance with said instructions, on the 23d of November last, at the bay of Teneriffe, and the third a manifesto signed at Vera Cruz on the 10th of January last past by the plenipotentiaries of the allied powers and the chiefs of the naval forces. In the latter we are assured that the allies have gone to that country in order to assist the Mexican people *to establish a good government*, and in the former enough is said to learn the wishes of France with regard to the said republic.

I have the honor to transmit you a copy of each of the documents referred to in this note, in case they should not previously, through another channel, have come to the knowledge of the government of the United States.

I avail myself with pleasure of this opportunity to renew to you, sir, the assurances of my very distinguished consideration.

M. ROMERO

Hon. WILLIAM H. SEWARD, &c., &c., &c.

Mr. Thouvenel to Rear Admiral la Gravière.

[Translation.]

PARIS, *November* 11, 1861.

ADMIRAL: The Emperor having called you to the command of the military forces which will be employed in obtaining from Mexico reparation for all our grievances, I have to make known to you in what manner you will have to act to fulfil his instructions.

The expedition which you are charged to direct has for its object to compel Mexico to perform obligations already solemnly entered into, and to give us guarantees of protection more efficacious for the persons and property of our citizens. The circumstances which have led us to resort to measures of coercion to attain this double object, imposed at the same time upon Great Britain and Spain to seek, through the use of rigorous measures, the satisfaction which grievances similar to our own demanded. It was natural that in this situation the three governments should think of combining their action against Mexico; and the understanding which was readily established between them upon this subject has resulted in the conclusion of a convention, signed at London on the 31st of October, and of which I have the honor to communicate to you the text herewith, in order that you may be guided in your conduct by the spirit of its several provisions. The three governments pledge themselves, as you will see, to prosecute in common and to the same ends the operations which it may be expedient to carry into effect. You will, therefore, have to concert them with the commanders-in-chief of the forces which Great Britain and Spain intend shall take part in them. It is from the co-operation of these several forces united that the three powers expect the result which they have deemed indispensable to prosecute in common. They have, moreover, provided for, without deferring on that account to act immediately, the eventual co-operation of the United States, to whom information of the convention of London will be given, with an invitation to accede thereto. It belongs to the secretary of the navy to furnish you with the military instructions which his department is alone competent to address to you; I shall confine myself to saying to you that the intention of the allied powers is, as indicated by the convention of the 31st of October, that the combined forces proceed to the immediate occupation of the ports situated upon the Gulf of Mexico, after having simply summoned the local authorities to make surrender thereof to them. The ports are to remain in their hands until the complete settlement of the difficulties to be solved, and the collection of custom dues will there be made in the name of the three powers, under the supervision of deputies appointed for that purpose. This measure will result in guaranteeing to us the payment of the sums and the several indemnities which are from this time, or which might subsequently be, carried to the account of Mexico as a claim of indemnity for the war; the question of the claims which each one of the allied governments will have to present requiring besides a special examination, there will be, by the terms of the convention, instituted a commission, to which will be specially assigned the duty of deciding with reference thereto, as also that of considering the mode of settlement which will best protect the respective interests. The government of her Britannic Majesty having appointed Sir Charles Wyke, the Queen's minister to Mexico, as a member of this commission, the government of the Emperor has likewise made choice, there to sit in his name, of its representative in Mexico, Mr. Dubois de Saligny. The character with which these two agents are clothed, not less than the practical knowledge they possess of the affairs of Mexico, naturally calls them to take part in the negotiations which must precede the re-establishment of regular relations. They will have to consult specially with, and also the commissioner designated by Spain, the commanders-in-chief of the allied forces, in order to draw up, after taking possession of the ports on the coast, the full statement of the conditions to which the Mexican government will be required to give its assent. In order to enable you to follow up all the negotiations and to sign all the acts and conventions to occur, I have the honor to send you herewith the full powers, in virtue of which his Majesty has appointed you his plenipotentiary, with the same title as Mr. Dubois de Saligny. It is besides well understood that full liberty is assured you as to all that relates to military operations, the movements of troops, the occasion and means of occupying such or such points of the Mexican territory; all these questions are specially left to your appreciation as well as to your initiation, and reserved for your sole decision.

The combined forces of the three powers having arrived upon the eastern shores of Mexico, you will have, as I have said, to demand the surrender into your hands of the ports on that coast. As a consequence of this step, two alternatives may occur: either resistance will be made to your summons, and then you will only have to arrange without delay with the allied commanders for the seizure by main force of these ports, or else the local authorities will decline to offer you a material resistance, but the Mexican government will refuse to enter into relations with you. The last news which have reached me from Mexico, and which announced the probable disarmament of the ports of Vera Cruz, would seem to cause us to foresee that such would in fact be the plan adopted by President Juarez. By reviving a tactic already employed by one of his predecessors in the war with the United States, he would, if necessary, retire into the interior of the country. The allied powers could not afford to let themselves be kept in check by such an expedient; neither could they continue to occupy indefinitely points of the coast if this occupation were not to furnish them a means of direct and immediate action upon the Mexican government. The interest of our dignity and considerations derived from the climacteric circumstances of the coast unite in demanding a prompt and decisive result. It is principally in view of this contingency that a body of disembarking troops is placed at your disposal, which, joined to the other military contingents, will give to the allies the means of extending the circle of their action. The government of the Emperor admits that, either to reach the Mexican government or to make more effectual the coercion upon it by the taking possession of its ports, you may find yourself under the necessity of combining a march into the interior of the country, which would lead, if necessary, the allied forces to the City of Mexico itself. I need scarcely add that another reason might determine you to do so; this would be the necessity of providing for the security of our citizens in case it should be threatened at any point whatever of the Mexican territory which could reasonably be reached.

The allied powers do not propose to themselves, I have said to you, any other object than that which is indicated in the convention; they forbid each other from intervening in the internal affairs of the country, and especially from exercising any pressure upon the wishes of the people as to the choice of their government. There are, however, certain hypotheses which present themselves to our foresight, and which it was our duty to examine. It might happen that the presence of the allied forces upon the soil of Mexico might induce the sane portion of the people, tired of anarchy, anxious for order and repose, to attempt an effort to constitute in the country a government presenting the guarantees of strength and stability which have been wanting to all those which have succeeded each other since the emancipation. The allied powers have a common interest and too manifest to see Mexico emerge from the state of social dissolution in which it is plunged, which paralyzes every development of its prosperity, sets aside for itself and for the rest of the world all the riches with which Providence has endowed a favored soil, and compels them to resort periodically to expensive expeditions to remind ephemeral and senseless powers of the duties of governments. This interest must induce them not to discourage the attempts of the nature of those which I have just indicated to you, and you should not refuse them your encouragements and your moral support if, from the standing of the men who should initiate them, and from the sympathy they should meet with among the mass of the people, they should offer chances of success for the establishment of a state of affairs of such a nature as to insure to the interests of the foreign residents the protection and the guarantees of which they have been deprived up to this time. The government of the Emperor relies upon your prudence and your judgment to appreciate, in conjunction with the commissioner of his Majesty, whose knowledge acquired by his residence in Mexico will be valuable to you, the events which may develop themselves under your eyes, and to determine the extent to which you may be called upon to take part therein.

THOUVENEL.

Rear Admiral la Gravière to his forces.

[Translation.]

ON BOARD THE MASSINA,
Teneriffe Bay, November 23, 1861.

SEAMEN AND SOLDIERS: We are going to Mexico. We have not only to seek there—as the gallant squadron of which many among you formed a part—the reparation of numerous and recent grievances; we shall have above all to demand, for the honor of our flag, for the security of our commerce, for the existence of our fellow-countrymen, guarantees more positive than those which are offered to us to-day.

We bear no animosity against the Mexican people. We know what we should expect from that noble and generous race, if it could put an end to its everlasting dissensions; but governments powerless to maintain internal peace will ever badly protect, whatever may be their flag, the security of foreigners. Our real enemy in Mexico is not this or that political faction—it is anarchy; anarchy is an enemy with which it is useless to treat.

Seamen and soldiers: In the new campaign which you are to undertake, you have as witness to your good right the sympathetic opinion of your country, the co-operation or the assent of the civilized world; you will soon have, in Mexico itself, the wishes of all good men.

Understand, therefore, the duties which this situation imposes upon you. Give to the people the example of order and discipline; teach them to honor the name of our glorious country, to envy the prosperity and the peace which we enjoy, and you may then repeat with just pride the words which were addressed to you some months since by our Emperor: "Wheresoever the flag of France shows itself, a just cause precedes it, a great people follows it."

JURIEN DE LA GRAVIERE,
Rear Admiral, commanding the French expeditionary forces
in the Gulf of Mexico.

Proclamation of the allies to the Mexicans.

VERA CRUZ, *January* 10, 1862.

MEXICANS: The representatives of England, France, and Spain fulfil a sacred duty in giving you to understand their intentions from the moment that they trod the ground of your republic. The faith of the treaties broken by the various governments which have succeeded each other among you, and the individual security of our citizens, continually menaced, have made necessary and indispensable this expedition.

They deceive you who would make you believe that behind our pretensions, as just as they are legitimate, come enveloped plans of conquest and restorations, and of interfering in your politics and government.

Three nations who accepted in good faith and acknowledged your independence have the right to expect you to believe them animated by no cowardly intentions, but rather by others more noble, elevated, and generous.

The three nations that we come representing, and whose first interest appears to be satisfaction of grievances inflicted upon them, have a higher interest, and one of more general and beneficial consequences; they come to extend the hand of friendship to a people to whom Providence has been prodigal of all its gifts, and which they behold with grief wasting its forces and extinguishing its vitality through the violent power of civil wars and of perpetual convulsions.

This is the truth, and those charged with the expression of it do it not with the voice of war and threats, but that you yourselves shall work out your own good fortune, in which we are all concerned.

To you, exclusively to you, without intervention of foreigners, belongs the task of constituting yourselves in a permanent and stable manner. Your labor will be the labor of regeneration, which all will respect, for all will have contributed to it, some with their opinions, others with enlightenment, and all and every one with their conscience. The evil is great, the remedy urgent. Now or never can you make your prosperity. Mexicans! listen to the voice of the allied powers, anchor of salvation in the destroying tempest through which you are rushing. Deliver yourselves up to their good faith and righteous intentions. Fear nothing from restless and turbulent spirits, which, should they show themselves, would be cowed by your firm and decided attitude. Meanwhile we shall preside over impassibly the glorious spectacle of your regeneration, guaranteed through order and liberty.

So will it be understood, we are sure, by the supreme government, to which we address ourselves; so will it be understood by the enlightened of the country, to whom we speak; and, as good patriots, you will all agree to the laying down of your arms and that reason alone shall be put forward, which is the power that ought to triumph in this the nineteenth century.

CHARLES LENNOX WYKE.
HUGH DUNLOP.
E. JURIEN DE LA GRAVIÈRE.
DUBOIS DE SALIGNY.
EL CONDE DE REUS.

Mr. Romero to Mr. Seward.

[Translation.]

MEXICAN LEGATION IN THE UNITED STATES OF AMERICA.

WASHINGTON, *April* 10, 1862.

Mr. SECRETARY: I have the honor to enclose to you, for the information of the government of the United States, a copy of a note addressed by Señor La Fuente, Mexican minister at Paris, to Monsieur de Thouvenel, under date of the 7th of March last, withdrawing the Mexican legation from Paris, asking his passports to leave France, and formally protesting, on behalf of the government of Mexico, against the conduct pursued by the French government in regard to that republic.

This opportunity is very agreeable to me to renew to you, sir, the assurances of my most distinguished consideration.

M. ROMERO.

Hon. WILLIAM H. SEWARD, &c., &c., &c.

PARIS, *March* 7, 1862.

MONSIEUR LE MINISTRE: It is not till after a long delay, and in consequence of the obstacles which the direct correspondence of this legation with the Mexican government has met with, that I have received the instructions sought by me of the President on the subject of my rule of conduct towards the government of the Emperor. His excellency has not only approved of the act whereby I suspended diplomatic relations with the French government—relations which itself had rendered impracticable—but has even acknowledged the justice of my observations on the dishonor which would have accrued to the republic in maintaining in this country a legation compelled to listen in silence to insults the most atrocious and declarations the most humiliating to the government and people of Mexico; a legation which could effect nothing towards restoring the good understanding which had been entirely destroyed, when peace became impossible by the resolution formed to overthrow republican institutions in Mexico, and substitute in their stead a monarchy for the benefit of a foreign prince. Such a design was fully apparent before it had been confirmed by the official documents recently published in Paris and London. On becoming convinced of the truth of this rumor I should have at once have had the honor of demanding my passports of your excellency had I not been restrained from doing so by the laudable hope that my government still cherished of being able to effect a convention with Mr. de Saligny, and later by the proclamation issued by his excellency the president in consequence of the iniquitous invasion of the territory of the republic made by the Spaniards, in violation of all the rules of the law of nations. By this public act his excellency offered to accede to all reasonable propositions made by the aggressors, while he bound himself to resist by all possible means such as were unjust or humiliating to the republic. This policy proved to me that, even to the last, my government left the way open to negotiations. It was not for me to close it by any act of mine.

But the rule of my official conduct is now fixed, and, in conformity with the express orders of my government, I hereby declare to your excellency that I break up the Mexican legation in France, and the protection of the natives of Mexico is confided to the good offices of his excellency Mr. Galvez, minister of Peru at the court of the Emperor of the French. I shall, therefore, be obliged to you, Monsieur le Ministre, to furnish me with passports to quit France for myself, my second secretary, Mr. Marcelino Orozco, and the members of my family.

From respect to justice and the dignity of my government I have to make a few remarks concerning this determination, which has been so long justified that it may appear rather tardy than precipitated.

France has deemed it right to employ force against Mexico. From this time diplomacy has nothing to do with this question.

Nevertheless, if it be demanded what was the cause of the commencement of hostilities, it may be replied that the motives openly enunciated are neither the just nor the true ones, and that beyond them must be sought the prime mover of this rupture.

From the beginning M. de Saligny assigned as a motive for breaking off relations with the Mexican government the law which decided to suspend for two years the payment of the foreign debt. But the Mexican government did not deny its obligations; it only postponed the fulfilment of them under the pressure of an imperious necessity, acknowledged by all, even by M. de Saligny, as is proved by his despatches addressed to your excellency. It did not have resource to the suspension of payments till all the sources, ordinary and extraordinary, of the public wealth were utterly exhausted; a fact which is also clear from the above despatches. It did not come, in short, to this hard extremity till after it had offered to its foreign creditors an arrangement which these last deemed satisfactory, and which was not carried into effect for the sole reason that obstacles were interposed by M. de Saligny in the name of the French creditors; a fact which shows that he was resolved at all hazards to keep in his own hands the power of breaking with the Mexican government.

The abrogation of this law was the sole condition imposed by M. de Saligny for resuming diplomatic relations with the government of the republic. It was, then, necessary to proceed to such extremes, and to exercise such rigor in treating with a nation ruined by civil war? What mighty interest would France have in the payment by instalments of less than two hundred thousand dollars, the amount of her acknowledged debt? Is it thus that she has acted towards other nations who are very far from finding themselves in a situation so deplorable as that of Mexico? And would it not have been preferable, more in conformity with the principles of justice and equity, to allow a little breathing to a friendly power engaged in the work of its social regeneration, and in the extermination of brigandage, a work of profound interest alike to natives and foreigners? For what purpose could it be judged right to rekindle the flame of the civil war, disastrous to the commerce and interests of French subjects in Mexico, with the view of overthrowing the government, and ruining its praiseworthy undertakings? Such animosity, from pecuniary motives, against an exhausted nation, has in it something so excessive, so unusual, that one must imagine other reasons in order to justify the expedition. If any credit is to be attached to recent official reports, what was due to French subjects, and of which the payment was reserved by the law of suspension, originated in the reparation of injuries committed against their persons and interests.

But no one knows better than your excellency, M. le Ministre, that our debt to France has been paid by the government of M. Juarez, even when France was acknowledging M. Miramon as president of Mexico, (a situation, perhaps, unique in history, where the title and honor of the government are accorded to one party, while the expenses are charged on another.) You know that in the midst of a civil war kindled by the government acknowledged by France, the constitutional president, M. Juarez, (the head of the unacknowledged government,) has paid the French debt with a punctuality; that even this payment was so advanced that there wanted not more than about two hundred thousand dollars to cancel the debt, and that, consequently, the constitutional government deserved some little commendation when, yielding to an insurmountable and evident necessity, it suspended payment for a time. And even if there were some grievances at the bottom of this debt in favor of France, it would still be undeniable, from the considerations above enumerated, that this suspension was no reason for pushing things to such extremities. But let me be allowed, also, to represent to you, M. le Ministre, that the debt in question, comprising, according to conventions and posterior declarations, every kind of responsibility, even affairs of *agiotage*, it was neither loyal nor just to assign as a sole source of its iniquities and injuries.

May I be permitted, M. le Ministre, to express my astonishment at learning from you that the government of the Emperor has millions to claim from that of Mexico. But under what title? On what proofs? No one knows of them. No discussion can take place on this subject from want of precise *data*, and yet the war begins. My government denies having contracted with M. de Saligny, the verbal engagement of which that minister speaks, on account of the forty thousand dollars of the convention Penaud; and this is not the first time that contradictions have arisen in the relations of M. de Saligny with the Mexican government. I should wish to suppose that M. de Saligny's prejudice against that government are not to be taken into account, and have already had the honor of pointing out to your excellency those prejudices which, if they show themselves so strongly in his correspondence with you, are brought into still bolder relief in his correspondence with the Mexican government. I am bound to suppose that his assertions are deemed by you worthy of credit, as are those of my government by me; but it results from them that Mexico can no longer cultivate friendly relations with this minister, seeing that these are no longer possible when one of the two parties has brought against the other a charge of falsehood. In such a case, your excellency must know, the simple consideration due to the government of a friendly power demands the removal of the minister.

Nevertheless, it is true that when it is desired to put an end to all friendly relations, and by a rupture and war, peaceful considerations are out of season.

In these documents other motives are assigned for this war, based on the insecurity of French subjects residing in Mexico, and M. de Saligny has forwarded a list of twenty-three outrages committed on their persons and property during a space of about nine months.

One word on the subject of this list. The greater part of the crimes pointed out can only be imputed to reactionary bands, against whom the government are actively engaged in war. In the relation of these excesses, there is clearly wanting one essential fact, the detail of the circumstances, which might entirely alter the case. It is not known from what sources the minister derives his information, a fact not without importance in a question of acts committed at such great distances. There is not the slightest proof, the vaguest indications that the Mexican government has been required to afford satisfaction in cases where it was due, according to the law of nations, and it is not even pretended that it has ever refused it. There is nothing to authorize such a supposition, while the government has ever shown its disposition to do what is right in claims of this nature.

In a difference so deplorable I will never weary in invoking the principles and usages which guide the international relations of all nations with regard to the crimes in question, although I may, perhaps, perceive that these usages have been cast aside in the case of Mexico. Nevertheless, it is not only a right but a duty to protest against the employment of force as a substitute for reason and justice. These last may sometimes make themselves heard even in the councils of governments who disregard them. At all events, they exalt the character of a nation which can recognize and fight for them. Thus, then, M. le Ministre, such rules and such usages being admitted, it is clear that in using its best exertions, as the Mexican government is doing to prevent and punish such crimes, no government incurs the responsibility of them or loses in reputation by them, nor can the weight of war be cast upon it on account of them. With what justice can a government be accused of violating the laws of humanity when the nation over which it rules, being distracted by civil war, certain misdeeds are perpetrated within its territory against the security of natives and foreigners? Assuredly the Italian government was not subjected to such harsh qualifications, nor to such hostile proceedings on account of the barbarous and cruel brigandage of Naples, sustained by the reactionary faction and combatted by the government, as is the case in Mexico. In France, even, where the nation enjoys profound peace and where the government exercises a power which enables it to act as it pleases, and with all the *apropos* of the moment, have we not just seen a long series of crimes brought to light, committed by a single individual for eight years?

Furthermore, Mr. de Saligny's despatches prove that the government had provided with promptitude for the safety of the inhabitants of the capital, a subject which had before given rise to complaints.

With regard to the attempt on the life of M. de Saligny, which is made to figure among the causes of the war, I have the honor to remind your excellency that the judicial inquiry, an account of which I remitted to you, fully explains the error into which that minister has fallen, and shows that the fancied cries of "*death*" were in reality acclamations in favor of France, and in reprobation of assassins of foreigners. The groups whence these cries issued were composed of Mexicans and Frenchmen reciprocating friendly sentiments. Who could ever have imagined that from all this would have arisen accusations and motives of war?

Really, M. le Ministre, when I call to mind the calumnies, as atrocious as absurd, that many journals in France, in England, and in Spain have permitted themselves to put on record against Mexicans, their society, and their government; when I see that in France, even in the high regions of power, my government is denounced as unscrupulous, and my countrymen as barbarous; when I find the good will and friendly cries of the latter towards France used against them in the bill of indictment, I cannot but entertain a conviction that national antipathies are to be found rather in Europe than among the inhabitants of Mexico.

I have two observations to make on the subject of this pretended attempt at assassination. From your despatches already published, it appears that you attach no credit to the investigation and the judicial sentence which I had the honor to communicate to you. Nevertheless, evidence taken before the tribunals is surely the best mode there as elsewhere, of arriving at the truth, both in cases of this nature and of all appertaining to a criminal jurisdiction. The government could not but abide by the issue, and were bound to accept the verdict, which they have every reason to believe was a true one.

The second remark I have to make is, that your despatches on this subject say: "Under other circumstances we should have demanded also *a full inquiry, and, in the event of failure, suitable reparation.* In the present state of affairs, * * * * *we can only add this fact to all those which impose* upon us the necessity *of having recourse to the employment of harsh measures against Mexico.*" So, then, a matter which, according to your own confession, deserves to be inquired into—a matter, the truth of which remains to be substantiated, you do not hesitate to enumerate among the motives of your resentment and your hostilities. On this occasion, Mr. le Ministre, I think I give a rare instance of moderation by forbearing to comment on these words.

The revolutions of Mexico are cast in the teeth of the government. Why, then, be silent about others still more disastrous and bloody? Was it on account of the enormity of the wrongs which had given rise to them, and the greatness of the benefit produced when they were suppressed? Now, I have the firm persuasion that few nations in the world have suffered so large an amount of evils as the Mexican from foreign domination, and few are the republics that have had to sustain, like ours, such cruel combats on the part of the privileged classes. With our revolutions we have achieved the national independence; the liberty of slaves; the destruction of our clerical military oligarchy, which multiplied seditions and menaced incessantly the existence of the republic; the liberty of conscience; civil marriage; the amelioration of the civil condition of foreigners, who have been placed on an equality with Mexicans; civil and political liberty; the elevation and fraternization of races which had long been kept in a state of abject degradation and even in perpetual antagonism by the Spanish government. And, since it is a question of intervention and of importing into Mexico a foreign monarchy, it is certainly not improper to add that we reckon among the benefits derived from our revolutions the establishment of republican institutions. Mexico loves them as dearly as France can love her empire, and to maintain the republic we have made and are prepared to make every kind of sacrifice.

Anarchy and *misgovernment*, such are the gratuitous charges brought against Mexico, and which serve as a theme for the expedition of the allied powers. But these recriminations refer rather to the political intervention than to the avowed motive of the triple alliance, that is to say, to the demands for reparation for guarantees, since this reparation and these guarantees might be accepted by the Mexican government, and the war would then be without object. But this language is clearly used to prevent an arrangement with the Mexican government. Indeed, Mr. the Admiral Jurien de la Gravière has affirmed, if I am rightly informed, that it is useless to treat with *anarchy*. Moreover, before all things, the Mexican nation has taken upon itself to reply to these charges. The war is at an end, leaving at most on the vast territory of the republic three or four reactionary bands, feeble and incessantly pursued, and not even the shadow of that great party is seen which was said to be favorable to intervention and the foreign monarchy. The States of the Mexican confederation which were described as disagreeing with the federal government furnish a contingent larger than that which was required of them; the majority of the rebel chieftains have given in their adhesion to the government, and are soliciting for the honor of fighting against the invaders of their country. Mexico has risen like one man to defend its liberties.

No, Mr. le Ministre, I repeat, none of the causes assigned either explains or justifies the violence of aggression, and even had the law for the suspension of payments, which is said to have worn out the patience of France, not been passed, Mexico would have met with no better treatment at her hands. This is not a mere supposition; it is an incontrovertible truth, demonstrated by facts anterior and posterior to that law. That law, indeed, was not in existence when Mr. de Saligny, even before being accredited to the president, permitted himself to begin his functions by treating the Mexican nation with a contempt of which there is no example on record, and personally embarrassing the action of the local authorities, under the pretext of protecting the sisters of charity, whom no one was attacking, who are not French, and with whom the French nation has nothing to do. This law did not exist when the same minister threatened the government and nation with certain ruin, if the propositions of Monsieur Jecker were not adhered to—a stock-jobbing affair concluded between him and the so-called government of Mr. Miramon.

It was then, as I have already stated to your excellency, that Mr. de Saligny wrote to the minister of foreign affairs that knowing he was protected by France, Mr. Jecker felt that he could attempt anything. This law was not passed when your excellency, in our first interview, informed me that your government had come to an understanding with that of England to treat Mexico with rigor; and you may remember that you assigned (in explanation of these threats and of the agreement entered into by the two states, and of that affair of Jecker, and other financial arrangements proposed by Mr. de Saligny and refused by Mexico) motives which assuredly have nothing in common with the law of nations and the duties of humanity, which the government of Mexico is accused of violating. This law was not then in existence, and your excellency opposed to my regular and official reception reasons which you subsequently were not able nor willing to sustain.

Since the promulgation of this law your excellency has formally refused to listen to the explanations that I was desired by my government to offer to that of the Emperor, as if the moments consecrated to giving, at least, an appearance of justification and love of peace were to France an intolerable sacrifice of time. Since the adoption of this law the government of the United States has offered to that of the Emperor to pay the interest of the French debt of Mexico, and as that debt does not produce any interest and was to be paid by instalments, the interest offered by the cabinet of Washington was a reasonable compensation for the delays in the payment of that part of the debt due, and a gratuitous benefit on what remains to be paid, but the government of the Emperor refused the arrangement.

If this law were indeed the true cause of the rupture and of hostilities, why, instead of being suspended by its abrogation, were warlike preparations increased?

Since its abrogation an essential change has taken place in the policy of the allied powers against the republic. Wrongs, satisfactions, and guarantees, are now secondary considerations, and the real motive is revealed. It is, in fact, a question of political intervention in Mexico, having for its object to force upon her as king a foreign prince. This revelation explains everything. The French government did not desire peace with Mexico. For a long time that government either through its head or by its agents, has not uttered a word, nor written a line about the republic, that was not inspired by anger and contempt, and this in defiance of reason and decorum. Such is the peace it left to Mexico— a miserable peace, and, whatever may be said to the contrary, it is Mexico and not France that has given reiterated proofs of an exemplery patience. The sympathies of France have for a long time been reserved for that ephemeral government which holds sway in Mexico, which she hastened to acknowledge, and supported with efficacy, leaving, as a charge to the present government, the liabilities which, even when just, could not be imputed but to its adversaries. But for this protection the civil war in Mexico, with all its horrors, would not have been thus prolonged. Her sympathies still remain with the partisans of this faction in Mexico, as well as with its agents who come to Paris to conspire against their country and to press the French government to invade it, as the discontented Greeks did at Suze, and the French emigrants at Coblentz.

It is evident, Mr. le Ministre, that in order to cover the political intervention and the importation of a foreign monarchy into Mexico, by means of the combined expedition, it is pretended that force is not to be employed, but that the wishes of the Mexicans are to be consulted and respected. A proclamation has also been issued by the allied powers, inviting the Mexicans to proceed at once to the work of their political regeneration. But even supposing this deference for public opinion to be sincere, who does not see clearly that this manifesto, emanating from the combined forces, is already the commencement of a political intervention? What has become of the respect due to the sovereignty and independence of nations, with this act calling in question and submitting to the ballot a government which Mexico has chosen by the universal suffrage of her citizens? This illegal summons is not only an intermeddling in the affairs of a nation, but a flagrant incitement to rebellion, to which a favor, a support, is granted that does not lessen the offence from its being only of a moral character; but I do not hesitate to add that from assent and sympathy they must pass to the use of violence, since the march of the expedition on the capital is already decided upon, and the ultimatum would thus be of such nature that it could not be accepted; besides as the chiefs of the invading forces might qualify at pleasure the national will, it would be they who would impose upon Mexico the form and constitution of the government.

We saw, in 1814, the powers allied against France protesting after the invasion, that they did not interfere in the question of the national government. Then also petitions and official deliberations appeared, which seem to be of a spontaneous character, in favor of the Bourbons, and the allies seem to yield to public opinion; but, your excellency knows better than I, France never suffered herself to be deceived by these appearances, and for her the restoration was still the act of the foreigner.

Mexico would as little be persuaded of the forbearance of the allies in any change of her government brought about those in the presence of the manifestations of a foreign force.

It was necessary to suppress history, to disregard proofs innumerable, and belie daily relations, to arrive at the conclusion that the government of Mexico is an unscrupulous government, and the country "barbarous," and yet this done in some of your official documents. It was necessary; for in what other manner could the enormous outrage be justified which is about to be committed upon us in open violation of the great principle of *non-intervention*, which was regarded as one of the most precious conquests of the new law of nations? This law has been violated by the commencement of hostilities and the occupation of Vera Cruz, in the name of the three powers allied against Mexico, without any demands having been made on the government, these being reserved for a later period. It is not possible that a cause can be just, or wear the semblance of justice, when its defenders have recourse to such means. What is the reason of these infractions and these wrongs perpetrated deliberately and without necessity? The weakness of Mexico? But she is not so weak as was Spain in the time of Napoleon I. Mexico may be conquered, but she cannot be subdued, nor will she be conquered without having given proofs of the courage and virtues that are denied her. Mexico, after having shaken off the monarchical dominion of Spain—a dominion secular and deeply rooted; Mexico, who would not have even her liberator for a king; Mexico, in short, who has just emerged victorious from a servile revolution against the remnant of an oligarchy which was weighing on her democracy, will never accept, at any price, a foreign monarchy. This monarchy it will be very difficult to create; still more difficult to maintain. Such an enterprise will be ruinous and terrible for us, but it will not be less so for its promoters. Mexico is weak, without doubt, in comparison with the powers that are invading her soil, but she possesses the consciousness of her outraged rights; the patriotism which will multiply her efforts, and the high convictions that in acquitting herself with honor in this perilous struggle, it will be given to her to preserve the beautiful continent of Christopher Columbus from the cataclysm with which it is threatened.

I protest aloud, Mr. le Ministre, in the name of my government, that all the evils that shall ensue from this unjustifiable war, caused either directly or indirectly by the action of the troops and the agents of France, will fall exclusively on the responsibility of its government. For the rest Mexico has nothing to fear, if Providence protects the rights of a people who maintain them with dignity

I have the honor, &c.,

DE LA FUENTE.

To his Excellency Monsieur DE THOUVENEL, &c., &c., &c.

WASHINGTON, *April* 10, 1862.

A true copy.

ROMERO.

THE PRESENT CONDITION OF MEXICO. 185

Mr. Seward to Mr. Romero.

DEPARTMENT OF STATE,
Washington, April 11, 1862.

SIR: Having completed my report to the President upon the subject of Mexican affairs, in compliance with a resolution of the House of Representatives for information and correspondence, I find, upon examination of the papers, that no acknowledgment has been made of your several notes of the 30th September, 30th October, 23d and 28th November, your confidential note of the 21st December, and your subsequent official communications of 24th January and 16th February.

As you were kind enough to place these notes in my hands in person, and to make them severally the subject of conversation at different times, it was not deemed necessary to make written acknowledgment of their receipt from time to time, whilst pending events seemed to promise a continuation of your valuable contributions to the history of Mexican complications

I desire, now, to acknowledge my sense of the importance and interest of the documents you have laid before me, and which have greatly elucidated the political embarrassments in which your country has been involved, and in which the United States feel so serious a concern; and I beg to assure you of my high sense of the industry, ability, and zeal which you have displayed, not only in sustaining the interests of your own government, but also in contributing so materially to the intelligent apprehension of those interests by the government of the United States.

I avail myself of this occasion to offer to you a renewed assurance of my high consideration.

WILLIAM H. SEWARD.
To Senor DON MATIAS ROMERO, &c., &c., &c.

The Ministers of Spain, France, and Great Britain to Mr. Seward.

[Translation.]

WASHINGTON, *November* 30, 1861.

The undersigned, envoys extraordinary and ministers plenipotentiary of their Majesties the Queen of Spain, the Emperor of the French, and the Queen of the United Kingdom of Great Britain and of Ireland, have the honor to transmit, herewith, to the honorable Secretary of State, the exact words [*le texte*] of a convention concluded at London on the 31st of October, between their respective sovereigns, with the view of obtaining through a common action the redress of their grievances against the republic of Mexico. As has been stipulated between the high contracting parties, the undersigned have received the order to invite the government of the United States to accede to this act; and in addressing this invitation to the honorable Secretary of State, they hasten to inform him that they are furnished with the necessary full powers to conclude and to sign, collectively or separately, with the plenipotentiary designated by the President of the United States, a similar convention.

Nothing would be more agreeable to the governments of Spain, France, and Great Britain than to see that of the United States receive favorably their proposition; and, requesting the honorable Secretary of State to be pleased to make known to them the decision of the President, the undersigned have the honor to tender to him the assurances of their very high consideration.

GABRIEL G. TASSARA.
HENRI MERCIER.
LYONS.

[Translation.]

LEGATION OF SPAIN AT WASHINGTON.

Her Majesty the Queen of Spain, his Majesty the Emperor of the French, and her Majesty the Queen of Great Britain and Ireland, being placed by the arbitrary and vexatious conduct of the authorities of the republic of Mexico under the necessity of exacting from those authorities a more efficient protection for the persons and property of their subjects, as well as the performance of the obligations contracted towards them by the republic of Mexico, have arranged to conclude a convention between each other for the purpose of combining their common action, and, to this effect, they have appointed as their plenipotentiaries, to wit: her Majesty the Queen of Spain, his excellency Mr. Don Xavier de Isturiz, (here follow his titles;) his Majesty the Emperor, his excellency the Count Flahant, (here his titles;) and her Majesty the Queen of Great Britain and of Ireland, the very honorable John Earl Russell, (his titles follow;) who, after having exchanged their powers, have agreed to adopt the following articles:

ARTICLE 1.

Her Majesty the Queen of Spain, his Majesty the Emperor of the French, and her Majesty the Queen of Great Britain and of Ireland, bind themselves to make, immediately after the signing of the present convention, the necessary arrangements to send to the shores of Mexico, land and sea forces combined, the effective number of which shall be determined in a further exchange of communications between their governments, but the total of which must be sufficient to enable them to seize and occupy the various fortresses and military positions on the Mexican sea-coast.

The commanders of the allied forces shall be, moreover, authorized to accomplish such other operations as may on the spot be deemed most suitable for realizing the end specified in the preamble of the present convention, and especially for insuring the security of foreign residents.

All the measures which are referred to in this article shall be taken in the name and on account of the high contracting parties, without distinction of particular nationality of the forces employed in executing them.

ARTICLE 2.

The high contracting parties bind themselves not to seek for themselves, in the employment of the coercive measures foreseen by the present convention, any acquisition of territory, or any peculiar advantage, and not to exercise in the subsequent affairs of Mexico any influence of a character to impair the right of the Mexican nation to choose and freely to constitute the form of its own government.

ARTICLE 3.

A commission composed of three commissioners, one appointed by each of the contracting powers, shall be established with full power to determine all questions which may arise from the employment and distribution of the sums of money which shall be recovered from Mexico, having regard to the respective rights of the contracting parties.

ARTICLE 4.

The high contracting parties desiring, moreover, that the measures which it is their intention to adopt may not have an exclusive character, and knowing that the government of the United States has on its part claims to enforce, like themselves, against the Mexican republic, agree that immediately after the signing of the present convention, a copy of it shall be communicated to the government of the United States, that that government shall be invited to accede to it, and that, in anticipation of such accession, their respective ministers at Washington shall be immediately furnished with full powers to conclude and to sign, collectively or separately, with the plenipotentiary designated by the President of the United States, a similar convention, with the exception of the suppression of the present article, to those which they sign on this date. But, as the high contracting parties would expose themselves, in making any delay in carrying into effect articles one and two of the present convention, to fail in the end which they wish to attain, they have agreed to not defer, with a view of obtaining the accession of the government of the United States, the commencement of the above-mentioned operations beyond the period at which their combined forces may be united in the vicinity of Vera Cruz.

ARTICLE 5.

The present convention shall be ratified, and the ratifications thereof shall be exchanged, at London, within the term of fifteen days.
In testimony whereof, the respective plenipotentiaries have signed it and have affixed to it the seal of their arms.
Done at London, in triple original, on the thirty-first day of the month of October, in the year of our Lord one thousand eight hundred and sixty-one.
[The seals and signatures of the three plenipotentiaries follow.]

Mr. Seward to Mr. Tassara, Mr. Mercier, and Lord Lyons.

DEPARTMENT OF STATE,
Washington, December 4, 1861.

The undersigned, Secretary of State of the United States, has the honor to acknowledge the receipt of a note which was addressed to him on the 30th day of November last, by Mr. Gabriel G. y Tassara, minister plenipotentiary of her Majesty the Queen of Spain; Mr. Henri Mercier, minister plenipotentiary of his Majesty the Emperor of the French; and the Lord Lyons, minister plenipotentiary of her Majesty the Queen of the United Kingdom of Great Britain and Ireland.
With that paper, the aforesaid ministers have submitted the text of a convention which was concluded at London on the 31st of October last, between the sovereigns before-named, with a view of obtaining, through a common action, the redress of their grievances against the republic of Mexico.
In the preamble the high contracting parties say that they have been placed by the arbitrary and vexatious conduct of the authorities of the republic of Mexico under a necessity for exacting from those authorities a more effective protection for the persons and properties of their subjects, as well as the execution of obligations contracted with them by the republic of Mexico, and have agreed to conclude a convention between themselves for the purpose of combining their common action in the case.
In the first article the high contracting parties bind themselves to make, immediately after the signing of the convention, the necessary arrangements to send to the shores of Mexico land and sea forces combined, the effective number of which shall be determined in a further exchange of communications between their governments, but the total of which must be sufficient to enable them to

seize and occupy the various fortresses and military positions of the Mexican sea-coasts; also that the commanders of the allied forces shall be authorized to accomplish such other operations as may, on the spot, be deemed most suitable for realizing the end specified in the preamble, and especially for insuring the safety of foreign residents; and that all the measures which are thus to be carried into effect shall be taken in the name and on account of the high contracting parties without distinction of the particular nationality of the forces employed in executing them.

In the second article, the high contracting parties bind themselves not to seek for themselves, in the employment of the coercive measures foreseen by the present convention, any acquisition of territory, or any peculiar advantage, and not to exercise in the subsequent affairs of Mexico any influence of a character to impair the right of the Mexican nation to choose and freely to constitute the form of its own government.

In the third article, the high contracting parties agree that a commission composed of three commissioners, one appointed by each of the contracting powers, should be established, with full power to determine all questions which may arise for the employment and distribution of the sums of money which shall be recovered from Mexico, having regard to the respective rights of the contracting parties.

In the fourth article, the high contracting parties expressing the desire that the measures which it is their intention to adopt, may not have an exclusive character, and recognizing the fact that the government of the United States, like themselves, has claims of its own to enforce against the Mexican republic, agree that, immediately after the signing of the present convention, a copy of it shall be communicated to the government of the United States, and that this government shall be invited to accede to it, and that in anticipation of such accession, their respective ministers at Washington shall be furnished with full powers to conclude and sign, collectively or severally, with a plenipotentiary of the United States, to be designated by the President, such an instrument.

But as the high contracting parties would expose themselves in making any delay in carrying into effect articles one and two of the convention to failure in the end which they wish to attain, they have agreed to not defer, with a view to obtaining the accession of the United States, the commencement of the stipulated operations beyond the period at which their combined forces may be united in the vicinity of Vera Cruz.

The plenipotentiaries, in their note to the undersigned, invite the United States to accede to the convention. The undersigned, having submitted the subject to the President, will proceed to communicate his views thereon.

First. As the undersigned has heretofore had the honor to inform each of the plenipotentiaries now addressed, the President does not feel himself at liberty to question, and he does not question, that the sovereigns represented have undoubted right to decide for themselves the fact whether they have sustained grievances, and to resort to war against Mexico for the redress thereof, and have a right also to levy the war severally or jointly.

Secondly. The United States have a deep interest which, however, they are happy to believe is an interest held by them in common with the high contracting powers and with all other civilized states, that neither the sovereigns by whom the convention has been concluded shall seek or obtain any acquisition of territory or any advantage peculiar to itself, and not equally left open to the United States and every other civilized state, within the territories of Mexico, and especially that neither one nor all of the contracting parties shall, as a result or consequence of the hostilities to be inaugurated under convention, exercise in the subsequent affairs of Mexico any influence of a character to impair the right of the Mexican people to choose and freely to constitute the form of its own government.

The undersigned renews on this occasion the acknowledgment heretofore given, that each of the high contracting parties had informed the United States substantially, that they recognized this interest, and he is authorized to express the satisfaction of the President with the terms in which that recognition is clearly embodied in the treaty itself.

It is true, as the high contracting parties assume, that the United States have, on their part, claims to urge against Mexico. Upon due consideration, however, the President is of opinion that it would be inexpedient to seek satisfaction of their claims at this time through an act of accession to the convention. Among the reasons for this decision which the undersigned is authorized to assign, are, first, that the United States, so far as it is practicable, prefer to adhere to a traditional policy recommended to them by the father of their country and confirmed by a happy experience, which forbids them from making alliances with foreign nations; second, 'Mexico being a neighbor of the United States on this continent, and possessing a system of government similar to our own in many of its important features, the United States habitually cherish a decided good will towards that republic, and a lively interest in its security, prosperity, and welfare. Animated by these sentiments, the United States do not feel inclined to resort to forcible remedies for their claims at the present moment, when the government of Mexico is deeply disturbed by factions within, and war with foreign nations. And, of course, the same sentiments render them still more disinclined to allied war against Mexico, than to war to be urged against her by themselves alone.

The undersigned is further authorized to state to the plenipotentiaries, for the information of the sovereigns of Spain, France, and Great Britain, that the United States are so earnestly anxious for the safety and welfare of the republic of Mexico, that they have already empowered their minister residing there to enter into a treaty with the Mexican republic, conceding to it some material aid and advantages which it is hoped may enable that republic to satisfy the just claims and demands of the said sovereigns, and so avert the war which these sovereigns have agreed among each other to levy against Mexico. The sovereigns need not be informed that this proposal to Mexico has been made, not in hostility to them, but with a knowledge of the proceeding formally communicated to them, and with the hope that they might find, through the increased ability of Mexico to result from the treaty, and her willingness to treat with them upon just terms, a mode of averting the hostilities which it is the object of the convention now under consideration to inaugurate. What has thus far been done by the American minister at Mexico, under those instructions, has not yet become known to this government, and the information is looked for with deep interest.

Should these negotiations offer any sufficient grounds on which to justify a proposition to the high contracting parties in behalf of Mexico, the undersigned will hasten to submit such a proposition to those powers. But it is to be understood, first, that Mexico shall have acceded to such a treaty; and secondly, that it shall be acceptable to the President and Senate of the United States.

In the meantime the high contracting parties are informed that the President deems it his duty to provide that a naval force should remain in the Gulf of Mexico, sufficient to look after the interests of American citizens in Mexico, during the conflict which may arise between the high contracting parties and that republic; and that the American minister residing in Mexico be authorized to seek such conference in Mexico with the belligerent parties, as may guard each of them against inadvertent injury to the just rights of the United States, if any such should be endangered.

The undersigned having thus submitted all the views and sentiments of this government on this important subject to the high contracting parties, in a spirit of peace and friendship, not only towards Mexico, but towards the high contracting parties themselves, feels assured that there will be nothing in the watchfulness which it is thus proposed to exercise, that can afford any cause for anxiety to any of the parties in question.

The undersigned has the honor to tender to the ministers of Spain, France, and Great Britain, the assurance of his very high consideration.

WILLIAM H. SEWARD.

Mr. Seward to Mr. Adams.

No. 71]
DEPARTMENT OF STATE,
Washington, August 24, 1861.

SIR: You will receive herewith an instruction which is this day sent from this department to Thomas Corwin, esq., the minister plenipotentiary of the United States residing in Mexico. The paper sufficiently explains itself. You will avail yourself of an early occasion to bring the subject therein presented to the attention of the British government, and ascertain whether it will consent to forbear hostilities against Mexico, so far as they may be dependent on the failure of the government of that country to pay the interest on the debts mentioned in the instruction, upon the condition and for the term therein mentioned; and if you find a favorable disposition on the part of her Majesty's government in that respect, you may ascertain how the stipulations contemplated can be entered into, reserving the unavoidable conditions which the instruction specifies.

I am, sir, respectfully, your obedient servant,
WILLIAM H. SEWARD.

CHARLES FRANCIS ADAMS, Esq., &c., &c., &c.

Mr. Adams to Mr. Seward.

[Extract]

No. 44.]
LEGATION OF THE UNITED STATES,
London, September 14, 1861.

SIR : * * * * * * * * *

There is a great demand, on the part of some of the commercial classes, for positive action in their behalf against Mexico. The decree of the authorities of that country, suspending the payment of debts to foreigners, followed, as it has been, by the protest and withdrawal of the representatives of France and England, is the pretext for a loud call upon the two governments for active intervention, involving the establishment of some permanent system in that country by force of arms.

It is proper to mention here that I have received from Mr. Corwin, at Mexico, a despatch, transmitting to me copies of all the official papers connected with the affair, and expressing great solicitude to learn the attitude about to be taken by the two great powers in consequence of it. I replied by return of mail, informing him that nothing had yet been determined on, so far as was publicly known, and expressing some doubts whether, in view of the practical obstacles in the way of a joint intervention to establish any power by common consent, more would be attempted than the customary plan of temporary occupation of some commerial ports, as security for the satisfaction of all pecuniary demands or to obtain the repeal of the obnoxious decree.

* * * * * * * * *

I have the honor to be, sir, your obedient servant,
CHARLES FRANCIS ADAMS.
Hon. WILLIAM H. SEWARD,
Secretary of State, Washington, D. C.

Mr. Adams to Mr. Seward.

[Extract.]

No. 46.]   LEGATION OF THE UNITED STATES,
London, September 19, 1861.

SIR: I have the honor to acknowledge the reception of the despatch No. 71, dated the 24th of August, with its enclosure, which was announced in my No. 45, of the 14th instant, sent last week, as having failed to come in its proper order. It is on the subject which I had already opened in my No. 44, of the 14th of this month. I applied at once to Lord Russell for an interview, in order that I might lay the view of the government before him, but as yet I have not been favored with a reply. The reason doubtless is that his lordship remains in Scotland taking advantage of the usual vacation at this season of the year, though retaining the general direction of the business of the office here. So that all papers undergo the delay of the transmission both ways before we hear of the action at this point.

The fact that a joint intervention in the domestic affairs of Mexico is contemplated by the three powers of Spain, France, and Great Britain is now beyond a doubt. Petitions praying such action on the part of this government have been put into circulation at the stock exchange, and have been extensively signed. The current of popular opinion here, so far as it may be gathered from the newspapers, all runs the same way. Spain seems to be eager to accept the advance in the movement, encouraged by its success in the case of Dominica, and by the hope of profiting by the present difficulties in the United States. Yet, in spite of all these concurring indications, I cannot repress a doubt whether any practical result satisfactory to all three of the parties will be arrived at. The establishment of a monarchy, which is the great object sought for by the commercial and religious interests in Mexico, can be sustained only with the active co-operation of a sufficient foreign military force to secure obedience. It will be productive of a great shock to the confidence of the other republican governments in America, and must inevitably press them into closer alliance. It will also be likely to draw them all into the political complications of this side of the Atlantic, by rendering counter combinations indispensible to the maintenance of a suitable balance of power. That all these possible consequences should have been entirely overlooked by the parties engaged in this crusade, and especially by Great Britain, which would seem to have less interest than the other two powers in producing them, is not a little surprising. It is scarcely to be imagined that she who is arming hundreds of thousands of her population, and indefinitely expanding her naval resources from mere apprehension of what may be intended on the part of her neighbor, can be very desirous of giving her aid to fortify a combination that may ultimately be turned with cumulative force upon her own borders.

Yet, in spite of all these considerations, the present indications are sufficiently alarming to render activity and vigilance eminently necessary on the part of all nations liable to be affected by this singular movement, and especially on the leading republican nation of the world, the United States. At no time since the adoption of the Constitution does there seem to have been a greater demand upon the capacities of the country in the direction of its foreign affairs than is now springing up in the midst of its internal difficulties. It is a source of great satisfaction to me to reflect that the care of them is reposed in such good hands.

* * * * * * * *

I have the honor to be, sir, your obedient servant,
CHARLES FRANCIS ADAMS.'
Hon. WILLIAM H. SEWARD,
Secretary of State, Washington, D. C.

Mr. Seward to Adams.

No. 94.]   DEPARTMENT OF STATE,
Washington, September 24, 1861.

SIR: This government has learned from information which leaves no room for doubt, that an armed movement is being prepared by the governments of Great Britain and France to proceed to Vera Cruz with a view to make demands of some nature upon the government of Mexico. There is also information, but not entirely reliable, that the government of Spain will join in this movement.

My despatch to you of the 24th day of August last will have shown you that this government takes so deep an interest in the permanence of the Mexican republic, that it is even not unwilling to render it some extremely good offices in its present exigencies.

The President desires you to inform the government of Great Britain that this government looks with deep concern to the subject of the armed movement to which I have thus directed your attention, and to ask Earl Russell for such explanations of it as her Majesty may feel at liberty to give, with a view to the satisfaction of the United States and the promotion of peace in this hemisphere. It is confidently believed that such explanations may not be unreasonably asked her in view of the intimations we have already given to our minister in Mexico in regard to an assumption of the payment of interest on the Mexican debt due to foreign bondholders.

It is perhaps necessary to say, that owing to some accidental delay, our foreign mail, which must have been sent by the Europa, has not yet been received, and therefore our information may be deemed very incomplete.

I am, sir, respectfully, your obedient servant,
WILLIAM H. SEWARD.
CHARLES FRANCIS ADAMS, Esq., &c., &c., &c.

Mr. Adams to Mr. Seward.

[Extracts.]

No. 50.]   LEGATION OF THE UNITED STATES,
London, September 28, 1861.

SIR: Scarcely had my despatch No. 46 been made up last Saturday to go to the department, when I received a note from Lord Russell in answer to my request for an interview. It was dated at Abergeldie Castle on the 19th of September, and expressed regret that he should not be able soon to be in

London to see me. But he added that if I would come up and pay him a visit in Scotland in the early part of the week, He should be "delighted" to see me there, and to confer with me touching any subject for which I desired the conference. Abergeldie is in the north of Scotland, and about five hundred miles by the road from London.   *   *   *   *   *   *

Accordingly I left London on Monday evening, the 23d, and by dint of travelling all night succeeded in reaching Abergeldie at about the same hour the next evening. It was too late for conversation with his lordship that night, but on Wednesday morning, the 25th, I was favored with abundant opportunity for full and free conversation, the substance of which I now propose to submit to your consideration.

I began by saying that I had been instructed to bring to his lordship's notice a matter that had excited great uneasiness in the minds of the authorities in the United States. I referred to the condition of Mexico, and to the rumors of certain movements making on the part of some of the powers of Europe in regard to her. The reason assigned for them was the late decree of the ruling party in that country, suspending the payment of interest on the debt to foreigners; but the proposed action was represented as going further than the practice heretofore customary in such cases, of occupation of certain ports as temporary security, in order to bring about some satisfactory arrangement. It was generally believed that it contemplated an actual intervention in the domestic affairs of that country, and even the imposition of a government over the people by the agency of an external military force. There seemed to be reason for supposing that Spain, at least, was preparing to transport troops and to send a navy with some such object. The disposition of France looked not altogether unfavorable to the same plan, and I had noticed in the newspapers that petitions were in circulation for signatures in London, and elsewhere, praying the co-operation of Great Britain to that end. It was this particular feature of armed intervention in the domestic affairs of Mexico that excited the alarm of my government. Had the matter been confined to a mere attempt to secure the payment of a debt, I did not know that it would have led to any extraordinary proceeding on the part of the United States. But as it looked now, it was an effort to introduce a new principle of action into American affairs. It was the inauguration of a policy on the part of some of the powers of Europe in opposition to which the government of the United States had committed itself forty years ago, and which that of Great Britain had not favored then nor at any time since. I said I trusted I need not enlarge on the consequences to which such a policy might lead, to the effect it would have in implicating America in all the struggles of Europe, from which it had always striven to keep aloof, and to bring on combinations not merely between the different States of North and South America, but also the formation of counter alliances by them all with the other States of Europe. This must be prompted by the instinct of self preservation if by nothing else. For there was no telling, if such a project were executed in the case of one American State, how soon it might be repeated in another. And the United States might, in their present difficulties, be made the subject of a similar experiment. For these reasons they were anxious to be prepared with some plan to remove the difficulty. To that end I had been directed to propose to her Majesty's government to postpone action for the present on her part, in order that the United States might be enabled to mature some arrangement with Mexico to provide for the payment of the interest on her debt, at least for a certain period, and thus remove the immediate cause of dissatisfaction. It was proposed to guarantee this payment by treaty, on such terms as might be agreed upon with Mexico. I had reason to believe that overtures had already been made by the minister of the United States in that country for a negotiation on that basis, which it was hoped might do away with any supposed necessity for the extraordinary measure presumed to be in agitation.

His lordship heard me very patiently to the end, and then drew out of his pocket a despatch from Lord Lyons, giving a pretty exact report of the particulars of the arrangement proposed by yourself in your paper of instructions to Mr. Corwin, a copy of which was furnished to me from the department. Of the conditions mentioned in it I had said nothing in my remarks, both in obedience to your directions and because they did not seem to me to be essential to the argument. Neither did his lordship make any especial reference to them in his reply. The objection that he made was that the proposed arrangement did not, by any means, meet the cause of complaint. Great Britain had much more to object to in the action of Mexico than the mere suspension of the interest on her debt. The conduct of the different parties in that country had been such as to render it difficult to keep any terms with the country at all. There was no safety to the lives or security to the property of English subjects. Some time since, when General Miramon was in power, a large sum belonging to English subjects, which had been put up to send by a conducta, had been taken by violence and divided among his adherents. No repayment had ever been made, or satisfaction given for this flagrant act of robbery, either by him or any one else, nor had the obligation of acknowledging the wrong been respected by those who came after him. The last act of suspension of the payment of interest on the debt was a wrong, but cumulative in its nature, and was not the only cause of complaint. Hence the plan of the United States, confined only to that one, did not seem quite co-extensive with the case.

His lordship then proceeded to remark that there was some misconception prevailing in regard to the precise condition in which the matter stood at this moment. He read extracts from the despatches of the British envoy at Madrid, reporting a conversation on the subject with the Spanish prime minister, O'Donnell, from which it would appear that the latter had not acknowledged any specific form of action as determined upon by Spain, and had gone so far as to concede that any scheme of forcing a government upon Mexico would be "chimerical," and that all efforts to do so would be "open to grave objection." It thus appears that, as yet, there is really no agreement at all between the English and Spanish government on this subject; and yet more, that the answer of Spain, thus made, was substantially drawn out in the form of a disavowal of an intention imputed by Great Britain, which the latter was not disposed to countenance. Furthermore, his lordship told me that he had expressed a desire that, before any action should be taken by either of the powers, the matter should be opened to the United States, and some plan, not of intervention, but of settlement, adopted with their co-operation. Of course this would require time. In this proposal France had concurred, *though not without hesitation.* Spain, on the other hand, had consented to wait, but not a great while. She would go forward alone to demand indemnity, if no result was obtained before the end of October or the first of November. Such was the present state of the question; and as a proof of it he showed me a telegram just received from the foreign office, in London, giving the contents of the last despatch from Spain to that effect. I replied that the course of Spain would not excite much surprise at home, for it had already been evident in the case of Dominica what motives stimulated her haste. The same intention to profit by our period of disorders was visible enough in this instance. I had little doubt she was meditating a restoration of her power in Mexico through the agency of the church and Spanish faction there. But I had been informed, from good authority, that any such scheme would only be likely to aggravate all existing difficulties there, instead of removing them. It would revive all old hatred and embitter a new contest. I trusted that I might be permitted to report to my government that Great Britain had had no participation in such projects, and, at least, that she contemplated no domestic intervention. To this he replied in the affirmative. I said this assurance would be a great relief to us in the United States. I had not supposed it could be otherwise. It was contrary to all my impressions of her system in the case of a former attempt of the same kind.

His lordship frankly admitted that such a proceeding was calculated to alarm the United States. To use the terms of Mr. O'Donnell, that it was "open to grave objection," was the least that could be said of it. It might, indeed, be that the exaggerated representations of the Spanish and priest party in Mexico were made to Spain to induce that country to effect its restoration to power by the intervention of troops. But there was no reason for believing any real good likely to come out of it. The truth was that there was little hope of the establishment of any stable form of government at all. Certainly the people were not prepared for any system like that of the United States. Hence it was that though intervention be admitted to be inadmissible, it yet remained to know what was best to be done. If Spain persisted in her intention of going forward, he supposed it would become necessary for Great Britain to take some action too. He believed that the United States had some claims likewise, which had been acknowledged in the treaty that had failed of ratification by the Senate. He should be very glad if any co-operation of all the powers could have the effect of sustaining any mode of government which the people of Mexico might themselves voluntarily establish.

I said that no country was more interested in the maintenance of a solid organization of government in Mexico than the United States. Everything that could fairly and honestly be done to favor the development of the spontaneous will of the people of that country might, I thought, be safely promised. But there we should stop. Whatever might have been the tendencies heretofore, the designs of the present administration were really friendly. Their good offices would be tendered in any way that might relieve Mexico from its present embarrassments. Yet if there were no question of domestic intervention involved, I presumed that the United States would not seek to interpose objections to any ordinary mode of gaining redress for the commission of flagrant wrongs.

Here the conversation ended on this subject. But the next morning, just before my departure, his lordship took me aside for a few minutes, to say that he had, in the interval, received a despatch from Lord Palmerston, in which he had taken the same view of the proposal of the United States that he did. That is, that the remedy did not cover the extent of the complaint. His lordship also had suggested that a counter proposition should be made to the United States. And he himself thought so favorably of it that he should direct a communication of it to be made, by instructions, to Lord Lyons, in his next despatch.

I said I was glad to receive the announcement, and should communicate it to my government. I believed that it would be ready cheerfully to entertain any proposition which avoided as a basis the principle of domestic intervention. And I understood, as the result of my interview, that no such proposition was in agitation.

* * * * * *

. I have the honor to be, sir, your obedient servant,
CHARLES FRANCIS ADAMS.
Hon. WM. H. SEWARD,
Secretary of State, Washington, D. C.

Mr. Adams to Mr. Seward.

No. 54.]   LEGATION OF THE UNITED STATES,
   London, October 4, 1861.

SIR: By reference to a leading article in the Times of this morning, you will at once perceive the condition of the negotiation in regard to Mexican affairs between the three powers, and the direction sought to be given to public opinion here on that subject. It is plain that Spain contemplates a movement in which Great Britain can have no sympathy. At the same time the representations from Mexico come worse and worse; and the statement that an attempt had been made on the life of M. de Saligny, the French minister, has had some effect in stiffening the attitude of the Emperor.

In the meanwhile, I have been in the receipt of a long confidential communication from M. Andres Oseguera, the gentleman heretofore mentioned as having had a conference with me, a report of which was contained in my despatch, No. 44, of the 14th September, substantially recapitulating the chief points of that conversation, but closing with a request for my good offices with Lord Russell, to procure for some representative of the Mexican authorities an opportunity to communicate with her Majesty's government in regard to the difficulties between the two countries. In consequence of this note, I called, on Monday last, to see M. Oseguera, and not finding him at home I asked him to call on me the next day, which he did. I then, in answer to his application, explained the change in my position, caused by the reception of later instructions from my government, expressed my desire to do anything in my power to pave the way to a better understanding between the two countries to which the United States were equally well wishers, and then defined the extent to which I was willing to accede to his request. I said that in view of the withdrawal of the British minister in Mexico from his relations with the government there, I should not venture to propose any acknowledgment or reception of a Mexican minister here. But if what he desired was that I should informally try the disposition of the head of the foreign office, to receive and listen to any representations that might be made to him by a person not clothed with any formal official character, but yet authorized to speak on behalf of the Mexican government, I signified my readiness to go thus far. I added that from some incidental expression of surprise let fall by Lord Russell in my last conversation with him, that there should be no representative of Mexico here, whilst there was one at Paris, I inferred that there might be an opening for the success of such an application. M. Oseguera replied that he should feel much obliged to me if I would take the course indicated; and he went on to mention a gentleman, heretofore the secretary of legation for Mexico at that place, Mr. Huicé, as the person whom M. La Fuente, the minister at Paris, would empower to act for his government, if agreeable to his lordship. I said that with this understanding I would proceed to make the overture.

Accordingly, the next day, that is, on Tuesday, the 1st of this month, I called at the foreign office, and in the absence of Lord Russell, who is still in Scotland, I had an interview with Mr. Hammond, one of the under secretaries. I explained to him my position in the premises, being that simply of a common friend making an effort to open the way to an understanding between two disagreeing parties. I had been asked to present the question whether Lord Russell would consent to receive an informal agent of the Mexican authorities. I was willing to go thus far from a belief that it would be agreeable to my government, and not from any express authority.

Mr. Hammond said that he would write to his lordship and communicate my message. He asked me if I knew how matters stood at Paris, and then mentioned the rumor of the attack on M. de Saligny, which I have already referred to. I said that I had heard nothing of it, neither did I believe M. Oseguera could have heard of it when I last saw him. I then took my leave.

I have the honor to be, sir, your obedient servant,
CHARLES FRANCIS ADAMS.
Hon. WILLIAM H. SEWARD,
Secretary of State, Washington, D. C.

Mr. Seward to Mr. Adams.

No. 99.] DEPARTMENT OF STATE,
Washington, October 10, 1861.

SIR: Your despatch of September 14, No. 44, was duly received. It treats two subjects, one the extraordinary proceedings of her Majesty's government in the matter of her consul at Charleston, Mr. Bunch, the other the attitude of Great Britain and France towards Mexico.

I shall consider only the latter subject in this paper.

My despatch No. 71, of the 24th of August last, has informed you of our overtures to Mexico, and our propositions concurrent therewith to Great Britain and France for an assumption on our part of the payment of interest on the Mexican bonds as a condition of forbearance on the part of those states to the Mexican republic.

My despatch No. 94, of the 24th ultimo, instructed you to ask explanations of her Majesty's government concerning the designs of the naval demonstration which rumor reports is about to be made by Great Britain and France against Mexico.

Since those instructions were given we learn, upon what seems to be sufficient authority, that the government of Spain is meditating a demonstration against Mexico, but it is not certainly known whether that demonstration is to be made alone or in concert with the designs of Great Britain and France. Some explanations have been informally given on this subject by the Spanish government to our minister at Madrid importing that no design of conquest is entertained by Spain in this movement. I shall, however, simultaneously with sending this despatch, instruct Mr. Schurz to recall the subject to the attention of the Spanish government, with a view, if possible, to induce it to practice forbearance. A copy of the communication to Mr. Schurz will accompany this despatch, and you will inform Lord Russell that this government is deeply anxious for the safety, peace, and prosperity of Mexico. Consulting the spirit rather than the letter of my previous instructions, and considering them enlarged so as to embrace the new danger with which Mexico is threatened, you will confer with him and ascertain whether any and what proposition that we can make to Spain, attended, if necessary, with a modification of our former proposition to Mexico and France and England, would receive the favorable consideration of the British government and engage its good offices to secure a forbearance of those three powers from hostile designs against the Mexican republic.

The negotiation on this subject is attended with embarrassments and delays. We have not yet received a reply from Mexico to our overtures already made. Operations may be definitively matured on the other side of the Atlantic while we are considering how we can most effectually and properly engage in preventing the necessity for them. I shall therefore expect you to consider carefully the whole case as you find it, and rather to propose to me what this government shall do than to wait for new suggestions from me in the premises.

I am, sir, your obedient servant,
WILLIAM H. SEWARD.
CHARLES FRANCIS ADAMS, Esq., &c., &c., &c.

Mr. Adams to Mr. Seward.

[Extract.]

No. 57.]
LEGATION OF THE UNITED STATES,
London, October 11, 1861.

SIR: I have the honor to acknowledge the receipt of the instructions contained in your despatch, No. 94, dated the 24th of September, to ask explanations of the government here as to the contemplated movements in respect to Mexico. My despatch, No. 50, addressed to the department four days after the date of yours, must by this time have come to hand, and have furnished some idea of the intentions of her Majesty's ministers; whilst the course indicated to me as about to be taken by Lord Russell, through the agency of Lord Lyons, will have brought to your notice the precise form of policy they have concluded to adopt. This position of things would seem to release me from the necessity of charging myself further with the matter, at least for the present. In the meanwhile the answer of Lord Russell to the petition presented to him from the merchants is published in all the papers, and seems to be giving a new turn to the public sentiment on the subject in London.

In my number 54, dated the 4th instant, I gave some account of an informal visit paid by me on the 1st instant to the foreign office, at the solicitation of M. Oseguera, of the Mexican legation at Paris, to learn whether his lordship would receive informally an authorized agent of Mexico. I have since received an unofficial note from Mr. Hammond, informing me that his lordship would receive such a person on his return to town about the 19th of the month. In the meantime, however, M. Oseguera sent me a note announcing that he had been recalled to Paris, and apprising me that the authorized person to whom he had referred would soon make himself known to me. But as yet I have seen nothing of him.

* * * * * * * * *

I have the honor to be, sir, your obedient servant,
CHARLES FRANCIS ADAMS.

Hon. WILLIAM H. SEWARD,
Secretary of State, Washington, D. C.

Mr. Seward to Mr. Adams.

[Extract.]

No. 100.]
DEPARTMENT OF STATE,
Washington, October 12, 1861.

SIR: Your despatch of September 19, No. 46, has been duly received. I have already in the latest instructions sent you (No. 99, of the 10th instant) anticipated the subject of Mexican affairs, and I need add nothing on that subject, except that I have transmitted a copy of the last-mentioned paper to Mr. Dayton, and requested him to be governed by its directions.

* * * * * * * * *

I am, sir, your obedient servant,
WILLIAM H. SEWARD.

CHARLES FRANCIS ADAMS, Esq., &c., &c., &c.

Mr. Seward to Mr. Adams.

No. 101.] DEPARTMENT OF STATE,
Washington, October 14, 1861.

SIR: Your despatch of September 28, No. 50, has been received.
It contains an account of your visit to Lord Russell, at his residence in Abergeldie castle, and your consultation with him there on the subject of the difficulties between Great Britain and France on the one part, and Mexico on the other part. The difficulties between Spain and Mexico were also treated of in the same conversation. The result was that a counter proposition would be sent to me. I do not see that a more favorable turn of this matter could have reasonably been expected

I am, sir, your obedient servant,
WILLIAM H. SEWARD.
CHARLES·FRANCIS ADAMS, &c., &c., &c.

Mr. Seward to Mr. Adams.

No. 106.] DEPARTMENT OF STATE,
Washington, October 19, 1861.

SIR: Your despatch No. 54, written under the date of October 4, has been received.

Your proceedings in behalf of Mr. Oseguera were prudent and just. I hope that he may be successful in averting the dangers which are impending over his unfortunate country.

I am, sir, your obedient servant,
WILLIAM H. SEWARD.
CHARLES FRANCIS ADAMS, &c., &c., &c.

Mr. Adams to Mr. Seward.

[Extract.]

No. 62.] LEGATION OF THE UNITED STATES,
London, October 24, 1861.

SIR: In my despatch, No. 57, dated the 11th of the present month, I had the honor to report the result of my informal application at the foreign office in behalf of a representative of the authorities of Mexico. I there stated that M. Oseguera, who had solicited my aid, had left London, and that the other person to whom in his note to me he had referred as about to take his place, had not made himself known to me. As the day appointed for the conference, the 19th, drew nigh, and as Mr. Hammond's private note to me seemed to assume that M. La Fuente himself was to be the person to call upon Lord Russell, I determined to write at once to M. Oseguera, at Paris, apprising him of this fact, and leaving it to M. La Fuente to determine what he should do in the premises. The effect was to bring M. La Fuente to London on Friday, the 18th of the month. In the meanwhile Lord Russell had requested a change of the time of the conference to that very day. So that, when M. La Fuente was announced as coming to see me at noon, it was not without some little trouble that I succeeded in making the appointment effective for that evening at a quarter before five o'clock.

M. La Fuente does not speak English, neither is he a very perfect master of French. As a consequence, it has not been easy to confer with him on the two occasions upon which he has been to see me, once before and once after his conference with Lord Russell. I did not gather from him that he had succeeded in eliciting anything more definite from his lordship than I had obtained myself. He seemed more anxious to make inquiries of me as to the nature of the proposition to be made to the United States, as well as to the rumored disposition of the latter to accept it. Lord Russell had been as silent to him in regard to his projects as he was to me. As to the other question, I pointed out the obvious impossibility that such a rumor should be true, inasmuch as the time necessary to receive a return from America had not elapsed. For the rest M. La Fuente seemed to be of opinion that any attempt by Spain to set up an authority in Mexico would certainly fail. I asked him whether there might not be a repetition of the drama played in Dominica, and a formal invitation to assume the power from certain self-constituted authorities of the priest and old Spanish parties in Mexico. He admitted the possibility, but he considered the preponderance of opposition so great over the broad surface of the country as to render the plan scarcely practicable. Yet he seemed utterly unprovided with any scheme to ward off the danger or to smooth the difficulties in which his country is involved. He is still in town, and he took leave expressing the hope of seeing me again before his return to France. I shall endeavor to call upon him before long.

On Thursday I returned the visit of Mr. Moreira, the Brazilian minister, and I seized the occasion casually to get his views upon this proceeding of Spain. I found him not disposed to give much credit to the notion that any establishment of authority was contemplated. He considered it far too visionary.

* * * * * * * * * *

Hon. WILLIAM H. SEWARD,
Secretary of State, Washington, D. C.

Mr. Seward to Mr. Adams.

No. 111.]
DEPARTMENT OF STATE,
Washington, October 28, 1861.

SIR: Your despatch of October 11, No. 57, has been received. I have thus far nothing from Lord Lyons on the subject of European intervention in Mexico. Of course I have nothing new to say on that subject. I hope the delay of movements is indicative of moderation.

I am, sir, your obedient servant,
WILLIAM H. SEWARD.
CHARLES FRANCIS ADAMS, Esq., &c., &c., &c.

Mr. Adams to Mr. Seward.

[Extracts.]

No. 66.]
LEGATION OF THE UNITED STATES,
London, November 1, 1861.

SIR: I have to acknowledge the reception of despatches from the department, No. 99 and No. 100, respectively dated the 10th and the 12th of October. They both relate to the Mexican question, upon which I have already made a report of my action in my despatches Nos. 50 and 62, the first of which, at least, must by this time be in your hands. It will clearly appear from the representation there made of the state in which the matter was left after my conference with Lord Russell, that it is utterly out of my power to propose a course of action for the government of the United States as suggested in your No. 99. As his lordship did not think fit to make me acquainted with the nature of the plan he was about to submit to your consideration through Lord Lyons, I must wait to learn it from you, as well as the reception which it has met with from the President. In the meantime, rumors continue to fly about in the newspapers of the adoption of a scheme of co-operation between the three governments, which, in my belief, are as yet the offspring of the wishes of interested parties rather than of established facts. There can be no doubt, however, that negotiation is actively in process for the attainment of some positive result, and that in the meantime the necessary force is ordered to be in preparation to execute what may be finally determined on.

Yesterday I had the honor of another visit from M. La Fuente. But it seemed to be rather for the purpose of gaining than imparting information. He had not yet received his despatches from home, or any authentic intelligence of the late events in Mexico. Indeed, he was indebted to me for a copy of the Mexican Extraordinary of the 27th of September, which I happened to have received the night before, confirming a report he had heard of a reactionary movement in the Sierra by the priest party, in conjunction with numbers of Spanish officers, and raising the Spanish flag. But he seems as much unprepared with any remedy as ever. The truth is that the condition of the country is such as positively to invite interference from abroad, and the great obstacle to it interposed by the ordinary position of the United States is so far diminished by their existing divisions as to give full play to the revival of ambitious national dreams in Spain. All this I can well understand. But the policy of Great Britain in appearing even indirectly to give countenance to them is not as yet clear to me. It may be that she proposes to take a part in order to retain a right to control the result. * * * * * * *

You will permit me here, however, to make a single remark in this connexion upon the importance of appearing to divest the United States of any personal and selfish interest in the action it may think proper to adopt. The view customarily taken in Europe is that their government is disposed to resist all foreign intervention in Mexico, not upon any principle, but simply because it is itself expecting, in due course of time, to absorb the whole country for its own benefit. Hence any proposal like that which I had the honor to receive, based upon the mortgage of portions of Mexican territory as security for engagements entered into by the United States, naturally becomes the ground of an outcry that this is but the preliminary to an entry for inevitable foreclosure. And then follows the argument that if this process be legitimate in one case, why not equally in all. As against Great Britain and France it would be difficult to oppose to this the abstract principle contained in what has been denominated the Monroe doctrine, however just in substance. But both those countries have of late years been disposed to give more and more weight to the doctrine of non-intervention in the internal government of nations where there may be a conflict with the general sentiment of the population. If this be acknowledged in the case of the smaller states of Italy, in Europe, it is difficult to understand how it can be denied in the more remote regions of the world. Certainly the states of America, north and south, are sufficiently distant from the theatre of contention on this side of the globe to entitle them to claim immunity from the danger of being swept by force into the vortex of its local passions. There can be no doubt that, as it regards Europe, the voice of all the independent American nations is the same. They want no dictation, nor any resumption of their old relations. If they fail in performing their honest engagements, they make themselves liable in their property, but not in their persons or their political rights. Any attempt to transcend that broad line of distinction is a mere appeal to force, which can carry with it no obligation one moment beyond the period when it may be successfully overthrown. And the principle is broad enough to make the maintenance of it in one country equally the cause of all the rest.

I have the honor to be, sir, your obedient servant,
CHARLES FRANCIS ADAMS.
Hon. WILLIAM H. SEWARD,
Secretary of State, Washington, D. C.

Mr. Adams to Mr. Seward.

[Extract.]

No. 68.]   LEGATION OF THE UNITED STATES,
London, November 8, 1861.

SIR: You will probably receive by the present opportunity a copy of the convention entered into by the three powers on Thursday, the 31st of October last, and signed at this place by Lord Russell, Count Flahault, and M. Isturiz. I have not yet seen it, but I am given to understand that it involves a joint possession of so much of Mexico as may be deemed necessary to secure a full reparation for all the injuries complained of, and leaves it open to the United States to become a party to the undertaking, if it shall think fit. I transmit herewith a copy of the London Morning Post of yesterday, which contains what may be regarded as a semi-official explanation of the views of this government on that subject.

I received another visit from M. La Fuente on Wednesday, and we talked the matter over again quite freely; but I did not discover that he had either any new views to present or additional information. I think he expresses more apprehension of a repetition of what he calls the "comedy of St. Domingo" than he did. But it seems to me that this is rendered less, rather than more, likely by the junction of the other two powers.

* * * * * * * *

I have the honor to be, sir, your obedient servant,
CHARLES FRANCIS ADAMS.
Hon. WILLIAM H. SEWARD,
Secretary of State, Washington, D. C.

LONDON, *Thursday, November* 7, 1861.

The Moniteur officially announces the fact, of which the better-informed class of persons in this country had been probably for some days aware, that the Mexican convention was concluded on Thursday last. This document was signed by Earl Russell, Count Flahault, and M. Isturiz, in this capital; and we believe that, as soon as we shall be able to lay the text before our readers, it will be found, both in its general tenor and in the specific provisions which it contains, to bear out the character which we assigned to the intervention when we first announced it in our impression of the 24th of September. We then showed that our case against the Mexican government was altogether exceptional, and was such as had no parallel in our grievances against any other state, whether in Europe or America. It was not simply that these grievances were of long standing, that the government of the country had become utterly demoralized, and that the rights which one state, according to international law, has against the other, were ignored, and their redress withheld. There had been both pecuniary wrongs and personal wrongs endured by the three parties to the convention of a nature altogether special and peculiar. There was, on the one hand, the personal protection due to British, French, and Spanish subjects who were denizens in Mexico; and there was, on the other hand, the property of bondholders, (chiefly English,) which had been formally secured upon mortgages of the public income, while the successive Mexican governments had diverted the latter from its due application. There can be no doubt that we are perfectly justified in insisting that a government in professed alliance with ourselves (as that of Mexico is) shall protect British subjects within its territories, and the same justification of course applies to France and Spain in their relations with the Mexican authorities. Neither can there be any doubt that we are equally justified in insisting upon the payment of our pecuniary claims where there has been a formal hypothecation of public income for their liquidation, and a fraudulent repudiation of the pledges thus entered upon, as well as, in a particular instance, a violent robbery of property secured under the seal of the British legation.

To deal first with the question of the personal security of the subjects of the three contracting powers in Mexico. The principle which we have always recognized as governing our relations with foreign countries is, that the foreign government is responsible for the acts of its subjects. So long as civil war lasted in that country, we should be ready to adopt this principle with some reservation in actual practice; and even when a government, imperfectly secure in its domestic authority, evinced a disposition to do its utmost in defence of British life and property, we should not be harsh in exacting a rigorous security for our subjects which could be hardly attainable in fact. But when this foreign government evinces an utter indifference to the lives of our fellow-subjects, our right of redress arises in all its force. Europeans have been unsafe even in the streets of the Mexican capital at midday; "Death to the foreigners" has been the common cry of the people; and when our representatives have demanded the redress to which we are entitled, they have been refused the very slightest assistance and protection for the future. We have, therefore, no alternative but to assume that the Mexican government, though not perhaps in actual complicity with the robbers and bandits by whom British subjects have been attacked, at any rate offers no opposition to their pillage. Let the government be as feeble as it may, we are entitled to require that it shall protect our subjects to the extent of its ability; and we cannot but charge upon its indifference, if not upon its complicity, much of the grievance which we have now to redress. If private wrongs of this kind ever call for public indemnification—if British subjects can ever demand security for their personal safety for the future—it is certainly in the present case of Mexico.

In turning from the more strictly personal to the more strictly pecuniary grievances which we have against Mexico, it may be fairly asked what is the good of a mortgage if it is not to operate as a security; and what becomes of the "security" if the mortgagors are not permitted to foreclose? A simple loan contracted by one country with another in itself imports a solemn obligation; and if there is any analogy whatever between international and municipal law in this respect, there ought to be a right of redress where the terms of the compact are fraudulently repudiated by the power which has incurred the debt. But if this be so with a simple loan, much more is it the case where there has been a formal hypothecation of sea-coast custom-houses as a security for the payment of interest due in consideration of it. Indeed, the very selection of seaport customs dues as a mortgage to a maritime power bears much of the character of an acknowledgment of the right of that power to interfere in the event of default taking place. To take an example from European states. We granted a loan to Turkey, in 1854, upon the security of the Egyptian tribute. Turkey, indeed, has faithfully met all her obligations. But, supposing that she had failed to pay the interest due upon this loan, either we should have had a distinct lien upon the Egyptian tribute, or the pretended security would have amounted to nothing at all. In the case of Mexico, however, there has been not only simple failure, but protracted failure, and a virtual repudiation which is obviously fraudulent, to say nothing of the open robbery committed by Miramon's government. We can hardly conceive, therefore, a wider misapplication of terms than to describe an insistance on the securities deliberately pledged by the Mexican government as equivalent to "a collection of bad debts," as it has been termed in one or two quarters. The customs revenue of the country warrants the supposition that the debts are capable of collection, and therefore good. The law of morality must bear in international jurisprudence an analogy to municipal jurisprudence if there is to be any confidence and security in transactions between one people and another. We, however, have yet to learn that there is any necessity for vindicating a convention which, at all events, cannot be duly criticized until its purport is fully known; and we believe that it will tend to establish a principle of morality between government and government which will impart fresh stability to all international transactions.

Mr. Seward to Mr. Adams.

No. 119.] DEPARTMENT OF STATE,
Washington, November 9, 1861.

SIR: Your despatch of October 24 (No. 62) has been received.
The rendering of your good offices to Mr. Oseguera is entirely approved. I wish, indeed, that it were possible for you or for me to do more than seems now to be practicable for the benefit of Mexico to assure her peace. As things stand, we can only be watchful of occasions for that purpose, and jealous of our own rights and interests.
We are waiting with some solicitude for the communication concerning the Mexican question promised you by Earl Russell.
I am, sir, your obedient servant,
WILLIAM H. SEWARD.
CHARLES FRANCIS ADAMS, Esq., &c., &c., &c.

Mr. Adams to Mr. Seward.

[Extract.]

No. 71.] LEGATION OF THE UNITED STATES,
London, November 14, 1861.

*　*　*　*　*　*　*　*　*

Before taking my leave I seized the opportunity to speak a word upon the subject of the confidential communication made in your No. 110. I asked whether his lordship was apprised of the facts there stated. He said yes. Lord Cowley had written to him about it. The proceeding did not seem to have a very definite shape. It was rather a suggestion than anything else.

And when asked whether Lord Lyons would be directed to follow suit, the answer had been in the negative.

I dropped the matter at that point, and went on to speak of the convention about Mexico. I said that what pretended to be the substance of that paper had already appeared in the journals, French and English, but as there was some discrepancy in the statements, I should feel myself much favored with the opportunity to have a sight of it. I presumed it had been already sent to my government, as I saw that an opening was left to it to become a party if it pleased. His lordship said the convention had not yet been signed. It probably would be in the course of the week, and I should have a copy of it. I then observed that M. La Fuente, who was still here, expressed great apprehension of the effects of it in destroying all that was left of authority in Mexico. On the other hand, the Spanish press did not pretend to conceal their confident expectation of a re-establishment of the national authority. His lordship replied that intervention was expressly disavowed in the treaty. As to the present existence of authority, there was none. If that which claimed it had acted with moderation, and had given notice of their embarrassments and acknowledged their obligations, it would have been something. But to proclaim coolly a refusal to pay an undeniable promise was intolerable. Sir Charles Wyke had written that the present mode was the only one by which to bring round any remedy for the evil, and so the government had concluded to adopt it.

I then took my leave of his lordship.

I have the honor to be, sir, your obedient servant,

CHARLES FRANCIS ADAMS.

Mr. Seward to Mr. Adams.

No. 128.]
DEPARTMENT OF STATE,
Washington, November 21, 1861.

SIR: Your despatch of November 1 (No. 66) has been received. It treats of the Mexican question. But thus far I have not received from Lord Lyons the note on that subject which we were authorized to expect. On the contrary, I hear informally that a convention has been concluded between Spain, France, and Great Britain, providing for concerted hostilities, and that this treaty is to be submitted to the United States, with consent that they shall become a party. I hear also that the treaty stipulates against any political designs, and confines the expedition merely to the redress of grievances.

I hear from Mexico at last. The Mexican government accepts our proposition to assume or guarantee her debt upon security to be given to us. But the British and French having virtually declined to accept this arrangement, the whole matter remains in a very unsatisfactory state, and I am unable to see at this moment what course we can take to afford relief or security to Mexico.

I am, sir, your obedient servant,

WILLIAM H. SEWARD.

CHARLES FRANCIS ADAMS, &c., &c., &c.

Mr. Seward to Mr. Adams.

No. 133.]
DEPARTMENT OF STATE,
Washington, November 25, 1861.

SIR: Your despatch of November 8 (No. 68) has been submitted to the President. Mr. Mercier, the minister of France, has unofficially communicated to me the treaty of Spain, France, and England in regard to Mexico, which I understand will be formally laid before us immediately by the three contracting powers.

I shall be able to give you the result of the President's deliberations upon it by the next mail; meantime it seems difficult to find out what can be done to avert the calamities which threaten our unhappy neighbor, though she has our sympathies guaranteed, as all just sympathies are, by enlightened views of interests of our·own.

I am, sir, your obedient servant,
WILLIAM H. SEWARD.
CHARLES FRANCIS ADAMS, Esq., &c., &c., &c.

Mr. Seward to Mr. Adams.

No. 148.] DEPARTMENT OF STATE,
Washington, December 18, 1861.

SIR: I transmit for your information the copy of a note, of the 4th instant, addressed by me to the diplomatic representatives of Spain, France, and Great Britain accredited to this government, relative to the proposed accession of the United States to the convention which was concluded at London on the 31st of October last between those powers for the redress of their grievances against the republic of Mexico.

I am, sir, your obedient servant,
WILLIAM H. SEWARD.
CHARLES FRANCIS ADAMS, Esq., &c., &c., &c.

Mr. Seward to Mr. Adams.

No. 161.] DEPARTMENT OF STATE,
Washington, January 8, 1862.

SIR: I have to acknowledge the receipt of your despatch (No. 71) of the 14th of November last.

I am, sir, your obedient servant,
WILLIAM H. SEWARD.
CHARLES FRANCIS ADAMS, Esq., &c., &c., &c.

Mr. Adams to Mr. Seward.

[Extract.]

No. 106.] LEGATION OF THE UNITED STATES,
London, January 24, 1862.

* * * * * * * * *

You will doubtless have had your attention drawn before this time to the course which the Mexican intervention is taking. On the reception of the news of the landing of the Spanish force and its occupation of Vera Cruz, the announcement is made of the outfit of a French force designed to follow up the advantage. It is no longer concealed that the intention is to advance to the capital, and to establish a firm government, *with the consent of the people*, at that place. But who are meant by that term does not appear. This issue is by no means palatable to the government here, though it is difficult to imagine that they could have been blind to it. Feeble murmurs of discontent are heard, but they will scarcely be likely to count for much in the face of the obligation under which the action of the Emperor in the Trent case has placed them. The military occupation will go on, and will not cease with the limits now assigned to it. It is not difficult to understand the nature of the fulcrum thus obtained for operations in a new and a different quarter, should the occasion be made to use it. The expedition to the city of Mexico may not stop until it shows itself in the heart of the Louisiana purchase.

* * * * * * * * *

Mr. Seward to Mr. Adams.

No. 191.]
DEPARTMENT OF STATE,
Washington, February 19, 1862.

SIR: Although I have adverted in other instructions to the subjects discussed in your despatch of January 24, (No. 106,) it is only now that I have found leisure to acknowledge the reception of that paper.

* * * * * * * * *

I shall carefully observe the progress of affairs in Mexico. If, indeed, our own Union were likely to fall, and the southern portion of the United States were to pass under a European protectorate, we could have small ground to hope that we could save Mexico from European reconquest and subjugation. But with reassurances of our own safety comes up to us an absolute confidence that no part of the continent will lose republican institutions and self-government.

We have acted, and shall continue to act, with frankness and justice towards the three powers who are invading Mexico, as well as with liberality to the government of Mexico itself. We do this distinctly relying on the assurances we have received from those powers that they will seek no political objects in their invasion. If they should forfeit these pledges their broken faith would be rewarded with only serious complications, ending in results disastrous to themselves.

But we will not allow ourselves to indulge apprehensions that could only be justified by distrust of the good faith of the three great states concerned.

I am, sir, your obedient servant,
WILLIAM H. SEWARD.

CHARLES FRANCIS ADAMS, Esq., &c., &c., &c.

Mr. Seward to Mr. Adams.

No. 198.]
DEPARTMENT OF STATE,
Washington, March 3, 1862.

SIR: We observe indications of a growing opinion in Europe that the demonstrations which are being made by Spanish, French, and British forces against Mexico are likely to be attended with a revolution in that country which will bring in a monarchical government there, in which the crown will be assumed by some foreign prince.

This country is deeply concerned in the peace of nations, and aims to be loyal at the same time in all its relations, as well to the allies as to Mexico. The President has therefore instructed me to submit his views on the new aspect of affairs to the parties concerned. He has relied upon the assurances given to this government by the allies that they were seeking no political objects and only a redress of grievances. He does not doubt the sincerity of the allies, and his confidence in their good faith, if it could be shaken, would be reinspired by explanations apparently made in their behalf that the governments of Spain, France, and Great Britain are not intending to intervene and will not intervene to effect a change of the constitutional form of government now existing in Mexico, or to produce any political change there in opposition to the will of the Mexican people. Indeed, he understands the allies to be unanimous in declaring that the proposed revolution in Mexico is moved only by Mexican citizens now in Europe.

The President, however, deems it his duty to express to the allies, in all candor and frankness, the opinion that no monarchical government which could be founded in Mexico, in the presence of foreign navies and armies in the waters and upon the soil of Mexico, would have any prospect of security or permanency. Secondly, that the instability of such a monarchy there would be enhanced if the throne should be assigned to any person not of Mexican nativity. That under such circumstances the new government must speedily fall unless it could draw into its support European alliances, which, relating back to the present invasion, would, in fact, make it the beginning of a permanent policy of armed European monarchical intervention injurious and practically hostile to the most general system of government on the continent of America, and this would be the beginning rather than the ending of revolution in Mexico.

These views are grounded upon some knowledge of the political sentiments and habits of society in America.

In such a case it is not to be doubted that the permanent interests and sympathies of this country would be with the other American republics. It is not intended on this occasion to predict the course of events which might happen as a consequence of the proceeding contemplated, either on this continent or in Europe. It is sufficient to say that, in the President's opinion, the emancipation of this continent from European control has been the principal feature in its history during the last century. It is not probable that a revolution in a contrary direction would be successful in an immediately succeeding century, while population in America is so rapidly increasing, resources so rapidly developing, and society so steadily forming itself upon principles of democratic American government. Nor is it necessary to suggest to the allies the improbability that European nations could steadily agree upon a policy favorable to such a counter-revolution as one conducive to their own interests, or to suggest that, however studiously the allies may act to avoid lending the aid of their land and naval forces to domestic revolutions in Mexico, the result would nevertheless be traceable to the presence of those forces there, although for a different purpose, since it may be deemed certain that but for their presence there no such revolution could probably have been attempted or even conceived.

The Senate of the United States has not, indeed, given its official sanction to the precise measures which the President has proposed for lending our aid to the existing government in Mexico, with the approval of the allies, to relieve it from its present embarrassments. This, however, is only a question of domestic administration. It would be very erroneous to regard such a disagreement as indicating any serious difference of opinion in this government or among the American people in their cordial good wishes for the safety, welfare, and stability of the republican system of government in that country.

I am, sir, your obedient servant,

WILLIAM H. SEWARD.

CHARLES FRANCIS ADAMS, Esq., &c., &c., &c.

THE PRESENT CONDITION OF MEXICO. 209

Mr. Adams to Mr. Seward.

[Extract]

No. 115.]   LEGATION OF THE UNITED STATES,
London, February 14, 1862.

SIR: You will receive by this steamer copies of the documents published by order of the British government relating to foreign affairs, numbered from 1 to 6. It is deserving of notice that the documents issued by the government of the United States in connexion with the President's message, on the same subject, have been also reprinted *in extenso* in a separate volume.

That portion of these papers relating to the Mexican imbroglio will, of course, attract your immediate attention. It would seem as if her Majesty's ministers were finding themselves already plunged far more deeply in the enterprise than they at first contemplated, and were on the point of being pushed into a complete abandonment of the long-established maxims of British policy. In this connexion I was led with some curiosity to examine Lord Russell's note to Lord Cowley of the 27th of September, giving an abstract of my conversation with him on this subject, and to compare it with my own report of the same, transmitted to you in my despatch, No. 50, of the 28th of the same month. In the earlier portion of the conference there is a substantial agreement, but it is worthy of note that the particular assurance given at its close, with authority to be communicated to you, is alluded to in his lordship's letter only as it may be found in the second of the two conditional bases of union directed to be presented to the consideration of the government of France.

The facts attending the present condition of the question, so far as I can gather them, are these: The Spanish government, impatient of delays, as indicated at the beginning, took the initiative, and despatched a much stronger force of troops to Mexico than had been contemplated by the other powers. Scarcely had they reached the country before new and material modifications of the original plans were given out to be rendered necessary by the emergency. On receiving the intelligence the French government, fearful of losing the whole control of the movement, at once ordered forth a re-enforcement of land troops, without, however, discouraging the change introduced into the plan of the expedition. It then became noised abroad that a distinct proposal had been made to the Archduke Maximilian of Austria to accept the position of king of the country, but by whom this proposal had been made did not clearly appear. The allegation now is, that it came from certain influential representatives of that country now in Europe. Very possibly Generals Almonte and Miramon may have been of the number, but at least no American could fail at once to see the vanity of such popular sentiment as they embody, or to comprehend the uses to which they have been put by persons who are ready to make that sentiment out of the bayonets of Europe. Of the motives for this action the conjectures of people widely differ. Some pretend to say that this offer to an Austrian prince was intended to secure the settlement of Italy by the surrender of Venetia and the temporal power of the Pope. Others affect to regard it as designed ultimately to establish a French principality all around the Gulf coast. However this may be, the fact of intervention is certainly avowed by Spain and France, and it finds its defenders even in Great Britain.

It remains only to examine the position of the latter power in connexion with the matter. We all remember the somewhat exaggerated egotism of George Canning, when he said, "I called that country into existence," as well as all the later policy which secured those regions as a field for British commerce and enterprise against a relapse under the narrow exclusiveness of Spain. We also know how earnestly England has proclaimed the doctrine of non-intervention

H. Ex. Doc. 100——14

in the domestic questions of European states that are seeking to make good their rights to establish their own institutions. Moreover, the distinctness with which Lord Russell, at our interview in September last, authorized me to declare this, as the principle of British action in regard to Mexico, is doubtless fresh in your recollection of my account of it; yet the fact is not the less clear to all the world that at this moment Great Britain actually occupies the post of holding the door, whilst her two associates, with her knowledge, go in, fully prepared, if they can, to perpetrate the act which she, at the outset, made them denounce, at the same time that she disavowed every idea of being made to participate in it. It is deserving of notice, in this connexion, that all the process which terminated in the convention between the three powers took place during the period of recess, when no cabinet consultations whatever are held. There is reason for believing that the business was conducted by Lord Russell, mainly under the direction of Lord Palmerston, and that many of the ministers were taken by surprise on learning that it was completed. I hear that some are not satisfied with the situation, and are anxious to retreat from it. Such is the present state of the question. In the meantime it is expected that the subject will be brought to the consideration of Parliament by the opposition in such a form as to compel the government to the adoption of a less equivocal line of policy.

* * * * * * *

I have the honor to be, sir, your obedient servant,
CHARLES FRANCIS ADAMS.
Hon. WILLIAM H. SEWARD,
Secretary of State, Washington, D. C.

Mr. Seward to Mr. Adams.

No. 204.] DEPARTMENT OF STATE,
Washington, March 10, 1862.

SIR: Your despatch of February 14 (No. 115) has been received.
The discussion of the intervention of the allies in Mexico which it contains has been found of great value.
I have already furnished you with full accounts of what this government has done in regard to it. Your own sagacity will enable you to discern the spirit in which we are acting upon that important subject.
Probably the great change that has occurred in the aspect of affairs here will not be without its beneficial influence in Mexico as well as in Europe.

* * * * * * *

I am, sir, your obedient servant,
WILLIAM H. SEWARD.
CHARLES FRANCIS ADAMS, Esq., &c., &c., &c.

Mr. Seward to Mr. Dayton.

No. 49.] DEPARTMENT OF STATE,
Washington, September 2, 1861.

SIR: I have to invite your attention to the enclosed copy of a despatch of the 24th ultimo, addressed by this department to the minister of the United States at Mexico, relative to the present state of affairs in that country.
I am, sir, respectfully, your obedient servant,
WILLIAM H. SEWARD.
WILLIAM L. DAYTON, Esq., &c., &c., &c.

THE PRESENT CONDITION OF MEXICO. 211

Mr. Dayton to Mr. Seward.

No. 49.] PARIS, *September* 25, 1861.

SIR: Despatches 49, 51, 52, 53, 54, and 55 were received yesterday, and their contents respectively noted.

I will, at the earliest opportunity, consult with the present minister at this court from Mexico, with a view to some concert of action in reference to the proposition in despatch 49.

Without some understanding with him as to the views of the Mexican government, it is not probable much can be accomplished.

With much respect, I am your obedient servant,

WM. L. DAYTON.

His Excellency WILLIAM H. SEWARD.
Secretary of State.

Mr. Seward to Mr. Dayton.

DEPARTMENT OF STATE,
Washington, October 11, 1861.

SIR: Your despatch of September 25 (No. 49) has just been received.

I transmit herewith a copy of my despatch No. 99 to Mr. Adams, relating to the impending designs of Spain, France, and Great Britain in regard to Mexico. You will please regard those instructions as addressed to yourself.

I am, sir, your obedient servant,

WILLIAM H. SEWARD.

WILLIAM L. DAYTON, Esq., &c., &c., &c.

Mr. Dayton to Mr. Seward.

No. 51.] PARIS, *September* 27, 1861.

SIR: Immediately after the receipt of yours in respect to the assumption by the United States of the interest at three per cent. on the debt due to the Mexican bondholders, I sought an interview with Mr. Fuentes, the minister who represents the present government of Mexico at Paris. Of course I was not ignorant of the condition of the diplomatic relations between France and Mexico, yet I felt that the aid of the Mexican minister might, in a certain event, be of service. I found him not only willing but anxious to co-operate with me in bringing about any arrangement which would relieve his unfortunate country from the threatened interference by England and France. His own interviews with Mr. Thouvenel had not been attended with any favorable result. I addressed a note to Mr. Thouvenel on the 25th soliciting an interview, which was promptly granted for the 27th. I have just returned from that interview. Mr. Thouvenel was already in possession of your proposition, made, he said, to Lord Lyons, in the absence of Mr. Mercier, and which he represented as substantially the same as that now presented by me. He gave me no reason to suppose the proposition would be accepted, but the contrary. He said you had not understood the character of the French claims, and that your proposition did not cover them at all. That those claims were not drawing interest as a *funded* debt, but the capital (25 to 30 millions of francs) was to be paid. This they intended to collect by taking possession of the ports of Vera Cruz and Tampico, and appropriating certain portions of the revenue to the payment of the capital of the debt, and the balance of the revenue, as I understood, was to go to the support of the government.

This was the plan intimated, though I think he said it was not definitely agreed upon. I told him that the government of the United States feared the complications to which this might lead, and was desirous that Mexico should remain an independent power on our continent. That we should view with great anxiety any course of action upon the part of foreign powers which looked to its extinction. He answered somewhat pointedly that, so far as he could judge from the past, its danger of extinction had been rather from the United States than elsewhere, to which, I am constrained to say, I made no very satisfactory reply. I told him, however, that the question now was of the future, not of the past. I said to him, further, that it seemed to me that if these foreign powers seized upon the revenues of Mexico, although no other forcible action was taken against her, that the government must, of necessity, fall to pieces; it could not exist without adequate means for its administration. To this he answered, that perhaps Mexico might find herself in the condition of China, the authorities of which, not long since, returned thanks to England and France for the *share* of revenue they allowed from certain ports in their possession, which was greater, as the authorities said, than they had ever received before. He assured me, however, that whatever England and France might do, it would be done in reference to realizing their money debt only, and that they had no purpose whatever to obtain any foothold in Mexico, or to occupy permanently any portion of its territory. He repeated this with emphasis. He furthermore stated, explicitly, that should Spain come in, as one of the powers acting in concert with France and England, for her claims, it would be with a distinct understanding that she, too, should not attempt to hold any part of the territory. I was somewhat particular in my inquiries upon this point, because I could not forbear the belief that Spain might look to a reassertion of her former rule over Mexico or some part of it.

Mr. Thouvenel said if I chose to put my proposition in writing he would examine it with care, and give me a written answer. I told him, however, as the proposition had already been communicated by Lord Lyons, and was distinctly understood, I did not think it necessary at present to go further. I may do so after conferring by letter with Mr. Adams, and ascertaining what are the dispositions manifested in England in reference to this offer. The amount of the Mexican debt held in England is so much larger than in France that perhaps (if the debt is all they seek) the proposition will be more favorably received there than here. If such should be so, I will then again present it formally to the French government, and, perhaps, with better prospects of success. I cannot but feel, however, that all these governments are disposed to take advantage of the present distracted condition of the United States. Should rebellion at an early day be suppressed, and leave us with a large and disciplined army on foot, and a navy increased, different dispositions may develop themselves. But I have no wish to comment upon this view of the question.

With much respect I have the honor to be, respectfully, your obedient servant,

WM. L. DAYTON.

His Excellency WM. H. SEWARD,
    Secretary of State, &c.

Mr. Seward to Mr. Dayton.

No. 68.] DEPARTMENT OF STATE,
Washington, October 19, 1861.

SIR: Your despatch of September 27, No. 51, was duly received. Your proceedings on the subject of the controversy between France and Mexico, and the tender you had been instructed to make on the part of this government, are entirely satisfactory. I learn from Mr. Adams that the British government and the French intend to make a counter proposition to the United States.

I am, sir, your obedient servant,
WILLIAM H. SEWARD.
WILLIAM L. DAYTON, Esq., &c., &c., &c.

Mr. Dayton to Mr. Seward.

[Extract]
No. 74.]
PARIS, *November* 6, 1861.

SIR: Your despatch No. 67, enclosing a copy of your despatch (No. 99) to Mr. Adams in reference to the affairs of France, Great Britain, and Spain, and Mexico, was duly received; but the matter was matured by the three governments first named before the arrival of this despatch, and was consummated by treaty on the 31st of October last. Had it come earlier, however, it would have been useless to solicit the kind offices of France with Spain when she wholly declined an acceptance of our propositions in reference to her own claims. Indeed, it seemed to me as if she had no disposition to have them settled by us. Steamers sail next Monday for the West Indies, where troops will be taken on board for the expedition. There will be quite an imposing fleet which these allies will have in the Gulf, as much, I fear, to watch the condition of things in our own country as to look after Mexico. But as the treaty has been, or immediately will be, sent over to you, with an invitation (somewhat late, as I told Mr. Thouvenel,) for the United States to participate, it is needless for me to dwell upon details. The French fleet, consisting, if I understood aright, of one large vessel-of-war, four frigates, two gunboats, and four advice boats, (small tenders,) will sail for the West Indies on Monday next to take troops, principally Spanish, I presume, from Cuba, and expect to reach Vera Cruz about the 25th of this month. Mr. Thouvenel said the United States had "griefs" to settle with Mexico as well as they. I availed myself of the occasion to say that I was happy that it was thought at least due to the United States that we should have an invitation (though somewhat late) to join in the expedition if we chose. I further told him I had been informed that it was a long time since suggested by Spain and Great Britain that the United States should be taken into conference on this subject, but that France had objected. He answered that this was not so, but it was directly the contrary; that France had first made the proposition as early as August last, as her correspondence with the British government would show.   *   *   *   *   *   *   *   *

With much respect, I have the honor to be your obedient servant,
WILLIAM L. DAYTON.
His Excellency WILLIAM H. SEWARD, &c., &c., &c.

Mr. Dayton to Mr. Seward.

[Extract.]

No. 62.] PARIS, *October* 16, 1861.

SIR: Despatches Nos. 59, 60, 61, and 62 are duly received, and contents noted. Despatch No. 60 applies to affairs between England, France, and Mexico. Immediately upon the receipt of your despatch No. 49, enclosing a copy of that which had been sent to Mr. Corwin, (which, I inferred, you intended should be acted upon by Mr. Adams and myself without further instructions,) I applied to Mr. Thouvenel for an interview. My despatch to you of the 27th of September last gives the result of that interview, and anticipates therefore the action required of me in your despatch No. 60. Mr. Thouvenel's statement of the purpose of the proposed action on the part of England and France towards Mexico was full and explicit, so far as the same had been understood or agreed upon between England and France.

Mr. Schurz, at Madrid, is satisfied that there is to be an attempt on the part of Spain to have one of the royal family of that country called upon by the people of Mexico to assume the throne. It is to be a call of the people of the same nature and got up in the same way as in the case of St. Domingo! But he has doubtless given you all information on this point. At his urgent request I have given him the information as to the contemplated action of England and France, which I received here. He was informed by Mr. Calderon that Great Britain and Spain were desirous of associating the United States with them on their proposed expedition to or against Mexico.

* * * * * * * *

With much respect I have the honor to be your obedient servant,

WM. L. DAYTON.

His Excellency WILLIAM H. SEWARD,
    Secretary of State, &c., &c., &c.

Mr. Seward to Mr. Dayton.

[Extract.]

No. 79.] DEPARTMENT OF STATE,
Washington, November 4, 1861.

SIR: Your despatch of October 16 (No. 62) has been received.

We cannot observe the proceedings in Spain, France, and Great Britain in regard to Mexico without deep concern. But their effects upon our own interests are likely to be only incidental.

* * * * * * * *

WILLIAM H. SEWARD.

WILLIAM L. DAYTON, Esq., &c., &c., &c.

Mr. Seward to Mr. Dayton.

[Extract.]

No. 85.] DEPARTMENT OF STATE,
Washington, November 23, 1861.
SIR: * * * * * * * * *
Mr. Mercier has just informally announced to us the execution of the convention between Spain, France, and Great Britain. We therefore have the subject under consideration.

I am, sir, your obedient servant,
WILLIAM H. SEWARD.

WILLIAM L. DAYTON, Esq., &c., &c., &c.

Mr. Dayton to Mr. Seward.

[Extract.]

No. 75.] PARIS, November 7, 1861.
SIR: * * * * * * * * *
Your despatch No. 68 informs me of Mr. Adams's communication of an intended counter proposition to be made by England and France to our government in respect to Mexican affairs. Of this I had heard before, and it made me less anxious as to the question here; for the fact that a counter proposition was to be made and answered would of necessity, as I thought, occupy time, and give the United States a chance for reflection and, perhaps, action. The prompt consummation of this matter in London has rather taken me by surprise. I fear that some misunderstanding of each other's meaning may have occurred upon the part of Mr. Adams and Earl Russell, or one of them. At all events, a point has been reached at a much earlier day than an intimation of such intended proposition led me to anticipate.

I am, sir, with respect, your obedient servant,
WM. L. DAYTON.

His Excellency WILLIAM H. SEWARD, &c., &c., &c.

Mr. Seward to Mr. Dayton.

No. 92.] DEPARTMENT OF STATE,
Washington, December 18, 1861.

SIR: I transmit for your information the copy of a note of the 4th instant, addressed by me to the diplomatic representatives of Spain, France, and Great Britain, accredited to this government, relative to the proposed accession of the United States to the convention, which was concluded at London on the 31st of October last between those powers, for the redress of their grievances against the republic of Mexico.

I am, sir, your obedient servant,
WILLIAM H. SEWARD.

WILLIAM L. DAYTON, Esq., &c., &c., &c.

Mr. Dayton to Mr. Seward.

[Extract.]

No. 103.] PARIS, *January* 15, 1862.

SIR: I have the honor to acknowledge the receipt of your despatch No. 92 with the copy of a note addressed to the representatives of Spain, France, and Great Britain, accredited to the government of the United States.

* * * * * * * * *

I have the honor to be, sir, your obedient servant,

WM. L. DAYTON.

His Excellency WILLIAM H. SEWARD,
    Secretary of State, &c., &c., &c.

Mr. Dayton to Mr. Seward.

[Extract.]

No. 113.] PARIS, *February* 13, 1862.

SIR: * * * * * * * *

I am not surprised to hear that more difficulty to the parties allied against Mexico is likely to arise than was contemplated. If serious resistance is made, it is not improbable that France may send out an increased force, and at an early day. It is now believed that her purposes, as respects the future of Mexico, conflict with those of Spain, and that each of these powers has a special object of its own to answer.

* * * * * * * * *

With much respect, your obedient servant,

WM. L. DAYTON.

His Excellency WILLIAM H. SEWARD,
    Secretary of State, &c., &c., &c.

Mr. Seward to Mr. Dayton.

No. 121.] DEPARTMENT OF STATE,
Washington, March 3, 1862.

SIR: We observe indications of a growing opinion in Europe that the demonstrations which are being made by Spanish, French, and British forces against Mexico are likely to be attended with a revolution in that country, which will bring in a monarchical government there, in which the crown will be assumed by some foreign prince. This country is deeply concerned in the peace of nations, and aims to be loyal at the same time in all its relations as well to the allies as to Mexico. The President has, therefore, instructed me to submit his views on the new aspect of affairs to the parties concerned.

He has relied upon the assurances given to this government by the allies that they were seeking no political objects, and only a redress of grievances. He does not doubt the sincerity of the allies, and his confidence in their good faith, if it could be shaken, would be reinspired by explanations apparently made in their behalf, that the governments of Spain, France, and Great Britain are not intending to intervene, and will not intervene to effect a change of the constitutional form of government now existing in Mexico, or to produce any political change there in opposition to the will of the Mexican people. Indeed, he understands the allies to be unanimous in declaring that the proposed revolution in Mexico is moved only by Mexican citizens now in Europe.

The President, however, deems it his duty to express to the allies, in all candor and frankness, the opinion that no monarchical government which could be founded in Mexico, in the presence of foreign navies and armies in the waters and upon the soil of Mexico, would have any prospect of security or permanence. Secondly, that the instability of such a monarchy there would be enhanced if the throne should be assigned to any person not of Mexican nativity. That, under such circumstances, the new government must speedily fall, unless it could draw into its support European alliances which, relating back to the first invasion, would, in fact, make it the beginning of a permanent policy of armed European monarchical intervention, injurious and practically hostile to the most general system of government prevailing on the continent of America, and this would be the beginning rather than the ending of revolution in Mexico.

These views are grounded upon some knowledge of the political sentiments and habits of society in America.

In such a case it is not to be doubted that the permanent interests and sympathies of this country would be with the other American republics.

It is not intended, on this occasion, to predict the course of events which might happen as a consequence of the proceeding contemplated, either on this continent or in Europe. It is sufficient to say that, in the President's opinion, the emancipation of this continent from European control has been the principal feature in its history during the last century. It is not probable that a revolution in a contrary direction would be successful in an immediately succeeding century, while population in America is so rapidly increasing, resources so rapidly developing, and society so steadily forming itself upon principles of democratic American government. Nor is it necessary to suggest to the allies the improbability that European nations could steadily agree upon a policy favorable to such a counter revolution as one conducive to their own interests. I will only remark that, however studiously the allies may act to avoid lending the aid of their land and naval forces to domestic revolutions in Mexico, the result would, nevertheless, be traceable to the presence of those forces there, although for a different purpose, since it may be deemed certain that, but for their presence there, no such revolution could probably have been attempted or even conceived.

The Senate of the United States has not indeed given its official sanction to the precise measures which the President has proposed for lending our aid to the existing government in Mexico, with the approval of the allies, to relieve it from its present embarrassments. This, however, is only a question of domestic administration. It would be very erroneous to regard such a disagreement as indicating any serious difference of opinion in this government or among the American people in their cordial good wishes for the safety, welfare, and stability of the republican system of government in that country.

I am, sir, your obedient servant,

WILLIAM H. SEWARD.

WILLIAM L. DAYTON, Esq., &c., &c., &c.

Mr. Seward to Mr. Dayton.

No. 126.] DEPARTMENT OF STATE,
Washington, March 10, 1862.

SIR: Your despatch of February 21 has been received. We are giving careful attention to affairs in Mexico. Whatever political designs may have found place, though disclaimed among the motives assigned for the expedition to that country, they seem likely to fail through three causes—want of agreement among the parties intervening, unlooked for resistance on the part of Mexico, and the changed aspect of public affairs in the United States.

I am, sir, your obedient servant,
WILLIAM H. SEWARD.
WILLIAM L. DAYTON, Esq., &c., &c., &c.

Mr. Seward to Mr. Dayton.

No. 135.]
DEPARTMENT OF STATE,
Washington, March 31, 1862.

SIR: I transmit extracts* from a despatch lately received from our very intelligent consul at Havana, which will direct your attention to the operations of the French government in Mexico.

We have acted with moderation and with good faith towards the three powers which invited our co-operation in their combined expedition to that disturbed and unhappy country. We have relied upon their disclaimers of all political designs against the Mexican republic. But we cannot shut out from our sight the indications which, unexplained, are calculated to induce a belief that the government of France has lent favoring attention to Mexican emissaries, who have proposed to subvert the republican American system in Mexico and to import into that country a throne, and even a monarch from Europe.

You will intimate to Mr. Thouvenel that rumors of this kind have reached the President and awakened some anxiety on his part. You will say that you are not authorized to ask explanations, but you are sure that if any can be made, which will be calculated to relieve that anxiety, they will be very welcome, insomuch as the United States desire nothing so much as to maintain a good understanding and the most cordial relations with the government and the people of France.

It will hardly be necessary to do more in assigning your reasons for this proceeding on your part than to say that we have more than once, and with perfect distinctness and candor, informed all the parties to the alliance that we cannot look with indifference upon any armed European intervention for political ends in a country situated so near and connected with us so closely as Mexico.

I am, sir, your obedient servant,
WILLIAM H. SEWARD.
WILLIAM L. DAYTON, Esq., &c., &c., &c.

Mr. Dayton to Mr. Seward.

[Extract.]

No. 131.]
PARIS, *March* 31, 1862.
SIR: * * * * * * *
"I then referred Mr. Thouvenel to your despatch, No. 121, in reference to the action of the allies towards Mexico. He said France could do no more than she had already done, and that was to reassure us of her purpose not to interfere in any way with the internal government of Mexico. That their sole pur-

---

* These extracts, being of a confidential character, are reserved.

pose was to obtain payment of their claims, and reparation for the wrongs and injuries done to them.

"I stated, in reply, that the President reposed entire confidence in those assurances, but, feeling great interest in the wellbeing of Mexico and its institutions, he felt that the occasion justified the expression of some general views in reference to the present and probable future of that country. To prevent misapprehension as to these views, I informed him that, although your despatch did not authorize me to give a copy, yet I would leave it in his hands to be read. This was accordingly done."

I am, sir, your obedient servant,

WM. L. DAYTON.

Mr. Schurz to Mr. Seward.

No. 15.] LEGATION OF THE UNITED STATES,
San Ildefonso, September 7, 1861.

SIR: Yesterday's papers, which reached us this morning, were filled with articles discussing the probability of an intervention of France and England in Mexico, and urging the Spanish government to join the two great powers in the enterprise. The tone of the ministerial journals led me to believe that an understanding had already been arrived at between those three governments, and I immediately called upon Mr. Calderon Collantes for the purpose of ascertaining what had been done and what was in contemplation.

I opened the conversation by referring to the above-mentioned newspaper articles and adding, that in everything that happened in Mexico, a state contiguous to our frontiers, the United States had a natural interest, and that it was a legitimate desire on our part to be informed of the plans which foreign powers might entertain with relation to that republic. As to the present case I had no instructions, nor even an expression of opinion from my government, but I addressed myself of my own motion to her Majesty's secretary of state, hoping that, in a matter of such importance, her Majesty's government would, with its accustomed frankness, communicate its intentions to a power as interested and at the same time as friendly as the United States. I desired to know whether an understanding had been arrived at between Spain, France, and England, as to an intervention in Mexico, and what were the objects of that intervention.

Mr. Calderon replied that he had no information as to the intentions of England and France, except from newspaper statements, and that neither her Majesty's representatives near the courts of France and England, nor the French and English legations here, had communicated with him on the subject. He was, however, bound to say that the present government of Mexico had given her Catholic Majesty's government just cause to complain. It had driven her Majesty's ambassador from the city of Mexico on groundless pretexts, and openly refused to fulfil treaty obligations solemnly stipulated by the preceding government of the Mexican republic. Spain was therefore amply justified in resorting to warlike measures for the redress of these grievances, but she had forborne so long in order not to expose herself to the imputation of interfering in favor of one of the political parties existing in the Mexican republic. It was, indeed, most desirable that the institutions of Mexico should be placed upon a solid and permanent basis, and that a government be established which might be relied upon to fulfil its treaty obligations and to do justice to foreign powers.

But it had always been a ruling principal with her Majesty's government not to interfere with the internal affairs of any state or nation. As to France and England he was inclined to think that they would act promptly and vigorously, and in that case it would be impossible for Spain to remain idle. If, however, Spain did take part in this intervention, it would be solely for the redress of her grievances, and not for the purpose of imposing new institutions upon the Mexican people against their own will.

I then gave Mr. Calderon to understand that enterprises like this, if undertaken without an understanding among all parties interested, were apt to lead to serious misunderstandings and difficulties, and he replied the European powers engaged in this matter, well knowing the interest the United States take in everything that concerns Mexico, would endeavor to come to an agreement (se mettre d'accord) with the United States government, and at all events, as far as Spain was concerned, we might rely upon her frankness and loyalty.

A large majority of the journals I have seen express themselves in favor of the measure, and I am inclined to think the war, if undertaken, will be popular with the Spanish people.

I am, sir, with great respect, your obedient servant,

C. SCHURZ.

Hon. WILLIAM H. SEWARD,
Secretary of State, Washington, D. C.

Mr. Schurz to Mr. Seward.

No. 17.] LEGATION OF THE UNITED STATES,
San Ildefonso, September 14, 1861.

SIR: On reading my despatch, No. 15, containing a report of my conversation with Mr. Calderon Collantes on the subject of Mexican affairs to this gentleman, he requests me to state to you a little more explicitly that his language in respect to endeavoring to come to an understanding with the United States must be understood as having reference only to the case that Spain, in connexion with France and England, should at any time conceive the project of interfering with the internal affairs and governmental instructions of that republic, in which case she would endeavor to come to an understanding on this subject with the United States. But she (Spain) claims and reserves the right to keep peace or to go to war with Mexico for the redress of her own grievances, without any previous understanding with the government of the United States; our government having been already informed, since the time of Mr. Dodge, that Spain had grievances to settle with Mexico which might make armed hostilities against that republic necessary. But that Spain, if these were undertaken, would go to that country solely with the object of redressing these grievances, and with no idea of conquest or forcibly changing the form of government there established.

I am, sir, with great respect, your obedient servant,

C. SCHURZ.

Hon. WILLIAM H. SEWARD,
Secretary of State, Washington.

Mr. Seward to Mr. Schurz.

No. 37.] DEPARTMENT OF STATE,
Washington, October 14, 1861.

SIR: The attitudes which Spain, France, and Great Britain are assuming towards Mexico have excited a very deep interest on the part of the United

States. You have given us what information you possess on the subject in your despatches Nos. 15, 16, and 17. Nevertheless, the objects and the character of the hostilities which Spain meditates against Mexico are only very imperfectly understood by us, though we do not doubt the entire frankness of the Spanish government in the communications it has made to you. We can well enough imagine that the Spanish government had not matured its own plans at the time when the conversations relating to them occurred between Mr. Calderon Collantes and yourself, and it seems still more probable that those plans might receive modifications at any time upon ascertaining the purposes and views of Great Britain and France in regard to expeditions of their own against Mexico.

I proceed, in the midst of this uncertainty, to give you the views and sentiments of the United States in regard to the expeditions in question, that you may make them known to Mr. Calderon Collantes.

The United States desire to be distinctly understood as deeming the freedom, integrity, and independence of Mexico important to the welfare of the Mexican people.

The United States, by reason of their position as a neighbor of Mexico, and the republican form of their constitution, similar to that of Mexico, deem it important to their own safety and welfare that no European or other foreign power shall subjugate that country and hold it as a conquest, establishing there a government of whatever form, independent of the voluntary choice of its people.

The United States, however, do not question the right of Spain, or of France, or Great Britain, to levy war against Mexico for the redress of injuries sustained by the invading state, and of the justice of the war such state may rightfully judge for herself.

Fourthly. The United States do not question the right of the invading states to combine as allies.

The United States having had some reason to suppose that the ground of the hostilities which Great Britain and France are preparing to institute against Mexico is the sequestration of the commercial revenues of that country, which had been pledged to the payment of the interest due upon bonds of the Mexican government held by subjects of Great Britain and France, have made overtures to those two powers and to Mexico, to relieve the controversy by assuming the payment of the interest on those bonds for a term of years. Thus far we have no answer from either party to that proposition.

We do not understand the grievances which Spain alleges against Mexico well enough to enable us to make any direct overtures to Spain in behalf of Mexico or to Mexico herself; but you will take an early opportunity to read this despatch to Mr. Calderon Collantes, whereby he may be assured of our desire, with the consent of the parties, to intervene with the tender of our good offices, and to express a willingness, but in no case without such assent, to assume some responsibility and incur some sacrifice to avert the necessity of a war between two nations, both of which, we trust, in common with the United States, would desire to remain at peace if they could do so consistently with their own convictions of honor and justice.

The declarations made by Mr. Calderon Collantes to you, as you have, with his consent, reported them to us, that if Spain should agree to enter into any arrangements with Great Britain and France, concerning any proceedings against Mexico, which might affect the political organization of that republic, she would seasonably consult us upon the subject; and that if she shall determine to proceed alone against Mexico, she will do so only to obtain a redress of grievances without any purpose or end of conquest, or of affecting the political relations of Mexico, are satisfactory to the President on the points thus presented, while they, at the same time, induce us to hope that the proposition, which on our behalf is now submitted, will be received in the friendly spirit in which it is made.

I will add only that in any case, whether Spain shall proceed alone or in conjunction with other powers in her hostilities to Mexico, on account of the nearness of that country to our own, we shall expect the utmost care to be taken on her part that no rights of American citizens in Mexico, nor any rights of this government in territories contiguous to the seat of war, shall be disturbed or affected. With that view we shall always have a naval force near the scene of possible conflict.

I am, sir, your obedient servant,
WILLIAM H. SEWARD.

CARL SCHURZ, Esq., &c., &c., &c.

Mr. Seward to Mr. Schurz.

No. 38.]
DEPARTMENT OF STATE,
Washington, October 14, 1861.

SIR: Your despatches of September 20, No. 20, and of September 21, No. 21, have just been received. I have anticipated the subject in a communication which will go simultaneously with this acknowledgment. I forbear from giving you the information of the proceedings in Great Britain, on the subject of affairs in Mexico, which I have received, because you are nearer London, and are probably at all times earlier informed of what occurs there than this government is.

I am, sir, your obedient servant,
WILLIAM H. SEWARD.

CARL SCHURZ, Esq., &c., &c., &c.

Mr. Schurz to Mr. Seward.

No. 26.]
LEGATION OF THE UNITED STATES,
Madrid, October, 4, 1861.

SIR: The negotiations between England, France, and Spain, relative to the expedition against Mexico, have not led to any positive result so far, and it appears somewhat doubtful whether they ever will. What I learn about them, through the public papers, and through my channels of private information, seems to confirm the correctness of the views I expressed in my despatch No. 21. As I predicted, England, desiring to limit the expedition to a mere collection of port duties, stands on one, and France and Spain, having further objects in view, on the other side. I had a conversation with Sir John Crampton to-day, in the course of which he assured me that he had no doubt England would firmly maintain the ground she had taken, and peremptorily refuse to engage in any enterprise beyond a mere redress of grievances. The semi-official journals of Madrid are declaiming fiercely against the selfish and narrow-minded policy advocated by the English press.

England, it seems, demands that, while the negotiations are going on, Spain shall suspend her preparations for the expedition. The ministerial papers have alternately stated that this request would be acceded to, and that the preparations would be pushed on with the utmost vigor. I am informed to-day, in a private way, that orders have been sent to the captain general of Cuba to suspend operations, and to delay the sending of agents into the Mexican territory until otherwise directed. But I am inclined to think, whatever she may be obliged to do at present to please her allies, she will not abandon her projects unless great changes at home should modify the character of her government. At all events, I would suggest to you that it will be necessary to watch her movements in the western hemisphere as closely as possible.

I am informed that Miramon, who has been living at Paris for some time, is shortly expected here. There can hardly be any doubt as to what he will come for.

I have solicited an interview with Mr. Calderon for the purpose of questioning him as to the plan the Spanish government means to carry out in Mexico. I shall send my report by next mail.

I am, sir, your obedient servant,
C. SCHURZ.
Hon. WILLIAM H. SEWARD,
   Secretary of State, Washington, D. C.

Mr. Schurz to Mr. Seward.

No. 27.]   LEGATION OF THE UNITED STATES,
                          Madrid, October 9, 1861.

SIR: Yesterday I had a conversation with Mr. Calderon Collantes, of which I will give you the principal points. I do not deem it necessary to write out a full report, partly because it was of a rather desultory character, and partly because we shall have to go over the same ground again, and then in a more formal manner, as soon as your despatch, No. 30, with accompanying documents, of which I have, to my great surprise, received notice through Mr. Calderon, will be in my hands.

I reminded Mr. Calderon of our conversation at St. Ildefonso concerning the intervention of Spain in Mexico, and added that, as it now seemed to be generally conceded that Spain intended to go beyond a mere redress of grievances, I desired to be informed by him what the plans of the Spanish government were. The government of the United States had a right to expect that no friendly power would undertake to effect important changes in a country bordering on the United States without consulting the government at Washington.

Mr. Calderon assured me that Spain intended nothing but to obtain satisfaction for the wrongs inflicted upon her by Mexico; that it was, indeed, very desirable that a solid government should be established there capable of giving guarantees for future good behavior, but that their internal arrangements should be left to the free choice of the Mexican people. On this point he confined himself to the assurances given me at San Ildefonso, and I may add that I give to those assurances the same interpretation.

I questioned him as to the progress of the negotiation between Spain, France, and England, and he replied that these negotiations had not yet come to a close; that Spain would wait a reasonable time, and that if within that time no agreement on a plan of joint action had been arrived at, Spain would act alone; that meanwhile orders had been sent to the captain general of Cuba to suspend, or rather not to commence, active operations, but that the preparations for the expedition were carried on with great activity, thus confirming the report I gave you in my despatch No. 26.

I asked him whether Spain intended to disembark troops and to operate in the interior of the Mexican republic. He replied that this was a military matter, of which he knew nothing. (There is, however, no doubt that such is the plan of the government.) He added that England had made the proposition to invite the United States to take part in the enterprise, and that Spain had seconded the proposition. He intimated that France was not in favor of it, and I doubt whether Spain is sincerely so. I addressed a letter to Mr. Dayton, informing him of this circumstance, and suggesting the propriety of speaking to Mr. Thouvenel about it.

The only comment I have to offer on Mr. Calderon's remarks is, that I deem the utmost vigilance on the part of the United States in the direction indicated in my despatch, No. 22, as necessary as ever, although the resistance offered by England may have rendered the execution of the plans entertained by the court of Spain more difficult than was at first anticipated. A skilful intrigue in Mexico, successfully carried through, might still render the Spanish government master of the situation.

The preparations for the expedition are not carried on as rapidly as was expected. The frigates Leattaci and Concepcion, which were to have sailed on October 1, are now announced to sail on October 13.

I am, sir, with the greatest respect, your obedient servant,

C. SCHURZ.

Hon. WILLIAM H. SEWARD,
Secretary of State, Washington, D. C.

Mr. Seward to Mr. Schurz.

No. 42.]　　　　　　　　　　DEPARTMENT OF STATE,
Washington, October 28, 1861.

SIR: Your despatch of October 4, No. 26, has been received.

The information which it gives us concerning the progress of the movement from Spain against Mexico is important as well as interesting. But it seems proper to reserve instructions until the result of your expected interview with Mr. Calderon Collantes shall be known here.

I am, sir, your obedient servant,

WILLIAM H. SEWARD.

CARL SCHURZ, Esq., &c., &c., &c.

Mr. Schurz to Mr. Seward.

No. 29.]　　　　　　　　　LEGATION OF THE UNITED STATES,
Madrid, October 15, 1861.

SIR: General Miramon, ex-president of the Mexican republic, arrived here a few days ago, accompanied by his family and a few Mexicans. I have endeavored to learn as much as possible about his movements and plans, and ascertained the following:

Miramon has had interviews with Mr. Calderon Collantes, General Narvaez, and several prominent statesmen, and it is very probable that there exists an understanding between him and the Spanish government.

In two or three days he will leave Madrid for Cadiz, and sail thence, as he and his friends say, directly for Mexico. He professes to be in great haste, and conversations between him and his friends, which have been reported to me, put it beyond a doubt that the object of his voyage is a political one. What this object is I have not been able to ascertain. He expresses himself frankly about the impossibility of maintaining a republic in Mexico, and says that it will be necessary to adopt another form of government. His idea is, that a constituent congress shall be convoked for the purpose of voting a constitutional monarchy and electing a king. This agrees with a plan which is now extensively discussed in the Spanish press.

It may be the policy of the Spanish government to avail itself of Miramon in Mexico, as it availed itself of Santana in San Domingo, although for a different object. The ministerial journals continue to indulge in high sounding declamations about the "mission of Spain" in Mexico, and some of them in bitter invectives against England.

I am, sir, your obedient servant,

C. SCHURZ.

Hon. WILLIAM H. SEWARD,
  Secretary of State, Washington, D. C.

Mr. Schurz to Mr. Seward.

No. 36.]   LEGATION OF THE UNITED STATES,
Madrid, November 3, 1861.

SIR: I have the honor to acknowledge the receipt of your despatches Nos. 35, 36, 37, and 38.

Immediately upon their arrival, I called upon Mr. Calderon Collantes, and read to him your despatch No. 37. I hasten to write for to-day's mail a short account of the conversation which followed.

Mr. Calderon expressed himself much gratified with the general tone of the despatch and the friendly intentions entertained by the government of the United States. He added that he had no knowledge of the proposition submitted by the United States to France and England. Spain was at present unable to entertain any offer of mediation between herself and Mexico; for the convention for joint action had just been signed by the representatives of the three powers, and Spain was not at liberty to act alone. Moreover, she had declined a similar offer made to her by France and England at the time when her resolution to proceed to hostilities had been made public. The financial question pending between Spain and Mexico might indeed have been arranged by mediation, but the point of honor, and especially the question of the guarantees to be given by Mexico for the rights and security of Spanish subjects residing in that republic, could not be settled by any mediation. Spain could not be satisfied with any reparation of affronts suffered or any guarantees for the security of her subjects unless they came in a direct way from the Mexican government itself.

I then endeavored, by putting questions and volunteering suggestions, to obtain from Mr. Calderon an explanation of the nature of the guarantees and reparations demanded by Spain, and of the manner in which they were to be obtained.

I asked Mr. Calderon whether Spain would make any formal and distinct demands on Mexico. Mr. Calderon replied by recounting the history of the outrages suffered by Spanish subjects at the hands of Mexicans and of the promises made by the Mexican government that the repetition of such outrages should be prevented. But the outrages had been repeated, again and again, and it was now the duty of Spain to see to it, that a state of things be established in Mexico which would afford sufficient protection and security to Spanish subjects.

I asked in what way Spain expected to bring about such a state of things in Mexico, since it seemed that Spain did not consider the present government of that republic able to give sufficient guarantees. Mr. Calderon replied that Spain did not mean to impose a new government upon Mexico; but that the appearance of the combined expedition in the Mexican waters, and the occupation of Vera Cruz and Tampico, would probably produce a moral effect sufficiently great to induce the Mexican people to rally around some man of power and authority capable of placing the government of that country upon a solid basis. *It might, for instance, give new strength and a new impulse to the conservative party in Mexico, and enable it to establish a strong government.*

I interposed the question, whether it was true, as the newspapers stated, that the allied powers intended to procure the convocation of a kind of constitutional convention in Mexico, and to constitute, in this way, a new government. Mr. Calderon replied that this plan had been discussed by the three powers, but that it had been definitively rejected.

I then asked in what way Spain meant to obtain her guarantees, in case the appearance of the combined expedition in the Mexican waters should not produce the anticipated moral effect on the Mexican people. Mr. Calderon replied, that the Spanish government had not fixed upon any definite plan of action to be carried out in that emergency. In general, the action of Spain would depend very much upon circumstances. Plenipotentiaries would be sent out with the expedition, and they would receive powers ample enough to shape their action according to emergencies.

I remarked that emergencies might arise which might render mediation between the three powers and Mexico admissible on the spot, and I had no doubt that the government of the United States would extend the tender of its good offices to such a case; I asked, therefore, whether Spain would empower her plenipotentiary to accept such tender on the spot, if thereby things could be satisfactorily arranged, and warlike measures avoided.

Mr. Calderon replied that this would not depend upon Spain alone; that the three powers would act jointly in every case; and that, therefore, no mediation could be accepted, except by common consent. The instructions to be given to the plenipotentiaries had, however, not yet been determined upon, and the matter might be taken into consideration. Mr. Calderon informed me that the invitation addressed by the three powers to the United States to accede to this convention was probably already on its way across the Atlantic, and that a good understanding was desired and anticipated. He added that in no case would Spain force a new form of government upon the Mexican people, nor would she suffer any other power to do so. He would, in this respect, be satisfied with the choice of the Mexican people, and it was indifferent to her whether they would establish a monarchy or preserve a republican form of government.

Mr. Calderon informed me further that all the papers relating to this affair would be submitted to the cortes, whose session will commence on the 8th instant, and that the policy of the government will be distinctly defined in the Queen's speech.   *   *   *   *   *

I am, sir, your obedient servant,

C. SCHURZ.

Hon. WILLIAM H. SEWARD,
Secretary of State, Washington, D. C.

Mr. Seward to Mr. Schurz.

No. 48.]

DEPARTMENT OF STATE,
Washington, November 9, 1861.

SIR: Your despatch of October 15 (No. 29) has been received. It is very interesting, and the information is conveys concerning the aspect of the Mexican question that presents itself to the public of Madrid is important.

I am, sir, your obedient servant,

WILLIAM H. SEWARD.

CARL SCHURZ, Esq., &c., &c., &c., *Madrid.*

Mr. Schurz to Mr. Seward.

No. 38.] LEGATION OF THE UNITED STATES,
Madrid, November 7, 1861.

SIR: In my despatch No. 29, dated October 15, I gave you some information concerning the movements of General Miramon. The statement that he would sail for Mexico from Cadiz has proved incorrect. He did, indeed, go to Cadiz with that intention, but for some reason, which I have not been able to ascertain, he returned to Madrid. Here he was received by General O'Donnell, and several other public men, with great distinction. He appeared publicly in O'Donnell's staff at the late field manœuvres of the garrison of Madrid. I am informed he will soon go to Paris, and then sail for Mexico. That there is an understanding between him and the leading men of the Spanish government as to the object of the expedition against Mexico can hardly be doubted.

I am, sir, your obedient servant,

C. SCHURZ.

Hon. WILLIAM H. SEWARD,
Secretary of State, Washington, D. C.

Mr. Seward to Mr. Schurz.

No. 51.] DEPARTMENT OF STATE,
Washington, November 11, 1861.

SIR: Your despatch of September 27 (No. 22) has been received. I have already advised you to the extent of our knowledge concerning the intentions of France and Great Britain in regard to the Mexican question. Thus far, we have not any direct communication from the government of either of those countries. It seems, therefore, only necessary for me to add, that the position you have taken upon that subject, as you have made it known to me, seems to be judicious and is approved.

I am, sir, your obedient servant,

WILLIAM H. SEWARD.

CARL SCHURZ, Esq., &c., &c., &c.

Mr. Seward to Mr. Schurz.

No. 56.] DEPARTMENT OF STATE,
Washington, November 23, 1861.

SIR: Your despatch of November 3 (No. 36) has been received. We are expecting daily direct communications from the Spanish, French, and British governments concerning their designs against Mexico.

Your proceedings in the matter, and your conversation with Mr. Calderon Collantes upon it, were judicious, and the tone of his replies was frank and liberal.

We wish a continuance of peace for Mexico only less than we desire a return of peace with union for ourselves. Without seeing just now what we can do to promote the former object, we shall persevere in our labors in that direction.

I am, sir, your obedient servant,

WILLIAM H. SEWARD.

CARL SCHURZ, Esq., &c., &c., &c.

Mr. Seward to Mr. Schurz.

No. 59.]　　　　　　　　　　　DEPARTMENT OF STATE,
　　　　　　　　　　　　　　Washington, December 6, 1861.

SIR: Your despatch of the 7th of November, No. 38, has been duly received. The prudence and diligence which you have exercised in keeping us well informed in regard to the subject of the policy of Spain towards Mexico are very highly appreciated.

　　　　I am, sir, your obedient servant,

　　　　　　　　　　　　　　　　WILLIAM H. SEWARD.

CARL SCHURZ, Esq., &c., &c., &c.

Mr. Seward to Mr. Schurz.

No. 60.]　　　　　　　　　　　DEPARTMENT OF STATE,
　　　　　　　　　　　　　　Washington, December 11, 1861.

SIR: Your despatch of November 14 (No. 41) has been received.

The light it throws upon the position of Spain, her sovereign, court, and general, in regard to Mexico, is exceedingly interesting, and I trust that we shall be able to make it useful.

I am charged by the President to express his decided approbation of the paper.

You will receive herewith a copy of my reply to the plenipotentiaries of the three powers on the subject of Mexico. We expect hourly to hear from Mr. Corwin, when we shall be able, perhaps, to follow up the policy indicated in that communication.

　　　　I am, sir, your obedient servant,

　　　　　　　　　　　　　　　　WILLIAM H. SEWARD.

CARL SCHURZ, Esq., &c., &c., &c.

CORRESPONDENCE

RESPECTING

THE AFFAIRS OF MEXICO.

PRESENTED TO BOTH HOUSES OF PARLIAMENT BY COMMAND OF HER MAJESTY.—1862.

TABLE OF CONTENTS.

No.	From whom and to whom.	Date.	Subject.
		1861.	
1	To Sir C. Wyke	Mar. 30	Instructions on proceeding to Mexico.
2	......do............	April 17	Murder of Mr. Bodmer. To demand redress.
3	Mr. Mathew	Mar. 26	Enclosing a note from Señor Zarco, the minister for foreign affairs, offering to secure religious liberty to foreigners in Mexico.
4	......do............	April 5	Correspondence with Señor Zarco relative to British claims. Observations.
5	......do............	April 19	Proposed settlement of the claim of Dr. Duval's family by a grant of nationalized property. He has accepted it.
6	To Sir C. Wyke......	May 30	Approval of proceedings with regard to the claim of Dr. Duval's family.
7	Mr. Mathew	May 12	General state of affairs. Arrival of Sir C. Wyke.
8	Sir C. Wyke..........	May 27	Conversation with Señor Guzman respecting the legation robbery. Government not prepared to repay the "conducta" money stolen by Señor Degollado.
9	......do............	....do....	Secularization of the church property. Position of the government.
10	......do............	June 24	Correspondence with the Mexican government relative to the robbery of $600,000 belonging to the bondholders from the British legation house.
11	......do............	....do....	Correspondence respecting the money taken from the Laguna Seca conducta.
12	......do............	June 25	Necessity for employing force to obtain redress from the Mexican government. Captain Aldham's views as to the course to be adopted.
13	......do............	June 27	Enclosing an extract from the "Mexican Extraordinary," giving an account of the outrages on British subjects.
14	......do............	June 28	State of the country. Military successes of the church party.
15	To Sir C. Wyke......	Aug. 21	Demands to be made on the Mexican government.
16	......do............	....do....	Her Majesty's government insist on the restoration of the $660,000 taken from the British legation.
17	Sir C. Wyke.........	July 11	Murder of Mr. H. M. Beale.
18	......do............	July 26	Stoppage of all payments on account of foreign debt. Correspondence with the government. Suspension of diplomatic relations.

Table of contents—Continued.

No.	From whom and to whom.	Date.	Subject.
		1861.	
19	Sir C. Wyke	July 28	Outrages by General Marquez. The country in a state of anarchy.
20	To Sir C. Wyke	Aug. 31	Approval of his having suspended relations.
21	Earl Cowley	Sept. 5	French government will send instructions to their minister, M. de Saligny, similar to those sent to Sir C. Wyke. Proposal that Spain should be invited to join in the proposed proceedings.
22	To Sir C. Wyke	Sept. 10	Her Majesty's government must hold the Mexican nation responsible for outrages on British subjects.
23	......do............	....do....	Approval of his conduct. Instructions as to breaking off relations.
24	Earl Cowley	....do....	Spanish government intend to occupy Vera Cruz and Tampico, but will act in concert with England and France.
25	......do............	Sept. 17	Explanations from the Spanish minister as to the intentions of his government.
26	Sir J. Crampton	Sept. 13	Views of the Spanish government with regard to Mexico.
27	......do............	Sept. 16	Expedition in preparation to act against Mexico. Spain desirous of joining Great Britain and France.
28	Lord Lyons	Sept. 10	Proposed convention between the United States and Mexico, by which the former were to pay the interest on the foreign debt in consideration of certain grants of land, &c.
29	To Sir J. Crampton	Sept. 23	Rights on Vera Cruz and Tampico custom-houses secured to the British government. Will Spain wait till France and Great Britain have agreed upon their plan of operations?
30	To Earl Cowley	....do....	Despatch from M. Thouvenel communicated by M. de Flahault. Proposal to seek the co-operation of the United States. Her Majesty's government wish to act in concert with the French government.
31	M. Isturiz	....do....	Intentions of Spain towards Mexico. Advantage of the joint action of the three powers.
32	Earl Cowley	Sept. 24	French government request to know the plan of action proposed by the British government. Objections to any plan for the United States undertaking to pay the interest on the foreign debt.
33	To Earl Cowley	Sept. 27	Explanation received from Mr. Adams as to the proposals the United States government wishes to make in regard to Mexico. Counter proposition made to him.
34	......do............	....do....	Enclosing a copy of Sir J. Crampton's despatch of the 13th instant.
35	To Sir J. Crampton	....do....	Conditions considered essential in any joint intervention in Mexico.
36	To M. Isturiz	....do....	Her Majesty's government will consider the proposals of the Spanish government.
37	To Lord Lyons	Sept. 28	Conversation with Mr. Adams. To speak in the same sense to Mr. Seward.
38	To Sir C. Wyke	....do....	In case of leaving Mexico to keep in communication with Admiral Milne. Instructions not yet determined on.

THE PRESENT CONDITION OF MEXICO. 231

*Table of contents—*Continued.

No.	From whom and to whom.	Date.	Subject.
		1861.	
39	Sir C. Wyke	Aug. 8	Letter addressed to Señor Zamacona justifying the suspension of relations.
40	......do............	Aug. 12	Enclosing extract from "Estafette," giving an account of the trial of the perpetrators of the legation robbery.
41	......do............	Aug. 23	Progress of events. Attempt on the life of the French minister. Correspondence with the government.
42	......do............	Aug. 24	Enclosing a decree imposing a tax of 1 per cent. on capital. Correspondence with British merchants.
43	......do............	Aug. 26	History of the British convention fund.
44	......do............	Aug. 27	State of affairs.
45	To Earl Cowley......	Sept. 30	Objections to forcible interference in the internal affairs of Mexico.
46	Earl Cowley	Oct. 2	Opinion expressed by M. Thouvenel as to interference in Mexico.
47	To Earl Cowley......	Oct. 5	The Queen prepared to enter into a convention with France and Spain with regard to Mexico. United States to be invited also to give their adhesion.
48	To Sir J. Crampton ..	....do....	To propose a joint convention as above.
49	Sir J. Crampton......	Sept. 21	Views of Marshal O'Donnell as to seeking the co-operation of the United States. He disclaims any intention of reconquering Mexico.
50	......do............	Sept. 24	Spanish government will respect the rights of Great Britain on the Vera Cruz and Tampico customs.
51	Earl Cowley	Oct. 10	French government ready to join the convention.
52	To Earl Cowley......	Oct. 12	Consider an engagement not to interfere by force in the internal policy of Mexico essential to the convention.
53	Earl Cowley	Oct. 18	Convention to be negotiated in London.
54	Sir J. Crampton	Oct. 9	Spanish government ready to sign a joint convention as to the establishment of an improved form of government in Mexico.
55	Lord Lyons..........	Oct. 14	Interview with Mr. Seward. Views of her majesty's government respecting Mexico communicated to him.
56	Sir C. Wyke.........	Sept. 29	State of affairs. Probable effects of foreign intervention.
57	To admiralty.........	Oct. 30	Reinforcements to be sent to the North American and West Indian squadron.
58	Lord Lyons..........	Oct. 17	Mr. Seward still anxious that the plan proposed by the United States for the payment of the foreign debt should be adopted.
59	To admiralty.........	Oct. 31	Naval force to be despatched to Vera Cruz. Instructions to be given to Admiral Milne and Maitland. Plan of operations.
60	To Sir C. Wyke......	....do....	Enclosing convention signed with French and Spanish ministers. To act as British commissioners. Instructions.
61	To Earl Cowley......	Nov. 1	Enclosing a copy of the instructions to Sir C. Wyke.
62	To Sir C. Wyke......	....do....	To proceed to Jamaica and join Admiral Milne. Further instructions to be sent.

Table of contents—Continued.

No.	From whom and to whom.	Date.	Subject.
		1861.	
63	To Earl Cowley	Nov. 1	Enclosing convention. Instructions to be sent to Sir C. Wyke.
64	To Sir J. Crampton	....do....	Do. do.
65	To Earl Cowley	....do....	Draft of further instructions to Sir C. Wyke.
66	To Sir J. Crampton	....do....	Enclosing draft of further instructions to Sir C. Wyke.
67	To Sir C. Wyke	....do....	Instruction as to interference in the internal affairs of Mexico.
68	Admiralty	....do....	Proposed rendezvous for allied fleets.
69	To Earl Cowley	....do....	Enclosing a copy of the above. M. de Flahault informed.
70	To Sir J. Crampton	....do....	Enclosing a copy of the above. M. Isturiz informed.
71	To admiralty	....do....	Arrangements for conveyance of Sir C. Wyke.
72	Sir J. Crampton	....do....	Spanish force to be sent to Mexico.
73	To admiralty	Nov. 6	Arrangements with regard to the French expeditionary force.
74	Earl Cowley	Nov. 5	M. de Saligny to be French commissioner and joint plenipotentiary with the French admiral. His instructions being prepared.
75	......do........	....do....	French government concur in draft of further instructions to Sir C. Wyke.
76	......do........	....do....	French government concur as to rendezvous. Amount of French force.
77	To Lord Lyons	Nov. 6	Enclosing copy of convention. To invite the adhesion of the United States government.
78	To admiralty	Nov. 7	Suggesting that the date of rendezvous should be settled by Admiral Milne with the French and Spanish commanders.
79	......do........	Nov. 8	In case of difference of opinion with regard to the negotiations, the opinions of Sir C. Wyke to prevail over that of Admiral Milne.
80	To Sir C. Wyke	Nov. 15	In case of operations against the capital, the British force not to advance beyond Vera Cruz.
81	......do........	....do....	As to operations on the Pacific coast.
82	To admiralty	....do....	Instructions to be sent to Admiral Maitland as to operations on the Pacific coast.
83	Earl Cowley	Nov. 14	Probability of the Spanish expedition having already started.
84	To Earl Cowley	Nov. 16	Copies of despatches to Sir C. Wyke and to admiralty of the 15th instant.
85	To admiralty	Nov. 18	Enclosing copy of despatch from Earl Cowley of the 14th instant.
86	Earl Cowley	Nov. 19	French expedition to stop at Teneriffe.
87	Sir J. Crampton	....do....	Appointment of General Prim as Spanish commander-in-chief and plenipotentiary.
88	Sir C. Wyke	Oct. 28	Monthly report on the state of affairs.
89	......do........	....do....	Negotiations with the Mexican government. Proposed convention for the settlement of British demands.
90	To Sir J. Crampton	Nov. 28	Informing him of Sir C. Wyke's negotiations. Her Majesty's government consider that the joint convention affords greater security for the due fulfilment of any Mexican engagements. What are the terms the Spanish government will require?

THE PRESENT CONDITION OF MEXICO. 233

Table of contents—Continued.

No.	From whom and to whom.	Date.	Subject.
		1861.	
91	To Earl Cowley	Dec. 2	Similar to the above. What are the terms the French government will require?
92	......do............	Dec. 4	Reduced force to be sent to Mexico.
93	To Sir J. Crampton...	...do....	Similar to the above.
94	Earl Cowley	Dec. 3	Terms to be demanded to be left to the decision of the French commissioners.
95	Lord Lyons..........	Nov. 29	Delay in presenting the convention to the United States government in consequence of the Spanish minister not having received his full powers and instructions.
96	......do.............	Dec. 3	Copy of note enclosing the convention, and inviting the adherence of the United States government.
97	Sir J. Crampton......	Dec. 10	Spanish government informed of the reduced force to be sent to Mexico.
98	......do.............	Dec. 15	Demands to be made by Spanish government on Mexico.
99	M. Isturiz...........	Dec. 22	Explanation respecting the sailing of the Spanish expedition from Cuba. The commander instructed to act in concert with the forces of the allies.
100	To Sir J. Crampton...	Dec. 24	Copy of the above.
101	......do.............	...do....	Sir C. Wyke to communicate to the Spanish commissioners the terms of the British demands.
102	Lord Lyons..........	Dec. 6	Note from Mr. Seward refusing to accede to the joint convention.
103	......do.............	Dec. 9	Copy of a joint note acknowledging Mr. Seward's note.
104	To M. Isturiz........	Dec. 24	Acknowledging note of 22d instant.
105	To Sir J. Crampton...	Dec. 27	Copies of despatches from Lord Lyons of the 3d, 6th, and 9th instant.
106	Sir C. Wyke.........	Nov. 25	Progress of his negotiations Convention signed with government, but thrown out by congress.
107	......do.............	Nov. 28	Address from British merchants and his reply.
108	......do.............	...do....	Reported intrigues of General Doblado.
109	......do.............	...do....	Proposed proceedings in consequence of the rejection of the convention. Has presented the British ultimatum.
		1862.	
110	Admiralty	Jan. 2	Particulars respecting the Spanish expedition.
		1861.	
111	Lord Lyons..........	Dec. 21	Proceedings of the United States minister in Mexico.
		1862.	
112	M. Isturiz...........	Jan. 13	Instructions given by governor-general of Cuba to the commander of the Mexican expedition.
113	To M. Isturiz........	Jan. 16	Receipt of the above. Cannot understand why Spanish expedition did not await the arrival of the British and French forces.
114	Earl Cowley	Jan. 17	French expedition to be reinforced.
115	M. Isturiz...........	Jan. 18	Further explanations respecting the Spanish expedition.
116	To Earl Cowley......	Jan. 20	Interview with M. de Flahault. French reinforcements to be sent. No further British force will be detached for Mexico.
117	To M. Isturiz........	Jan. 23	Not satisfied with his explanations, but accept the assurance that the Spanish government will observe the terms of the joint convention.

Table of contents—Continued.

No.	From whom and to whom.	Date.	Subject.
		1862.	
118	To Sir J. Crampton	Jan. 19	Representations to be made respecting the Spanish expedition.
119	Earl Cowley	Jan. 24	Rumor respecting Archduke Maximilian being made king of Mexico.
120	To Sir C. Wyke	Jan. 27	Instructions as to any change of the Mexican government. Measures to be taken on the Pacific coast.
		1861.	
121	Sir C. Wyke	Dec. 14	Intends to proceed to Vera Cruz. British interests left in charge of the Belgian minister.
122	......do	Dec. 29	Arrival at Vera Cruz. Reasons for not proceeding to Jamaica.
123	......do	....do....	Proceedings of the Spanish at Vera Cruz. Aspect of affairs.

CORRESPONDENCE RELATING TO MEXICAN AFFAIRS.

No. 1.

Lord J. Russell to Sir C. Wyke.

[Extract.]

FOREIGN OFFICE, *March* 30, 1861.

A passage to Vera Cruz having been ordered for you on board the contract packet appointed to leave Southampton on the 2d of April, you will embark on board that vessel, and on your arrival at Vera Cruz proceed at once to Mexico. You will probably find Mr. Mathew already in diplomatic communication with the constitutional government; for her Majesty's government can hardly doubt that it will have willingly acceded to the conditions on which the re-establishment of friendly intercourse has been made to depend.

The instructions addressed to Mr. Mathew, both before and since the final triumph of the liberal party, made the recognition by Great Britain of the constitutional government contingent upon the acknowledgment by that government of the liability of Mexico for the claims of British subjects, who, either in their persons or in their property, for a long series of years can be proved to have suffered wrong at the hands of successive governments in Mexico.

If Mr. Mathew should not have obtained any such concession from the constitutional government before your arrival, you must use your own discretion as to the time at which you should present your credentials. It is, of course, desirable that the re-establishment of regular diplomatic intercourse with Mexico should not be delayed; but it might happen that the manifestation of any undue eagerness on your part to bring about such a state of things might encourage the constitutional government to withhold the preliminary concession which Mr. Mathew was instructed to require.

Her Majesty's government have all along declared that they had no desire to prejudge the quarrel between the two parties who have been long arrayed against each other in Mexico, or to side with one party against the other. Had the party of General Miramon shown a due regard for international obligations and for the rights of British subjects, the British legation would not have been withdrawn from the city of Mexico. That step was forced upon her Majesty's government by continual disregard of the rights of British subjects and of the obligations of international engagements, which rendered it impossible for her Majesty's government to continue to hold relations with the constituted authorities. But if the newly-established government should evince a disposition to act on different principles, you will state to it, without hesitation, that the friendly feelings of her Majesty's government for Mexico have undergone no change, notwithstanding the grievous wrongs which British subjects have sustained at the hands of the successive governments of that republic; that the policy of the British government with regard to Mexico is a policy of non-intervention, and that the British government desire to see Mexico free and independent, and in a position to regulate the civil administration of the country, to maintain internal peace, and to discharge its international duties without the active intervention of any foreign power whatever. Her Majesty's government cannot doubt that such assurances as these will induce the Mexican government to rely with confidence on the disinterestedness of any advice or suggestions which you may see occasion to offer to it, though I would caution you against obtruding such advice upon it, and still more against entering into any contest with the representative of any other power for exclusive influence over the councils of the government.

I would, moreover, particularly caution you against taking any part in the political questions which may arise between contending parties in the state. A British minister can never safely interfere in such matters; but, as the representative of a country possessing liberal institutions, and therefore desiring to see other nations enjoying the same blessing, he will always be looked upon with respect, and will have more real influence for good in proportion as he keeps aloof from the factions or disputes of rival parties in the state.

Your earliest attention after your arrival in Mexico must be given to the question of British claims. You are aware that it has not been the custom of her Majesty's government, although they have always held themselves free to do so, to interfere authoritatively on behalf of those who have chosen to lend their money to foreign governments, and the Mexican bondholders have not been an exception to this rule. The constitutional government, however, while established at Vera Cruz, under the presidency of Señor Juarez, concluded with Captain Dunlop two years ago an arrangement by which it was stipulated that twenty-five per cent. of the customs receipts at Vera Cruz and Tampico should be assigned to the British bondholders, and sixteen per cent. to the holders of convention bonds. That convention was confirmed and extended by the arrangement lately made by Captain Aldham. The claims of the bondholders, therefore, to the extent provided for in those arrangements, have acquired the character of an international obligation, and you should accordingly insist upon the punctual fulfilment of the obligations thus contracted.

The bondholders, moreover, have sustained a grievous loss by the robbery of a large sum of money belonging to them which had been deposited for security in the house of her Majesty's legation, and if Mr. Mathew should not have succeeded before your arrival in making a satisfactory arrangement for the early restitution of the amount thus plundered, you will insist upon such arrangement being immediately entered into with yourself. Her Majesty's government will not admit as an excuse for hesitation in this respect the plea that the robbery was committed by the late government; for as regards this, as indeed all other claims, her Majesty's government cannot admit that the party who committed the wrong is alone responsible. Great Britain does not recognize any party as constituting the republic in its dealings with foreign nations, but holds the entire republic, by whatever party the government of it may from time to time be administered, to be responsible for wrongs done to British subjects by any party or persons at any time administering the powers of government.

Her Majesty's government do not, indeed, anticipate any determined refusal on the part of the constitutional government to afford redress in this particular case; but if you should meet with any such resistance, you will apprise the Mexican government that you are authorized and enjoined at once to call upon her Majesty's naval forces to support, and, if necessary, to enforce, your demand for reparation. The fact that the scene of the outrage was the residence of the British mission gives her Majesty's government a special right to enforce reparation in this particular case.

The robbery committed by General Degollado, when acting under the orders of the government established at Vera Cruz, on a conducta of specie on its way to the coast, in which specie British subjects were largely interested, stands next in order as an act of violence for which reparation must be obtained; and I do not doubt that there will be no hesitation in making good the losses sustained by that transaction.

It is unnecessary for me on this occasion to go through the list of claims of British subjects which it will be your duty to press for settlement. Mr. Mathew has been instructed to present a list of such claims to the ministers of the republic and to demand a settlement of them.

You will find on examining this list that the several claims, although differing in degree, are all of a nature to require reparation, and it will be your duty to arrange with the Mexican government the manner in which such reparation shall be made. Whatever arrangement you may make should be recorded in a convention. For this purpose her Majesty has been pleased to grant you a full power under the great seal.

The general British claims may probably be classed under two heads: those the validity of which has been recognized, and those the validity of which is still to be ascertained.

As regards the first class, the convention should be confined to providing for the manner in which the amounts already agreed upon should he paid; for her Majesty's government will not allow cases already examined and determined to be reopened for prospective benefit either of British parties or of the Mexican government.

As regards the second class, the convention should provide for examining the claims and for the liquidation of such as may be pronounced valid, either in whole or in part, on the same principle and in the same manner as may be stipulated in regard to the first class. Whether the examination of such claims shall be made by a mixed commission or not must be left to your discretion to determine.

As regards the first class of claims, they should be severally specified in the convention, with the sums payable in respect of each; but such enumeration will, of course, not be practicable as regards the second class, which must remain open for the insertion of any claims brought forward before a specific day.

As regards the time at which either class of the claims shall be paid, her Majesty's government are aware that some degree of indulgence may be necessary. The troubles which have for many years past distracted the republic have, as a natural result, impoverished the country, and made it difficult for the constitutional government to raise at once funds sufficient to provide for the immediate wants of the civil administration, and for the liabilities of the country towards foreign creditors and claimants. But you must be careful not to allow any temporary forbearance which you may show in pressing for the liquidation of British claims to be construed into indifference. So far from that, you will lose no opportunity of pointing out the necessity of taking measures for developing the resources of the country, on the ground that the result of such development will be to supply the treasury not only with the means of meeting the expenses of the civil government, but also with those for satisfying all international claims.

An opinion has got abroad that the constitutional government will probably adopt some measure in regard to ecclesiastical property which will place at its disposal a large sum of money.

It is not the part of her Majesty's government to say whether this act should be sanctioned or not, but if by any measures of the Mexican government, which they consider right and expedient, the public treasury should be immediately or prospectively replenished, her Majesty's government may fairly urge that British claimants should have the benefit of such a state of things, and obtain an earlier settlement of their outstanding claims.

The only question affecting the internal polity of Mexico, in regard to which her Majesty's government would feel warranted in offering advice unsolicited, is that of freedom for religious worship. Putting aside all considerations of a moral character, which are so strongly in favor of a general liberty of conscience, it is impossible to doubt that Mexico would find great political advantage in throwing down the barrier which now prevents Christians of different sects from settling in the country, and in thereby encouraging the immigration from other countries of persons whose activity and skill would contribute to improve the resources of the country.

I enclose a despatch on this subject which I addressed to Lord Cowley in July last.

You are so well acquainted with the peculiarities of the Spanish character that it is needless for me to dilate on the best means of dealing with the people with whom you may be brought into contact. They are to be influenced by moderate language and considerate demeanor, but they resist and defy attempts to intimidate or coerce.

But it may be that with all your tact and forbearance you will fail to obtain a hearing for well-founded representations on behalf of British subjects; and in such cases you may, by referring quietly to the presence of her Majesty's ships-of-war on the coasts of Mexico, leave the Mexican government to infer that those ships are available for your support if your just demands should be rejected, or if the engagements entered into with you should be disregarded.

As regards the question of article 10 of the convention of 1826, you will find that the construction of that article has been a fruitful source of discussion between the two governments, more especially during the rule of General Miramon, when forced loans, under one denomination or another, but more usually, of late, under that of a tax on capital, were continually attempted to be levied on her Majesty's subjects. You will judge how far any overture on your part for clearing up doubts in regard to this article, and for securing for British subjects exemption from all extraordinary contributions, under whatever denomination they may be levied, would meet with a favorable reception on the part of the Mexican government, and if you see a probability of such being the case, you will frame and refer home for consideration the draft of an additional article to the convention of 1826, to which the Mexican government would be likely to agree.

If any differences should arise between the Mexican government and foreign powers you will not hesitate to employ such influence as you may possess for preventing those differences from leading to an open rupture. But in taking such a course you must be careful not to assume for yourself, or for your government, any responsibility, and you must avoid any uncalled for assumption of mediation.

With the representatives of foreign states accredited to the republic you will endeavor to live in harmony. You will always bear in mind that neither in Mexico nor in any part of the world do her Majesty's government seek any exclusive political influence, nor any commercial advantages which they are not ready to share with all the nations of the earth. The only object at which they aim is to secure for this country its proper place in the family of nations, and their only desire is to employ any influence which Great Britain may possess for the promotion of general peace and the development of commercial industry.

Enclosure in No. 1.

Lord J. Russell to Earl Cowley.

[Extract.]

FOREIGN OFFICE, *July* 17, 1860.

I have to state to you that her Majesty's government do not at all pretend to impose religious toleration as a basis in Mexico.

But it appears to her Majesty's government that to restrict a quiet and obedient subject of the state from worshipping God in such manner as he thinks most acceptable to his Creator, whether alone or in communion with others, is a barbarous abuse of power. All that the civil magistrate can ask is obedience in civil matters, and the right of religious freedom is so natural and so obvious that it is probable Mexico never will be tranquil so long as men are punished for entertaining a belief different from that of the government. When, therefore, there is a question of renewing our offer of mediation, her Majesty's government will express in a separate despatch their conviction that a tyranny over men's consciences ought to be abandoned by the government of Mexico.

No. 2.

Lord J. Russell to Sir C. Wyke.

FOREIGN OFFICE, *April* 17, 1861.

SIR: I have received from Mr. Mathew and from her Majesty's consul in Mexico an account of the barbarous murder of Mr. Edward Bodmer, the British vice consul at Tasco, whilst endeavoring to save the life of a Mexican citizen, who was assaulted by some soldiers belonging to a section of General Vicario's army. I have now to instruct you to urge the Mexican government to spare no efforts to bring the perpetrators of this atrocious outrage to justice, and you will at the same time demand ample reparation for the widow and family of Mr. Bodmer.

I am, &c.,

J. RUSSELL.

No. 3.

Mr. Mathew to Lord J. Russell.

MEXICO, *March* 26, 1861.

MY LORD: I have received a note, of which I have the honor to enclose a translation, from Senor Zarco, expressing the desire of the Mexican government to secure to her Majesty's subjects in Mexico the rights of worship according to their conscience, by an additional, or more correctly I believe, by a separate article to the international treaty.

A similar communication has, I understand, been addressed to the ministers of the United States and Prussia, who inform me that they entertain no doubt that the proposal will be gladly accepted by their respective governments.

From the class of persons who are likely to be attracted to this country, in mining and other pursuits, by the prolongation of peace, I believe that to no nation will this privilege be more important than to her Majesty's subjects, and I venture to assure myself that your lordship will receive with much satisfaction the proposal of the Mexican government for insuring this right under the guarantee of treaties.

I have, &c.,

GEORGE B. MATHEW.

Enclosure in No. 3.

Señor Zarco to Mr. Mathew.

[Translation.]

MEXICO, *March* 25, 1861.

The undersigned, &c., has the honor to address Mr. Mathew by special com mand of his excellency the president, and to inform him that the constitutional government of Mexico is desirous to afford foreigners full protection and security with proper guarantees, and that consequently it is ready to add an additional article to the treaty already existing between Great Britain and Mexico, whereby it shall be stipulated that foreigners may carry out freely, publicly, and under the protection of the law, their several forms of religion, and worship God according to the dictates of their own conscience.

The preliminary steps in this matter can be entered upon in this capital, should Mr. Mathew be provided with the powers necessary for such transactions; otherwise at the court of St. James, so soon as the representative of Mexico shall have presented his credentials.

The undersigned, &c.

FRANCISCO ZARCO.

No. 4.

Mr. Mathew to Lord J. Russel.

MEXICO, *April 5*, 1861

MY LORD: In a recent and prolonged conversation with Señor Zarco, minister for foreign affairs, relative to British claims, that gentleman earnestly assured me of the desire entertained by his government to meet my just demands on behalf of her Majesty's subjects in every manner that the deplorable financial condition of Mexico would admit; and further expressed the readiness of the Mexican government to do whatever your lordship might deem proper for preventing a recurrence of the exactions lately suffered by British subjects from misinterpretation or deficiencies in the international treaty, from which many of the existing reclamations have arisen.

I thought it, therefore, desirable to address him a brief note on these subjects, in order to be enabled to submit to your lordship some definite proposals and views.

The unsettled condition and future prospects of Mexico, and the experience of the last three years, render it, I feel convinced, of obvious importance that all articles of disputed interpretation in the treaty should be clearly defined, and that such additions should be made to it as your lordship may think conducive to the security of her Majesty's subjects, and to the advantage of British interests.

I have much pleasure in being able to lay before your lordship, by the enclosed translation of Señor Zarco's reply, the official declaration of the desire of the Mexican government to meet these objects.

This government, as your lordship will observe, propose to refer all British reclamations, not yet recognized by it, to the examination and final decision of a mixed commission, and to assign for the gradual discharge of all English claims thus or previously admitted a stated portion of their revenues.

It is distinctly understood that this proposal which I have now to submit to your lordship's consideration has no reference to the special agreement already entered into by the Mexican government for the repayment of the British money seized in the "conductas" at Lagos and Tampico, nor to the negotiation in progress between the Mexican government and the agent of the boudholders for the restoration of the money plundered at this legation.

Señor Zarco proceeds to state the willingness of his government to define or extend, as your lordship may think best, in the usual manner, the privileges to be mutually enjoyed by British and Mexican subjects respectively, and makes, in the name of the Mexican government, the declaration that they stipulate from the present moment for the extension of the right of exemption from forced loans in the ninth article to exemption from extraordinary contributions, from which her Majesty's subjects have so severely suffered.

He observes that he has proposed by a separate note (the subject-matter of my despatch of the 26th of March) to secure to her Majesty's subjects, by a separate article, the free right of public worship, and he transmits a copy of the now existing law for that object, which I have the honor to enclose.

I think your lordship will not disapprove of my having thus taken the earliest opportunity of bringing these matters to issue. I am not aware of any other points in the international treaty calling for notice, except that of intestate estates; but I may at the same time bring to your consideration the questions affected by the late proposed and, I imagine, discarded treaty with the United States, of any exclusive rights of transit for merchandise or of isthmus jurisdiction.

I have, &c.

GEORGE B. MATHEW.

Enclosure 1 in No. 4.

Mr. Mathew to Señor Zarco.

MEXICO, *March* 22, 1861.

The undersigned refers with much pleasure to his recent conversation with his excellency Señor Don Francisco Zarco respecting some proposed mode of liquidation, by mutual arrangement, of the heavy claims of British subjects against Mexico, and he would be glad to be enabled to transmit, for the consideration of his government, the views entertained by his excellency and the Mexican cabinet.

The consideration of this subject naturally led to remarks upon certain alleged doubts with regard to the wording of the present international treaty between Great Britain and Mexico, upon infractions of which many of the British claims are founded, which his excellency Señor Zarco informed him had attracted the serious consideration of his government.

The undersigned would have great satisfaction at the same time, therefore, in laying before his government any general suggestions which his excellency Señor Zarco may think fit to communicate to him, with the view of securing, beyond the possibility of doubt or question, in Great Britain and in Mexico, to the natives of each country, the rights and privileges to which the two governments have declared them entitled in civil and religious matters.

The undersigned, &c.

GEORGE B. MATHEW.

Enclosure 2 in No. 4.

Señor Zarco to Mr. Mathew.

[Translation.]

NATIONAL PALACE, *Mexico, March* 27, 1861.

The undersigned, &c., has the honor of acknowledging the receipt of the note which Mr. Mathew, &c., was pleased to address him, under date of the 22d instant, in which, referring to a recent conversation he had with the undersigned respecting British claims, he expresses a desire to know what are the intentions of the Mexican government as to their liquidation and settlement.

The undersigned, who has already expressed to her Majesty's chargé d'affaires how sincere is the wish of the Mexican government to offer every kind of security for faithfully complying with the treaties, and to attend to all claims founded in justice, has also laid before him the great difficulties which at this moment impede an immediate and satisfactory settlement; difficulties which are the natural consequences of a three years' civil war, and by which the public treasury has been drained, and the burdens weighing upon the revenue have been greatly increased.

The undersigned has been gratified by perceiving that her Britannic Majesty's worthy representative has justly estimated the good will of the Mexican government, and is not unconscious of the obstacles which are but superficially noticed in this note.

The undersigned has requested from the finance department a circumstantial statement of the assignments of the duties of the maritime custom-houses granted for the payment of foreign claims; and as soon as this statement is made out he will have the honor of submitting it to her Britannic Majesty's chargé d'affaires, in order that he may be pleased to take it into his consideration. In the meantime the undersigned can inform his excellency that the desire of the Mexican government is to examine all British claims in order to ascertain their exact amount, to submit all that may be pending and not yet recognized (should her Britannic Majesty's government concur) to the scrutiny and decision, without appeal, of a mixed commission, whose organization would be the subject of arrangement between the two governments, and to assign for the payment of all claims thus admitted all that part of the national revenues that can be disposed of, reserving only what is absolutely necessary for covering the estimated expenditure, into which every economy, compatible with the existence of government, has been already commenced to be introduced.

The undersigned would truly wish to be able to make more flattering promises to her Britannic Majesty's chargé d'affaires, but he prefers (and thinks it more consonant with rectitude) to use only the sincere language of truth, and to state that only which is within the limits of possibility in the present circumstances of the country.

The government of the undersigned recollect with satisfaction that Mr. Mathew, on the day of his official reception, offered them the full moral support of Great Britain, and they confidently hope, from the sentiments of justice and benevolence which animate the government of her Britannic Majesty, that they will see in this statement a proof of good faith, and of the sincere desire of the Mexican government to meet their just and well-founded reclamations.

The undersigned takes leave to observe that when peace has been consolidated in the republic, and the government has been enabled to direct their attention to the improvement of all the branches of the public administration, the increase of their revenues will be gradual and progressive, and the product, therefore, of whatever assignments may have been made of these revenues will be greater for the payment of British claims.

The undersigned likewise observes that a general arrangement and the formation of a common fund would have the advantage of offering a greater degree of equity to British claimants, for they would thus avoid preferences in favor of some and to the detriment of others, occurrences which might take place independently of the desire of the Mexican government, and even of the British legation, who occasionally recommend and give ear to certain cases without being able to do the same for all the cases of like nature.

As Mr. Mathew, in the note to which the undersigned has the honor of replying, has been pleased to suggest the propriety of laying down the clear meaning of some of the articles of the existing treaty of friendship between Great Britain and Mexico, the infraction of which has caused many of the reclamations, the government of the undersigned perceives no sort of inconvenience in making with that of Great Britain such declarations as may seem best suited to prevent for the future all species of doubt or questions of interpretation, so that the natives of each country may enjoy when resident in the other clear and defined rights.

Although, in order to arrive at this result, it may be needful to open negotiations, and to give the proper instructions to plenipotentiaries, the government of the undersigned declare that from the present moment they agree, with respect to the stipulations in the 10th article of the treaty of December 26, 1826, to extend the exemption from forced loans to extraordinary contributions, limiting their obligation of paying to such contributions as may be legally established in accordance with the constitution of the republic, and to those which the States may impose in conformity with their particular laws and their municipal regulations.

The government of Mexico are prepared, with regard to any explanation or modification of any other articles of the treaty, to take into consideration any proposals or suggestions made on the part of Great Britain; and in considering such they will entertain no other view than that of maintaining and of strengthening more and more the friendly relations that happily exist between the two countries, reserving to themselves the right of proposing on their part the modifications which, on a careful examination, they may deem conducive to the maintenance of these relations and the legitimate interests of the republic.

With respect to the question of granting to the natives of both countries reciprocally the right of religious liberty, the undersigned has already made known to Mr. Mathew in his note of the 25th instant that the government of Mexico is willing to secure, by an additional article to the treaty, the necessary stipulation for insuring to British subjects the free exercise of their worship, and the right of adoring God according to the inspirations of their conscience.

Foreign residents in Mexico enjoy this right since the triumph of the legitimate government, who have proclaimed, defended, and sustained the great principle of religious liberty; and such is the desire of the government to see it carried out fully into practice, that they have not awaited in proclaiming it for the suggestion of friendly powers, and they will concede the liberty of worship to all mankind, even though they should know that on this point due reciprocity had been denied to Mexican citizens in any other country of the world.

In order that Mr. Mathew may form an exact idea of the principles which on this point serve as a guide to the government of the republic, and which he may communicate to that of her Britannic Majesty, the undersigned has the honor to enclose a copy of the decree of the 4th December last, which regulates the liberty of worship in this country, and whose provisions the undersigned hopes may be the basis accepted by the government of Great Britain for the stipulation proposed by the undersigned in his note of the 25th instant.

The undersigned, &c.

FRANCISCO ZARCO.

No. 5.

Mr. Mathew to Lord J. Russell.

MEXICO, *April* 19, 1861.

MY LORD: A public and religious ceremony having been announced to take place at Tacubaya in commemoration of the murders of prisoners and other persons committed there in the month of April, 1859, by order of Generals Miramon and Marquez, I deemed it a fitting moment to call the consideration of the

Mexican government to the claim of the widow and family of the unfortunate Dr. Duval.

Señor Zarco, in a note of which I have the honor to enclose a translation, informed me that the president was willing to assign nationalized property of the value of $25,000 for their benefit. Conscious of the all but impossibility under which the government labored of finding other means, I conceived it important to the interest of Dr. Duval's family to place the offer of Señor Zarco in the hands of a respectable person, Mr. Knight, as their representative to carry it into effect; but at the same time I deemed it right to guard myself in my reply, of which a copy is herewith transmitted, against the possible presumption of having admitted the disclaimer contained in Señor Zarco's note of pecuniary responsibility on the part of the government.

I have, &c.

GEORGE B. MATHEW.

Enclosure 1 in No. 5.

Señor Zarco to Mr. Mathew.

[Translation.]

MEXICO, *April* 12, 1861.

The undersigned, &c., in reply to Mr. Mathew's note respecting certain indemnity for the family of Dr. Duval, has the honor to inform him that, notwithstanding their desire to meet his wishes in the present instance, the Mexican government neither are nor can be held responsible, whether they be judged by international law, the laws of Mexico itself, or by the general principles of justice, for the crimes of certain people calling themselves a government, and lately in possession of the capital, much less when such crimes come under the category of murders, as in the case of the unfortunate Dr. Duval. Consequently, the undersigned cannot but feel that Mr. Mathew will perceive how impossible it would be for the present government, with the principles they hold, to impose upon the country the payment of such indemnities as could not fail to give rise to a responsibility quite inadmissible.

Nevertheless, the constitutional government, from feelings of humanity and justice, would not be indisposed to grant some kind of voluntary indemnity in such instances as the present one, and, as regards the family of Dr. Duval, would be willing to set aside house property to the amount of $25,000, the sum specified by Mr. Mathew, an arrangement which could be carried out either in actual houses or in covenant property, the latter having been secularized.

The undersigned, &c.

FRANCISCO ZARCO.

Enclosure 2 in No. 5.

Mr. Mathew to Señor Zarco.

MEXICO, *April* 18, 1861.

The undersigned, &c., begs to acknowledge the notes addressed to him by his excellency Señor Don Francisco Zarco, &c., under dates of the 12th, 13th, 15th, and 16th instant.

He feels most fully assured of the sentiments of reprobation with which the government of whom his excellency is a justly distinguished member must regard any acts of outrage and exaction from which her Majesty's subjects in Mexico may have suffered, and for which they naturally look to that country for the compensation due to them, still less can he doubt the indignation with which they must view such atrocious and cowardly acts of assassination as that of which the unfortunate Dr. Duval was a victim, deeds whose advisers and perpetrators will yet, he trusts, meet condign punishment.

The undersigned has received with sincere gratification the notification that his excellency the president has determined to assign immediately property of the value of $25,000 for the benefit of Dr. Duval's widow and family, and has requested Mr. Knight, as their agent and friend in this capital, to wait upon his excellency Señor Zarco, and to concert with him all necessary steps for carrying his excellency's benevolent commands into immediate effect.

The undersigned, &c.

GEORGE B. MATHEW.

No. 6.

Lord J. Russell to Sir C. Wyke.

FOREIGN OFFICE, *May* 30, 1861.

SIR: Her Majesty's government approve Mr. Mathew's proceedings as reported in his despatch of the 19th ultimo, with reference to the proposed assignment of national property of the value of $25,000 to the widow of the late Dr. Duval.

I am, &c.

J. RUSSELL.

No. 7.

Mr. Mathew to Lord J. Russell.

[Extract.]

MEXICO, *May* 12, 1861.

There has been but little change in the affairs of Mexico for the last two months. Señor Prieto was succeeded in the ministry of finance by Señor Mata, whose previous nomination as minister to England I had the honor of notifying to your lordship, and who has only agreed to fill the office until the meeting of congress. The death of Señor Lerdo de Tejada, the ablest, if not the only financier in the republic, has been severely felt at the present crisis.

It seems doubtful whether Señor Mata will proceed to London; the name of Señor Gomez Farias has been mentioned to me by Señor Zarco, in the event of a new appointment.

Señor Fuente, a lawyer of some note, left Mexico by the last packet on a mission to Paris, and probably to Spain, his departure having been long delayed by the difficulty of procuring even the small sum of money necessary for his journey and support.

To this complete deficiency of resources must be attributed the continued existence and increase, in various parts of the country, of guerilla bodies under the Spaniards Cobos and Vicario, and under the infamous Marquez, who pursues still his course of murder and rapine.

Two petty attempts to create disturbances in this capital were discovered and put down in time.

In other respects public tranquillity has not been disturbed, and however faulty and weak the present government may be, they who witnessed the murders, the acts of atrocity and of plunder, almost of daily occurrence, under the government of General Miramon and his counsellors, Señor Diaz and General Marquez, cannot but appreciate the existence of law and justice.

Foreigners, especially, who suffered so heavily under that arbitrary rule, and by the hatred and intolerance towards them, which is a dogma of the church party in Mexico, cannot but make a broad distinction between the past and the present.

President Juarez, though deficient in the energy necessary for the present crisis, is an upright and well-intentioned man, excellent in all the private relations of life, but the mere fact of his being an Indian exposes him to the hostility and sneers of the dregs of Spanish society, and of those of mixed blood, who ludicrously arrogate to themselves the higher social position in Mexico.

I have already made known to your lordship my opinion of the objectionable nature of the federal constitution now in force; and I have not concealed my fear for the future peace of Mexico, from the utter want of patriotism among the higher classes, and from the demoralization and restlessness produced among all by the prolonged state of civil warfare. A desire for change is already stated to exist in certain quarters, and the idea of the selection of a military dictator has been put forward; but it is scarcely needful to observe that such a step would be no palliation of the present wants, and no preventive of the future dangers of the country.

General St. Anna was the ablest man of that class that Mexico has produced, and the temporary good effect of his energetic character is unquestionable; but that due appreciation of equal justice, of social rights, and of peaceful prosperity, by which alone nationality can be maintained, cannot be created by the strong hand of arbitrary power.

The hope of Mexico rests upon the maintenance of peace. A wise basis of civil and of religious liberty has been laid down, and peace only is needed for the development of constitutional principles, and for the gradual enlightenment of the people.

But seeing, as I do, so many native and foreign elements at work to disturb the existing state of things, I cannot but entertain a conviction that unless the present government or principles of government are in some way avowedly upheld by England or the United States—by a protecting alliance, or by the declaration that no revolutionary movements would be permitted in any of the seaports on either ocean—further deplorable convulsions will afflict this unfortunate country, to the heavy injury of British interests and commerce, and to the disgrace of humanity.

I do not believe it possible that the church party, or that the former rule of intolerance and of gross superstition can ever be restored to power; so far, at least, has been secured by the result of the last civil war—the first contest for principles, it may be remarked, in this republic. But the result of the intrigues of various parties with different views and hopes, and the difficulties and embarrassments purposely brought to bear upon a weak and bankrupt government, may cause an early dismemberment of the republic, and its division into many petty States.

The most imminent peril, however, to Mexico, and one which will equally press on any future as on the present government, is the deplorable state of its finances. On the one hand, the supreme government have no power to raise taxes, save with the consent of the States, (and the country, though possessed of great internal wealth, is, for the present year or more, utterly ruined and exhausted by the late war;) and on the other, the resources now receivable by the government are avowedly unequal to more than half the amount of the expenditure actually requisite.

The chief revenues arise from the import duties, and not only are these gradually but surely diminishing, from the smuggling consequent on the high duties so unwisely imposed on cottons and woollens, and other goods of general consumption, but at this moment in Vera Cruz, the chief port of the republic, no less than 77 per cent. are claimed by foreign creditors. Of this amount—

27 per cent. are assigned to the London bondholders.
24 per cent. to the "British convention," which numbers very few English holders.
10 per cent. extra to replace arrears.
10 per cent. to replace the money at the mint of Guanaxuato.
8 per cent. for the French convention.

——
77

The Mexican government has been accused, and not without some reason, of having frittered away the church property recently nationalized; but it must be remembered that, while forced contributions, plunder, and immense supplies from the church and its supporters have enabled Generals Zuloaga and Miramon to sustain the civil war for three years, the constitutional government abstained from such acts, and have the sole robbery of the conducta at Lagos, towards the close of the war, to answer for. Their resources, during this lengthened period, were drawn from advances by individuals, on bonds for far larger sums, payable at the close of the war, and from the actual sale of a great part of this property at 25, 20, and even 15 per cent. of its supposed value.

The advantageous disposal of the remainder was most detrimentally affected by the circulation of reports calculated to prevent the restoration of confidence, and the consequent investment of money in the purchase of nationalized property; and the government have consequently been obliged by their necessities, after trying in vain every better mode of sale, to dispose of the property on "pagarés" (or. promissory notes) to be paid off by instalments extending over several years.

These "pagarés," again, they are compelled to sell by auction, at a heavy discount, to provide for the daily subsistence of the troops, and the maintenance of the government.

From the foregoing details your lordship will at once understand the precarious condition of Mexico; and that, without some foreign interposition, the dismemberment of the republic and a national bankruptcy appear all but inevitable.

The session of the Mexican congress, after some preliminary time spent in verifying the elections, was opened on the 10th; and I have the honor to enclose copies of the speeches of President Juarez, and of the president of the congress, on that occasion.

I am sorry to say that I entertain but little hope of much practical advantage from their deliberations; indeed, I know not that much is in their power, especially with regard to the most pressing danger, the financial position of Mexico.

The bondholders might, perhaps, save their capital by submitting to a temporary suspension of interest; and the establishment of a more equitable tariff, which the government are pledged to me to urge upon the congress, may lay down a better future basis of revenue.

But Mexico should, whatever her distress, at least commence at home; and the holders of the immense internal debt should be the first to suffer for the ruin their own folly has caused or abetted. I much fear that the republic has not produced men of sufficient energy and honor to adopt this course, unsustained by some foreign interposition.

The effort will always be made to make the foreigner the chief sufferer from the undoubtedly bankrupt state of the country.

One of the first acts of the congress will be to verify the election of the president, which has recently taken place throughout the country: unless one of the candidates has a majority of all the votes cast, the congress selects; and it is thought very possibly that by this course Señor Juarez, though highest on the list of candidates, may be defeated, and that General Ortega may be named.

Her Majesty's envoy extraordinary and minister plenipoteniary, Sir Charles L. Wyke, and Mr. Johnston, arrived safely in this capital on the 9th instant.

No. 8.

Sir C. Wyke to Lord J. Russell.

[Extract.]

MEXICO, *May* 27, 1861.

In a long conversation I had with Señor Guzman I dwelt on the astonishment that would naturally be felt by her Majesty's government when informed that no steps had yet been taken for the payment of the $660,000, which we must insist on being refunded to the parties from whom it had been stolen. I added that the honor of the Mexican government was directly concerned in this matter, and therefore fully expected to hear from him some explanation.

Don Leon Guzman was profuse in his professions of being willing to do all that could in justice be required of him, but whenever I attempted to get him out of generalities, he avoided the difficulty by stating that until I was formally installed as her Majesty's minister here, he could not officially treat the question with me, but again expressed his willingness to render every satisfaction when the proper time for so doing should arrive. As soon after the departure of the mail as possible I shall put his sincerity to the test.

The term of delay granted for the repayment of the money stolen from the "conducta" by General Degollado expires on the 11th of next month, and I have every reason to believe that they are not prepared to meet the demand that will then be made upon them.

No. 9.

Sir C. Wyke to Lord J. Russell.

[Extract.]

MEXICO, *May* 27, 1861.

It will be very difficult, if not impossible, to give your lordship a correct idea of the present state of affairs in this unfortunate country, so utterly incomprehensible is the conduct of the government which at present presides over its destinies.

Animated by a blind hatred towards the church party, the present government has only thought of destroying and dissipating the immense property formerly belonging to the clergy, without, however, at the same time taking advantage of the wealth thus placed at their disposal to liquidate the many obligations which at present weigh them down and cripple their resources.

The church property has generally been supposed to be worth between 60,000,000 and 80,000,000 Spanish dollars, the whole of which appears to have been frittered away without the government having anything to show for it. A considerable amount has, doubtless, been spent in repaying advances at exorbitant interest, made to the liberal party when they were fighting their way to power; but still enough ought to have remained after satisfying their creditors to have left them very well off, and in a better position as to their pecuniary resources than that held by any other government.

Since their declaration of independence, according to a decree issued by them some time ago, anybody denouncing church property has the right to purchase it on the following terms: 60 per cent. of the value of such houses or lands are to be paid in bonds of the internal debt, (which bonds are in reality only worth 6 per cent.,) and the remaining 40 per cent. in "pagarés" or promises to pay hard cash, at sixty, and even eighty months' sight. The pagarés," of course, were subsequently discounted at an enormous sacrifice, as the government was pressed for money, and willing to pay any nominal value to obtain it without delay. In this way $27,000,000 worth of church property has been squandered in this city alone and the government, now without a sixpence, is endeavoring to raise a loan of $1,000,000 to pay their current expenses.

The church party, although beaten, are not yet subdued, and several of their chiefs are within six leagues of the capital, at the head of forces varying from 4,000 to 6,000 men. The notorious Marquez is one of these, and he has lately defeated several bodies of government troops sent against him.

The religious feelings of a fanatic population have been shocked by the destruction of churches and convents all over the country, and the disbanded monks and friars wandering about amongst the people fan the flame of discontent, which is kept alive by the women, who, as a body, are all in favor of the church.

Those well acquainted with the country watch this movement with anxiety, and say that, unless promptly checked, it will lead to the downfall of the present government, and renew again all the horrors of a civil war.

In the meantime congress, instead of enabling the government to put down the frightful disorder which reigns throughout the length and breadth of the land, is occupied in disputing about vain theories of so-called government on ultraliberal principles, whilst the respectable part of the population is delivered up defenceless to the attacks of robbers and assassins, who swarm on the highroads and in the streets of the capital. The constitutional government is unable to maintain its authorty in the various States of the federation, which are becoming *de facto* perfectly independent, so that the same causes which, under similar circumstances, broke up the confederation of Central America into five separate republics are now at work here, and will probably produce a like result.

This state of things renders one all but powerless to obtain redress from a government which is solely occupied in maintaining its existence from day to day and therefore unwilling to attend to other people's misfortunes before their own. The only hope of improvement I can see is to be found in the small moderate party who may step in perhaps before all is lost, to save their country from impending ruin. Patriotism, in the common acceptation of the term, appears to be unknown, and no one man of any note is to be found in the ranks of either party. Contending factions struggle for the possession of power only to gratify either their cupidity or their revenge, and in the meantime the country sinks lower and lower, whilst its population becomes brutalized and degraded to an extent frightful to contemplate.

Such is the actual state of affairs in Mexico, and your lordship will perceive therefore that there is little chance of justice or redress from such people, except by the employment of force to exact that which both persuasion and menaces have hitherto failed to obtain.

No. 10.

Sir C. Wyke to Lord J. Russell.

[Extract]

MEXICO, June 24, 1861.

In my despatch of the 27th ultimo I stated that I should take an early opportunity of testing the sincerity of Don Leon Guzman, the new minister for foreign affairs, with reference to his assertion to me that the Mexican government were most anxious to atone, by any means in their power, for the outrage committed at the British legation in November last.

My interview with him took place on Saturday, the 1st instant. He said that legal measures had been instituted against the persons who had stolen the $660,000 on that occasion, and that, if they were condemned by the courts, their property would be confiscated, and the proceeds thereof employed towards paying off that sum.

This I told him I had nothing whatever to do with, having merely to insist on the repayment of the money stolen, without in any way being concerned in the means by which it was to be procured.

I pointed out to Señor Guzman that the speedy repayment of the sum above mentioned was essential, not only for the honor and credit of the Mexican government, but also for the maintenance of friendly relations between the two countries.

Don Leon then assured me that before the departure of the next mail he should be able to furnish me with such explanations relative to this matter as would prove satisfactory to her Majesty's government.

With regard to the money robbed from the "Laguna Seca" conducta, he informed me that it should be paid at the end of the four months named as the term for liquidating this claim.

On the Monday following, that is to say, the 3d of June, appeared in most of the newspapers a decree issued by the president, under the authority of the congress, whereby all payments to the creditors of the national treasury were suspended for the space of one year, with the exception of the claim commonly known as that of the "Laguna Seca," and of the diplomatic conventions.

As the claim arising out of the legation robbery was not specified in the list of exceptions to non-payment, I addressed a note to Señor Guzman on the subject, copy of which, together with a translation of his reply, I have the honor to enclose.

Not deeming the latter satisfactory, I again wrote to him on the 7th instant, in order to maintain the position I had taken, as well also as to prove to him that I was perfectly justified in demanding an explanation as to the omission of all mention of the legation robbery claim in the decree of the 29th ultimo, which I herewith enclose for your lordship's information. Copy of this note I likewise transmit, together with translation of his reply, in which he endeavors to establish by inference the principle that the actual perpetrators of the legation outrage are alone responsible for the wrong done on that occasion.

Seeing the necessity of at once checking this attempt to shift the responsibility from off the shoulders of the Mexican government, I again addressed Señor Guzman on the 14th instant, which note had the effect of producing a reply, showing considerable temper, and in which it is plainly asserted that they will do nothing that they are not strictly bound to perform by the agreement made with Mr. Mathew at the time of his recognition of the Juarez government.

The tone of this communication was, taking into consideration the general style of their official correspondence, anything but courteous, and it therefore called forth a reply from me couched in even stronger terms than my note of the 14th instant. I have the honor to enclose copy of this despatch, which has remained unanswered up to the present moment, owing, I suppose, to the resignation of the Guzman administration.

In order to avoid all confusion, I will treat of the "Laguna Seca" claim in a separate despatch, enclosing therein the correspondence which has taken place with reference to it between the Mexican government and her Majesty's legation.

Enclosure 1 in No. 10.

Sir C. Wyke to Señor Guzman.

MEXICO, *June* 3, 1861.

SIR: In the second article of a decree bearing the president's signature, and dated the 29th ultimo, but which was only brought to my notice this morning, I perceive that the payment of all claims against the national treasury, except those guaranteed by diplomatic conventions, and the one commonly known as that of the "Laguna Seca," is to be suspended for the period of twelve calendar months.

Without entering into the grave questions that may arise out of the practical operation of this decree, I will simply call your attention on the present occasion to the omission of all mention in it of the claim caused by robbery from her Majesty's legation of the sum of $660,000 belonging to the English bondholders.

The settlement of this claim, which so nearly affects the honor and credit of the Mexican government, cannot surely be intended to be postponed until after the expiration of the term mentioned in said decree for the suspension of payment.

Your excellency will greatly oblige me by clearing up all doubt on this subject, for the question involved is one of the greatest importance, as nearly affecting those good relations between our respective governments which it is our duty as well also, I am sure, our mutual desire to maintain.

I avail, &c.

C. LENNOX WYKE.

Enclosure 2 in No. 10.

Señor Guzman to Sir C. Wyke.

[Translation.]

MEXICO, *June* 6, 1861.

The undersigned, &c., has the honor of replying to the note of his excellency the British minister under date of the 3d instant, in which his excellency is pleased to ask for an explanation of the omission to include among the exceptions to the decree of the 29th of May last, upon the subject of a general suspension of treasury payments, the $660,000 belonging to the London bond holders, and stolen by the rebels from her Britannic Majesty's legation.

In doing so, the undersigned has the honor to inform Sir Charles Wyke that the suspension of payments does not and could not include the 660,000 in question, and consequently there was no necessity to make any exception in this case.

By the arrangement made in the matter of the $660,000 the Mexican government has assigned for their payment the property of the responsible parties, and only in the event of such property proving insufficient for the purpose did it engage itself to treat of and settle amicably the reimbursement of the whole sum. Inasmuch, then, as the money is not being paid by the national treasury, the suspension of payments referred to does not and cannot affect it.

Were, indeed, the treasury eventually called upon to make good any deficiency, the suspension of payments could never prove an obstacle in the way of its carrying out such an arrangement.

In offering these explanations, which he doubts not will appear satisfactory to Sir C. L. Wyke, the undersigned, &c.

LEON GUZMAN.

Enclosure 3 in No. 10.

Decree.

Le citoyen Benito Juarez, Président Intérimaire Constitutionnel des Etats-Uni Mexicains, à tous leurs habitants faisons savoir:

Que le Congrès Souverain de la nation a bien voulu décréter ce qui suit:—

ARTICLE 1. L'Exécutif est autorisé à mettre en cours forcé des titres ("escrituras") de capitaux nationaux imposés sur immeubles ruraux et urbains, en quantité suffisante pour lui procurer le 1,000,000 piastres auquel se réfère le Décret du 20 du courant, avec un escompte pouvant s'élever jusqu'au deux pour cent. mensuel.

ART. 2. Sont suspendus, pour une année, les paiements aux créanciers du Trésor national, à l'exception de celui de la conduite de Laguna Seca, et des conventions diplomatiques; pendant ce temps, le Congrès de l'Union rendra les lois de crédit public, de suppression des douanes intérieures et "alcabalas," de réforme de Tarif et d'établissement de la contribution directe.

ART. 3. L'Exécutif présentera une initiative d'arrangement pour la suspension des conventions diplomatiques, en rendant compte du résultat an Congrès pour son approbation.

ARTICULO 4. En dehors des exceptions qu'établit l'article 2 l'Exécutif ne pourra faire d'autres paiements que ceux d'administration.

Donné dans la Salle des Séances du Congrès de l'Union, le 29 Mai, 1861.

JOSE MARIA AGUIRRE,
Député Président.
GUILLERMO VALLE,
Député Secrétaire.
E. ROBLES GIL,
Député Secrétaire.

Pourquoi j'ordonne, &c.

PALAIS DU GOUVERNEMENT FÉDÉRAL À MEXICO, *le* 29 *Mai*, 1861.

Au Citoyen JOSÉ MARIA CASTAÑOS,
Ministre des Finances et du Crédit Public.

Enclosure 4 in No. 10.

Sir C. Wyke to Señor Guzman.

MEXICO, *June* 7, 1861.

SIR: I have the honor to acknowledge receipt of your excellency's communication bearing yesterday's date, in reply to my despatch of the 3d instant, in which I requested you to inform me why all mention of the legation robbery had been omitted from that article of the decree of the 29th ultimo which specifies the exceptions that are to be made to the suspension of payment of all claims against the national treasury for the space of twelve calendar months.

In the second paragraph of your above-named despatch, your excellency informs me that the decree of the 29th could not affect the case of the legation robbery, and that consequently there was no necessity to mention the claim arising therefrom in the list of exceptions to the general rule of a suspension of payments; and yet, in the concluding sentence of the third paragraph, you inform me that if the means adopted for the liquidation of this claim should prove insufficient, that then the national treasury would make up the deficit.

Seeing that this must eventually be the case, your excellency will easily understand why I was anxious to obtain the assurance which you have now given me, that the payment shall be made out of the national treasury, for the means you have hitherto adopted to repay the money stolen have not produced the desired result.

As I had the honor of stating to you in our recent conversation with reference to this matter, the prompt settlement of this claim equally affects the honor of both governments, an opinion in which you fully concurred, at the same time assuring me that before the departure of the next European mail you would be able to prove to me the honorable intentions of your government in doing all in their power to satisfy the just demands of that of her Majesty.

Fully trusting in that assurance, I will no longer dwell upon a subject the importance of which is well known to your excellency; indeed, I should not again have alluded to it, were it not for my desire to prevent the possibility of any misunderstanding arising with reference to it.

I avail, &c.

C. LENNOX WYKE.

Enclosure 5 in No. 10.

Señor Guzman to Sir C. Wyke.

[Translation.]

MEXICO, *June* 12, 1861.

With your excellency's note of the 3d instant, which the undersigned had the honor of receiving on the 4th, the question raised by your excellency about no exception having been made in the decree of the 29th for the robbery committed by the rebels at the British legation should have terminated. But, like your excellency, the undersigned is desirous of preventing any misunderstanding upon this point, and considers himself, therefore, under the necessity of explaining matters.

Now there is a palpable difference between asserting, as did the undersigned, that, in the event of the legation robbery not being covered by the property of the perpetrators thereof, the Mexican government were under an obligation to treat about and arrange the reimbursement of the moneys taken, and positively affirming that under similar circumstances the deficiency would have to be covered by the national treasury.

The undersigned hinted, indeed, at the possibility of such a contingency, but he never did, nor could he, say that it was a certainty; such a statement was out of the question, inasmuch as it is not possible to give a positive assurance about any matter which has to be treated of and settled, before the treatment and settlement shall have taken place.

With regard to the loyal intentions of the Mexican government, of which the

undersigned has assured your excellency—your excellency at the same time being pleased to acknowledge them—the undersigned can state that stringent orders have been given for expediting the judicial inquiries which have been instituted, so as to permit of the money stolen from the legation being repaid by whatever property of the responsible parties has been or may be embargoed.
The undersigned, &c.
LEON GUZMAN.

Enclosure 6 in No. 10.

Sir C. Wyke to Señor Guzman.

MEXICO, *June* 14, 1861.

SIR: Unwilling as I am to prolong a correspondence which I fear will lead to no practical result for some time to come, yet I cannot pass over in silence your excellency's note of the 12th instant, written in reply to mine of the 7th, without at once protesting against the doctrine therein attempted to be established by inference, to the effect that the actual perpetrators of the legation outrage are alone responsible, in their persons and property, for the wrong done on the 17th of November last.

Now, according to every principle of international law having reference to cases in any way similar to the one in point, her Majesty's government is perfectly justified in holding the State of Mexico (I use the word in its largest sense) responsible for the insult done to their legation, and the robbery of British property committed on that occasion, without in any way occupying themselves with the mere individuals who acquired so unfortunate a notoriety by a crime which it should have been the first duty of the present government to punish and atone for.

It was an express stipulation on the part of her Majesty government, before recognizing that of President Juarez, that this obligation should be complied with, and Mr. Mathew, late her Majesty's chargé d'affaires, was so fully convinced of the sincerity of his excellency's then cabinet in this matter, that he at once proffered the recognition he had to offer, without waiting to see the accomplishment of a duty which was binding, in honor as well as justice, on the parties who had inherited the advantages as well as the responsibilities of their predecessors.

If Mr. Mathew's confidence has been misplaced, that can in no way affect the rights of her Majesty's government in this matter, which, as represented by me, I now again insist on, as well for the principle involved as for the interests of the parties concerned.

When I had the honor of communicating verbally with your excellency on this subject, I had hoped that you had clearly understood the view taken of this question by her Majesty's government, and the more so as, according to those principles of international law now universally acknowledged, there is only one way of looking at it.

I avail, &c.

C. LENNOX WYKE.

Enclosure 7 in No. 10.

Señor Guzman to Sir C. Wyke.

[Translation.]

NATIONAL PALACE, *Mexico, June* 15, 1861.

The undersigned, &c., has the honor to address himself to his excellency Sir Charles Lennox Wyke, &c., and to inform him that, without insisting upon continuing the correspondence that his excellency was pleased to commence, and which, according to the declaration in his note of the 14th instant, he does not desire to prolong, the undersigned must take notice of the protest that his excellency makes "against the doctrine which is attempted to be established by inference, to the effect that the actual perpetrators of the legation outrage are alone responsible in their persons and property for the wrong done on the 17th of November last."

Without entering into a question which is irrelevant, and confining himself to his note of the 12th instant, the undersigned finds himself compelled to explain matters by observing that in his said note of the 12th no doctrines were laid down, but facts were recalled; facts consigned in an agreement concluded between the agent accredited by the English government and the minister of foreign affairs of the Mexican government.

The government of the undersigned is disposed to treat questions of right on the ground of justice and reason, but will not prejudice them, nor allow them to be prejudiced, by introducing them incidentally and out of their place, or contrary to established forms. Thus, then, and without its being understood that the doctrines noted down by his excellency are accepted or rejected, the undersigned has the honor to assure him that in the matter of the legation robbery he will be strictly bound by the agreement entered into by the representatives of both governments, without discussing whether it be good or bad, inasmuch as the opportunity of so doing has passed.

The undersigned hopes that his excellency will do him the justice to admit that he cannot occupy himself in this note with the other questions that his excellency introduces into his note, because, if upon this principle we were to go on mixing up questions indiscriminately, their solution would become more and more intricate and eventually impossible. If, on the contrary, we give to each one the independent place its nature requires, its solution will be as easy as it will be prompt.

The undersigned, &c.

LEON GUZMAN.

Enclosure 8 in No. 10.

Sir. C. Wyke to Señor Guzman.

MEXICO, *June* 18, 1861.

SIR: I have the honor to acknowledge receipt of you excellency's note of the 15th instant, a careful perusal of which leads me to infer that you think you have a right to complain of the tone of my communication of the 14th, to which it is a reply.

In that despatch I endeavored, in terms as clear and concise as possible, to put the question which has given rise to the present correspondence in its proper light, and in doing so I conceive I was fulfilling a duty imperative on me to perform, as no possible misunderstanding as to the views of her Majesty's government with reference to this matter must arise, as far as it lies in my power to prevent it.

On the 17th of November last an outrage was committed by the *de facto* government of Mexico on the legation of a friendly power, which was not only a disgrace to its perpetrators, but a direct act of felony on the subjects of that power; and this crime up to the present moment remains unatoned for.

It is not by the vain promises of an agreement, never yet acted up to, that such a scandal can either be forgotten or forgiven, and therefore I should be deceiving you were I not clearly to point out that her Majesty's government will hold the republic of Mexico and its government directly responsible for what is complained of.

In succeeding to the offices of your predecessors, you have inherited their responsibilities, and international law renders these as binding on you as if the last three years' civil war had never existed, and you had peaceably succeeded to the places of the former administration. The continuance of the good relations now existing between our respective governments renders the clear understanding of this principle absolutely necessary, and therefore no false delicacy shall prevent my insisting upon it, however ungracious it may appear on my part thus repeatedly urging it upon your excellency's attention.

You inform me that no doctrine was laid down in your excellency's note of the 12th, but that acts were therein recalled, "acts consigned in an agreement concluded between the accredited agents of our respective governments."

I have looked in vain in that communication for the mention of any act of reparation, and have found only promises of redress to the effect that the personal property of the individuals who committed the outrages shall, if condemned by the legal authorities, be held liable to indemnify the losses sustained by British subjects on the occasion referred to.

Now, in the first place, the legal process which you mention has, up to the present moment, resulted in absolutely nothing; and in the second, had it even produced the full effects which you desired, the pecuniary resources thus obtained would have proved quite inadequate to cover the loss sustained, as it is notorious that the value of the united property of all the parties concerned in the legation robbery would not exceed one-sixth part of the money stolen on that occasion.

Your excellency informs me that your government is disposed to treat questions of right on the grounds of justice and reason, but will not allow them to be prejudiced by being introduced incidentally and out of place, in violation of established form.

It is in complete accordance with the rule that you have thus laid down that I now again call upon your government to treat this grave question on the principles of justice and right, by adopting serious measures for repairing the wrong done instead of repeating promises which have hitherto led to nothing, and which never can lead, as already pointed out, to anything but a partial reparation of an insult and an injury to the nation which I have the honor to represent.

I see no use whatever in prolonging a correspondence on this subject, which must be treated according to the well-defined principles of international law, and not according to the partial wishes of one of the parties interested in it.

Having thus placed you in possession of the views of her Majesty's government with reference to this question, I avail, &c.,

C. LENNOX WYKE

No. 11.

Sir C. Wyke to Lord J. Russell.

MEXICO, *June* 24, 1861.

MY LORD: On the recognition of the Juarez government by Mr. Mathew it was agreed on with them that the remainder of the money due from the robbery of the "Laguna Seca" conducta should be repaid within four months from the date of such recognition.

The term having expired on the 11th instant, I then addressed a note to Señor Guzman on the subject, copy of which I have herewith the honor to enclose, together with the translation of his excellency's reply, by which your lordship will perceive that the difficulty of the situation and the penury of the treasury are urged as excuses for not fulfilling their engagement by the payment in specie of the debt owing. Such being the case he offers compensation in the shape of convents, farms recently belonging to the church, or even the national palace itself; and if these should not suffice, his excellency proposes that each individual claim shall be admitted to the full amount in payment of duties on any future importations made by any of the parties having such claims. Nothing can apparently be fairer than such a proposal, but to anybody actually on the spot its unsatisfactory nature is at once apparent for the following reasons:

Were this government to be upset and the church party to return to power, any such grants as those above named would at once be repudiated; and the remission of duties, which is the most plausible of the proposals made, might at any moment be set aside by a decree founded on the urgent necessities of the government for ready money to carry on their current expenses.

On my communicating a copy of Señor Guzman's note of the 12th, through Consul Glennie, to the parties interested, they, after due consideration, refused the offer made on these grounds; at the same time saying that what they wanted was ready money to meet the engagements which had devolved on them in consequence of the robbery of the "Laguna Seca" conducta, which refusal I conveyed to Señor Guzman in a note dated the 22d instant, copy of which I have now the honor to enclose.

Knowing the utter impossibility of obtaining ready money from a government which is actually penniless, I recommended the parties interested not to refuse listening to any further proposals that the Mexican commissioners might have to make them, and they, in compliance with my recommendation, have accordingly named two members of their body to represent them in the conferences now about to take place with reference to this matter. Thus stands the case at present, and I fear that in this instance also the interests of British subjects will again be sacrificed to the reckless folly and bad faith of this government.

I have, &c.

C. LENNOX WYKE

Enclosure 1 in No. 11.

Sir C. Wyke to Señor Guzman.

MEXICO, *June* 11, 1861.

SIR: A few days ago I had the honor of explaining to your excellency the present position of what is generally known as the "Laguna Seca" conducta claim, and as on that occasion I gathered from your excellency's remarks that the Mexican government considered itself bound to carry out in all sincerity the arrangements for repayment laid down in Señor Zarco's note to Mr. Mathew of the 12th of February last, I request your excellency to inform me, at your earliest convenience, to whom the sufferers by the above-named robbery are to apply, at the ports of Vera Cruz and Tampico, for the sum of money forcibly taken from them by Señor Degollado at Laguna Seca.

This sum, as I believe your excellency is aware, amounts, with interest, to $285,569 38, and I may further add that every British subject interested in the question is furnished with, and ready to produce, the documents necessary to prove the legitimacy of his particular reclamation.

I avail, &c.

C. LENNOX WYKE.

Enclosure 2 in No. 11.

Señor Guzman to Sir C. Wyke.

[Translation.]

MEXICO, *June* 12, 1861.

The undersigned, &c., has the honor to reply to the note of his excellency Sir C. Lennox Wyke, &c., under date of yesterday, and to inform him that the government of Mexico always has been and ever will be ready to fulfil its engagements with British subjects. This is more especially the case with respect to the funds seized by General Degollado at Laguna Seca, so much so that even when the government was compelled to make a general suspension of payments care was taken not to include therein the funds in question.

The government has spared no effort to get together sufficient moneys for meeting the debt, the payment of which, with the fullest intention of acting up to their engagements, they had fixed for the 11th instant. The difficulties, however, of the moment, combined with the penury of the treasury—facts which are now publicly notorious, and have doubtless come to the knowledge of your excellency—have rendered of no avail the efforts of government, and frustrated their best intentions; still good security has been given, and no small portion of the Laguna Seca credits taken as cash-payments.

Thus, then, the undersigned is under the painful necessity of informing your excellency that it will be quite impossible for the government to fulfil, at the specified time, their engagements in the matter of Laguna Seca, and they are consequently placed in the painful position of having to enter into some fresh arrangement with the parties interested therein.

If the financial crisis was of less import, if the government could count upon their actual resources being sufficient to cover even a portion of their most pressing liabilities, they would assign part of those resources for the settlement of the above preferential claim. Owing, however, to the extreme scarcity of money, and to the certainty that for the moment cash-payments are quite out of the question, they prefer avowing honestly their actual position to hazarding some new promise, which they would find themselves under the painful necessity of breaking.

The government recognizes the just rights of the creditors, and are resolved upon making every possible sacrifice in order to satisfy them. Government can dispose of convents and other valuable property. These, and even the national palace, are at the creditors' disposal; they may take their choice, and whatever they select shall at once be consigned to them at an equitable and conventional price.

These same creditors, moreover, can count upon their credits being admitted as cash in any transactions, whether on account of duties, or otherwise, which they may have with government.

THE PRESENT CONDITION OF MEXICO.   259

In order satisfactorily to arrange their business, Mr. Deputy Mata and Señor Zarco have been appointed commissioners to treat with the parties interested, who, on their part, may likewise talk over the matter with those gentlemen, and make whatever propositions they may deem suitable, always remembering that the government will leave nothing undone to bring the question at issue to an amicable and successful termination.

The undersigned, &c.

LEON GUZMAN.

Enclosure 3 in No. 11.

Sir C. Wyke to Señor Guzman.

MEXICO, *June* 22, 1861.

SIR: On the receipt of your excellency's note of the 12th instant I communicated a copy of it to those persons directly interested in the question to which it referred.

It was only yesterday that I was made acquainted with their views on the subject, which I will now put you in possession of as briefly as possible. They naturally cannot accept the plea of poverty put forward to excuse the non-payment of so sacred an obligation as that contracted by the Mexican government with her Majesty's late chargé d'affaires on the occasion of that government receiving the formal recognition of Great Britain, when the repayment within the space of four months of the money belonging to British subjects that had been stolen from the conducta of the Laguna Seca was one of the express conditions on which that recognition depended. Since that engagement was entered into several millions of hard dollars have passed through the hands of the Mexican government, so that they cannot, with anything like reason, plead their poverty as an excuse for not having provided the funds necessary to meet the demand now brought against them.

It is clear that as specie was stolen money should be repaid, for it is with currency alone, or good bills to the same amount, that the engagements of the sufferers in this affair can be duly met. Farms, convents, or even the national palace itself, may be valuable property in its way, and yet not at all suit the wants of those who, as in the present instance, would not be able to convert it into ready money for their immediate necessities.

For these reasons the parties interested cannot accept the offer of indemnification made to them in your excellency's letter to me above mentioned, and must hold the Mexican government responsible for all loss and prejudice accruing to them through that government failing to repay the money owing within the time specified.

As, however, it would not be courteous absolutely to refuse the offer made in your excellency's letter of the 12th, I have recommended the parties interested to name two amongst their number to wait on the commissioners appointed by your excellency, in order to learn from those gentlemen what further steps the Mexican government intends taking with a view of satisfying this pending claim against them.

I have just learned that Mr. Whitehead and Mr. Watson have been appointed by the English merchants to confer with your commissioners, Don José M. Mata and Don Francisco Zarco, and I trust that, in the conferences about to be held between them, some means may be found for protecting the interests, and at the same time satisfying the just demands, of those persons in whose name I have had the honor to address you.

I avail, &c.

C. LENNOX WYKE.

No. 12.

Sir C. Wyke to Lord J. Russell.

[Extract.]

MEXICO, *June* 25, 1861.

A perusal of my preceding despatches and their enclosures will prove to your lordship that no further reliance can be placed on the promises or even the formal engagements of the Mexican government.

If the old church party succeeds in driving from power the present ultra liberal administration, we shall then be even still worse off, as will be seen by the enclosed copy of a decree recently sent to me by ex-President Zuloaga, who, with his lieutenant, Marquez, is at the head of a considerable armed force, which, after twice defeating the government troops, is at this very moment attacking the gates of the city of Mexico.

It will thus be seen that, with the contending parties, we have not a chance of obtaining justice from either as long as we confine ourselves to remonstrating instead of employing coercion.

Under such circumstances it appears to me that only two courses are open to us, viz: either to withdraw the mission altogether from a country where its dignity is compromised, and where, consequently, it has become useless, or else to support its influence by such means as will compel obedience to our just demands, and obtain that redress for the wrongs and grievances of British subjects which they are lawfully entitled to claim.

There is but one way of obtaining such redress, and that is by employing her Majesty's naval forces simultaneously at the ports on both coasts of this republic, when the moral effect produced would equal the material pressure, and insure prompt compliance with any conditions which we might choose to impose.

Captain Aldham, who during the last three years has gained a very clear insight into the Mexican character, and the manner of evading their engagements so peculiar to their officials, is of opinion that the time for leniency is past, and that if we mean to protect the lives and properties of British subjects coercive measures must now be employed.

Before he left the station I consulted with him upon the best means of using such coercion should it become inevitable, and I will now convey his views to your lordship in as few words as possible.

He thinks that a blockade is not advisable, on account of the large force that would be required for that purpose on so extensive a line of coast, to say nothing of the commercial difficulties to which it would give rise, besides the fact that by so blockading we should actually be robbing ourselves of the percentage on the duties levied at Vera Cruz and Tampico.

This plan, then, presenting so many objections, Captain Aldham is of opinion that the next best thing to be done is to take possession of the custom-houses of Vera Cruz, Tampico, and Matamoros, on the Atlantic; and of either Acapulco, Mazatlan, or San Blas, on the Pacific; to lower the duties on all goods landed at those places; and to pay ourselves by the percentage to which we are entitled, but which we now never obtain, owing to the rascality of the Mexican authorities, who either suspend payment altogether, or only give us one-fifth of what we ought to receive. Reducing the tariff would naturally largely increase the importations, and thus enable us rapidly to pay off long arrears of what is now owing to us, and which we shall never obtain without some measure of this sort being adopted.

It may be urged against this plan, that the Mexican government would place a line of interior custom-houses for levying other duties, and thus partially defeat the object we have in view. But this objection is easily set aside by anybody really knowing the country, as the badly paid and venal officers serving on this second line would not be able to resist the temptations which the importers at the ports who had paid only a low entrance duty would know how to throw in their way; besides, the Mexican traders themselves would not allow such an impost to be levied, and would, for their own interests, force the goods into the interior, when, by their sale, they would realize large profits.

In order to take and hold these places, Captain Aldham considers that a squadron of from six to ten vessels-of-war should be employed; some of these should be of the frigate class, and others gunboats drawing not more than from seven to eight feet of water.

Vera Cruz and Tampico are the most important places on the Atlantic, owing to their trade and the specie shipped there, and these are the only places on either coast which would, in Captain Aldham's opinion, require any force to take possession of. Two frigates at the anchorage, and a garrison of 300 men for the Castle of San Juan de Ulloa, would be sufficient to hold the former town, it being completely commanded by the castle which is roomy and airy, and not unfitted, Captain Aldham says, for a British garrison.

Tampico lies some seven miles up the river, which has seldom more than six to ten feet of water on the bar. There would be no difficulty in taking the place, and a garrison of from 100 to 200 men, with one or two gunboats, he thinks enough to hold it.

On the Pacific coast, Acapulco is probably the most important place for trade; Mazatlan comes next, and then San Blas.

The former has a good anchorage, but its climate is unhealthy. Mazatlan could easily be garrisoned by a small force, and there is high ground overlooking the town already fortified.

San Blas is an open roadstead, and unsafe in the rainy season; it is of importance from its trade and the specie shipped there.

For the object we have in view, I think taking one or two of these places quite sufficient, and the naval officer in command on that coast could use his discretion as to which of them he should occupy.

Should her Majesty's government adopt a course which I am convinced will prevent all future difficulties with Mexico, the sooner measures are taken for carrying this plan into execution the better, for the sake of putting a stop to an accumulation of grievances and claims which will go on increasing until this government is taught that it cannot set every principle of justice at defiance with impunity.

The French have only a small debt of $190,000 to recover, which is being chiefly paid off by 25 per cent. of the import duties levied at Vera Cruz on cargoes brought in French ships. The Spanish claim 8 per cent. on all import duties for some claim of theirs which is in suspense, and therefore the interest thereon is not paid. Besides this they have what is known as the Padre Moran claim of $825,000, which receives about a sixth of the sum assigned to the British convention.

I mention these obligations to foreign governments because they would gladly see our occupation of these ports, from a knowledge that, under our administration, justice would be awarded to all, and that the money thus collected would be fairly distributed amongst the various claimants.

From the moment that we show our determination no longer to suffer British subjects to be robbed and murdered with impunity we shall be respected, and every rational Mexican will approve of a measure which they themselves are the first to say is necessary, in order to put a stop to the excesses daily and hourly committed under a government as corrupt as it is powerless to maintain order, or cause its own laws to be executed.

Enclosure in No. 12.

Decree.

[Translation.]

Felix Zuloaga, general of brigade and president *ad interim* of the Mexican republic, to its inhabitants. Be it known—
That in virtue of the full powers with which I am invested, I have been pleased to decree the following:

ARTICLE 1. The party in Mexico that at present assumes the title of government, not possessing any character of legality, all its acts are null and void, and for the same reason the government of Tacubaya does not recognize any engagements that may be entered into with the government that has intruded itself into power.

ART. 2. Every individual who shall lend to the faction denominated "Constitutional" any sort of help, whether as a loan or in any other manner, shall pay afterwards to the government of Tacubaya double the quantity that he may have furnished, and will remain subject to the penalties which he may have incurred, as settled by the law, as an enemy of his country.

ART. 3. All foreigners, of whatever nationality they may be, are included in the preceding articles.

Given at headquarters, at Tepeji del Rio, this 4th of June, 1861.

FELIX ZULOAGA.

Don ANTONIO ANDRADE,
   Under Secretary of State charged with the Department.

I have the honor to communicate the above to your excellency for your information, and for the due fulfilment of the same.

God and order!

J. ANTO. ANDRADE.

TEPEJI DEL RIO, *June* 4, 1861.

No. 13.

Sir C. Wyke to Lord J. Russell.

MEXICO, *June* 27, 1861.

MY LORD: Although the enclosed extract from this day's "Mexican Extraordinary" gives an account of the outrages perpetrated on British subjects which is not accurate in all its details, I still think it worthy of your lordship's notice, as showing at a glance the amount of wrong done, which still remains to be atoned for.

The list is unfortunately by no means complete, but I forward it as it is, in order that your lordship may form an idea of the indignation felt by the English community in Mexico at being subjected to such brutality, without ever obtaining redress from the successive governments of this republic, each of which invariably asserts that it is not responsible for the acts of its predecessor.

I have, &c.

C. LENNOX WYKE.

Enclosure in No. 13.

Extract from the "Mexican Extraordinary" of June 27, 1861.

FOREIGN INTERESTS IN MEXICO.—No. 2.

British claims of the small and most distressing class.

On the 25th of last month we referred at some length to the condition of British interests in Mexico. We now resume the subject, and shall notice on this occasion a portion of the most flagrant outrages which have been perpetrated upon British residents, leaving for another occasion the publication of more, and our own lengthened remarks. The robbery of the legation and the various "conductas" are subjects fresh in the memory of every one, and as these outrages affect the interests of the wealthy and influential, they are likely to absorb that attention which should, we submit, be shared by the humbler sufferer. Our mission is to lay facts before the world and thus to excite action, and it little matters whether it be from motives of duty or from shame, so long as our proper protectors are made to move. In continuation we give a brief notice of some of the objects of our present article:

Mr. Bodmer's case.—This gentleman, who was her Majesty's vice-consul at Tasco, was shot in the balcony of his house whilst endeavoring to save an unfortunate Mexican from ill-treatment at the hands of some of Vicario's troops, who had made a sudden irruption into the town. Mr. Bodmer was a man universally respected; upon three several occasions had he saved the city of Tasco from being sacked by one or other of the contending parties. He held a very lucrative appointment in the mine of the Pedregal, and has left a widow and three children, totally unprovided for.

Mr. Burnand's case.—This gentleman was the first to establish a manufactory of glass in this country.
In the year 1852 he erected on some property, situated about five leagues from the city of Mexico, a manufactory on a very considerable scale, and had just got it into working order, when the whole of the premises were arbitrarily taken possession of by Santa Anna, and it was not until the end of 1856, when Comonfort came to the head of affairs, that the property was restored to him, but in so dilapidated and ruined a condition that it was two years before he could place the factory in a proper state to resume operations. In March 1860 the factory was attacked by a portion of the liberal forces and sacked, and on the 2d of April of the same year another body of men belonging to the same party entered the premises at night, attacked Mr. Burnand, inflicted on him sixteen sabre cuts, broke three of his ribs, left him for dead, and effectually destroyed all that had been spared by their predecessors. The life of Mr. Burnand was for a long time despaired of, his left arm had to be amputated, and he is now a man wreck. The shock was so great that his poor wife lost her senses, and his eldest daughter has now since been subject to epileptic fits. From being a man of considerable property, Mr. Burnand has been reduced almost to a state of starvation. Maimed, mutilated, and reduced in health, it is no longer in his power by his own exertion to provide for his unfortunate family, and all he has to look to is the reparation that may be exacted from the Mexican nation for these repeated and fearful outrages. Should this case fall under the observation of her Majesty's ministers, as we trust it will, surely immediate steps will be taken to relieve this gentleman and his family from the utter state of destitution into which they have been plunged.

Dr. Duval's case.—Dr. Duval was an Englishman, born at Kensington, near London. When the constitutional forces entered Tacubaya, on the 22d of March,

1859, he was at the head of the medical staff, a position he retained until the day of his death. On the 11th of April, Marquez entered Tacubaya at the head of the reactionary forces, and, in taking possession of the hospital of San Diego, promised most solemnly that the lives of the sick and wounded, as well as those of the medical men, were safe. At half-past 7 o'clock of the same evening, however, in spite of this assurance, and in violation of the ordinary laws of civilized warfare, Dr. Duval, in company with seven other medical men, was taken out and shot. He was not allowed to communicate with any of his countrymen, and it was not until the following morning that this monstrous murder became generally known. Notwithstanding the most strenuous efforts made by the Miramon government, with the connivance of Mr. Otway, to justify this horrid proceeding, so damning was the evidence that the British government could do no otherwise than insist upon some pecuniary compensation for the widow and child of their murdered citizen.

The amount fixed was $25,000, but no steps were taken to exact this sum from the murderers during their continuance in power, nor has the same, as far as we can learn, been paid.

Mr. Newall's case.—Mr. Newall, an inhabitant of Zacatecas, a member of one of the oldest and most respected firms in the country, as agent for Mr. Davis, of San Luis Potosi, received the sum of $15,950, and gave the usual receipt. This receipt fell into the hands of Marquez, who sent for Mr. Newall, and required of him, at once, to hand over the money. Mr. Newall replied that it was impossible for him to do so, as the money was not his. The general then called in a guard and said, "Take this man, put him in 'capilla,' (the place assigned to criminals for the few hours previous to their execution,) and without further orders shoot him to-morrow morning before six o'clock." Mr. Newall was marched off, thrown into "capilla," and would, no doubt, have been shot, had not some of his friends raised the money amongst themselves, and paying it into the hands of Marquez, obtained his release.

The English government showed their appreciation of the conduct of a citizen, who, at the risk of his life, refused to betray a trust reposed in him by another, by awarding him the very magnificent sum of £500, the estimated value of a British merchant's life in Mexico.

Mr. Pitman's case.—Mr. Pitman, of the firm of Simpson & Pitman, of San Luis Potosi, was imprisoned and made to pay the sum of $5,100, under the following circumstances:

When the constitutional forces were in possession of San Luis, Mr. Pitman, in the usual course of business, upon the admission of goods, paid the duties to the properly constituted authorities. Subsequently Miramon, the leader of the church faction, took possession of the town, and he demanded the payment over again of the same duties. Mr. Pitman, for refusing this exaction, was thrown into prison, and would have been marched off as a common soldier, had he not, to avoid the latter alternative, paid the amount.

Mr. Davis's case.—This gentleman, in June, 1858, was assessed at $2,000 in a forced loan imposed upon the merchants of San Luis Potosi by General Miramon. This amount he refused to pay, as contrary to existing treaties. He was seized by Miramon, thrown into prison, subsequently marched off as a common soldier with the troops sent against the opposite faction, and only rescued by a friend who paid the $2,000, and obtained his release.

Cases of Messrs. Whitehead and Potts.—These gentlemen were both banished from the country for expressing their horror at the atrocities that followed the massacre at Tacubaya, on the 11th April, 1859.

Application was made to Mr. Otway in writing, pointing out to him the imminent peril to which Englishmen were exposed if abandoned to the unbridled and savage will of Miramon and Marquez, who, without even a form of trial, slaughtered so many innocent victims at Tacubaya, and in cold blood, rather more than two years ago. Amongst the murdered men was Dr. Duval, an English surgeon, who, with other medical men, was dragged from the bedside of the wounded, while amputating the shattered limbs and stanching the gushing arteries of numbers of poor creatures, who, from want of assistance, perished during that memorable and dreadful night. Lamentation brought them no aid. Marquez and Miramon had murdered the only ones who could give them comfort, and they bled to death!

Another English victim was, at the same time, waiting the moment of execution. George Selly, a peaceable resident of Tacubaya, was seized and forced from his house, and, as poor Dr. Duval, without trial or inquiry, was taken out to be shot, but was miraculously saved by the timely interference of a Mexican officer, who met him on his way to the place of execution.

As has been already mentioned, a brief statement of these horrors, signed by almost every Englishman here, was laid before Mr. Otway, imploring him to use his influence to check these cruelties, and asking protection for Englishmen from the grasp of these sanguinary men; and, strange as it may seem, this document, by means better known than explained, made its appearance in the palace, where it was translated and published in pamphlet form, and the Miramon government accused the signers of having published it. The consequence of this was that orders were issued for the immediate banishment of five of those whose signatures appeared on the petition, Messrs. Potts and Whitehead being of the number.

Remonstrances and repeated denials on their part to Mr. Otway of all knowledge or complicity in the affair were unavailing; so, to satisfy the wishes and assist a zealous partisan in carrying out his treacherous designs against those he was paid to protect, the order was enforced, and these gentlemen left the country and laid their cases before Lord John Russell, who, on becoming acquainted with the outrage, demanded the withdrawal of the passports and fair indemnities.

The amounts of these reclamations have been fixed in both cases in accordance with instructions from home, and demands have been made upon the Mexican government, and even payment promised; but, as these demands have not been insisted upon, the subject has remained where it was a year ago, whilst millions of dollars have been allowed to find their way into the pockets of people to whom the nation owed nothing. Those whose interests have been almost ruined by violence and plunder meet with but indifference and neglect.

Mr. Jones's claim.—In the year 1826 Mr. R. Lancaster Jones was secretary to her Britannic Majesty's consul general in Mexico. On the solicitation of the governor of the State of Jalisco, and according to the popular spirit of the day in England, he went to Guadalajara and established a school on the Lancasterian system. The Mexican government, permanently to secure his services, guaranteed him a fixed salary of $2,000 a year. From 1826 to 1834 this salary was paid, but in the latter year Mr. Jones was turned out of his employment without any pretext and left destitute.

The case was brought under the notice of the British legation, and in the year 1852 an arrangement was come to by which the Mexican government acknowledged the justice of the case and their indebtedness to Mr. Jones in $28,000. Not one dollar of this sum was ever paid to Mr. Jones, who died some years back in very distressed circumstances. The amount, with interest, is now claimed by the widow and children.

A more cruel case it is almost impossible to conceive. A man holding an honorable and lucrative employment was, from purely philanthropic motives, induced to give it up, upon the promise of an annuity of $2,000 a year. After the interval of eight years the annuity is withheld, and the man and his family are left in absolute want. The robbery of a "conducta" may be a more striking event, and may more internally affect the interests of British merchants, but can it be a comparison, in point of hardship, with the case of Mr. Jones? And yet, forsooth, this injured man and his family have been allowed to drag through twenty-six years of suffering, and up to the present moment no steps have been taken by our government to compel the payment of a sum which the Mexican government, in a settlement with her Majesty's legation, have themselves admitted to be due.

George Selly.—Was residing in Tacubaya at the time the constitutional forces retired on the 11th April, 1859. About 12 o'clock on that day, whilst at breakfast with his wife and child, was seized in his own house and conducted to San Diego, and there confined with Duval and the other victims of the famed massacre, whose fate he providentially escaped. He was kept there until the middle of the next day, and then led in triumph, at the head of the prisoners, through the streets of Mexico; was then taken to the citadel, locked up in a filthy dungeon, and there kept until the following day, when he was led out, in company with two others, and marched to Tacubaya to be shot, and providentially saved by the interference of a Mexican general, who met him on his way and who prevailed upon the officer in command to defer the execution, which gave time for the interference of Mr. Otway to take steps.

The pretext for this barbarous treatment was that George Selly had mixed himself up with the liberal party; this was disproved by the evidence of twenty-two of the most respectable inhabitants of Tacubaya, and the utmost that could be laid to his charge was, that during the continuance of the liberal forces in Tacubaya, he, as a means of livelihood, supplied the mess of four of the officers. After much delay, from the unrighteous opposition of Mr. Otway, his government, more than a year back, declared that "Selly's entire innocence had been amply vindicated, and had established his claim to be compensated for the indignities to which he has been exposed." For this fearful outrage a sum of $2,500 has, it is said, been asked as compensation, but no steps taken to enforce payment. Selly is a poor man.

The case of Mr. Lynch.—On the 11th June, 1858, General Miramon, commanding the reactionary forces at San Luis Potosi, imposed a forced loan upon the merchants of that town. Mr. Pitman, an English merchant residing in that town, was assessed at $10,000, and required to pay the amount before night of the same day (11th June) on pain of imprisonment. The assessment in this case appears to have been excessive, as firms possessing larger capitals had been assessed in much smaller sums. Mr. Pitman called upon the general to remonstrate with him upon these arbitrary proceedings, but was unable to see him. He was, however, informed by others that it was Miramon's determination to carry out the loan, and that all who refused to pay, natives or foreigners, would be marched off as common soldiers with the troops about to leave that night. Mr. Pitman then applied to Mr. Chabot, the English consul, but all that gentleman's exertions on his behalf proved unavailing.

Mr. Pitman and his lady, fearing personal violence, took up their residence in Mr. Chabot's house, leaving his establishment in charge of Mr. Lynch, his confidential clerk, never for one moment supposing that any outrage would be committed against this latter gentleman. At six o'clock, however, of the following morning, the house was entered by order of Miramon. Mr. Lynch was taken to prison, and would have been marched off as a common soldier, had not Mr. Pitman requested Mr. Chabot to pay $6,000, the amount to which the assessment had been reduced, and so obtained his release.

Case of Mr. R. J. Perry.—On the 18th October, 1858, this gentleman was arbitrarily arrested and thrown into prison by General Zuloaga, then president of the capital, and kept in close confinement for several days, without being allowed to communicate with his consul, friends, or counsel. He was detained in prison and under arrest twenty-eight days, without being brought to trial, or any charge or accusation being made against him; without being consigned to any judge, or any declaration taken from him, and even without being informed of the cause of his arrest; and, finally, he was expelled the country at a few hours' notice, without being accused of any crime or misdemeanor.

The consequence was, that he was suddenly obliged to close, settle, and wind up, at any sacrifice, or abandon all his accounts and business transactions to a considerable magnitude he had pending in this country after a continued residence in it for nearly eighteen years. Those outrageous proceedings have caused his total ruin, and he now finds himself, after having spent the best years of his life in acquiring, by his honest industry, comparative affluence, reduced to want and ruin.

On his arrival in England he applied to the British government for protection and redress, and after overcoming innumerable difficulties, has lately returned to this country under authority and at the suggestion of the foreign office, with the view of prosecuting his claim there, but as yet has done so without any result.

The alleged pretext for his prosecution was his supposed sympathy with the party now in power; the real motive or cause, as is well known here, being private matters of too delicate a nature to be made the subject of our comment.

Mr. Worrall's case.—Mr. Worrall was assessed for a forced loan, and on applying at the legation for advice, was shown by Mr. Otway a despatch from Lord Malmesbury, which recommends British subjects to pay such forced loans under protest and on compulsion. In consequence of having made this protest, Mr. Worrall was arrested a few days afterwards in the public streets of Mexico, by Lagarde, and sent off to Vera Cruz next morning, having thus to abandon heavy private interests in this country.

On submitting his claim for indemnity at the foreign office, Lord Malmesbury wrote him stating "that there was no justification for the conduct of the Mexican government in your case, and that it was his lordship's intention to instruct her Majesty's minister in Mexico to require that you shall be properly compensated for the treatment you have undergone and the losses you have sustained."

Although a convention was signed by Mr. Otway in March, 1859, assigning Mr. Worrall an indemnity, and although this government even directed Mr. Worrall, through the foreign office, to apply to Messrs. Barings for its amount, yet no money was remitted, and up to the present moment not a dollar has been paid.

Very little encouragement is given to British subjects standing up for treaty rights if the present case is a fair instance of home protection.

Claim of Messrs. Bates, Jamison & Co.—This claim is now represented by Messrs. Bates, Barton & Co., of the city of Mexico, and is for a sum of $8,815 02, the unpaid balance of a government order for $98,000 for import duties illegally exacted. The interest has been only calculated up to the month of April, 1859.

Mr. Charles B. Lambley.—Plunder of his house, on two separate occasions, by soldiers under the command of chiefs of the constitutional party.

Mr. Thomas Gillow.—Repeated embargoes of wagons, mules, and horses for the transport of cannon and military stores. As this claimant farms a very considerable estate, it is unnecessary to point out how serious must have been all consequential damages, in addition to those of the mere embargo.

Mr. John Innes.—Plunder of his store at Ejutla, in the department of Oajaca, by soldiers of the central government party, under the command of Cobos. There are a number more claims of the same character preferred by Englishmen resident in Oajaca, of which we have not yet received full details.

Mr. Daniel Owen.—Plunder of his goods by soldiers of the central government, under the command of General Echeagaray, on the 17th April, 1858.

Mr. John Sumner.—Plunder of his house at Tlalpam, on the 17th October

1858, by a party of soldiers under the command of the constitutional chief, Don Ignacio Delgado.

Mr. Thomas Fuller.—Embargo by General Pueblita in November, 1856, of wagons, mules, and effects belonging to Mr. Fuller's extensive carrying establishment, thereby disabling him from fulfilling a contract with the Real del Monte Mining Company for carrying ore from that company's mines at Pachuca to their ore depot at Real del Monte. The loss of this contract, in itself a most profitable one, is attested by the certificate of the director of the Real del Monte Company. It entailed upon Mr. Fuller very heavy additional expenses, as he had to maintain upwards of one hundred pack-mules without work. Subsequently he was compelled to break up a very profitable carrying business, and sell the mules he was unable to maintain, in consequence of the loss of his contract, for a little more than half their original cost. In fact, this cruel outrage created such an embarrassment in the affairs of Mr. Fuller as to bring him to the verge of ruin, from which he has not recovered, and for which his claim will be very insufficient compensation.

Mr. William Hooper.—Plunder of effects, consisting of wearing apparel, books, papers, accounts, and mathematical and other scientific instruments, by a body of revolutionary troops during the sacking of the city of Culiacan, department of Sinaloa, in the month of March, 1852, as attested by the judge of that city, Don Eustaquio Buelua, in a judicial document under date of 10th March, 1856.

Mr. Elliot Turnbull.—This claim originated in the forcible entry of a large body of troops into Turnbull's hacienda, about ten miles from the city of Puebla, in the month of May, 1858, and of robberies and destruction of property committed by them. Mr Turnbull was especially recommended by her Majesty's ministers to obtain the necessary proofs. These proofs are now in his possession, and consist of sworn declarations of several witnesses to the act, taken before the judge of the district.

Extra duties illegally exacted.

Messrs. Graham, Geaves & Co.	$10,623 74
Messrs. Bates, Barton & Co.	4,929 87
Messrs. Watermeyer, Kauffman & Co.	5,545 22
Messrs. J. J. Schmidt & Co.	5,246 82

These claims originated in the following manner: By a sudden and unexpected decree issued by the general government on the 31st of May, 1858, an extra 10 per cent. "internation" duty, and 20 per cent. import duty, were imposed on all goods coming from Vera Cruz. This imposition, contrary to the express stipulations of the existing tariff, was at once most energetically protested against by her Majesty's minister. The decree, although not repealed, was never again acted upon by the Mexican government—a clear admission of its illegality.

The number of instances in which foreign governments have demanded and compelled restitution of sums thus illegally exacted are too well known to require enumeration, and it is unnecessary for us to point out how impossible it would be to carry out successfully any commercial transactions under a system of tariff at any moment admitting of sudden and arbitrary changes by the Mexican government, or the illegality of their act: the sums exacted during the temporary operation of the decree still remain unpaid.

These sums, requiring no further proof or verification than the production of custom-house receipts, ought, we submit, to be considered as admitted claims.

Matamoros Fire Claim.—This is a claim for goods destroyed by fire at Matamoros in October, 1851. The goods were warehoused in a house occupied by the government forces under General Avalos. The town was suddenly attacked by Carbajal, at the head of the rebel forces. The block of houses in which the goods were placed formed a prominent point in the line of defence, and was fortified and held by a portion of the government troops. It was subsequently set fire to by the rebels, and the whole of the goods were destroyed. No notice was given by General Avalos of his intention to fortify the block, nor was any time given or opportunity afforded for the removal of the goods. A certificate of General Avalos proves the occupation and fortification of the premises for the purposes of defence, and their destruction by fire.

No valid objection has ever been raised by the Mexican government to this claim, and their liability to make good the losses inflicted upon the losers, Messrs. Bates, Jamison & Co., under such circumstances, cannot admit of a doubt. The principle has been so clearly laid down in numberless cases, that to hold a different doctrine would be subversive of the very first principles of international law. To admit of a different principle in a country like Mexico, ever torn by internecine strife, would be to place the property of neutrals unconditionally at the mercy of military chiefs. The decree issued by President Juarez upon the occasion of the bombardment of Vera Cruz by General Miramon, in the month of April last year, providing for the indemnification of neutrals whose property had suffered by that bombardment, places the question beyond dispute. The subject has been frequently urged upon the consideration of the Mexican government, but hitherto without results.

The claim now put forward by Messrs. Bates, Barton & Co., as successors to Bates, Jamison & Co., is for—

226 packages of merchandise destroyed under the circumstances above detailed, of the value of	$37,144 04
And interest, at 6 per cent., to April, 1859..................	20,389 07
Total..	57,524 11

The foregoing list of claims against the Mexican nation, although it does not contain all, presents such a frightful catalogue of murder, spoliation, and robbery, that, except it was vouched for on the most solemn and truest grounds, would be scarcely credited; scarcely credited, indeed, as having happened in a so-called civilized country against the subjects of a friendly nation; and yet this catalogue of outrage is still very incomplete, for many individuals, such as Staines, Egerton, Gibson, and others, have lost their lives by attacks in the streets, in their dwelling-houses, and on the public roads.

Justice has, indeed, here iron hands and leaden feet, but they are never lifted in favor of the defenceless foreigner; some little show of inquiry, a constant and incessant persecution of witnesses, and never-ending expenses and outlay to, perhaps, some spirited prosecutor, ending in a mockery of investigation and an impunity for crime, are generally the utmost attained.

Who can ever tell of the bitter dying anguish of these neglected victims, and how in their awful moments of desertion the hopeless conviction haunted them that no inquiry would be made of their fate, and no punishment fall on their assassins?

And who can tell what desolation the love of fathers, sons, and brothers may have caused in some far-away homestead; how, instead of gladdening news, they have found that the angel of desolation has passed by and rendered their hearths desolate!

In the name of humanity outraged we call for energy in redress against this wholesale trampling on treaties and international laws, and exactions from a country that professes to belong to the family of nations, a regard to the ordinary tenets of humanity, and a concordance with the creed of civilization.

No. 14.

Sir C. Wyke to Lord J. Russell.

[Extract.]

MEXICO, *June* 28, 1861.

The past month has been fertile in events not only tragic in themselves, but terrible also from affording convincing proof of the degradation to which this unfortunate republic has been reduced by the vindictive spirit of contending factions.

My correspondence by last mail informed your lordship that the church party was still in arms, led by ex-President Zuloaga and his lieutenant general, Marquez, who, at the head of between 2,000 and 3,000 men, were enabled not only to hold their ground, but actually to drive the government troops before them, and ravage the whole valley of Mexico.

On the 2d instant news reached this city that Marquez had seized and shot Señor Ocampo, one of the leading men of the liberal party, and recently their minister for foreign affairs, who for the moment had retired from public life, and was living quietly on his estate in the country. This intelligence caused the greatest excitement here, and gave rise to threats of vengeance against those unfortunate members of the church party who were confined in the prisons of this city.

The feeling of hatred against them became so strong that their relatives flocked to the different legations and implored our intercession with the government to protect the lives of the prisoners against the fury of the rabble. The French minister, as doyen of the diplomatic corps, called a meeting of the different foreign agents resident here, when it was unanimously agreed that we should seek an interview with the president, calling on him in the name of humanity to save these unfortunate persons, and at the same time to vindicate the authority of his government against the attempts of that violent party in the State which meditated the commission of such a crime.

His excellency received us very graciously, and stated that we need not be under the least anxiety, as he had already given orders for the guards to be doubled at the different prisons, besides adopting other measures to frustrate the evil intentions of those who wished thus to disgrace themselves and the country to which they belonged.

The president kept his word, for that very night when the rabble rushed to the prisons they were kept in check by the military, and obliged to disperse without effecting their object.

This interview took place on the 4th instant, and there were present at it, besides the president and the secretary of state for foreign affairs, the ministers of France, England, Prussia, the United States, and the chargé d'affaires of Ecuador.

In the congress stormy debates followed, and General Degollado, another distinguished member of the liberal party, asked for a command in order to pursue Marquez, and revenge the death of his former colleague. His request was granted in the midst of the greatest enthusiasm, and in a few days he marched at the head of a division towards Toluco in pursuit of the enemy. Whilst reconnoitring with a small party on the 16th instant, he was surprised by General Galvez, his party was dispersed and cut to pieces, and he himself killed.

The news of this event on reaching Mexico only added fuel to the fire, and General Ortega marched at the head of a strong body of government troops to repair the disaster. Marquez retired before him from the 14th to the 23d. The pursuit was hotly maintained, and General Valle, the most promising officer of the liberal party, marched with 1,500 men to try and intercept Marquez and force him to action. The latter by a masterly manœuvre joined Galvez, and with the united forces fell upon Valle, utterly routed and dispersed his forces, took him prisoner, shot him, and then hung his body on a tree. But one of the government officers escaped to tell the tale; the others, with many of the poor soldiers, were butchered after the action.

These tidings spread terror in this community; the national guard was called out, and the city has been declared under martial law. On the 25th a party of 400 of Marquez's men forced their way into the suburb of San Cosmé, and at one time it was thought would have captured the city, as they were supposed to be the vanguard of a much larger force. After carrying away some of their party who were prisoners in that part of the town, they retired with the loss of only one man killed and a few wounded.

These events, by proving the miserable improvidence of the present government, have completely discredited President Juarez, and his retirement is now looked upon as an absolute necessity for the good of the commonwealth. As a preparatory step towards it, General Ortega has been elected vice-president, in order to succeed to the presidential chair when Juarez resigns. Ortega, I fear, will do no better.

Congress has voted $10,000 apiece for the heads of Marquez and half a dozen other chiefs of the church party; but there is no probability of the money being called for, which is so far fortunate for the credit of congress, as that sum is not at present to be found in the national treasury.

I do not enter into details of persons carried off from here by Marquez to be either shot or ransomed, because by so doing I should only unnecessarily increase the length of this despatch, but will merely add that nothing I can write would give your lordship a correct idea of the miserable and disgraceful disorder which now reigns here, and which is only another proof, if one were wanted, of the utter incapacity of these people to govern themselves.

The church party are daily gaining ground, and, it is feared, may eventually succeed in capturing this city and driving the present government again into the provinces, thereby renewing all the horrors of a civil war which has devastated this unfortunate country for the last three years.

The Guzman ministry resigned ten days ago, and such are the difficulties of the situation that no men have been yet found who are willing to take their places. In the meantime business is brought to a standstill, and any note one has to address to the foreign department remains unanswered.

No. 15.

Earl Russell to Sir C. Wyke.

FOREIGN OFFICE, *August* 21, 1861.

SIR: I have received and laid before the Queen your despatches of the 24th, 25th, 27th, and 28th of June, and I have to convey to you the entire approval of her Majesty's government of your conduct as therein reported.

Her Majesty's government have read, with much concern, your account of the deplorable condition of Mexico, but her Majesty's government cannot accept that condition as an excuse for the want of good faith shown by the late acts of the Mexican government, and by the tone of Señor Guzman's correspondence with you.

It appears to her Majesty's government to be useless to continue negotiations with that government, either as regards the repayment of the proceeds of the conducta robbery, or the money stolen from the British legation, or the non-fulfilment of the Aldham and Dunlop compacts; and her Majesty's government will, accordingly, in such manner as they shall deem most suitable, adopt more active measures to obtain redress.

I have now to instruct you to demand, in the first instance, of the government of Mexico, that in the ports of Vera Cruz and Tampico commissioners shall be placed, who shall be named by the British government, for the purpose of appropriating to the powers having conventions with Mexico the assignments which those conventions prescribe, which shall be paid out of the receipts of the maritime custom-houses of the republic; including, in the sums to be paid to the British government, the amount of the conducta robbery and the money stolen from the British legation.

You will also require that the commissioners shall have the power of reducing by one-half, or in any less proportion, the duties now levied at those ports.

If these terms are not complied with you will leave Mexico with all the members of your mission.

I am, &c.

RUSSELL.

No. 16.

Earl Russell to Sir C. Wyke.

FOREIGN OFFICE, *August* 21, 1861.

SIR: With reference to your despatch of the 24th of June, and its several enclosures, I have to state to you that her Majesty's government must insist on the restoration of the $660,000 stolen from her Majesty's legation, and that if that money is not restored friendly relations between the two governments cannot be maintained.

I am, &c.

RUSSELL.

No. 17.

Sir C. Wyke to Lord J. Russell.

MEXICO, *July* 11, 1861.

MY LORD: By the enclosed extract from this day's "Mexican Extraordinary" your lordship will perceive that another British subject has been murdered, under circumstances of peculiar atrocity.

The deceased's nephew, after searching in vain throughout the village of Tacubaya for some sort of legal authority to take a deposition on the spot, and perform the usual formalities necessary in such a case, was obliged to have the body removed into this city, when he reported to the British consul what had taken place, requesting him to acquaint the authorities therewith in order that some steps might be taken for the apprehension of the offenders.

Mr. Glennie had considerable difficulty in overcoming the apathy of the officials, both military and civil, for murder has now become a matter of such everyday occurrence that it excites little or no attention. At length, however, he succeeded, and, the usual forms having been gone through, the body was next day interred, Mr. Walsham, Mr. Glennie, and a numerous body of British residents following it to the grave.

On becoming aware of what had occurred, I addressed, in the absence of any minister for foreign affairs, a note to the official mayor of that department, copy of which I have herewith the honor to enclose, together with a translation of his reply thereto, by which your lordship will perceive that they were shamed into affording some protection to a place that ought never to have been left defenceless, and also that they promised to take measures for detecting the authors of this atrocious crime.

It is impossible to give your lordship an idea of the state of anarchy and disorder into which this country is plunged under the misrule of this incompetent government. The high roads all over the republic are swarming with robbers, and murders are constantly committed in the most frequented streets of the capital, without the culprits ever being, in any one instance, either captured or punished.

I shall spare no effort to ascertain who were poor Beale's assailants; but, if I even succeed, there is not a chance of their being brought to justice, for crime is now triumphant, and no judge would dare, under existing circumstances, to vindicate the law, which, in matters of criminal jurisdiction, has become a dead letter.

I have, &c.,

C. LENNOX WYKE.

Enclosure 1 in No. 17.

Extract from the " Mexican Extraordinary" of July 11, 1861.

NEWS TOPICS.—The daily events of Mexico have become so alike that one is induced to ask, on getting up in the morning, "Who has been robbed?" "Who has been murdered?"

Since our last publication the event that has caused most sensation has been the murder of Mr. H. M. Beale, one of the very oldest British residents of Mexico, at his residence at the village of Naples. The news of this melancholy event reached here early on the morning of the 7th, and caused that degree of horror and alarm (not surprise) which similar events are likely to create amongst people who exist in a state of anxiety for their own lives and property.

The facts of this murder are as follows: About 11 o'clock on the night of the 6th a force of some twenty-five or more men on horseback made their appearance in the village of Naples. They were well armed, and came in with a trumpet sounding. Soon after entering the place (which, by the way, is an embryo village of five or six houses) they made a descent upon the house of Mr. Beale, which is the principal one, and commenced to fire at the windows and doors. All the inmates of the house appear to have been in bed. Mr. Beale was awakened, and, it is believed, was wounded by the first discharge. He at once got up, and rushing to the room of an old lady (Mrs. Wylie) who was stopping with him, took her to the roof of the house for safety. He then descended to the lower floor, and, being unarmed, spoke with the assailants, who had then broken into the house, and offered them the liberty to take what they might wish, supposing, as he had a right to do, that he could have no mortal enemies, and that their object was merely to rob.

In reply to his offer and assurance that he had no arms, he was told that they only sought his life "as a foreigner," their mission being to kill foreigners, and not to rob. This declaration was followed by some remonstrance on his part, when he was struck upon the head with a sword, and the work of assassination commenced, amid the most frightful oaths, and cries of "Death to foreigners!"

At the time of the attack there was another foreigner in the house, but he made his escape from a window, and fled to Tacubaya, where he gave notice to a friend of Mr. Beale, (Mr. Bueron,) who proceeded to Naples. When he arrived he found the place deserted by the murderers, and poor Beale quite dead. The body was brought to this city the same day, and examined by physicians named for the purpose by the government. The wounds were numerous, made by fire-arms, swords, knives, &c. The head was laid open in two places, and disfigured by bruises, cuts, and gunshot wounds, in the most horrible manner. In the breast were four wounds, two by fire-arms, and two by knives or swords. Both arms had wounds, and two deep incisions, apparently made by sword thrusts, were found in the lower part of the body. The corpse altogether presented a most shocking spectacle, not that alone of the victim of murderers, but of cowardly fiends who had wreaked upon it their most envenomed hatred. The funeral of Mr. Beale took place the day following, and, notwithstanding a drenching rain, the attendance was numerous.

The victim of this atrocity was a British subject of many years' residence in this country, who had always been noted for his pacific and inoffensive character. He had never taken any part in the politics of the country, and it is not known that he ever so much as expressed an opinion in favor of one party or the other. When warned a few days before his death of the existence of danger, he laughed at the idea, and urged his entire neutrality as a guarantee that no one would molest him. He was a hard-working man, and the new village where he resided owed its name and existence to his untiring industry and enterprise. He was a charitable man, as is well known by everybody, for, although unmarried, he had a considerable family made up of poor orphan children, who were fed, clothed, and cared for through his industry. His last act of kindness to Mrs. Wylie proves the true character of the deceased more than anything else. His first thought was to save the aged and infirm, and then go to face the danger.

The death of this unfortunate man has, with reason, created a deep feeling of alarm amongst the foreign residents of this place, who cannot longer look upon their situation but as precarious in the extreme. Had many others fallen as Mr. Beale has fallen, there might have been some explanation of the act—that they had been partisans, meddlers with the affairs of the country, or some of the many base reasons which have been advanced to palliate the murder of others of our countrymen. But here nothing of the kind can be advanced. Mr. Beale was "a foreigner," (a British subject,) and for being such has been murdered. The fact cannot be changed. We have not only the testimony of a child who witnessed the murder of Mr. Beale, and heard the threats of the assassins, but we have the fact that the houses of other foreigners in the same place were broken into, inquiries made for the owners, and, when they were found absent, the repetition of the same cries of "Death to foreigners!" and threats to come back and murder them also. It was providential that no others shared the fate of Mr. Beale.

The authors of this atrocity are supposed to be of the clergy forces scattered through the valley. This is natural to suppose, although the fact will probably never be proved. It matters little, however, of what force or party they are. It is alarming enough to know they have murdered one of our countrymen, and have threatened to serve all of us in the same way, and that they are still at large to do as they please.

Nothing has been done, as far as we can learn, to bring the criminals to justice, and we fear that it will be the fate of this case to pass like those of Staines, Gibson, Duval, Egerton, Bodmer, and others—one wail of horror, a home and hearth desolated, one or two formal stereotyped protests, and eternal silence. Surely we are an abandoned people. But the most terrible part of our abandonment is the anxiety, which no foreigner can free himself of, as to who may be the next victim.

Enclosure 2 in No. 17.

Sir C. Wyke to Señor Magarola.

MEXICO, *July* 8, 1861.

SIR: I yesterday learnt with feeling of horror and indignation, which I will not attempt to describe, the barbarous murder of a British subject named Beale, at a farm called "Napoles," by a party of thirty or forty men, who, after destroying their victim, left the house without removing a single article from it, thereby proving that their sole motive was vengeance against a man universally known as kind-hearted and inoffensive, and who had never taken any part in the dissensions which distract this unfortunate country.

His son-in-law, who lives in Tacubaya, on hearing what had occured, searched in vain throughout the village for some legal authority to proceed to the spot with him in order to verify the facts and draw up a *procès verbal* duly proving the crime, and the circumstances under which it had been committed. Failing in his object, he next applied to the British consul in this city, who, on addressing the authorities here, was informed that the corpse must be brought into Mexico, as there was no person competent in Tacubaya to perform the legal formalities necessary to be fulfilled in such a case as this.

It is perfectly incredible that the government should thus leave a place like Tacubaya, within three miles of the capital, inhabited by thousands of people, and containing much valuable property, totally destitute of any authority whatever, either civil or military, to protect the lives of those who have every right to claim the protection of a government which is bound to watch over them.

In bringing this dreadful case to your notice I must request that you will immediately inform me what steps have been taken for the detection and punishment of the assassins who have committed this murder, and let me know at the same time what measures have been adopted to prevent outrages of a similar nature being again perpetrated in a place close to the gates of the capital.

If I had supposed Tacubaya had been thus left defenceless I should have warned all my countrymen to leave a place which everybody thought was under the direct and immediate protection of the general commanding the district. In conclusion I must again urge on you the necessity of giving me an immediate reply to the demand I now address you, not only for the sake of justice to the deceased, but also for the due protection of those British subjects still resident in the actual vicinity of the city.

I avail, &c.

C. LENNOX WYKE.

Enclosure 3 in No. 17.

Señor Magarola to Sir C. Wyke.

[Translation.]

NATIONAL PALACE, *Mexico July* 8, 1861.

SIR: Before receiving your excellency's note of this day's date the government had been informed of the assassination committed on the person of the

British subject Beale, and had, in consequence, ordered all the necessary measures for the investigation of the deed and the prosecution of the culprits so soon as they should be arrested.

The government itself, full of indignation at this crime, desires that its authors should suffer condign punishment, and has again given orders to the general-in-chief and to the governor of the district to take active measures, and to inform this department of what has already been done, and what it is their intention to do, not only in this case, but also about the matter which your excellency was pleased to lay before me.

As soon as the information referred to has been received in this department I shall have the pleasure to transmit it to your excellency, assuring you in the meanwhile that this government will spare no effort, as far as it may be in its power, to give its protection to the life and property of the inhabitants of the district.

I avail, &c.,

LUCAS DE PALACIO Y MAGAROLA.

No. 18.

Sir C. Wyke to Lord J. Russell.

[Extract.]

MEXICO, *July* 26, 1861.

After a perusal of the despatches I had the honor of addressing to you by the last mail, your lordship will, probably, not be surprised to learn that this government, encouraged by the apparent impunity with which they stopped payment of the assignments stipulated for by the agreements entered into with Captains Dunlop and Aldham, should have gone a step further, and suspended all payments assigned to their foreign claimants by the British, French, and Spanish conventions.

This scandalous and dishonest act was announced in a new financial law issued by congress on the 17th instant, and published in newspapers and placards in the form of a decree by the president's order on the 19th.

In this document, of which I have now the honor to enclose a translation, your lordship will perceive by article 1 that all payments, including the assignments destined for the London bondholders and the foreign conventions, are suspended for the space of two years. By article 13 the "contra registro," or duty on consumption of all foreign merchandise, is doubled within the federal district during the government's good pleasure, to enable them by these means, and those proposed by a tax on tobacco, to pay off in preference the debts contracted since the 29th of May last, as well as those they may incur for the expenses entailed on them in maintaining the public peace, or, in other words, carrying on the civil war.

These are the two articles of the decree that directly affect foreigners; the others bear more upon native interests, such as articles 12 and 13, by which the government is authorized to place an impost on tobacco, and to augment by 50 per cent., up to the end of December next, the excise duties on national products within the federal district, comprising an area of eighty-nine square miles, with a population of about 300,000 souls.

The "Junta," mentioned in article 6, is what we should term a special finance committee appointed for the reduction of the national debt by means of funds accruing from property formerly belonging to the church and other corporate bodies. Two members of the Junta are to be named from the different creditors of the

State; but those foreigners to whom such an appointment has been offered have refused it with indignation.

Such is the scheme by which this government propose to free themselves from their engagements towards foreign powers, and to procure money sufficient to enable them to go on in the old scrambling disorderly way, living from hand to mouth by augmenting duties, levying contributions, and repudiating engagements which they are bound in honor to fulfil.

The same evening that this decree was published I wrote a note to Señor Zamacona, minister for foreign affairs, asking him whether it was really authentic, as I could not bring myself to believe that the government actually meant thus to set at defiance an international obligation such as the British convention, which could not be put on one side at the will of one of the contracting parties, unless with the sanction of the other, and this too without in any way announcing their intention of doing so to this legation.

In his reply of the 21st, herewith enclosed, your lordship will perceive the very lame attempt he makes to account for this important omission, for even the visit to which he refers was made twenty-four hours after the decree had been placarded in the streets of this capital.

The second note, dated the 21st, translation of which I likewise enclose, is the one announcing the publication of the decree, to which he alludes in the first note as having been already sent to me, but which in reality only reached me an hour and a half after I had received the other. My letter of the 22d refutes the arguments he uses to justify the decree, and contradicts the insinuation that I must have known of its being about to be issued. My note of the 23d is an answer to the official announcement of the decree, by which I solemnly protest against it, and warn Señor Zamacona that unless this obnoxious measure is withdrawn in forty-eight hours I shall suspend all further official intercourse with the Mexican government until I receive instructions from her Majesty's government with reference to this matter.

The full forty-eight hours having expired without my having received any answer whatever to this communication, I again addressed him on the evening of the 25th, formally suspending my relations as I had threatened to do. An hour later I received two notes from his excellency, by the former of which he endeavors to make out that there is no necessity whatever for the step I have taken, and requested me, therefore, still to maintain my official relations with this government; this was in answer to my note written on the evening of the 23d, and the latter, in reply to the one of the 25th, complains that the full term of forty-eight hours was not accorded, for my note, which was written the day before at 5 o'clock, had not been received by him until 7 p. m. As in the first of these Señor Zamacona states the impossibility, according to his view of the case, of withdrawing the decree, I could not, after the announcement of my determination, reply to him officially, and I therefore answered some incorrect statements contained in his note by a private letter, copy of which I have the honor likewise to enclose.

It is very evident by the tone of these communications that they are now alarmed at the turn affairs have taken; but their wretched vanity and pride will prevent them from taking any step to remedy the evil, and therefore I see no chance of the measure being withdrawn.

Your lordship will thus perceive that it has become impossible any longer to suffer the illegal and outrageous proceedings of a government which neither respects itself nor its most solemn engagements.

It is only by adopting coercive measures that we can force them to give up a system of violent spoliation, which in reality is nearly as prejudicial to themselves as to those foreigners who are so unfortunate as to have brought their capital and industry to a country so misgoverned.

On the publication of the decree, the British merchants resident here addressed a letter to me, praying for my interference in their behalf, against the increase of duties on all foreign articles of consumption thus imposed on them. I enclose copy of their letter, together with my reply thereto.

As long as the present dishonest and incapable administration remains in power, things will go from bad to worse; but with a government formed of respectable men, could such be found, the resources of the country are so great that it might easily fulfil its engagements, and increase three-fold the amount of its exportations, not only of the precious metals, but of those productions for which they receive British manufactured goods in exchange. Mexico furnishes two-thirds of the silver now in circulation, and might be made one of the richest and most prosperous countries in the world; so that it becomes the interest of Great Britain to put a stop, by force if necessary, to its present state of anarchy, and insist on its government paying what it owes to British subjects. The moderate party, which is now cowed by the two opposing ultra factions in the State, would then raise its head, and encouraged by adopting the measures I pointed out as necessary in my last month's correspondence, probably establish by themselves such a government as we require; but without this moral support they fear to move, and hence the continuation of the deplorable state of things now existing.

M. de Saligny, the French minister here, has acted in concert with me throughout this affair, and although the interests he has to defend are trifling in comparison to ours, he has used even stronger language than I have, for he does not merely suspend, but actually breaks off all official intercourse with the government, unless they rescind the decree of the 17th instant.

I have not the least hesitation in saying that unless her Majesty's government take the most decided measures for proving to this government that it cannot thus act with impunity, British subjects resident here will remain defenceless, and their property be at the mercy of a set of men who disregard their most solemn engagements, whenever such interfere with either their caprice or rapacity.

From the tone of their notes to me anybody not on the spot would imagine that dire necessity had alone compelled them thus to act, whereas in reality, 6,000,000 of hard dollars have actually passed through their hands within the last half year, to say nothing of the immense amount of church property in this district alone which has been dissipated in a manner, according to public rumor, utterly discreditable to the members of the government.

Awaiting your lordship's instructions, I have, &c.

P. S.—I have herewith the honor to transmit translations of another long private note from Señor Zamacona, containing only a repetition of the same sort o arguments he has used before. When I reply to it I shall merely acknowledge reception of a communication which in no way really affects the question at issue.

Enclosure 1 in No. 18.

Decree.

[Translation.]

The citizen Benito Juarez, constitutional President of the United Mexican States, to the inhabitants, know ye:

That the sovereign congress of the union has deemed it well to address me the following decree:

ARTICLE 1. From the date of this law, the government of the union will recover the complete product of the federal revenues, deducting from them only the expenses of the administration of collecting, and all payments are suspended for two years, including the assignments for the loan made in London and for the foreign conventions.

ART. 2. The maritime custom-houses and all the other collecting offices of the federal revenues will surrender all their products into the general treasury, being exclusively subject to the orders of the ministry of finances. On the 15th and on the last day of each month they will forward to the ministry a statement of their receipts and disbursements.

ART. 3. Within the term of one month the government will form and publish an economical estimate of all public expenses, based on the estimate of the 31st December, 1855, conveniently reduced. The government is to subject itself to this economical estimate from the day of its publication, and congress only has the faculty of making changes afterwards.

ART. 4. The payments in this estimate are to be made in the following manner:
1. The armed force in campaign and in garrison. The material of war. The invalids and disabled soldiers. These payments are to be made complete, but no surplus can be admitted.

2. The civil list in active service and the military list not in service. These payments, if under three hundred dollars, are to be made complete; if above three hundred dollars they are to be made in strict and equal proportion.

3. The classes pensioned by the nation are to be paid in strict and equal proportion, if the classes above mentioned have been paid before, as is ordered by the decree.

ART. 5. If an order, not included in the estimates, is sent to the general treasury by government, an observation must be made by a communication of the government; if repeated, the treasurer is to communicate it immediately to congress. If the treasurer does not make the observations here mentioned, he is to be destituted immediately.

ART. 6. A superior committee of hacienda is instituted, composed of one president and four members named by government, with the sanction of congress. Two of them, at least, must be creditors of the nation.

ART. 7. The attributes of the junta are the following:—
1. To pay the loan made in London and the foreign conventions;
2. To pay the creditors not comprised in the law of the 30th November, 1850;
3. To pay legal and posterior credits against the nation up to the 30th June of this year, including those comprised in the law of the 17th December, 1860;
4. To receive the payment of what is due to the nation, if it be unknown to the collecting offices;
5. To administer and sell the nationalized clergy property, and to execute all the attributes of the law of disamortization and nationalization.
6. To make arrangements, with the sanction of government, with all the persons interested in, or that have any business relative to, nationalized property;
7. To distribute all the funds collected amongst the creditors of the nation. The product of the suppressed convents is to be applied to the creditors of the conducta of Laguna Seca, and after covering the estimates of the nunneries, the remainder is to be distributed to the creditors in the foreign conventions.

ART. 8. In order that the junta may be able to fill the attributes conferred upon it by government, the following is assigned to it:—
All the "pagarés" existing in the special disamortization office; the product of all pending redemption; the capitals not redeemed belonging to the nation, the buildings of the suppressed convents, the lands and all existing materials. In the States and territories all the lands, convents, and buildings comprised in the law of nationalization, and all the products, except the 20 per cent. belonging to the same States and territories. The buildings and capitals expressly excepted by government are not comprised in this article.

ART. 9. All this property will form a fund distinct of public credit; the employers in the district, the chiefs ("gefes superiores") of the finance department in the States and territories are to forward immediately to the junta the titles, deeds, notices, and corresponding documents.

ART. 10. In the special law published for the conversion of public debt, the part to be delivered by the States is to be fixed and regulated.

ART. 11. The government is authorized to publish a decree taxing tobacco; this tax is to be collected for the federal treasury in all the republic.

ART. 12. The government is authorized to increase, during the remaining months of this year, the alcabala of one-half per cent. more on national products, excepting the articles of agricultural and manufacturing industry specified in the decree of the 24th September, 1855.

ART. 13. The duty of "contra-registro" on foreign goods is increased to double in the district; this increase is to be paid as long as the government may deem it necessary to fulfil the object of the following article.

ART. 14. With the new product of the alcabala, the "contra-registro" and the tax imposed upon tobacco, the government will pay with preference all the debts contracted from the 29th of last May, and all those that it may contract for the re-establishment of public tranquillity, leaving extant all the orders that have been given on account of "refacciones" for the payment of the money taken in Laguna Seca.

ART. 15. The governors of States and the employés of the collecting department have no intervention whatever in the federal revenues.

ART. 16. The government is authorized to reform and organize within one month all the offices on such a base that their estimates be reduced, and is authorized to increase the salaries of some employés, and to reduce their number.

Given in the sessions hall of the congress of the union, on the 17th of July, 1861.

GABINO BUSTAMANTE, *Deputy President.*
FRANCISCO CENDEJAS, *Secretary.*
E. ROBLES GIL, *Deputy Secretary.*

For which I order that it be printed, published, circulated, and given due respect.

Given in the national palace in Mexico, the 17th July, 1861.

BENITO JUAREZ.

Enclosure 2 in No. 18.

Sir C. Wyke to Señor Zamacona.

MEXICO, *July* 19, 1861.

SIR: A printed paper, as strange in compilation as in the nature of its contents, was this day hawked about the principal thoroughfares of the city, and has now, I see, been reprinted in the columns of this evening's "Siglo."

According to the wording of this document, it would appear that congress has thought fit to make a free gift of other people's property to the government of the republic by suspending for the space of two years the payment of all assignments, as well to the London bondholders as to the parties interested in the foreign conventions.

Until I hear from you to the contrary, I am bound to consider this announcement in the light of a falsehood; for I cannot bring myself to believe that a government which respects itself could sanction a gross violation of its most sacred obligations to other nations, and then proclaim the fact of their having done so in a manner which, if possible, aggravates the offence.

That the representatives of those nations who are thus slighted and injured should be allowed to learn, in the first instance by handbills circulated in the streets, that you have repudiated your engagements, is as unaccountable as the policy which could dictate a measure alike fatal to the character and credit of the republic.

I will not dwell on other obnoxious paragraphs of this publication, as at present I cannot believe it to be authentic; for when your excellency did me the honor of calling on me to-day, you in no way alluded to a subject which would otherwise surely have formed the chief topic of your conversation.

Awaiting a reply at your earliest convenience, I avail, &c.

C. LENNOX WYKE.

Enclosure 3 in No. 18.

Señor Zamacona to Sir C. Wyke.

[Translation.]

MEXICO, *July* 21, 1861.

The undersigned, minister for foreign affairs, has had the honor of receiving from his excellency Sir Charles Lennox Wyke, her Britannic Majesty's envoy extraordinary and minister plenipotentiary, the note in which his excellency requests to be informed whether the decree of the federal congress providing for a total suspension of payments, not excepting those of the London bondholders and diplomatic conventions, is or is not authentic.

His excellency's request might have been looked upon as anticipated by the explanation the undersigned had the pleasure of making yesterday at the legation only a few minutes after the note, to which this is a reply, had been sent to the foreign office, indeed while it was yet on its way there; but the private character of that explanation renders it incumbent upon the undersigned to recapitulate a portion of it in the present communication.

In the first place, he begs to assure Sir Charles Wyke that so soon as the decree of yesterday was made known to him through the department of finance, he proposed to bring it at once to the cognizance of his excellency, though anxious that this step should be preceded by a visit, at which it was the intention of the undersigned to give Sir Charles Wyke a fuller and more detailed explanation of the decree in question, its purport, and probable results, than was compatible with the limits of an official note. In the meanwhile, however, the decree was duly and formally published and printed in the daily newspapers, and this will account for his excellency the British minister having seen it before he received either an explanatory communication or visit from the undersigned.

Sir Charles Wyke will now allow the undersigned the liberty of stating that he does not consider his excellency has formed a correct estimate of this decree, when he says the congress therein makes a free gift to the government of other people's property. Her Majesty's worthy representative likewise goes on to qualify the act of congress as a total suspension of payments for the space of two years; still it will not escape his keen judgment that the application of the term " free gift" to what is merely the act of ratifying certain obligations, and specifying the mode of fulfilling the same, amounts to a misnomer.

Neither can the undersigned agree with Sir Charles Wyke in his opinion that the decree in question is a violation of Mexico's most sacred obligations towards other nations. Such a phrase would imply the idea of a voluntary and deliberate act; whereas the republic, in suspending the payments due to the diplomatic conventions, yielded not to the dictates of its own free will, but solely to the force of circumstances, which have rendered it morally and physically impossible for the nation to continue making those payments which have hitherto been made by means of the most strenuous exertions. When, then, such efforts have been unavailing, the government may be permitted to say so without any want of respect either for itself or for those nations with whom they may have engagements.

To every obligation there is attached the tacit condition of possible fulfilment or non-fulfilment, and nobody has ever been judged faithless to his engagements, for having, when compelled to suspend payment, stated the simple fact of such engagements being incompatible with possibility.

Of such a nature is the statement contained in the decree that has now passed congress, and her Majesty's minister should not be astonished that it did so pass congress, or that it was afterwards published without the previous consent of the diplomatic representatives in their character of protectors to foreign creditors, for it must be treated of as the mere declaration of a simple fact, in no way tending to the modification or prejudice of the interests connected with the public debt.

It will not have escaped the clear judgment of Sir Charles Wyke, acquainted as is his excellency with the actual situation of the republic, that the suspension of payments which has lately been decreed, which only expresses what has long been the public feeling, and has formed the subject of confidential conversations with some members of the corps diplomatique, as well also as with some of those most interested in the foreign debt, has been brought about by an imperious necessity, which did not admit of any preliminary arrangement or adjustment. The government had to choose between two evils—either to respond to public opinion by adopting the only existing means of preserving order and reorganizing the whole administrative system, or to look quietly on and leave society to become an easy prey to the prevailing anarchy.

Government, considering the preservation of order to be its first duty, and believing that for the positive good of all who had interests at stake in the country some one plan should be undertaken which would tend to consolidate those same interests, presumed they might count, to a certain extent, upon the assent of the creditors.

Sir Charles Wyke, then, will thus understand why the undersigned, holding as he does these opinions, can neither look upon the decree originating this note as repudiating national engagements, nor as prejudicial to the good fame and credit of the republic.

In order the better to understand the true force and purport of the decree, the undersigned would beg to refer her Majesty's minister to the note which has been addressed to the legation for the purpose of announcing to his excellency the act of congress; and if Sir Charles Wyke considers that in the visit which the undersigned had the honor of paying yesterday at the mission he was only performing such an act of courtesy as should always precede any official or confidential conferences upon matters of business, his excellency will cease to wonder at the absence of special reference to the subject of this communication during the conversation which then took place.

The undersigned, &c.

MANUEL DE ZAMACONA

Enclosure 4 in No. 18.

Señor Zamacona to Sir C. Wyke.

[Translation.]

MEXICO, *July* 21, 1861.

The undersigned, &c., has the honor to inform his excellency Sir C. Lennox Wyke, &c., that the decree which forms the enclosure to this note has passed the federal congress of the republic, and that the undersigned brings it to the cognizance of his excellency on account of its connexion with the diplomatic conventions and their payments.

From the known ability and sound sense of her Britannic Majesty's minister, the Mexican government are led to hope that his excellency, so far from seeing in the above decree any cause for alarm on account of those interests which are under the protection of the British legation, will, on the contrary, perceive in this act of the legislature a proof that the republic is anxious to arrive at an estimate of their resources; to organize those resources in the most profitable manner; to cut at the root of such abuses as have hitherto brought censure upon the government, the supreme power being the first to submit to the restrictions and other conditions necessary for this object; and, at the same time, to place the engagements and obligations of the nation upon such a footing as will insure them in future a sure and lasting inviolability.

To fulfil faithfully their international compacts, the Mexican government have made almost superhuman efforts, and can show results of no ordinary kind; such, for instance, as the present balance-sheet of the Mexican debt, whereby it is seen that no very notable change has been brought about therein by the continuous state of revolution. During this crisis, on the contrary, the position of foreign creditors has improved. In the midst of its greatest embarrassments the nation has gone even so far as to increase the rate of interest for paying off the public debt, and has thus deprived itself of the very means which were at its disposal for terminating the civil war; in other words, the nation has paid its creditors their gold with the blood of its citizens.

Since the revolution began the republic has been thirsting after peace, order, and security; yet the government, fully convinced though they were of being able to right themselves if only they could count upon any means that would really admit of action, hesitated long before laying hands upon the funds destined for the payment of their foreign debt. So great, indeed, was their respect for these funds that they preferred to sacrifice their obligations to Mexicans, to trample under foot the most cherished principles of their country, nay, even to imprison persons of the highest respectability, in order to obtain resources from the sums paid for their release, rather than touch a cent of the assignments destined for the diplomatic conventions and the London debt.

So hateful an expedient, although it has served to prove their good faith towards other nations, has not been and never can be efficacious; so that the government has now to start afresh, as they should do, upon different principles, and with the fixed purpose of thoroughly reorganizing their plan of administration, and of having recourse, not to temporary expedients, but such a system of taxation as from its nature will, while adding fresh vigor to government, abolish once and for all the old system of forced imposts.

To carry out this principle the republic has need of its entire revenue and of conscientious and practical persons to administer the same; and this is the intention of the law which the undersigned has the honor of placing in Sir Charles Wyke's hands.

The present government of the republic has to meet, on the one hand, the demands of society and civilization for order, and guarantees, on the other, those of the foreign creditors for nearly the entirety of the public revenue. So circumstanced, no government could hesitate as to the course to be taken.

The nation, then, has yielded to the cry of society and civilization, has given way before a pressure too heavy for it to bear, but it has done so merely in order to recover strength and then return to the charge.

The government of the undersigned originated the measures contained in the enclosed decree; and possibly they are the first rulers in the country who have religiously and honestly undertaken seriously to consider the nature of their obligations, and to discover the best means of meeting them.

It is impossible for Mexico to attempt any administrative reform, or the re-establishment of peace and order, if she has to support the burden of the national debt.

To enable her, however, to remove whatever has led to those numerous questions which have so incessantly occupied the attention of foreign representatives and the finance department, and to do away with the system of forced imports—to enable her to free herself from the necessity of breaking through her own liberal principles and overtaxing foreign imports—to enable her, in short, to procure some portion of the money now paid by the maritime custom-houses towards the extinction of the debt—it is necessary she should be allowed a short respite wherein to recover herself, as well as the full use for a few days of her entire revenue. In that case, by proper management and economy, public order and tranquillity would be re-established, and the revenue of the country, with the exception of what was absolutely requisite for the proper protection of society, set apart to meet the payment of arrears.

The government of the undersigned considers that a debtor, so long as he is actuated by honorable feelings and a full determination to carry out his engagements, does not forfeit his dignity in presenting himself to his creditor and frankly confessing he is, though temporarily so, unable to pay his debts; and the sole object which that government now has in view is to prove to the world that they are really and truly resolved upon attempting administrative reforms in the country, as the only means left likely to produce any amelioration in its political condition. They perfectly understand that they have to struggle against the unfavorable impression caused by the abuses and irregularities allowed in former times; yet it does not escape them that they have inherited this fresh difficulty in addition to the others which they have now to combat, though they are not ashamed of such difficulties, inasmuch as this is no exceptional case in the annals of Mexican revolutions, nor is it the work of the present administration.

A nation, like an individual, has the right to ask to be judged by its own acts, and not according to preconceived prejudices or partial comparisons.

When the president of the republic convened the members of the present government they each and all, with heartfelt sincerity and honesty of purpose, hailed the idea of at once fearlessly grappling with the difficulties of the problem upon the solution of which depended the great question of reform. They saw that the nation lacked not the material elements of such a work, but merely their proper organization. Nor were moral elements wanting; for were there not proofs to the contrary in the general longing for the time when, upon the spurious and self-interested promises of a frivolous and corrupt minority, there should be built up lasting institutions, under whose protecting influence Mexicans and foreigners alike would deem their honor, lives, and property secure? The government saw that the nation was weary of its state of anarchy; that it cursed the abuses and the recklessness which had brought upon it discredit and ruin. They saw, in fact, that the majority in the country asked but honesty of purpose from the ruling power, and they did not hesitate to consecrate their efforts exclusively to respond to so just a call.

The cabinet, of which the undersigned is a member, takes pride in its firmness of purpose, and considers that it merits the sympathy and co-operation of foreign representatives, whose presence in the republic is not solely for the protection of specified interests or nationalities, since their mission is equally one dedicated to the cause of humanity and civilization.

Sad, indeed, would it be if history had one day to recount how that this country, after the most trying vicissitudes, came to be ruled over by men who, without any supernatural gifts, and animated solely by their patriotism and their experience, shrunk not from making one final effort—an effort such as never yet had been made—to establish in Mexico the rule of reason and morality, yet that this effort was shipwrecked on the prejudices and scepticism of the most enlightened nations of the world in respect to Mexico's future and Mexico's capabilities for reform.

Every impartial person must look upon what is now passing as a proof of the energy and loyalty which Mexico is displaying in her endeavors to attain that position which reason and prudence dictates. Government, at the outset, has procured and dedicated to the interests of the public debt all the national property. They have initiated a system of economy which is already in operation; and as a result thereof, have imposed upon themselves and their subordinates such restrictions and self-denial as have never yet been imposed by any former administration. They have further been occupied with the details of a programme based upon those principles of economy which experience has proved to be necessary. Great progress, too, has been made towards establishing public order and tranquillity by the steps taken by government for tracing out clearly the position which the States hold in respect to the supreme federal power. Moreover, the Departments of State now are denied to those who would hold office simply to speculate in the gains of the reigning disorder and confusion, and the present rulers of Mexico would sooner sink under their difficulties than yield an inch of the ground on which they have taken their stand in defence of reform and morality.

All those who have interests in the country, all indeed who would see civilization on the increase, should aid the government in attaining the objects they have in view, instead of throwing obstacles in their way. The great European powers are extending their sympathies at the present hour to those countries who are striving to join the rest of mankind in the great work of civilization, and Mexico would fain hope that she is not alone to be excepted.

The very creditors of Mexico themselves should, the undersigned thinks, in their own interests, feel that great encouragement is given to them at the present moment; for it is not the republic alone that is now concerned in the proper regulation of the public debt under surer guarantees, and in the necessity of consolidating the same. The creditors of the nation have even a higher interest at stake, inasmuch as by no other means than those already mentioned can they expect to obtain greater advantages than those they now possess, notwithstanding that they have gradually acquired for themselves almost the entire revenue of the country.

This very circumstance is regarded, and with reason, as a proof of non-stability, while it equally produces distrust in people's minds, a state of things no less prejudicial to the republic generally than to its creditors.

Upon this point natural instinct cannot be deceived. As matters now stand, whether in respect to the country or the creditors, it might be possible that the drain upon the revenue could be continued for the space of a few months, but it would be possible only at the price of certain ruin, alike to the country and the creditors.

Had the government hesitated to adopt the measures for a radical financial reform, to which sufficient reference has already been made, they would have been either compelled, against their principles and inclination, to impose fresh taxes upon foreign importations, or quietly to submit to every interest connected with social order being swallowed up in the flood of anarchy—an idea too horrible to be thought of.

To avoid either of these extremes the government, guided by their conscience and feelings of patriotism, suggested the plan contained in the enclosed decree. If, as it is to be hoped, it should meet with support and sympathy from other nations, Mexico would be able to raise her voice and proclaim aloud that she had entered upon the one road that could lead to her salvation. Should it be otherwise, the nation must perish, and with her all those interests which are so closely connected with her future prosperity. Be this as it may, the government that in these stormy days rules over the destiny of Mexico, will have had the honor and glory of initiating and doing battle for the only means left that could save their country.

The undersigned would feel obliged to her Majesty's envoy extraordinary if his excellency would transmit a copy of this note to his government, and avail himself, &c.

MANUEL DE ZAMACONA.

Enclosure 5 in No. 18.

Sir C. *Wyke to Señor Zamacona.*

MEXICO, *July* 22, 1851.

SIR: In reply to your communication bearing yesterday's date, which I have just had the honor to receive, I will endeavor to answer seriatim the objections you have to offer to the statements contained in my note to your excellency of the 19th instant.

You state the reasons why the financial decree was not sooner communicated to this legation, and say that you were anxious personally to explain to me the motives which had originated it; but what I complained of was, that it should have passed into a law without the intention even of carrying it into execution ever having been announced to me.

When two parties bind themselves to perform certain stipulations, neither of them has the right to free himself from such obligations without having first of all obtained the consent of the other contracting party. With regard to what you say about the impropriety of my calling this act of the congress a giving away of other peoples property without their consent, permit me to observe that I am perfectly justified in making that assertion, for in matters of this nature time is often equivalent to money, and the arbitrary act of stopping all payments for the space of two years is depriving the parties interested of their money for that space of time, which is a dead loss of so much value to them.

The imperious necessity which you urge as an excuse for the act cannot in any way justify the manner in which you have made yourselves sole judges of that necessity, without first of all urging it on the forbearance of your creditors, in order to obtain their consent to what you were about to do.

A starving man may justify, in his own eyes, the fact of his stealing a loaf on the ground that imperious necessity impelled him thereto; but such an argument cannot, in a moral point of view, justify his violation of the law, which remains as positive, apart from all sentimentality, as if the crime had not had an excuse. If he was actually starving, he should have first asked the baker to assuage his hunger, but doing so of his own free will, without permission, is acting exactly as the Mexican government has done towards its creditors on the present occasion.

Although, as your excellency truly observes, the law just published does not certainly affect the rights of the parties interested, yet it does most positively touch their material interests by depriving them of payments on which they had counted to fulfil their other engagements.

With regard to the hope of immediate relief which you seem to entertain from the operation of this measure, I am convinced that it will, on the contrary, greatly aggravate the actual difficulties under which you are now laboring, and that for reasons so evident that I will not now advance them.

I am not aware that the project of this law was shown to other diplomatic agents, but I certainly never heard of it before under its present form, and therefore, as far as I am concerned, the case stands exactly as I have stated it.

With regard to the light in which your excellency views this question, as expressed in your above-named note, you will, I am sure, excuse me for stating that it cannot be treated of partially, without also taking into consideration the opinions of those who directly suffer from the practical operation of such ideas as emanating from yourself and the other members of the government who submitted the project to the congress.

With respect to what you mention about a note addressed by your excellency to this legation with reference to this matter, I must inform you that it has never reached me, and that, therefore, I had a full right to complain, as I did in my communication to you of the 19th, of having first of all heard of this extraordinary measure of the government by seeing it in printed bills placarded through the public streets of the capital.

I have, &c.

C. LENNOX WYKE.

P. S.—Since writing the foregoing lines, the note of your excellency alluded to above as missing, has been put into my hands, it having reached this legation an hour and a half later than the one to which this is a reply.

C. L. W.

Enclosure 6 in No. 18.

Sir C. Wyke to Señor Zamacona.

MEXICO, *July* 23, 1861.

SIR: Your excellency's note of the 21st instant reached me yesterday afternoon, by which I learn that the decree forming its enclosure has passed the federal congress of the republic, and that you forward it to me as directly bearing on the stipulations of the diplomatic convention for the payment of British claims concluded between Great Britain and Mexico in the year 1851.

I have already so fully explained to you, in my notes of the 19th and 22d of this month, what I think of this decree, and the manner in which it has been issued, that any further observations of mine with reference to it would only be superfluous, and prolong a correspondence which should never have been called for at all.

As to the appeal you make to the indulgence and forbearance of her Majesty's government, in order to obtain their sanction to a measure which is of itself sufficient forever to deprive you of their confidence, I need only remind you that such indulgence has already been too far abused by the utter failure of all your engagements in the affairs of the Calle de Capuchinas and Laguna Seca for it to be again extended to those who, instead of feeling grateful for it, only seem to count on its exercise in order to free themselves from every obligation, however binding it may be.

Apart from these considerations, however, the carrying out of ·this financial law, so far from benefiting the nation, will only plunge it into tenfold greater difficulties by largely increasing its obligations to its creditors, and at the same time striking at the root of its credit and commercial prosperity.

That which is in itself wrong can never come right, for it is a well known axiom that spoliation, as a source of revenue, soon exhausts itself.

It is not by such means that the resources of the country can be augmented, but by a determination to make every sacrifice, and incur every privation, with a view of maintaining your honor and fulfilling your engagements. This determination, once adopted and manfully put in practice, would at once inspire confidence and rally round you those whose sympathies you now appeal to in vain, because they doubt, from past experience, both your prudence and your sincerity.

In using language thus strong you must not attribute to me a desire to offend, which is, indeed, far from my intention, but I have a duty to perform both to my own government and to that to which I am accredited, which impels me fearlessly to tell the truth and warn you against the inevitable consequences of a step alike fatal to your own interests, as well as to those of my countrymen affected by that law.

It now only remains for me to protest most solemnly, as I hereby do, against this decree, at the same time that I hold the republic responsible for all and every damage and prejudice caused by it to the interests of those whom I represent in this matter; and further to warn your excellency that, unless the said decree is withdrawn within forty-eight hours from this present time, I shall, until I receive fresh instructions, suspend all official intercourse with the Mexican government, as any longer maintaining such under existing circumstances would be incompatible with the dignity of the nation I have the honor to represent.

In compliance with your request, I will transmit a copy of your excellency's note of the 21st instant to her Majesty's government.

I avail, &c.,

C. LENNOX WYKE.

Enclosure 7 in No. 18.

Sir C. Wyke to Señor Zamacona.

MEXICO, *July* 25, 1861, 5 *p. m.*

SIR: The day before yesterday, at this hour, I had the honor of informing your excellency that, if the decree of the 17th instant was not withdrawn within forty-eight hours I should feel it my duty to suspend all official intercourse with the Mexican government until I should receive instructions from her Britannic Majesty's government as to the next step to be taken in the matter, which not only implies the breach of a solemn international compact, but also carries with it so great a slight as almost to amount to a direct insult to the nation I have the honor to represent.

The term having now expired within which I should have received a reply, and none having reached me, I take your silence as a refusal of my demand; and I therefore, from this time forward, suspend all official relations with the government of this republic until that of her Majesty shall adopt such measures as they shall deem necessary under circumstances so unprecedented.

I have, &c.,

C. LENNOX WYKE.

Enclosure 8 in No. 18.

Señor Zamacona to Sir C. Wyke.

[Translation.]

MEXICO, *July* 25, 1861.

The communication which his excellency her Britannic Majesty's minister was pleased, under yesterday's date, to address to the undersigned upon the subject of the decree of the sovereign congress proclaiming a total suspension of payments, not excepting those of the diplomatic conventions and the London debt, has rendered it incumbent upon the undersigned to make certain explanations, without which it might be supposed that his government had accepted as irrefutable some of the facts and statements therein adduced by Sir Charles Wyke.

Once for all, then, the undersigned rejects the notion entertained by his excellency in his notes of the 19th and 22d instants, that the decree of the 17th implies an act of spoliation.

This act of the legislature carries with it no legal right whatever to rob foreign creditors of what belongs to them. The nation, in whose house of representatives the decree in question was carried with scarcely a dissenting voice, has never sought to disavow the rights which have accrued to others from international compacts. Still she has been forced to declare that, for some time to come, such rights cannot continue to be a drain upon the revenue of the maritime custom-house, for that revenue, the only one government possesses for immediate purposes, does not suffice for the actual exigencies, temporary though they be, of the country and society, and at the same time for the payment of the interest and principal of the public debt. Government have obligations to perform both towards society and their creditors. They cannot perform both at once, and consequently, by the decree which has originated this note, government have done nothing more than place those obligations in their legitimate order, without attacking or disavowing any of them.

His excellency her Majesty's envoy extraordinary, while attempting to clothe the act of congress in the garb of spoliation, has in one of his former notes employed a simile, the inaptitude of which is strikingly perceptible. His excellency compares the government at this moment to a person who, impelled by hunger, assaults and robs a provision merchant. Now, two ruling principles are implied in such an act, one of aggression, the other of robbery, neither of which can even be assumed in respect to the conduct of government towards its creditors. Of not a sixpence have these same creditors been deprived; and if one had to employ a simile to qualify the conduct of government, it would be rather that of a father overwhelmed with debts, who, with only a small sum at his disposal, scarcely sufficient to maintain his children, employed it in the purchase of bread instead of in the payment of his bills. Were her Britannic Majesty's representative a member of the family, would his excellency be eager to qualify his father's conduct by the name of spoliation?

In every-day life one is accustomed to see people who suspend payment, owing to pecuniary embarrassments, yet nobody seeks to call them thieves. Now, in the decree upon which her Britannic Majesty's minister passes so severe a sentence, not a single word is there which can give rise to the idea of thieving propensities. Payments, it is true, are stopped, because government cannot pay out of the funds assigned to it. They are stopped because the nation, to be orderly and at the same time methodical in the accounts of the public debt, wants, as soon as possible, a government; yet still, with feelings of loyalty and with a solicitude worthy both of being more justly appreciated, she has given her creditors a two-fold guarantee—firstly, in the plan itself, so complete, so impartial, a plan wherein looms a prospect of solid stability; and, secondly, in the

H. Ex. Doc. 100—19

assignment of a special fund of several millions, (most of which can shortly be realized,) whereby, even during the period of suspension, (in their case nominal,) the foreign creditors will obtain even better security than what was given them in the maritime custom-houses.

It is not, M. le Ministre, about sacrifices or money that Mexico is haggling; that which she is defending are the principles of order; that which she is longing for is system and organization, without which she is lost; and she is searching after prudence and method, so that she may never again be accused of slovenliness and mismanagement by those who regard as a national vice what is but a phenomenon inseparable from a state of revolution.

It is well, too, to state accurately the attitude of Mexico before her creditors, both as it was and is; for it is not such a one as his excellency her Majesty's envoy describes in his last note. To judge therefrom, our republic has never been aught than an indigent debtor, who, from time immemorial, has responded with ingratitude and bad faith to the undeniable generosity and indulgence of her creditors.

The undersigned shuts his eyes purposely to the history of the foreign debt, for neither would he wish to employ the bitter tone of Sir Charles Wyke's note, nor give the slightest indication of Mexico's belonging to the set of faithless debtors who, to avoid payment, dispute the legality of their obligations. Mexico, on the contrary, recognizes in a high degree her engagements, and will abide by them, moreover, without taking exception at the antecedents of the original contract.

But the undersigned is convinced that, when this correspondence shall have come to light, all who are familiar with the history of our external debt, all who are acquainted with the primary elements of the British convention, and know how the parties interested therein were allowed the advantages of increased interest in the midst of a ruinous civil war, and in the days of Mexico's hardest struggle, will see something strange in the allusion of his excellency her Majesty's minister to the indulgence of which the foreign creditors were so prodigal, but which the republic so systematically abused.

Had the demands of the creditors been somewhat fewer, then, perhaps, the fulfilment of international engagements might have come within the range of possibility. Mexico, however, has been like those fields where the harvests have been out of proportion to the fertility of the soil, and the day comes when the land becomes impoverished, yields nothing, and is obliged to lie fallow for one or two years.

The undersigned considers he should not pass over in silence the charge which is made against his government of having failed to fulfil their engagements in respect to the funds seized at the British legation by functionaries of the reaction, and to the money-convoy "occupied" at Laguna Seca.

In the first case, government, with the consent of the legation, engaged simply to make the perpetrators of the act responsible, and if such means did not lead to the desired result, viz, indemnity, to discuss others which might do so. No one, then, can say that until now government has not fulfilled their engagement in this case.

As for the affair of Laguna Seca, when government undertook to repay, within the space of four months, what remained unpaid of the amount "occupied" out of the "conducta," they did so at a time when they could not foresee that the remnant of the reaction would turn refractory, and oblige them to enter upon an expensive campaign, which would upset all their financial calculations.

Notwithstanding this, however, they have made every kind of sacrifice, monetary and otherwise, to keep intact this special debt—to an extent, indeed, that has left them in possession of but a small available surplus. No one who does justice to the Mexican nation can refuse to acknowledge the exemplary manner in which she has endeavored to satisfy her creditors, to the unstable disparagement of national interests.

The actual amount assigned for the payment of the foreign debt during the residence of the constitutional government at Vera Cruz, and that, too, at a time when the re-establishment of peace was being laboriously worked out, and when, consequently, the country could ill-sustain the heavy demands made upon it, speaks volumes in itself.

The little faith manifested by his excellency Sir Charles Wyke as to the results of the financial law, and the small value he puts upon the guarantees it gives to foreign creditors, do not seem to be shared in by the parties themselves who are interested in the diplomatic conventions, since it is only within the last few days that government had all but concluded an arrangement with them, the basis of which would not have interfered with their present rate of interest, but it could not be perfected owing to her Majesty's envoy extraordinary having refused to sanction it.

The same may be said of the creditors in the matter of the Laguna Seca "conducta." Guided by natural instinct—so infallible a rule where individual interests are concerned—they did not, like Sir Charles Wyke, entertain any doubts about the prudence and sincerity of the government. And touching these said doubts, amounting, as they do, to an insult, his excellency will permit the undersigned to exhort him to commune with his conscience, and ask it whether or not the tone of his excellency's last communication is such as should be used by a creditor, calling himself generous and indulgent, towards a friend who is in his debt and overwhelmed by difficulties.

It cannot escape the enlightened understanding of his excellency the representative of Great Britain that, in demanding from the government of the undersigned the withdrawal, within forty-eight hours, of the late decree, he simply demands an impossibility. Neither could the government initiate the withdrawal, for it would be equivalent to initiating the reign of anarchy and a general dissolution of society; nor could congress, who had carried this law almost by acclamation, and who were convinced of its vital importance to the republic, listen for a moment to such a proposition.

The protest with which his excellency her Majesty's envoy extraordinary concludes his note appears to the undersigned so much the more superfluous, as in his very first note upon this subject the undersigned had, so to speak, also protested, but against the supposition that the last act of congress in any way affected the lawful rights of the persons interested in the public debt.

The undersigned will further take the liberty of stating, with all due deference and respect to Sir Charles Wyke's sound judgment, that, very far from seeing in the suspension of relations, now announced by his excellency as representative of Great Britain. an act due to the honor and dignity of England, he thinks it not improbable that all nations who consider the matter impartially will look upon this step as absolutely uncalled for; and he therefore trusts that his excellency, while awaiting the instructions to which he alludes, will continue his friendly relations to this government, for the interruption of which there can be no possible cause, while their maintainance will surely contribute to the satisfactory solution of the present difficulty.

The undersigned, &c.

MANUEL DE ZAMACONA.

Enclosure 9 in No. 18.

Señor Zamacona to Sir C. Wyke.

[Translation.]

MEXICO, *July* 25, 1861.

The undersigned, &c., has this moment had the honor of receiving from his excellency Sir C. Lennox Wyke, &c., the note in which his excellency is pleased to announce the suspension of his relations with the government of Mexico.

Sir Charles Wyke must have received the communication which the undersigned had the honor of addressing at 5 o'clock this afternoon; this will prove the utter absence of any motive for a suspension of relations between the government of Great Britain and that of the Mexican republic.

Neither can there be any cause for the resolution taken by Sir Charles Wyke, in the expiration of the forty-eight hours fixed by his excellency in his note of the 23d instant, (as the term to be allowed to government for answering the ultimatum,) inasmuch as it was only 7 o'clock in the evening of the 23d that the above note was received at government house.

The undersigned, in calling attention to his last communication, avails, &c.

MANUEL DE ZAMACONA.

Enclosure 10 in No. 18.

Sir C. Wyke to Señor Zamacona.

[Private.]

MEXICO, *July* 26, 1861.

DEAR SIR: At 7 o'clock yesterday evening, that is, two hours after the expiration of the forty-eight hours in which I had required a reply to my note of the 23d instant, I received yours dated the 25th, to which, consequently, I can only reply by a private letter, as its contents have in no way changed the resolution which both the French minister and myself have been driven to adopt by the extraordinary and unjustifiable conduct of the Mexican government with reference to the decree of the 17th instant.

A careful perusal of your above-mentioned note has convinced me that mine of the 23d, to which it is a reply, has not been properly translated to you, as you put some things into my mouth which I never said, and so twist the sense of others as to give them a totally different meaning from what they really convey.

Passing by this, however, I will only revert to the really essential part of your note, which is the refusal to rescind a financial scheme, the maintenance of which, besides plunging the republic into further pecuniary difficulties, will have the effect of bringing it into collision with the two first maritime powers of the world, and that, too, in a quarrel which you have originated, and where, permit me to say, you are quite in the wrong.

As I am in thus writing to you unfettered by the reserve imposed in an official correspondence, I may tell you frankly that you are leaning on a broken reed when you trust to the sympathy of those whose interests Mexico has systematically sacrificed to her own. This is proved by the history of the foreign debt as applicable to the bondholders, which it would be well that you should carefully study, and you will then see that the repeated engagements made with them have, up to the present moment, always been either entirely evaded or only partially executed, as, for instance, when, after consenting to a reduction of interest of from five per cent. to three per cent. on the condition of receiving certain payments from the duties levied in the Pacific ports, they do not receive one sixpence from that source, and are only very partially paid from the Atlantic custom-houses.

I will not dwell on the long and dreadful list of murders committed on my unfortunate countrymen, which, with one exception, I believe, have remained unpunished from the date of your independence down to the recent dreadful butchery of poor Mr. Beale at Napolis.

Do you think that these lamentable facts are calculated to gain our sympathy or inspire us with confidence in a people who thus violate their engagements with us, and kill our fellow-subjects with perfect impunity?

It is really time that the government of Mexico should open their eyes to the natural consequences produced by such conduct, and should become aware of the unfavorable opinion entertained of them in Europe.

Whose fault is it that the country has been deluged in blood ever since the declaration of its independence but that of its own citizens, in constantly making revolutions and carrying on a series of fratricidal wars amongst themselves, which have reduced one of the finest countries in the world to misery, and so degraded its population as to make them dangerous, not only to themselves, but to everybody coming into contact with them?

You appeal to the generous sentiments of creditors towards an unfortunate debtor bowed down by his difficulties, forgetting that that debtor, with only common prudence within the last six months, might, at this moment, be actually free from debt, had he not wilfully and recklessly squandered the millions he then had at his disposal.

As to the mode of payment proposed to certain British claimants, to which you allude in your yesterday's note, it was so impracticable as to be unacceptable to all of them when its real nature was pointed out to them.

With regard to what you say about the Laguna Seca robbery and the legation outrage, it is useless for the Mexican government to deceive itself by calling the former an "occupation of funds," and the latter a deed performed by the "functionaries of the reaction." The first was a theft and the second an unheard-of violation of international law, committed by a government recognized by every European nation, and for both these crimes, as yet unatoned for, Great Britain will surely hold this republic fully responsible.

I have already extended this letter to an undue length, and must therefore conclude, but before doing so let me again urge you, for your own sakes, to retrieve the fatal error you have made with regard to this decree by immediately withdrawing it, for otherwise all official intercourse between this legation and your government becomes impossible, and you will remain with the responsibility attaching to an act which, both in form and substance, is perfectly unjustifiable.

Trusting that you will receive what I have now written in the spirit which really dictated these lines, I will take leave of a subject which is a much more serious one than seems to be supposed by the Mexican government.

In a second note of yours received yesterday, you complained that my note, written at 5 o'clock on the 23d, only reached you at 7 o'clock on that day, and that consequently, in writing to you yesterday at 5 o'clock, you had had only forty-six, instead of forty-eight hours' delay before the suspension of official relations. This I regret, but it was not my fault, as on both days I despatched my note from here at half-past five in the afternoon. In point of fact, however, the two hours thus lost are of no importance, as you refuse to withdraw the obnoxious decree.

Believe me, &c.,

C. LENNOX WYKE.

Enclosure 11 in No. 18.

Messrs. Graham, Geaves & Co., and others, to Sir C. Wyke.

MEXICO, *July* 23, 1861.

SIR: We, the undersigned, British merchants, beg leave most respectfully to solicit your excellency's powerful assistance under the following circumstances:

By article 13 of the government decree of July 17, which has been recently published, (copy of which we enclose,) the duty styled "contra-registro" is increased from 20 to 40 per cent. on the amount of import duty.

This double "contra-registro" duty is recoverable immediately, and therefore even goods which were forwarded last month (and but for the unprecedented bad state of the roads would have arrived before the decree in question was issued) are also subject to the increase referred to, and which is the more unjust and severe as goods have been sold to arrive under the existing tariff, and consequently a dead loss is at once sustained.

It is to be observed, also, that, as this additional duty is recoverable in the federal district, or in the capital of the republic only, all the other States are exempt from the charge, and consequently offering a further inducement to the illegitimate trader through the northern frontier, to the extra detriment, not to say ruin, of the Vera Cruz merchant.

We would further beg leave to point out, for the consideration of your excellency, that the measure now adopted by government is in every way analogous to the one of the year 1839, when the duty then called "consumo" duty was increased from 16⅔ to 50 per cent., but which, through the influence of her Majesty's legation, was abolished; and we believe to be correct in stating that a diplomatic convention was made at the time between Sir Richard Pakenham and the Mexican government, to the effect that no increase of duties affecting British commerce could from that time forward be enforced, except with a prior notice of six months, a record of which, if we may be allowed to remark, will probably be found in the archives of her Majesty's legation for the years 1840–'41, and there exists an acknowledged, though unsettled claim, at the present day, for that increase of duty, which had been exacted on British goods during the first six months.

We have, &c.,

GRAHAM, GEAVES & CO.,
And others.

Enclosure 12 in No. 18.

Sir C. Wyke to Messrs. Graham, Geaves & Co., and others.

MEXICO, *July* 24, 1861.

GENTLEMEN: I have to acknowledge receipt of your letter bearing yesterday's date, by which you request my assistance to prevent the execution of article 13 of the decree of the 17th instant, by which a double "contra-registro" duty is not only levied on goods imported into the federal district, but is also claimed from the date of the decree.

I fully concur in the justice of your observations on the subject, for the tax is not only injurious to the legitimate commerce of the country, but is also, in my opinion, a shameful robbery of those merchants who have sold their goods "to arrive." I should not, therefore, have hesitated in protesting against the immediate application of the double "contra-registro" duty, but, as you are probably aware, the decree in question contains infractions of international engagements of a most serious character; and I have therefore, on these grounds, whilst protesting against the decree, declared to the Mexican government that if it is not withdrawn within forty-eight hours I shall suspend all official intercourse with them until I receive further instructions with reference to this matter from her Majesty's government.

I am, &c.,

C. LENNOX WYKE.

Enclosure 13 in No. 18.

Señor Zamacona to Sir C. Wyke.

[Translation.]

MEXICO, *July* 27, 1861.

MY DEAR SIR: I have had the honor of receiving your letter of yesterday, and I am glad that it gives me the opportunity of asking you to listen once more to the voice of one who is as sincere as he is honorable; of one whose love for his country is only excelled by this love of justice and reason; of one who is confident that you will be brought to do justice to the intentions of the Mexican government, for, as if by inspiration, he knows you to be possessed of similarity of sentiment with himself.

It cannot be that, talented and generous as you are, you have yet thought it strange that government should refuse to withdraw the decree of the 17th instant. Your conscience must tell you, M. le Ministre, that it is an impossibility you ask of government, for how could they entertain your proposition? The mere preliminaries for the suspension of a law which had passed congress would take up more time than what you have allowed for deciding whether or not our official relations were to be maintained. This single fact would account for the position taken up by government, as well as for their determination to meet boldly dangers and difficulties even greater than those which you have had the goodness to warn me against.

Such a step as the one you now propose if taken by Mexico could not but prove suicidal to her political standing as a nation, for it would be equivalent to the surrender of her constitution and her sovereignty into the keeping of the foreign diplomatic body, and that too in a matter where my inmost conviction tells me that justice is on our side.

Still, as in the correspondence which has passed between us during the last few days I had seen the opposite doctrine sustained and heard the conduct of my government qualified repeatedly as unjustifiable, I began to distrust my own convictions about equity and common sense, so much so that I sought to justify myself and my country by a reference to international law; and I can only say, now that the work of reference is over, that my former convictions are only the more confirmed.

I perceive, M. le Ministre, that writers on international law hold it to be a general principle, that any change of circumstances or the positive inability of one of the parties in a contract to fulfil the same does of itself nullify a bond; and since I likewise, in my turn, may be permitted to avail myself of the advantages of a private letter, I will take the liberty of doing what might be considered in the light of pedantry were I writing to you officially, and make certain quotations which bear upon this question.

Grotius and Corcellus hold that "the obligation which results from a compact becomes null and void so soon as its fulfilment becomes impossible." Wheaton too has the following passage: "Treaties may be avoided, even subsequent to ratification, upon the ground of the impossibility, physical or moral, of fulfilling their stipulations. Physical impossibility is where the party making the stipulation is disabled from fulfilling it for want of the necessary physical means depending on himself." In Martens we read, "Physical impossibility in a nation to fulfil treaty engagements absolves it from the obligations of the compact, but not from the obligations to make indemnity should it be proved that the physical impossibility could have been foreseen, or that it was caused by the nation itself." And Heffter has the following remarkable sentence: "The contracting party may refuse to fulfil his engagements when their fulfilment becomes impossible and is likely to remain so, even though the contract be violated, more especially if private duties or the rights and well-being of a people are concerned."

I could go on quoting, but I should exceed the limits of this note were I to bring forward the numerous authorities upon this recognized principle of international law.

There is, M. le Ministre, something inexplicably harsh in denying the right of Mexico to the sympathy of her creditors, and in saying that she has systematically sacrificed their interests to her own.

I had already, before receiving your advice, studied the history of the English debt, and my research has shown me that from the very date of the London loan the republic has been a loser, its actual loss amounting to something like $8,000,000; that when bonds were issued in the year 1824 she did nothing less than make good at par what she could have made good at 50 per cent.; that later on she lost several millions in the failure of those British firms who had been mixed up in the business, yet that still, notwithstanding the civil war which has for years been raging in the country, she has made the bondholders such remittances as cannot but have filled their pockets beyond what could have been expected, considering the circumstances of the country. But this refers solely to the exterior debt, which perhaps has suffered less than anything else from the vicissitudes Mexico has had to undergo, since, at all events, this particular debt has been attended to with something like the very care and method which the government is desirous of employing in respect to the entire public debt.

While her Majesty's legation is talking about the history of the exterior debt, it would be well if, instead of turning their attention solely to the question of the London loan, which has no diplomatic character whatever, they looked into the matter of the British convention and stated frankly who really have been the sufferers in this business, and who have had to make sacrifices and undergo hardships. Let them say whether or not the republic has come off scot-free, when in the midst of her difficulties she has gone on punctually paying the assignments of the British convention and even increasing the rate of interest on those assignments.

In one of my last official communications I mentioned to you that feelings of delicacy prevented my entering into the details of the convention question. I can, however, in a private letter call your attention to the kind of elements composing this diplomatic arrangement, and to the consequences resulting therefrom; indeed, it is only a few days ago that an English paper in this capital brought the matter to light, and proved nothing less than that Mexico had been paying for some tobacco concern at the rate of two ounces for each box of cigars.

As to the complaints which you have made about the robberies and murders that of late have been committed in the republic, though they have not solely been committed upon the persons of Englishmen, but equally upon Mexicans, nobody need have less cause to blush than those who, like the present government, are giving the most positive proofs of how much they are taken up with this subject, and of their anxiety to put a stop at any price to such atrocities, and who were actually on the point of procuring the means of carrying out their intentions when those means were protested against by the British legation.

Who, you ask, is to blame for the present state of affairs and for the wars which have been desolating the republic? I will tell you in all frankness, M. le Ministre, and you must not be astonished at what I am going to say.

If, as I suppose, you are well acquainted with what has happened since the date of our independence, you will find that the origin of the evil can be traced to circumstances over which neither our race in general, nor this generation in particular, had any control. It was no work of theirs; while, as for what has taken place within the last few years, foreign diplomatic agents are in a great measure responsible for having recognized and given moral support to a handful of rebels who were utterly repudiated by the nation at large. Such, at all events, is public opinion.

In your last letter you still hold to the general but exaggerated notion, that many millions of the late church property have been needlessly squandered away. My opinion upon this point, M. le Ministre, may be considered worth something, for no journalist has advocated more strenuously than I have done the necessity of a proper and organized administration of the property in question; yet I am sure that if the matter were reduced to figures, and the actual value of the church property put on paper, with the positive depreciation that value has undergone owing to the civil war; and if, moreover, there be taken into consideration the sums paid from this source towards the extinction of the national debt, the discount at which government has' been compelled to transact their negotiation in order to realize this property and the surplus which still remains, I am sure, I repeat, that the charge of having squandered away millions will be found exaggerated.

I cannot understand why you should qualify as impracticable the arrangement which the parties interested in the British convention had entered into with government. This, or any other analogous one, would be very feasible upon the bases laid down in the decree of the 17th for the guidance of the special finance committee. This decree has in no way sacrificed the rights of the public debt; and nothing is asked for either by the government, the congress, or the country but the permission to attempt the pacification of the country and carry out their administrative reform. They claim but this.

With respect to what you are pleased to say about the conduct of the chiefs of the federal army in having "occupied" certain funds at Laguna Seca, I will simply ask you whether you conceive the word "robbery" implies the idea of a future indemnity, such as was made voluntarily and at a great sacrifice on this occasion, as is proved by the trifling sum which still remains unpaid.

As for the outrage at the British legation, I must correct a slight error you have made in referring to this act. It is not true that the authors of this outrage at the time of its commission, were recognized by the representatives of friendly powers.

I thank you, in conclusion, most sincerely for the kind language you employ, while exhorting me to facilitate the renewal of our relations by the withdrawal of the decree of the 17th instant; but it appears to me that the interest you profess in the matter would have lost none of its weight, and would have gained in dignity, had you accompanied it, by way of incentive, with some proposition for an arrangement not incompatable with the honor of the nation, and less unfeasible than the essentially impracticable one you have already made us.

Hoping that you will have the goodness to consider well the observations I now offer, and flattering myself that they may lead to the re-establishment of our official intercourse, for the interruption of which there is as yet no motive, I beg, &c.

MANUEL DE ZAMACONA.

No. 19.

Sir C. Wyke to Lord J. Russell.

MEXICO, *July* 28, 1861.

MY LORD: Since this day last month, when I had the honor of writing to your lordship, describing the state of affairs in this unfortunate country, matters here have only been going from bad to worse, and every day's experience only more clearly proves the imbecility and bad faith of a government now generally detested, and against which various conspiracies are on foot.

Marquez, at the head of about 4,000 men, still ravages the country, burning villages and levying contributions, without mercy, on the unfortunate inhabitants of whatever district he passes through, whilst the government troops, under the command of General Ortega, go running about the country in the hope of catching the rebels, who elude their pursuit apparently with the greatest facility.

On the 28th of last month, Marquez, with a force amounting to nearly 5,000 men, marched upon Real del Monte, at which place there are some very valuable mines belonging to a mixed English and Mexican company. Having easily overcome the government troops stationed near the place, his people rushed tumultuously into the village, burst open the doors of the houses, which they pillaged without mercy, ill-treating the inhabitants, and breaking the prison gates in order to liberate more than ninety of the worst criminals in the republic, who had been condemned to work in the mines. Fortunately no lives were lost, but the surgeon of the company, Dr. Griffin, received a sword-cut through the face, and the 160 English miners employed in the works were all more or less ill-treated, besides being robbed of their property to the amount, in the aggregate, of $3,898, a serious loss to these poor men, some of whom were thus deprived of their hard-earned savings to the amount of $200 and $300 each. Marquez himself levied a contribution on the company of $80,000, besides occasioning them a loss, during the three days he staid there, by the stoppage of works, stealing of horses, &c., amounting to the value of $20,000.

I enclose copy of a letter dated the 16th instant, which I have only just received, signed by the director and all the Englishmen employed there, by which your lordship will see that these poor people write to ask me what guarantee there is for the safety of their lives and property.

Marquez has, I hear, since then threatened another visit to the place, for the purpose of levying fresh contributions. Other bands, under Mejia and Velez, hold the roads leading to the interior of the republic, and carry out the same system of pillage and murder, having recently razed to the ground the town of Huichapam, and put to death many of its inhabitants.

The horrible murder, at Napoles, of poor Mr. Beale, a British subject, I have already mentioned to your lordship in a separate despatch, and I need only add, that notwithstanding the incessant applications made to this government by both myself and her Majesty's consul, the murderers remain still at large, ready to destroy the next unprotected foreigner whom they may surprise in an insolated place. The fate of this poor man is like that of Staines, Gibson, Duval, Bodmer, and a long list of others, whose deaths still remain unatoned for and unavenged.

Señor Comonfort, ex-president of the republic, has arrived at Monterey, in Nuevo Leon, where it is said the governor has made a "pronunciamento" in his favor, which will very likely be joined in by the neighbouring States, and probably aided by a party in this capital, who are thoroughly disgusted with the weak and tyrannical government of Señor Juarez.

Señor Llave has taken possession of the government of Vera Cruz, and this

State, it is thought, would immediately separate from the union in the event of a rupture with foreign powers.

The general dissolution of all authority in this wretched country has so much alarmed foreigners resident here that they are obliged to look to their own efforts to protect their lives and properties, and, with this object in view, are about to arm and organize themselves into a compact body for mutual defence. This measure has been sanctioned by their several representatives, and consented to by the government, on the express condition stipulated for by my colleagues and myself—that they were to remain strictly neutral in all the quarrels of the nation, and only act against those who actually attacked them.

I have, &c.,

C. LENNOX WYKE.

Enclosure in No. 19.

The Sub-Director and Miners employed at Real del Monte to Sir C. Wyke.

REAL DEL MONTE, *July* 16, 1861.

SIR: We, the undersigned, British subjects, residents of Real del Monte and Pachuca, take the liberty of addressing you on a most momentous question, in a word, to ask you, as her Majesty's representative, what guarantee we have for the safety of our lives and property.

Without referring to antecedents, such as the constant entrance of parties of rebels, or anti-government forces, whereby we have been kept in a perpetual state of alarm and anxiety, we at once beg to call your serious attention, and through you that of the English government, to what we suffered lately by the inroad of the forces under Marquez.

Our houses were forcibly entered, our females insulted, our lives threatened, and our property robbed to a large extent, to say nothing of the heavy losses occasioned to the company, of which we have the honor to form part, in forced loans, horses and arms taken, and the complete paralyzation of all works for days, thereby; as our interests are so mixed up with the prosperity or otherwise of the said company, such a loss as they have sustained lately must be felt by all.

On former occasions two Englishmen were killed, and on this one was wounded, several were fired at, beaten, and narrowly escaped with their lives, and all this without the least provocation or slightest show of resistance on our part.

We have the honor to subjoin a list of most of the property lost by the English residents here; the original list, which is in the company's office, bears the signature of General Cobos, as approved by him.

We have, &c.

STEWART J. AULD, *Sub-Director.*
RICHD. SKINFILL, *Mine Manager*
G. M. MURRAY, *Treasurer.*
WM. R. U. GRIFFIN, *Surgeon.*

(Here follow 129 signatures of English miners.)

No. 20.

Earl Russell to Sir C. Wyke.

FOREIGN OFFICE, *August* 31, 1861.

SIR: I have received and laid before the Queen your despatches to that of the 28th ultimo, inclusive.

I have to inform you that your conduct, as stated in your despatch of the 26th ultimo, is approved by her Majesty's government. Further instructions will be sent, and, in the meantime, you will act on my instructions of the 21st of August.

I am, &c.,

RUSSELL.

No. 21.

Earl Cowley to Earl Russell.

[Extract.]

PARIS, *September* 5, 1861.

M. Thouvenel said that he was so desirous of acting in complete unison with her Majesty's government in Mexican affairs, that he had determined on furnishing M. Dubois de Saligny with instructions completely identical with those transmitted by your lordship to Sir Charles Wyke.

His excellency then requested me to ask your lordship whether it might not be advisable to ask the association of the Spanish government in any measures which might be taken with regard to Mexico. His excellency observed that should a hostile demonstration become necessary, Spain possessed resources at the Havana which might be of great assistance to Great Britain and France.

No. 22.

Earl Russell to Sir C. Wyke.

FOREIGN OFFICE, *September* 10, 1861.

SIR: With reference to your despatch of the 11th of July, reporting the murder of Mr. Beale, and to your despatch of the 28th of that month, enclosing a representation from British miners at Real del Monte, I have to state to you that such atrocious outrages upon life and property committed towards British subjects cannot be extenuated by any condition of anarchy or civil war which may exist in Mexico, and that her Majesty's government must hold the Mexican nation answerable for such infamous proceedings.

I am, &c.,

RUSSELL.

No. 23.

Earl Russell to Sir C. Wyke.

FOREIGN OFFICE, *September* 10, 1861.

SIR: I have received your despatches of the 26th and 28th of July, and I have to convey to you the entire approval of her Majesty's government of your conduct as therein reported.

The suspension for two years of all payments in discharge of debt, at a time when the Mexican government can afford to spend 6,000,000 dollars in six months, is a shameless breach of faith, which cannot be in the slightest degree excused by the pretences put forward by Señor Zamacona in its defence.

Señor Zamacona asserts that the present government of Mexico are actively employed in maintaining internal and social order, in reorganizing the administration of the republic, in introducing rigid economy into all the branches of the public service, and in vigorously putting an end to the civil war and restoring internal peace to the country. But it is notorious that every one of these assertions is directly the reverse of the truth. It is well known that life and property are nowhere safe, not even in the streets of the capital; that the administration is as corrupt and as reckless of any interests but their own personal advantage as any that has heretofore governed in Mexico; that great anarchy and disorder prevail in all the departments of the government; and that so far from their having applied the resources of the state to a vigorous suppression of the civil war, the opposite party under the adherents of Miramon were, by the last accounts, in great force within a short distance of the capital, and not unlikely to become its masters.

Her Majesty's government, it is needless to say, cannot accept such excuses for the wrongs of which her Majesty's subjects in Mexico have been the victims, and therefore, if the proposals contained in my despatches of the 21st ultimo are not accepted by the Mexican government, you will finally break off relations, and put yourself in communication with Rear-Admiral Milne, who will receive instructions from the admiralty on this subject.

I am, &c., RUSSELL.

No. 24.

Earl Cowley to Earl Russell.

PARIS, *September* 10, 1861.

MY LORD: A communication has been made by the Spanish ambassador to this government that orders have been sent to the captain-general at the Havana to take possession of Vera Cruz and Tampico for the protection of Spanish interests in Mexico.

The Spanish government at the same time professes its desire to act in concert with Great Britain and France.

I have, &c., COWLEY.

No. 25.

Earl Cowley to Earl Russell.

[Extract.]

Paris, *September* 17, 1861.

I met the Spanish ambassador at M. Thouvenel's this morning, who immediately turned the conversation on the affairs of Mexico, expressing the hope that the governments of Great Britain, France, and Spain, would concert measures for common action in order to obtain the satisfaction due to them from the Mexican government.

I replied to M. Mon that I had heard from M. Thouvenel.that the Spanish government had the intention of acting alone in this matter, and had already given orders for the occupation of Vera Cruz and Tampico; that having transmitted this information to her Majesty's government, Sir John Crampton had been instructed to make inquiries of the Spanish government, and that Marshal O'Donnell had denied that any orders of the kind had been given; I should be glad, therefore, to ascertain how this matter really stood.

M. Mon replied that I must be aware that the Spanish government had more than once meditated the employment of force to obtain the satisfaction due to them in Mexico, but that they had much rather act in concert with Great Britain and France. It would only be in case of the refusal of those two powers to co-operate with Spain that she would proceed to act alone.

I related to M. Thouvenel what had passed between myself and M. Mon, observing that the Spanish ambassador's language to me did not quite tally with what his excellency had stated, the last time I had seen him, had been M. Mon's language to himself.

M. Thouvenel answered that he had not intended to convey more to me than that orders had been transmitted to the Havana to make every preparation for an expedition against Mexico, the Spanish government hoping to employ it in co-operation with British and French ships. M. Thouvenel proceeded to express the hope that her Majesty's government would not refuse this co-operation, observing that 3,000 Spanish infantry could be sent from the Havana.

I should mention that when the Spanish ambassador urged the joint action of the three governments, I stated to him the value which her Majesty's government must attach to freedom of religious profession and worship. M. Mon said that he considered that questions of that nature ought to be left to the decision of the Mexican government. He abjured at the same time, on the part of Spain, all desire to impose any particular government on Mexico; all she desired was a government chosen by the Mexicans, which would make itself respected and would scrupulously fulfil engagements taken with foreign powers.

No. 26.

Sir J. Crampton to Earl Russell.

San Ildefonso, *September* 13, 1861.

My Lord: In a late conversation with Marshal O'Donnell his excellency spoke of the present deplorable condition of Mexico.

Spain, he remarked, had suspended her diplomatic relations with the Mexican government, and he perceived both France and England had taken the same step. But would this be sufficient? He thought not. The motives of the three governments in following this course were evidently the same, viz: to enforce redress for the intolerable wrongs inflicted upon their respective subjects by the anarchical governments which succeeded each other in that distracted country.

It appeared to him, therefore, to be both possible and very desirable that England, France, and Spain should come to an understanding as to the adoption of some common course in enforcing upon Mexico the observance of her international duties.

"With respect to Spain," the marshal added, "the number of our subjects in Mexico is so great, and the interests involved so considerable, that I have no hesitation in telling you that we at all events must take decided measures to protect them. In short, we shall go there, not certainly with any view of conquest or exclusive advantage, but for the protection of our rights."

I observed that I was not at present in possession of the precise views of her Majesty's government as to what had lately taken place in Mexico, or the remedies which would be applicable to what seemed an almost hopeless state of affairs. I was, however, aware that British subjects had suffered repeated acts of oppression and denial of justice in Mexico, and I had seen it reported that our diplomatic relations with that country had been suspended. I would not fail, consequently, to acquaint your lordship with what has now fallen from his excellency on this matter.

On pursuing the subject I did not find Marshal O'Donnell prepared to suggest any definite plan of action on the part of the powers whose joint intervention he recommended. His excellency remarked, however, that the notion which had at different times been put forward of establishing by foreign intervention a constitutional monarchy in Mexico was, in his opinion, very chimerical, and he seemed entirely to concur in the justness of a remark which I made in regard to this matter, viz: that any engagement which should bind England, France, and Spain to a permanent intervention and tutelage of any sort in the internal affairs of a country so situated as Mexico would be liable to grave objections.

I am the more particular in drawing your lordship's attention to this opinion of Marshal O'Donnell, because a large portion of the Spanish press has lately been advocating an intervention of this sort, and the establishment of a monarchy in Mexico, and indulging in wild speculations as to the recovery by Spain of her ancient possessions in America and the "Indies."

I have, &c.,

JOHN F. CRAMPTON.

No. 27.

Sir J. Crampton to Earl Russell.

SAN ILDEFONSO, *September* 16, 1861.

MY LORD: Upon the receipt of your lordship's telegram of the 14th instant, informing me that Lord Cowley had reported that the Spanish ambassador at Paris had announced that the captain-general of Cuba had been ordered to take possession of Vera Cruz or Tampico for the protection of Spanish interests in Mexico, and that the Spanish government at the same time proposes to act in concert with England and France, I immediately waited upon Marshal O'Donnell and requested him to inform me whether this announcement had been made.

His excellency replied that, with respect to the desire of Spain to adopt a common course with France and England for obtaining satisfaction from Mexico for the wrongs inflicted upon their respective subjects, both M. Mon and M.

Isturiz had been instructed in the same terms to express this desire to the French and British governments, and to add that if those governments declined to adopt the coursep roposed, Spain would nevertheless feel it necessary to take, singly, such measures as might be necessary to vindicate her rights. As regarded the statement that the captain-general of Cuba had been ordered to take possession of Vera Cruz or Tampico, or to undertake any military operations against Mexico, it must have originated in a misapprehension, because he could assure me that no such orders had been given.

It was the wish of the Spanish government, the marshal added, to act in concert with France and England, in regard to this matter, and he had desired to ascertain the disposition of the two governments to do so previously to deciding upon the measures which would be necessary to effect the object in view.

All that the Spanish government had done, therefore, was to take such preparatory measures as were necessary to place them in a position to act efficaciously when the proper time came. With this view orders had been given to reinforce the garrison of Cuba by an addition of 4,000 troops, and to increase the naval force of Spain in the West Indies. The amount of the army in Cuba would be raised to about 25,000 men, and the naval force (the present amount of which his excellency did not mention) would be increased by the presence of the four screw frigates in which it was proposed to embark the troops from Spain. Two of these frigates were now about to sail; the remaining two would be ready at the end of the present month.

With regard to military operations against Mexico the marshal remarked that nothing could be undertaken before the commencement of November. The yellow fever prevailed at Vera Cruz and other parts of the coast during the present month, and the hurricanes which never failed to take place in the Gulf of Mexico during the equinox put any such operations out of the question before that period. There would, consequently, be ample time for the Spanish government to ascertain whether the French and English governments were disposed to act in concert with them, and to take measures for so doing in case those governments should agree to adopt that course.

I have, &c.,

JOHN F. CRAMPTON.

No. 28.

Lord Lyons to Earl Russell.

WASHINGTON, *September* 10, 1861.

MY LORD: Mr. Seward told me this morning that he had authorized the United States minister in Mexico to conclude a convention with that republic, in virtue of which the United States should assume the obligation to pay three per cent. interest on the foreign debt of Mexico during the period for which the payment of the interest on this debt is suspended by the recent decree of the Mexican government. The lands, minerals, &c., of certain provinces of Mexico were to be pledged to the United States, as a guarantee that Mexico would repay to them, with six per cent. interest, the sum which they would thus advance for her.

The particulars of the scheme were, Mr. Seward said, to be communicated to the governments of Great Britain and France, and the validity of the convention was to be conditional upon those governments engaging not to take any measures against Mexico to enforce the payment of the interest of the loan until time had been given to submit the convention to the ratification of the United States

THE PRESENT CONDITION OF MEXICO. 305

Senate at the session which begins in December next. It was also to be a condition that if the convention should be ratified by the United States Senate, Great Britain and France should engage not to make any demand upon Mexico for the interest, except upon its failing to be punctually paid by the United States.

The inducement to the United States to take upon themselves the payment appeared to be the extreme importance to them of the independence of Mexico. So far as I could ascertain, the instructions to the American minister with regard to this convention do not direct him to propose an alliance offensive and defensive between the two republics, nor, indeed, any other stipulations than those I have mentioned.

 I have, &c.,

                     LYONS.

No. 29.

Earl Russell to Sir J. Crampton.

FOREIGN OFFICE, *September* 23, 1861.

SIR: With reference to the affairs of Mexico, I have to state to you that it is most desirable that complications in this question should be avoided.

Certain rights on the customs of Vera Cruz and Tampico have been secured to her Majesty's government by convention.

To secure these and other rights the government of Mexico has been invited to give the control of those customs to British commissioners, who, it is understood, should also pay to other nations the sums due to them, and secured on the same customs.

No orders have as yet been given by her Majesty's government for the employment of force in Mexico, and they would be glad to know if the Spanish government will agree to postpone their action till England and France can have time to confer as to acting in concert.

 I am, &c.,

                     RUSSELL.

No. 30.

Earl Russell to Earl Cowley.

FOREIGN OFFICE, *September* 23, 1861.

MY LORD: The Count de Flahault has communicated to me the substance of a despatch from his government on the affairs of Mexico.

In this despatch M. Thouvenel, referring to the instructions recently given by the two powers to their representatives in Mexico, and which, if the demands presented therein to be made on the Mexican government are acquiesced in, will admit of the resumption of official relations on their part with the government of the republic, proceeds to say that it is necessary to provide for the two contingencies, of a refusal on the part of the Mexican government, or of the overthrow of the Juarez government before the English and French ministers receive their instructions.

M. Thouvenel then adverts to the measures of coercion to which, in the first case, the two governments might have recourse, and to the importance of coming to an early understanding on that point; and he goes on to say that, even supposing the second contingency to be realized, the two governments would, nevertheless, have to devise means for obtaining redress of grievances, and for insuring the payments of the debts which have been formally acknowledged.

M. Thouvenel is, however, of opinion that the two governments should carry their common understanding still further, and devise means for promoting the political reorganization of Mexico; and M. Thouvenel expresses his willingness to take as a basis the measures formerly suggested by her Majesty's government, as affording the best means of arriving at the pacification of the country, namely, the publication of a general amnesty, and the convocation of an extraordinary congress. He expresses his opinion, however, that the cabinet of Madrid should be invited to concur in the course to be taken by the two powers, and that the cabinet of Washington should also have the opportunity afforded to it of joining the other powers.

Finally, M. Thouvenel adverts to a communication just made to him by the Spanish ambassador of the intended despatch of a Spanish force from the Havana to the coast of Mexico, and of the readiness of the court of Madrid to act in concert with France and England.

Upon this matter I wish you to observe to M. Thouvenel that the demands of Great Britain upon Mexico are founded upon two principles:

1. The right to require security for the lives, and respect for the property of British subjects in Mexico.

2. The right to exact the fulfilment of obligations contracted towards Great Britain by the government of Mexico.

On these two principles are founded the claims urged by Sir C. Wyke. The British government is ready to prosecute these claims by its own means, or to join with other powers who have claims founded on similar principles regarding their own subjects.

Her Majesty's government are glad to find by M. Thouvenel's despatch that the government of his Imperial Majesty takes the same view of this matter, and her Majesty's government will willingly enter into concert with the government of France as to the course to be pursued. Her Majesty's government also fully concurs with M. Thouvenel in thinking that before any active steps are taken in this matter by the European powers, an offer of co-operation ought to be made by them to the government of the United States. The interest of the United State in the peace and prosperity of Mexico is such that her Majesty's government agree with M. Thouvenel in thinking that full communication should be made to the United States government.

It does not appear that the Spanish government have as yet sent any precise orders for the immediate employment of their forces in Mexico. There is, therefore, time for deliberation and concert.

With respect to the measures to be taken for the future peace and tranquillity of Mexico, her Majesty's government are ready to discuss the subject with France, Spain, and the United States. But it is evident that much must depend on the actual state of affairs at the time when our forces may be ready to act on the shores of Mexico. The measures suggested some time ago by her Majesty's government appear to be inapplicable to the present state of affairs.

I am, &c.,

RUSSELL.

No. 31.

M. Isturiz to Earl Russell.

[Translation.]

LONDON, *September* 23, 1861.

MY LORD: The despatches which I.have lately received from my government announce to me an important fact.

The injuries which the republic of Mexico seems determined to inflict upon us being unceasingly repeated, and all the measures of consideration which Spain is always inclined to adopt, so far as honor will permit, having been exhausted, the government of the Queen my august sovereign has at length resolved to obtain by force the reparation that is due to it.

The despatches of my government also inform me that Sir John Crampton, the representative of Great Britain in Madrid, is already aware of this resolution, and of the sentiments which dictate it, so that I might almost dispense with communicating it to your excellency.

However, it has appeared proper to me not to omit it, so that your excellency may be fully informed of this affair through the most direct channel.

The government of the Queen, my mistress, has therefore made arrangements to operate energetically in Mexico, and hopes to obtain the satisfaction that it claims, although it does not disguise from itself that the result of any demonstration of this sort would be more permanent if other governments, those of England and France, for example, having injuries to avenge, should think proper to unite their forces to those of Spain.

A combination of this kind would perhaps avert the repetition of such scandals, and contribute to the recognition by the Mexicans of the necessity of constituting a government which would give security at home, and sufficient guarantees abroad.

With this object, I have, &c.,

XAVIER E. ISTURIZ.

No. 32.

Earl Cowley to Earl Russell.

[Extract.]

PARIS, *September* 24, 1861.

I had the honor to receive, this morning, your lordship's despatch of yesterday's date, giving me the substance of a communication which had been made to you by Count de Flahault on the affairs of Mexico, and stating the willingness of her Majesty's government to concert with the French and other governments recognizing the same principles of action as her Majesty's government, the course which should be pursued by them in that country.

M. Thouvenel, on my communicating to him your lordship's despatch, expressed his concurrence in the views of her Majesty's government, but he remarked that as your lordship seemed to be of opinion that the measures suggested some time ago for the pacification of Mexico were inapplicable to the present state of affairs, he should be glad to receive from you the plan of action which you now propose to follow.

I inquired of M. Thouvenel whether he was in possession of any intelligence, either from Washington or from Mr. Dayton, of a proposal made by the United

308   THE PRESENT CONDITION OF MEXICO.

States government to that of Mexico with regard to the payment of the interest on the Mexican foreign debt; and finding that no intelligence on the subject had reached his excellency, I stated to him the substance of Lord Lyons's despatch to your lordship of the 10th instant. M. Thouvenel expressed the opinion that these proposals of the United States must be dealt with before the other governments interested in the Mexican question could settle any plan of common action, and he expressed himself very anxious to know the opinion of her Majesty's government. It might not be possible, he said, to prevent the United States offering money to Mexico, or to prevent Mexico receiving money from the United States, but neither England nor France ought in any way to recognize the transaction.

I said that I trusted that, in case of Mr. Dayton making any representation on this subject, M. Thouvenel would abstain from all reply until I should be in a position to inform him of the views of her Majesty's government, and his excellency promised me to follow this course.

No. 33.

Earl Russell to Earl Cowley.

FOREIGN OFFICE, *September* 27, 1861.

MY LORD: I received from Mr. Adams on the 25th instant an explanation of the proposals the United States wish to make to Great Britain and France in the affairs of Mexico.

He said that the United States government were considerably alarmed at the statements made in the newspapers regarding an intervention in Mexico, which was supposed to be in the contemplation of Great Britain, France, and Spain.

The United States government were aware that Great Britain, France, and Spain, as well as the United States, had many grievances to complain of on the part of the government of Mexico; but a direct intervention, with a view to organize a new government in Mexico, and especially the active participation of Spain in such an enterprise, would excite strong feelings in the United States. It would be considered as that kind of direct interference in the internal affairs of America to which the United States had always been opposed. In fact, there was a sort of understanding that so long as European powers did not interfere in America, the United States might abstain from European alliances; but if a combination of powers were to organize a government in Mexico, the United States would feel themselves compelled to choose their allies in Europe, and take their part in the wars and treaties of Europe.

The United States government thought that such a necessity would be avoided if Great Britain and France would accept the payment of interest by the United States of the debt due by Mexico to Great Britain and France; this advance to be continued only for a time till Mexico should be able to defray her own obligations.

I replied by relating to him, in the first place, what had taken place in Mexico itself. I then stated the overture of M. Thouvenel, including the proposal to make offers to the government of the United States to act in co-operation with us on this subject. That we had replied we had but two objects in view: 1. Security to the persons and property of British subjects. 2. The fulfilment of all the obligations of Mexico to her Majesty. Mr. Adams, I continued, would see that our demands embraced not only the payment of interest on a debt which might be settled by naming a fixed sum, be it more or less, but also comprehended satisfaction for the injuries done to British subjects; that we could hardly transfer these obligations to the United States without raising an indefinite number of questions of detail, upon which Great Britain and Mexico would have to appeal to the equity of the United States; that I thought it the interest of our two countries to have as few entangling questions and clashing interests as possible. I should be afraid that our friendly relations might be endangered if we increased the number of points upon which we might come into collision; that, without giving him a final answer, I could tell him at once that I thought the proposition of his government open to very grave objections.

Without entering further upon its merits, however, I had a counter proposition to make, which I thought deserved the serious consideration of his government, to whom I begged it might be submitted.

I was as apprehensive as he was of an attempt to build upon the foundation of debts and injuries a claim to organize a new government in Mexico; that I was convinced that, of all countries, Mexico was the one where intervention in its internal affairs would bring the most severe disappointment upon its authors; that the factions in that country were too hostile to each other and too sanguinary in their tempers to be recognized by a small force of Europeans in the name of order and moderation. But might not the evils we both feared be guarded against by defining terms of co-operation with Spain which would exclude interference in the internal affairs of Mexico? Would not this be a better course than leaving Spain to seek her own vindication and afterwards opposing the results of her operations?

I read to Mr. Adams part of Sir John Crampton's despatch of the 13th instant, to show him that Marshal O'Donnell was by no means desirous of undertaking the reconquest of the Indies.

Mr. Adams promised me that he would communicate this view to his government.

Her Majesty's government are of opinion that if any combined operations are to be taken against Mexico they should be founded on these two bases:

1. The combined powers of France, Great Britain, Spain, and the United States feel themselves compelled by the lawless and flagitious conduct of the authorities of Mexico to seek from those authorities protection for the persons and property of their subjects and a fulfilment of the obligations contracted by the republic of Mexico towards their governments.

2. The said combined powers hereby declare that they do not seek any augmentation of territory, or any special advantage, and that they will not endeavor to interfere in the internal affairs of Mexico or with the free choice of its form of government by its people.

You will read this despatch to M. Thouvenel, and give him a copy of it.

I am, &c.,

RUSSELL.

No. 34.

Earl Russell to Earl Cowley.

FOREIGN OFFICE, *September* 27, 1861.

MY LORD: With reference to my preceding despatch of this day's date, I transmit herewith, for your excellency's information, copy of a despatch from her Majesty's minister at Madrid* upon the subject of the state of affairs at Mexico, and which is alluded to in my above-mentioned despatch.

I am, &c.,

RUSSELL.

---

* No. 26.

No. 35.

Earl Russell to Sir J. Crampton.

FOREIGN OFFICE, *September* 27, 1861.

SIR: I enclose a copy of a note which Mr. Isturiz has sent me.*

Her Majesty's government have many injuries to complain of in regard to Mexico, especially the atrocious robbery committed in the house of her Majesty's legation at Mexico, and against which the Spanish minister in Mexico protested in vain.

Her Majesty's government would willingly co-operate with those of France and Spain in enforcing redress for these wrongs. There are, however, two conditions which her Majesty's government deem essential:

The first is, that the co-operation of the United States should be invited.

The second is, that the combined powers should not interfere by force in the internal government of Mexico.

Her Majesty's government would be happy to see the Mexicans constitute a government "which would give security at home and sufficient guarantees abroad." But her Majesty's government are persuaded that any attempt to effect this desirable purpose by force of arms would fail in its purpose. If the force were Spanish, one of the contending parties would be fiercely opposed to it; if it were English, the opposite party would be as strongly its antagonist. Nor is any other foreign force likely to be received with favor. The Mexicans themselves can alone put an end to the anarchy and violence which have torn Mexico to pieces during the last years.

I trust this view is in accordance with the sentiments of the Duke of Tetuan and the government of her Catholic Majesty.

I am, &c.,

RUSSELL.

No. 36.

Earl Russell to M. de Isturiz.

FOREIGN OFFICE, *September* 27, 1861.

SIR: I have the honor to acknowledge the receipt of your note of the 23d instant, acquainting me with the course which your government propose to pursue with a view to obtaining satisfaction for the injuries inflicted on Spanish subjects in Mexico, and pointing out the advantage of concerted action on the part of England, France, and Spain, for the purpose of putting an end to the present state of affairs in that republic; and I beg leave to assure you, in reply that the question shall be duly considered by her Majesty's government.

I am, &c.,

RUSSELL.

---

* No. 31.

No. 37.

Earl Russell to Lord Lyons.

FOREIGN OFFICE, September 28, 1861.

MY LORD: I transmit to your lordship herewith a copy of a despatch which I have addressed to Earl Cowley,* giving his excellency an account of a conversation which I have had with Mr. Adams respecting the proposal of the government of the United States in regard to Mexico, referred to in your despatch of the 10th instant, and I have to instruct your lordship to speak to Mr. Seward in the same sense as that in which I spoke to Mr. Adams.

I am, &c.,

RUSSELL.

No. 38.

Earl Russell to Sir C. Wyke.

FOREIGN OFFICE, September 28, 1861.

SIR: I have to state to you, with reference to my despatches of the 21st of August and of the 10th of September, that if circumstances should have caused you to quit the territory of the Mexican republic, you are at liberty to use your own discretion as to the direction in which you shall proceed, keeping, however, in the neighborhood of Admiral Milne, and having means of ready communication with him.

You will, of course, give notice to Rear-Admiral Milne; but that officer will not yet have received the instructions from the admiralty to which I alluded in my despatch of the 10th of this month, inasmuch as her Majesty's government are still in communication with the governments of other powers having similar interests in Mexico to those of this country, as to the course which should be pursued under the existing state of things in that republic.

I am, &c.,

RUSSELL.

No. 39.

Sir C. Wyke to Lord J. Russell.

MEXICO, August 8, 1861.

MY LORD: In the postscript of my despatch of the 26th ultimo I stated that I should merely acknowledge receipt of the private note I had just received from Señor Zamacona, but on reflection I thought it better not to leave unanswered the false and incorrect statements it contained, and I therefore replied to him on the 30th ultimo, copy of which note I have now the honor to enclose for your lordship's information.

I have, &c.,

C. LENNOX WYKE.

*No. 33.

Enclosure in No. 39.

Sir C. Wyke to Señor Zamacona.

[Extract.]

MEXICO, *July* 30, 1861.

I can really see no good reason for continuing a correspondence which cannot in any way alter, as you seem to suppose it may do, the resolution I have adopted to suspend all official relations with your government; yet, out of courtesy to one so well entitled to it as yourself, I will not leave unanswered your note of the 27th, with the premise, however, that having fulfilled this duty, all further communications relative to this matter must cease.

It is remarkable that, mutually desirous as we are of stating the truth, we should each feel the greatest astonishment at the other's entertaining so diametrically opposite an opinion upon a subject which, on being calmly considered, can only be looked at in one point of view.

If you feel surprise that I should have demanded the repeal of the decree of the 17th instant, how much greater must mine have been on finding that your government had dared to issue it without consulting with me as the representative of that power which was the other contracting party to a convention which said decree shamefully violated.

I cannot appreciate the false pride which, according to what you state, was the principal reason for not complying with what I demanded; for when either a nation or an individual is in the wrong, it is not dishonorable to confess it, and to offer reparation for the offence given. Had your government withdrawn the decree, they would not have been disgraced by giving way, as you assert, to the dictation of foreign diplomacy, but they would simply have retrieved a false step, and, in doing so, relieved themselves from an amount of responsibility of which at present they seem to have no idea.

In order to sustain your argument you make a number of quotations from various authors who have written on international law; but apart from the fact that such quotations are valueless without their context, there is one amongst them that directly condemns a measure which you have always said was meant to relieve the State from its pecuniary difficulties. De Martens, you say, states that the party violating an engagement is liable to indemnify the other party where such breach of contract has been caused by the offender's fault.

Now, the government of President Juarez on coming to power was possessed of ample means to liquidate all the engagements binding on the republic, but by their wilful recklessness and want of common prudence they dissipated their resources, and then fell into the difficulties from which they are now vainly endeavoring to extricate themselves by repudiating their obligations; they therefore clearly become liable to indemnify Great Britain, and thus, as I have all along told you, you aggravate instead of mitigate the evil of your poverty by the decree of the 17th.

You go on to say that many of your misfortunes have been occasioned by diplomatic agents here having acknowledged a government which you dislike; and, in reply, I can only once more observe that such agents were obliged, on the principle now universally recognized, to acknowledge a real *bona fide de facto* government holding the capital and the archives of the nation.

As for your remarks about church property, let me remind you that it is difficult to overcome the inexorable logic of facts by a few well-turned phrases; we all know what that property was, and we are now equally well aware that your government is in a state of penury, and with respect to the means proposed for paying the English claimants, I thought I had already told you that they had been condemned, on reflection, by the parties themselves, and not through any obstacle that I had thrown in the way.

In the matter of the Laguna Seca "conducta," I repeat that I am justified in calling robbery the act of taking by force that which belongs to another and not returning it; promises and fair words go for nothing in such a case as this; and I also beg again to assert that the government which committed the legation outrage was a *de facto* government recognized by the agents of European powers resident here.

Under these circumstances, and with the greatest desire to meet your wishes, allow me here to observe that I can really find nothing in your note but what confirms me still more in a resolution forced on me by the obstinacy of your government, and which my duty likewise absolutely compelled me to adopt.

If you had studied the history of the Mexican debt to the English bondholders with the attention that it really deserves, you would have learnt that the latter have in reality sacrificed, in order to relieve the republic at various times, the enormous sum of upwards of $59,000,000. The last great concession made was in 1850, when the interest was reduced from five to three per cent., a transaction which your own financial agent, Señor Payno, boasts of in his statement of 1852 as having benefited the republic to the amount of $25,581,570.

You have further thought fit to attack the nature of the British convention, and I must therefore remind you that it was founded entirely on British claims, the justice of which the Mexican government acknowledged in signing that act, and that if a great many of the bonds are now held by Mexicans instead of Englishmen, it has so come about in the natural course of money transactions on 'change, where bonds and shares pass from hand to hand according to the wants of buyers and sellers.

With regard to what you say in reply to my complaint of so many Englishmen having been butchered with impunity by your countrymen, it is no satisfaction to me to learn as a set-off that some Mexicans have also been murdered by their fellow-citizens without the crime having been punished.

These crimes, and the senseless wars carried on here since the declaration of your independence, are to be attributed to the bad passions of a vitiated population, which alone can be held responsible for a state of things unparalleled in the annals of the civilized world.

I cannot, in justice to myself, conclude this letter without telling you frankly that I consider the mere fact of my having under existing circumstances expressed an interest in the solution of the present question, ought to have saved me from the reproof of having proposed to your government what was incompatible both with my own and their dignity; and excuse me for adding that such a proposition as I have made to you does not necessarily become undignified and impracticable simply because you, an interested person, are pleased to say so.

No. 40.

Sir C. Wyke to Lord J. Russell.

[Extract.]

MEXICO, *August* 12, 1861.

In my despatch of the 27th of May last I pointed out to your lordship the nature of the terms accepted by Mr. Mathew on his recognition of the Juarez government, for the repayment of the $660,000 robbed from the British legation in the month of November last, by which that government promised to reimburse the money so stolen, by confiscating for that purpose the private property of all those persons found guilty, by a legal sentence, of participating in that outrage.

The enclosed extract from Saturday's "Estafette" gives an account of the sentence which has been passed on three of the persons implicated, viz: Don Isidro Diaz, Francisco Montéro, and Teofilo Marin, the first of whom was minister of justice and legal adviser to General Miramon.

The wretched quibble by which the accused are declared innocent of robbery, while found guilty of "occupying" funds belonging to the English bondholders, is quite in character with all that is now occurring here, and proves the utter degradation of a government whose judges even make use of a slang phrase, such as "ocupacion" has become, in order not to employ the word properly qualifying a crime which, instead of punishing, they seek to palliate by such unworthy means.

This sentence will, of course, have the effect of absolving Marquez and all others implicated in the robbery, as it frees them from the danger of criminal prosecution for what is now designated as merely a civil misdemeanor, the only punishment for which is dismissal from offices long ago forfeited by all the parties engaged in this affair.

As far as we are concerned, therefore, in our relations with the Mexican government the case stands thus:

They deny their responsibility for any acts of their predecessors, whose private property they say should be confiscated to repay the money stolen; and when measures are apparently taken for that purpose, the judge who tries the case declares that the accused are only guilty of a misdemeanor, and, therefore, that their property is safe from confiscation for so trifling an offence, for which they can only be proceeded against by civil process, as for the recovery of a debt, which under the circumstances would be an absurdity. We thus neither obtain justice nor compensation, unless her Majesty's government are determined to obtain both, by employing the only means likely to succeed with a government so utterly unprincipled as this.

Enclosure in No. 40.

Extract from the "Estafette" of August 10, 1861.

Les Proces Politiques.—Le juge de district a rendu sa sentence dans le procès intenté à. MM. Isidro Diaz, Francisco Montero, et Teofilo Marin. L'acquittement a été prononcé sur le chef de vol des fonds de la convention Anglaise.

Les considérans sur lesquels s'appuie cette décision judiciaire méritent d'être connus; aussi reproduisons nous ici le texte de la sentence:

"Juzgado de district de Mexico.—En la ville de Mexico, le 3 Août, 1861, le citoyen Licencié Jesus Maria de Herrera, deuxième Suppléant de Juzgado de district de la capitale de la république: vu les pièces du procès intenté à MM. Francisco Montero, Isidro Diaz, et Teofilo Marin, pour vol des fonds de la convention Anglaise (tels sont les termes contenus dans l'acte d'accusation) commis le 17 Novembre, 1860, dans la maison située Rue de Capuchinas et portant le No. 11, a déclaré:

"Considérant que la saisie ('ocupacion') de fonds publics ou particuliers éxécutée par des individus qui sont en état de rébellion contre le gouvernement légitime, ou, en d'autres termes, que le fait de s'emparer par la violence de valeurs appartenant à des particuliers ou à des corporations, aux etats ou au trésor public de la féderation, constitue un cas expressément prévu par les lois du pays, et notamment par la loi du 22 Février, 1832, déclarée en pleine vigueur par l'Article 58 de la loi du 6 Décembre, 1856, proscrivant les peines encourues pour délits contre la nation, contre l'ordre et la paix publique;

"Considérant que ces faits entraînent pour leurs auteurs et les complices de ces derniers, non la responsabilité criminelle, mais une responsabilité purement civile, ('responsabilidad puramente civil,') attendu que la susdite loi de Février, 1832, se borne à les déclarer responsables solidairement dans leurs biens propres ('responsables de mancomun iu solidum con sus bienes propios,') sans autre peine que le perte des honneurs et des emplois dont, au moment de consommer la saisie ('ocupaciones') jouissaient les individus en révolte contre le gouvernement;

"Considérant qu'en raison de ce qui précède, il existe une différence substantielle entre les saisies ('ocupaciones') de fonds publics ou particuliers opérées par les agents de la rébellion dans le but de favoriser et soutenir celle-ci, et les vols commis par des individus n'ayant pas ce caractère et n'ayant d'autre but que de tirer un avantage personnel de l'argent dont ils s'emparent; attendu que le premier cas constitue simplement un délit politique qui aux yeux de la loi n'a d'autre conséquence que la responsabilité purement civile ('responsabilidad puramente civil,') tandis que le second constitue un délit de l'ordre commun qualifié de vol et dont les auteurs et leurs complices sont désignés sous le nom de voleurs ('ladrones') et méritent les peines qui résultent non seulement de la responsabilité civile mais des délits criminels;

"Considérant comme étant comprise dans la première catégorie la saisie des fonds destinés au paiement des créanciers Anglais, exécutée par ordre des chefs rebelles Miramon et Marquez, le 17 Novembre, 1860, dans la maison portant le No. 11 de la Rue de Capuchinas de cette ville, attendu que ce fait a tous les caractères définis par la loi du 22 Février, 1832;

"Considérant que, en raison de ce qui précède, les auteurs et complices de la saisie doivent être considérés simplement comme passibles de la responsabilité civile ('responsabilidad civil') pour le seul fait de la saisie, dans les termes indiqués par la susdite loi, attendu que la responsabilité criminelle ne résulte que des délits de l'ordre commun qui ont pu se commettre à l'occasion de la saisie, soit qu'ils consistent dans la violence exercée contre les personnes en les maltraitant, en les blessant, ou en leur donnant la mort, soit qu'ils se rapportent aux choses, en forçant les serrures, en brisant les coffres ou en violant les scellés destinés à protéger les valeurs saisies;

"Considérant qu'il résulte, soit du procès-verbal inscrit aux feuillets 7, 8, 9, et 10 du dossier principal, et dressé par 'l'escribano Negreiros' sur les faits qui se passèrent lors de l'occupation des fonds des créanciers Anglais, le 17 Novembre, 1860, soit des déclarations fournies par MM. Antonio Barreda et Ricardo Ituarte, enregistrées aux feuillets 4 et 12 du dossier des preuves, ainsi que de celles fournies par MM. Ignacio de la Barrera et Juan Ramirez, feuillets 7 et 9 verso du dit dossier; que M. Francisco Montero n'est pas intervenu, et même n'était pas présent lorsque, pendant l'accomplissement de la saisie ('ocupacion') les délits dont il est question ont pu se commettre, attendu que, bien que sa signature figure au procès-verbal, le notaire ne fait pas figurer son nom parmi ceux des personnes qui ont été témoins des faits expressément énoncés dans le corps de ce document; d'autre part qu'il faut donner à cette insertion la valeur attribuée aux déclarations de MM. Andres Maria Peza, Luis Carrion, et Angel Bunenabad, inscrites aux feuillets 5 verso, 6 recto, 8 recto et verso, et 11 recto et verso du susdit dossier des preuves, c'est-à-dire, que le fait s'est borné à recevoir la somme saisie, et que M. Francisco Montero n'a pas été présent à l'accomplissement des faits, attendu qu'il est prouvé qu'il se présenta au lieu de la saisie après que les fonds avaient été enlevés et transportés dans la cour de la maison portant le numéro 11;

"Considérant que ce simple fait ne rend pas M. Francisco Montero responsable des actes plus ou moins criminels qui ont pu s'accomplir avant et pendant la saisie ('ocupacion') dans l'enceinte des pièces où se trouvaient déposées les fonds de la convention Anglaise, et qu'il constitue l'exercice d'une des attributions naturelles de son emploi de commissaire de l'armée réactionnaire, ce qui constitue la responsabilité politique qui incombe, d'après la constitution et les lois en vigueur, à tous ceux qui servent les gouvernements émanés de la rébellion;

"Considérant que cette dernière responsabilité même ne pèse pas sur le susdit Don Francisco Montero, attendu que les circulaires publiées par le gouvernement national les 8 Mars et 30 Avril de la présente année bornent l'action de la justice aux chefs ('cabecillas') de rébellion et à ceux qui en qualité de ministres d'etat ont servi les administrations illégitimes de Miramon et de Zuloaga, et que les circulaires amnistient ('amnistiando') tous les autres employés d'un ordre secondaire, au nombre desquels doit être placé le commissaire général de l'armée ('comisario general del ejercito');

"Considérant qui s'il est vrai qu'il peut résulter contre M. Francisco Montero un motif plus grave de responsabilité du fait de sa présence dans la maison où les fonds ont été saisis, par cela seul qu'il les a reçus (circonstance pleinement prouvée dans le procès,) il n'en est pas de même en ce qui concerne M. Isidro Diaz et M. Teofilo Marin, auxquels, bien qu'il n'existe contre eux aucune preuve relativement à la saisie des fonds de la convention Anglaise, le juge chargé de l'instruction de la cause a attribué une responsabilité de simple probabilité ('mera probabilidad'), suppléant par le fait de la présomption ('conciencia de hombre') à l'absence de preuves légales et authentiques;

"Considérant enfin qu'il est impropre ('impropia') et contraire aux termes exprès de la loi du 22 Février, 1832, de qualifier de vol par bande ('robo en cuadrilla'), comme il a été fait dans l'acte d'accusation, la saisie des fonds destinés au paiement des créanciers Anglais, attendu les faits énoncés dans les premiers motifs; d'où il résulte que la loi du 5 Janvier, 1857, relative au jugement des voleurs, des homicides, des auteurs de voies de fait et des vagabonds ('ladrones, homicidas, heridores y vagos') ne pouvait pas servir de guide dans l'instruction du procès et dans la décision, vu qu'elle ne traite pas de délits communs ('responsabilidades comunes') qui sont du ressort de la justice ordinaire, mais de délits politiques et civils ('politicos y civiles'), lesquels sont exclusivement du ressort des tribunaux de la fédération, aux termes des lois spéciales du 22 Février, 1832, et du 6 Décembre, 1856;

"Il devait absoudre et il a absout en ce qui concerne cette accusation, conformément aux dispositions de la susdite loi du 22 Février, 1832, MM. Francisco Montero, Isidro Diaz et Teofilo Marin, et il devait déclarer et a déclaré le premier passible de la peine prescrite par la dite loi en ce qui concerne les emplois et charges honorifiques dont il pouvait jouir au moment de la saisie ('ocupacion') des fonds de la convention Anglaise; et ce sans préjudice du droit des tiers et notamment de ceux du trésor public dont le représentant légal sera fondé à procéder judiciairement.

"Cette sentence sera communiquée au Promoteur F'scal, aux accusés et à leurs défenseurs; après quoi elle sera portée devant le tribunal supérieur, pour être approuvée, modifiée, ou revoquée, selon la justice. Ainsi par les présentes il a été jugé définitivement, rendu sentence, ordonné et signé.

"En foi de quoi j'ai signé.

"Lic. JESUS MARIA DE HERRERA.
"A. GILBERTO MORENO, *Secrétaire.*"

No. 41.

Sir C. Wyke to Lord J. Russell.

MEXICO, *August* 23, 1861.

MY LORD: On the 14th instant General Ortega returned to this capital with the division under his command, amounting to between 3,000 and 4,000 men, after having had two days' previously a night skirmish at Jalatlaco with the forces of General Marquez, who retreated, leaving some guns and about eighty prisoners in the hands of the enemy.

Ortega, who was heartily tired of the campaign, and anxious to return to this city with a view of intriguing against Juarez and getting himself elected president, magnified this affair into an important victory, and declared that the reactionary forces were annihilated and the rebellion put down. So far from this being the case, however, we have since learnt that Marquez is still at the head of 4,000 men, and that Megia, another chief of the same faction, has nearly 3,000 cavalry and infantry under his orders. These forces are in the centre of the country, and interrupt all direct communication between this place and the interior of the republic. The partisans of Ortega were noisy in their joyful demonstrations in honor of this so-called victory, and paraded the streets at night with music and a torchlight procession. At about 10 o'clock a large party of them drew up in front of the French legation, where they remained about twenty minutes, shouting " Death to the French minister and death to all Frenchmen!"

In the course of the same evening a shot was fired at M. de Saligny, the French minister, whilst he was walking up and down an interior corridor of his house. The ball struck and flattened against a pillar near which he was passing, fortunately without injuring him, as the fragment of detached stone hit him on the right arm.

On his colleagues being made acquainted with this infamous attempt on his life, a meeting of the corps diplomatique was held at Mr. Corwin's, the American minister, for the purpose of addressing the government collectively, not only with reference to this attack on one of the members of their body, but also to remonstrate against the demonstration before the French legation having been allowed to take place without any interference whatever on the part of the police.

I have the honor to enclose herewith copies of the correspondence which took place between the corps diplomatique and this government, which, as usual in all cases of outrage, has hitherto led to no result whatever beyond specious promises of redress.

Since this event General Ortega has been sworn in as head of the supreme court of justice, which gives him the legal right of succession to the presidency in the event of anything happening to Juarez, who, by his utter incapacity, has proved himself so unworthy of the post he now holds. A meeting of the congress has been summoned for the 30th instant, when it is supposed an effort will be made to get rid of him, and elect General Ortega in his stead.

I have, &c.,

C. LENNOX WYKE.

Enclosure 1 in No. 41.

The representatives of the United States, Belgium, Ecuador, and Prussia, to Señor Zamacona.

MEXICO, *le* 16 *Août*, 1861.

M. LE MINISTRE: L'envoye extraordinaire de France vient de nous informer que le 14 de ce mois à 10 heures du soir, une bande d'une vingtaine de musiciens, accompagnée d'un attroupement populaire, dans lequel se trouvaient plusieurs soldats en uniforme, s'est arrêtée devant la porte de la légation de France, en poussant les cris de " Mueran los Franceses!" " Muera el ministro de Francia!"

cris qui ont duré dix à quinze minutes, sans que la police se soit présentée pour faire cesser ce désordre et cet outrage public.

En portant ce fait à la connaissance de votre excellence, nous devons insister sur la nécessité q'une enquête, sévère sur la punition des coupables, et surtout celles des agents de police, qui n'ont rien fait pour réprimer un pariel excés.

Nous devons aussi signaler à votre excellence un autre fait qui, san avoir le même caractère de publicité, est plus grave encore et aurait pu avoir des conséquences funestes. Deux heures avant l'attroupement susmentionnée, un coup de feu a été tiré sur la personne du ministre de France pendant qu'il se promenait seul dans la gallérie intérieure de son hotel.

Nous espérons que cette nouvelle tentative d'assassinat mettra enfin un terme à l'insouciance avec laquelle le gouvernement a paru tolérer jusqu'ici les assassinats d'étrangers, qui se répètent presque journellement sans que les autorités prennent les mesures suffisantes pour leur répression.

Agréez, &c.,

THOMAS CORWIN.
E. DE WAGNER.
FRACO. DE EN PASTOR.
AUGT. KINT ROODENBECK.

Enclosure 2 in No. 41.

Señor Zamacona to M. de Wagner.

[Translation.]

GOVERNMENT HOUSE,
Mexico, August 17, 1861.

The undersigned receives at this moment, which is 4 in the evening, the note which the minister of the United States, in conjunction with the representatives of Prussia, Belgium, and Ecuador, has been pleased to address to him, in which he denounces to him the hostile demonstration which, he says, took place at the door of the French legation, and the attempt at assassination of which he declares the French minister to have been the object a little while before.

Notwithstanding all the gravity of those acts, and the publicity which is attributed to one of them, the collective note to which this is a reply has been the first information relative to this matter received by the undersigned, who certainly deplores profoundly, that in treating of events of such gravity the French minister should not have employed a more expeditious manner of informing the government, and thus have enabled it to investigate immediately into the real state of the case, and punish the guilty if it appeared that there were any. The information has been given to the government after three days, and in a note drawn up apparently since yesterday.

In order to repair this delay, the undersigned has immediately transmitted the note which he answers to the ministry of justice, in order that a serious judicial investigation may be made concerning the facts which are denounced to him. The judge to whom this is intrusted will doubtless share the interest felt by the president for the investigation of the truth of what has taken place, and it is to be hoped that the result of this measure will not give occasion for the imputation to be repeated to the government, that it is indifferent to the personal security of foreigners.

And with reference to this offensive imputation, the undersigned, on seeing it stated in the note which he answers, has experienced two most bitter impressions: one that is natural to whoever feels himself the object of an unjust reproach, and the other that which is felt in seeing persons generally benevolent and discreet serve as a medium for accusations which perhaps have their origin in illwill and hasty judgments. It cannot have escaped the perspicacity of Baron de Wagner what superhuman efforts the Mexican government has made, and is making, for the re-establishment of peace and order, with which will come the remedy for all the evils experienced at the present time, not only by the foreigners resident in the republic, but also by the Mexicans. But the guardian spirit of the government is most evident with reference to the former, and in proof thereof could be cited the measures that it has taken in consequence of the attack upon Captain Aldham, of the English navy, and of the assassination of Mr. Beale; measures which, on account of the suspension of relations with the representative of Great Britain, have not been able to be communicated to him.

In answering with this statement the aforesaid collective note of the diplomatic corps, the undersigned, &c.,

MANUEL MA. DE ZAMACONA.

Enclosure 3 in No. 41.

M. de Wagner to Señor Zamacona.

MEXICO, *ce* 21, *Août*, 1861.

Le soussigné, ministre résident de Prusse, a eu l'honneur de recevoir l'office de son excellence M. de Zamacona du 17, relatif aux attentats commis à la légation de France.

Le soussigné s'est empressé de s'associer à la démarche collective du 16 de ce mois, espérant qu'elle offrirait au gouvernement Mexicain l'occasion de reprouver hautement ces odieux attentats, et d'en poursuivre les auteurs. L'opinion que le soussigné et les autres membres du corps diplomatique ont énoncée sur l'attitude du gouvernement Mexicain à l'égard des nombreux assassinats qui se commettent, est basée sur des faits comme ceux qui se trouvent consignés sur la feuille ci-jointe. Cette opinion, qui est trés général, se maintiendra tant qu'on se borne à ordonner seulement des enquêtes sans que les malfaiteurs soient, en effet, poursuivis, attrapés, et punis.

Le soussigné ignore si les crimes énumérés dans l'annexe ont reçu leur châtiment. Si les lois et les juges ne sont pas assez sévères, les facultés extraordinaires du gouvernement doivent y suppléer; car si les assassins, les malfaiteurs, et les voleurs de toute espèce restent impunis, les conséquences seront aussi funestes pour les victimes que pour la république.

Le soussigné, &c.,

E. DE WAGNER.

Enclosure 4 in No. 41.

Statement of outrages committed upon foreigners in Mexico.

Assassinat du vice-consul d'Angleterre, Bodmer, à Tasco.
Do. du Sieur Richard Rule à Pachuca.
Do. du Dr. Gibson près d'Acapulco.
Do. du Sieur Stephen Bennett à Pachuca.
Do. du Sieur Beale à Napoles.
Do. de Madame Chaurier entre Pachuca et Mexico.

Attentat avec blessures mortelles contre le Capitaine Aldham.
Do. du Sieur Rojas contre le Consul Allsopp à Tépic.
Do. contre M. Lettsom, chargé d'affaires d'Angleterre, près de Tacubaya.
Do. contre M. Burnaud à Cuajimalpa.
Les auteures de ces attentats n'ont pas été punis.

Attentat avec blessures mortelles commis dans la rue de San Juan de Letran, sur M. Charles Wagner, attaché à la légation de Prusse.
Attentat contre MM. Brecker, pére, fils, et neveu, au moulin de Belen, près de Tacubaya, vols et déprédations.
Attentat et vol commis sur Guillaume Hulvershorn dans la rue de Capuchinas par trois voleurs à cheval.
Attentat et enlèvement du Sieur Heidlmann près de Cuernavaca.
Attaque de la diligence et vol du ministre de Prusse près d'Ayotla et du Peñon.
Attaque nocturne contre le brasseur Strüttmayer près d'Alameda.
On ignore le résultat des enquêtes, et si les malfaiteurs on été punis.

Attentats commis contre des Français en 1861.

Louis Gaudry, marchand tailleur à Mexico, rue San Francisco, fut assailli par plusieurs bandits devant la porte de son habitation, et blessé d'un coup de poignard, le Janvier, 1861.
François Barateigt, cordonnier à Mexico, fut assailli à 7 heures du soir dans la rue de la Providence par six hommes. Il fut blessé d'un coup de poignard, puis dépouillé même d'une partie de ses vêtements, 21 Janvier.
Louis Majérus, petit marchand, alors établi à Tacubaya. Ayant eu affaire à Puebla dans la fin de Janvier, il y fut assassiné et dépouillé dans la rue le second jour de son arrivée dans cette ville. La police l'ayant ramassé baigné dans son sang, il supplia les agents de le transporter à son logement, où il se serait fait soigner. La loi, lui repondit-on, exigeat qu'il allât en prison pour être interrogé et de là à l'hôpital. Tandis que le pauvre blessé était ainsi trainé comme pièce de conviction d'un crime demeuré impuni, la chambre d'auberge dans laquelle il avait laissé ses bagages fut complètement dévalisée, et il a fallu que ses amis de Puebla lui fournissent du linge, des habits, et de l'argent pour se rendre à son domicile.
Ajoutons que le juge qui fut chargé de l'instruction de cette affaire s'est constamment refusé à remettre à Majérus, ni au vice-consul de France, aucun document constatant les faits, notoires à Puebla.
En Février les Sieurs Augustin Coffe et Alexandre Bordemann furent maltraités, blessés et injustement emprisonnés par les autorités de Minatillon. Ces sevices durèrent jusqu'au 22 Avril, qu'un bâtiment de guerre vint les prendre pour les mener à Vera Cruz.
Pierre Maurel, hotélier à Rio Frio, puis au Palmas, sur la route de Puebla, a été deux fois pillé, puis enlevé par des brigands, en Janvier et Avril.
Pierre Lement, assassiné le 11 Mars à Pinar, entre Puebla et Perote, au lieu où deux jours auparavant avait été tué Mr. Yorke.
Louis Mathieu Bonhomme, propriétaire rural, fut assassiné à Velmonte, sur la route de Durango, à dix-huit lieues de cette ville, le 3 Avril.
Alexis Maurice, conducteur de charriots, a été enlevé, maltraité, et plusieurs fois mis à rançon par des brigands en Avril, Juin, et Juillet.
Lucien Fix, administrateur d'une hacienda de M. de la Torre, dans le territoire d'Iturbide, enlevé le 18 Avril par des brigands, et relâché moyennant rançon après des jours de souffrances.
Madame Eugénie Maison, assassiné près Cordova le 12 Mars et décédée le 21 Avril.

Pierre Lacoste, commerçant, assassiné à Rosas, sur la route de Queretaro à Mexico, à dix-huit lieues de la capitale, le 9 Mai.

Auguste Firmin Davesne, maître meunier, assassiné le 18 Mai, dans le moulin du Battant à trois lieues de Mexico. Les assassins, qui furent même reconnus et désignés à la justice, se promènent tranquillement dans le pays, et y gaspillent en paix le produit du crime, car ils ont dû se partager 5,000 à 6,000 piastres.

Benjamin Jaffré, contre-maître au moulin du Battant, assailli par les brigands qui voulurent tuer Davesne; il fut blessé à la téte de plusieurs coups de crosse et laissé sans connaissance le 18 Mai. Aujourd'hui guéri de ses blessures.

Jean Baptiste Delaporte, assassiné à Otumbilla, à huit lieues de Mexico, le 2 Août. Les assassins, qui sont parfaitement connus et tous voleurs de profession, n'ont point été inquiétés jusqu'ici.

Louis Guerrier, jeune artisan demeurant à Mexico, fut enlevé dans le village de San Autonio, le 26 Juin. Après avoir été grièvement blessé par les brigands armés qui l'avaient trouvé sur la route, et les avoir péniblement suivis pendant une journée et une nuit, il a pu s'échapper et rejoindre sa famille.

Jean Caire, propriétaire rural, a été enlevé sur sa propriété de Salazar, le 2 Juin. Relâché moyennant rançon.

Louis Acho, fils, enlevé de l'hacienda de son père, près Puebla en Juin. Relâche moyennant $1,000.

Jaques Loudais, commerçant, attaqué et blessé par des brigands dans la rue de San Clara, le 21 Juillet.

Joseph Louis Thinesse, tailleur, dépouillé et roué de coups par des soldats du gouvernement, à un quart de lieue de Cuernavaca, le 24 Juillet.

Paul Dairo, marchand colporteur, assassiné à Huichilaque à deux lieues de Cuernavaca, le 2 Août.

Jaques Bernard, commerçant, attaqué par quatre soldats dans la rue de Zuleta, blessé de coups de sabre et volé, le 28 Juillet.

Benoit Deffis, négociant à Temascaltepec, enlevé par des soldats dits pronouncés, emprisonné, maltraité de toute façon, et relâché après trois jours de souffrance, et sa maison pillée, le 28 Juillet.

Pierre Duhart, seul employé de la maison Echenique, de Temascaltepec, enlevé et traité comme M. Deffis, et la maison également pillée par les mêmes, le 28 Juillet.

Henri Hanville, mineur à Temascaltepec, se trouvant absent le 28 Juillet a été pillé.

Adrien Daste, directeur de mines, a eu ses chevaux volées.

Auguste Daussart, brasseur, a été attaqué par plusieurs bandits, et a été blessé dans rue San Francisco, le 11 Août.

Joseph Agand, maître meunier, au moulin del Sacono, commune de Tlalmanalco, près de Chalco. Le 17 Août courant dix hommes de la garde de sûreté de Chalco sont venus demander les écuries du moulin pour l'usage de la petite garnison. Après s'être introduits dans l'établissement sous ce pretexte, et avoir placé des sentinelles au dehors, ils ont trouvé un autre prétexte pour attirer le Sieur Agand et quelques autres employés dans la chapelle du moulin, où ils les ont enfermés. Après quoi ils ont pillé le moulin, sans oublier les effets personnels du Sieur Agand et des domestiques. Cinq des soldats bandits ont été reconnus par l'alcalde de Tlalmanalco, qui les a désignés au préfet, mais inutilement.

Le 18 Août courant, M. Victor Prudhomme, industriel fort inoffensif de Mexico, a été brutalement frappé au visage par un lieutenant colonel qui passa rapidement à côté de lui un pistolet à la main, lancant en même temps l'épithète de "estrangero."

H. Ex. Doc. 100——21

No. 42.

Sir C. Wyke to Lord J. Russell.

[Extract.]

MEXICO, *August* 24, 1861.

I have the honor to enclose translation of a decree issued the night before last by this government, imposing a tax of 1 per cent. on all capital exceeding 2,000 dollars, to be paid to the government as follows: One-third on the day following the publication of the decree, another at the end of eight days, and the remaining third at the expiration of a fortnight. Those persons not complying with these stipulations are to be punished by fines of 50 per cent. on such contributions. Nothing can possibly be more arbitrary or unjust than this, as many persons during the whole of yesterday remained in ignorance that such a decree had been published and placarded during the night at the corners of two or three of the principal streets of the capital. This tax at first was only to be levied within the district of Mexico, but by an additional decree, published yesterday, I hear it is to be levied on the capital, wherever it may be, of all inhabitants of the district whose fortunes may exceed the sum mentioned.

On this being known, the British merchants here addressed a letter to me on the subject, which I have the honor to enclose, together with my reply thereto.

Were this principle once admitted, the door would be open to all sorts of illegal exactions on the part of a government so rapacious and utterly unprincipled as this. Finding that their decree of the 17th ultimo, suspending the convention payments, did not produce as much as they expected, they are now determined to obtain funds by forced contributions, for this tax is nothing else under another form. I was glad to find that all my colleagues here took the same view of the case as I did, and recommended their countrymen respectively to resist the payment of this impost, except on compulsion and under protest. Mr. Corwin, the United States minister, alone refrained from doing so, and although urged by us, in a meeting which took place to-day at his house, to join the Prussian minister and the chargés d'affaires of Belgium and Ecuador in remonstrating with the government on the injustice of this measure, we could not persuade him to do so, although he must be aware that had he acted with us, this government would never dare, in their present precarious position, to set at defiance the remonstrances of the whole corps diplomatique.

Baron Wagner, the Prussian minister, yesterday called on Señor Zamacona, and recommended him at once to withdraw the decree, or not to apply it to foreigners resident here, as he knew that, with the exception of the Americans, they had all been recommended by their representatives only to pay the tax on compulsion and under protest.

The government again urges necessity as their excuse, saying that, as the commercial body of Mexico would not advance them the sum of 400,000 dollars a month for their expenses, on the guarantee of the maritime custom-houses, an offer which they had made and which had been refused, they had no other alternative but to do what they have done.

If one once acknowledges their right to tax capital for 1 per cent., they may, when next in want of money, levy 10, 15, or 20 per cent. on it, and thus ruin the whole commercial body here.

Were the money thus obtained spent in restoring order, or in affording protection to the lives and properties of those so taxed, there would be some excuse for so arbitrary a measure; but, instead of this, the disorder reigning here becomes every day greater, whilst many of the smaller shopkeepers are utterly bankrupt from the paralyzation of all trade.

Under these circumstances, I trust your lordship will approve of the advice I have given to the English merchants here, and the more so, as it is in strict accordance with the instructions issued to my predecessors when a similar tax was imposed by the former government.

Enclosure 1 in No. 42.

Decree.

[Traduction.]

Le citoyen Juan José Baz, gouverneur du district fédéral, à ses habitants faisons savoir:
Qu'il m'a été adressé, par le ministère des finances et du crédit public, le décret suivant:
Le citoyen Benito Juarez, président constitutionnel des etats-unis Mexicans, à leurs habitants faisons savoir:
Qu'en vertu des facultés que concède au gouvernement le décret du 4 Juin dernier, j'ai décrété ce qui suit:
Article unique.—Il est établi, dans le district, une contribution de un pour cent sur les capitaux qui excèdent $2,000; elle sera payable de la manière suivante, à la direction générale des contributions directes: un tiers le jour qui suivra la publication du présent décret, un autre tiers dans les huit jours, et le dernier tiers dans les quinze jours.
De ceux qui ne verseront pas leurs cotes dans les délais exprimés, on les exigera, au moyen de la faculté économico-coactive, avec les surcharges que fixent les lois en vigueur.
Pourquoi j'ordonne, &c.
Donné au Palais National, à Mexico, le 21 Août, 1861.

BENITO JUAREZ.

Au citoyen JOSÉ H. NUÑEZ,
Secrétaire d'Etat et des Finances et du Crédit Public.

Et je vous le transmets pour son accomplissement.
Dieu et liberté!
Mexico, le 21 Août, 1861.

JOSÉ H. NUÑEZ.

Au citoyen GOUVERNEUR *du District.*

Et pour qu'il arrive à la connaissance de tous j'ordonne qu'on l'imprime, qu'on le publie, &c.
Mexico, le 22 Août, 1861.

JUAN JOSÉ BAZ.
JOSÉ M. DEL CASTILLO VELASCO,
Secrétaire.

Enclosure 2 in No. 42.

Messrs. Graham, Geaves & Co., and others, to Sir C. Wyke.

MEXICO, *August* 23, 1861.

SIR: We beg to call your attention to a decree which has appeared in some of the papers this morning, by which a contribution of 1 per cent. is imposed upon all capitals exceeding $2,000.

At a time when we had great hopes that reparation would be demanded by her Majesty's government for similar exactions under the late administration, we cannot but express our surprise at the present illegal demand of the Mexican government; but we consider that the form of the present decree may probably be understood to exclude foreigners. You will observe by the annexed copy of the decree in question that the 1 per cent. is to be levied in the federal district only, and does not therefore come under the denomination of the general taxation of the country to which we are bound to contribute.

The first payment of one-third of the amount is to be paid in this very day, under the heaviest penalties in case of delay, and we therefore beg that you will favor us with your opinion as to whether we are obliged to contribute to a system of taxation against which so many objections have already been raised by her Majesty's legation on previous occasions, and which in the present case appears clearly most unjust, both on account of its partial action and of the illegal principle, now renewed, of imposing forced loans upon us at the will of government, under the false name of taxes.

We beg to add that the fixed taxes under a very heavy assessment have already been exacted from us in advance, and are paid up to the 31st of December next. Should the right of government be now admitted to the present capital tax, our past experience proves that we are sure to be called upon every few days for further contributions, which, as we all know, are purely required for war purposes.

We have, &c.,

GRAHAM, GEAVES & Co.,
And others.

Enclosure 3 in No. 42.

Sir C. Wyke to Messrs. Graham, Geaves & Co., and others.

MEXICO, *August* 23, 1861.

GENTLEMEN: In reply to your communication bearing this day's date, asking my opinion as to whether you are obliged to pay the new tax of 1 per cent. on capital, against the principle of which, when similar taxes were formerly levied, her Majesty's legation, you say, had protested; I would recommend you only to pay said tax on compulsion and under protest, after duly notifying the same to those persons authorized to levy it.

I am, &c.,

C. LENNOX WYKE.

No. 43.

Sir C. Wyke to Lord J. Russell.

MEXICO, *August* 26, 1861.

MY LORD: The question of the British convention has been brought under the consideration of her Majesty's government so frequently, and always, hitherto, as a cause of complaint on the part of those interested in it, that I regret excessively again to recur to the subject.

I am compelled, however, to do so on the present occasion, not only because the Mexican government have of late publicly attacked the convention, but because there are certain matters of importance connected with it which require, I consider, some explanation on my part, in order to clear up the doubts which have been and still are entertained with respect to the origin and management of this fund.

Before I proceed to the discussion of this now complicated question, I would mention that, in order to avoid as much as possible a continued repetition of figures in the body of this despatch, I have had drawn up in the mission the enclosed memorandum, which I trust may be found useful for purposes of reference, if at any future period the Mexican government or private individuals carry their complaints and accusations directly before the foreign office.

I will now endeavor to trace the history of the convention from its commencement. In 1842 her Majesty's minister at Mexico, Mr. Pakenham, concluded a diplomatic arrangement for the payment of certain recognized claims; and in 1851 it was evident that, so far from having carried out this arrangement, the Mexican government had incurred additional liabilities, which they were equally unable to meet, and which rendered a fresh arrangement of some sort absolutely necessary.

Hence it was that Mr. Doyle, on the 4th of December, 1851, signed the convention which has given rise to so many and such needless difficulties, and in which were included as well the claims under the Pakenham convention as other credits which had been severally recognized by the British and Mexican governments.

The creditors met at the national treasury, and, after the usual preliminaries on both sides, it was agreed that the claims, amounting to $4,984,914, should be treated as a consolidated fund, to be paid off upon the generally received principles of debtor and creditor; that is to say, the government obliged themselves to pay interest on this consolidated fund at the rate of 3 per cent. per annum, with a sinking fund of 5 per cent.; it being further stipulated that five years after the ratification of the convention the interest was to be raised to 4 per cent., and the sinking fund to 6 per cent.

For this purpose the Mexican government were supposed—I say supposed, for reasons which will hereafter appear,—to mortgage to us 12 per cent. per annum of their entire customs revenue, upon the condition that if this assignment of 12 per cent. more than sufficed for the interest and sinking fund, the commissioner appointed by the creditors for receiving their money was to return to the treasury any surplus, whereas in the contrary case, the treasury was to meet any deficit by the first drafts they received from any of their maritime custom-o uses.

The manner in which this 12 per cent. of import duties was mortgaged to us I will explain in its proper place, for it has seriously affected us, and, indeed, may be said to have been the origin of all subsequent troubles.

It so happened, to continue my narrative, that at the end of the first year, *i. e.*, in December, of 1852, the stipulated custom-house assignments were not forthcoming, consequently it became necessary to call upon government to fulfil their engagements upon this point; and on the 27th of November of the same year a sub-convention (copy of which is enclosed herewith, as meriting your lordship's attention) was signed by Mr. Doyle, whereby a further custom-house assignment of 3 per cent. was set aside solely for paying this deficit, to cease so soon as the deficit was made good.

To all intents and purposes, however, the original assignment of 12 per cent. now became 15 per cent. permanently, because, although this increase of 3 per cent. was originally only meant to cover a particular class of arrears, it never did so; on the contrary, arrears went on accumulating instead of diminishing, more assignments were asked for and granted, and ultimately we were supposed to have mortgaged to us 29 per cent. of import duties, wherewith to satisfy interest and sinking fund, the interest, by an arrangement made by Mr. Otway, having been increased from 4 to 6 per cent., while the sinking fund remained, as stipulated in the 5th article of the original convention, at 6 per cent. per annum.

Such is the history of the British convention; and it will now be my duty to explain, as far as may be, the complications and difficulties which have ensued, and which in many cases could, and most certainly should, have been avoided.

First in the list of complainants come the government themselves, who were the other contracting party to the Doyle convention, and they begin by attacking the very elements of the convention, which they allege to be suppositious, and lay especial stress upon the introduction into the arrangement of what are commonly known as the "tobacco bonds."

To avoid entering here into a lengthy and unnecessary discussion upon a question which for many years occupied the attention of her Majesty's government, I will simply state, though for the sake of reference I beg to enclose a short account of this particular grievance, that Messrs. Martinez del Rio, who are naturalized British subjects, and the present agents of the convention, became possessors, under a guarantee from the supreme government, of certain of these "tobacco bonds," to the amount of about $2,500,000. Their tenure thereof had been sanctioned by her Majesty's government, and when afterwards the Mexican government, in spite of their guarantee, attempted to dispute the right of tenure, Mr. Doyle received positive instructions from home to support Messrs. Martinez, and to insist upon justice being done to them. A plan of settlement was proposed, but though partly initiated by the Mexican government, never carried into effect.

This happened in 1849, and it seemed only natural that two years later what had now assumed the character of a claim, and might almost be said to have formed a convention of itself, should be admitted into the new compact concluded by Mr. Doyle in 1851.

This is the first objection to the convention, and I cannot help thinking that it must be looked upon as perfectly groundless.

Next in order follow the complaints raised by certain private individuals who, either after the fashion of a Mr. Grant, one of convention bondholders, attack the convention generally, or like Messrs. Bourdillon and Moran, (the latter being in no way connected with the convention of that name to which I shall have occasion to refer,) paid agents for claims not included in the convention, persist in affirming that their clients' interests have been damaged by the illegitimate uses to which the convention custom-house assignments have been turned.

In 1852, as your lordship will have observed, a special increase of 3 per cent. on the customs revenue was allotted to pay off a particular deficit, with the proviso that it was to cease as soon as the deficit was made good. A Mr. Dalton, whose case has been before the foreign office since 1857, had, I believe, obtained from the Mexican government the reversion of this 3 per cent. whenever it again became government property, and in 1860 his agents, Messrs.

Bourdillon and Moran, did their utmost to procure this reversion, upon the ground that the original object for which the 3 per cent. of import duties was assigned had long ago been accomplished, and that the convention had no further right to it.

The Mexican government were only too glad to seize such an opportunity, and eagerly acquiesced in the assertion that the 3 per cent. had reverted to them, upon what plea I cannot say, for, so far from laying any claim to it, they had themselves sanctioned its running on as part and parcel of the convention custom-house assignments, had even of their own free-will added a something to it, as will be seem by article 2 of Mr Otway's convention, which forms enclosure No. 4 of this despatch, and never thought of its reversion until Messrs. Bourdillon and Moran, Mr. Dalton's agents, appeared on the stage in 1860.

Be this, however, as it may, the enclosed document will, I feel assured, set the matter to rights; for thereby and subsequent, be it remarked, to the application of Mr. Dalton's agents it becomes evident that this person could in no way interfere with the British convention, and, indeed, I know that he himself had proposed to the Mexican government a new arrangement for the payment of what was owing to him.

At any rate, however, our priority of claim to this said 3 per cent. cannot be questioned, for it is proved (memorandum, paper D) that notwithstanding the gradual, though in reality merely nominal, increase of our custom-house assignments from 12 to 29 per cent., not even the original assignment of 12 per cent. has ever yet been paid up.

If, then, we have never received in full the first assignment of all, it surely cannot be illogical to infer that we have not obtained anything over and above that first assignment, and consequently that, inasmuch as the above-mentioned additional assignment has never yet been paid, it cannot possibly have fulfilled the object for which it was granted.

There is one point which both the Mexican government and these private individuals appear to have overlooked when attacking the convention; they do not remember that, be the elements of a convention or compact what they may, they cannot suffer change for good or bad, when once that convention or compact has been ratified, unless it be with the full consent of both contracting parties; and it ill becomes any Englishman, especially at the present moment, to attempt to overthrow a diplomatic arrangement which had obtained the sanction and support of his government, and when the very stipulations thereof compensate him, as in the case of Mr. Grant, for losses which would never have been made good to him but for the intervention of her Majesty's legation.

I now come to the real and most serious difficulty connected with this convention, and would that its solution were simpler; yet I am at a loss to conceive how the actual error which led to this difficulty escaped the observation of my predecessors, or was allowed to be perpetuated up to the present date by the very agents of the fund, whose duty it most certainly was to have had it rectified.

It so happened that two days after the ratification of Mr. Doyle's convention, *i. e.*, on the 6th of December, 1861, Señor Sayas, the Spanish minister in Mexico, signed on behalf of some of his countrymen a convention almost identical with our own. The interest on the debt thereby recognized was the same, the sinking fund the same, and it was equally stipulated in both conventions that a certain government order, which was to authorize the custom-house to set aside the proper proportion of custom-house assignments for the payment of the said interest and sinking fund, "should be considered as having been inserted in and as forming part" of the convention for which it was intended.

The Sayas or, as it is generally called, the Padre Moran convention, was only for a sum of $983,000, whereas, as I have already stated, ours represented $4,984,914, yet, strange to say, the government order, which was to be looked upon as quite as sacred as any part of either convention, was one and the same in each case. This order shall, however, speak for itself; and your lordship will observe that the 12 per cent. of import duties, which, as I stated above, was supposed to have been mortgaged to us, is by the order set aside for the purpose of satisfying the conditions of both the Padre Moran and the British conventions; no division of the 12 per cent. is made therein, no proper proportion thereof is defined, the 12 per cent. stands there as much the property of the one as of the other convention.

Now, even supposing, for the sake of argument, that the Mexican government had intended there should be but one order, and that 12 per cent. of the import duties was to suffice for paying the interest and sinking fund of both conventions, one might have expected to discover in the order some clear definition of the proportion that the 12 per cent. was to bear to each convention.

It was, however, otherwise, and the consequence is that our own and the Spanish convention have, as it were, been merged into one. The agencies of the two conventions, which once were separate, have ceased to be so. Messrs. Martinez del Rio from the very beginning were recognized as the sole agents for both, though, in point of fact, that of Padre Moran, as a Spanish convention, became a dead letter, and, to all intents and purposes, might as well have never existed, since all applications to this legation for support and protection have been made by Messrs. Martinez del Rio in their capacity as agents for the British convention.

Up till now we have been allowed to slumber on in the full assurance that the original, as well as every additional custom-house assignment was ours. Such, however, has not been the case; from 1851 to 1860 her Majesty's government, this legation, and British ships-of-war, have been laboring on behalf not only of British but of Spanish interests, for out of every assignment we have received, with the exception of that obtained by Captain Aldham, a sixth part has regularly been handed over by Messrs. Martinez del Rio to the sister convention, while no violation of contract has ever taken place; but we, and we alone, have been appealed to by them for redress, and it was not until early in 1861 that Messrs. Martinez del Rio breathed a word that could imply the fact of their having thus practically and systematically amalgamated the two conventions. Why, or wherefore, they should have made an exception to their general line of conduct in the case of the Aldham convention I am unable to say. It is sufficient that they did so, and it appears to me that the letter, copy of which I herewith enclose, addressed by them to Mr. Mathew, in reference to this subject, is proof enough that a doubt must always have existed in their minds as to the propriety of claiming British protection for a convention with which we had nothing in the world to do.

It is useless for these gentlemen to assert that in issuing one order the Mexican government intended the two conventions to draw from one and the same fund, that the proportion of the custom-house assignments to those conventions was naturally in the ratio of the two debts, and that consequently their conduct can be justified.

If such, indeed, was the intention of the Mexican government, surely it could not also have been their intention to make one convention responsible for what belonged to another convention, and that other convention of a totally different nationality. This would have been absurd, and I fear, therefore, that but one construction can be put upon the whole affair; the order on the custom-houses was simply a piece of trickery on the part of the Mexican government, nobody took the trouble to counteract it, and we alone have been the dupes to our own prejudice, but to the profit of others.

There is one fact which cannot be disputed. A certain order, the very essence, if I may use the expression, of both conventions, but which does not exist at the time of ratification, becomes by anticipation an actual part of both. By that order, not a separate one, be it remarked, for each convention, 12 per cent. of import duties is to be set apart for satisfying the demands of both conventions; consequently there enters an idea of partition, the entire 12 per cent. being the sole property of neither convention: we, therefore, have no right to the whole, nor has the Spanish convention any right to it, but we have been made responsible for the whole, and our agents have applied to us for protection when the whole was not given to us; moreover, Mr. Doyle in his sub-convention states positively that the whole is ours in virtue of the actual convention, while the actual convention proves it is not ours by article IV, for that article and the original custom-house orders are, I might almost say, synonymous terms, and the latter distinctly states that it is not ours.

The 12 per cent. of import duties then is ours, and is not ours: it is ours, because we have claimed it and our claim has not been questioned; it is not ours, because whenever it has been obtained a sixth part has always been taken away from us.

It is now perhaps too late to remedy the evil that has been done, but henceforward it will be our fault if Spain does not look after Spanish, and England after English interests, whenever the moment arrives for reinstating the conventions in the position they lost through the government decree of the 17th ultimo, which amongst other payments suspended those belonging to diplomatic arrangements.

Far be it from me to make any direct accusation against those who have been principally to blame in this matter, but I cannot acquit Messrs. Martinez del Rio of great and culpable negligence. As agents of the British convention fund they ought to have known that whatever may have been the object of the Mexican government in issuing but one custom-house order for two conventions, it never could have been intended that the British legation alone was to see that order carried out, to the prejudice of its own and the profit of Spanish interests; it was their bounden duty to have called the attention of the legation to the existing state of affairs, and they left that duty undone.

I need not, of course, assure your lordship that in thus accusing Messrs. Martinez del Rio of great negligence, I have no intention or wish whatever to cast a slur upon their character as honorable men: still I feel that, in the interests of all parties concerned, it would be much better, for obvious reasons, to place the agency in other hands; and I do not think I can recommend to your lordship a better or fitter person to succeed Messrs. Martinez del Rio than Mr. Consul Glennie, who is now auditor of the fund, and who, I feel sure, has the esteem of all those who are connected therewith. It appears to me, too, that it would be more becoming for the convention to have its agency in our consulate, and I cannot help thinking that such an appointment as the one I have now the honor of proposing to your lordship would tend greatly to diminish the existing causes of complaint.

I have only now further to call your lordship's attention to the fact that there are but few Englishmen holders of convention stock at the present time; it has passed on 'change into other hands, principally Mexican, and I have, for purposes of reference, accompanied my memorandum on the convention with a list of those who were bondholders when the first dividend took place, as well as of those who are now holders of convention stock; and it is worthy of remark, that even during the first six months after the ratification of the Doyle compact, bonds were eagerly bought up in the money market, so great was at that time the confidence inspired by an agreement for the due fulfilment of which Great Britain was supposed to be a responsible party.

Such, my lord, is the account of the British convention, past and present; its length may, perhaps, seem to require some apology on my part. Had I, however, curtailed it, I much fear I should have failed in the original object I had in view, and that so far from being useful at a future period for reference, this despatch and its enclosures would merely have added to the difficulties connected with the convention.

While, then, I sincerely trust that, in its present state, this will not be found to be the case, may I request your lordship, should my proposals meet with your approbation, to be good enough to send me such instructions as will admit of immediate action, not only as regards the future agency of the British convention, but also as regards the restoration of the Spanish convention to the protection of its rightful owners?

Everything connected with the so-called British convention has got into such a tangle of confusion, that it would have been impossible for me to have understood the actual state of the case without the assistance of Mr. Walsham, whose experience here, joined to the untiring assiduity he has displayed in elucidating the whole question, and putting the numerous enclosures of this despatch into proper order, have been of the greatest service in enabling me to transmit a statement which I hope may hereafter prove useful for reference, whenever the subject of this convention and its numerous complications shall again be brought under the notice of the foreign office.

I am, &c.,

C. LENNOX WYKE.

Enclosure 1 in No. 43.

Memorandum on the British convention.

On the 15th of October, 1842, Mr. Pakenham signed a convention with the Mexican government, in which it was stipulated that certain recognized claims, amounting to about $250,000, should be formed into a consolidated fund, to be paid off, capital and interest, by a percentage on the import duties at the maritime custom-houses of Vera Cruz and Tampico.

This convention was not carried out by the Mexican government; and on the 4th of December, 1851, Mr. Doyle signed a fresh one, in which not only the claims under the Pakenham convention, (see annexed paper A,) but others, which had been recognized by both the English and Mexican governments, and had indeed formed separate diplomatic arrangements, were included, (see papers B and C.)

By Mr. Doyle's convention the claims, amounting to $4,984,914, were likewise formed into a consolidated fund, the Mexican government obliging itself to pay thereupon 5 per cent. as sinking fund, and 3 per cent. as interest, until the debt should be paid off.

To meet this 5 per cent. and 3 per cent., it was agreed that a certain portion of the annual customs revenue should be set apart, and half-yearly dividends take place; and it was further stipulated that in 1857 the sinking fund should be raised to 6 per cent., and the interest to 4 per cent.

Now it so happened, that two days after Mr. Doyle had signed his convention, Señor Sayas, Spanish minister in Mexico, also signed a convention on behalf of some Philippine missionaries, which is generally known as the "Padre Moran" convention, and which, singularly enough, was made upon exactly the same basis as our own. Its consolidated fund was $983,000, the sinking fund 5 per cent., and the interest 3 per cent.

This 5 per cent. and 3 per cent. were to be increased respectively to 6 per cent. and 4 per cent. at a stated period, and to be satisfied, as in our case, by yearly custom-house assignments, whenever it could be found out what amount of assignment would be necessary.

Instead, however, of fixing this amount at the time of ratification, the Mexican government only did so some two months afterwards by a custom-house order setting apart 12 per cent. of import duties for paying the sinking fund and interest of both conventions, but unfortunately without specifying in what proportion this 12 per cent. was to be made.

At first each convention had its own agent in Mexico, but later on Messrs. Martinez del Rio, naturalized British subjects, took charge of both, and from that time it would seem the Padre Moran convention lost its nationality; for we, though until now unaware of the fact, have always collected its portion of custom-house assignments, as will hereafter appear.

The original custom-house assignment for both conventions was 12 per cent. At the end of 1852 it had not been paid, and to meet the deficit the Mexican government assigned an additional 3 per cent. until it should be made good; but this 3 per cent. had simply reference to the English part of the deficit, as appears from Mr. Doyle's sub-convention (forming enclosure No. 3 in the despatch,) for there is no evidence that any steps were taken in this direction by the Spanish representative; yet as Messrs. Martinez del Rio had previously, on their own responsibility, apportioned to the Padre Moran convention a sixth part of what the custom-house did pay in 1852, so also they now made over a sixth part of the additional 3 per cent.

In 1852, therefore, the state of the conventions was—

British convention.—Sinking fund, 5 per cent.; interest, 3 per cent.; custom-house assignment, 12 per cent., and 3 per cent. for arrears.

Padre Moran convention.—Sinking fund, 5 per cent.; interest, 3 per cent.; custom-house assignment, 12 per cent., and 3 per cent. for arrears.

In 1857, the interest and sinking fund of both conventions became, as originally stipulated therein, sinking fund, 6 per cent.; interest, 4 per cent.; the only difference in the custom-house assignment being that the 3 per cent., originally intended to pay off a particular class of arrears, was now merged into the body of assignments, which therefore stood at 15 per cent.

In 1858 the Mexican government, apparently of their own free will, increased this 15 per cent. to 16 per cent., and Mr. Otway, in the same year, had the interest of the British convention raised to 6 per cent.

Thus, at this period, the following was the progress made in both conventions:

British convention.—Sinking fund, 6 per cent.; interest, 6 per cent.; custom-house assignment, 16 per cent.

Padre Moran convention.—Sinking fund, 6 per cent.; interest, 4 per cent.; custom-house assignment, 16 per cent.

In 1859 the arrears on the sinking fund had accumulated to $1,800,000, and it was then that Captain Dunlop, senior naval officer in the Gulf of Mexico, obtained an additional 8 per cent. of import duties; and in 1860, when the custom-houses of Vera Cruz and Tampico had seized assignments to the amount of $350,000, Captain Aldham, who had succeeded Captain Dunlop, made a further convention, by which 5 per cent. more of import duties was to be set aside, though only in the custom-houses of Vera Cruz and Tampico. Both the 8 per cent. of Captain Dunlop and the 5 per cent. of Captain Aldham were to cease as soon as they had respectively satisfied the $1,800,000 arrears, and $350,000 ("occupation") above referred to. It is certain that Captain Aldham's 5 per cent. was upon all import duties from all vessels at the ports of Vera Cruz and Tampico. The 8 per cent., however, of Captain Dunlop would appear to refer to the custom-houses generally, and to have been upon all import duties from all except French vessels.

Both the 8 per cent. and the 5 per cent. were solely for the specific object above referred to, and were to cease directly that object was attained, so that the regular custom-house assignment upon all import duties from all vessels was, as has been stated, only 16 per cent.; and yet if the statement (see paper D) made by Messrs. Martinez del Rio be correct, even the original assignment of 12 per cent. has never been paid, much less that of 16 per cent.

Between 1852 and 1861 the proper amount of interest had been paid upon the consolidated fund of the British convention, viz: $1,744,604 14, and nearly the proper amount of interest upon the consolidated fund of the Padre Moran convention, viz: $320,197 99, instead of $344,961 50; (see papers E and F,) whereas the sinking fund of the two conventions, which during the same period stand at $2,592,165, British convention; $511,160, Padre Moran convention, have only respectively been paid $810,634, and $157,280. Of course convention stock has frequently changed hands in the money market, and this will account for so many of the present holders of bonds being foreigners.—(See paper G.)

Table showing the various changes which have taken place in the British and Padre Moran conventions between 1851 and 1860.

Sinking fund and interest to be paid to British convention.	Custom-house assignments to satisfy both conventions.	Sinking fund and interest under Padre Moran's convention.
Mr. Doyle's convention.		
1851. Sinking fund, 5 per cent. Interest, 3 per cent.	12 per cent	Sinking fund, 5 per cent. Interest, 3 per cent.
1852. Sinking fund, 5 per cent. Interest, 3 per cent.	12 per cent. and 3 per cent, (arrears.)	Sinking fund, 5 per cent. Interest, 3 per cent.
1857. Sinking fund, 6 per cent. Interest, 4 per cent.	15 per cent	Sinking fund, 6 per cent. Interest, 4 per cent.
Mr. Otway's convention.		
1858. Sinking fund, 6 per cent. Interest, 6 per cent.	16 per cent	Sinking fund, 6 per cent. Interest, 4 per cent.
Captain Dunlop's convention.		
1859. Sinking fund, 6 per cent. Interest, 6 per cent.	24 per cent	Sinking fund, 6 per cent. Interest, 4 per cent.
Captain Aldham's convention.		
1860. Sinking fund, 6 per cent. Interest, 6 per cent.	29 per cent	Ceased to participate in extra assignments.

MEXICO, *August* 20, 1861.

A.

Pakenham convention, Agent P. de Ansoategui; concluded by Mr. Pakenham, on the 15th of October, 1842, with the consent and approbation of both the British and Mexican governments, as is proved by the despatches marked in the margin.

Original capital	$287, 412 09
Interest to November 30, 1850	160, 804 45
	448, 216 54
Amount paid off to same date	291, 654 95
Balance included in Doyle convention	156, 561 59

Parties representing Pakenham convention:

Jecker, Torre & Co	$67, 246 59
Manning & McIntosh	52, 573 71
Viuda Echeverria é hijos	27, 813 57
Drusina & Co	13, 717 27
J. J. de Rozas	12, 203 12
Aguero Gonzalez & Co	13, 850 56
Alexander Grant	54, 483 03
C. A. Fornachon	2, 332 00
Martinez del Rio, Brothers	32, 561 79
Domingo de Ansoategui	4, 067 70
G. J. Martinez del Rio	250 00
Bates Jamison & Co	1, 600 00
E. J. Perry	3, 862 75
Ernesto Masson, for G. & J. Campbell	500 00
Thomas H. Worrall	350 00
	287, 412 09

B.

Diplomatic arrangement commenced on behalf of Messrs. Montgomery, Nicod & Co., by Mr. Pakenham, continued by Mr. Doyle in 1843–'44, and concluded by Mr. Bankhead in 1844.

Amount of capital on January 1, 1843	$1, 036, 489 25
Paid as "refaccion," on May 27 and September 23	112, 980 00
	1, 149, 469 25
Interest up to December 3, 1851	845, 743 70
	1, 995, 212 95
Amount received up to same date	842, 491 77
Balance included in Doyle convention	1, 152, 721 18

Parties interested in above arrangement:

Martinez del Rio, Brothers	$563,127 22
Stephen Miller	11,402 67
D. Manterola, for Echeverria	22,748 04
C. de Luchet	65,427 11
B. Maqua	121,878 81
Frederick Montgomery	116,728 02
W. Mackintosh	3,000 00
M. Mead	119,728 02
M. Moreda	22,805 34
J. B. Jecker	2,624 02
	1,149,469 25

C.

Diplomatic arrangement concluded by Mr. Doyle with the Mexican government in 1849, on behalf of Messrs. Martinez del Rio, agents at that time for what was known as the "tobacco claims;" liquidated up to December 3, 1851.

Amount of "tobacco bonds"	$2,745,000 00	
Amount of "interior debt" bonds	717,000 00	
		$3,462,000 00
Amount received		384,000 00
Capital unpaid on December 31, 1851*		3,078,000 00
Due for interest to same date	601,727 91	
Less received from the treasury	4,095 84	
		597,632 07
Balance included in Doyle convention		3,675,632 07

*Parties interested in the above arrangement:

Martinez del Rio Brothers	$1,003,348 97
J. S. Bengough	251,899 03
J. A. de Bertegui	841,122 61
Benito Maqua	354,053 55
Muriel Brothers	155,974 87
Edward J. Perry	31,837 33
Rafael Beraza	18,521 85
Manuel Escandon	156,749 65
Viuda de Echeverria	138,158 25
F. Fagoaga	74,627 32
Aguero Gonzalez y Ca	43,005 47
J. Rodriguez de S. Miguel, for Madame Arismendi	8,601 10
	3,078,000 00

THE PRESENT CONDITION OF MEXICO. 335

D.

Statement of the amount received from all the custom-houses on account of the convention fund, from 1852 to 1859.

1852..	$261,914 24
1853..	406,198 26
1854..	540,514 26
1855..	343,107 52
1856..	301,917 05
1857..	104,087 25
1858..	130,593 16
1859..	420,149 87
	2,508,481 61

The annual estimated produce of the import duties is from $7,000,000 to $8,000,000, but even taking the very low figure of $5,000,000, it will be seen that in no one year has the original assignment of 12 per cent. been paid.

E.

BRITISH CONVENTION—Original capital, $4,984,914 84.

Date.	Sums that ought to have been paid on account of—		Date.	Sums actually paid on account of—	
	Capital.	Interest.		Capital.	Interest.
June 4, 1852	$124,622 87	$74,773 72	July 31, 1852	....	$74,773 72
Dec. 4, 1852	124,622 87	74,773 72	Dec. 4, 1852	$60,084 84	74,773 72
June 4, 1853	124,622 87	73,872 45	Sept. 5, 1853	....	73,872 45
Dec. 4, 1853	124,622 87	73,872 45	Dec. 30, 1853	175,939 05	73,872 45
June 4, 1854	124,622 87	71,233 37	June 5, 1854	....	71,233 37
Dec. 4, 1854	124,622 87	71,233 37	Dec. 28, 1854	300,839 61	71,233 73
June 4, 1855	124,622 87	66,720 77	June 15, 1855	124,622 87	66,720 77
Dec. 4, 1855	124,622 87	64,851 43	Dec. 20, 1855	....	64,851 43
June 4, 1856	124,622 87	64,851 43	July 12, 1856	....	64,851 43
Dec. 4, 1856	124,622 87	64,851 43	Dec. 27, 1856	149,148 47	64,851 43
June 4, 1857	149,547 45	83,485 60	Jan. 25, 1858	....	83,485 60
Dec. 4, 1857	149,547 45	83,485 60	May 20, 1858	....	83,485 60
June 4, 1858	149,547 45	125,228 40	May 12, 1859	....	125,228 40
Dec. 4, 1858	149,547 45	125,228 40	Sept. 14, 1859	....	125,228 40
June 4, 1859	149,547 45	125,228 40	Jan. 5, 1860	....	125,228 40
Dec. 4, 1859	149,547 45	125,228 40	Apr. 12, 1860	....	125,228 40
June 4, 1860	149,547 45	125,228 40	July 16, 1860	....	125,228 40
Dec. 4, 1860	149,547 45	125,228 40	May 1, 1861	....	125,228 40
June 1, 1861	149,547 45	125,228 40	July 12, 1861	....	125,228 40
Total...	2,592,155 75	1,744,604 14		810,634 84	1,744,604 14

F.

Padre Moran's Convention—Original capital, $983,000.

Date.	Sums which ought to have been paid on account of—		Date.	Sums actually paid on account of—	
	Capital.	Interest.		Capital.	Interest.
June 4, 1852	$24,575 00	$14,745 00	July 31, 1852	----------	$14,745 00
Dec. 4, 1852	24,575 00	14,745 00	Dec. 4, 1852	$9,830 00	14,745 00
June 4, 1853	24,575 00	14,597 55	Sept. 5, 1853	----------	14,597 55
Dec. 4, 1853	24,575 00	14,597 55	Dec. 30, 1853	34,060 95	14,597 55
June 4, 1854	24,575 00	14,086 63	June 5, 1854	----------	14,086 63
Dec. 4, 1854	24,575 00	14,086 63	Dec. 28, 1854	59,324 05	14,086 63
June 4, 1855	24,575 00	13,196 78	June 15, 1855	24,575 00	13,196 78
Dec. 4, 1855	24,575 00	12,828 15	Dec. 20, 1855	----------	12,828 15
June 4, 1856	24,575 00	12,828 15	July 12, 1856	----------	12,828 15
Dec. 4, 1856	24,575 00	12,828 15	Dec. 27, 1856	29,490 00	12,828 15
June 4, 1857	29,490 00	16,514 40	Jan. 25, 1858	----------	16,514 40
Dec. 4, 1857	29,490 00	16,514 40	May 20, 1858	----------	16,514 40
June 4, 1858	29,490 00	24,771 60	May 12, 1859	----------	24,771 60
Dec. 4, 1858	29,490 00	24,771 60	Sept. 14, 1859	----------	24,771 60
June 4, 1859	29,490 00	24,771 60	Jan. 5, 1860	----------	24,771 60
Dec. 4, 1859	29,490 00	24,771 60	Apr. 12, 1860	----------	24,771 60
June 4, 1860	29,490 00	24,771 60	July 16, 1860	----------	24,771 60
Dec. 4, 1860	29,490 00	24,771 60	May 1, 1861	----------	24,771 60
June 4, 1861	29,490 00	24,771 60		----------	----------
Total	511,160 00	344,969 59	----------	157,280 00	320,197 99

G.

Convencion Inglesa, 1o dividendo, Julio 31 de 1852.

Martinez del Rio Hermanos	$1,670,000 00
G. J. Martinez del Rio	15,000 00
J. P. Martinez del Rio	12,000 00
E. J. Perry	51,000 00
Alejandro Grant	97,000 00
Rafael Beraza	22,000 00
	1,867,000 00
J. A. de Beistegui	1,006,000 00
B. DeMacua	546,000 00
J. S. Bengough	301,000 00
Manuel Escandon	187,000 00
Muriel Hermanos	186,000 00
Viuda de Echeverria é hijos	182,000 00
J. B. Echave, por Testamentaria de D. Manterola	129,000 00
J. B. Echave, por Testamentaria de J. M. Echeverria	23,000 00
McCalmont Geaves y Ca., Testamentaria de F. Montgomery	117,000 00
McCalmont Geaves y Ca., por la Compañia Unida	9,000 00
J. B. Jecker	103,000 00

THE PRESENT CONDITION OF MEXICO. 337

Jecker, Torre, y Ca., por C. de Luchet	$65,000 00
Id..........id..Gme. Cochran	28,000 00
Id..........id..M. Moreda	22,000 00
Id..........id..Estevan Miller	11,000 00
J. M. Flores, Testamentaria de F. Fagoaga	90,000 00
Agüero Gonzales y Ca	57,000 00
Schmidt, Higson y Ca	13,000 00
C. Whitehead	7,000 00
J. Rodriguez de S. Miguel	10,000 00
J. J. de Rosas	7,000 00
C. G. Kauffmann	6,000 00
Benjamin Laurent	5,000 00
Concurso de Guillermo de Drusina y Ca	3,000 00
C. A. Fornachon	2,000 00
Manning y Mackintosh	2,000 00
Bates, Jamison, y Ca	914 84
Convencion Inglesa	4,984,914 84
Convencion Española (names not given)	983,000 00

Names of proprietors or agents given in the account of the 2d dividend of the Spanish convention, made December 4, 1852.

M. J. de Lizardi	$368,625 00
Cayetano Rubio	245,750 00
McCalmont Geaves & Ca., por M. de Embil y Ca	184,312 50
Jecker, Torre, y Ca	184,312 50
	983,000 00

CONVENCION INGLESA, 19o dividendo, Julio 12 de 1861.

Martinez del Rio Hermanos	$417,876 63
E. J. Perry	50,880 00
José de Ansoategui	45,254 66
	514,011 29
Carlos Byrn	1,117,698 94
Hermenegildo de Viya	50,000 00
Id...por Viya Hermanos	97,103 45
Id...por Francisco Giffard	200,603 46
Id...por Rafael Beraza	18,480 00
Id...por J. de Muñoz y Muñoz	5,793 10
Francisco G. de Luzarraga	368,000 00
Francisco Morphy	206,724 14
Graham Geaves y Ca	88,908 89
Id......por F. Montgomery	98,280 00
Antonio M. Priani	170,000 00
J. B. Echave	20,000 00
Id....por Testamentaria de D. Manterola	108,360 00
Id....por J. M. Echeverria	19,320 00

H. Ex. Doc. 100——22

Viuda de Echeverria é hijos	$120,103 02
N. Davidson	100,000 00
Manuel Soriano	100,000 00
Alejandro Graut	100,000 00
Agüero Gonzales y Ca.	38,880 00
Miguel Buch	50,000 00
Francisco Buch	10,000 00
Raymundo Mora	69,613 98
Martin Carrera	68,275 86
Manuel M. Rubio	55,600 00
Benjamin Barton	43,000 00
J. J. Schmidt y Ca., por Schmidt, Higson, y Ca	10,920 00
Teodore Chavez	46,551 73
Manuel Hernandez	38,000 00
Jorge S. Whitehead	36,666 62
C. y J. Whitehead	3,242 23
J. B. Jecker y Ca., por Guillermo Cochran	23,520 00
Id .... por Estevan Miller	9,240 00
Francisco Colina	30,000 00
Juan Antonio de Beistegui	25,000 00
Juan Antonio de Beistegui por Testamentaria de Azurmendi	3,754 19
J. Velasquez de Leon	26,827 59
José C. Murphy	24,512 81
G. R. Glennie	14,600 00
P. Echeverria, por Menores Echeverria	12,432 00
A. Pamanes	9,793 10
C. G. Kauffman	8,400 00
J. Rodriguez de San Miguel	8,400 00
J. J. de Rosas	5,880 00
J. M. Landa, por E. Mugaburu	1,383 61
Convencion Inglesa	4,174,280 00

Convencion Espanola.

Carlos Byrn	$309,645 00
Francisco J. de Luzarraga	254,822 50
Juan Antonio de Beistegui	154,822 50
Miguel Bringas	103,240 22
Francisco Morphy	3,189 78
	825,720 00

Enclosure 2 in No. 43.

THE PAKENHAM CONVENTION, SIGNED OCTOBER 15, 1842.

Whereas it is expedient that a definite arrangement be concluded for the payment of certain sums acknowledged to be due by the Mexican government to subjects of her Britannic Majesty, the discharge of which has, in some

Por cuanto es conveniente que se concluya un arreglo definitivo para el pago de ciertas cantidades reconocidas por el gobierno Mexicano á favor de varios súbditos de su Magestad Británica, cuyo pago, en algunos casos en

cases in the whole, and in others in part, been hitherto prevented by unforeseen circumstances; the government of the Mexican republic have, from a desire to meet the wishes of that of Great Britain, consented to conclude with her Majesty's minister plenipotentiary a formal agreement for the above purpose; wherefore the undersigned, her Britannic Majesty's minister plenipotentiary, having met in formal conference, by previous appointment, in the office of foreign affairs, the minister of that department and the minister of finance, they have agreed to the following articles:

la totalidad, y en otros en parte, no ha podido hasta ahora verificarse por circunstancias imprevistas, el gobierno de la república Mexicana, dispuesto de conformarse con los deseos del de la Gran Bretaña, ha convenido en concluir con el ministro plenipotenciario de su Magestad un convenio formal para el objeto indicado: á cuyo fin, reunidos en conferencia formal citada previamente en el ministerio de relaciones exteriores y gobernacion, los infrascritos ministros del citado ramo y del de hacienda, con el espresado ministro plenipotenciario de su Magestad Británica, han convenido en los articulos siguientes:

ARTICLE I.

Of the import duties accruing at the ports of Vera Cruz and Tampico, from and after the date of the present agreement, there shall be set apart two per cent. in the former and one per cent. in the latter port, to be applied to the payment of the sums acknowledged to be due up to this date to British subjects. The proceeds of these appropriations shall be paid over to the agent of the parties interested in them, to be distributed in proportion to their respective credits.

The duties already disposed of by the government in their whole amount previously to the date of this agreement are not included in these appropriations, it being understood that the portion of the duties assigned by the present article shall not henceforward be disposed of for any other object.

ARTICULO I.

De los productos de los derechos de importacion que se causaren en los puertos de Vera Cruz y Tampico, desde la fecha del presente convenio en adelante, se separará un dos por ciento en el primero, y el uno por ciento en el segundo, que se aplicará á pago de las cantidades reconocidas hasta el dia á favor de súbditos Británicos. Los productos de estas asignaciones se entregarán al agente que designen los interesados en ellas, para que las distribuya en justa *prorata* con proporcion al monto de los creditos que representen.

No se comprenden en estas asignaciones los derechos de que en totalidad haya dispuesto el gobierno con anterioridad á la fecha de este convenio, entendiendose que en lo sucesivo no se dispondrá para otro objeto de la parte de derechos consignada por el presente articulo.

ARTICLE II.

Such of the said credits as have hitherto gained interest by virtue of pre-existing agreements shall continue to gain interest at the rate in each case stipulated; and such as have not hitherto been entitled to interest shall hereafter be entitled to it at the rate of twelve per cent. per annum.

ARTICULO II.

Los creditos que hasta el dia han ganado interes á virtud de convenios pre-existentes, seguirán gozandolo segun la cuota estipulada en cada caso; y los que hasta ahora no lo han disfrutado, tendrá derecho á el á razon de un doce por ciento anual.

Article III.

It is moreover agreed that the interest accruing up to this date, and not yet discharged, shall be computed and added to the respective capitals; and this new capital shall be entitled to interest at the rate of twelve per cent. per annum up to the date of its discharge.

Article IV.

In order to prevent any doubt or misapprehension as to the description of credits to be entitled to the benefit of the present agreement, it is declared that its application shall extend only to such credits as have been acknowledged by the Mexican government through the interference of the British mission, including the sums exacted from time to time from the subjects of her Majesty under the head of forced loans.

Article V.

It is formally declared by the parties to this agreement that it shall be considered as having the same force and effect, and being equally binding, as a convention between the two governments.

In witness whereof we, the ministers aforesaid, have signed it, and sealed it with our respective seals.

Done at Mexico, this fifteenth day of October, one thousand eight hundred and forty-two.

[L. S.] R. PAKENHAM.
[L. S.] J. M. DE BOCANEGRA.
[L. S.] G. INGUERAS.

Articulo III.

Se conviene ademas que los intereses vencidos hasta esta fecha, que no han sido satisfechos, se liquidarán y agregarán al capital respectivo, y este nuevo capital disfrutará tambien del beneficio del doce por ciento de interes anual hasta su pago.

Articulo IV.

En obvio de cualquiera duda ó mala inteligencia en cuanto á la clase de creditos que han de disfrutar de las ventajas del presente convenio, se declara que ellas se aplicarán solamente á los creditos que han sido reconocidos por el gobierno de Mexico á solicitud de la legacion Británica, entre los que comprenden las cantidades exigidas en diversas épocas á súbditos de su Magestad en clase de prestamos forzosos.

Articulo V.

Se declara solemnemente por ambas partes que el presente convenio se considerará de la misma fuerza y valor que una convencion entre los dos gobiernos, y que será igualmente obligatorio.

En fé de lo cual los espresados ministros lo firmamos, y sellamos con nuestros sellos respectivos.

Fecho en Mexico, á quince de Octubre, de mil ochocientos cuarenta y dos.

[L. S.] J. M. DE BOCANEGRA.
[L. S.] G. INGUERAS.
[L. S.] R. PAKENHAM.

Enclosure 3 in No. 43.

SUB-CONVENTION, SIGNED BY MR. DOYLE, NOVEMBER 27, 1852.

In virtue of the convention signed on the 4th of December, 1851,* between the minister for foreign affairs of the Mexican republic and her Britannic

En virtud de la convencion que se firmó el dia 4 de Diciembre de 1851* por el excelentisimo señor ministro de relaciones de la república Mexicana y

---

a See Enclosure 5 in No. 43.

Majesty's chargé d'affaires in that republic, it was agreed that twelve per cent. of the sums received at the maritime custom-houses should be set apart for the payment of the three per cent. interest and of five per cent. destined to pay off the capital of the sums included in that convention, and that "if at the end of the year the amounts due for interest and for paying off the capital should not be covered, the general treasury, without waiting for any further orders, was to pay the amount due with the first drafts it received from the maritime custom-houses."

It has been ascertained that, in consequence of the revolutionary movements which have been for some time existing, and which unfortunately still exist in various parts of the republic, there will be a large deficit on the 4th proximo in the amount necessary to pay the sums stipulated upon in the aforesaid convention. With the view, however, of proving the entire good faith with which the Mexican government is resolved to carry the convention of the 4th of last December into effect, and which has been partially delayed on the present occasion by the unforeseen circumstances above-mentioned, a formal conference by previous appointment took place this day in the office of foreign affairs, the minister of that department, the minister of finance, and her Britannic Majesty's minister plenipotentiary being present, when the following agreement was come to, namely:

That for the payment of the sums which may be ascertained to be due in the liquidation to be made on the 4th of next December, of the three per cent. interest, and of the five per cent. destined to pay off the capital under the English convention, there be set apart from that date a further sum of three per cent. of the import duties in the maritime custom-houses of Vera Cruz, Tampico, Acapulco, Manzanillo, Altata, and Guaymas, and in those of San Blas and Mazatlan, as soon as they return to the obedience they owe to the

el encargado de negocios de su Magestad Británica en dicha república, se convenió que se separaria un doce por ciento de los derechos de importacion en las aduanas marítimas para pagar el tres por ciento de reditos y cinco por ciento de amortizacion de las sumas comprendidas en esa convencion, y que "si al fin del año no estuvieran cubiertas los intereses y el cinco por ciento de amortizacion, la tesorería general, sin necesidad de nueva orden, cubriria el deficit con la primeras libranzas que recibiera de las aduanas marítimas."

Mas habiendose reconocido que, á consecuencia de los movimientos revolucionarios que de algun tiempo á esta parte se han presentado, y que por desgracia todavia existen actualmente en varios puntos de la república, habrá un deficit considerable para completar la suma que corresponde al dividendo que se debia pagar el dia 4 del proximo Diciembre conforme á la citada convencion; y con el fin de manifestar la absoluta buena fé que el gobierno Mexicano quiere mostrar en el cumplimiento de la convencion del 4 de Diciembre ultimo, y que en esta ocasion se ha diferido parcialmente por las circunstancias imprevistas ya mencionadas, se citó una conferencia formal, la cual se ha efectuado el dia de hoy en el ministerio de relaciones, estando presentes los señores ministros de relaciones y de hacienda, y el señor ministro plenipotenciario de su Magestad Británica, y se convinó en el arreglo siguiente:

Se destina para el pago de la cantidad que por la proxima liquidacion resulte deberse á la convencion Inglesa, por el tres por ciento de reditos y cinco por ciento de amortizacion correspondientes al año que termina el 4 de Diciembre proximo, un tres por ciento mas de lo que tiene señalado de los derechos de importacion que se causen en las aduanas marítimas de Vera Cruz, Tampico, Acapulco, Manzanillo, Altata, y Guaymas, y en las de San Blas y Mazatlan, cuando vuelvan el orden.

342   THE PRESENT CONDITION OF MEXICO.

This increase of three per cent. will cease as soon as the deficit is made good. [L. S.] PERCY W. DOYLE.	Este aumento del tres por ciento cesará en cuanto esté cubierto el deficit espresado. [L. S.] M. YANEZ.

Enclosure 4 in No. 43.

THE OTWAY CONVENTION, SIGNED AUGUST 10, 1858.

At a conference held between the undersigned minister plenipotentiary of her Britannic Majesty and the minister for foreign affairs of the Mexican republic, with the object of drawing up in due form the new arrangements relative to the fulfilment of the convention of 4th December, 1851, for the payment of claims of British subjects against the national treasury, which, by approval and sanction of his excellency the acting president of the republic, were agreed to on the 31st of last month, in conformity with the contents of the confidential note addressed by the latter to the former on the same date, bearing in mind the previous circumstances of this transaction, the explanations in various conferences with reference thereto, the statement given in writing on the 23d of the same month by Messrs. Martinez del Rio Brothers, as parties interested in the same convention and agents thereof, and moreover all that which was stated verbally by Messrs. Martinez del Rio in the last conference as to the losses and injuries sustained in consequence of the delays and want of punctuality in the payments, the large amount which on this account is due to them, and the rights to which, in virtue of the said convention, they are entitled, especially those conceded by article VII, of which they might take advantage, as the case provided against has now arisen, being desirous of not carrying matters to this extremity, but, on the contrary, to conciliate inasmuch as possible the interests of the creditors with the distressed position of the national finances in consequence of the circumstances in which the country	Reunidos los infrascritos ministro de relaciones esteriores de la república Mexicana y ministro plenipotenciario de su Magestad Británica con el objeto de extender en debida forma los arreglos relativos al cumplimiento de la convencion de 4 de Diciembre de 1851, sobre pago de créditos de súbditos Ingleses contra el erario nacional que, con aprobacion de su excelencia el presidente interino de la república quedaron acordados desde el 31 del mes proximo anterior, segun la nota confidencial que el primero pasó al segundo en la misma fecha, teniendo en consideracion los antecedentes de este negocio, lo manifestado en diversas conferencias acerca de él, lo espuesto por escrito en 23 del mismo por los Señores Martinez del Rio, Hermanos, como interesados y agentes de la referida convencion, y cuanto de palabra espresó el Señor Martinez del Rio en la última conferencia sobre los daños y perjuicios que han sufrido con ocasion de las dilaciones y falta de puntual cumplimiento en el pago, la crecida suma que por tal motivo se les debe, y los derechos que por tal convencion les competen, especialmente los que les dejó á salvo el articulo VII, de que pudieran hoy hacer uso por haber llegado el caso previsto en él deseando no llevar las cosas á este estremo, sino conciliar cuanto sea posible los intereses de los acreedores con el estado angustioso del erario por las circunstancias en que actualmente se encuentra la nacion, y aprovechando los buenos sentimientos que siempre han mostrado los espresados acreedores, animado el gobierno por su parte de los mas sinceros deseos de proteger, cuanto esta á su alcance,

finds itself, and profiting by the favorable disposition always evinced by the said creditors, and, at the same time, the government being on their part animated by the most sincere desire to protect, in as far as may be in their power, the interests of British subjects, have agreed as follows:

Article I.

For the exact fulfilment, strict observance, and inviolability of the convention of December 4, 1851, regarding British claims, and with the view of repairing in some degree the injuries sustained by the parties therein concerned from the want of the punctual payment of the quotas assigned, all dividends which from this time forward shall be declared on account of interest, shall be so at the rate of six per cent. per annum in lieu of three and four as hitherto stipulated.

Article II.

The payments will continue to be made on the terms stipulated in the aforesaid convention, setting aside for that purpose the assigned quota of sixteen per cent. of the import duties of the maritime custom-houses, without any alteration or change whatever, and remitting the same in bills, as agreed upon, for delivery to Messrs. Martinez del Rio Brothers.

Article III.

The amounts which have been omitted to be paid to the parties interested, and to which they have a just and indisputable right, will be made good to them whenever the government shall possess sufficient means, it being impossible to effect this at the present moment, in consequence of their urgent necessities and limited resources.

Article IV.

The aforesaid convention of the 4th of December, 1851, and all the provisions necessary for its exact fulfilment,

los intereses de los súbditos Británicos, han acordada los articulos siguientes:

Articulo I.

Para el exacto cumplimiento, estricta observaucia, é inviolabilidad de la convencion de 4 de Diciembre, de 1851, sobre creditos Ingleses, y reparar de alguna manera los perjuicios que han sufrido los comprendidos en ella por falta de pago puntual de los cuotas señaladas, todo dividendo que se haga desde esta fecha en adelante por cuenta de reditos será á razon de seis por ciento al año en vez del tres y cuatro que estaba estipulado.

Articulo II.

Los pagos continuarán haciendose en los términos espresados en dicha convencion, separandose al efecto en las aduanas maritimas sin variacion la cuota fijada de diez y seis por ciento de los derechos de importacion, remitiendose en libranzas, como esta dispuesto, para su entrega á los Señores Martinez del Rio, Hermanos.

Articulo III.

Las cantidades que han dejado de pagarse á los interesados, á que tienen derecho justo é indisputable, les serán satisfechas cuando el gobierno tenga recurros bastantes, no pudiendo verificarse desde luego por sus urgentes atenciones y las escasezes del erario.

Articulo IV.

Quedan en todo su vigor y fuerza la citada convencion de 4 de Diciembre de 1851, y las disposiciones que se

remain in full force and vigor without further alteration or change than what is expressly laid down and stipulated in the present agreement as to the increase of interest, without its being in any way thereby understood to be modified, changed, altered, or with less force and vigor than heretofore, inasmuch as that which is now agreed to is for the sole object and purpose, as already stated, of confirming and ratifying the inviolability and punctual observance thereof; it will, consequently, hold the same force as though it had been literally inserted in the same, and Article VII thereof extended to the present agreement.

In witness whereof, we, the said minister plenipotentiary of her Britannic Majesty and minister for foreign affairs of the republic of Mexico, have signed the present protocol, and have affixed thereto our respective seals.

Done in the city of Mexico on the tenth day of the month of August, in the year of our Lord one thousand eight hundred and fifty-eight.

[L. S.]   L. C. OTWAY.

hubieren dictado para su exacto cumplimiento sin mas diferencia que lo espresamente estipulado en el presente convenio sobre aumento de redito, no entendiendose por esto inovada, alterada, ó con menos valor que antes; pues lo pactado ahora es como se ha dicho para confirmar y asegurar su inviolabilidad y puntual observancia; tendrá por tanto la misma fuerza que si literalmente se hallara inserto en ella; haciendose estensivo á este arreglo lo contenido en su Articulo VII.

En fé de lo cual los espresados ministro de relaciones esteriores de la república Mexicana y ministro plenipotenciario de su Magestad Británica, hemos firmado y sellado con nuestros sellos respectivos al presente protocolo, en la ciudad de México, á diez de Agosto, de mil ochocientos cincuenta y ocho.

[L. S.]   J. M. DE CASTILLO Y LANZAS.

Enclosure 5 in No. 43.

THE DOYLE CONVENTION, SIGNED DECEMBER 4, 1851.

Habiendo el gobierno de la república Mexicana hecho presente la imposibilidad en que se encuentra de cumplir ciertos convenios y arreglos que existen entre el gobierno Mexicano y varios súbditos Británicos, celebrados bajo la garantía de la legacion de su Magestad Británica, porque la penuria del erario federal lo ha obligado á suspender el pago de las cuotas á que por aquellos convenios y arreglos estaba obligado; despues de largas y repetidas conferencias en que se han examinado detenidamente el estado de las rentas de la república, las cuantiosas obligaciones que sobre ellas pesan, y la conveniencia comun de fundar un arreglo sobre condiciones exiquibles y no sobre unas de dificil ó incierto cumplimiento que ademas del perjuicio que causarian á los acreedores podrian comprometer la conservacion de la buena armonía que existe entre los gobiernos de ambos paises, deseando el de Mexico hacer justicia á las demandas de sus acreedores hasta donde se lo permiten sus recursos y la obligacion y derecho de conservarse, y convenidos los acreedores en hacer el sacrificio de sus reclamos bajo las bases de un arreglo tan equitativo como lo permita la situacion pecuniaria del gobierno contándose con la garantía y seguridad de que será exactamente cumplido, los infrascritos ministro de relaciones de los Estados Unidos Mexicanos, autorizado por el decreto de diez y siete de Octubre del corriente año, y encargado de negocios de su Magestad Británica, reunidos en conferencia diplomática han convenido en los artículos siguientes:

ARTICULO I.

Los reclamantes interesados en las convenciones y arreglos existentes que corren con el nombre de la casa de Martinez del Rio hermanos, de Montgomery Nicod y Compañia, representados, por la casa de Jecker y Compañia y de convencion Pakenham firmada el 15 de Octubre de 1842, se presentarán á la tesorería general para hacer la liquidacion de sus créditos con arreglo á este convenio, y la citada oficina lo verificará precisamente dentro del término de treinta dias contados desde el de su fecha.

ARTICULO II.

El gobierno Mexicano se obliga á pagar anualmente cinco por ciento de amortizacion de ese fondo consolidado, y tres por ciento de interes anual calculado sobre la disminucion progresiva que ocasiona la amortizacion.

ARTICULO III.

El pago de las cantidades anuales que se destinan á la amortizacion é intereses de los créditos comprendidos en el presente convenio se verificará por semestres vencidos, en manos del comisionado que al efecto nombraren los acreedores comprendidos en él. Para hacer efectivas las estipulaciones contenidas en el artículo anterior, el gobierno Mexicano se obliga á consignar sobre el producto de los derechos de importacion que se cobren en las aduanas establecidas en los puertos de la república, un tanto por ciento bastante para cubrir el monto del cinco por ciento de amortizacion, y del tres por ciento de interes que se señala á los créditos comprendidos en el presente convenio. Para que en ningun tiempo pueda diferirse ó suspenderse el pago de ese cinco y tres por ciento, el gobierno Mexicano se obliga á pasar una órden á los administradores de la espresada renta, señalándoles la cuota de los derechos espresados que deben remitir en libranzas separadas á la tesorería general á favor de dicho comisionado, las cuales libranzas deberán serle entregadas en cuanto las reciba la espresada tesorería.

Si al fin del año no estuvieren cubiertos los intereses y el cinco por ciento de amortizacion, la tesorería general, sin necesidad de nueva órden, cubrirá el déficit con las primeras libranzas que reciba de las aduanas maritimas; y el comisionado, por su parte, si hubiese recibido mayor cantidad que la que importen los espresados intereses y amortizacion anual, devolverá á la tesorería general el escedente.

ARTICULO IV.

El ministro de relaciones de la república pasará al encargado de negocios de su Magestad Británica una copia de la órden que por el de hacienda se trasmita á los administradores de aduanas en cumplimiento del artículo anterior, la cual se considerará como si estuviese inserta y formará parte del presente convenio.

ARTICULO V.

Deseando el gobierno Mexicano dar pruebas inequívocas de la justicia y equidad con que se propone proceder en este arreglo, se obliga á mejorar la condicion de sus acreedores, aumentando despues del quinto año, contado desde esta fecha, el interes concedido al capital y á su amortizacion. En consecuencia, se obliga á pagarles el cuatro por ciento anual de interes y el seis por ciento anual de amortizacion al cumplirse dicho quinto año, de tal manera que este aumento empiece á correr desde el sesto.

ARTICULO VI.

Como el congreso Mexicano está tratando de hacer una ley para el pago de la deuda interior, los interesados comprendidos en el presente convenio quedan cada uno de ellos en libertad de trasladar sus créditos al fondo que en virtud de ella se creare, haciendo saber su resolucion al ministro de relaciones, quien la communicará á la legacion de su Magestad Británica.

Articulo VII.

Queda espresamente estipulado y convenido que en caso de quebrantarse, suspenderse, ó diferirse por el tesoro Mexicano el cumplimiento de cualquiera de las obligaciones que contrae en presente convenio, queda este de hecho anulado, y convenciones existentes.

En fé de lo cual los espresados ministro de relaciones y encargado de negocios de su Magestad Británica lo firmamos y sellamos con nuestros sellos respectivos, en la ciudad de México, á 4 de Diciembre de 1851.

[L. S.] PERCY W. DOYLE.
[L. S.] JOSÉ F. RAMIREZ.

THE SAYAS OR PADRE MARAN CONVENTION, SIGNED DECEMBER 6, 1851.

Habiendo hecho presente el gobierno de la república Mexicana la imposibilidad en que se encuentra de cumplir ciertos convenios y arreglos que se celebraron entre el mismo gobierno y el Reverendo Padre Moran, apoderado de las Misiones Apostólicas de Filipinas, de la orden de Santo Domingo, bajo la garantía de la legacion de su Magestad Católica, porque la penuria del erario federal le ha obligado á suspender el pago de las cuotas que por aquellos se asignaron para la estincion de varios créditos, despues de largas y repetidas conferencias en que se han examinado detenidamente el estado de las rentas de la república, las cuantiosas obligaciones que sobre ellas pesan, y la conveniencia comun de fundar un arreglo sobre condiciones exequibles y no sobre unas de difícil ó incierto cumplimiento, que ademas del perjuicio que causarian á los acreedores podrian suscitar dificultades entre los gobiernos de España y de Mexico; descando este último hacer justicia á las demandas de sus acreedores hasta donde se lo permitan sus recursos, y obligacion y derecho de conservarse, convenido Don Cayetano Rubio, dueño actual de los créditos que pertenecieron á las espresadas misiones, en hacer el sacrificio de sus derechos entrando en una transaccion bajo las bases de un arreglo tan equitativo como lo permita la situacion pecuniaria del gobierno Mexicano, y con la garantía y seguridad de que será exactamente cumplido, los infrascritos ministro de relaciones de los Estados Unidos Mexicanos, autorizado por el decreto de 17 de Octubre del corriente año, y enviado extraordinario y ministro plenipotenciario de su Magestad Católica, reunidos en conferencia, han convenido en los articulos siguientes :

Articulo I.

Don Cayetano Rubio, actual poseedor de los dréditos que pertenecieron á los padres misioneros dominicos, comprendidos en los arreglos y convenios que corren con el nombre de su apoderado el Reverendo Padre Moran, se presentará á la tesorería general para hacer la liquidacion de los espresados créditos con arreglo al presente convenio, y la citada oficina la verificará precisamente dentro del término de treinta dias contados desde él de su fecha.

Articulo II.

El gobierno Mexicano se obliga á pagar annualmente cinco por ciento de amortizacion de ese fondo consolidado, y tres por ciento de interes anuel calculado sobre la diminucion progresiva que ocasione la amortizacion.

Artículo III.

El pago de las cantidades anuales que se destinan á la amortizacion ó intereses de los créditos comprendidos en el presente convenio, se verificará por semestres vencidos en manos de Don Cayetano Rubio. Para hacer efectivas las estipulaciones contenidas en el articulo anterior, el gobierno Mexicano se obliga á consignar sobre el producto de los derechos de importacion que se cobren en las aduanas establecidas en los puertos de la república un tanto por ciento bastante para cubrirse el monto del cinco por ciento de amortizacion y del tres por ciento de interes que se señala á los creditos comprendidos en el presente convenio. Para que en ningun tiempo pueda diferirse ó suspenderse el pago de ese cinco y tres por ciento, el gobierno Mexicano se obliga á pasar una órden á los administradoes de la espresada renta, señalandoles la cuota de los derechos espresados que deben remitir en libranzas separadas á la tesorería general á favor de dicho Señor Rubio, las cuales libranzas deberán serle entregadas, en cuanto las reciba la espresada tesorería.

Si al fin del año no estuvieren cubiertos los intereses y el cinco por ciento de amortizacion, la tesorería general, sin necesidad de nueva orden, cubrirá el déficit con las primeras libranzas que reciba de las aduanas marítimas, y el Señor Rubio por su parte, si hubiere recibido mayor cantidad que la que importen los espresados intereses y amortizacion anual, devolverá á la tesorería general el escedente.

Artículo IV.

El ministro de relaciones de la república pasará al ministro plenipotenciario de su Magestad Católica una copia de la órden que por el de hacienda se transmita á los administradores de las aduanas, en cumplimiento del artículo anterior, la cual se considerará como si estuviese inserta, y formará parte del presente convenio.

Artículo V.

Deseando el gobierno Mexicano dar pruebas inequívocas de la justicia y equidad con que se propone proceder en este arreglo, se obliga á mejorar la condicion del crédito á que se refiere, aumentando despues del quinto año, contado desde esta fecha, el interes concedido al capital y á su amortizacion. En consecuencia, se obliga á pagar al Señor Don Caytano Rubio, el quatro por ciento anual de interes, y el seis por ciento anual de amortizacion, al cumplirse dicho quinto año, de tal manera que este aumento empiece á correr desde el sesto.

Artículo VI.

Como el congreso Mexicano está tratando de hacer una ley para el pago de la deuda interior, Don Cayetano Rubio queda en libertad de trasladar los créditos á que se refiere el presente convenio al fondo que en virtud de ella se creare, haciendo saber su resolucion al ministerio de relaciones, quien la comunicá á la legacion de su Magestad Católica.

Artículo VII.

Queda espresamente estipulado y convenido, que en caso de quebrantarse, suspenderse ó diferirse por el tesoro Mexicano el cumplimiento de cualquiera de las obligaciones que contrae en el presente convenio, queda este de hecho anulado, y el Señor Rubio restituido en el goce de los derechos adquiridos en los arreglos y convenciones celebradas con el Reverendo Padre Moran.

En fé de lo cual, espresados Ministro de relaciones de la república Mexicana, y enviado estraordinario y ministro plenipotenciario de su Magestad Católica, lo firmamos y sellamos con nuestro sello respectivo, en la ciudad de Mexico, á seis de Diciembre de mil ochocientos cincuenta y uno.

[L. S.]   JOSÉ F. RAMIREZ.
[L. S.]   JUAN ANTONIO Y ZAYAS.

[Translation which, *mutatis mutandis*, will serve for both conventions.]

The Mexican government having declared the impossibility of its fulfilling certain conventions and agreements which exist between it and various British subjects, entered into under the guarantee of her Britannic Majesty's legation, on account of the state of penury of the federal treasury, which has caused it to suspend the payment of certain quotas set apart for the payment of those conventions and agreements, after long and repeated conferences, in which the state of the revenue of the republic has been carefully looked into, the numerous obligations by which it is bound, and the advantage to both parties to enter into an arrangement founded on conditions which can be carried out, and not on such as may be of difficult or uncertain execution, which besides the prejudice they would cause to the creditors themselves, might compromise the preservation of the good harmony which exists between the governments of both countries; and being, moreover, desirous of doing justice to the demands made by its creditors, as far as its resources and the obligation and right it has to preserve its existence will permit, and its creditors being willing to make the sacrifice of their demands in favor of an arrangement based upon as equitable terms as the situation of the finances of the country will permit, counting upon the guarantee and security that it will be faithfully carried out, the undersigned, minister for foreign affairs of the United States of Mexico, authorized by the decree of 17th October of the present year, and her Britannic Majesty's chargé d'affaires, having met together in a diplomatic conference, have agreed upon the following articles:

ARTICLE I.

The creditors interested in the existing conventions and arrangements known under the name of the house of Martinez del Rio Brothers; of Montgomery, Nicod & Co., represented by the house of Jecker & Co.; and of the convention signed by Mr. Pakenham on the 15th of October, 1842—shall present themselves at the general treasury to settle the amount of their credits, according to the terms agreed upon in this convention, and that amount shall be fixed precisely within the term of thirty days, counted from the day on which this convention is signed.

ARTICLE II.

The Mexican government obliges itself to pay yearly a sum of five per cent. for the purpose of paying off the capital of this consolidated fund, and three per cent. a year for interest upon it, calculated on the gradual decrease of the amount of the fund caused by the paying off of the capital.

ARTICLE III.

The payment of the sums destined to pay off yearly the capital and interest of the credits included in the present convention shall take place every six months through a commissioner appointed for that purpose by the creditors interested in the convention.

To render effective the stipulations contained in the preceding article, the Mexican government obliges itself to assign from the produce of the importation duties collected in the custom-houses established in the ports of the republic, so much per cent. as may be sufficient to cover the amount necessary for paying the five per cent. destined to pay off the capital and the three per cent. interest allotted to the credits included in the present convention.

To prevent any delay or suspension at any time taking place in the payment of the five and three per cent. above mentioned, the Mexican government obliges itself to send an order to the collectors of the aforesaid revenue, stating to them the amount of the aforesaid duties to be sent in separate drafts to the general treasury in favor of the aforesaid commissioner, which drafts are to be made over to him as soon as they are received at the treasury.

If at the end of the year the amounts due for the interest and for paying off the capital are not covered, the general treasury, without waiting for any further order, shall pay the amount due with the first drafts it receives from the maritime custom-houses; and the commissioner, on his part, if he should have received more than is ncessary for paying off the yearly amount of the capital, and the interest agreed upon, shall return the surplus to the treasury.

ARTICLE IV.

The minister for foreign affairs of this republic shall send to her Britannic Majesty's chargé d'affaires a copy of the order which the minister of finance sends to the collectors of the custom-houses in fulfilment of the preceding article, which article shall be considered as having been inserted in and forming part of the present convention.

ARTICLE V.

The Mexican government being desirous of giving unequivocal proofs of the justice and equity with which it intends to act in this arrangement, obliges itself to better the condition of its creditors, by increasing from the fifth year, counted from the present date, the interest granted for the capital, and the sum allotted for paying it off.

It consequently obliges itself to pay four per cent. interest a year, and to allow six per cent. a year for paying off the capital from the end of the fifth year, that is to say, that this increase is to take place from the beginning of the sixth year from the present date.

ARTICLE VI.

As the Mexican congress is about to pass a law for the purpose of paying off the internal debt, the persons interested in the present convention are all and each one at liberty to transfer their credits into the fund which may be created for the above purpose, making their intention known to the minister of foreign affairs, who will communicate it to her Britannic Majesty's legation.

ARTICLE VII.

It is especially stipulated and agreed that, in the event of any part of the obligations contracted by the present convention being broken through, or their fulfilment delayed or suspended by the Mexican treasury, this convention becomes at once thereby annulled, and the creditors restored to the possession of the rights acquired in the conventions and arrangements already existing.

In witness whereof we, the aforesaid minister for foreign affairs of the Mexican republic, and her Britannic Majesty's chargé d'affaires, have signed and sealed the above convention with our respective seals.

Done at Mexico, the fourth day of December, one thousand eight hundred and fifty-one.

[L. S.]   PERCY W. DOYLE.
[L. S.]   JOSÉ J. RAMIREZ.

Enclosure 6 in No 43.

Custom-house order which formed part of the Doyle and Padre Moran conventions, though not issued till two months after the ratification of the two conventions.

SECRETARIA DE ESTADO Y DEL DESPACHO DE HACIENDA, SECCION 2, NUM. 37.

Para que tengan su puntual cumplimiento las convenciones celebradas en 4 y 6 de Diciembre del año próximo pasado con el Señor Encargado de Negocios de su Magestad Británica y el excelentisimo Señor Enviado Extraordinario de su Magestad Católica sobre la amortizacion gradual y pago de intereses á razon de 3 por ciento anual de los créditos reconocidos por el gobierno á favor de varios súbditos Ingleses, y del que tienen contra el erario las misiones de Filipinas representadas por el Reverendo Padre Fr. José M. Moran, y perteneciente hoy á Don Cayetano Rubio, el excelentisimo Señor Presidente ha tenido á bien disponer que esa tesoreria general prevenga á las aduanas maritimas que de los derechos de importacion que se causen en ellas, separen el 12 por ciento que es lo que por ahora se necesita para la indicada amortizacion y pago de réditos; remitiendo su importe sin demora de ninguna clase á esa tesoreria general en libranzas pagaderas á los plazos del arancel á favor de los Señores Martinez del Rio hermanos, quienes las recibirá de esa oficina para dar á su importe la aplicacion correspondiente como comisionados nombrados al efecto por los respectivos acreedores, llevándose por easa propia tesoreria la cuenta respectiva de las sumas que se abonen en cuenta de los mencionados créditos, prévia la correspondiente liquidacion de su monto. Como por las circunstancias en que aun se encuentra el Estado de Yucatan no es posible que por ahora se haga en las aduanas maritimas de Campeche y Sisal la separacion del indicado 12 por ciento por la diminucion que sufririan los recursos destinados á las tropas ocupadas en la guerra contra los indigenas, el excelentisimo Señor Presidente ha dispuesto que entretanto las espresadas aduanas pueden hacer la remision del repetido 12 por ciento den únicamente noticia á esa tesorería, cada mes, de lo que importe la misma cuota para que lo reintegre la aduana de Vera Cruz por cuenta de la parte libre para el gobierno de los derechos de importacion. Deseando el excelentisimo Señor Presidente que lo estipulado en las mencionadas convenciones sea exactamente cumplido como exige el decoro de la nacion, ha dispuesto que V. SS. encarguen muy particularmente á los administradores de las aduanas maritimas respectivas, la puntual observancia de las prevenciones precedentes sin distraer para ningun otro objeto las cantidades pertenecientes al fondo de que se trata, en el concepto de que su excelencia verá con desagrado cualquiera omision ó descuido que note en el particular, y tomará en el caso las providencias que convengan. Todo lo que de órden suprema comunico á V. SS. para su inteligencia y fines indicados.

Dios y libertad.

MÉXICO, *Febrero 9 de* 1852.

(Firmado)   M. DE ESPARZA.

Señores MINISTROS DE LA TESORERIA GENERAL.

[Translation]

DEPARTMENT OF FINANCE, SECTION 2, No. 37.

MEXICO, *February* 9, 1852.

To give full force and effect to the conventions which were concluded respectively on the 4th and 6th of December, 1851, by her Britannic Majesty's chargé d'affaires and her Catholic Majesty's envoy extraordinary, in reference to the sinking funds and three per cent. interest, destined to pay off gradually certain British claims which have been recognized by the government, as well as those of the Philippine missionaries, represented by the Reverend Francis J. Moran, and now in the hands of Mr. Rubio, his excellency the president has been pleased to ordain that the general treasury do make known to the maritime custom-houses that 12 per cent. of the import duties is to be set apart for the present requirements of the sinking funds and interest of both conventions, the amount produced by this 12 per cent. to be remitted without any kind of delay to the general treasury by bills payable, as the custom-house tariff directs, in favor of Messrs. Martinez del Rio, the appointed agents of the respective creditors, who will receive these bills from the treasury and apply them to the purposes for which they are intended, the treasury having, previous to their liquidation, taken an account of the several sums thus handed over for the payment of the above-mentioned credits.

Owing to the present state of Yucatan, it will be impossible for the moment to set aside 12 per cent. of import duties in the maritime custom-houses of Campeche and Sisal, as this would tend to diminish the resources required for the maintenance of the troops now engaged in the Yucatan war, and consequently his excellency the president has further ordained that, until the said custom-houses are in a position to make this assignment of 12 per cent. they are simply to notify to the treasury every month the amount that it has actually produced, and the equivalent will then be paid from the free portion of the revenue at the custom-house of Vera Cruz.

The president wishes that the stipulations of the above-mentioned conventions should be carried out in a manner befitting the national honor. The authorities, therefore, of the several custom-houses must be especially enjoined punctually to carry out the conditions of this order, and in no case to employ for other purposes the moneys belonging to the convention funds, as any omission or shortcomings on their part would cause his excellency displeasure, and oblige him to act accordingly.

All which I am commanded to communicate to the general treasury for their guidance in carrying into effect the above order.

God and liberty.

M. DE ESPARZA.

The COMMISSIONERS OF THE GENERAL TREASURY.

Enclosure 7 in No. 43.

Messrs. Martinez del Rio to Mr. Mathew.

MEXICO, *May* 24, 1861.

SIR: We beg leave to request that you will have the goodness to inform us whether the additional five per cent. assigned in virtue of the arrangement made by Captain Aldham for repaying the amount taken by the Mexican government is to be applied exclusively to the British convention, or to that of the Padre Moran as well?

As the money seized by the Mexican government belonged to the two conventions, and the extra assignment was intended to repay that money, we are in doubt how the said five per cent. is to be considered, and shall feel much obliged by your informing us in what manner we are to act.

We have, &c.,

MARTINEZ DEL RIO,
Agents for the British Convention.

Enclosure 8 in No. 43.

Mr. Mathew to Messrs. Martinez del Rio.

MEXICO, *May* 24, 1861.

GENTLEMEN: In reply to your letter of this date, I have no hesitation in stating that the steps taken by Captain Aldham, at my request, with respect to the repayment of the sums due to the British convention, referred solely to that fund and not to the convention of the Padre Moran, of which you happen to be also agents, and which is, I believe, under Spanish protection.

I am, &c.,

GEORGE B. MATHEW.

Enclosure 9 in No. 43.

The Minister of Finance to Messrs. Martinez del Rio.

[Translation.]

MEXICO, *June* 14, 1860.

In reply to your communication of the 5th instant, respecting certain bonds issued to Mr. Henry Dalton by the general treasury as if belonging to the British convention, the supreme government has desired me to tell you that there are documents existing in this department proving that, by the consent of Mr. Dalton himself, the bonds which were issued to him could in no way affect the British convention fund; consequently, this gentleman may present himself before the supreme government whenever he likes to do so, and establish the right of his claim, it being understood that such claim, be its present condition what it may, cannot affect the interests of the aforesaid convention.

God and liberty.

TOVAR.

No. 44.

Sir C. Wyke to Lord J. Russell.

MEXICO, *August* 27, 1861.

MY LORD: During the past month the position of affairs has not materially changed in this country, where the hatred and contempt felt for the government

THE PRESENT CONDITION OF MEXICO.

seem daily to increase. Murders and robberies continue to be perpetrated with the greatest impunity, and the precincts of a legation have not saved the French minister from an attack on his life, as already reported to your lordship in a former despatch.

On the 3d instant the diligence arrived from Pachuca containing a wounded Frenchman, who subsequently died, and the dead body of poor Mrs. Chawner, a pretty young Englishwoman of only twenty-four years of age, who, with her husband, was coming to Mexico from the mines of Real del Monte, where he has been employed for some time past as a laborer. They were attacked by robbers at about six leagues from this city, who, having been beaten off by the other passengers, have not again been heard of. Since then, an Englishman of the name of Mathews has been stabbed in one of the most frequented streets of this capital, and other foreigners have been similarly assaulted, but no further deaths have occurred that I am aware of. In all these cases the assailants have come off with perfect impunity, and the government has not even had the decency to express regret for these outrages, which they are apparently unwilling or unable to prevent.

A more disgraceful state of things than that now existing here it is impossible to conceive in any country pretending to call itself a civilized nation. Mrs. Chawner was the daughter of Stephen Bennett, who was murdered at Pachuca in the month of April last.

General Ortega, who, at the head of a considerable force, has for the last two months been vainly endeavoring to put down the rebellion, at length surprised Marquez at Jalatlaco on the night of the 12th or 13th instant, when he succeeded in capturing some guns and making seventy or eighty prisoners, Marquez escaping in the confusion, with the rest of his forces.

Instead of following up his success, Ortega immediately returned to Mexico, and thus left Marquez at liberty to reorganize his defeated troops and effect a junction with Mejia, and they both now hold their old position with between 6,000 and 7,000 men.

The friends of Ortega have taken advantage of his pretended success to bring him forward as a candidate for the presidency, and, as all parties are thoroughly disgusted with Juarez, it is not improbable that they may succeed, if any legal means can be found of getting rid of the latter. Congress has been summoned to meet on the 30th, when, doubtless, some effort will be made in the sense indicated.

In the meantime Don Ignacio Comonfort, ex-president of the republic, has arrived at Monterey, and is supposed to be intriguing with Doblado, Vidaurri, and several other governors of States in that part of the country, to put himself at the head of a coalition which would be strong enough, could Marquez and Mejia, as chiefs of the reactionary party, be got rid of, to upset Juarez and counteract Ortega. Many people assert that Doblado, who is governor of Guanajuato, and, as such, at the head of 8,000 men, is working for himself and using Comonfort as a tool; but I believe nobody here knows really what is going on, except that all feel certain that something is about to occur, for the present state of things cannot last much longer.

The civil war now raging, and the weakness of the government, have encouraged the Indian population to rise against the whites at Ixmiquilpam, about twenty leagues from here, where they have committed dreadful atrocities, thus adding a new element of discord and misery to those already existing. This movement, if not at once checked, may lead to terrible results, as the immense majority of the inhabitants of this republic belong to the Indian race, which, if properly led, is quite strong enough utterly to exterminate the degenerated and vitiated descendants of the old Spanish conquerors.

The tax on capital now being levied, of which I have treated in a separate despatch, has only tended still further to discredit the government and increase the number of its enemies, as nobody now can tell when he may not be called on to supply the necessities of an administration which is as rapacious as it is dishonest and incapable.

The decree of the 17th ultimo has had the effect of paralyzing all business at Vera Cruz, where the merchants refuse to remove their goods from the custom-house, and the government is thus deprived of the duties which they expected to obtain free from any encumbrance.

All the respectable classes look forward with hope to a foreign intervention as the sole means of saving them from ruin, and preventing a dissolution of the confederation, as well as a general rising of the Indians against the white population. If either Great Britain or France adopt coercive measures to obtain redress for the violation of the conventions, and the many other grievances we have to complain of, then the moderate party may take courage and be able to form a government which would afford some hope for the future; but without such moral support and assistance they are afraid to move, and will remain the victims of the two contending factions, whose dissensions have already caused so much misery and bloodshed.

I have, &c.,

C. LENNOX WYKE.

No. 45.

Earl Russell to Earl Cowley.

[Extract]

FOREIGN OFFICE, *September* 30, 1861.

To forcible interference in the internal affairs of an independent nation her Majesty's government are, on principle, opposed. It remains to be considered whether Mexico forms an exception to the general rule.

Undoubtedly, in regard to the evils to be remedied, few cases of internal anarchy, bloodshed, and murder can exceed the atrocities perpetrated in Mexico. But, on the other hand, there is no case in which a remedy by foreign interference appears so hopeless.

The contending factions are spread over a vast extent of country; they do not obey any one, two, or three chiefs, but are split into fragments, each of which robs, pillages, and murders on its own account. No foreign army would be likely to establish any permanent or pervading authority over these scattered bodies.

In the next place, the Spanish troops, which form the most available force for the occupation of any forts or positions which may be taken, are peculiarly an object of dislike and apprehension to one of the two parties which divide the country. This dislike arises from a fear that the power of a dominant church might be restored, with the abuses and religious intolerance which accompany it. For opposite reasons British interference would be just as odious to the church party.

I may add to these reasons the universal alarm which would be excited, both in the United States and in the southern States, at the contemplation of European interference in the domestic quarrels of an American independent republic.

Without at all yielding to the extravagant pretensions implied by what is called the Monroe doctrine, it would be, as a matter of expediency, unwise to provoke the ill-feeling of North America, unless some paramount object were in prospect and tolerably sure of attainment.

The Spanish government are of opinion that the successful action of Great

Britain, France, and Spain, to enforce their just demands, would induce the Mexicans to institute a government more capable than any which has lately existed to preserve the relations of peace and friendship with foreign powers. Should such be the indirect effect of naval and military operations, her Majesty's government would cordially rejoice; but they think this effect is more likely to follow a conduct studiously observant of the respect due to an independent nation, than to be the result of an attempt to improve by foreign force the domestic institutions of Mexico.

No. 46.

Earl Cowley to Earl Russell.

[Extract.]

PARIS, *October* 2, 1861.

M. Thouvenel having been in the country when I received your lordship's instructions to communicate to him your despatch of the 27th ultimo, containing an account of a conversation which you had had with Mr. Adams on the affairs of Mexico and the views of her Majesty's government as to the course which should be pursued, I sent him a copy of it.

An opportunity for seeing him did not occur until to-day, and I had in the meantime received your lordship's despatch of the 30th ultimo, relating to the employment of a foreign force in that country, which I read to his excellency before our conversation commenced.

M. Thouvenel said that he had made no proposal to impose, or to influence by an armed force, an arbitration in the internal affairs of Mexico. He had thought it very likely that the employment of force for those legitimate purposes which the British and French governments had in view might encourage the well-disposed part of the Mexican people, who might feel the gall of the yoke to which they were subjected, to profit by the moment to throw it off and to substitute something better in its place; and he must confess that, should such turn out to be the case, he did not see why a movement of the kind, if it proved to be decidedly popular, should not receive the support of the powers who had come to Mexico to seek from an acknowledged bad government redress for injuries done to their subjects and for violated engagements towards themselves.

While, therefore, partaking in principle your lordship's views, and admitting the inexpediency of forcible interference in the internal affairs of an independent nation, he drew a distinction between forcible interference and the indirect encouragement, arising out of the presence of forces called to those shores for other purposes, given to the Mexican people to emerge from an odious tyranny.

No. 47.

Earl Russell to Earl Cowley.

FOREIGN OFFICE, *October* 5, 1861.

MY LORD: I have to acquaint your excellency that the Queen is prepared to enter into a convention with France and Spain, the object of which would be to secure the fulfilment by the government of Mexico of its obligations towards the respective governments, and to obtain redress for injuries done in Mexico to their respective subjects.

In the opinion of her Majesty's government it would be proper to insert in any such convention a stipulation providing that the forces of the contracting parties shall not be employed for any other objects than those which I have specified, and especially that they shall not interfere with the internal government of Mexico.

Her Majesty's government consider that the government of the United States should be invited to adhere to any such convention; but they would not think it necessary that, in anticipation of meeting with the concurrence of the United States, the three powers should defer the commencement of the contemplated operations against Mexico.

If the government of the Emperor should be willing to enter into such a convention as I have described, a draught of it shall forthwith be sent to your excellency for communication to M. Thouvenel.

I have directed Sir John Crampton to make a similar overture to the Spanish government.

I am, &c.,

RUSSELL.

No. 48.

Earl Russell to Sir J. Crampton.

FOREIGN OFFICE, *October* 5, 1861.

SIR: I have to acquaint you that the Queen is prepared to enter into a convention with France and Spain, the object of which would be to secure the fulfilment by the government of Mexico of its obligations towards the respective governments, and to obtain redress for injuries done in Mexico to their respective subjects.

In the opinion of her Majesty's government it would be proper to insert in any such convention a stipulation providing that the forces of the contracting parties should not be employed for any other objects than those which I have specified, and especially that they should not interfere with the internal government of Mexico.

Her Majesty's government consider that the government of the United States should be invited to adhere to any such convention; but they would not think it necessary that, in anticipation of meeting with the concurrence of the United States, the three powers should defer the commencement of the contemplated operations against Mexico.

If the government of her Catholic Majesty should be willing to enter into such a convention as I have described, a draught of it shall forthwith be sent to you for communication to Marshal O'Donnell.

I have directed Earl Cowley to make a similar overture to the French government.

I am, &c.,

RUSSELL.

No. 49.

Sir J. Crampton to Earl Russell.

SAN ILDEFONSO, *September* 21, 1861.

MY LORD: On the receipt of your lordship's telegram I lost no time in making the inquiry therein directed, as to whether the Spanish government would object to ask the United States to act in concert with England and France in relation to the affairs of Mexico.

Marshal O'Donnell, without saying anything which implied an opinion that the co-operation of the United States in this matter would in itself be objectionable, observed that the government of that country was probably too much engrossed in its internal affairs to be able at the present moment to direct its attention elsewhere; and added that the Spanish government, which had already displayed great patience under extraordinary provocation, could at all events not now postpone the measures which it had determined to adopt, and which were called for by the country in vindication of its rights.

Spain, the marshal observed, by inviting England and France to join with her in a common line of action in Mexico, had given sufficient proof that she did not desire to secure to herself any exclusive advantages in that country, and still less that she designed to avail herself of its distracted condition with a view to the conquest or reannexation of any part of it.

In his opinion nothing could be more detrimental to the true interests of Spain than the recovery of her ancient possessions in America; whatever may have been the sentiments of former governments of Spain, a sounder view of this matter was now, he thought, well established in the minds of all persons who had duly reflected upon the subject. With regard to Cuba and the Philippines it was different, because their insular position and other circumstances still rendered their position advantageous to the mother country; but to seek to extend her dominion on the continent of America would be a most mistaken policy for Spain, even if circumstances were to favor its practicability. The recent acquisition of Spain in Santo Domingo might, his excellency remarked, appear to be a deviation from this principle; but the proximity of Santo Domingo to Cuba rendered it a point from which the safety of the latter might be menaced were it to fall into the hands of parties hostile to Spain.

I took occasion to remark that, although I was not in possession of your lordship's views upon this subject, further than they might be inferred from the question I had just put to his excellency, there were circumstances which, in my opinion, rendered it desirable that the government of the United States should, at all events, be invited to act in concert with the European powers in regard to Mexico. The extreme jealousy felt by every political party in America in regard to intervention or interference of any sort by European powers in the affairs of the New World was well known. Her Majesty's government, it was true, could never recognize what was commonly called the "Monroe doctrine," nor did I believe that any other European government was likely to subscribe to it. But the repeated announcement of this maxim by successive Presidents of the United States as a fundamental principle of their policy, and its eager acceptance as such by the American people, rendered it sufficiently evident that European intervention in the affairs of Mexico would be viewed by them as an infringement of an imagined right, and if now undertaken without their being consulted, and at a time when it would appear to them that advantage was taken of their internal troubles to make light of their influence, and perhaps to realize projects repugnant to their political sympathies, a strong feeling of resentment would not fail to be created, in which both sections of the now divided Union would concur. Although this feeling might not, under present circumstances, manifest itself in measures of actual hostility, influences could, nevertheless, be brought to bear by parties in the United States upon the affairs of Mexico, sufficiently powerful to cause embarrassment to Spain or any other European power which had a political object to achieve in that country.

Marshal O'Donnell did not deny that there was some force in these considerations, and replied that as it was no part of the design of Spain to take advantage of the powerless condition of the United States with a view of either reconquering Mexico or of re-establishing monarchy there, he did not see that there existed any positive objection to the concurrence of the United States in the measures proposed by Spain. With regard to the expediency, however, of a proposal to that effect being made by Spain to the United States, he would request me to speak with M. Calderon Collantes, when the question would be brought by that minister under the immediate consideration of the cabinet.

On communicating with M. Calderon Collantes I found his excellency in no way indisposed to take the subject into consideration, and he promised shortly to inform me of the decision of the cabinet. M. Calderon did not seem to anticipate any objection to the proposal of her Majesty's government to invite the United States to join in a common line of action with Great Britain, France, and Spain. His excellency, however, made the same reserve as Marshal O'Donnell had done, viz: that Spain could in no case postpone her action in order to secure the co-operation of the American government.

I have, &c.,

JOHN F. CRAMPTON.

No. 50.

Sir J. Crampton to Earl Russell.

[Extract.]

SAN ILDEFONSO, *September* 24, 1861.

I took the earliest opportunity after the receipt of your lordship's telegram to call Marshal O'Donnell's attention to the rights of her Majesty's government upon the customs revenue of Vera Cruz and Tampico.

These rights, I observed, were sanctioned by a convention with Mexico; and her Majesty's government had claimed of the Mexican government that the customs of those ports should be placed under the control of British commissioners with a view to the satisfaction of British claims, it being understood that those commissioners should also pay the sums due by Mexico to other nations, and which were guaranteed by mortgage on the revenues of the same customs.

I added that I made this communication by direction of her Majesty's government, in order to avoid any misunderstanding which might arise in regard to the rights of Great Britain at Vera Cruz and Tampico in case Spain should find it necessary to take military possession of those ports.

Marshal O'Donnell replied that in case it was found necessary to occupy Vera Cruz and Tampico, and that such occupation was effected by the combined action of England, France, and Spain, as he hoped would be the case, the three powers would have no difficulty in apportioning their respective claims upon the customs revenues there collected under their authority. If, on the other hand, Spain were to act alone and to hold possession of Vera Cruz and Tampico, she would not on that account be the less ready to recognize, and to the best of her power enforce, the legitimate rights which Great Britain and other friendly powers might have previously acquired there. As matters now stood, it appeared that Mexico, by an act of her congress, had repudiated the claims of all nations upon her custom-house revenues, and consequently the blockade or military occupation of her ports by Spain could not, by causing a suspension of commerce, place the interests of the parties to whom their customs revenue was pledged in a worse position than they now were; but if Spain were thus enabled to enforce her own claims, she would undoubtedly respect those of other nations.

Marshal O'Donnell expressed the opinion that if England, France, and Spain were to combine their forces no resistance would be attempted by Mexico. If Spain acted alone it might be otherwise, and this made him desire that a common line of action might be agreed upon.

This being his view, I inquired whether the Spanish government would not consent to defer its action until Great Britain and France could concert together as to the best measures to be taken.

Marshal O'Donnell replied that paramount considerations rendered it impossible for Spain to consent to delay the measures she had decided upon beyond the period which he had previously mentioned to me, viz: the beginning of November, before which time naval or military operations on the coasts of Mexico could not be undertaken, on account of the prevalence of the yellow fever and the West India hurricanes.

The grievances of which the Spanish government had to complain were of long standing, and they had waited with patience for more than six months in the vain hope of some satisfaction for them being afforded, and more especially for the indignity offered in the dismissal of the Spanish minister from Mexico. Cortes would assemble in the course of next month, and the Spanish government would be unable to justify themselves before that body and the nation if they were to defer, beyond what was rendered necessary by material obstacles, the vindication of its rights and dignity.

This inevitable delay would, however, he expressed the hope, afford time for England and France to concert together, and with Spain, the measures necessary for combined action.

Marshal O'Donnell renewed to me on this occasion the assurances he had formerly given, that Spain had no views of conquest upon Mexico, and that he was entirely opposed to the notion of re-establishing, by foreign influence, a monarchical form of government in that country, or otherwise meddling with the internal administration of its government.

No. 51.

Earl Cowley to Earl Russell.

[Extract.]

PARIS, *October* 10, 1861.

I saw M. Thouvenel this afternoon on the subject of the proposed convention for regulating the joint action of Great Britain, France, and Spain in the expedition to be undertaken against Mexico, and I read to him your lordship's despatch of the 5th instant upon this subject received this morning.

M. Thouvenel said that he was quite ready to join her Majesty's government in signing a convention for the purposes recited by your lordship; that he agreed entirely in the principles which your lordship had laid down as those which should guide the action of the allied powers.

M. Thouvenel disclaimed, as he had done on a former occasion, any desire to impose any particular form of government in Mexico.

No. 52.

Earl Russell to Earl Cowley.

[Extract.]

FOREIGN OFFICE, *October* 12, 1861.

I have received your excellency's despatch of the 10th instant, reporting your conversation with M. Thouvenel on the course which her Majesty's government proposed should be adopted towards Mexico by the governments of England, France, and Spain, as explained to you in my despatch of the 4th instant.

I have to state to your excellency that her Majesty's government consider an engagement not to interfere by force in the internal affairs of Mexico to be an essential part of the convention.

I understand from Sir John Crampton that, while reserving to themselves the right of exerting moral influence for the establishment of a better order of things in Mexico, the Spanish government agree with her Majesty's government that force ought not to be used for that purpose.

No. 53.

Earl Cowley to Earl Russell.

[Extract.]

PARIS, *October* 18, 1861.

SIR: M. Thouvenel informs me that the Emperor is willing that M. de Flahault should negotiate the treaty concerning Mexico in London, and full powers will be sent to him on Tuesday next.

No. 54.

Sir J. Crampton to Earl Russell.

[Extract.]

MADRID, *October* 9, 1861.

On the receipt of your lordship's telegram of the 5th instant I sought an interview with Marshal O'Donnell, as well as with M. Calderon Collantes, and stated that her Majesty's government were prepared to enter into a convention with France and Spain for the purpose of obtaining reparation from Mexico for the injuries received by their respective subjects, and for securing the fulfilment of the obligations entered into by Mexico towards their respective governments.

I observed that her Majesty's government proposed that it should be provided by an article of the convention, that the forces of the contracting parties are not to be employed for any ulterior object, and especially that they are not to interfere with the internal government of Mexico. I said that her Majesty's government desire that the government of the United States should be invited to adhere to the convention; adding, however, that her Majesty's government did not consider that any delay in the commencement of active operations ought to be permitted on this account.

Marshal O'Donnell replied that the proposal of her Majesty's government should be immediately submitted to the consideration of the cabinet.

This was accordingly done, and M. Calderon Collantes, on the 8th instant, communicated to me the views of her Catholic Majesty's government in regard to the proposed convention.

The Spanish government, M. Calderon said, were very willing to conclude with England and France a convention for the objects which I had stated to him on the part of her Majesty's government.

They agreed to the insertion of an article in the convention to the effect that the forces of the high contracting parties should not be employed for any ulterior object. Spain, his excellency remarked, had no such object in view; she neither sought to reconquer any part of Mexico nor to re-establish a monarchical government there in favor of any European prince or other person; nor had she any intention of endeavoring to place one or the other of the contending factions in Mexico at the head of the government of the republic. The Spanish government felt no difficulty, therefore, in concurring with her Majesty's government in the opinion that no armed intervention in the internal government of Mexico should be attempted.

The only point, consequently, in regard to which he could perceive any shade of difference in the views of her Majesty's government and those of Spain in this respect was that her Catholic Majesty's government was of opinion that, considering the great influence which must necessarily be exercised by the very presence of the combined forces of England, France, and Spain upon the internal state of Mexico, it would be well that they should endeavor to profit by the impression which could not fail to be created thereby upon the Mexican people, to exercise a moral influence upon the contending parties, with a view of inducing them to lay down their arms, and come to an understanding for the formation of a government which would offer some guarantee to the allies for the fulfilment of the engagements of Mexico towards their respective governments, for a better observance of her international duties in future, and one which would afford some prospect, at least, of a cessation of the miseries to which that unfortunate country had so long been exposed. This, his excellency said, he thought the three powers were bound in honor to attempt, both on the grounds of humanity and of policy; and perhaps more on the ground of humanity than of policy. It was not generally borne in mind, M. Calderon remarked, that at the bottom of the civil strife in Mexico there was a contest between two races. The Spanish race was at all times in a minority in that country; and, from natural causes, the disproportion between it and the original Indian race was continually increasing. If these causes continued to operate unchecked by the moral superiority of the European element, and were aggravated by a continual recurrence of intestine struggles, there could be no doubt that the germs of civilization which had been originally planted by Spain would be crushed out, and the country would relapse into something of the same condition in which it was found by Hernan Cortez. This was a consummation which he thought the European powers ought to make at least an effort to prevent.

I remarked, in reply, that I did not doubt her Majesty's government would entirely concur with his excellency in thinking that the object which he proposed to himself was both a politic and a humane one; and if by moral influence was meant the offer of advice to the Mexican government to refrain from civil strife, her Majesty's government would, I felt sure, not hesitate now to do, conjointly with Spain and France, what they had done singly on more than one occasion. If, however, more than this was intended by the Spanish government, I confess I felt at a loss as to the means of effecting any real change in the state of Mexico without the application of actual force, or without exerting the influence of the intervening powers in favor of one or the other of the contending factions. Besides this, it appeared evident to me that the object proposed, if it were to be effected at all, must be the work of time, and, consequently, could not be effected within any definite period. I would, therefore, inquire whether the Spanish government contemplated the continuance of the occupation of the Mexican ports until such time as a government such as they should desire to see established in Mexico should be constituted.

M. Calderon replied, certainly not; the Spanish occupation would be limited to what was necessary for obtaining the redress of wrongs inflicted upon Spanish subjects, and satisfaction for acts inconsistent with the rights and dignity of the Spanish government; and would, if possible, not be prolonged beyond the period at which the climate would render the stay of the troops and vessels dangerous to their health and safety.

No. 55.

Lord Lyons to Earl Russell.

[Extract.]

WASHINGTON, *October* 14, 1861.

I had the day before yesterday the honor to receive your lordship's despatch of the 28th ultimo, relative to the affairs of Mexico.

I had, a few hours later in the day, an interview with Mr. Seward. In the course of conversation he introduced the subject of Mexico. I found that he had not yet received Mr. Adams's report of the conversation which he held with your lordship on the 25th ultimo, concerning the proposal of the United States to assume the payment of the interest of the Mexican debt to Great Britain and France.

He told me that he had already sent instructions to the United States ministers in London and Paris which would enlarge their powers of negotiation, and which would in particular enable them to engage that the United States should provide for the interest of the debt to Spain, and also for the satisfaction, to a certain extent, (as I understood,) of the general claims of Great Britain, France, and Spain, upon Mexico. He was, he said, on the point of sending similar instructions to the United States minister at Madrid. He had been informed that the Spanish government having heard that England and France were about to intervene in Mexico, had determined to be beforehand with them, and had already prepared an expedition, which was ready to sail from Cuba. Would it not be wise to avoid the complications which could not but follow such an expedition, by assenting to an arrangement which would provide for the material interests of the three European powers, and postpone to a more favorable moment difficult and dangerous questions ?

I said to Mr. Seward that I presumed that he would receive in the course of the day reports from Mr. Adams and Mr. Dayton of the manner in which his proposals had been received by your lordship and M. Thouvenel. He would, I observed, find that grave objections to them were entertained both in London and in Paris. I proceeded, in obedience to your lordship's instructions, to speak to Mr. Seward in the sense in which your lordship had spoken to Mr. Adams, as set forth in your despatch to Earl Cowley, dated the 27th ultimo. I said in particular that her Majesty's government were as apprehensive as Mr. Seward himself could be of an attempt to build upon a foundation of debts due and injuries inflicted by Mexico a pretension to establish a new government in that country. Her Majesty's government thought, however, (I proceeded to observe,) that the most effectual mode of guarding against this danger would be for Great Britain, the United States, and France to join Spain in a course of action the objects and limits of which should be strictly defined beforehand. This certainly appeared more prudent than to allow Spain to act alone now, and afterwards to oppose the results of her operations if she should go too far.

Mr. Seward appeared to be unwilling to abandon his own plan, which would, he said, have the advantage of rendering all interference on the part of European powers in the affairs of Mexico entirely superfluous.

No. 56.

Sir C. Wyke to Earl Russell.

[Extract.]

MEXICO, *September* 29, 1861.

During the past month nothing of any particular importance has taken place here. The opposition, after endeavoring to get rid of President Juarez, has been crippled by the desertion of twelve of its members, and parties in congress have become equalized, and each now prevents the other from carrying any measure of an important character.

General Ortega, after his unsuccessful campaign against Marquez, was deprived of his command, and has now returned to his native State of Zacatecas, of which he is governor. His rival, General Doblado, has succeeded him as commander-in-chief of the forces, and is about, in his turn, to attack Marquez and the other chiefs of the reactionary party, who still remain at the head of between 7,000 and 8,000 men, with which they have hitherto completely baffled all the efforts of the government to subdue them.

The executive has lost all real authority over the different States of the confederation, which are now virtually independent, and, whenever it suits them, set at defiance any orders they may receive from the supreme government.

Some anxiety is beginning to be felt as to the measures likely to be adopted by England and France, in consequence of the violation of the diplomatic conventions; but these people console themselves with the reflection that "when the day cometh sufficient is the evil thereof."

Should the different ports be occupied by our naval forces, they propose to withdraw the custom-houses further inland, with a view of levying duties on all goods proceeding from the coasts to the capital. This is a project which they will find some difficulty in carrying out, from their utter want of system and regular organization.

With the moral support given by our occupation to the moderate and respectable party, they will probably be strong enough to turn out the present administration and form a government which would be glad to treat with us, and thus re-establish those friendly relations with foreign powers so necessary to the real welfare of the republic.

No. 57.

Earl Russell to the Lords Commissioners of the Admiralty.

FOREIGN OFFICE, *October* 30, 1861.

MY LORDS: I am commanded by the Queen to signify to your lordships her Majesty's pleasure, that with a view to the operations on the coast of Mexico, to be carried out by the combined forces of England, France, and Spain, her Majesty's squadron on the North American and West Indian station should, as soon as convenient, be re-enforced, and a detachment of 700 supernumerary marines should be embarked on board the squadron.

I am, &c.,

RUSSELL.

No. 58.

Lord Lyons to Earl Russell.

WASHINGTON, *October* 17, 1861.

MY LORD: Mr. Seward mentioned to me yesterday that he had received a despatch from Mr. Adams, stating that he had waited upon your lordship in Scotland, and communicated to you the proposal that the United States should assume the payment of the interest on the foreign debt of Mexico. Mr. Seward told me that Mr. Adams reported that your lordship had not agreed to the proposal, but had stated your intention to make a counter proposal. This, Mr. Seward said, was perhaps as favorable a reception of his plan as could be expected at the first moment.

He proceeded to inform me that he had received a communication from M. Tassara, the Spanish minister here, stating that the expedition which Spain was prepared to send against Mexico was intended solely to seek redress for the wrongs suffered by Spain herself, and not at all to interfere with the internal affairs of Mexico, or to change the form of government in that country.

Mr. Seward added that M. Tassara had further informed him that it was under consideration whether Spain should make the expedition alone or in conjunction with England and France. If the latter course were adopted, the concert of the United States would (M. Tassara had assured Mr. Seward) be invited by the three powers.

Mr. Seward appeared to be very unwilling to admit that his own proposal to assume the payment of the interest of the debt was not likely to be accepted either in London, Paris, or Madrid.

I have, &c.,

LYONS.

No. 59.

Earl Russell to the Lords Commissioners of the Admiralty.

FOREIGN OFFICE, *October* 31, 1861.

MY LORDS: I have the honor to acquaint your lordships that I have this day signed, on behalf of her Majesty, with the plenipotentiaries of France and Spain, a convention having for its object the adoption of measures of coercion against

Mexico for the protection of the persons and properties of the subjects of the respective States, and for securing a fulfilment of the obligations contracted by the republic of Mexico towards the sovereigns of Great Britain, France, and Spain.

In pursuance of the provisions of this convention the contracting powers propose to employ on the coast of Mexico a sufficient naval and military force, and I am accordingly to signify to your lordships her Majesty's pleasure that a force consisting of two line-of-battle ships, four frigates, and an adequate number of smaller vessels, should be sent to Vera Cruz, and that a body of supernumerary marines, to the amount of 700 men, should be embarked on board those ships, with a view to their being landed and employed on shore, if circumstances should require it.

I am further to signify to your lordships her Majesty's pleasure that the admiral, or other senior officer in command of this force, should be instructed to place himself in communication with the officers commanding the French and Spanish forces, and in concert with them to demand:

1. Full satisfaction and reparation for the wrongs suffered by the three nations; and
2. That the forts of Vera Cruz should be at once delivered up to the forces of the three nations as a guarantee for the performance of such conditions as may be agreed upon.

I have further to state to your lordships that it is the intention of the three powers severally to name a commissioner to frame, in concert with the officer commanding the naval forces of the three powers, the articles an assent to which will be demanded of the Mexican government, or of the persons exercising authority in Mexico; and that Sir Charles Wyke, her Majesty's envoy extraordinary and minister plenipotentiary, will be empowered to act as commissioner on behalf of her Majesty, and with that view he will be instructed to embark on board the ship of the British admiral, or of the officer in command of her Majesty's forces.

The troops and marines of the combined forces will remain in possession of the forts of Vera Cruz and other forts, if taken, until further order.

Her Majesty has been pleased, likewise, to signify her pleasure that Rear-Admiral Maitland should be instructed to possess himself of the harbor of Acapulco, or any other port on the Pacific coast of Mexico, with the exception of Mazatlan, which he may consider necessary to occupy with a view to secure the objects of the convention; but Mazatlan is not to be occupied without special orders.

I enclose, for your lordships' information, a copy of the convention* under which these operations are to be carried out, although some days must elapse before the ratifications of it can be exchanged.

I am, &c.,

RUSSELL.

No. 60.

Earl Russell to Sir C. Wyke.

FOREIGN OFFICE, *October* 31, 1861.

SIR: I transmit to you herewith confidentially, inasmuch as the ratifications of it have not yet been exchanged, a copy of a convention* which I have signed this day with the plenipotentiaries of France and Spain respecting the

---

* Enclosure in No. 60.

measures of coercion which England, France, and Spain are prepared jointly to adopt for the protection of the persons and properties of their respective subjects in Mexico, and for securing the fulfilment of the obligations contracted by the republic of Mexico towards the respective sovereigns.

I also enclose a copy of a letter which I have addressed to the lords commissioners of the admiralty,* signifying her Majesty's pleasure as to the measures to be taken on the part of her Majesty in fulfilment of the engagements undertaken by her in this convention; and in conformity with what is stated in my letter, I have to instruct you to embark on board the ship of the admiral or of the senior officer commanding her Majesty's ships, and at the proper time to undertake the duties of commissioner on behalf of her Majesty under the convention, and to frame, in concert with Admiral Milne, and with the commissioners of France and Spain, and the officers commanding the naval forces of those two countries, the articles an assent to which will be demanded of the Mexican government, or of the persons exercising authority in Mexico.

You will instruct her Majesty's consuls at the ports which may be determined on, to collect, in concert with the French and Spanish consuls at those ports, the customs duties, and to pay them over according to such rules as the commissioners may jointly lay down.

I am, &c.,

RUSSELL.

Enclosure in No. 60.

Convention between her Majesty, the Queen of Spain, and the Emperor of the French, relative to combined operations against Mexico, signed at London, October 31, 1861,†

Sa Majesté la Reine du Royaume Uni de la Grande Bretagne et d'Irlande, sa Majesté la Reine d'Espagne, et sa Majesté l'Empereur des Français, se trouvant placées par la conduite arbitraire et vexatoire des autorités de la république du Mexique dans la nécessité d'exiger de ces autorités une protection plus efficace pour les personnes et les propriétés de leurs sujets, ainsi que l'exécution des obligations contractées envers elles par la république du Mexique, se sont entendues pour conclure entre elles une convention dans le but de combiner leur action commune, et, à cet effet, ont nommé pour leurs plénipotentiaires, savoir :

Sa Majesté la Reine du Royaume Uni de la Grande Bretagne et d'Irlande, le très honorable Jean Comte Russell, Vicomte Amberley de Amberley et Ardsalla, pair du Royaume Uni, conseiller de sa Majesté Britannique en son conseil privé, principal secrétaire d'état de sa Majesté, pour les affaires, etrangères;

Sa Majesté la Reine d'Espagne, Don Xavier de Isturiz y Montero, chevalier de l'ordre insigne du toison d'or, grand croix de l'ordre royal et distingué de Charles III, de l'ordre impérial de la légion d'honneur de France, des ordres de la conception de Villaviciosa et Christ de Portugal, sénateur du Royaume, ancien président du conseil de ministres et premier secrétaire, d'état de sa Majesté Catholique, et son envoyé extraordinaire et ministre plénipotentiaire près sa Majesté Britannique;

Et sa Majesté l'Empereur des Français, son excellence le Comte de Flahault de la Billarderie, sénateur, général de division, grand croix de la légion d'honneur, ambassadeur extraordinaire de sa Majesté Impériale près sa Majesté Britannique;

Lesquels, après s'être communiqué réciproquement leurs pleins pouvoirs respectifs, trouvés en bonne et due forme, sont tombés d'accord pour arrêter les articles suivants:

*No. 59.   †Ratifications exchanged at London November 15, 1861.

Article I.

Sa Majesté la Reine du Royaume Uni de la Grande Bretagne et d'Irlande, sa Majesté la Reine d'Espagne, et sa Majesté l'Empereur des Français, s'engagent à arrêter aussitôt après la signature de la présente convention, les dispositions nécessaires pour envoyer sur les côtes du Mexique des forces de terre et de mer combinées dont l'effectif sera déterminé par un échange ultérieur de communications entre leurs gouvernements, mais dont l'ensemble devra être suffisant pour pouvoir saisir et occuper les différentes forteresses et positions militaires du littoral Mexicain.

Les commandants des forces alliées seront, en ontre, autorisés à accomplir les autres opérations qui seraient jugées, sur les lieux, les plus propres à réaliser le but spécifié dans le préambule de la présente convention, et notamment, à assurer la sécurité des résidents étrangers.

Touts les mesures dont il s'agit dans cet article seront prises au nom et pour le compte des hautes parties contractantes, sans acception de la nationalité particulière des forces employées à les exécuter.

Article II.

Les hautes parties contractantes s'engagent à ne rechercher pour elles-mêmes, dans l'emploi des mesures coercitives prévues par la présente convention, aucune acquisition de territoire ni aucun avantage particulier, et à n'exercer, dans les affaires intérieures du Mexique, aucune influence de nature à porter atteinte au droit de la nation Mexicaine de choisir et de constituer librement la forme de son gouvernement.

Article III.

Une commission composée de trois commissaires, un nommé par chacune des puissances contractantes, sera établie avec plein pouvoir de statuer sur toutes les questions que pourrait soulever l'emploi ou la distribution des sommes d'argent qui seront recouvrées au Mexique, en ayant égard aux droits respectifs des trois parties contractantes.

Article IV.

Les hautes parties contractantes désirant, en outre, que les mesures qu'elles ont l'intention d'adopter n'aient pas un caractère exclusif, et sachant que le gouvernement des Etats Unis a, de son côté, des réclamations à faire valoir, comme elles, contre la république Mexicaine, conviennent qu'aussitôt après la signature de la présente convention, il en sera communiqué une copie au gouvernement des Etats Unis; que ce gouvernement sera invité à y accéder; et qu'en prévision de cette accession leurs ministres respectifs à Washington seront immédiatement munis de pleins pouvoirs à l'effet de conclure et de signer, collectivement ou séparément, avec le plénipotentiaire designé par le Président des Etats Unis, une convention identique, sauf suppression du présent article, à celle qu'elles signent à la date de ce jour. Mais comme les hautes parties contractantes s'exposeraient, en apportant quelque retard à la mise à exécution des Articles I et II de la présente convention, à manquer le but qu'elles désirent atteindre, elles sont tombées d'accord de ne pas différer, en vue d'obtenir l'accession du gouvernement des Etats Unis, le commencement des opérations sus mentionnées au delà de l'époque à laquelle leurs forces combinées pourront être réunies dans les parages de Vera Cruz.

Article V.

La présente convention sera ratifiée, et les ratifications en seront échangées à Londres, dans le délai de quinze jours.

En foi de quoi les plénipotentiaires respectifs l'ont signé, et y ont apposé le sceau de leurs armes.

Fait à Londres, en triple original, le trente-unième jour du mois d'Octobre, de l'an de grace mil huit cent soixante-un.

[L. S.]   RUSSELL.
[L. S.]   XAVIER DE ISTURIZ.
[L. S.]   FLAHAULT.

[Translation.]

Her Majesty the Queen of the United Kingdom of Great Britain and Ireland, her Majesty the Queen of Spain, and his Majesty the Emperor of the French, feeling themselves compelled by the arbitrary and vexatious conduct of the authorities of the republic of Mexico to demand from those authorities more efficacious protection for the persons and properties of their subjects, as well as a fulfilment of the obligations contracted towards their Majesties by the republic of Mexico, have agreed to conclude a convention with a view to combine their common action, and, for this purpose, have named as their plenipotentiaries, that is to say:

Her Majesty the Queen of the United Kingdom of Great Britain and Ireland, the right honorable John Earl Russell, Viscount Amberley of Amberley and Ardsalla, a peer of the United Kingdom, a member of her Britannic Majesty's privy council, her Majesty's principal secretary of state for foreign affairs;

Her Majesty the Queen of Spain, Don Xavier de Isturiz y Montero, knight of the illustrious order of the golden fleece, grand cross of the royal and distinguished order of Charles III, of the imperial order of the legion of honor of France, of the orders of the conception of Villaviciosa and Christ of Portugal, senator of the kingdom, late president of the council of ministers, and first secretary of state of her Catholic Majesty, and her envoy extraordinary and minister plenipotentiary to her Britannic Majesty;

And his Majesty the Emperor of the French, his excellency the Count de Flahault de la Billarderie, senator, general of division, grand cross of the legion of honor, his Imperial Majesty's ambassador extraordinary to her Britannic Majesty;

Who, after having reciprocally communicated their respective full powers, found in good and due form, have agreed upon the following articles:

Article I.

Her Majesty the Queen of the United Kingdom of Great Britain and Ireland, her Majesty the Queen of Spain, and his Majesty the Emperor of the French, engage to make, immediately after the signature of the present convention, the necessary arrangements for despatching to the coasts of Mexico combined naval and military forces, the strength of which shall be determined by a further interchange of communications between their governments, but of which the total shall be sufficient to seize and occupy the several fortresses and military positions on the Mexican coast.

The commanders of the allied forces shall be, moreover, authorized to execute the other operations which may be considered, on the spot, most suitable to effect the object specified in the preamble of the present convention, and specifically to insure the security of foreign residents

All the measures contemplated in this article shall be taken in the name and on account of the high contracting parties, without reference to the particular nationality of the forces employed to execute them.

ARTICLE II.

The high contracting parties engage not to seek for themselves, in the employment of the coercive measures contemplated by the present convention, any acquisition of territory nor any special advantage, and not to exercise in the internal affairs of Mexico any influence of a nature to prejudice the right of the Mexican nation to choose and to constitute freely the form of its government.

ARTICLE III.

A commission composed of three commissioners, one to be named by each of the contracting powers, shall be established with full authority to determine all questions that may arise as to the application or distribution of the sums of money which may be recovered from Mexico, having regard to the respective rights of the three contracting parties.

ARTICLE IV.

The high contracting parties desiring, moreover, that the measures which they intend to adopt should not bear an exclusive character, and being aware that the government of the United States on its part has, like them, claims to enforce upon the Mexican republic, agree that immediately after the signature of the present convention a copy thereof shall be communicated to the government of the United States; that that government shall be invited to accede to it; and that in anticipation of that accession their respective ministers at Washington shall be at once furnished with full powers for the purpose of concluding and signing, collectively or separately, with the plenipotentiary designated by the President of the United States, a convention identic, save the suppression of the present article, with that which they sign this day. But as by delaying to put into execution articles first and second of the present convention the high contracting parties would incur a risk of failing in the object which they desire to attain, they have agreed not to defer, with the view of obtaining the accession of the government of the United States, the commencement of the above-mentioned operations beyond the time at which their combined forces can be assembled in the neighborhood of Vera Cruz.

ARTICLE V.

The present convention shall be ratified, and the ratifications thereof shall be exchanged at London within fifteen days.

In witness whereof the respective plenipotentiaries have signed it, and have affixed thereto the seal of their arms.

Done at London, in triplicate, the thirty-first day of the month of October, in the year of our Lord one thousand eight hundred and sixty-one.

[L. S.] RUSSELL.
[L. S.] XAVIER DE ISTURIZ.
[L. S.] FLAHAULT.

No. 61.

Earl Russell to Earl Cowley.

FOREIGN OFFICE, *November* 1, 1861.

MY LORD: I transmith to you herewith a copy of a despatch which I have addressed to Sir C. Wyke,* directing him to repair to Jamaica, and from thence to proceed to join the admiral wherever he may be.
I am, &c.
RUSSELL.

No. 62.

Earl Russell to Sir C. Wyke.

FOREIGN OFFICE, *November* 1, 1861.

SIR: I have to instruct you forthwith to repair to Jamaica with all the members of her Majesty's mission.
Admiral Milne has been directed to send a ship-of-war without delay to Vera Cruz, to receive you on board and convey you and your suite to Jamaica; and subsequently to convey you and one of the attachés of her Majesty's mission from Jamaica to Bermuda, or wherever the admiral may be.
You will leave the rest of the mission at Jamaica until you require their services.
In joining the admiral you will embark on board the flag-ship.
The admiral will deliver to you the further instructions for your guidance, which will be sent to his care.
I am, &c.
RUSSELL.

No. 63.

Earl Russell to Earl Cowley.

FOREIGN OFFICE, *November* 1, 1861.

MY LORD: I transmit to your excellency herewith a copy of convention† which I yesterday signed with the plenipotentiaries of France and Spain, on the subject of the measures to be adopted towards Mexico.
I also enclose drafts of the instructions which, in order to give effect to the provisions of this convention, I have, by the Queen's commands, addressed to the board of admiralty and to her Majesty's minister in Mexico.‡ I have communicated copies of these drafts to the French ambassador and Spanish minister.
I shall instruct Sir Charles Wyke, by the mail of to-morrow, to repair to Jamaica, and there await further instructions.
Her Majesty's naval forces, of which the expedition, so far as this country is concerned, is to be composed, are already, or will be shortly, at Bermuda; and I will inform Count Flahault, and will enable your excellency to apprise M. Thouvenel in what manner and at what place it may, in the opinion of the

---

* No. 62.   † Enclosure in No. 60.   ‡ Nos. 59 and 60.

THE PRESENT CONDITION OF MEXICO. 371

board of admiralty, be advisable that the three squadrons should unite, so as to proceed in company to the coast of Mexico.
It will remain for the three powers to instruct their ministers at Washington to make to the government of the United States the communication contemplated by the 4th article of the convention. Her Majesty's government propose to send their instructions to Lord Lyons by the mail of the 9th of November.
I am, &c.
RUSSELL.

P. S.—Sir C. Wyke will receive his further instructions on board the admiral's ship.

No. 64.

Earl Russell to Sir J. Crampton.

FOREIGN OFFICE, *November* 1, 1861.

SIR: I transmit to you herewith a copy of a convention* which I yesterday signed with the plenipotentiaries of France and Spain on the subject of the measures to be adopted towards Mexico.
I also enclose drafts of the instructions which, in order to give effect to the provisions of this convention, I have, by the Queen's commands, addressed to the board of admiralty and to her Majesty's minister in Mexico.† I have communicated copies of these drafts to the French ambassador and Spanish minister.
I shall instruct Sir C. Wyke, by the mail of to-morrow, to repair to Jamaica, and there await further instructions.
Her Majesty's naval forces of which the expedition, so far as this country is concerned, is to be composed, are already, or will be shortly, at Bermuda; and I will inform M. de Isturiz, and will enable you to apprise the Spanish government, in what manner and at what place it may, in the opinion of the board of admiralty, be advisable that the three squadrons should unite, so as to proceed in company to the coast of Mexico.
It will remain for the three powers to instruct their ministers at Washington to make to the government of the United States the communication contemplated by the 4th article of the convention.
Her Majesty's government propose to send their instructions to Lord Lyons by the mail of the 9th of November.
I am, &c.

RUSSELL.

No. 65.

Earl Russell to Earl Cowley.

FOREIGN OFFICE, *November* 1, 1861.

MY LORD: With reference to my previous despatch of this day's date,‡ I enclose, for your excellency's information, and for communication to M. Thouvenel, a draft of a further instruction which it is my intention to address to Sir Charles Wyke with reference to the 2d article of the convention respecting the measures to be taken towards Mexico. §
I am, &c.

RUSSELL.

*Enclosure in No. 60.   † Nos. 59 and 60.   ‡ No. 63.   § No. 67.

No. 66.

Earl Russell to Sir J. Crampton.

FOREIGN OFFICE, *November* 1, 1861.

SIR : With reference to my previous despatch of this day's date, I enclose, for your information, and for communication to the Spanish government, a draft of a further instruction which it is my intention to address to Sir C. Wyke with reference to the 2d article of the convention respecting the measures to be taken towards Mexico.*

I am, &c.

RUSSELL.

No. 67.

Earl Russell to Sir C. Wyke.

FOREIGN OFFICE, *November* 1, 1861.

SIR : You should be most careful to observe with strictness article 2 of the convention signed yesterday between Great Britain, France, and Spain, by which it is provided that no influence shall be used in the internal affairs of Mexico calculated to prejudice the right of the Mexican nation freely to choose and establish its own form of government.

Should any Mexican, or any party in Mexico, ask your advice on such subjects, you will say that any regular form of government which shall protect the lives and properties of natives and of foreigners, and shall not permit British subjects to be attacked or annoyed on account of their occupations, their rights of property, or their religion, will secure the moral support of the British government.

I am, &c.

RUSSELL.

No. 68.

The Secretary to the Admiralty to Mr. Hammond.

ADMIRALTY, *November* 1, 1861.

SIR : Earl Russell having expressed his desire to be furnished with the views of my lords commissioners of the admiralty as to the most convenient rendezvous for the combined English, French, and Spanish squadrons about to be sent to Mexico, I am commanded by their lordships to acquaint you as follows :

The Spaniards having a good harbor at Havana, on the direct road to Vera Cruz, will probably assemble at that port.

The French ships going from Europe will most likely touch at Guadalupe; but as that island and Martinique are a long way from the entrance of the Gulf of Mexico, it seems probable that the French squadron would go on to Havana, or rather to Jamaica, as the more direct route, the latter island having the safe harbor of Port Royal, where water, coals, and provisions can be filled up.

---

* No. 67.

The English ships would also naturally assemble at Port Royal, and, assuming that the joint French and English squadrons meet there, the best rendezvous that could be given for the Spanish squadron to join them would be fifteen miles northwest of Cape St. Antonio, at the western end of Cuba. This cape is moderately high, and has a revolving light on it visible twenty miles, so that by night or by day it could be easily kept in sight. It is 175 miles, or one day's sail from Havana, and 540 miles, or three days' sail from Port Royal; and when the day of departure from Port Royal is fixed an aviso or despatch-vessel might be sent on the day before from Port Royal to Port Sagua, on the south coast of Cuba, (whence, no doubt, there is telegraphic communication to Havana,) to apprise the Spanish admiral.

From Cape St. Antonio to Vera Cruz the distance is 650 miles, or rather more than three days' sail; but there is no place on the coast of Mexico at which a convenient rendezvous could be given, and it seems desirable that the combined squadrons should approach the coast in company.

When the "nortes" or "northers" blow, the anchorage of Anton Lizardo, about twelve miles southeast of Vera Cruz, will be found a safe shelter, with space for a large fleet.

I am, &c.

W. G. ROMAINE.

No. 69.

Earl Russell to Earl Cowley.

FOREIGN OFFICE, *November* 1, 1861.

MY LORD: I transmit to your excellency herewith, for communication to M. Thouvenel, a copy of a letter which I have received from the board of admiralty respecting the manner in which the junction of the allied squadrons on their way to the coast of Mexico should be effected.*

The Count de Flahault has been informed of the substance of this letter.

I am, &c.

RUSSELL.

No. 70.

Earl Russell to Sir J. Crampton.

FOREIGN OFFICE, *November* 1, 1861.

SIR: I transmit to you herewith, for communication to the Spanish government, a copy of a letter which I have received from the board of admiralty respecting the manner in which the junction of the allied squadrons on their way to the coast of Mexico should be effected.*

M. de Isturiz has been informed of the contents of this memorandum.

I am, &c.

RUSSELL.

° No. 68.

No. 71.

Earl Russell to the Lords Commissioners of the Admiralty.

FOREIGN OFFICE, *November* 1, 1861.

MY LORDS: Her Majesty has been pleased to direct that a man-of-war should be at once sent to Vera Cruz to bring Sir C. Wyke and the members of his mission to Jamaica.

Sir C. Wyke and one of his attachés should be conveyed from Jamaica to Bermuda, or wherever Admiral Sir A. Milne may be, and received on board his flag-ship, leaving the rest of the mission at Jamaica.

I am, &c.

RUSSELL.

No. 72.

Sir J. Crampton to Earl Russell.

[Extract.]

MADRID, *November* 1, 1861.

Marshal O'Donnell, in reply to my question as to the number of Spanish ships and troops intended to be sent on the expedition, replied that, as nearly as he could at present judge, the squadron would consist of 12 or 14 vessels, of different sizes, carrying altogether about 300 guns. These would be accompanied by two large steam transports, and the number of troops would amount to between 4,000 and 5,000 men.

No. 73.

Mr. Hammond to the Secretary to the Admiralty.

FOREIGN OFFICE, *November* 6, 1861.

SIR: I am directed by Earl Russell to request that you will acquaint the lords commissioners of the admiralty that he communicated to the French ambassador the substance of your letter of the 1st instant, respecting the place at which the junction of the allied squadrons, about to proceed to Mexico, should be effected; and that the French ambassador has informed me to-day that the French naval expedition will take its departure from France on Monday next, and will touch at the French colonies in the West Indies, and probably at Jamaica, on its way to Havana, where it is expected to arrive between the 15th and 20th of December.

Arrangements have already been made for its obtaining provisions and supplies at Havana, which, it is calculated, it will require four or five days to embark, so that the French expedition will probably be able to proceed on the 20th or 25th of December to the point off Cape St. Antonio, at which it was proposed in your letter that the squadrons should unite.

I am, &c.

E. HAMMOND.

No. 74.

Earl Cowley to Earl Russell.

PARIS, November 5, 1861.

MY LORD: M. Dubois de Saligny is to be the French commissioner under article third of the convention of the 31st ultimo. He will also be named first plenipotentiary with Admiral Jurien de la Gravière to frame, in concert with the plenipotentiaries of Great Britain and Spain, the demands to be made on the Mexican government. His instructions are not yet ready, but M. Thouvenel about to occupy himself on them.
I have, &c.

COWLEY.

No. 75.

Earl Cowley to Earl Russell.

PARIS, November 5, 1861.

MY LORD: I have communicated to M. Thouvenel, as instructed by your lordship's despatch of the 1st instant,* the draft of a further instruction, enclosed therein, which it is your lordship's intention to address to Sir Charles Wyke with reference to article 2 of the convention, respecting the measures to be taken towards Mexico, and his excellency expressed his full concurrence in them.
I have, &c.

COWLEY.

No. 76.

Earl Cowley to Earl Russell.

PARIS, November 5, 1861.

MY LORD: M. Thouvenel had already received from M. de Flahault, before I could communicate them to his excellency, the observations of the board of admiralty respecting the manner in which the junction of the allied squadrons on their way to the coast of Mexico should be effected, to which your lordship's despatch of the 1st instant† relates.

His excellency said that he had already spoken with the minister of marine, and had found that arrangements had been made for the French squadron to take its final departure for Mexico from the Havana, whence it could put to sea in company with the Spanish squadron. There was no objection to Cape St. Antonio as the rendezvous of the allied squadrons.

The French squadron will leave Toulon on Monday next, but will call at Algiers to embark 500 Zouaves. The French admiral will then be enabled to land about 2,500 men.
I have, &c.

COWLEY.

° No. 65. † No. 69.

No. 77.

Earl Russell to Lord Lyons.

FOREIGN OFFICE, *November* 6, 1861.

MY LORD: I transmit to you herewith a copy of a convention* between her Majesty the Queen of Spain and the Emperor of the French, for combined operations against Mexico, which was signed at London on the 31st of October.

Your lordship will perceive that by article IV of this convention the contracting parties engage to communicate a copy of it to the government of the United States, and to invite that government to accede to it; and that, in anticipation of its consenting to do so, the representatives of the three powers at Washington shall be immediately furnished with full powers authorizing them, either jointly or separately, to conclude and sign with the plenipotentiary who may be named by the President of the United States an identical convention, with the omission merely of article IV.

I have accordingly to instruct your lordship to make a proposal to that effect to the Secretary of State of the United States, in such form as may be agreed upon between yourself and the French and Spanish ministers, and you will receive the requisite full power to enable you, either jointly with them or separately, to sign the convention with a plenipotentiary of the United States.

You will take care not to conclude this matter, either in form or substance, without coming to a complete and clear understanding with the French and Spanish ministers.

I am, &c.

RUSSELL.

No. 78.

Mr. Hammond to the Secretary to the Admiralty.

FOREIGN OFFICE, *November* 7, 1861.

SIR: I am directed by Earl Russell, with reference to my letter of yesterday, to request that you will acquaint the lords commissioners of the admiralty that his lordship would suggest that Rear Admiral Milne should be instructed to assemble the ships of his squadron at Port Royal, Jamaica, and should settle with the commanders of the French and Spanish squadrons, which will assemble at the Havana, on what date the British squadron shall appear off Cape St. Antonio to effect a junction with them.

I am, &c.

E. HAMMOND.

No. 79.

Earl Russell to the Lords Commissioners of the Admiralty.

FOREIGN OFFICE, *November* 8, 1861.

MY LORDS: With reference to my letter of the 31st of October, signifying to your lordships the Queen's commands as to the instructions to be given to

---

* Enclosure in No. 60.

Rear Admiral Milne for the guidance of his conduct in regard to affairs of Mexico, and more particularly to that passage in those instructions in which I refer to "the intention of the three powers severally to name a commissioner to frame, in concert with the officers commanding the naval forces of the three powers, the articles, an assent to which will be demanded of the Mexican government, or of the persons exercising authority in Mexico," I have the honor to state to your lordships that Admiral Milne should be informed that, in the event of any difference of opinion between himself and Sir Charles Wyke as to the terms in which those articles should be framed, the opinion of Sir Charles Wyke, so far as Great Britain is concerned, should prevail.

I am, &c.

RUSSELL.

No. 80.

Earl Russell to Sir C. Wyke.

[Extract.]

FOREIGN OFFICE, *November* 15, 1861.

The instructions of the Emperor of the French are similar in substance to those which I have transmitted to you.

The French government have contemplated a case of which I had not taken notice. It is supposed that the Mexicans may withdraw from Vera Cruz, destroying their fortifications, and refuse to enter into any agreement or negotiation whatever. In such a case the French government maintain that the allied powers could not allow themselves to be baffled; they could not permit their subjects to be ill-treated and defrauded, nor three powerful governments to be defied with impunity.

The French government in such a case, therefore, suppose that the allied forces would march on Mexico, and there require the reparation which had not been obtained on the coast. I have nothing to say against this reasoning or the measures in contemplation.

But, as regards her Majesty's forces, you are aware that no land forces have been directed to join the British portion of the expedition. A body of seven hundred marines is the whole force set apart for this service which can be employed on shore for any length of time. Neither the constitution of this force nor its amount would allow of its being employed in a march upon Mexico.

You will, therefore, if such a case should arise, decline to direct the marines to take part in the operations against Mexico; but it is essential that uniformity should be preserved in the demands to be made upon the *de facto* authorities of Mexico.

I do not think it necessary to give you more detailed information. Her Majesty's government have entire reliance upon your judgment and discretion. They would be unwilling to fetter that discretion by minute directions upon hypothetical cases. They would prefer, in regard to operations of much difficulty, where concert is necessary and the aspect of affairs may vary from day to day, to leave you to the guidance of your own judgment, enlightened as that judgment will be by local information and experience. Her Majesty's government are confident that Sir A. Milne and yourself will, in the performance of your present arduous duties, be guided by that zeal for the public service and by that judgment and discrimination of which you have both given satisfactory proofs.

No. 81.

Earl Russell to Sir C. Wyke.

FOREIGN OFFICE, *November* 15, 1861.

SIR: I enclose for your information and guidance a copy of a further letter which I have addressed to the lords commissioners of the admiralty,* modifying to a certain extent that part of my previous letter of the 31st of October which related to operations on the Pacific coast of Mexico.

Her Majesty's government are of opinion that if the Mexican authorities should accede to the terms which will be proposed to them, and should put the allied forces in possession of Vera Cruz, it may be unnecessary to undertake operations on the Pacific coast; but, at all events, they think it best, before any such operations are commenced, that you, in conjunction with Admiral Milne, and with the ministers and commanders of France and Spain, should have the opportunity of determining whether such operations are desirable.

If such is the case, you will apprise Rear Admiral Maitland of the result of your deliberations, and in requesting him to proceed to execute the contingent instructions with which he is furnished by the lords of the admiralty, you will further inform him of the steps which he should take for collecting the duties of customs at the ports which he may occupy, and of the manner in which he should dispose of the money which he may thereby raise.

It is possible that the Mexican government, not opposing the occupation of Vera Cruz by the allies, may decline to enter into any convention, and may divert their exports to the ports on the Pacific. This is a contingency for which the instructions to Admiral Maitland are intended to provide.

I am, &c.

RUSSELL.

No. 82.

Earl Russell to the Lords Commissioners of the Admiralty.

FOREIGN OFFICE, *November* 15, 1861.

MY LORDS: With reference to that part of my letter to your lordships, of the 31st of October, in which I conveyed to you her Majesty's pleasure in regard to the operations to be undertaken by Rear Admiral Maitland on the coast of Mexico, in execution of the convention between England, France, and Spain, I have the honor to acquaint your lordships that her Majesty has been pleased to direct that the previous instruction should be so far modified as to subject Rear Admiral Maitland's action to the information that he may receive from Sir Charles Wyke.

It will, therefore, be, in the first instance, sufficient that your lordships should direct Admiral Maitland to occupy Acapulco, or other ports on the Pacific coast of Mexico, with the exception of Mazatlan, on receiving information from Sir Charles Wyke that such an operation is desirable for the purposes of the convention; and I will instruct Sir Charles Wyke, in the event of his making such a communication to Admiral Maitland, to acquaint him with the further steps which it may be advisable to take on obtaining possession of the ports in question.

I am, &c.

RUSSELL.

---

* No. 82.

THE PRESENT CONDITION OF MEXICO. 379

No. 83.

Earl Cowley to Earl Russell.

PARIS, *November* 14, 1861.

MY LORD: The French ambassador at Madrid has informed M. Thouvenel that intelligence had been received by the Spanish government that the Spanish expedition against Mexico was to have put to sea on the 24th ultimo.
Marshal Serrano, the governor of Cuba, had taken this determination in ignorance of the negotiations pursuing between the British, French, and Spanish governments to undertake this expedition in common; but, according to calculations made by the latter, it seemed probable that the despatches to Marshal Serrano, informing him of this circumstance, would have reached his excellency before the 24th ultimo, and would have prevented the departure of the Spanish squadron.
I have, &c.
COWLEY.

No. 84.

Earl Russell to Earl Cowley.

FOREIGN OFFICE, *November* 16, 1861.

MY LORD: I enclose, for your excellency's information, and for communication to the French government, copies of communications, as marked in the margin,* which I have addressed to the admiralty and to Sir Charles Wyke, on the subject of the projected operations against Mexico.
I am, &c.
RUSSELL.

No. 85.

Mr. Hammond to the Secretary to the Admiralty.

FOREIGN OFFICE, *November* 18, 1861.

SIR: I am directed by Earl Russell to transmit to you, for the information of the lords commissioners of the admiralty, a copy of a despatch from her Majesty's ambassador at Paris, respecting the time of departure of the Spanish squadron for the coast of Mexico.†
I am, &c.
E. HAMMOND.

---

*Nos. 80, 81, and 82.   † No. 84.

No. 86.

Earl Cowley to Earl Russell.

PARIS, *November* 19, 1861.

MY LORD: I fear that some longer time may elapse than is expected by her Majesty's government before the French squadron destined for Mexico can reach the Havana, as Admiral Jurien de la Gravière has insisted on all the vessels composing it rendezvousing in the first instance at Teneriffe.

I have, &c.

COWLEY.

No. 87.

Sir J. Crampton to Earl Russell.

[Extract.]

MADRID, *November* 19, 1861.

I have the honor to transmit, in translation, an extract from the official "Gazette" of this day's date, containing two royal decrees, the one appointing General Prim to be commandant-in-chief of the expeditionary corps to Mexico; the other appointing him to be plenipotentiary for the settlement of the questions pending with the republic of Mexico.

Enclosure 1 in No. 87.

Extract from the Madrid "Gazette" of November 19, 1861.

[Translation.]

WAR DEPARTMENT.

Royal Decree.

In consideration of the qualifications of Lieutenant General Don Juan Prim, Marquis of Castillejos, I name him commandant-in-chief of the expeditionary corps to Mexico.

Given in the palace, November 3, 1861.

(Signed by the royal hand.)

LEOPOLDO O'DONNELL,
 Minister of War.

Enclosure 2 in No. 87.

Extract from the Madrid "Gazette" of November 19, 1861.

[Translation.]

DEPARTMENT OF STATE.

Royal Decree.

In consideration of the peculiar qualifications of Don Juan Prim, Count of Reus, Marquis of Castillejos, I appoint him my plenipotentiary for the settlement of the questions pending with the republic of Mexico.

Given in the palace, November 17, 1861.

(Signed by the royal hand.)

SATURNINO CALDERON COLLANTES,
Minister of State.

No. 88.

Sir C. Wyke to Earl Russell.

MEXICO, *October* 28, 1861.

MY LORD: During the past month nothing worthy of note has taken place to change either for better or worse the chronic state of misery and disorder into which this unfortunate country has fallen, from the incapacity of its rulers, and the bitter spirit of party hatred which animates its contending factions.

Marquez and the other chiefs of the reactionary party, after having for a while withdrawn from the immediate vicinity of Mexico, have retraced their steps, and are now within twenty leagues of the capital with a force variously estimated at between 3,000 and 4,000 men.

A few days ago Marquez paid a second visit to the mining establishment of Real del Monte, in which English capital to a large amount is invested, and levied another forced contribution there to the amount of $50,000. Before he had time to do more mischief he was attacked by the government forces under General Tapia, who forced him to retreat, with the loss of six guns and the greater part of his badly armed infantry. He appears to have retired, however, in pretty good order, and having got between the government troops and the capital, actually intercepted and captured Tapia's despatches, giving an account of the late victory.

The action of congress is entirely nullified by the opposition, which, without any real policy of their own, counteract every measure supported by government from a feeling of personal hostility to the president, whom they wish to displace, without apparently having chosen anybody to succeed him, should their efforts eventually be crowned with success.

Every day's experience only tends to prove the utter absurdity of attempting to govern the country with the limited powers granted to the executive by the present ultra-liberal constitution, and I see no hope of improvement unless it comes from a foreign intervention, or the formation of a rational government composed of the leading men of the moderate party, who, however, at present are void of moral courage and afraid to move, unless with some material support from abroad.

I have, &c.

C. LENNOX WYKE.

No. 89.

Sir C. Wyke to Earl Russell.

[Extract.]

MEXICO, *October* 28, 1861.

I was much gratified in learning, by the receipt of your lordship's despatches of the 21st and 31st of August last, that the line of conduct I adopted in negotiating with this government to obtain the repayment of the $660,000 stolen from the legation, and the $400,000 from the Laguna Seca conducta, as reported in my correspondence of the months of June and July last, had been entirely approved of by her Majesty's government.

The instructions contained in your lordship's despatch of the 21st of August enabled me to act in the only way that can be successful with a government which, from the patient forbearance hitherto shown by her Majesty's government, had come to the conclusion that they could commit any and every outrage with impunity.

I was unwilling to use the power with which your lordship had invested me by sending in an ultimatum, without first of all trying to reason them into the necessity of complying with the demands which, just in themselves, would soon be urged in such a manner as to compel the government of the republic to listen to them with attention.

With this object in view, I wrote a note to Señor de Zamacona, the minister for foreign affairs, informing him that I had received by the English mail, which had just arrived, instructions from her Majesty's government, the tenor of which I was anxious to acquaint him with. He immediately replied that he would call on me at 4 o'clock the same day, at which hour he duly arrived at the legation.

On my informing him of the nature of your lordship's instructions, and even reading them to him, in order that no doubt should exist on the subject, he was as much astonished as alarmed, and expressed an earnest wish that I should not communicate with him in writing on a subject so serious until he had acquainted the president and his colleagues, the other ministers, with the actual state of the case, after which he would call on me again and acquaint me with the views of his government.

Eight days elapsed without my seeing him, and he then returned to negotiate with me for the settlement of a question the gravity of which he had at length become fully aware of. From that day to this, that is to say, during three weeks, he has been with me for two hours at least out of every twenty-four, urging the impossibility of complying with your lordship's demands, and trying to obtain better terms than those I insisted on.

I told him that I was willing in every way to spare their *amour propre* and extreme susceptibility as far as was consistent with my duty, but that the essential substance of what was required must be conceded, or else I should withdraw the mission from the republic, which would thus have to bear the responsibility of a refusal.

The two principal objections to be overcome consisted in the repayment of the $660,000 robbed from the legation, and the appointment of interventors at the different ports; the first, because it involved the necessity of their practically recognizing a principle they had hitherto always repudiated, viz., their responsibility for the acts of the other government; and the second, because the presence of such agents was looked on as a national humiliation, which it would be disgraceful in them, as a government, to consent to.

Added these was the all but impossibility of their procuring resources which would enable them to comply with our demands. At this juncture Mr. Corwin, the United States minister, informed them that he had instructions to negotiate a convention with them, by which, on their giving certain guarantees, such as pledging the remains of their church property, waste lands, &c., the American government would engage to pay 3 per cent. interest annually on their English debt, for the space of five years, provided at the end of that time Mexico would repay the money so advanced with 6 per cent. interest thereon.

Señor de Zamacona at once wished to hand me over to my American colleague, who, he felt sure, would guarantee the payment of the interest on the English debt, and thereby settle the very disagreeable questions existing between his government and this legation. He seemed so pleased with this new solution of his pressing difficulties that it was quite painful to wake him out of his happy day-dream by the declaration that such a combination could not be entertained, and that his government alone must be held responsible for what it owed us.

After he had recovered from the perception of this unpleasant truth, he reflected that the money would still be forthcoming, and that he had only first of all to receive it from the United States in order to pay it back again to Great Britain. This point once settled, we set to work again, when he immediately stumbled over the insurmountable difficulty of the appointment of interventors for the reasons already stated, and, as if that was not sufficient, declared the impossibility of finding funds from which to pay the legation and Laguna Seca robberies.

To this I replied, that if they refused our conditions, we should appoint the interventors, and by seizing their ports with a naval force, pay ourselves and their other creditors out of the duties levied at such ports. This brought him back again to the point from which we had diverged, and he then said, with some degree of truth, that, independent of the difficulty of getting the president to look at the question in its proper point of view, it was useless to wound the susceptibilities of the nation, as any agreement he made with me which had that result was certain to be repudiated by the congress, and would utterly defeat the object we had in view. I then persuaded him that what I required could easily be reconciled with the national honor, and even prove highly advantageous to the pecuniary interests of the republic, by giving it another form and putting aside the name of "interventor" altogether. This point at length settled, as I will hereafter explain, the next question was where the money was to come from wherewith to pay the sums before referred to, as 59 per cent. of their import duties being mortgaged to us alone, it was clear it could not be taken from the remaining 41 per cent. out of which they have to pay the French convention and other assignments to foreign creditors.

Some time ago they made over 20 per cent. of some extra duties, called "mejoras materiales," to Don Manuel Escaudon for the purpose of aiding him to construct a railroad between this city and Vera Cruz. Now as this railroad plan is little better than a chimera, and they have no right to squander their money in this way whilst leaving their debts unpaid, I suggested the propriety of stopping Don Manuel's allowance, and employing one-half of it towards the liquidation of their debt to us, and keeping the other for their own more pressing necessities.

I will not any longer take up your lordship's time by detailing the means by which, in long and weary interviews, I day by day gained my ground, until at length I think I may say I have carried my point, and brought Señor Zamacona to agree to a settlement of the difficulty on terms which, although slightly modified in form from what your lordship instructed me to demand, will still in substance, I trust, prove satisfactory to her Majesty's government.

Our interviews only terminated this afternoon; and as soon after the departure of the English mail as possible, I shall draw up the articles of a convention embodying the following agreement:

1. Repayment of the legation and Laguna Seca robberies, with 6 per cent. interest on the first and 12 per cent. interest on the second, by the additional 10 per cent. on extra import duties above referred to as "mejoras materiales."

2. The payment of arrears of interest due to the London and convention bondholders to be made good by consigning 30 per cent. of the import duties at all the ports for the former, and 29 per cent. for the latter, until said arrears are paid off, when the percentage on such duties will again revert respectively to 25 and 12 per cent. as heretofore.

3. Such sums owing to both classes of bondholders as were in the hands of the custom-house authorities at the time of the suspension of payments caused by the law of the 17th of July last, shall be paid out of the aforesaid 10 per cent. extra duties styled "mejoras materiales," which, as already stated, are set aside for paying the claims arising out of the legation and Laguna Seca robberies; and these payments shall be made of said extra duties when the losses caused by those robberies have been reimbursed.

4. The consuls at the different ports shall be authorized to claim the inspection of any books, accounts, documents, or manifests in the respective custom-houses, as they consider necessary to verify the receipts and accounts of the same; and, finally, any commercial house paying duties to the government on goods imported without first of all receiving the receipts from the bondholders' agents for their percentage on such duties shall, as well as the custom-house authorities, render themselves liable to be sued by law for the recovery of double the amount of such duties.

5. Before signing the convention containing the above stipulations, the government will address me an official note engaging to use their best efforts to carry a measure through congress for the alteration of the tariff, whereby the duties on English manufactured goods shall be reduced to nearly one-half of what is now levied on them.

Such, my lord, is the outline of the convention which I hope to sign with this government in the course of the ensuing month; and if I succeed in doing so, I think the bondholders will have every reason to be satisfied with the bargain made for them.

As it would have been impossible for this government to fulfil such engagements without the pecuniary aid afforded to them by the American government, and as that aid will not be forthcoming until the month of January next, the stipulations of this convention will not come into force until that period, dating from the 1st day of the month.

The extended power given to our consuls, together with the agent's right to prosecute all parties defrauding the bondholders of their proper percentage on the duties, are advantages only to be equalled by those arising from extending the collection of such percentage to all the ports in the republic, instead of its being confined to Tampico and Vera Cruz.

The reduction in duties will also have an immense effect in largely increasing our commercial relations with this country, which have hitherto been cramped by the enormous duties levied on our manufactured goods.

With these people one must never count on anything until it is actually done; therefore I must not boast of my success until the convention is actually signed, which I hope it will be within the next fortnight.

As it was under the pressure of fear that this government has yielded, it becomes absolutely necessary for our future prestige and influence here that a respectable naval force shall soon make its appearance in the waters of Vera Cruz, and in the event of the Mexican government ever failing to comply with the engagements which they have entered into, I should be authorized to employ such naval force as I could then procure from Jamaica or elsewhere, in order to force them to perform their duty, without waiting until I could obtain instructions from home to that effect.

With such power placed in my hands I should be able to prevent much mischief, as well as future annoyance to her Majesty's government.

I cannot speak in terms of sufficient praise of my American colleague, Mr. Corwin, who throughout this transaction has acted with me most cordially, having refused to negotiate his convention with this government until he learnt from me that I had settled all pending difficulties with them, as he was determined that the money to be advanced by his government should be applied for the purpose it was intended, and not uselessly squandered, as it otherwise would have been, to no purpose.

As the interest due on the French convention is a mere trifle in comparison to ours, I have strongly urged this government to satisfy the just reclamations of the French legation with respect to its suspension, and they have assured me that they will use their best efforts to come to some satisfactory arrangement of this question with M. de Saligny.

No. 90.

Earl Russell to Sir J. Crampton.

FOREIGN OFFICE, *November* 28, 1861.

SIR: I received last night, from Sir Charles Wyke, a despatch dated the 28th of October, the substance of which I propose now to communicate to you.

I should explain, in the first instance, that in the proceedings reported in this despatch Sir Charles Wyke was engaged in carrying out the instructions contained in my despatch to him of the 21st of August, of which a copy is herewith enclosed for your information,* and from which you will learn the nature of the demands which he was at that time instructed to make on the government of Mexico in the name of her Majesty's government.

On the receipt of this instruction Sir C. Wyke placed himself in communication with the Mexican authorities, with the view, if possible, to avoid the necessity of presenting an ultimatum.

The two principal difficulties which Sir C. Wyke had to meet in the course of the discussions which followed were, first, the objection to the repayment of the sum robbed from her Majesty's legation; and, secondly, the proposed appointment of interventors at the ports.

The objection to the first of these demands was grounded on the principle that the actual authorities do not hold themselves responsible for the acts of their predecessors; and as regards the interventors, it was urged that such an arrangement would be regarded as a national humiliation which it would be disgraceful for the Mexican government to consent to.

The impossibility of raising funds to meet the pecuniary demands of her Majesty's government was also urged upon Sir C. Wyke. But a proposal made by the minister of the United States placed the matter in a new aspect.

That minister informed the Mexican authorities that he had instructions to negotiate a convention with them by which, on their giving certain guarantees, such as pledging the remains of the church property, waste lands, &c., the American government would engage to pay 3 per cent. per annum on the Mexican debt to England for the space of five years, provided that at the expiration of that period Mexico would repay the money so advanced, with 6 per cent. interest thereupon.

The difficulties raised as to the repayment of the legation and Laguna Seca robberies, and as to the appointment of interventors, came next under discussion;

---

* No. 15.

but Sir C. Wyke states that he eventually carried his point, and that he thinks he may say that he has brought Señor Zamacona, with whom the discussion was carried on, to agree to a settlement on terms which, though slightly modified from those proposed, might still prove satisfactory to her Majesty's government.

The terms thus arrived at are contained in the articles herewith enclosed for your information,* and which Sir C. Wyke proposed immediately to embody in the form of a convention, which he states that he hoped he should succeed in inducing the Mexican government to sign in the course of last month.

As it was understood that it would be impossible for the Mexican government to fulfil such engagements without the pecuniary aid afforded to them by the American government, and as that aid was not to be forthcoming until the month of January next, it was arranged that the stipulations of the proposed convention should not come into force until the 1st of January, 1862.

Such is the state of the case as reported by Sir C. Wyke; but with reference to the fact that the convention was not yet signed, and that the terms agreed upon had only been conceded under the pressure of fear, Sir C. Wyke has urged the presence of a naval force at Vera Cruz, and that he should be authorized, in case of necessity, to have recourse to force to compel a compliance with the British demands as then made.

Sir C. Wyke has further urged the Mexican government to satisfy the claims of the French legation as regards the suspension of interest due on the French convention, and the Mexican government have assured him that they would use their best efforts to come to some satisfactory arrangement with M. de Saligny.

Having stated the history of these negotiations, and the result which has been reached, I have now to communicate to you the view which her Majesty's government take of this transaction.

The terms obtained by Sir Charles Wyke fulfil, generally speaking, the separate requirements of Great Britain; but no security is obtained that those terms will be observed any better than former stipulations and engagements.

That security, if to be found at all, is to be found in the convention which her Majesty has concluded with France and Spain.

The advantage of having obtained the consent of the Mexican government to these conditions consists, first, in the precision with which Sir Charles Wyke has drawn up the British demands; and, secondly, in the assent of the Mexican authorities to the terms thus laid before them.

The task of the British commissioner is thus rendered easy, and the work of our respective missions will be facilitated.

It would greatly add to the facility and abridge the time of negotiation if the government of the Queen of Spain should be able to communicate to her Majesty's government the terms which they would think it necessary to require for the reparation of the wrongs they have sustained at the hands of Mexico, and the safety of their subjects for the future.

I am, &c., RUSSELL.

No. 91.

Earl Russell to Earl Cowley.

FOREIGN OFFICE, *December* 2, 1861.

MY LORD: I received on the 27th instant, from Sir C. Wyke, a despatch dated the 28th of October, the substance of which I propose now to communicate to you.

* See page 117.

I should explain, in the first instance, that in the proceedings reported in this despatch Sir C. Wyke was engaged in carrying out the instructions contained in my despatch to him of the 21st of August, of which a copy is herewith enclosed for your information,* and from which you will learn the nature of the demands which he was at that time instructed to make on the government of Mexico in the name of her Majesty's government.

On the receipt of this instruction Sir C. Wyke placed himself in communication with the Mexican authorities, with the view, if possible, to avoid the necessity of presenting an ultimatum.

The two principal difficulties which Sir C. Wyke had to meet in the discussions which followed were, first, the objection to the repayment of the sum robbed from her Majesty's legation; and, secondly, the proposed appointment of interventors at the ports.

The objection to the first of these demands was granted on the principle that the actual authorities do not hold themselves responsible for the acts of their predecessors; and, as regards the interventors, it was urged that such an arrangement would be regarded as a national humiliation, which it would be disgraceful for the Mexican government to consent to.

The impossibility of raising funds to meet the pecuniary demands of her Majesty's government was also urged upon Sir C. Wyke, but a proposal made by the minister of the United States placed the matter in a new light.

That minister informed the Mexican authorities that he had instructions to negotiate a convention with them, by which, on their giving certain guarantees, such as pledging the remains of the church property, waste lands, &c., the American government would engage to pay 3 per cent. per annum on the Mexican debt to England for the space of five years, provided that at the expiration of that period Mexico would repay the money so advanced, with 6 per cent. interest thereupon.

The difficulties raised as to the repayment of the legation and Laguna Seca robberies, and as to the appointment of interventors, came next under discussion; but Sir C. Wyke states that he eventually carried his point, and that he thinks he may say that he has brought Señor Zamacona, with whom the discussion was carried on, to agree to a settlement on terms which, though slightly modified from those proposed, might still prove satisfactory to her Majesty's government.

The terms thus arrived at are contained in the articles herewith enclosed for your information,† and which Sir C. Wyke proposes immediately to embody in the form of a convention, which he states that he hoped he should succeed in inducing the Mexican government to sign in the course of last month.

As it was understood that it would be impossible for the Mexican government to fulfil such engagements without the pecuniary aid afforded to them by the American government, and as that aid was not to be forthcoming until the month of January next, it was arranged that the stipulations of the proposed convention should not come into force until the 1st of January, 1862.

Such is the state of the case, as reported by Sir C. Wyke; but with reference to the fact that the convention was not yet signed, and that the terms agreed upon had only been conceded under the pressure of fear, Sir C. Wyke has urged the presence of a naval force at Vera Cruz, and that he should be authorized, in case of necessity, to have recourse to force to compel a compliance with the British demands as there made.

Sir C. Wyke has further urged the Mexican government to satisfy the claims of the French legation as regards the suspension of interest due on the French convention, and the Mexican government have assured him that they would use their best efforts to come to some satisfactory arrangement with M. de Saligny.

Having stated the result of these negotiations, and the result which has been

*No 15.   † See page 117.

reached, I have now to communicate to you the view which her Majesty's government take of this transaction.

The terms obtained by Sir C. Wyke fulfil, generally speaking, the separate requirements of Great Britain. But no security is obtained that those terms will be observed any better than any former stipulations and engagements.

That security, if to be found at all, is to be found in the convention which her Majesty has concluded with France and Spain.

The advantage of having obtained the consent of the Mexican government to these conditions consists, first, in the precision which Sir C. Wyke has drawn up the British demands; and, secondly, in the assent of the Mexican authorities to the terms thus laid before them.

The task of the British commissioners is thus rendered easy, and the work of our respective missions will be facilitated.

It would greatly add to the facility and abridge the time of negotiation if the government of the Emperor of the French should be able to communicate to her Majesty's government the terms which they would think it necessary to require for the reparation of the wrongs they have sustained at the hands of Mexico, and the safety of their subjects for the future.

I am, &c.,

RUSSELL.

No. 92.

Earl Russell to Earl Cowley.

FOREIGN OFFICE, *December* 4, 1861.

MY LORD: In the present state of our relations with the United States, her Majesty's government propose to send one line-of-battle ship and two frigates only to form part of the expedition to Mexico.

The number of supernumerary marines will be 700.

I am, &c.,

RUSSELL.

No. 93.

Earl Russell to Sir J. Crampton.

FOREIGN OFFICE, *December* 4, 1861.

SIR: In the present state of our relations with the United States, her Majesty's government propose to send one line-of-battle ship and two frigates only to form part of the expedition to Mexico.

The number of supernumerary marines will still be 700.

I am, &c.,

RUSSELL.

No. 94.

Earl Cowley to Earl Russell.

PARIS, *December* 3, 1861.

MY LORD: I have communicated to M. Thouvenel your lordship's despatch, No. 1324, of yesterday's date, in which your lordship informs me of the negotiations which have taken place between Sir Charles Wyke and the Mexican minister for foreign affairs for the settlement of British claims on the Mexican government.

M. Thouvenel did not make any other remark than that he regretted that he could not communicate to her Majesty's government the terms which the imperial government would require for the reparation of the wrongs they have sustained, and for the safety of French subjects in future. He had not himself the necessary information to enable him to form an opinion, and he had been unable, therefore, to furnish any instructions on this head to Admiral Jurien de la Gravière, which he had much desired to do. All that he could say was, that the greater part of the French claims were provided for by the convention which the Mexican government had set aside; and, with regard to the others, he must leave it to the discretion of the commissioners to examine into and settle their amount.

I have, &c.,

COWLEY.

No. 95.

Lord Lyons to Earl Russell.

WASHINGTON, *November* 29, 1861.

MY LORD: M. Mercier and I received last week our instructions and full powers with regard to inviting the accession of the United States to the convention for combined operations against Mexico, which was signed in London on the 31st of last month. But the full powers and instructions for M. Tassara, the Spanish minister, have not yet reached him. M. Mercier and I have therefore been obliged to defer addressing to the government of the United States the formal invitation to accede to the convention. M. Mercier, however, on the 23d ultimo told Mr. Seward that instructions had been received by me and by himself, and that we should be glad to make the invitation, either collectively or separately, as he pleased; in fact, to make it in whatever form he thought most convenient.

Mr. Seward said that he presumed the invitation would be in writing, but that he was indifferent about the point of form. He did not give any hint of the nature of the answer which he should make on behalf of the United States government.

M. Tassara expects to receive his instructions to-morrow or the next day.

I have, &c.,

LYONS.

No. 96.

Lord Lyons to Earl Russell.

WASHINGTON, *December* 3, 1861.

MY LORD: With reference to my despatch of the 29th ultimo, I have the honor to inform your lordship that on the following day M. Tassara, the Spanish minister, received the instructions and full powers necessary to enable him to join M. Mercier and me in inviting the government of the United States to accede to the convention for combined operations against Mexico, which was signed in London on the 31st of October last. We lost no time in addressing a collective note to Mr. Seward, inviting, in the name of the governments of Great Britain, France, and Spain, the accession of the United States to the convention. I have the honor to enclose a copy of the note. No answer has yet been made to it.

I have, &c.,

LYONS.

Enclosure in No. 96.

MM. Tassara and Mercier and Lord Lyons to Mr. Seward.

WASHINGTON, *ce* 30 *Novembre*, 1861.

Les soussignés, envoyés extraordinaires et ministres plénipotentiaires de leurs Majestés la Reine d'Espagne, l'Empereur des Français, et la Reine du Royaume Uni de la Grande Bretagne et d'Irlande, ont l'honneur de transmettre ci-joint à l'honorable Secrétaire d'Etat le texte d'une convention conclue à Londres le 31 Octobre entre leurs souverains respectifs, dans le but d'obtenir par une action commune le redressement de leurs griefs contre la république du Mexique.

Ainsi qu'il a été stipulé entre les hautes parties contractantes, les soussignés ont reçu l'ordre d'inviter le gouvernement des Etats-Unis à accéder à cet acte; et en adressant cette invitation à l'honorable Secrétaire d'Etat, ils s'empressent de l'informer qu'ils sont munis de pleins pouvoirs nécessaires à l'effet de conclure et de signer collectivement ou séparément avec le plénipotentiaire désigné par le Président des Etats-Unis une convention identique.

Rien ne serait plus agréable aux gouvernements d'Espagne, de France, et de la Grande Bretagne que de voir celui des Etats-Unis accueillir favorablement leur proposition, et en priant l'honorable Secrétaire d'Etat de vouloir bien leur faire connaître la décision du Président, les soussignés, &c.

GABRIEL J. TASSARA.
HENRI MERCIER.
LYONS.

No. 97.

Sir J. Crampton to Earl Russell.

MADRID, *December* 10, 1861.

MY LORD: On the receipt of your lordship's despatch of the 4th instant, I immediately informed Marshal O'Donnell that, in the present state of our relations with the United States, her Majesty's government proposed to send one line-of-battle ship and two frigates only, to form part of the expedition to Mexico.

I have, &c.,

JOHN F. CRAMPTON.

No. 98.

Sir J. Crampton to Earl Russell.

MADRID, *December* 15, 1861.

MY LORD: I have communicated to M. Calderon Collantes the substance of your lordship's despatch of the 28th ultimo, giving the history of the negotiations between Sir C. Wyke and the Mexican government, and the result which had been reached; and acquainting me, at the same time, with the view which her Majesty's government take of this transaction.

I told M. Calderon Collantes that the terms obtained by Sir Charles Wyke fulfil, generally speaking, the separate requirements of Great Britain; but I added that the agreement which had been thus come to with the Mexican government in no way altered the position of her Majesty's government as regards the convention which Great Britain had concluded with France and Spain.

That convention, I observed, affords in fact the only security that the terms agreed upon by the Mexican government on this occasion shall be better observed than former stipulations and engagements.

The advantage, therefore, of having obtained the consent of the Mexican government to these conditions consists in the precision with which the British demands have been stated, and the assent of the Mexican authorities to the terms laid before them.

The task of the British commissioners was, I remarked, thus rendered easy, and the work of our respective missions would be facilitated; but it was the opinion of her Majesty's government that it would greatly add to that facility if the government of the Queen of Spain should be able to communicate to them the terms which her Catholic Majesty's government would think it necessary to require for the reparation of the wrongs they had sustained at the hands of Mexico, and the safety of their subjects in future.

M. Calderon replied that he entirely entered into the views of her Majesty's government in this respect, and that, as far as Spain was concerned, nothing could be easier than to state with precision the terms which she on her part would require of the Mexican government. These terms are, in fact, embodied in the convention concluded with Miramon, and confirmed by the treaty Mon-Almonte, which had been repudiated by the succeeding government of Mexico upon the same monstrous principle which the Mexican government had attempted to oppose to the demands of Sir C. Wyke, viz: that the actual authorities do not consider themselves responsible to foreign nations for the acts of their predecessors. Upon the fulfilment of these engagements the Spanish government would insist, and all that they would demand in addition to them would be the infliction of due punishment upon the perpetrators of the assassinations which had since been committed upon Spanish subjects.

This, he considered, however, to be a capital point; for if the Mexican government was unable or unwilling to administer justice in such flagrant cases, what hope could we entertain of their fulfilling other engagements? If the lives of British subjects had in any instance been sacrificed, he presumed that as a matter of course the punishment of the assassins would be made by her Majesty's government a primary condition to any arrangement with the Mexican government.

In conclusion, M. Calderon expressed the opinion that the readiest way of coming to the understanding proposed by her Majesty's government, with a view to facilitating the negotiations, would be that the commissioners of Spain and England should be instructed by their respective governments to communicate to each other the terms which each would think it necessary to insist upon in satisfaction for past wrongs, and as security for the future observance of international duties by Mexico.

I have, &c.,

JOHN F. CRAMPTON.

No. 99.

M. Isturiz to Earl Russell.

LONDRES, 22 *de Diciembre de* 1981.

MY LORD: Cuando se celebró el convenio de 31 de Octubre para arreglar la accion mancomunada de Inglaterra, España, y Francia en la república de Méjico, tuve el honor de advertir á vuestra excelencia, de parte de mi gobierno, que si no llegaban á tiempo las órdenes que iban á enviarse al capitan general de Cuba, era posible que la expedicion Española saliese del puerto de la Habana sin aguardar la llegada de las otras escuadras.

Debo ahora manifestar á vuestra excelencia, de órden del gobierno de la Reina mi augusta soberana, que las últimas noticias de Cuba recibidas en Madrid, correspondientes al 26 de Noviembre, hacen todavia mas posible la eventualidad de que se trata. Parece efectivamente que dispuesta hacia ya tiempo en la Habana y lista para darse á la mar la expedicion Española, ignorándose allí si se habia firmado el convenio entre Inglaterra, España y Francia, siendo por consiguiente desconocido cual seria el punto designado para la reunion de las tres escuadras; y ocasionando gastos enormes el mantener la prolongacion indefinida de una expedicion militar tan considerable, el capitan general de Cuba, movido por estas poderosas consideraciones, hacia ánimo á aquella fecha de disponer la inmediata salida de las fuerzas Españolas con direccion á Vera Cruz.

Al dar aviso á vuestra excelencia de estos hechos, apenas necesito añadir que si realmente han llegado á verificarse, el Comandante de la expedicion Española habrá llevado órdenes de ponerse en todo de acuerdo con las fuerzas de las dos potencias amigas y aliadas que pudieran hallarse en las aguas de Mejico; y de todos modos, dado el caso de que el gefe Español haya roto las hostilidades y ocupado á Vera Cruz y el Castillo de San Juan de Ulloa, esta ocupacion se entenderá hecha en nombre de las tres potencias coaligadas hasta que lleguen las escuadras de Inglaterra y Francia y se resuelva lo mas conveniente de comun acuerdo.

Con este motivo, &c.

XAVIER E. ISTURIZ.

[Translation.]

SPANISH LEGATION,
London, December 22, 1861.

MY LORD: When the convention of the 31st October was concluded for determining the joint action of England, Spain, and France, in the republic of Mexico, I had the honor to acquaint your excellency that if the orders which were to be transmitted to the captain general of Cuba should not reach him in time, it was possible that the Spanish expedition might leave the port of Havana without waiting for the arrival of the other squadrons.

I have now to inform your excellency, by order of the government of the Queen my august sovereign, that the last intelligence from Cuba received in Madrid, reaching to the 26th November, shows this event to be still more likely. It appears, in fact, that the Spanish expedition had been for some time prepared at the Havana, and was ready to put to sea, as it was unknown there whether or not the convention between England, Spain, and France had been signed, and it was therefore unknown what place would be fixed upon for the meeting of the three squadrons; and as the indefinite procrastination of so considerable a military expedition would occasion enormous expense, the captain general of Cuba, moved by these weighty considerations, was hastening, at that date, the immediate departure of the Spanish forces to Vera Cruz.

In making known these facts to your excellency, I need scarcely add that if this should have really taken place, the commandant of the Spanish expedition will have had orders to put himself, in everything, in accordance with the forces of the two friendly and allied powers which may be in the waters of Mexico; and, at all events, supposing that the Spanish commander has commenced hostilities and taken possession of Vera Cruz and the Castle of San Juan de Ulloa, this possession will be understood as taken in the name of the allied powers, until the squadrons of England and France shall arrive, and the most advisable action shall be determined by common accord.

I have, &c.,

XAVIER E. ISTURIZ.

No. 100.

Earl Russell to Sir J. Crampton.

FOREIGN OFFICE, *December* 24, 1861.

SIR: I enclose, for your information, a copy of a note which I have received from M. Isturiz,* as to the course which would be pursued if the Spanish fleet should have left the Havana for Mexico before the arrival of the allied squadrons.

I am, &c.,

RUSSELL.

No. 101.

Earl Russell to Sir J. Crampton.

FOREIGN OFFICE, *December* 24, 1861.

SIR: With reference to the concluding paragraph in your despatch of the 15th instant, I have to state to you that Sir C. Wyke will be instructed to act in the manner proposed by Señor Collantes, and to communicate to the commissioners of Spain the terms which, so far as British interests are concerned, her Majesty's government would think it necessary to insist upon as satisfaction for past wrongs, and as security for the future observance of international duties by Mexico.

I am, &c.,

RUSSELL.

° No. 99.

No. 102.

Lord Lyons to Earl Russell.

WASHINGTON, *December* 6, 1861.

MY LORD: I have the honor to enclose a copy of a note addressed to M. Tassara, M. Mercier, and to me, by which the government of the United States announces its refusal to accede to the convention for combined operations against Mexico, which was signed in London on the 31st of October last.

The note was sent last night to M. Tassara, without any intimation that similar notes had not been sent to M. Mercier and me. It consequently did not occur to M. Tassara to communicate it to us; and it was only accidentally that I learnt of its existence just in time to procure a copy for my messenger of to-day.

I have, &c.,

LYONS.

Enclosure in No. 102.

Mr. Seward to MM. Tassara and Mercier and Lord Lyons.

WASHINGTON, *December* 4, 1861.

The undersigned, Secretary of State of the United States, has the honor to acknowledge the receipt of a note which was addressed to him on the 30th day of November last, by M. Gabriel G. Tassara, minister plenipotentiary of her Majesty the Queen of Spain; M. Henri Mercier, minister plenipotentiary of his Majesty the Emperor of the French; and Lord Lyons, minister plenipotentiary of her Majesty the Queen of the United Kingdom of Great Britain and Ireland.

With that paper the aforesaid ministers have submitted the text of a convention which was concluded at London on the 31st October last, between the sovereigns before named, with the view of obtaining, through a common action, the redress of their grievances against the republic of Mexico.

In the preamble the high contracting parties say that they have been placed, by the arbitrary and vexatious conduct of the authorities of the republic of Mexico, under a necessity for exacting from the authorities a more effective protection for the persons and property of their subjects, as well as the execution of obligations contracted with them by the republic of Mexico, and have agreed to conclude a convention between themselves, for the purpose of combining their common action in the case.

In the first article the high contracting powers bind themselves to make, immediately after the signing of the convention, the necessary arrangements to send to the shores of Mexico land and sea forces combined, the effective number of which shall be determined in a further exchange of communications between the governments, but the total of which must be sufficient to enable them to seize and occupy the various fortifications and military positions of the Mexican seacoast. Also, that the commanders of the allied forces shall be authorized to accomplish such other operations as may, on the spot, be deemed most suitable for realizing the end specified in the preamble, and especially for insuring the safety of foreign residents. And that all the measures which are thus to be carried into effect shall be taken in the name and on account of the high contracting parties, without distinction of the particular nationality of the forces employed in executing them.

In the second article the high contracting parties bind themselves not to seek for themselves, in the employment of the coercive measures foreseen by the present convention, any acquisition of territory, or any peculiar advantage, and not to exercise, in the subsequent affairs of Mexico, any influence of a character to impair the right of the Mexican nation to choose, and fully to constitute, the form of its own government.

In the third article the high contracting parties agree that a commission, composed of three commissioner, one appointed by each of the contracting powers, shall be established, with full power to determine all questions which may arise from the employment and distribution of the sums of money which shall be received from Mexico, having regard to the respective rights of the contracting parties.

In the fourth article the high contracting parties, expressing the desire that the measures which it is their intention to adopt may not have an exclusive character, and recognizing the fact that the government of the United States, like themselves, has claims of its own to enforce against the Mexican republic, agree that immediately after the signing of the present convention a copy of it shall be communicated to the government of the United States, and that this government shall be invited to accede to it, and that, in anticipation of such accession, their respective ministers at Washington shall be provided with full powers to conclude and sign, collectively or severally, with a plenipotentiary of the United States, to be designated by the President, such an instrument. But as the high contracting parties would expose themselves, in making any delay in carrying into effect Articles I and II of the convention, to peril in the end which they wish to attain, they have agreed not to defer, with a view to obtaining the accession of the United States, the commencement of the stipulated operations beyond the period at which their combined forces may be united in the vicinity of Vera Cruz.

The plenipotentiaries in their note to the undersigned invite the United States to accede to the convention. The undersigned having submitted the subject to the President will proceed to communicate his views thereon.

First, as the undersigned has heretofore had the honor to inform each of the plenipotentiaries now addressed, the President does not feel himself at liberty to question, and he does not question, that the sovereigns represented have undoubted right to decide for themselves the fact whether they have sustained grievances, and to resort to war with Mexico for the redress thereof, and have a right, also, to levy the war severally or jointly.

Secondly, the United States have a deep interest, which, however, they are happy to believe is an interest held by them in common with the high contracting powers and with all other civilized states, that neither of the sovereigns by whom the convention has been concluded shall seek or obtain any acquisition of territory, or any advantage peculiar to itself, and not equally left open to the United States and every other civilized state, within the territories of Mexico; and especially that neither one nor all of the contracting parties shall, as a result or consequence of the hostilities to be inaugurated under the convention, exercise in the subsequent affairs of Mexico any influence of a character to impair the right of the Mexican people to choose, and freely to constitute, the form of its own government.

The undersigned renews on this occasion the acknowledgment heretofore given, that each of the high contacting parties had informed the United States, substantially, that they recognized this interest; and he is authorized to express the satisfaction of the President with the terms in which that recognition is clearly embodied in the treaty itself.

It is true, as the high contracting parties assume, that the United States have, on their part, claims to urge against Mexico. Upon due consideration, however, the President is of opinion that it would be inexpedient to seek satisfaction of these claims at this time, through an act of accession to the convention.

Among the reasons for this decision which the undersigned is authorized to assign, are, first, that the United States, so far as it is practicable, prefer to adhere to a traditional policy recommended to them by the father of their country, and confirmed by a happy experience, which forbids their making alliances with foreign nations. Secondly, Mexico being a neighbor of the United States on this continent, and possessing a system of government similar to our own in many of its important features, the United States habitually cherish a decided good will towards that republic, and a lively interest in its security, prosperity, and welfare.

Animated by these sentiments, the United States do not feel inclined to resort to forcible remedies for their claims at the present moment, when the government of Mexico is deeply disturbed by faction within, and exposed to war with foreign nations; and, of course, the same sentiments render them still more disinclined to allied war against Mexico than to war to be urged against her by themselves alone.

The undersigned is further authorized to state to the plenipotentiaries, for the information of the sovereigns of Spain, France, and Great Britain, that the United States are so earnestly anxious for the safety and welfare of the republic of Mexico that they have already empowered their minister residing there to enter into a treaty with the Mexican republic, conceding to it some material aid and advantages which, it is hoped, may enable that republic to satisfy the just claims and demands of the said sovereigns, and to avert the war which those sovereigns have agreed among each other to levy against Mexico. The sovereigns need not be informed that this proposal to Mexico has been made, not in hostility to them, but with a knowledge of the proceedings frankly communicated to them, and with the hope that they might find, through the increased ability of Mexico to result from the treaty, and her willingness to treat with them upon just terms, a mode of arresting the hostilities which it is the object of the convention now under consideration to inaugurate.

What has thus far been done by the American minister at Mexico under these instructions has not yet become known to this government, and the information is looked for with deep interest.

Should these negotiations offer any sufficient ground on which to justify a proposition to the high contracting parties in behalf of Mexico, the undersigned will hasten to submit such a proposition to those powers. But it is to be understood, first, that Mexico shall have acceded to such a treaty; and, secondly, that it shall be acceptable to the President and Senate of the United States.

In the meantime the high contracting parties are informed that the President deems it his duty that a naval force should remain in the Gulf of Mexico, sufficient to look after the interests of American citizens in Mexico during the conflict which may arise between the high contracting parties and that republic; and, secondly, that the American minister residing in Mexico be authorized to seek such conference in Mexico with the belligerent parties as may guard either of them against inadvertent injury to the just rights of the United States, if any such shall be endangered.

The undersigned having thus submitted all the views and sentiments of this government on this important subject to the high contracting parties in a spirit of peace and friendship not only towards Mexico, but towards the high contracting parties themselves, feels assured that there will be nothing in the watchfulness which it is thus proposed to exercise that can afford any cause for anxiety to any of the parties in question.

The undersigned, &c.

WILLIAM H. SEWARD.

No. 103.

Lord Lyons to Earl Russell.

WASHINGTON, *December* 9, 1861.

MY LORD: I have the honor to transmit to your lordship a copy of a collective note, by which M. Tassara, M. Mercier, and I have acknowledged the receipt of Mr. Seward's note of the 4th instant, conveying the refusal of the United States government to accede to the convention of the 31st· October for combined operations against Mexico.

I purpose to communicate a copy of Mr. Seward's note to Sir Charles Wyke, sending it under flying seal to Vice-Admiral Sir Alexander Milne.

I have, &c.,

LYONS.

Enclosure in No. 103.

MM. Tassara and Mercier and Lord Lyons to Mr. Seward.

WASHINGTON, *ce* 7 *Décembre*, 1861.

Les soussignés, envoyés extraordinaires et ministres plénipotentiaires de leurs Majestés la Reine d'Espagne, l'Empereur des Français et la Reine du Royaume Uni de la Grande Bretagne et d'Irlande, ont l'honneur d'accuser réception à l'honorable Secrétaire d'État de la note qu'il a bien voulu leur adresser sous le date du 4 de ce mois, en réponse à celle par laquelle ils lui ont communiqué le texte de la convention conclue à Londres entre leurs souverains dans le but de régler par une action commune leurs différends avec la république Mexicaine, et ont invité le gouvernement des Etats Unis à accéder à cet acte. Ils vont s'empresser de transmettre cette réponse à leurs cours respectives.

Les soussignés, &c.

GABRIEL J. TASSARA.
HENRI MERCIER.
LYONS.

No. 104.

Earl Russell to M. de Isturiz.

FOREIGN OFFICE, *December* 24, 1861.

M. LE MINISTRE: I have the honor to acknowledge the receipt of your note of the 22d instant, in which, in pursuance of instructions from your government, you have had the goodness to communicate to me the course which will be pursued if the Spanish fleet at the Havana should have left for Mexico prior to the arrival of the allied squadrons, and should have taken possession of Vera Cruz.

I am, &c.,

RUSSELL.

No. 105.

Earl Russell to Sir J. Crampton.

FOREIGN OFFICE, December 27, 1861.

SIR: I enclose for your information copies of despatches from Lord Lyons,* reporting the answer which the government of the United States have returned to the invitation adressed to it to accede to the convention of the 31st of October for combined operations in Mexico.

I am, &c.,

RUSSELL.

No. 106.

Sir C. Wyke to Earl Russell.

[Extract.]

MEXICO, November 25, 1861.

By the last mail I was enabled to give your lordship some idea of the effect produced upon President Juarez and his cabinet by the instructions contained in your lordship's despatches of the 21st and 31st of August last, while I at the same time explained to your lordship for what reasons and to what extent I had taken upon myself the responsibility of modifying those instructions.

The result of these modifications was, as I had the honor of stating in my despatch of the 28th ultimo, that I obtained a starting point from which to commence my operations with some chance of success. It would, of course, have been far easier to demand from this government a plain "yes" or "no" to the ultimatum I was instructed to present to them, but I felt sure her Majesty's government, determined though they were to obtain from Mexico the satisfaction that had been so long denied them, would prefer doing so by ordinary means to employing force.

In order, therefore, to obtain what was required, I did not hesitate to adopt a line of conduct which, by being somewhat more palatable to the susceptible Mexicans, would not in reality interfere with the requirements of her Majesty's government.

Your lordship will have seen that, even under these circumstances, it was only after the greatest trouble I obtained the outline of a convention that was embodied in my despatch of the 28th ultimo, above alluded to. Since that time my difficulties have greatly increased.

I nevertheless continued my negotiations with this government through the medium of their minister for foreign affairs, with whom I consented to treat unofficially at the legation, and it will now be my duty to lay before your lordship the results which have been arrived at.

First of all comes the reduction of the tariff. I had informed Señor Zamacona that unless the government consented to a *bona fide* reduction it would be useless for us to think of negotiating a convention having for its basis the old system of duties; that her Majesty's government insisted upon this point, and that it would be far better for his government to yield with a good grace than eventually to be forced into compliance with our demands.

This, in the eyes of the minister for foreign affairs, seemed an insurmountable difficulty, for, said he, congress will be certain to throw out any bill that carries

---

* Nos. 97, 103, and 104.

with it even the semblance of foreign interference. This I know to be too true, and I therefore proposed that the reduction should come apparently from congress itself, as a voluntary act resulting from the report of the mixed commission which some time back had been named for examining into the state of the present tariff.

This idea struck Señor Zamacona as a good one, and he promised to do his best to have it carried out. Fresh obstacles, however, soon presented themselves, while intrigues of every kind were being practiced to prevent congress sanctioning any reformation whatever in the tariff.

Luckily at this moment the finance department was offered to a person of considerable merit, socially and politically, Señor Gonzales Echeverria, who had just returned from Europe for the purpose of settling his affairs in the country previous to leaving it for good.

When, however, Señor Echeverria looked into the state of his department he found everything in such hopeless confusion that he refused to undertake the charge. I was then asked to see him as a last hope. During our interview I was so much struck with his good common sense, and with the clear notion he had formed of his country's condition, that I tried to persuade him to accept office. At first he refused, telling me that it was too late to do any good, and that he was convinced nothing but foreign intervention could now save Mexico; but I am happy to say that I at least got him to consent to my request.

His acceptance of office, added to my carefully abstaining from menacing congress in any way, and to Señor Zamacona's untiring exertions, seem to have produced the desired effect, for when the tariff commission a few days ago presented to congress their proposed reform it was duly taken into consideration, and, though not accepted as it stood, was not *de facto* rejected.

According to the existing tariff, goods, besides paying high import duties, were compelled to satisfy endless additional duties after leaving the custom-house, and before coming into the market. The commission therefore proposed a reduction of 50 per cent. on the import duties, and a further reduction, though not of an equal amount, on the additional duties.

I at once, upon this plan of reform becoming known, called a meeting of the British merchants here, in order to obtain their opinion in the matter. They, one and all, owned that the reduction was very much in favor of trade generally, but Mr. Whitehead, agent for the London bondholders, considered that as the assignments due to the body he represented came out of the import duties, and as those duties were to be diminished by one-half, whereas the additional duties, which were not taxed with assignments, were not reduced in the same proportion, he would be the loser, inasmuch as it would require the introduction of double the amount of goods annually to enable government to pay the bondholders their assigned quota of import duties, and that such an event could hardly be expected with the additional duties at so high a figure.

I explained that so long as Mexico, by reducing her tariff, really benefited trade, we had no right to insist upon her effectually crippling herself for the sake of being able actually to square the balance-sheet of the bondholder, or fix the exact ticket to be placed on each separate piece of shirting that came into the country.

Congress, however, threw out the proposal for a reduction of fifty per cent., and passed a law, copy of which I beg to enclose herewith, by which government was authorized to reform the tariff upon a basis of forty per cent. reduction on the import duties, and to reduce the additional duties by about forty-two per cent., making a clear reduction on all duties to which foreign goods are liable of somewhat more than forty-one per cent.

This plan was preferable to the first for many reasons; though it was not quite so beneficial for trade generally, yet it affected pretty equally both the bondholder and the merchant, and had the immense advantage of taking the tariff reform out of the hands of congress, and placing it under the sole control of government.

When Señor Zamacona asked me if I would consent to the system of reduction on the above basis, I told him I could have no objection to it if government would add a clause clearly specifying that neither as regarding import, export, or additional duties, would any change whatever be allowed without at least six months' notice being given.

Here a fresh dispute arose, as it appeared to the minister for foreign affairs that my request implied a doubt as to the honesty of his government. I insisted, however, upon this clause as a *sine qua non*. Had I not done so the government might at any moment have added to their list of additional duties upon the plea of necessity, and so entirely annulled the advantages of the new tariff system.

Besides the above clause, I have obtained a further one, providing for the tariff coming into operation within four months of its publication. The government wanted it to come into operation two months after date, while the merchants required six months' law, so that I had no alternative but to take a period between the two.

This, my lord, is the outline of the proposed new tariff; it will not be possible to have the tariff itself worked out in detail for this mail, and I can therefore merely give your lordship an idea of the result that will be produced by enclosing a comparative statement of duties payable on a supposed cargo under the old and new systems; by which it will be seen that a cargo of merchandise which is now liable to $100,000 import duties, and to $81,000 additional duties, would, under the new system if honestly carried out, be subject to $60,000 import duties, and $46,500 additional duties; thus paying $106,500 for all duties, instead of $181,000, this being equivalent, as I stated above, to a reduction on the whole duties paid by foreign merchandise of somewhat more than forty-one per cent.

The tariff question being thus satisfactorily disposed of, I set to work again on the proposed convention, but found, as I anticipated, that in the interval fresh difficulties had sprung up, and that it would be absolutely necessary to modify the plan that we had originally proposed. This was a matter of comparative indifference to me, provided I obtained the essential points necessary to be secured.

I will not weary your lordship by giving a detailed account of daily interviews with Señor Zamacona, in which as soon as one difficulty was got rid of another sprung up, and this in endless succession, until finally, on the 21st instant, I succeeded in persuading Señor Zamacona to sign with me a convention, copy of which I have herewith the honor to enclose.

In Article I the long-disputed question of the payment of those sums of money robbed from the conducta and the British legation is at length satisfactorily settled, by an extra assignment corresponding to ten per cent. of the import duties, to be taken out of that portion of the additional duties commonly known under the denomination of "mejoras materiales."

In Article II, six per cent. on the $660,000 stolen from the legation, and twelve per cent. on the money still due from the conducta robbery, is secured by an assignment on the same fund, to date from the time the money was taken.

In Article III, all treaties, conventions, and agreements heretofore concluded between the two high contracting parties are declared to be binding in their totality on both parties, and the supreme decrees of the 14th of October, 1850, and the 23d of January, 1857, are likewise to remain in full force and vigor in all that concerns the London bondholders.

Article IV settles the manner of payment of such sums of money owing to the London bondholders and the convention bondholders as were in the hands of the custom-house authorities at the time all payments were suspended by the law of the 17th of July, together with six per cent. interest thereon.

Article V secures the interests of the French convention and the arrears due on other claims as arranged by Admiral Penaud; after the payment of which the quota belonging to the British convention bondholders shall be augmented, as before agreed on, by two per cent. additional.

Article VI gives the British consuls and bondholders' agents at all the ports in the republic the real *bona fide* powers of interventors, without outraging the national feelings, as would have been done by the means proposed in the ultimatum.

Article VII secures the due and punctual payment to the bondholders of their proper share of the duties to be paid on every cargo arriving in a manner never before obtained, thereby saving the immense loss inflicted on them by the irregular way in which these payments have hitherto been made to them.

Article VIII settles the date from which the several assignments above alluded to shall commence.

Article IX frees the Mexican government from the responsibilities of a debtor from the time these several assignments are paid to the agents of the bondholders at the several ports.

Article X stipulates that in all concerning either the appointment of interventors with fuller powers, or the payment of assignments such as those above alluded to, no advantage shall hereafter be accorded to any foreign nation that is not by the same act also accorded to her Majesty's government.

Such, my lord, is the convention that was duly signed and sealed on the 21st instant by Señor Zamacona and myself after the exchange of a couple of notes, copies of which I have the honor herewith to enclose.

The object of these communications was, on his part, to secure the passing of the convention through Congress, as by the tone of them it would appear that the government had been acting from a spirit of justice, instead of being under the undue pressure of menaces from this legation. On mine, it was to aid him in this laudable effort, as well also as to secure an official declaration from this government, binding them to the reduction of the tariff which I had in reality made the basis of my operations.

I conceive that by the arrangement above detailed I had secured all the real objects we had in view, and that with the great advantage of obtaining them by means of persuasion instead of by the employment of force.

That a display of such force would have been temporarily necessary to carry it out I think probable; but that once made, and the determination of her Majesty's government not to be trifled with thus exemplified, all would have gone on smoothly, and we should thus have obtained all we required.

How the arrangement I had thus concluded has been nullified by congress having thrown out the convention by a large majority must form the subject of a separate despatch, in which I will detail all that has taken place here since its rejection.

Had it been ratified by that body I should have made it the foundation for a final settlement with this government of all pending claims, as well as for obtaining compensation for the relatives of such British subjects as have been murdered here up to the present time with impunity. Such an arrangement I could, I doubt not, have made during the presence in these waters of a powerful English squadron, but now the obstinacy of the legislature has destroyed my combinations, and reduces the settlement of these questions to the future employment of brute force.

H. Ex. Doc. 100——26

Enclosure 1 in No. 106.

Law fixing the bases for the reduction of the tariff.

Le citoyen Benito Juarez, président constitutionnel des Etats-Unis Mexicains, à leurs habitans faisons savoir:

Que le secrétariat du souverain congrès de l'union m'a adressé le décret suivant:

Le congrès de l'union a cru devoir décréter ce qui suit:

ARTICLE I. Le gouvernement est autorisé à dresser un nouveau tarif des douanes maritimes et frontières en opérant, dans celui qui est en vigueur, toutes les réformes que l'expérience a démontré être indispensables pour concilier les intérêts du trésor, du commerce, de l'agriculture, et de l'industrie.

ARTICLE II. En agissant ainsi, il se soumettra aux bases suivantes:

1. Il dictera toutes les mesures indispensables afin que le travail ne fasse pas défaut aux agriculteurs, aux industriels, et aux artisans.

2. Il pourra réduire jusqu'à, un quarante pour cent les droits d'importation que paient actuellement les articles étrangers, conformément au tarif en vigueur.

3. Il établira les droits additionnels suivants:

Le municipal, tel qu'il est aujourd'hui;

Celui de "mejoras materiales," trente pour cent sur les droits d'importation;

Celui d'internation, quinze pour cent sur les mêmes droits;

Celui de "contra-registro," trente pour cent sur les mêmes droits;

Celui de deux et demi pour cent pour le ministère de fomento.

ARTICLE III. Le tarif que dressera le gouvernement, suivant les régles établies dans l'article qui précède, ne pourra être modifié, en tout ou en partie, tant que le congrès ne dictera pas de nouvelles bases, en vertu de ses facultés constitutionnelles.

Donné dans le salon des séances du congrès de l'union, à Mexico, le 15 Novembre, 1861.

MANUEL DUBLAN, *Député Président.*
JUAN N. GUZMAN, *Député Secrétaire.*
M. M. OVANDO, *Député Secrétaire.*

Pourquoi j'ordonne que le présent soit imprimé, publié, mis en circulation et dûment exécuté.

Palais du gouvernement fédéral, á Mexico, le 18 Novembre, 1861.

BENITO JUAREZ.

Au citoyen JOSÉ GONZALEZ ECHEVERRIA,
Ministre des Finances et du Crédit Public.

Enclosure 2 in No. 106.

Schedule showing the amount of duties that would be paid under the reduced tariff voted by congress, by a cargo of merchandise which now pays $100,000 import duties:

UNDER THE PRESENT SYSTEM.

Import duties.................................	$100,000	
Additional duties:		
Mejoras materiales........................	$20,000	
Internation................................	10,000	
Contra-registro...........................	30,000	
Railway or amortization..................	15,000	
Departmental.............................	6,000	
	81,000	
Total amount of duties...................		$181,000

UNDER TARIFF VOTED BY CONGRESS.

Import duties................................	60,000	
Additional duties:		
Mejoras materiales.......................	18,000	
Internation...............................	9,000	
Contra-registro...........................	18,000	
2½ per cent. of ministry of fomento......	1,500	
	46,500	
Total amount of duties...................		106,500
Showing a reduction of...................		74,000

Equal to 41⅛ per cent. on the whole duties.

MEXICO, *November* 25, 1861.

HORACE JOHNSON

Enclosure 3 in No. 106.

Convention between her Britannic Majesty and the republic of Mexico for the settlement of various questions now pending between the two governments.

Desirous of putting an end to the present suspension of diplomatic relations between the British legation and the government of Mexico by an arrangement removing the cause of such suspension, and at the same time settling certain other questions in which the government of her Majesty and that of the republic are mutually interested, they have resolved to conclude a treaty for that purpose, and have named as their plenipotentiaries—that is to say, her Majesty the Queen of the united kingdom of Great Britain and Ireland, Sir Charles Lennox Wyke, knight commander of the most honorable order of the bath; her Majesty's envoy extraordinary and minister plenipotentiary to the republic of Mexico; and his excellency the president of the republic of Mexico, Señor Don Manuel Maria de Zamacona, minister for foreign affairs, &c., &c., &c.; who, having communicated to each other their respective full powers, found in good and due form have agreed upon and concluded the following articles:

ARTICLE I.

The sums still remaining due to British subjects of the moneys abstracted from the conducta at the Laguna Seca, as well as the six hundred and sixty thousand dollars forcibly taken from the British legation in the month of November last, shall be repaid to the lawful owners thereof by an assignment made for that purpose by the Mexican government corresponding to ten per cent. of the import duties, to be taken from that portion of the additional duties commonly known under the denomination of "mejoras materiales."

ARTICLE II.

The rate of interest due from the time when the money was taken to be paid on both these sums from the same fund shall be as follows: namely, six per cent. per annum on the six hundred and sixty thousand dollars, and twelve per cent. per annum on the remainder of the money due to British subjects from the moneys abstracted from the conducta at the Laguna Seca.

ARTICLE III.

All treaties, conventions, and agreements heretofore concluded between the two high contracting parties shall remain binding in their totality on both parties in all affecting British and Mexican interests; and the supreme decrees of the fourteenth of October, one thousand eight hundred and fifty, and the twenty-third of January, one thousand eight hundred and fifty-seven, do likewise remain in full force and vigor in all that concerns the London bondholders.

ARTICLE IV.

Such sums of money owing to the London bondholders and convention bondholders as were in the hands of the custom-house authorities at the time all payments were suspended by the law of the seventeenth of July last, shall be paid to the owners thereof, together with six per cent. interest thereon, out of the same fund that is set apart for the legation and Laguna Seca claims, when those shall have been liquidated.

ARTICLE V.

Nothing contained in this convention shall in any way interfere with the stipulations of other agreements or conventions by which the goods imported in French vessels are exempt from contributing to British assignments until the French convention shall have been wholly paid off, as well as the arrears due on other claims, as arranged with Admiral Penaud, have also been liquidated, when the quota belonging to the British convention bondholders shall be augmented, as agreed on, by two per cent. additional.

ARTICLE VI.

The British consular agents and agents of bondholders at the different ports of the republic shall be entitled to exact the production of all custom-house books and papers as may have reference to their clients' interests, and to call for ships' manifests, bills of lading, and all other documents which, for the above-named purpose, they may consider it necessary to examine.

Every month a statement of the duties incurred, and of the liquidation of the assignments due to the London bondholders and the convention bondholders at each of the custom-houses, shall be delivered to the British consul resident at the port, and in those places where there is no British consul, such statements shall be given to the agents of the respective funds, provided there be any such on the spot.

Article VII.

In order to insure with every certainty the fulfilment of the conditions contained in the preceding articles, the assignments made over to the British creditors shall henceforth be represented by certificates to be issued by the ministry of finance, according to the regulations which shall be framed by said ministry, and no importer will be permitted in future to pay the duties on his cargo without at the same time paying said assignments, which shall not be paid in cash or in any other form except in the said certificates, under the penalty of a second payment of double the amount, one-half in certificates, and the other in cash, which latter half shall be given to the informer of the fraud.

The minister of finance shall deliver a sufficient quantity of said certificates to the representatives of both classes of bondholders in Mexico, who shall be required to keep enough of them on hand, both in this city and the ports, to enable the importers to obtain them with the facility required.

For greater security these certificates must be signed by the representatives of the aforesaid bondholders, as well as by the aforesaid agents, and after liquidation they shall be remitted by the collectors of the maritime and frontier custom-houses directly to the minister of finance, for the purpose of enabling the government to take due note thereof in forming the account current of the respective debts.

Article VIII.

The assignment of ten per cent. of the duties alluded to in article I for the purposes above specified shall commence from the date of the signature of this convention; and the assignments belonging to the London bondholders and to the convention bondholders, secured to them by article III, shall begin from the first day of January, one thousand eight hundred and sixty-two.

Article IX.

It is understood that the Mexican government shall be free from the responsibility of a debtor to a creditor in so far as concerns any such sums as shall have been paid by them at the end of each month to the agents of the respective bondholders, when a liquidation of the sums so paid and received is duly made out and signed by the authorities of the custom-houses and the agents at the ports.

Article X.

In settling with the other foreign creditors of the republic the difficulties to which the law of the 17th of July last has given rise, no advantage shall be accorded to them with regard to the time at which the payment of the assignments shall be renewed, nor as regards the control that they may have in the custom-houses, which shall not by the same act be conceded to the British creditors.

Article XI.

The present convention shall be ratified by her Britannic Majesty and by the congress of the Mexican republic, and the ratifications shall be exchanged at London as soon as possible within the space of six months.

In witness whereof the respective plenipotentiaries have signed the same, and have affixed thereto their respective seals.

Done at Mexico this twenty-first day of November, in the year of our Lord one thousand eight hundred and sixty-one.

|L. S.| C. LENNOX WYKE.
|L. S.| MANUEL MA. DE ZAMACONA:

Enclosure 4 in No. 106.

Sir C. Wyke to Señor Zamacona.

MEXICO, *November* 20, 1861.

SIR: The result of the various conferences I have had with your excellency appears to be that no real difficulty now exists to prevent our coming to a perfect understanding on the subject which gave rise to those conferences, in a manner alike satisfactory to the governments we have the honor respectively to represent.

In order to attain so desirable an end, and to remove the evils caused by the law of the 17th of July last, as well also as to prevent any future disagreement arising from the consequences thereof, it becomes necessary now to put in writing what we have already verbally agreed on, and to settle by a formal instrument the due execution of the following conditions:

1. Delivery by your government of the money robbed from the British legation in the month of November last, amounting to the sum of $660,000, as well also of what was abstracted from the Laguna Seca conducta, which originally amounted to $400,000, but part of which has since been restored to its rightful owners.

2. That all arrears due to the bondholders arising from the suspension of payments of custom-house duties formally consigned to them by the Dunlop and Aldham compacts, as well as the British convention, shall be refunded, of course including the payments already deposited in the hands of the custom-house authorities at the time of such suspension of payments, but which had not yet been made over to the agents of said bondholders.

3. The payment of interest on all sums above specified, from the date of their abstraction or detention, as compensation to the owners thereof for the loss and inconvenience to which they have been subjected by these arbitrary proceedings.

4. That the British consular agents at the ports shall be authorized by the government to examine the books and render an account of the receipts of the several custom-houses there, such agents receiving directly the assignments for the bondholders from the importers, in a manner hereafter to be agreed on between us.

As I believe we are entirely of the same opinion with reference to the advantages to be obtained by a reduction of the tariff, I trust that your government, with this object in view, will adopt some measure of reform in this branch of your administration so comprehensive in its nature as entirely to remove the evils caused by the present high rate of duties, which are as prejudical to foreign commerce as they are to the best interests of the republic.

By a frank acceptance of these conditions no obstacle will then remain to prevent a renewal of official intercourse between your government and this legation, which, without such an arrangement, will be finally broken off, and thus lead to consequences fatal to the friendly relations which it is so desirable to maintain between the two countries.

Awaiting your reply, I have, &c.

C. LENNOX WYKE.

Enclosure 5 in No. 106.

Señor Zamacona to Sir C. Wyke.

[Translation.]

GOVERNMENT HOUSE, *November* 21, 1861.

The undersigned, minister for foreign affairs, has had the honor to receive the note, dated yesterday, which his excellency the English minister, Sir Charles Lennox Wyke, was pleased to write him.

The undersigned after his repeated conferences with his excellency her Britannic Majesty's minister is as much convinced as his excellency that there does not really exist any difficulty for the re-establishment of the ordinary relations between Mexico and Great Britain. He is entirely of the opinion of Sir Charles Wyke as to the great interest that the two countries have in maintaining and drawing still closer their relations; and the sincere desire to re-establish them has doubtless given rise to the conciliatory spirit that has reciprocally prevailed in the conferences held for that purpose, and which has so much contributed to attain it.

The question pending since a year, relative to the abstraction made in November last by the usurpers of the public power of a sum belonging to the holders of Mexican bonds in London, and deposited in the Calle de Capuchinas, gives this government an opportunity of showing its conciliatory and willing spirit, and its desire to terminate all the difficulties pending with Great Britain. Notwithstanding that the government of the republic has protested against the responsibility that might be laid to its charge on account of that odious attempt, it has also protested its desire to prevent as far as possible the losses that the holders of bonds have thereby suffered, and therefore agrees to facilitate to them the reimbursement of the sum robbed, if the said holders of bonds cede to the republic their action for indemnity from the produce of the property of the perpetrators of the crime that has been or may be sequestrated. This concession, with which the government of Mexico responds to those which his excellency her Britannic Majesty's minister has made in the arrangement of this affair, removes one of the principal difficulties pending between the two nations. This government does not then make any objection to the acceptance of the conditions contained in the note of his excellency Sir Charles Wyke, bearing yesterday's date.

As regards the tariff at present in force in the republic, the undersigned believes that, in fact, a reform in this matter in a liberal sense will be equally beneficial to the nation as to the foreign commerce; and as this government is authorized by congress to make it, it is at present occupied in carrying out this work. By means of it will be removed the ills which, as indicated by her Britannic Majesty's minister, are caused by the amount of the duties at present levied on goods imported; and his excellency will perceive it, by simply knowing that the government, following the rules that the congress has laid down for it, and the principles of liberal political economy, will carry out the following bases in the new tariff that will be published in a few days:

That the reduction on the import duties is to consist in 40 per cent. on the present amounts.

That when the reform, which is to be put into operation four months after its publication, has been once made, no change shall be able to be made in the import, export, or additional duties, without informing the commercial body six months beforehand.

And that in the new tariff shall not be included the article that figured in the project lately presented by the committee of finance of the congress, which authorized the States of the coast to place duties on the export of their own products.

The undersigned indulges in the same belief as that entertained by his excellency her Britannic Majesty's minister, that after the declaration contained in this note, and after the points to which it refers have been consigned in a formal act, for which this government is ready, there will not be any obstacle to prevent the renewal of relations between it and that legation, and drawing still closer those bonds of sympathy and common interest which unite the two nations.

The undersigned, &c.

MANUEL MA. DE ZAMACONA.

No. 107.

Sir C. Wyke to Earl Russell.

MEXICO, *November* 28, 1861.

MY LORD: I have the honor to enclose herewith an address signed by some English merchants and other persons resident in this city, which, although addressed to me, I am requested to forward to her Majesty's government.

I likewise transmit my reply thereto, to which I beg leave to call your lordship's attention, as it disposes of the principal grievance there complained of.

I have, &c.

C. LENNOX WYKE.

Enclosure I in No. 107.

Messrs. Graham, Geaves & Co., and others, to Sir C. Wyke.

MEXICO, *November* 25, 1861.

SIR: We, the undersigned British merchants, and others, consider it our duty to address you at the present moment in defence of the interests which have been confided to us, as also to express our opinion in the present critical state of affairs.

The particulars which we have been able to learn regarding the convention you had agreed upon with the Mexican government being rather vague and imperfect, we are hardly able to judge of the ultimate advantages which might have accrued to British commerce had the said convention been ratified by congress; but in the absence of any official communication on the subject we are necessarily led to believe that the version given by the principal journal of this city, "El Siglo," is, at least, tolerably correct, although we must confess that we doubt of its entire authencity, being, as we are, unwilling to believe that any arrangement can have been contemplated which only provided for the redress and liquidation of the larger and more prominent claims, to the exclusion of the numerous smaller, but equally deserving, claims of British residents in this country.

By the English papers which have lately arrived, we have also been made acquainted with the answer which Earl Russell addressed on the 3d of October to Messrs. Rothschild, and other merchants of England interested in the Mexican trade, in answer to their petition asking for that protection for the lives of their fellow countrymen, and for their own property in Mexico, which Englishmen have a right to expect from their government.

THE PRESENT CONDITION OF MEXICO. 409

We have followed with the utmost care and anxiety every step of your negotiations with the Mexican government, and we now beg most respectfully to manifest our decided opinion that whilst we consider the course you have pursued since your arrival in Mexico as entirely in accordance with the intentions expressed by Earl Russell, and whilst we fully acknowledge the great exertions which you have personally made to secure every advantage compatible with what we understand to be your instructions, we cannot but regard the views taken by the home government as entirely erroneous with respect to the actual state of the country, and their proposed measures as altogether insufficient to obtain either redress for past outrages or to insure any sort of confidence or security for the future.

You have obtained the passing of an act of congress which authorizes the reduction of the tariff, but it cannot be denied that this innovation will be quite as advantageous to Mexico as it will be to England, and therefore it cannot be looked upon as a concession which Mexico makes, but simply as an important improvement which the country has resolved upon in consequence of the suggestion made by England to this effect.

There are two points at issue in the present case: the first being the due reparation, as far as practicable, of the numerous outrages upon Englishmen and upon the English flag; the second, the adoption of such measures as may check the recurrence of such outrages, and by degrees put a stop to the anarchy and consequent ruin which has been spreading over this country for several years.

We fully comprehend that the home government look upon the whole question with repugnance, caused principally by the difficulties which surround every plan of action, and consequently we refrain from entering into the consideration of the second point; for, on the one hand, we feel perfectly confident that you are fully impressed with the importance of the question, and that your own personal views must coincide with ours, whilst the limits to which we desire to reduce this note could never suffice to enter into such a vast and complicated question.

As Englishmen, however, we think it our duty to use every effort in our power, and to avail ourselves of every privilege which our constitution grants us, to induce her Majesty's government to exact that reparation for the past which may at least prove that our countrymen's blood is not to be wantonly shed, and England sneered at without the country which has tolerated such atrocities being made to atone for them.

We maintain that the assassination of a British consul and numerous fellow-countrymen, the marching through the streets of Englishmen as prisoners of war under the most unwarrantable circumstances, the robbery of English property by armed forces, headed by leading men of the acknowledged governments, and other acts of almost equally atrocious character, are not to be atoned for by the simple payment of an insignificant sum of money; we maintain that England cannot allow a Mexican minister of finance to appropriate sums of money assigned to her under the most solemn diplomatic conventions without demanding something more than the mere repayment of the sums so taken. The ministers who authorize these acts know full well that it requires three or four months at least before the action of her Majesty's government can be brought to bear against them, and they invariably take care to resign their posts before the expiration of such time; they care little for the reclamations which their successors may have to deal with; but is it anything more than common justice to demand that the whole administration, or the country, should be made aware that similar outrages must be atoned for a little sooner or later?

When all our grievances arose from the acts of one party in the country, we understood too well that nothing could be done; but when we witnessed the seizure of the bondholders' funds by the church party, and the seizure of the Tampico conducta by the constitutional party, we had every reason to consider that the chief difficulty towards exacting reparation was removed; nor can there be any essential difference between one *de facto* government robbing money deposited in the hands of the bondholders' agent and the next administration robbing their assignments on the coast.

We do not wish you to believe that we in any way ask for impossibilities, nor that we wish to take up certain cases as pretexts to force her Majesty's government into useless and difficult military expeditions; we do not even pretend that in a country like Mexico the punishment of the precise perpetrators of the crime should be insisted upon; but we see little difficulty to the penalty being paid by the country.

After seeing that her Majesty herself considered the question worthy of being mentioned in her speech from the throne; after being assured that the matter was and had been long under consideration; and after waiting for perhaps the most propitious moment that could possibly present itself, we are bound to say that the conduct of England is likely to impress foreign nations with but a very poor and inadequate amount of respect or consideration if the whole list of outrages is to be atoned for, and even passed over in silence, on receipt of a sum of money. Some of our number are interested in the British convention fund, many of us have private claims against the Mexican government, whilst others are only indirectly interested in any settlement or treaty which may be made; but we all unite to express, in the most respectful but at the same time in the most emphatic terms, that we look upon the precise percentage of duties which may be exacted as of no importance whatever compared to the question of the securities and guarantees which may and, as we submit, ought to be demanded, and more particularly to the just and, so to speak, national reparation on the part of Mexico for past outrages, which, if committed by a private individual, would be classed as criminal in the highest degree.

The principle of allowing any outrages to be committed for nothing more or less than a certain price is surely too dangerous a one to be tolerated by England. The sacred character of international treaties would by this means be entirely destroyed; and it is not merely the lives and property of English residents in Mexico, but of those in remote countries all over the world, that would be exposed to dangers which our government is bound to ward off and protect us from, instead of tolerating them with comparative impunity. English miners, merchants, and colonists would, in one word, find themselves in a weaker and more difficult position than the natives of almost any other nation. Surely this cannot be the state of things which an English cabinet can take any pride in creating or countenancing, nor can it be expected that British subjects can quietly and passively wait for such a result to be produced; and it is therefore that we wish through you to impress upon her Majesty's government that no arrangement should be entered into which does not embrace full reparation for every just British claim, whatever may have been its origin, atonement for the violation of treaties, and ample guarantees for the future security of persons and property of British subjects resident within the republic.

In conclusion, we beg to repeat that this present address is not directed to you personally, and that we have the highest motives for respecting and appreciating your own exertions since your arrival as her Majesty's minister; but we most earnestly solicit that you will communicate our views to her Majesty's government, and at the same time trust that your experience of Mexico will induce you to support and advance our petition as the only means of obtaining any permanent improvement in the foreign trade of this country.

We have, &c.

GRAHAM, GEAVES & CO.,
And twenty-eight others.

THE PRESENT CONDITION OF MEXICO. 411

Enclosure 2 in No. 107.

Sir C. Wyke to Messrs. Graham, Geaves and Co., and others.

MEXICO, *November* 28, 1861.

GENTLEMEN: A careful perusal of your communication dated the 25th instant, which only reached me late in the afternoon of yesterday, has left me in doubt as to your precise object in requesting me to forward it to her Majesty's government.

It is not by an expression of your fears and anxieties in vague and general terms that any good result can be arrived at; such an address as the one you have sent should, to have any real value, embody the decided opinion, founded on your long experience here, as to the remedy to be applied with a view of removing the evils of which you so justly complain.

Had you consulted with me personally and pointed out your wishes more distinctly, a more definite end might have been attained, and I should have been better enabled to forward those wishes, by supporting them, than I now am by the mere receipt of such a letter as yours on the eve of the mail's departure for England.

The convention of the 21st instant, to which you allude, was concluded for the purpose of binding this government and nation to fulfil their engagements, in a positive and practical manner, to a large body of British subjects who have an immense stake in this country, and whose interests have hitherto been shamefully disregarded, from the fact of their being in part protected merely by agreements and memorandums passed between some of our naval officers and certain local authorities at the port of Vera Cruz, such authorities being at the time in open rebellion against a government to which we had an accredited minister at this capital. As some amongst your number were the sufferers by having no better guarantee than this, you could only have been benefited by exchanging it for the adequate protection of a solemn international obligation such as a convention, which also secured the repayment of the moneys stolen from British legation and the conducta, with 6 per cent. on the former and 12 per cent. on the latter, in compensation for the inconvenience to which the owners of such moneys have been subjected by the arbitrary and unjustifiable acts of two successive governments.

These payments, and the due fulfilment of the engagements set aside by the law of the 17th of July last, it was imperative for the honor of her Majesty's government should in the first instance be obtained, and hence the conclusion of the convention above alluded to, which satisfactorily terminated a separate and distinct question, and would have naturally cleared the way for a settlement of the other British claims arising out of the numerous acts of violence against life and property, hitherto perpetrated with impunity against our fellow-subjects.

You little know me, gentlemen, or the instructions I have received from her Majesty's government, if you suppose that with a British squadron in the waters of Vera Cruz I should not obtain such reparation and compensation as is just and fair to demand of the Mexican government for such outrages.

With regard to the opinion you express, that the views of her Majesty's government with respect to the actual state of this country are entirely erroneous, and the measures they propose adopting to obtain redress insufficient, I altogether differ from you, and I trust events will prove that I am not wrong in doing so.

You allude to the murder of a British consul and numerous other countrymen, the marching through the streets of Englishmen as prisoners of war, the robbery of English property by armed forces, &c., its being atoned for by the simple payment of an insignificant sum of money; and further state that a minister of finance cannot be allowed to appropriate sums of money belonging to English subjects without demanding something more than the mere repayment of the sums so taken. The outrages on life and person you thus describe took place before my arrival in this country, and I am not aware that they have, or are likely to be, atoned for by the payment, as you state, of an insignificant sum of money.

With regard to the money taken from British subjects in the way you mention, something more will be exacted than repayment, in the shape of interest thereon, more or less in amount according to the circumstances of each particular case.

Reparation for all these outrages will be exacted by her Majesty's government, not from any particular set of men who happened to be in power when they were committed, but from the country, which is held responsible for them, and I really cannot see, therefore, what you wish for more.

My foregoing remarks will have explained to you that the convention I lately concluded with Señor Zamacona was never intended to settle these grievances, but was merely a preliminary step for removing those amongst them which, from their magnitude, were of the first importance; this fact I had clearly stated to some amongst you, whose signatures I was therefore surprised to see to the letter to which this is a reply.

You say that, by my having obtained the passing of an act of congress authorizing the reduction of the tariff, I have only persuaded them to do that which is as advantageous to themselves as it is to us, and therefore it cannot be looked on as a concession which Mexico makes.

If you were aware of the many days and hours' labor it has taken me to persuade them of this fact, you would, I think, set more value on a concession which would never have been obtained unless it had formed the basis of the convention I have so often alluded to.

This advantage, as well as the abrogation of the law of the 17th of July by congress, has been the result of my negotiations, which will now, therefore, I hope, appear to you in a less unfavorable light than when you addressed me on the 25th instant.

I thank you, gentlemen, for the kind manner in which you mention the humble services I have been able to render to you since my arrival in this country, but in doing so I venture to hope you will in future believe that there is not one amongst you who is more jealous of the honor of his country than is England's representative in this republic.

Your address, together with this reply to it, shall be forwarded to her Majesty's government by to-morrow's mail.

I have, &c.

C. LENNOX WYKE.

No. 108.

Sir C. Wyke to Earl Russell.

[Extract]

MEXICO, *November* 28, 1861.

General Doblado, governor of the State of Guanaxuato, who is at the head of about 8,000 men, is said to be on the eve of making a "pronunciamiento" with a view of getting himself elected president; but from the extreme caution of the man's character, I think that he is hardly likely to expose himself to the risk of failure which he thus would undoubtedly have to incur.

No. 109.

Sir C. Wyke to Earl Russell.

[Extract.]

MEXICO, *November* 28, 1861.

In my despatch of the 25th instant I had the honor of laying before your lordship, in detail, the business which had occupied my attention since the departure of the last European mail.

My labors, as your lorpship will have seen, terminated in my having obtained a considerable reduction in the existing tariff, and in having signed such a convention as promised to place our relations with the Mexican government on a somewhat better footing than they have been for some time past.

It is to be sincerely regretted that congress was so carried away by party feeling as not to perceive the error they were committing in throwing out a convention which, both in form and substance, avoided, as far as possible, any attack upon the honor and *amour propre* of the nation, and yet held out to Mexico the means of coming to an equally satisfactory settlement of the difficulties with France and Spain whenever these two powers demanded redress at their very doors.

Congress, as if frightened at what it had done, passed a resolution on the 23d instant abolishing the law of the 17th of July, and stating that the convention assignments should be again paid, as heretofore, to both classes of bondholders, as well also as those sums due to them at the time the suspension of payments was decreed.

As this would, of course, not satisfy me, I had no choice left but to present at once to government an ultimatum, and demand my passports in case it was refused.

On the presentation of my ultimatum Señor de Zamacona resigned, the minister of war having done so the day before; and there is now a probability of the other members of the cabinet doing so likewise, unless congress retraces its steps, for the government have sent back the convention to be reconsidered by them as a last resource.

To-day I had a visit from Señor Lerdo de Tejada, the leader of the opposition in congress, who called to ask me whether I would consent to any modification in the convention, as, if I would agree to modify the articles concerning the repayment of the legation and conducta robberies, and the powers given to enable our consuls to act as interventors, he would engage to pass it through congress, and then accept the vacant post of minister for foreign affairs, which, under such circumstances, he thought the president would confer upon him.

My answer was a simple one, and to the effect that, having already made every concession possible in my negotiations with Señor de Zamacona, I could make no others. On receiving this answer Señor Lerdo de Tejada retired, and with him disappeared every hope of the convention's ratification.

I have only now again to express to your lordship my high sense of Mr. Corwin's conduct through the whole business; he has stood by me in the most honorable manner, and on learning the rejection of my convention by congress, refused, in the most positive manner, to advance the government one dollar of the proposed American loan. Nor can I pass over in silence the services of Señor de Zamacona, the minister for foreign affairs. He, at all events, has been sincere in trying to second my late endeavors, and his resignation of office proves that there is an exception to every rule, even as regards Mexico and the Mexicans.

I shall start for Vera Cruz with the members of my mission as soon as I can conveniently do so, leaving Mr. Consul Glennie in charge of the archives, and with him that most excellent public servant, Don Rafael Beraza, so that the merchants here shall not suffer by my absence in the courier arrangements. Havana will probably be the place where I shall await your lordship's instructions, but wherever I may settle to go, I will not fail to remember the instructions contained in your lordship's despatch of September 28, in reference to the admiral on the station.

P. S.—Since writing the above I have received the enclosed letter from the Mexican foreign office, by which your lordship will see that I am requested to wait for the answer to my ultimatum until the new minister for foreign affairs is appointed.

Enclosure 1 in No. 109.

Propositions voted by congress abrogating the law of July 17, 1861.

LA DEROGATION DE LA LOI DU 17 JUILLET.—Voici le texte de la proposition présentée et adoptée, le 23 du courant, par le congrès qui l'a dispensée des formalités du réglement; elle a pour auteurs MM. les Députés Sebastian Lerdo de Tejada, Manuel Ruiz, Mariano Riva Palacio, Montes, Dublan, Linares, Piño y Ramirez, Baz, Suarez Navarro et Chico Sein.

Article 1. Sont dérogées les dispositions de la Loi du 17 Juillet de la présente année qui se réfèrent aux conventions diplomatiques et à la dette contractée à Londres.

Art. 2. Le gouvernement mettra immédiatement en voie de paiement les assignations respectives, conformément aux dispositions et aux réglements antérieurs à la dite Loi.

Art. 3. Le gouvernement remettra immédiatement au congrès une notice des sommes qui existaient au moment de l'expédition de la Loi et de celles qu'il aura reçues depuis, appartenant aux dites assignations, en initiaut les lois qu'il jugera nécessaires pour rembourser les dites sommes aux créanciers des conventions et de la dette contractée à Londres, et pour procurer au trésor les fonds dont il manque pour cet objet.

Economique.—Une commission du congrès déclarera au président de la république la convenance que le gouvernement, en publiant la présente Loi, expose et explique officiellement les raisons de justice qu'il a eues pour rendre celle du 17 Juillet, et les motifs pour lesquels elle est dérogée, en ce qui touche aux conventions et à la dette contractée à Londres.

Enclosure 2 in No. 109.

Sir C. Wyke to Señor Zamacona.

MEXICO, *November* 24, 1861.

SIR: The rejection of the convention of the 21st instant by congress on the night of Friday last has, I regret to say, put a term to those measures of conciliation by which, after six weeks' incessant labor and sacrifices, we had sought to remove the serious differences between the two countries.

Under these circumstances I have but one course left open to me, and that is,

without delay to present to your excellency the ultimatum of her Majesty's government, requiring the acceptance of the following conditions, viz:
1. Immediate abrogation of the law of the 17th of July last.
2. That in the ports of the republic commissioners, to be named by her Majesty's government, shall be placed for the purpose of appropriating to the powers having conventions with Mexico the assignments which those conventions prescribe shall be paid out of the receipts of the maritime custom-houses, including in the sums to be paid to the British government the amount of the conducta robbery and the money stolen from the British legation in the month of November last.
3. That the commissioners shall have the power of reducing by one-half, or in any less proportion that they think fit, the duties now levied under the existing tariff.

If these terms are not complied with, I shall find myself under the necessity of quitting the republic, with all the members of my mission, leaving the government of Mexico responsible for the consequences that will ensue.

I have, &c.

C. LENNOX WYKE.

Enclosure 3 in No. 109.

Señor Arias to Sir C. Wyke.

[Translation]

GOVERNMENT HOUSE,
Mexico, November 28, 1861.

The undersigned, charged temporarily with the ministry of foreign affairs, has the honor to answer the note which his excellency Sir Charles Lennox Wyke, &c., has been pleased to address to the said ministry, under date of the 24th instant, in which he communicates the conditions, the acceptance of which is demanded by her Britannic Majesty's government, in order to terminate the suspension of diplomatic relations, to which the law of the 17th of July last gave rise.

The undersigned must, first of all, make his excuses to his excellency Sir Charles Wyke for the delay which he will perceive in this answer, but which will, however, have already been explained, if he knows that the minister charged with this department withdrew from it, having previously resigned, almost at the very moment that the said note of the legation was received, and if he knows also that the supreme government is making every effort with the congress, in order to settle the difficulties which unfortunately have arisen between Great Britain and the republic of Mexico.

The chief magistrate of the republic is most anxious that this should take place, and his excellency Sir Charles Wyke will not doubt it if he remembers the recent proofs which the Mexican government has given of its desire for a peaceful and reasonable settlement of the difficulties pending with Great Britain.

In order to obtain this result the chief obstacle has been removed by the abrogation of the law of July 17th; and in consideration of this, and that there will soon be a new minister to take charge of the present negotiation, the undersigned confidently hopes, from Sir Charles Wyke's honest intentions and benevolent sentiments, that he will be good enough to wait only until the new minister to be named may give the due answer to the aforesaid note of his excellency, and to suspend for the moment any resolution which may alter the position which the question now has.

The undersigned, &c.

JUAN A. D. ARIAS.

No. 110.

The Secretary to the Admiralty to Mr. Hammond.

ADMIRALTY, *January* 2, 1862.

SIR: I am commanded by my lords commissioners of the admiralty to send you herewith, for the information of Earl Russell, a copy of a letter from Commodore Dunlop, dated the 5th ultimo, and of its enclosures, reporting the sailing of the Spanish expedition from Havana for Vera Cruz on the 30th November and the 1st and 2d of December last.

I am, &c.

C. PAGET.

Enclosure 1 in No. 110.

Commodore Dunlop to the Secretary to the Admiralty.

"CHALLENGER," *at Havana, December* 5, 1861.

SIR: I have the honor to transmit herewith, to be laid before the lords commissioners of the admiralty, copy of a letter and its enclosures which I have this day addressed to Rear Admiral Sir A. Milne, K. C. B., commander-in-chief, reporting the sailing from Havana of the Spanish expedition for Vera Cruz.

I am, &c.

HUGH DUNLOP.

Enclosure 2 in No. 110.

Commodore Dunlop to Rear Admiral Sir A. Milne.

"CHALLENGER," *at Havana, December* 5, 1861.

SIR: I have the honor to acquaint you that the Spanish expedition for Vera Cruz sailed from this place in three divisions on 30th ultimo and 1st and 2d instants under the command of Rear Admiral Rubalcava, who sailed on the 1st instant, with his flag in the paddle-steamer "Isabel la Catolica."

Enclosed is a list of the vessels forming the expedition.

The troops embarked amount to 6,000 of all arms, under the command of Don Manuel Gassett. The names of the principal staff officers are enclosed.

I am, &c.

HUGH DUNLOP.

P. S.—I shall transmit a copy of this letter and its enclosure to the secretary of the admiralty.

H. D.

THE PRESENT CONDITION OF MEXICO. 417

Enclosure 3 in No. 110.

List of ships-of-war and transports composing the Spanish expedition to Mexico.

Class.	Name.	Guns.	Horse-power.	Captains.
Paddle corvette	Isabel la Catolica°	16	500	Don Carlos del Camino
Do	Francisco de Asis	16	500	Don Nicolas Chicarro
Paddle sloop	Blasco de Garay	6	350	Don Me. Diaz Herrera
Do	Pizarro	6	350	Don Juan Pita la Vega
Paddle gunboat	Guadalquiver	1	100	Don Adolfo Navarite
Paddle transport	Velasco	4	440	Don José Carranza
Screw frigate	Princessa de Asturias	60		Don José Alvarado
Do	Concepcion	37		Don Ml. McCrohin
Do	Lealtad	50		Don Pedro del Castillo
Do	Blanca	42		Don Ml. de la Rigada
Do	Berenguela	37	380	Don José R. de Arrias
Do	Petronila	37	380	Don R. M. Venalet
Screw transport	Ferrol	2		Don Pablo Lugo Vinas
Do	Numero Tres	2		Don Ramon Bran
Sailing transport	Santa Maria	2		Don Aleyo Rodriguez
Do	Marigalante	2		Don Sunico
Screw transport	Cubana, (No. 1)			
Do	Cuba, (No. 11)			
Do	Cardenas, (No. 9)			
Do	Maisi, (No. 7)			
Paddle transport	Pajara del Oceano, (No. 5)			
Sailing transport	Sunrise, (No. 2)			
Do	Teresa, (No. 4)			
Do	Favorita, (No. 6)			
Do	Paquita, (No. 8)			
Do	Palma, (No. 10)			

° Flag-ship.

Enclosure 4 in No. 110.

List of the principal staff officers of the Spanish expedition to Mexico.

Commander-in-chief, Don Manuel Gasset; second in command, Brigadier General Don Carlos de Valgos; chief of the staff, Colonel Don Juan Vidarte, of Bobadilla; colonel commandant of artillery, Marques de la Concordia; colonel commandant of engineers, Don Nicolas Valdes y Fernandez; commissary general, Don Baltasar Llopisy y Caparros; surgeon general, Don Joaquin Rosell y Fio; colonel commandant of 1st, Brigadier Don Francisco Aparicio y Pardo; colonel commandant of 2d, Brigadier Don Vincente Diaz de Caballas; colonel commandant of artillery, Don Antonio Fernandez Cuevos; colonel commandant of engineers, Don Andres Gortia, of Goyeneche. 2d battalion, Cazadores de Baileu y Union; 1st battalion, Napoles; 1st battalion, Cuba; 4 companies 1st battalion, Napoles; 4 companies of 2d battalion, Rey.

H. Ex. Doc. 100——27

No. 111.'

Lord Lyons to Earl Russell.

WASHINGTON, *December* 21, 1861.

MY LORD: In my despatch of the 10th September last I informed your lordship that instructions had been sent to Mr. Corwin, the United States minister in Mexico, to conclude a convention with the Mexican government, in virtue of which the United States should assume the obligation to pay the interest on the foreign debt of that country.

Mr. Seward told me this morning that Mr. Corwin had not concluded the proposed convention, but had sent, in lieu of it, a draught of a convention providing for the United States advancing to Mexico a very large sum to enable her to discharge her obligations to foreign creditors. Mr. Seward said that if Mr. Corwin had sent a convention in the terms of his draught, already signed, the President would, no doubt, have recommended it to the Senate for ratification. Since, however, a draught only had been sent, it had been determined, in conformity with a plan occasionally adopted in important cases, to ask the Senate beforehand whether it advised the President to conclude a treaty on the terms proposed.

Mr. Seward proceeded to say that Mr. Corwin would, in all probability, have signed the treaty at once, had he not been displeased by the rejection, by the Mexican congress, of a "very proper" treaty negotiated by Sir Charles Wyke. Mr. Corwin had, Mr. Seward said, given Sir Charles Wyke all the support in his power, and had declined to conclude his own treaty when he found that the treaty made by Sir Charles had been rejected.

I told Mr. Seward that I had received a private letter from Sir Charles Wyke, speaking in the highest terms of Mr. Corwin.

Mr. Seward observed that, as the draught of the treaty was before the Senate in secret session, it would not be right for him to acquaint me with the exact sum to be advanced by the United States, or with other details.

I have reason to suppose that Mr. Corwin was instructed not to engage for the payment of money by the United States unless the Mexican government should previously come to such an arrangement with Great Britain as should render it pretty certain that the money would not be paid in vain; that it would not fail to prevent the combined expedition, or at all events to prevent Great Britain taking part in it.

Some of the details of Mr. Corwin's draught have transpired, or at any rate very confident assertions are made concerning them. It is stated that the sum to be advanced is, in all, $9,000,000; $500,000 to be paid at the expiration of thirty days from the ratification of the treaty, and a like sum at the expiration of each successive period of thirty days, until $5,000,000 have been advanced; the remaining $4,000,000 to be advanced in half-yearly payments of $2,000,000, the first to be made six months after the payment of the last sum of $500,000.

As security the American government is to have a mortgage on all the public lands, minerals, &c., of Lower California, Chihuahua, and two other provinces bordering on the United States. A commission composed of three Mexicans and two Americans is to assume the administration of the land, &c., thus mortgaged.

It is understood, however, that Mr. Corwin will still be instructed to abstain from signing the treaty, unless there be a reasonable prospect of its attaining the object the United States government have in view, that of removing the combined fleets to a distance from the Gulf of Mexico and the coasts of this country.

I have, &c.,

LYONS.

No. 112.

M. Isturiz to Earl Russell.

LEGACION DE ESPAÑA EN LONDRES,
13 *de Enero de* 1862.

MY LORD: El gobierno de la Reina mi augusta soberana me comunica con fecha 7 del actual las instrucciones que apenas recibió en 13 de Diciembre las órdenes necesarias para el cumplimiento de la convencion firmada en Londres el 31 de Octubre último, se apresuró á remitir el capitan general de Cuba á los gefes del ejército y escuadra de la expedicion que habia enviado á Méjico, en virtud de órdenes anteriores y en completa ignorancia de los pormenores y arreglos que fueron consecuencia de la citada convencion.

A mi vez tengo el honor de transmitir á vuestra excelencia una copia de estas instrucciones, cuyo tenor es sin duda el mas á propósito para asegurar, de acuerdo con lo estipulado en 31 de Octubre, la accion mancomunada de las tres potencias en la república de Méjico.

Con este, &c.,

XAVIER E ISTURIZ.

[Translation.]

SPANISH LEGATION,
London, January 13, 1862.

MY LORD: The government of the Queen my august sovereign communicated to me on the 7th instant the instructions which the captain general of Cuba, so soon as he received on the 13th December the orders necessary for carrying out the convention signed in London the 31st October last, hastened to transmit to the heads of the army and squadron of the expedition which he had sent to Mexico, in furtherance of preceding orders, and in entire ignorance of the details and arrangements made in consequence of that convention.

I have now the honor to forward to your excellency a copy of those instructions, the tenor of which is doubtless most suitable to secure, in accordance with what was stipulated on the 31st October, the joint action of the three powers in the republic of Mexico.

I have, &c.,

XAVIER E ISTURIZ.

Enclosure in No. 112.

Instructions addressed by the captain general of Cuba, on the 13*th of December,* 1861, *to the heads of the Spanish expedition to Mexico.*

1. Si al recibo de este despacho no se hubiesen emprendido ya operaciones militares deberá suspenderse toda agresion, permaneciendo las tropas á bordo si en ello no hay inconveniente ó peligro; si en efecto lo hubiese procurarán V.EE. desembarcar y formar un campamento atrincherado, donde permanecerá la division á la defensiva sin proceder á agresion de ningun género y protegida por la escuadra.

2. Si como lo afirman todas las noticias aqui recibidas, han sido abandonados por los Mejicanos la plaza de Vera Cruz y el Castillo de San Juan de Ulua, y las tropas han ocupado ya ambos puntos, deberán V.EE. conservarlos, rechazando

los ataques de que pudiera ser objeto, pero sin tomar nunca la iniciativa de operacion alguna militar.

3. En los dos supuestos precedentes esperarán la llegada del nuevo general ministro plenipotenciario, á quien supongo se le han comunicado por el gobierno todas las instrucciones necesarias acerca de la conducta ulterior de la expedicion. Con la llegada del Señor Prim concidirá probablemente la de los almirantes Francés é Inglés, y en semejante caso cumple solo á V.EE. atenerse á los acuerdos de las tres potencias.

4. Si la plaza y el castillo estuviesen en aptitud de defenderse y el ataque se hubiese emprendido, se procederá como convenga al cumplimiento de las nuevas órdenes de su Magestad si el honor de nuestras armas lo permite, y sinó se llevará á cabo lo que pueda ser necesario á la gloria del nombre Español.

5. Si el bloqueo se hubiese establecido al recibo de esta comunicacion declararán V.EE. en suspenso sus efectos hasta la llegada de los aliados. No prescindirán sin embargo de la posesion de la aduana si ya estuviesen en ella; pero la entregarán inmediatamente á disposicion de los plenipotenciarios luego que estén reunidos.

Como V.EE. han podido comprender, las cinco disposiciones precedentes se reasumen en un pensamiento general reducido á conservar un perfecto *statu quo* hasta que lleguen los representantes de las potencias aliadas.

A la discrecion de V.EE. corresponde, dado el estado de cosas que yo no puedo conocer desde aqui, armonizar lo que se ha hecho con lo demas que deba hacerse, evitando conflictos y complicaciones con las potencias firmantes del convenio.

Dios, &c.

FRANCISCO SERRANO.

[Translation.]

1. If, at the receipt of this despatch, no military operations shall have been undertaken, all aggression must be suspended, the troops remaining on board ship if there shall be no inconvenience or danger therein; but if in fact there should be any, you will land and form an entrenched camp, where the division will remain on the defensive, without proceeding to an attack of any sort, and under protection of the squadron.

2. If, as it is asserted by all the information hitherto received, the place of Vera Cruz and the Castle San Juan de Ulloa have been abandoned by the Mexicans, and both points are in occupation of the troops, you will maintain them, repulsing any attacks that may be made against them, but without ever taking the initiative of any military operation.

3. In these two supposed cases you will await the arrival of the new general minister plenipotentiary, to whom, I presume, all the instructions necessary for the ulterior conduct of the expedition will have been communicated by the government. The arrival of Señor Prim will probably coincide with that of the French and English admirals, and in such case you will have to attend only to the concurrent resolves of the three powers.

4. If the place and the castle shall be in a defensive attitude and the attack shall have been commenced, you shall proceed according to the new orders of her Majesty, if the honor of our arms allow it, and if not, you will complete what may be requisite for the glory of the Spanish name.

5. If the blockade shall be established on the receipt of this communication, you will declare the effects thereof to be in suspense until the arrival of the allies. Nevertheless, you will not give up possession of the custom-house, if you shall be in possession of it; but you will immediately place it at the disposal of the plenipotentiaries so soon as they shall have met.

As you will have understood, the five preceding articles may be summed up

THE PRESENT CONDITION OF MEXICO. 421

in one general idea, of maintaining a perfect *statu quo* until the arrival of the representatives of the allied powers. It is left to your discretion, according to the state of things which I cannot be acquainted with from this place, to harmonize what is done with what remains to be done, avoiding conflicts and complications with the powers who have signed the agreement.
God preserve, &c.
FRANCISCO SERRANO.

No. 113.

Earl Russell to M. Isturiz.

FOREIGN OFFICE, *January* 16, 1862.

M. LE MINISTRE: I beg leave to thank you for your note of the 13th instant, in which you communicate to me the instructions addressed by the captain general of Cuba to the commander of her Catholic Majesty's military and naval forces in Mexico.
I have at the same time the honor to inform you that, whilst those instructions are considered satisfactory by her Majesty's government, they have not yet been able to understand why the Spanish expedition set out before the arrival of the British and French forces.
I am, &c.,
RUSSELL.

No. 114.

Earl Cowley to Earl Russell.

[Extract.]

PARIS, *January* 17, 1862.

M. Thouvenel informed me this afternoon that the Emperor had determined to re-enforce the expeditionary corps sent to Mexico. M. de Flahault, his excellency said, would be instructed to state the reasons of this determination to your lordship, and he (M. Thouvenel) hoped that it would not be opposed by her Majesty's government.

No. 115.

M. Isturiz to Earl Russell.

LEGACION DE ESPAÑA EN LONDRES,
18 *de Enero de* 1862.

MY LORD: He tenido el honor de recibir la comunicacion de vuestra excelencia fecha 16 del actual, en respuesta á la dota que le dirigí el dia 13, trasladándole las instrucciones enviadas por el capitan general de Cuba à los gefes de la expedicion de Méjico. Manifiesta en ella vuestra excelencia que considera satisfactorias aquellas instrucciones, pero que el gobierno de su Magestad Británica no ha podido comprender aun porqué salió de Cuba la expedicion Española antes de la llegada de las fuerzas Inglesas y Francesas. Creia haber explicado suficientemente este punto en mi nota de 22 de Diciembre último; pero puesto que todavia necesita aclaraciones, diré á vuestra excelencia que, segun los despachos del capitan general de Cuba, las órdenes para suspender la expedicion, enviadas por la via de Nueva York con la esperanza de que llegasen mas pronto á su destino, no fueron recibidas en Cuba hasta la mitad de Diciembre, y que el capitan general, ignorante de los pormenores del tratado y del punto fijado para la reunion de las escuadras y temoroso de llegar tarde á Vera Cruz, juzgó oportuno no demorar la salida de una expedicion que hacia mucho tiempo que se hallaba lista de todo punto. Si en la conferencia que tuve el honor de celebrar con vuestra excelencia el dia 7 del corriente se hubiese tocado esta duda, hubiera yo tenido el mayor gusto en desvanecerla, como espero lo quedará ahora con estas francas explicaciones.

Con este, &c.,

XAVIER E ISTURIZ.

[Translation.]

SPANISH LEGATION,
London, January 18, 1862.

My LORD: I have had the honor to receive your excellency's communication dated the 16th instant, in reply to the note which I addressed you on the 13th, transmitting to you the instructions sent by the captain general of Cuba to the heads of the expedition to Mexico. In that communication your excellency informs me that you consider those instructions satisfactory, but that her Britannic Majesty's government could not yet understand why the Spanish expedition left Cuba before the arrival of the English and French forces. I thought I had sufficiently explained this point in my note of the 22d of December last, but since it still requires explanation, I have to inform your excellency that according to the despatches of the captain general of Cuba the orders to suspend the expedition, which were sent *via* New York in the hope that they would the sooner reach their destination, were not received in Cuba till the middle of December, and that the captain general, unacquainted with the details of the treaty, and with the point fixed for the meeting of the squadrons, being also fearful of arriving too late at Vera Cruz, thought it right not to delay the departure of an expedition which had been for a long time ready in every point. If this doubt had been mentioned at the interview which I had the honor to have with your excellency on the 7th instant, I should have already had very great pleasure in clearing it up, as I hope will be done by this frank explanation.

I have, &c.,

XAVIER E ISTURIZ.

No. 116.

Earl Russell to Earl Cowley.

[Extract.]

FOREIGN OFFICE, *January* 20, 1862.

I saw Count Flahault yesterday. His excellency informed me that he was instructed to state that the French government considered it necessary to send an additional land force to Mexico. I had been prepared for this communication by your excellency's despatch of the 17th of January.

Count Flahault went on to say that the precipitate step taken by General Serrano in commencing operations, without waiting for the forces of France and England, was calculated to enhance the difficulties of the expedition; that it now seemed inevitable that the allied forces must advance into the interior of Mexico, and not only would the force at present agreed upon be insufficient for such an operation, but the operation itself would assume a character in regard to which the Emperor could not allow the French force to be in a position of inferiority to that of Spain, or to run the risk of being compromised.

His Imperial Majesty has therefore determined to send a re-enforcement of between 3,000 and 4,000 men to Mexico.

I told Count Flahault that I very much regretted this step: I had no objection to offer on behalf of her Majesty's government to the validity of the argument that the forces of France should not be inferior in number to those of Spain. I would, therefore, only observe that it would not be possible for her Majesty's government to detach any greater amount of troops for operations on shore than the force of marines already sent to the Mexican coast.

No. 117.

Earl Russell to M. Isturiz.

FOREIGN OFFICE, *January* 23, 1862.

M. LE MINISTRE: In acknowledging the receipt of your excellency's communication of the 18th January last, I have to state to your excellency that although her Majesty's government are not entirely satisfied with the explanation offered by your excellency as to the departure from Cuba of the Spanish expedition to Mexico before the time agreed upon between the three powers, they are willing to accept your excellency's declaration that it has been the intention of her Catholic Majesty's government to act in conformity with the provisions of the treaty of the 20th of November, 1861.

I am, &c.,

RUSSELL.

No. 118.

Earl Russell to Sir J. Crampton.

FOREIGN OFFICE, *January* 19, 1862.

SIR: Although her Majesty's government are satisfied, from the explanations given by M. Isturiz, that the government of her Catholic Majesty has given instructions to her Catholic Majesty's commanders at Havana in conformity with the agreements entered into with her Majesty and his Majesty the Emperor of the French, yet the proceedings of Marshal Serrano are calculated to produce some uneasiness.

The departure of the Spanish expedition from Havana, and the military occupation of Vera Cruz, to say nothing of the tone of the proclamation issued by the Spanish government, demonstrate that a combined expedition, at a great distance from Europe, is subject to the discretion at all times, to the rashness sometimes, of the separate commanders and diplomatic agents.

I wish you to read to Marshal O'Donnell and M. Calderon Collantes the preamble and the article of our convention which define what our intervention is intended to do, and what it is not intended to do.

You will point out that the allied forces are not to be used for the purpose of depriving the Mexicans of their undoubted right of choosing their own form of government.

Should the Mexicans choose to constitute a new government which can restore order and preserve amicable relations with foreign nations, her Majesty's government will be delighted to hail the formation, and to support the consolidation, of such a government. If, on the contrary, the troops of foreign powers are to be used to set up a government repugnant to the sentiments of Mexico, and to support it by military force, her Majesty's government could expect no other result from such an attempt than discord and disappointment. In such a case the allied governments would only have to choose between withdrawing from such an enterprise with some shame, or extending their interference beyond the limits, scope, and intention of the triple convention.

You will explain to Marshal O'Donnell that this apprehension on our part does not arise from any suspicion of the good faith of the government of her Catholic Majesty; but commanders acting at a distance require to be very closely watched, lest they should commit their principals to unwarrantable proceedings.

You will read this despatch to M. Calderon Collantes.

I am, &c.,

RUSSELL.

No. 119.

Earl Cowley to Earl Russell.

[Extract.]

PARIS, *January* 24, 1862.

I have heard from so many quarters that the language of officers going with the re-enforcements to Mexico is, that it is for the purpose of placing the Archduke Maximilian upon the throne of that country, that I have thought it necessary to question M. Thouvenel upon the subject.

I inquired of M. Thouvenel whether any negotiations had been pending between this government and that of Austria with reference to the Archduke Maximilian. His excellency replied in the negative. He said that the negotiations had been carried on by Mexicans only, who had come over for the purpose and gone to Vienna.

No. 120.

Earl Russell to Sir C. Wyke.

FOREIGN OFFICE, *January* 27, 1862.

SIR: I have received and laid before the Queen your despatches from the 18th to the 28th November.

Since I last wrote to you, the Emperor of the French has decided to send 3,000 more troops to Vera Cruz.

It is supposed that these troops will march at once with the French, and a part of the Spanish troops already there, to the city of Mexico.

It is said that the Archduke Ferdinand Maximilian will be invited by a large body of Mexicans to place himself on the throne of Mexico, and that the Mexican people will gladly hail such a change.

I have little to add to my former instructions on this head. If the Mexican people, by a spontaneous movement, place the Austrian archduke on the throne of Mexico, there is nothing in the convention to prevent it.

On the other hand, we could be no parties to a forcible intervention for this purpose. The Mexicans must consult their own interests.

I have to add to my former instructions respecting the admirals in the Atlantic and Pacific, that you will make no objection to the withdrawal of the marines from Vera Cruz when the unhealthy season shall arrive.

You will also not object to any measures which may be concerted between the senior British naval officer at Vera Cruz and Admiral Maitland for the occupation or blockade of any or all the Mexican ports on the Pacific which it may be thought necessary, for the purposes of the convention, to occupy or to blockade. Acapulco, San Blas, and Mazatlan, are the ports chiefly alluded to in this instruction.

I am, &c.,

RUSSELL.

No. 121.

Sir C. Wyke to Earl Russell.

MEXICO, *December* 14, 1861.

MY LORD: I have the honor to acknowledge receipt of your lordship's despatch of the 1st of November last, instructing me to proceed to Jamaica, with all the members of her Majesty's mission here, as soon as Admiral Sir Alexander Milne could send a vessel-of-war to Vera Cruz for that purpose.

Having just heard of the arrival of her Majesty's ship "Ariadne" at that port, I yesterday wrote to Señor Doblado, the newly-appointed minister for foreign affairs, requesting to be furnished with my passports, to enable me to leave the territory of the republic.

I have the honor to enclose copy of my letter to his excellency, together with his reply thereto.

I quit Mexico for Vera Cruz the day after to-morrow, leaving Mr. Consul Glennie in charge of the archives of the legation; and in the event of hostilities taking place between her Majesty's forces and those of the republic, I have requested M. Kint de Roodenbeeck, the Belgian chargé d'affaires, to take British subjects and their interests here under his protection.

I herewith enclose copy of the communication which I addressed to him with reference to this matter, together with his reply thereto.

I shall wait at Vera Cruz for the English mail, which ought to arrive there on the 27th instant, and immediately after its arrival shall proceed on to Jamaica to join the admiral, who expects to be there in the first week of January.

I have, &c.,

C. LENNOX WYKE.

Enclosure 1 in No. 121.

Sir C. Wyke to Señor Doblado.

MEXICO, *December* 13, 1861.

SIR: The ultimatum of her Majesty's government, which I presented to that of the republic on the 24th ultimo, having remained up to the present moment unanswered, no other course is now open to me than to demand my passports, so as to enable me and the other members of her Majesty's mission to leave Mexico.

Mr. Glennie, the English consul here, will remain in charge of the archives of the legation, as well also as of British subjects and their interests in the republic. Should, however, hostilities hereafter unfortunately ensue between the forces of our respective governments, it will then become necessary to place my country-men and their property here under the protection of a neutral flag, for which purpose I have requested M. Kint de Roodenbeeck, the Belgian chargé d'affaires, to take charge of them, which, from the intimate relations of friendship existing between the governments of Belgium and Great Britain, he has most willingly consented to do.

This I consider necessary more as a matter of form than for any other reason, so convinced am I that under such circumstances the government of Mexico will consider it as a point of honor to afford every protection and guarantee to British subjects whose interests may oblige them to remain as residents within the territory of the republic.

In order to avoid great inconvenience both to the Mexican government as well as to the whole commercial body, I shall leave Don Rafael Beraza here to direct, as heretofore, the courier service of this legation, which I am sure will continue to receive every protection and assistance from your government.

My intention is to leave this city for Vera Cruz on Monday next, and I should feel obliged if your excellency would give the necessary instructions in the proper quarter to furnish me with a proper escort for our due protection on the road.

I have, &c.,

C. LENNOX WYKE.

Enclosure 2 in No. 121.

Señor Doblado to Sir C. Wyke.

[Translation.]

GOVERNMENT HOUSE, *Mexico, December* 14, 1861.

The undersigned, minister for foreign affairs, has had the honor to receive the note of his excellency Sir Charles Wyke, &c., dated the 13th instant, in which he is pleased to state that, as his ultimatum of the 24th ultimo has not been answered, the legation will be under the necessity of leaving Mexico; adding that Mr. Glennie, British consul, remained charged with the protection of the British subjects, and that in the unfortunate event of a rupture, this commission was intrusted to the Belgian chargé d'affaires, but rather as a form than for any other motive, since his excellency rests assured that Mexico will, as a point of honor, give every sort of guarantee to British subjects, and concludes by announcing that Don Rafael Beraza will remain in this capital in order to superintend the couriers of the legation, which legation intending to leave next

Monday, he requests that the necessary escort should be furnished him, in order to protect him on his journey.

Complying with the request of his excellency, the undersigned has the honor to annex herewith the necessary passport, at the same time that he hastens to transmit to him a copy of the circular issued on the 5th instant by the supreme government of the republic, in which the desires of that legation are anticipated, assuring, as it does, guarantees to all the foreigners residing in the country, even in the unfortunate event of a rupture.

The orders are given for the placing of the escorts that have to protect the person of his excellency, Sir Charles Wyke, up to Vera Cruz, and the postmaster general is agreed that Don Rafael Berazá should remain charged with the transmission of the correspondence of the legation.

The citizen president being authorized in every possible way by the supreme congress to make treaties with friendly nations without the necessity of obtaining the approval of that body, he has still the hope of renewing the negotiations with his excellency the British minister that were interrupted, always on the understanding, as is indispensable, that that legation should be sufficiently authorized by the government of her Britannic Majesty, for Mexico is disposed to do whatever may be compatible with justice and the national dignity.

The undersigned, &c.

MANUEL DOBLADO.

Enclosure 3 in No. 121.

Circular addressed to governors of States.

MINISTÈRE DES RELATIONS,
Mexico, le 5 Décembre, 1861.

La situation délicate où en est venue la république avec les puissances étrangères met la nation et le gouvernement dans le devoir impérieux de veiller plus que jamais à ce que les garanties concédées aux étrangers par les lois du pays et le droit des gens soient respectées d'une manière inviolable.

La justice du Mexique dans ses différends avec quelques unes de ces puissances offre une probabilité que les conflits seront écartés, lorsqu'on examinera de plus près les motifs puissants qui sont venus s'interposer accidentellement comme une difficulté dans le développement des relations cordiales que le Mexique a désiré, même au prix de grands sacrifices, cultiver et resserrer avec les nations amies.

Une preuve de ces désirs est la franche et généreuse hospitalité avec laquelle le pays a reçu dans son sein les enfants de ces nations, en leur concédant les plus grandes franchises dans l'exercice du commerce, de l'agriculture, de l'industrie et des arts. Si quelquefois des événements qui ont porté préjudice, non seulement aux étrangers, mais encore aux nationaux dans une mesure beaucoup plus grande, le Mexique n'a jamais cessé néanmoins de manifester son amour pour la justice et la civilisation, ni de faire tout ce qu'exigent ces dernières, dans l'intérêt de son nom et de son décorum.

Cependant, des difficultés inattendues obligent aujourd'hui la nation à donner de nouvelles preuves et de plus grands témoignages de loyauté et d'honneur aux puissances étrangères, et à démentir, par des actes d'humanité et d'illustration, la note de semi-barbares qu'on déverse sur elle, grâce aux manœuvres exécrables et aux informations mensongères de spéculateurs sans conscience et de quelques enfants dénaturés du Mexique qui feraient sa honte, s'il n'était certain que les nations, comme les familles, ne peuvent être responsables devant la véritable civilisation de l'ingratitude et des vices personnels d'une minorité d'hommes qui, dans tous les pays et dans tous les temps, ont prétendu ternir l'éclat des sociétés les plus éclairées.

En considération de ce qui précède, le citoyen président a bien voulu décider que je vous recommande, comme j'ai l'honneur de le faire, de veiller, aujourd'hui plus que jamais, par tous les moyens que vous suggérera votre prudence, votre circonspection et votre patriotisme, à ce que les garanties concédées aux étrangers par les traités et par le droit des gens deviennent efficaces, en écartant ainsi tout motif ou tout prétexte qui pût les engager à ne pas conserver la stricte neutralité à laquelle ils sont obligés dans les questions pendantes avec le gouvernement respectif. Il appartient à votre jugement et à votre tact bien connus de diriger vers un but profitable l'exaltation du patriotisme, et d'empêcher que les excitations populaires dans les conflits de la nation ne débordent contre les étrangers laborieux et pacifiques, auxquels on doit entière protection, de même qu'on doit appliquer strictement la loi aux turbulents et aux séditieux.

Il est superflu de vous démontrer combien la situation actuelle serait aggravée par des désordres qui, dans les circonstances du moment, viendraient justifier dans une certaine mesure les inculpations que l'on fait au Mexique, et combien, au contraire, contribuerait au bon succès de sa défense l'attitude digne d'un peuple qui soutient, dans son indépendance, et son décorum, son amour pour l'humanité et la civilisation.

En accomplissant l'ordre du citoyen président, il m'est agréable de vous reitérer, &c.

Dieu, liberté et réforme.

JUAN DE D. ARIAS.

Au Citoyen GOUVERNEUR *de l'Etat de* ———.

Enclosure 4 in No. 121.

Sir C. Wyke to M. de Roodenbeeck.

MEXICO, *December* 13, 1861.

SIR AND DEAR COLLEAGUE: On quitting Mexico I leave Mr. Glennie, our consul here, in charge of the archives of the legation, as well also as of the in-interests of those British residents in the republic whose affairs, either public or private, will not permit them to leave the country at the present time.

For the moment such protection will prove sufficient; but in the event of hostilities hereafter occurring between her Majesty's forces and those of this republic, it will become necessary that Englishmen and their property here should be placed under the protection of a neutral flag.

With this object in view, and taking into consideration the intimate and friendly relations existing between our respective governments, I know nobody more fitting to take charge of British interests than yourself, provided you would not object to do so under the circumstances I have named; in which case, with full confidence in your tact and judgment, I should feel certain that my countrymen would receive every protection and assistance which you may have it in your power to afford during the absence from this capital of a British legation.

I have, &c.,

C. LENNOX WYKE

Enclosure 5 in No. 121.

M. de Roodenbeeck to Sir C. Wyke.

LÉGATION DE BELGIQUE,
Mexico, le 14 *Décembre,* 1861.

MONSIEUR ET CHER COLLÈGUE: J'ai reçu la dépêche en date d'hier par laquelle vous m'avez fait l'honneur de m'informer, que lors de votre départ de Mexico vous confierez les archives de la légation de sa Majesté Britannique et les intérêts de vos nationaux à M. Glennie, votre consul dans cette résidence; mais que si des actes d'hostilité devaient avoir lieu entre les forces de la Grande Bretagne et celles du Mexique vous désirez que les nationaux Anglais et leurs propriétés soient placés sous la protection du pavillon et de la légation Belges.

Je m'empresse de vous manifester, Monsieur et cher collègue, que je serai heureux de faire tout ce qui sera en mon pouvoir pour que durant l'éloignement de la légation de sa Majesté Britannique, vos compatriotes et leurs propriétés soient parfaitement respectés. N'importe dans quelle éventualité, ils trouveront auprès le légation du Roi mon auguste souverain la même protection et la même assistance que mes propres nationaux.

Je saisis, &c.,

T'KINT DE ROODENBEECK.

No. 122.

Sir C. Wyke to Earl Russell.

[Extract.]

VERA CRUZ, *December* 29, 1862.

I arrived here on the evening of the 24th from Mexico, intending to leave this place in her Majesty's ship "Ariadne" for Jamaica immediately after the arrival of the English mail, which I fully expected would have brought your lordship's replies to my official correspondence of the 29th of October last. The steamer "Clyde" arrived at this port the day before yesterday, without, however, having brought any despatches for me, so that I conclude they have been sent to Jamaica under the admiral's address. Yesterday morning Captain Von Donop, of her Majesty's ship "Jason," called to show me a letter from Commodore Dunlop, dated the 23d instant, from the Havana, by which I learnt that it was not the admiral's intention to proceed to Jamaica as announced, but that he was expected with the squadron at the Havana on the 26th instant *en route* for Vera Cruz.

Under these circumstances, had I proceeded even at once to that place in the "Ariadne," I should probably have crossed without meeting him on the way.

This consideration induced me to remain where I was; and by way of avoiding any further uncertainty, I immediately despatched Mr. Walsham in the "Ariadne" with a letter for the admiral, begging his excellency at once to forward to me my despatches in case the present critical state of our relations with the United States should prevent his coming on here, as Captain Von Donop thought it not at all improbable that he would now return to the north.

As this place has been in possession of the Spaniards since the 17th instant, there could be no impropriety in my remaining here, as I am no longer residing in a town under the authority of the Mexican government.

The English and French squadrons are expected here three or four days hence, but they may be detained for a week or ten days more in consequence of the heavy northerly gales which so frequently blow on this coast at the present season.

Until the admiral's arrival, or Mr. Walsham's return, I of course remain ignorant of the nature of your lordship's instructions, as well also of the stipulations of the convention which I hear has been signed by the plenipotentiaries of England, France, and Spain.

No. 123.

Sir C. Wyke to Earl Russell.

[Extract.]

VERA CRUZ, *December* 29, 1861.

On my arrival here, a few days ago, I found that Vera Cruz had formally been taken possession of, on the 17th instant, by a Spanish force, under the command of General Gasset, composed of 6,500 men and 300 horses. They were brought here from the Havana in twenty-six transports and vessels-of-war, commanded by Admiral Rubalcava, who having summoned the place to surrender, both castle and town were delivered up to him without resistance. All the Mexican authorities, with many of the inhabitants, retired into the interior, and nothing has since occurred to disturb the peaceable occupation of the town, which the Spaniards hold in the name of the allies as well as their own, until the arrival of the English and French admirals.

They have formed an administration for the service of the custom-house, post office, town council, &c. All duties levied are to be divided hereafter, according to the claims of each nation on the government of the republic.

On arriving here, the governor of the town immediately sent me a guard of honor, which I dispensed with, and both himself and the general-in-chief offered their services to me in the kindest manner. The day following I called on them, and they, as well as the admiral, then assured me that everything they had done was considered by them as a mere temporary measure employed until the arrival of the allies.

Their troops are a very fine body of men, and are kept under strict discipline, so that no complaints have been made against them by the inhabitants of the town.

The Mexicans are fortifying some very strong mountain passes, where they mean to resist the march of the allies on the capital; but as long as the Spaniards keep within their lines here they do not intend to molest them, except by cutting off, as far as they can, all supplies of provisions from entering the town. As fresh meat was becoming scarce here a few days ago, General Gasset was about seizing on three of the neighboring villages to obtain cattle, but I strongly advised him not to take such a step before the arrival of the French and English forces, as by so doing he would only bring on a collision with the Mexican forces outside the town, which it was most advisable to avoid, owing to the bitter feeling still existing in this country against the Spaniards. The general most readily yielded to my wishes, and although the troops were already out and under arms, he consented to change his projected expedition into a mere military promenade, to be made round the outer works of the town.

I at the same time wrote to General Uraga, commanding the Mexican forces outside, strongly advising him to allow provisions to enter the town for the sake

THE PRESENT CONDITION OF MEXICO. 431

of his own countrymen shut up in it, and also to avoid any hostile movement until the arrival of the allied squadrons in this harbor. This suggestion was also well received, as the general replied that he would do all in his power to carry out my wishes.

I am most anxious to give time for the formation of a respectable government, who will understand that it is for their interest to receive the intervention in a friendly and not a hostile spirit, so as to aid them to re-establish order, and take the opinion of those who alone are entitled to have a voice in the matter. Hitherto the men of property and intelligence have been completely silenced and domineered over by the rabble, who elected from their own class the members of a congress which, besides being a disgrace to the country, rendered anything like good government impossible.

The nation are now thoroughly frightened at the formidable coalition formed against them, and will be more disposed to grant what we want before blood has been shed and their passion excited, than they will be when once engaged in a struggle with the Spaniards.

The rejection of my convention by the congress, as described in my last month's correspondence, had the effect of breaking up the late cabinet, and the crisis which then ensued brought General Doblado forward, who would only consent to form a government on the condition of having full powers conferred on him by congress, authorizing him to settle pending questions with the three powers as he deemed best. Having obtained these he adjourned the assembly until April next, and now remains unfettered to make the best arrangement he can with us.

He is a man of such talent and influence in the country that the reactionary chiefs began to lay down their arms and give in their adhesion on his appointment becoming known, and he is now engaged in forming his cabinet from the best men he could find, irrespective of their political opinions.

His first act was to entreat me not to leave Mexico, as he was, he said, now able to conclude an arrangement with me that would give England positive guarantees for the due fulfilment of their engagements towards us. As this overture was made to me after the arrival of last month's mail bringing English newspapers in which it was positively stated that a convention was about being signed, binding the three powers to a joint intervention in Mexico, I could not, of course, take advantage of an offer which, under other circumstances, I should have gladly availed myself of.

Everything depends on the manner in which matters are managed here at first. If the intervention is properly received it will prove a blessing to the country; but, on the other hand, violent measures at first will spoil all, and engage us in an undertaking the difficulties of which can hardly be overrated.

Fortunately, the Spanish commander, both military and naval, appear to be men of great prudence and discretion, and up to the present moment they have shown a spirit of justice and conciliation which speaks highly in their favor.

In a long conversation I had with Admiral Rubalcava the day before yesterday, he expressed his opinion on this subject in terms nearly identical to those I have now used in giving my own.

I have the honor to enclose an extract from the "Trait d'Union," in which your lordship will find the summons of the Spanish admiral demanding the surrender of the town, as well as the president's address to the nation on the present state of affairs.

Enclosure in No. 123.

Extract from the "Trait d'Union" of December 19, 1861.

LA SOMMATION DU CHEF DE L'ESCADRE ESPAGNOL.

COMMANDANCE GÉNÉRALE DE FORCES NAVALES DE SA MAJESTÉ CATHOLIQUE DANS LES ANTILLES.

M. LE GOUVERNEUR: La longue série d'outrages infligés au gouvernement de sa Majesté Catholique par celui de la république Mexicaine, les violences réitérées, commises contre des sujets Espagnols et l'obstination aveugle avec laquelle le gouvernement du Mexique s'est refusé constamment à écouter les justes réclamations de l'Espagne, toujours présentées avec la modération et le décorum propres à une nation aussi noble ("hidalgo,") ont mis mon gouvernement dans le cas de rejeter tout espoir d'obtenir, par la voie de la conciliation, un règlement satisfaisant des graves différends existant entre les deux pays. Le gouvernement de sa Majesté Catholique, résolu, cependant, à obtenir réparation complète ("cumplida") pour tant d'outrages, m'a ordonné de commencer mes opérations en occupant la place de Vera Cruz et la château de San Juan de Ulùa, qui seront conservés, comme gage ("prenda pretoria") jusqu'à ce que le gouvernement de sa Majesté s'assure que, dans l'avenir, la nation Espagnole sera traitée avec la considération qui lui est due, et que les pactes qui seront célébrés entre les deux gouvernements seront religieusement observés.

Vous me communiquerez, par l'intermédiaire de M. le Consul Français, chargé de représenter les intérêts commerciaux de l'Espagne, dans le délai le vingt-quatre heures, comptées du moment où vous recevrez la présente sommation, si vous êtes ou non disposé à me livrer la place et le château; dans l'intelligence que si la réponse est négative, ou si je n'ai reçu aucune réponse à l'expiration du délai, vous pouvez dès ce moment considérer les hostilités commencées, et l'armée Espagnole débarquera dans ce but.

Je ne dois pas vous cacher que s'il est vrai que je fais la présente sommation seulement au nom de l'Espagne, suivant les instructions que j'ai reçues, l'occupation de la place et du château servira également de garantie pour les droits et les réclamations qu'auront à faire valoir contre le gouvernement Mexicain, les gouvernements de la France et de la Grande Bretagne.

Il me reste à vous faire observer que la mission de forces Espagnoles ne se rattache en rien à la politique intérieure du pays ("en nada se roza con la política interior del pais"): toutes les opinions seront respectées; on ne commettra aucun acte censurable, et du moment où nos troupes occuperont Vera Cruz, les chefs Espagnols répondront de la sûreté des personnes et des intérêts de ses habitants, quelle que soit leur nationalité. Il vous appartient ainsi qu'aux autres autorités de donner des garanties aux étrangers jusqu'à ce que la dite occupation se réalise, soit pacifiquement, soit de vive force. Si les sujets Espagnols et les autres étrangers étaient persécutés et maltraités, les forces qui composent cette expédition se verraient dans la dure mais impérieuse nécessité de recourir aux représailles.

J'entretiens l'espoir que, quelle que soit votre résolution, vous agirez avec la prudence qu'on doit attendre, et vous pénétrant que les forces Espagnoles, toujours humaines, toujours nobles et loyales, même avec leurs ennemis, ne feront pas le premier pas dans la voie des violences réprouvées même en cas de guerre, vous éviterez toute sorte de crimes dont le seul résultat serait de rendre plus difficile, sinon impossible, le règlement des questions internationales pendantes.

Je profite, &c.

Vapeur "Isabel la Catoiica," et mouillage d'Anton Lizardo, le 14 Décembre, 1861.

JOAQUIN GUTIERREZ DE RUBALCAVA.

M. le GOUVERNEUR *de l'Etat de Vera Cruz, &c.*

THE PRESENT CONDITION OF MEXICO. 433

Le Gouvernement Suprême à M. le Gouverneur de l'Etat de Vera Cruz.

MINISTERE DES RELATIONS EXTÉRIEURES ET DE GOBERNACION.

Le citoyen président, à qui j'ai rendu compte de la communication officielle que vous a adressée le commandant des forces navales Espagnoles, et de celle que vous avez envoyée à ce chef réponse, m'ordonne de vous dire de suivre ponctuellement les instructions qui vous ont été données par anticipation, pour le cas, aujourd'hui réalisé, de la rupture ouverte des hostilités de la part des sujets de l'Espagne, et de laisser, en matière militaire, l'action libre au citoyen Général Uraga, qui commande-en-chief l'armée Mexicaine, afin qu'il agisse également, dans so sphère, conformément aux instructions détaillées qui lui ont été données.

Il serait peu convenable pour le gouvernement de la république de s'adresser à un chef qui, passant par dessus les formes du droit des gens, commence par intimer la reddition d'une place. Le cri de guerre que la nation a lancé spontanément, marque au gouvernement le chemin qu'il doit suivre, et ce ne sera pas le citoyen president de la république qui reculera devant une invasion étrangere, avec d'autant plus de raison que, dans la circonstance, le Mexique ne fait que repousser la force par la force, en vertu de son droit naturel incontestable.

Je vous adresse également, par disposition suprême, un exemplaire du décret et de la circulaire qui sont envoyés aujourd'hui, par extraordinaire, aux citoyens gouverneurs des etats, en vous recommandant de seconder, avec l'énergie et l'activité que commandent les circonstances, la pensée du gouvernement; le citoyen president ne doute pas qu'à l'aide de cette fidèle exécution, l'invasion qui menace de détruire notre liberté et notre indépendance sera repoussée.

Liberte et réforme!

Mexico, le 17 Décembre, 1861.

MANUEL DOBLADO.

AU CITOYEN GOUVERNEUR DE L'ETAT DE VERA CRUZ.

Circulaire aux Gouverneurs d'Etats.

MINISTERE DES RELATIONS EXTÉRIEURES ET DE GOBERNACION.

Par ordre du citoyen président, j'ai l'honneur de vous remettre copie des communications officielles échangées entre le commandant des forces Espagnoles à Vera Cruz et le citoyen gouverneur de cet etat, ainsi que du décret et manifeste que le magistrat suprême de la république a cru devoir publier aujourd'hui, pour que les etats se préparent à la défense de l'indépendance.

Aprés avoir épuisé les moyens d'un arrangement pacifique entre l'Espagne et le Mexique, le gouvernement de la république, fort de la conscience de sa justice et ressentant l'impulsion de l'opinion populaire prononcée pour la guerre, accepte celle qu'ont commencée les forces Espagnoles d'une manière si inusitée, parceque son droit de repousser la force par la force est incontestable, et il proteste, devant le monde civilisé, que la responsabilité des événements postérieurs retombera toute entière et uniquement sur le gouvernement de la Reine d'Espagne qui a fait siennes, d'une maniére si inconsidérée, les injustes accusations sur lesquelles out entendu spéculer les ennemis de la liberté du Mexique.

Malgré nos dissensions intestines, le sentiment pour l'indépendance et la haine contre les anciens dominateurs du pays se maintiennent vivants, bien que la seconde soit atténuée par l'effet des lumières et de la civilisation du siècle.

Le citoyen président, en arborant le drapeau de la nationalité Mexicaine, ne fait que suivre le torrent de l'opinion générale, et a la plaisir de voir groupés

H. Ex. Doc. 100————28

autour de lui, au jour du conflit national, la plupart des Mexicains qui restaient désunis pour cause d'opinions politiques, mais qui ont abandonné les partis intestins au premier appel de la patrie.

Bien que le gouvernement ait tout droit d'expulser du territoire de la république les Espagnols qui y résident, il n'a pas voulu le faire quant à présent, car il a confiance en ce que ces derniers, répondant à la génerosité avec laquelle on les traite, observeront la stricte neutralité que leur position leur conseille. Le citoyen président a donné ainsi un noveau témoignage de la prudence avec laquelle il s'est conduit dans ses relations extérieures, en prouvant, par des faits irréfutables, qu'il n'a pas la faute si ces relations en sont venues au malheureux état dans lequel elles se trouvent actuellement.

Le citoyen président espère donc qu'en donnant une prompte et stricte exécution au décret dont j'ai parlé dès le début, vous mettrez en marche, aussitôt que possible, le contingent de force armée qui vous est signalé, et que vous userez en outre de toutes les ressources que vous permet votre gouvernement pour mettre l'etat de votre digne commandement dans l'attitude imposante qui lui correspond, en excitant par tous les habitants du même etat, afin qu'ils contribuent à la défense commune, et pour que, dans le cas malheureux où l'ennemi pénétrerait dans l'intérieur, tous les habitants du pays se lèvent en masse et opposent, avec leur épée et leur constance, une muraille invincible à l'audace de nos envahisseurs.

Que la mémoire d'Hidalgo, de Morelos et de Guerrero soit un exemple pour les Mexicains, et que la bannière qui flottera dans les rangs de notre armée, à l'heure du combat, ait pour inscription: "Vive l'Indépendance! Vive la République!"

Liberté et réforme.

MEXICO, *le* 17 *Décembre*, 1861.

MANUEL DOBLADO.

AU CITOYEN GOUVERNEUR DE L'ETAT DE ———.

www.ingramcontent.com/pod-product-compliance
Lightning Source LLC
Chambersburg PA
CBHW051729300426
44115CB00007B/517